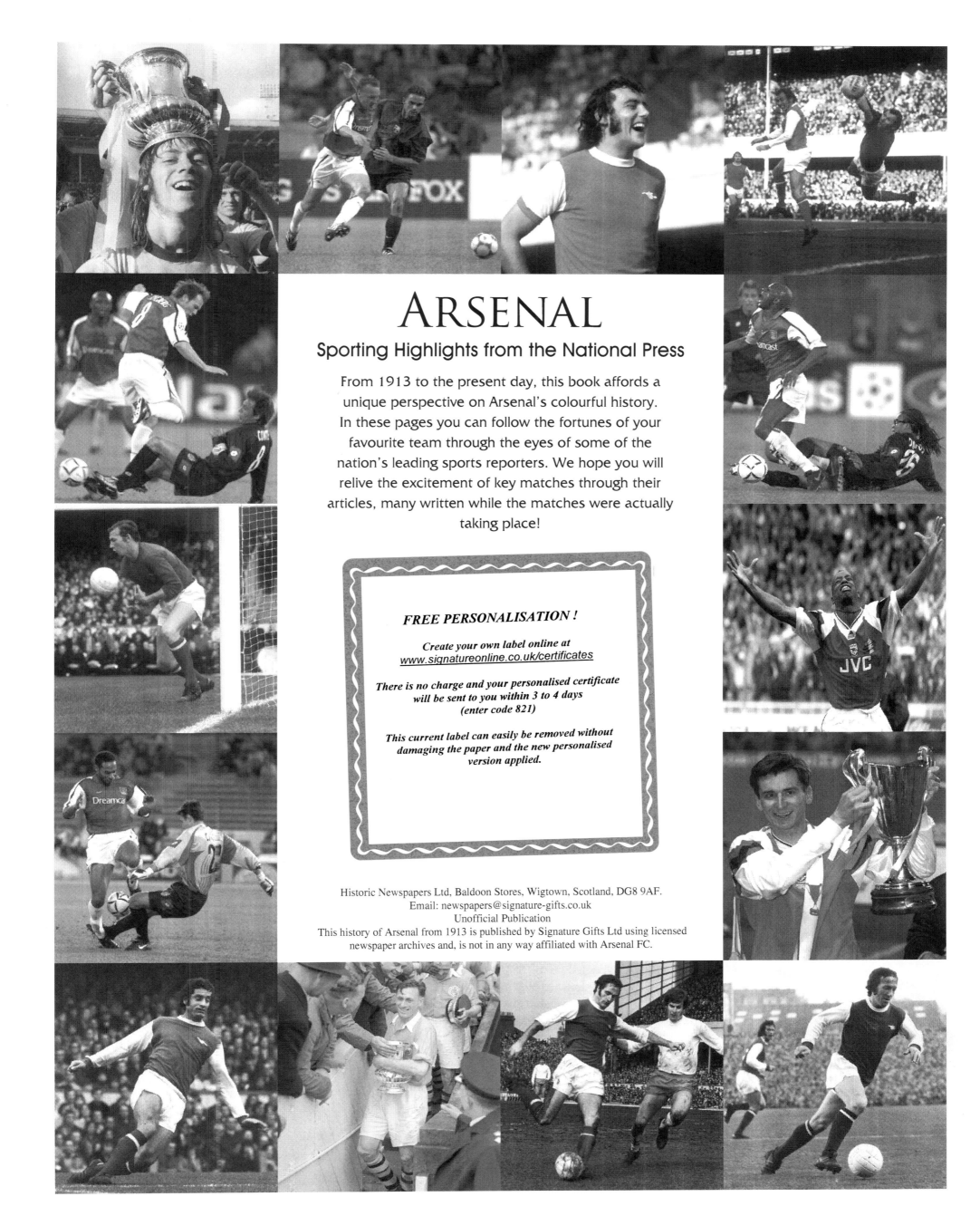

ARSENAL

Sporting Highlights from the National Press

From 1913 to the present day, this book affords a unique perspective on Arsenal's colourful history. In these pages you can follow the fortunes of your favourite team through the eyes of some of the nation's leading sports reporters. We hope you will relive the excitement of key matches through their articles, many written while the matches were actually taking place!

FREE PERSONALISATION !

Create your own label online at
www.signatureonline.co.uk/certificates

There is no charge and your personalised certificate will be sent to you within 3 to 4 days
(enter code 821)

This current label can easily be removed without damaging the paper and the new personalised version applied.

Historic Newspapers Ltd, Baldoon Stores, Wigtown, Scotland, DG8 9AF.
Email: newspapers@signature-gifts.co.uk
Unofficial Publication
This history of Arsenal from 1913 is published by Signature Gifts Ltd using licensed newspaper archives and, is not in any way affiliated with Arsenal FC.

The headlines and stories featured in this book have been reproduced by scanning original newspapers from our historic newspaper archive. As some of these newspapers are now very old, this may result in some of the reproduced pages being a little faded. From 2006, we have used the digitised images sent to us directly by the Daily Mirror, which significantly enhances the print reproduction.

Published by Historic Newspapers
PO Box 453
Harpenden
AL5 9AL

ISBN-13: 978-0-9552803-2-0

MODERATE SPORT AT DERBY RACES.

Powder and Shot Wins Doveridge Hurdle—Another Amusing Contest.

GATWICK AND HAYDOCK TO-DAY

Thanks to a decided improvement in the weather there was an all-round increase in the attendance at Derby yesterday. The sport, too, showed a slight improvement, but the meeting by no means realised the expectations of the executive.

Quite the most interesting race of the afternoon was the Doveridge Handicap Hurdle, five horses being supported at odds varying from 7 to 2 to 6 to 1. The Birmingham winner, Mint Tower, was favourite, and he was very unlucky not to win. He was hampered at each of the last two obstacles, and Payne had almost to pull up, with the result that Powder and Shot won comfortably from Star of Fortune.

Barnet Fair fell, and despite the fact that Mr. Drake was knocked down again on trying to rise, he miraculously escaped injury. Hamilton ran much better than the final placings would suggest.

Willaura and St. Felicien gave way to Blue Banner in the Devonshire Hurdle, but his public form did not suggest that he held much chance, and he was less fancied than either Recorder or Hainesby. Recorder would undoubtedly have won but for a blunder at the last hurdle, which gave Mr. Drake on Hainesby a chance, of which he availed himself, to win luckily by three parts of a length.

E. R., favourite for the Quarndon Steeplechase, had no difficulty in winning, despite the fact that his jockey lost an iron about half way. The rider of Gallerani, who nearly came to the ground at the first hurdles, also lost an iron.

The Hunters' Steeplechase, for horses which had been regularly hunted during the season 1911-12 or 1912-13, attracted the largest field of the afternoon. The event excited far more interest than any other race at the meeting, and there was quite a crowd to see the horses in the paddock.

The favourite was Abakur, who was ridden by the fine Irish rider, Mr. O'Brien Butler, and to the delight of his supporters had no difficulty in winning. Sandy, who finished second, is engaged in the Grand National. Last Beck, Ridley and Debden Mystery failed to finish.

The wind-up would have been quite farcical had it not involved an accident to E. Rollason, who was injured by the fall of Hinemoa. The other three horses refused, and though Bill Brendan was ultimately got over, he got rid of his rider at the last fence but one, through the bridle breaking.

Bill Brendan then galloped across the cricket pitch, but L'Estrange ultimately secured him, and, remounting, completed the course. Knockroe followed on, but the judge did not wait to see him finish.

SELECTIONS FOR TO-DAY.

GATWICK.	HAYDOCK PARK.
2. 0.—SIMON PURE II.	2. 0.—DUSTMAN.
2.30.—MISERE.	2.30.—MIDAS.
3. 0.—GROWLER.	3. 0.—KATHA.
3.30.—BLACK PLUM.	3.30.—SALAMIS.
4. 0.—AN DER WIEN.	4. 0.—TIBET CHIEF.
4.25.—HANNIBAL.	4.30.—BANFF.

Special Selection.
GROWLER.

GREY FRIARS.

DERBY RACING RETURNS.

2.0.—QUARNDON S. 'CHASE. 2m.—E.R. (Mr. H. Brown), 1; WINGFIELD (W. Smith), 2; BUZZY (Mr. George), 3. Also ran: Lynchpin, Calais Green, Comfort and Gallerani. Betting.—6 to 4 E.R., 7 to 2 Buzzy, 4 Comfort, 10 Gallerani, 100 to 8 others. Two; bad. (Pape.)

2.30.—DOVERIDGE H'CAP HURDLE. 2m.—POWDER AND SHOT (Driscoll), 1; STAR OF FORTUNE (Mr. O'Brien Butler), 2; MINT TOWER (W. Payne), 3. Also ran: Angel's Path, Gallivant, Connie Ediss, Flanagan, Hamilton, Barnet Fair and Van Zandt. Betting.—7 to 2 Mint Tower, 9 to 2 Powder and Shot and Star of Fortune, 5 Gallivant, 6 Angel's Path, 10 Hamilton, 100 to 8 others. Length and a half; half. (Withington.)

3.0.—DEVONSHIRE MAIDEN HURDLE. 2m.—HAINESBY (Mr. Drake), 1; RECORDER (Newey), 2; BLUE BANNER (F. Mason), 3. Also ran Lord Dennis. Betting.—10 to 11 Recorder, 9 to 4 Hainesby, 7 to 2 Blue Banner, 25 Lord Dennis. Three-quarters; head. (Moran.)

3.30.—HUNTERS' H'CAP S'CHASE. 3m.—ABAKUR (Mr. O'Brien Butler), 1; SANDY (Mr. Drake), 2; WARDSTOWN (Mr. F. A. Boll), 3. Also ran Ridley, Debden Mystery, Enoch, Aberrant, Duston, Last Beck, Bright Light III., Spinning Coin, Foolhardy and Mighty Ocean. Betting—3 Abakur, 6 Sandy and Spinning Coin, 8 Mighty Ocean and Aberrant, 10 others. Six; half. (Clayton.)

4.0.—FOUR-YEAR-OLD H'CAP HURDLE 2m.—BUOY AND GULL (Mr. Harrison), w.o. (Wilson.)

4.30.—SHIPLEY HALL S'CHASE. 2m.—BILL BRENDAN (L'Estrange), 1. Also ran: Hinemoa, Servetus and Knockroe. Betting—4 to 6 Hinemoa, 9 to 4 Bill Brendan, 10 Knockroe, 100 to 8 Servetus. Finished alone. (Private.)

TO-DAY'S PROGRAMMES.

GATWICK.

2.0.—ROSTRUM S. 'CHASE, 85 sovs; 2m.

	yrs	st	lb		yrs	st	lb
Simon Pure II.	a	12	0	Scribo	a	12	0
Upstart	6	12	0	Pitsea	a	12	0
Florial	a	12	0				

2.30.—EWELL SELLING HURDLE, 85 sovs; 2½m.

	yrs	st	lb		yrs	st	lb
Captain Kite	a	11	10	Enthusiastic Lad.	a	11	5
Bumpkin	a	11	10	Tilshead	5	11	1
aThe Alant	a	11	10	Steinbok	5	11	1
Wenden II.	a	11	10	G.A.P.	5	11	1
Prieska	a	11	10	Newnham	5	11	1
Misere	a	11	10	Macdowry	4	10	10
Greator	a	11	10	aPichincha	4	10	5
Dr. Mitchell	5	11	[illegible]	Manque	4	10	5
Dinna Ken	a	11	[illegible]				

3.0.—INTERNATIONAL HURDLE (h'cap), 400 sovs; 2m.

	yrs	st	lb		yrs	st	lb
Lady Madcap	a	12	11	Dark Collar	6	11	5
Wild Aster	a	12	6	aBernstein	4	11	4
aBronzewing III.	a	12	0	Ulster	5	10	11
Minstrel Park	5	12	0	Colonist	4	10	10
aGeneral's Pride	6	11	11	[illegible]ockland	5	10	7
aGrowler	5	11	10	a[illegible] Dolin	4	10	3
aSir Oracle	6	11	9	[illegible]'s Favour	a	10	0
Moscato	a	11	7	S[illegible]on	4	10	0
aElstead	6	11	6	D[illegible]in Bay	4	10	0
War Dance	5	11	5				

3.30.—MARCH 'CHASE (h'cap), 85 sovs; 3m.

	yrs	st	lb		yrs	st	lb
Moonstruck	a	12	10	Circassians Pride	a	11	1
aPeriwinkle II.	a	12	7	Sent[illegible]	a	10	12
Bridge IV.	a	12	2	Rhim[illegible]na S[illegible]ark	a	10	11
Black Plum	a	11	13	Sheer Pluck	6	10	10
aAbbott's Choice	a	11	13	Lowfield	6	10	4
Big Foot	a	11	7	Violet Charlesworth	a	10	0
Spinning Coin	a	11	5	Velindre	6	10	0
Finnigan	5	11	4	aGrey Leg IV.	6	10	0
aDurrain	a	11	4				

4.0.—MODERATE H'CAP HURDLE, 85 sovs; 2m. 7f.

	yrs	st	lb		yrs	st	lb
Garinish Island	a	12	7	Tagra	5	11	0
Captain Dreyfus	5	11	12	St. Bruno	5	11	0
Catherine	6	11	6	Wavelass	6	10	13
Nemo	6	11	6	Responsible	4	10	13
William the First	a	11	3	Mas[illegible]er Fo[illegible]es	4	10	12
Celtic King	6	11	1	Brentwood	5	10	11
Caldwell	5	11	1	An der Wien	5	10	10
aCerisaie	5	11	1	Authority	5	10	5
Watershield	a	11	0	Solomon's Glory	4	10	3

RUGBY TOPICS.

Referee's Blunder in an International—Gloucester's Championship.

I am afraid that the Irish fifteen are in for a beating next Saturday. There has been nothing in their play to suggest their ability to overcome Wales at Swansea. I recall a game on that enclosure when Ireland were robbed of a victory through a blunder by an English referee. As my readers know, I deprecate any questioning of a referee's decision, but there was an awful row on this occasion.

Some thirty thousand Welshmen knew that their side had won by a fluke and could hardly raise a cheer at the finish. But they heartily cheered the Irishmen when they were driven from the ground. Yet, as the referee observed after the match, "If I made a mistake it was the mistake of an honest man. And it will be a bad day for Rugby when paid referees come into the game." I quite agree, but there was a terrible rumpus after that match.

So Gloucestershire have won the county championship for the second time. The previous occasion was in the season of 1909-10. Prior to that Gloucestershire had got in the second stage of the competition, and were beaten by Lancashire.

I have frequently been asked whether so and so would have been a great player under modern conditions. That is and must necessarily be a difficult question to answer. My own view is that a player who is really great has in him the elements enabling him to adapt himself to any kind of game.

That point was delightfully demonstrated in the person of Arthur James Gould, of Welsh fame. Arthur, whom I have had the pleasure of playing against, and whom I know personally, had quite an unique experience. He first of all played full back for Wales, then centre in the old three three-quarter game, and later on on the present lines.

He was away in India for two seasons, came back, and played as well as ever. The style of play was a matter of indifference to him. In the four three-quarter game he allowed himself a certain amount of personal liberty that would not be permitted a younger player. But it was a case of custom nodding to a great king. And there could be no doubt that Arthur Gould was an exceptional player.

Whether he is the greatest three-quarter Wales ever produced must always be a matter of opinion, but, personally, I regard him as such. He was a top sawyer under two distinct styles, and was in the same position when the game was in a state of transition.

In Welsh football the nearest approach to Gould has been W. J. Trew, who has, I understand, decided to give up the game. In the matter of accidents he has been none too lucky, and the plucky player generally gets most of the hard knocks. Trew was in the first flight of backs, whether as stand-off half or centre quarter. He had a natural genius for the game, and could play in any position. I have no doubt he would have made a good forward as a booker. As a full back he would easily have made a name for himself. As it is, he goes down in archives as one of the many men who have helped to make the Swansea club famous.

TOUCH JUDGE.

SCOTLAND'S XI. FOR DUBLIN.

The following team was selected at Glasgow yesterday to represent Scotland against Ireland at Dublin on March 15:—

Brownlie (Third Lanark); Gordon (Rangers) and Walker (Swindon); Mercer (Hearts), Thomson (Sunderland) and H. Low (Sunderland); Bennett (Rangers), McMenemy (Celtic), Reid (Rangers), Croall (Falkirk) and Robertson (Sheffield Wednesday).

ENGLAND'S CALCUTTA CUP TEAM

The following players have been selected to represent England against Scotland in the match for the Calcutta Cup at Twickenham on March 15:—

W. R. Johnston (Bristol); C. N. Lowe (Cambridge U.), F. N. Tarr (Leicester), R. W. Poulton (Harlequins), V. H. M. Coates (Bath); F. E. Oakeley (Royal Navy), W. J. A. Davies (Royal Navy); N. A. Wodehouse (United Services), J. E. Greenwood (Cambridge U.), L. G. Brown (Oxford U.), C. H. Pillman (Blackheath), J. A. King (Headingley), J. A. S. Ritson (Northern), G. Ward (Leicester), and A. N. Other.

TO-DAY'S MATCHES.

Brighton and Hove Albion v. Brentford (Southern League).
Portsmouth v. Millwall (Southern Alliance).
Watford.—Hertfordshire v. Middlesex (Southern Counties championship, semi-final).
Aldershot.—4th Middlesex Regiment v. 1st East Yorkshire Regiment (Army Cup, semi-final).
Bournemouth.—Hampshire v. Paris League.

RUGBY RULES.

Portsmouth.—United Services v. Aldershot Command.
Greenwich.—Royal Naval College v. University College Hospital.

ARMY RACQUETS.

The remaining two matches in the first round made up the second day's play in the Army doubles championship at Prince's Club, Knightsbridge, yesterday. The first match—that between 1st Battalion King's Royal Rifles and 4th Battalion Rifle Brigade—did not provide a very brilliant exhibition of the game, and, although the King's Royal Rifles won by four games to one, they did not play up to usual form.

The match between the Royal Engineers and 1st Battalion Rifle Brigade was much more close, and it was not until the full seven sets had been decided that the Engineers ran out winners. There were many splendid rallies, the feature of which was the fine service and smashes of Hedley and Williams for their respective sides.

4.25.—TYRO STEEPLECHASE, 85 sovs; 2m.

	yrs	st	lb		yrs	st	lb
aArable	a	12	3	Schemer IV.	a	11	0
Wavespray	6	11	10	Como	5	10	7
Avernus	6	11	10	Marbles	5	10	7
Cowper's Oak	5	11	3	Lord Marcus	5	10	7
Red Admiral	6	11	3	John Redmond	5	10	7
aTarmac	6	11	3	Cassock	4	10	3
Hannibal	5	11	3	Hawkins	4	10	3
Carmeen	a	11	3	Mr. Preedy	4	10	3
Proposal	6	11	0	Self Defence	4	10	0
Floridor	a	11	0				

HAYDOCK PARK.

2.0.—PADDOCK S. 'CHASE, 70 sovs; 2m.

2.30.—MARCH H'CAP 'CHASE, 80 sovs; 2m.

	yrs	st	lb		yrs	st	lb
Bloodstone	a	13	1	Seisdon Prince	a	10	4
Wavelet	6	10	13	Top o' the Morn	a	10	1
Claydon	a	10	10	Purdysburn	a	10	1
Miss Picton	a	10	6	aThistlecock	6	10	0
aSetanius	a	10	6	Shavington Belle	5	10	0
Midas	a	10	4				

3.0.—COUNTY S. 4-Y-O HURDLE, 70 sovs; 2m.

3.30.—GOLBORNE MAIDEN HURDLE, 200 sovs; 2m.

	yrs	st	lb		yrs	st	lb
Dilwyn	5	11	10	Blue Banner	4	10	7
Set Free	6	11	7	Plumstead	4	10	7
Stronvar	a	11	7	Star of Fortune	4	10	7
aDustcap	6	11	7	Ben Trovato	4	10	7
Salamis	6	11	7	Crack Shot	4	10	7
Jaseur	5	11	3	aMarshland II.	4	10	7
aRomeo	5	11	3	aMelburg	4	10	7
aHowdyedo	4	10	7	Silver Jack	4	10	7

4.0.—WEDNESDAY S. HURDLE, 70 sovs; 2m.

4.30.—CLUB STEEPLECHASE, 70 sovs; 2m.

LATEST LONDON BETTING.

LINCOLNSHIRE HANDICAP.—100 to 8 Uncle Pat (t, o) and Long Set (t, o), 100 to 6 Le Touquet (t, o), 25 Cigar (t, o) and Cuthbert (t, o), 100 to 3 Sobieski (t, o).

GRAND NATIONAL 'CHASE.—100 to 7 Blowpipe (t).

THE FUTURE OF WOOLWICH ARSENAL.

Statement by Mr. Norris on the Reasons for the Removal of the Club to Highbury.

THE GLASGOW MEETING.

Last night, at the Connaught Rooms, Mr. G. H. Norris, the chairman of the Woolwich Arsenal club, made a statement regarding the future of the club, and more particularly with regard to their proposed removal to Islington next season.

Mr. Norris pointed out that it was impossible for the club to pay its way any longer in the district. There was a time, he said, when there were no other attractions of the same kind in London, and in those days the club had a prosperous time. But it was impossible to get people to go to Plumstead nowadays, with other League clubs in the metropolis.

The following are the gates for the home matches this season: Sunderland £248, Manchester City £228, Everton £198, Blackburn Rovers £195, Notts County (Christmas Day) £235, Liverpool £234, Sheffield United £200, Oldham Athletic £227, Bradford City £247, and in the second round of the English Cup, against Liverpool, £343. On those gates, said Mr. Norris, it was impossible to make both ends meet.

They proposed, said Mr. Norris, to go to Highbury, which he described as the apex of an equilateral triangle, with a line drawn from Clapton Orient and Tottenham Hotspur grounds as the base. Highbury was four miles from Tottenham and four miles from Homerton, and Homerton was four and a half miles from Tottenham.

Going on to point out what Woolwich had done for League football in London, Mr. Norris said that they had been twenty years in the Football League, and they hoped to get back some of the patronage of the football public which had been transferred from Woolwich Arsenal to other clubs.

The Woolwich club had voted for Chelsea, Fulham, Clapton Orient and Tottenham being admitted to the League, when they applied for membership. He also said that, they had no knowledge or intimation that any protest would be raised at the Glasgow meeting to their proposed scheme.

Mr. Norris pointed out that the 'Spurs' ground is situated in the County of Middlesex, and in the area governed by the Edmonton Board of Guardians, the population being 500,000. The new ground of the Arsenal Club is in the County of London, and the population tapped by the three clubs would be some two and a half millions.

Mr. Norris also denied that Mr. T. A. Deacock had promised to join the board of directors, but he was understood to say that Mr. Deacock would be welcome as a colleague if he cared to throw in his lot with the Arsenal.

In endorsing the remarks of Mr. Norris, Mr. W. Hall, a director of the Woolwich club and a member of the Management Committee of the League, said that he took no part in the debate at the meeting of the Management Committee, whose decision was come to simply after the ex parte statements of the gentlemen who represented the Tottenham and Clapton clubs at the Glasgow meeting.

Without giving anything away in his speech, Mr. Norris made out a strong case for the removal of the club. In a way it is difficult to see how it will affect the other bodies: It has been the experience when professional football has been establishd in any quarter that a new public has been created for the game. Chelsea is a case in point.

It would be a thousand pities if a club like the Arsenal had to put up its shutters for lack of support, seeing that for twelve years they were the only members in town of the Football League, and most people will wish the Arsenal good luck in their plucky endeavour to keep the flag flying under the most disastrous conditions in recent years.

HOSPITAL SOCCER CUP FINAL.

In a hard game at Chiswick Park yesterday, St. Bartholomew's beat St. Thomas', the holders, in the final of the Hospital Cup by 2 goals to 1. The better side in all respects, Bart's thoroughly deserved success. They had to work desperately for the lead, and for a long time it seemed as if a draw would be the result.

St. Thomas's began with some attacks, and were dangerous when Walker and Chaplin tried shots. Bart's soon settled down to the stronger game, and Soutter scored with a splendid left-foot shot. It was not long before St. Thomas's equalised, Walker utilising a centre by Cooke.

After change of ends Bart's forwards played splendidly. Waugh, in the centre, worked with special effect, and he was credited with the winning goal after beating two or three opponents.

HOME SCOTS v. ANGLO-SCOTS.

At Glasgow last night the Scottish Selection Committee chose the following elevens for the trial match between Home Scots and Anglo-Scots, to be played at Glasgow on March 18:—

Home Scots.—Brownlie (Third Lanark); McNair (Celtic), Dodds (Celtic); Mercer (Hearts), Logan (Falkirk), Nellies (Hearts); Templeman (Airdrieonians), Walker (Hearts), Robertson (Falkirk), Croall (Falkirk) and Smith (Rangers).

Anglo-Scots.—Campbell (Liverpool); Walker (Swindon), Taylor (Burnley); Halley (Bradford), Low (Newcastle), Campbell (Sheffield W.); Stirling (Middlesbrough), McTavish (Newcastle), McLean (Sheffield W.), Wilson (Sheffield W.), and Donnachie (Oldham).

'VARSITY BOAT RACE PRACTICE.

Considerable interest was taken in the morning work of the Cambridge crew yesterday owing to the uncertainty as to the constitution of the crew. Fortunately no further changes were necessary, the crew being seated in the same order as on Monday afternoon—Fisher (bow), Swann, Roper, Askwith, Clark, Shove, Buxton and Tower (stroke).

The Light Blues were accompanied by a London Rowing Club scratch eight stroked by H. Lumb. Captain Gibbon took his crew down to Wandsworth, and by the time they got back to Hurlingham the boat had shipped a lot of water. The crew baled some of it out, and then rowed half a minute against the scratch crew, but did not gain much.

Oxford went down to the lower end of Hurlingham, and then returned to Putney Bridge, where they rowed a minute at 34 in fairly good form. Later they pulled 18 strokes in a half-minute burst.

In the afternoon both crews did some important work. Oxford were out first, and they paddled right away up to Mortlake, with three or four "easies" en route. They turned opposite the Ibis boathouse, and prepared to row from the Ship at Mortlake to Hammersmith Bridge.

Horsfall rowed 18—35 in the half and full minute, and then dropped the rate to 29. The crew reached Barnes Bridge in 2m. 50s. At Chiswick Steps (reached in 7m. 5s.) a Thames scratch crew picked up the Dark Blues. Opposite The Doves Horsfall spurted and, finishing with a burst at 34, reached the bridge just clear of the scratch crew in 11m. 15s.—a fairly good performance on the moderate ebb tide.

Cambridge were out soon after their rivals. They paddled up to the lower end of Chiswick Eyot and then turned and prepared to row from Hammersmith Bridge to Putney Bridge. The conditions were not favourable—a head wind and rough water from Harrod's to the last bend. Tower rowed 18—33 in the half and full minute, getting his men off the mark in very lively fashion. He then rowed 28, and reached the Mile Post in 3m. 34s. They quickened to 29 along the boathouses, and finished at 32 in 8m. 39s.

DRAW FOR DAVIS CUP.

The draw for the eliminating competition in the international lawn tennis tournament for the Dwight Davis Cup, at present held by the British Isles, was made yesterday in the offices of the Lawn Tennis Association.

The draw is: Australasia versus United States of America, Germany versus France, South Africa versus Canada, Belgium a bye.

SPRING OF GOLF.

Prominent Professionals and Their Matches—Tom Ball's Putting.

Spring is the golfer's season of hope, inspiration and experiment; and to the pessimistic people who declare that winter has yet to begin in earnest there surely must be gladness in the reflection that the programme of professional exhibition matches opens next Saturday. That is a sure sign of the coming of spring.

The chief event will take place at Prestatyn, in Flintshire, where Edward Ray and Harry Vardon will renew activity after four months of hibernation. They will contest a single in the morning, and will be joined in a four-ball match in the afternoon by W. J. Leaver, of Worsley, and the local professional. Ray and Vardon look like playing a big part in this year's golf. Both have been showing excellent form in recent practice, and with the help of the confidence born of their joint supremacy in the chief tournaments of 1912, they will be difficult to beat.

James Braid, who has a goodly list of engagements, has found something like his old game, judging by his doings at Le Touquet during the past few weeks. The only thing seriously wrong with Braid's golf last year was the putting; it prevented him from giving Ray a hard run for the championship, and it cost him many strokes with monotonous regularity. He suffered just about the worst and longest attack of the "jumps" which had ever assailed him. The impotency of a crack golfer when, in this condition, he tries to hole four-foot putts is one of the most remarkable phenomena in the whole scheme of sport. The only first-class player whom I have heard declare that he has never been off his putting in his life is Tom Ball.

TWO HOURS' PUTTING PRACTICE.

He attributes his maintenance of steadiness on the greens solely to constant practice. In the early stages of a season he practises putting for two or three hours at a stretch, day after day. Even in the winter, when there is nothing very particular to be won, he seizes odd half-hours for his pursuance of the work of remaining infallible on the green. He is about the one noted golfer who believes in swaying when putting. At least, I fancy that G. Pulford, another deadly putter, who finished third in the open championship of 1907, has this swaying habit, but it is not so pronounced as in the case of Ball, who allows his body to follow the club in a manner which is startling to the worshipper of the orthodox motionless body and pendulum swing with the arms.

Ball is convinced that his method encourages a smooth impact and a rhythmic follow-through, and it suits him so well that he is most certainly justified in adopting it.

George Duncan is assured of many opportunities of distinguishing himself during the coming season. He is booked for a large number of exhibition matches and tournaments, and, being by nature confident, he ought to do well. He is at the top of his form, as witness four recent rounds of 73, 70, 73 and 70, which he played in two days at Deal. In the list of the year's events one does not notice the names of J. H. Taylor and Alexander Herd with the frequency which would be reasonable. Both are fine players to watch; Herd, with his irrepressible energy in the waggle and general tendency towards dashing, rather than careful golf, and Taylor, with his incisive hitting, particularly of iron shots.

TAYLOR'S SHOT.

"Give it the back of the left hand" is an old and no doubt valuable piece of advice regarding the manner of striking the ball; Taylor seems to give it both hands and both forearms and a flick of both wrists. There is nobody who starts more calmly and invests the shot with more power than Taylor, just as he hits the ball.

Of late there has been some discussion on the subject of the master eye in golf. It has been argued that everybody has one eye which is more important than the other in the business of focussing the ball, and presumably the idea is to study the question as to which is your predominant optic and make the most of it.

E. W. B. Scratton, the old Cantab and English international, would seem to have discovered his by chance. I am informed that in the match between Royal West Norfolk and Cambridge University at Brancaster, last Saturday, Mr. Scratton played with his left eye completely bandaged. It was undergoing medical attention (indeed, the doctor had ordered him to give up golf for a while), but he resolved to see what he could do with the use of the right eye only. He did so well that he halved with C. Gardiner Hill, the Cambridge captain.

At times Mr. Scratton found the distances rather hard to judge, and he gave up three holes, but his score for the other fifteen holes was one over 4's—very hot golf for a man with only half his ordinary powers of vision on such a testing links as Brancaster.

R. E. HOWARD.

FLY-WEIGHT CHAMPIONS.

Who Is to Meet Smith for the Lonsdale Belt?—McCormick's Next Match.

It has been decided that a match for the fly-weight championship shall take place at the National Sporting Club in April. It is also practically decided that Sid Smith, who is now very well and strong, will be one of the two principals to it. Who the other man will be cannot be told until next Tuesday.

Bill Ladbury has the first chance, but Ladbury is matched to box Jim Berry, the Northumberland fly-weight, at the New Cross Baths on Monday night, and it is just possible that Berry may emulate Johnny Best's success over Hughes and relegate Ladbury to the rear rank. Berry is capable of doing such a thing, or his record belies his class. On Monday night he knocked out a good bantam in Billy Atkin, and he has previously defeated Curley Walker, Bill Beynon, Bat McCarthy, Joe Wilson, Peter Cain, and others of high class.

If Ladbury proves to be the winner it will be he and Smith who will have a go for the championship belt in April, and when the match is made both will be asked to refrain from other matches until they have decided the most important one. Should Berry triumph over Ladbury it will then be left to Johnny Best to oppose Smith, and the little Scotsman has well earned the honour.

Having looked over Tom McCormick in his full maturity at the National Sporting Club on Monday night, I was deeply impressed by his skill as a boxer—more particularly his almost perfect defence—but was surprised to note the absence of power in his punching. McCormick is a most adept boxer, but quite harmless. There is not the slightest doubt in my mind that he will out-box anything of his pounds and inches in the country, but as he will never do any damage to a good, strong tear-away man, he will always be more or less susceptible to defeat at the hands of a hard-punching, though less skilful, boxer.

George "Binks" Cohen, the London amateur welter-weight, whose battles with Charley Mitchell, jun., at the old Arena, and Mr. Sol Adler, at the N.S.C., were classics in their way, is now located in New York. Yesterday I received a letter from him, stating that he had agreed to box the American amateur 10st. 5lb. champion within a few weeks, and was expecting another match subsequently with Ivan Kahn, the California amateur, whom Adler defeated at Chandos Hall a few years back.

F. M.

Last night's billiards scores were: At Soho-square—Smith, 4,421; Aiken, 4,002. At Leicester-square—Falkiner, 5,393; Stevenson, 3,002.

The final of the Oxford University inter-college hockey tournament was decided at Oxford between St. John's College and Hertford College yesterday, and ended in a win for the former by 2 goals to 1.

A charity "Soccer" match has been arranged between representative teams of the Stock Exchange Athletic Club and the London Banks' Football Association, to be played on April 12 at Tufnell Park. The proceeds will be given to the funds of the Lord Mayor Treloar Cripples' Hospital and College, Alton, Hants.

At a council meeting of the L.F.A. last evening the secretary reported that the eight matches in the Charity Cup competition this season had yielded £191 7s. 10d. The following eight clubs were selected to take part in next season's Charity Competition: London Caledonians, Nunhead, Dulwich Hamlet, Clapton, Ilford, West Norwood, Leytonstone and Shepherd's Bush.

HALF A MILLION AT LEAGUE FOOTBALL.

Many Away Victories in First League—Sunderland Defeated.

'SPURS CONTINUED SUCCESS.

Preston and Burnley, the Promoted Clubs, Both Beaten—Four Goals for Bentley.

Football's opening Saturday was favoured by fine weather and enormous crowds turned out to see the more important matches. There were five first-class league matches in London, and at these alone the attendance numbered no fewer than 130,000.

All over the country in the thirty important League games under the auspices of the English and Southern Leagues the attendances were returned at 521,000. Of course, these are only a part of the enormous army of football enthusiasts who go to the numerous matches under the Soccer, Rugby and Northern Union codes of rules. It would probably be safe to say that over a million spectators saw Saturday's games.

Some of the play was exceptionally interesting. Clubs that did badly last year started out well last Monday and kept it up on Saturday, and some of the top sawyers of the last campaign came a cropper. The uncertainty of football is truly one of its chief charms.

Biggest attendance of the lot was at Stamford Bridge, where estimates of the crowd vary from 60,000 to 70,000. That supporters of both clubs, the 'Spurs and Chelsea, were eager to see their favourites doubtless accounted for this exceptional gate. The first League match ever played in Islington between Woolwich Arsenal and Leicester Fosse on the Arsenal's new home at Highbury attracted 20,000 people, in spite of the fact that the stand accommodation is not finished.

Sunderland, the champions, had 40,000 to see the match with Newcastle, and at the matches at Manchester, Bradford, Sheffield and Blackburn there were gatherings of 30,000 or over. It is a wonderful tribute to the popularity of our national game, and when it is remembered that there must have been over 20,000 other games under amateur conditions played it becomes positively amazing.

Londoners were chiefly interested in the match at Stamford Bridge. Last season both clubs were under a cloud and both kept out of the last two places in the League table by a mere trifle. Both have made strenuous efforts to strengthen their sides, the 'Spurs' management realised that it was scoring forwards they lacked, have got a fine front line together, and in their two matches up to now have demonstrated that there is little wrong with the old defence, and they have now proved their ability to get goals.

WALDEN'S CLEVER WORK.

Their brilliant victory by 3 goals to 1 over Chelsea on Saturday by no means exaggerates their superiority. They were faster and cleverer all through and quite deserved even more goals. Walden, the ex-Northampton right winger, was always too good for Downing and Sharp, who had a very unhappy afternoon.

Steel, as I have always contended he would, made a fine centre half, and Webster and Collins, the backs, had much less work thrown on them than was the case last year, when the forwards were all at sixes and sevens. It is early as yet, but there is every prospect of Tottenham having a great season.

After Bauchop had headed against the bar of the Chelsea goal, Grimsdell, from the half back line, scored first goal for the 'Spurs, and ten minutes later Cantrell shot the second from a free kick. Cantrell got the Tottenham third goal halfway through the second half, and just on the finish Halse, who played well but was badly supported by the rest of the Chelsea forwards, got through for the home team.

Matches between Sunderland and Newcastle rarely turn out as anticipated. The form of the opening day of the season quite led most people to expect a victory for the champions. Newcastle, however, visited Roker Park and won by 2 to 1. Sunderland were, of course, without the suspended Thomson, and also had to take the field without Mordue, who is suffering from a bruised knee.

Sunderland took the lead after seven minutes' play through Holley, but Hall equalised just before the interval. In the second half Low missed a penalty kick for Sunderland, and eight minutes from the finish King scored for Newcastle. A feature of a fast, hard match was the play of Cuggy at centre half for Sunderland, and the clever tactical work of McCracken, at back, for Newcastle.

Another side to gain a rather surprising victory was Blackburn Rovers, who triumphed by no fewer than six goals to two over Liverpool at Blackburn. The Rovers played brilliant football all through, the work of the wing men being particularly good. Shea, the old West Ham man, got four of the goals, and Latheron and Bradshaw the other two.

Mitchell, who scored twice for Liverpool, worked hard all through and wanted a lot of watching, but he was the only outstanding player in the Liverpool team.

CROMPTON GOOD AS EVER.

By the way, it will interest all footballers to know that Crompton, the veteran Rovers and English captain, played a wonderfully good game. Seasons come and go, but Crompton seems as good as ever.

Sheffield United, after being whacked at home by the 'Spurs on the opening day, visited Derby and surprised the County by winning there by 5 goals to 3. Two surprise goals early on by Fazackerley and Gillespie disheartened the Derby men, and when Kitchen scored before the interval it looked a walk-over for Sheffield.

But Derby played better after the interval, and although Fazackerley early on added to the United's lead, first Barnes and then the evergreen Bloomer scored for Derby. Gillespie put the issue beyond doubt, however, by adding a fifth for Sheffield, although before the close Bloomer found the net again for Derby.

Manchester United created something of a surprise by winning at Owlerton. The Wednesday scored the first point, through Birkenshaw, and Turnbull equalised before the interval. Spoors put the ball through his own goal from a well-placed centre by Meredith, who played finely throughout. How these veterans do last! Sheffield never recovered from this disaster, and in the closing stages West added another goal.

Bolton Wanderers ran the rule over Oldham Athletic and found out the weaknesses in the team with a vengeance. Lillycrop, their importation from Barnsley, got a couple of goals, and Smith, Feebury, Jones and Vizard also found the net, what time Woodger and Donnachie scored for Oldham.

BRILLIANT BOLTON FORWARDS.

It was another case of brilliant forward play wearing down the defence opposed to it, for at one time in the first half Oldham, whose forwards were quite good, held a lead of 2 to 1. Charlie Roberts, the new Oldham captain, who was transferred from Manchester United, was not a conspicuous success.

It was a very hard game at Manchester, where the City shared a couple of goals with Middlesbrough. My Manchester correspondent says "The game was more remarkable for strenuous play than anything else. It was too fast and too scrappy to be satisfactory." Taylor got Manchester's goal in the first half, and a blunder by Goodchild, who ran out of his goal, enabled Carr to equalise in the second half.

Hardy played a magnificent game in goal for Aston Villa at Bradford, and it was largely through his efforts that the match ended in a pointless draw. The Bradford forwards simply bombarded him, while Mellors, the Bradford goalkeeper, enjoyed the fun as a spectator, and doubtless wished he could act the part of a sixth forward.

Both the clubs promoted from the Second Division at the end of last season met with defeat. Preston were a bit unlucky in losing at Liverpool, where Mitchell kept a fine goal for Everton. There was no score in the first half, but after change of ends Jefferis went right through the Preston defence while they were appealing for offside and scored, and towards the end Bradshaw got through again. There was little to choose between the teams on the run of the play, and Osborne, the Preston outside left, might easily have scored with two or three rasping shots that Mitchell kept out.

In an interesting game at West Bromwich the Albion proved too good for Burnley and won by 4 to 1. Bentley had a regular field day, as he scored all four of the Throstles' goals. The ex-Derby and Bolton forward, who took Pailor's place at centre forward, shot three goals in the first half and one afterwards. Burnley, who were without Bellamy, who sprained his ankle, in the second half, scored their goal through Freeman, who lifted the ball over Pearson's head into the net when the Albion goalkeeper ran out to stop him.

P. J. MOSS.

SECOND LEAGUE MATCHES.

Arsenal's Win on their New Ground—Bradford Triumph at Birmingham.

Most interest in the Second League matches was centred in Woolwich Arsenal's debut on their new ground at Highbury, where, before an excellent crowd of 20,000, they gained a deserved victory by 2 goals to 1 over Leicester Fosse.

Quite the most pleasing feature was the success of Hardinge, the Kent cricketer, formerly associated with Sheffield United. Hardinge did not score a goal, but he got through a lot of work, his dribbling and passing being very clever.

Leicester had the best of the first half, and after eighteen minutes Benfield scored with an unstoppable shot. Jobey headed an equalising goal just before the interval, and half an hour after the resumption had the misfortune to be so badly injured that he had to be carried off on a stretcher.

In spite of this disadvantage, the Arsenal, showing improved form carried all before them during the last ten minutes. They scored once only, however, Devine giving them a victory from a penalty kick. The Arsenal defence was certainly unsteady to begin with, but the whole team finished in splendid style.

Clapton Orient's single goal victory over Fulham at Homerton was not a great one, but was well deserved on the run of the game, the result being due as much to Fulham's poor play as to the winners superiority. The only goal came from a penalty just prior to the interval, McFadden taking the kick.

Dash there was in plenty about the Orient forwards, but they lacked finishing power, and Hunter, the old Manchester United forward, ought to have scored more than once. Still, when he is more used to his colleagues' play Hunter will probably make an efficient leader.

Forrest, from Northumberland, should strengthen the Orient half-back line. Fulham had an experimental left wing in Russell and Torrance, and during the last quarter of an hour the whole forward line played finely, but for the rest of the game the attack was quite disjointed, and altogether the display was little, if any, better than that of the previous Monday against Bury.

FOREST BEATEN AGAIN.

Nottingham Forest's second failure within four days has already caused serious doubts as to the merits of the reconstituted eleven. Their display against Wolverhampton, who won 3—1, again lacked effective combination. Brooks and Lloyd scored for the Wolves in the first half, and Derrick for the Forest and Harrison (Wolverhampton) got through afterwards.

Two very smart performances were those of Bradford and Wolverhampton Wanderers, who secured away victories at Birmingham and Nottingham respectively. It was due to their sound defence that Bradford beat Birmingham by 2 goals to 1.

Their first goal—the only one of the opening half—was a lucky one, Little scoring after Tinkler had miskicked. Subsequently Jones equalised, and in the closing stages Howie gave Bradford the lead. A draw would have been a more fitting result.

Huddersfield Town's display at Leeds-road in drawing 1—1 with Bury was distinctly disappointing, for the team never seemed able to settle down. Weak at half back, their forwards received little support, and it was well for them that Blackman and Bullock were in such good form. Mann scored for Huddersfield and Cameron equalised with a long shot.

In one respect Blackpool did well to draw with Hull City at Blackpool after being two goals down, but if they had accepted half their chances in the second half they would have won easily. McCurry and Stevens scored for Hull, and Brown and Gillow brought the scores level.

An interesting game at Lincoln ended in a draw of two goals each. In the opening half Barnsley scored twice without response, Moore putting on both goals—one from a penalty. Afterwards Lincoln City played up in fine style, and drew level through Brindley and McCubbin. In the closing stages of the game Moore, of Barnsley, and Jackson, of Lincoln City, were sent off the field for fighting.

Grimsby Town and Notts County played a goalless draw at Grimsby. Play in the first half went on very even lines, but following change of ends Grimsby did most of the attacking. Try as they would, however, their forwards could not penetrate a sound defence.

Bristol City again showed brilliant form, and by defeating Stockport County by 5 to 0 at Bristol, brought their total of goals to nine for two matches. All the scoring took place in the first half, when Chapple (3), Broad and Fuge got through. Lunn, the Stockport goalkeeper, was injured before the interval, and had to be carried off.

Glossop were beaten by 3 to 0 at Leeds, but there were not so many goals difference between the teams on the run of the play. Spiers scored in the first half, and just before the end McLeod put on two more goals in quick succession.

TO-DAY'S MATCHES.

Four interesting First League matches are down for decision this afternoon. Two of them are to be decided in town, Chelsea entertaining West Bromwich Albion and Tottenham Hotspur receiving a return visit from Sheffield United. In the first match last Monday the 'Spurs won at Bramall-lane by 4 goals to 1. The game at Stamford Bridge is timed to start at five o'clock, and that at White Hart-lane a quarter of an hour later.

In the other matches Blackburn Rovers visit Burnley and Manchester United are at home to Sunderland.

THE LEAGUE.—Division I.

Chelsea v. W. B. Albion. | Burnley v. Blackburn Rvs.
'Spurs v. Sheffield United | M'chester U. v. Sunderland

SOUTHERN ALLIANCE.—Brentford v. Portsmouth.

LONDON LEAGUE.—Millwall R. v. Fulham R. Clapton O. R. v. West Ham R.

OTHER MATCH.—Portsmouth v. United Services League.

P. G. Wyatt, the North Middlesex professional, holed the sixteenth hole on his course on Saturday in one stroke. Wyatt is playing fine golf, and only a few days ago returned a 63, which is a record for the green.

SPIRITED SOUTHERN LEAGUE CONTESTS.

Swindon's Fine Victory at West Ham—Reading Defeat Millwall.

SOUTHEND START WELL.

London's Southern League teams did very badly on Saturday, only one out of the four winning. Crystal Palace easily defeated Portsmouth on their own ground by virtue of cleverer forward play and a strong defence. Hewitt scored twice and Smith once before James replied for the visitors.

Swindon accomplished a great performance in winning at West Ham after being behind at the interval. Leafe, of Sheffield United, made his debut in the West Ham forward line. Swindon scored first through Wheatcroft, but Leafe scored twice for his side, and it was not until Fleming was brought down illegally early in the second half that Swindon drew level, Tout converting the penalty kick.

After Fleming, who played a great game all through, had put Swindon ahead, Hilsdon missed a penalty.

Much was expected of Millwall at Reading, but although they showed plenty of dash they were beaten by 3 goals to 1. Davis scored first for Millwall, but goals from Burton and Pinfield gave Reading the lead, and after the interval Foster scored a third.

Plymouth Argyle have started the season in fine style. Following upon their win at Portsmouth in the week, they beat Cardiff City at home by 2 goals to 1. Here, again, the losers were the first to score, through Harvey, but Bower and Kirkpatrick put the Argyle in front before the interval. Although there was no scoring in the second half both teams played bright football, with the Argyle slightly superior.

PROMOTED CLUB'S SUCCESS.

Southend, one of the teams to gain promotion last year, started the season in great style by winning at Watford. Wileman scored for Southend before the interval from a penalty, and after Ashbridge had equalised Wilson shot the winning goal. With a little more finish in the forward line Watford would probably have won.

A great improvement will have to be shown by Queen's Park Rangers if they wish to regain the Southern League championship they lost to Plymouth last season. After being beaten at Swindon they went down before the moderate Gillingham side on Saturday by a goal, scored by Gilligan. The Rangers forwards were very weak and their efforts disjointed.

Southampton defeated Exeter City at the Dell, but although they were the better team the margin of two goals in their favour did not represent the play. Exeter had the better of the exchanges in the first half, but after the interval Small gave the Saints the lead with a long shot and Smith added a second.

In a poor game at Coventry the home team defeated Brighton by 2 goals to 1. The game right through was dull and scrappy, and the chief feature was the goalkeeping of Whiting, for Brighton. Parkes and Davison scored for Coventry and Simpson for the Albion.

Norwich followed up their good display against Watford during the week by some good football against Northampton at Norwich. Wolstenholme and King scored for their respective sides, and only the splendid defence of Northampton kept the home forwards out and the game ended in a draw.

Bristol Rovers lost at Merthyr by a goal to nothing in a game which was chiefly noticeable for the soundness of the defence on either side. McKie scored the only goal five minutes after change of ends.

SOUTHERN LEAGUE JUNIORS.

Stoke opened their season in the Second Division of the Southern League with a drawn game against Croydon Common at Stoke.

Stoke had Arvill at outside left and Croydon fielded full side. In the first half Stoke were more aggressive, and after twenty-five minutes Pentland scored. In the second half Croydon had the better of matters and Hutchens equalised from a penalty.

Barry won their first match as members of the Second Division against Mid-Rhondda by 2 goals to 1 at home, and fully deserved the points. Sherwood scored twice for Barry and Mason for the visitors.

Aberdare were easily beaten at Llanelly by 3 goals to nil. The play was exciting all through, and during the first half Osborne scored. The second half was all in favour of Llanelly, who bombarded the visitors' goal.

Swansea defeated another new side, Caerphilly, by 2 goals to 0. Mardy won by a similar margin against Treharris and Pontypridd lost to Newport by 3 goals to 1.

THE WORLD OF SPORT.

Abe Mitchell, the famous artisan golfer, who has announced his intention of becoming a professional, will make his debut in that capacity at the opening of the new St. George's Hill Golf Club, Weybridge, on October 2.

At the Blackfriars Ring, on Saturday night, Willie Farrell (Southwark) beat Petty-Officer Roche (Deptford) on points in a fifteen rounds boxing contest. Sid Smith and Arthur Ireland meet in a twenty rounds contest at the Ring this evening.

The English v. Scots bowling match of the English Bowling Association was successfully held on Saturday on the Forest Hill and Brownswood Clubs' greens. The Scots won each section of the match, being 120 to 118 at Forest Hill, and 126 to 103 at Brownswood. They thus hold the Earl of Rosebery's cup for twelve months.

Mr. A. Vicker's Izme won the Royal Motor-Yacht Club's second eliminating trial in Southampton Water on Saturday, and was selected as the third boat for the British team. Izme covered the 30 1-3 sea miles in 4h. 4m. 33s. The American challenger Ankle Deep has arrived at Southampton, and Disturber III. is expected to-day, together with the two French boats.

Playing on the links of the Royal North Devon Club at Westward Ho on Saturday, in the Kashmir Cup competition, which is open to all members of amateur clubs, H. H. Hilton, besides winning the event, was responsible for a record round of the course. His score was 74 plus 86, equals 160, the 74 being two strokes better than the previous record for the course.

SATURDAY'S FOOTBALL RESULTS IN BRIEF.

THE LEAGUE.—Division I.

Newcastle	2	Sunderland (h)	1
M'chester C. (h)	1	Middlesbrough	1
Bolton W. (h)	6	Oldham A.	2
Tottenham H.	3	Chelsea (h)	1
Bradford C. (h)	0	Aston Villa	0
W. B. Albion (h)	4	Burnley	1
Everton (h)	2	Preston	0
Sheffield U.	5	Derby Co. (h)	3
Blackburn R. (h)	6	Liverpool	2
Manchester U.	3	Sheffield W. (h)	1

THE LEAGUE.—Division II.

Wolv. Wan.	3	Notts Forest (h)	1
Lincoln C. (h)	2	Barnsley	2
Blackpool (h)	2	Hull City	2
Clapton O. (h)	1	Fulham	0
Huddersfield (h)	1	Bury	1
Woolwich A. (h)	2	Leicester Fosse	1
Leeds City (h)	3	Glossop	0
Bradford	2	Birmingham (h)	1
Grimsby (h)	0	Notts County	0
Bristol City (h)	5	Stockport	0

SOUTHERN LEAGUE.

Swindon	3	West Ham (h)	2
Gillingham (h)	1	Q. P. Rangers	0
Crystal Pal. (h)	3	Portsmouth	1
Norwich C. (h)	1	Northampton	1
Southend	2	Watford (h)	1
Plymouth (h)	2	Cardiff City	1
Coventry (h)	2	Brighton	1
Reading (h)	3	Millwall	1
Southa'pton (h)	2	Exeter City	0
Merthyr T. (h)	1	Bristol R'v's	0

SOUTHERN LEAGUE.—Division II.: Llanelly (h) 3, Aberdare 0; Newport (h) 2, Pontypridd 1; Stoke (h) 1, Croydon Common 1; Swansea 2, Caerphilly (h) 0; Barry (h) 2, Mid-Rhondda 1; Mardy (h) 4, Treharris 0.

SCOTTISH LEAGUE.—Rangers (h) 5, Aberdeen 1; Airdrieonians (h) 0, Partick 0; Celtic 2, Hibernians (h) 1; Raith Rovers 1, Clyde (h) 0; Dundee 1, Motherwell (h) 0; Falkirk (h) 0, Heart of Midlothian 0; Morton (h) 4, Hamilton 2; Queen's Park (h) 3, Kilmarnock 1; Third Lanark 2; St. Mirren (h) 1.

ATHENIAN LEAGUE.—Barnet and Alston (h) 1, Tufnell Park 1; Luton Clarence (h) 4, Grays Athletic 0; Rest of League 4, Catford Southend (champions) 2.

ISTHMIAN LEAGUE.—Ilford (h) 2, Nunhead 2; London Caledonians 1, Shepherd's Bush (h) 0.

SOUTH-EASTERN LEAGUE.—Tottenham R. (h) 3, Chelsea R. 0; Woolwich R. 4, Brighton R. (h) 2; Peterborough (h) 2, Bristol City R. 1; Leicester Fosse R. (h) 1, Reading R. 1; Portsmouth R. (h) 2, Southampton R. 0; West Ham R. 3, Swindon R. (h) 0; Brentford R. 3, Croydon Common R. (h) 1; Norwich R. 2, Northampton R. (h) 0; Fulham R. (h) 2, Clapton O. R. 1; Q.P. Rangers R. (h) 4, Gillingham 0.

SOUTHERN ALLIANCE.—Luton 3, Brentford (h) 2.

SOUTH ESSEX LEAGUE.—Leyton (h) 2, Colchester 1; Custom House 1, Romford (h) 0, Shoeburyness Garrison (h) 2, Barking 2.

KENT LEAGUE.—Division I.: Crystal Palace R. 5, Sittingbourne (h) 1; Gravesend 2, Woolwich A (h) 0; Royal Naval Depot (h) 1, Chatham 1; Northfleet United (h) 2, Tunbridge Wells Rangers 1; Millwall R. (h) 6, Maidstone 1; Bromley 5, Rochester (h) 1; Southend R. (h) 4, Sheppey United 2. Division II.: Depot Royal Marines (h) 3, Ashford Railway Works 0, Depot Royal West Kent Regiment 4, Cray Wanderers (h) 0.

OTHER MATCHES.—Metrogas (h) 9, West Norwood 4; Leytonstone (h) 2, Clapton 1; Page Green O.B. (h) 7, Ilford 0; Hampstead Town (h) 5, East Ham 1; Croydon 4, Chelmsford (h) 2; Cardiff Corinthians 2, Swansea Town (h) 1.

RUGBY RULES.

CLUB MATCHES.—Leicester (h) 17, Bedford 3; Gloucester (h) 7, Bream 3; Swansea (h) 17, Swansea League 3.

ARSENAL SCORE THEIR GREATEST CUP VICTORY

Aston Villa Beaten by 2 to 0 at Highbury

SUNDERLAND OUT

Three London Clubs Now in the Last Eight

The Arsenal gained their greatest Cup victory in the replayed tie with Aston Villa at Highbury yesterday, when they beat the famous Birmingham side by 2 goals to 0. Sunderland, another of the favourites, made their farewell appearance at Manchester, where the United beat them by 2 to 1 Other features were:—

Football.—Bury beat West Bromwich Albion in a League game by 2 to 0.

Racing.—Master Billie, a stable companion to Silvo, engaged in the Grand National, won the Newbury Chase.

The Coldstream Guards retained the Army rackets doubles championship at Princes Club.

HOW VILLA FELL

Not Up to Form in Cup Replay with Arsenal

Aston Villa failed to live up to their reputation at Highbury yesterday, and Arsenal had a comparatively easy task in qualifying to meet Swansea in the sixth round.

The Londoners won by two clear goals. The first, which followed an exciting opening, was obtained within three minutes of the start. Yet even so, both goals had been seriously imperilled before that, Aston Villa's twice.

J Brain.

Arsenal in the first minute forced a corner, and Spiers twice had to clear. Then play quickly went to the other end, where a slight delay on Kirton's part before shooting lost a great opportunity.

The ball was swung to Lawson. Moss, who endeavoured to challenge his progress, slipped and fell Lawson tricked Mort and put the ball square across the goal and Dr. Paterson cut across, took it on the run and scored easily.

In the seventeenth minute of the game Buchan shot hard near the post Spiers dived and partly saved; but before he could get it away Brain flicked the ball out of the goalkeeper's hand and walked it into the net.

That ended the scoring but not the excitement. Arsenal's half backs, and Blyth in particular, were in great form, and prevented the Villa forwards from settling down.

In spite of this Arsenal hardly deserved to be two goals up at the interval. The Villa played clever football up to a point, but near goal showed none of their usual incisiveness.

HARPER'S DIVE

To be frank, they shot badly, and it was not until the second half was well advanced that one saw anything of Capewell. In the second half he drove in a couple of beautiful shots in quick succession, from one of which Harper made a great dive to effect a sensational save.

York was the Villa's best forward. He was always threatening, and Kirton supported him well, but there was something of a wrangle between Buchan and Walker in which neither player showed up really well.

Arsenal's defence was fine throughout, in spite of an uncertainty about Mackie at one stage of the game Brain, for the most part, was able to outmanœvre Dr Milne, and Lawson, young though he is, was a shining example to some of his older colleagues.

So great was the crowd that the gates were closed when 55,400 people had paid £4,020 for admission, but nearly half as many again were left struggling in vain to enter the ground.

Had the accommodation at Chelsea or Tottenham been super-imposed on the Arsenal ground it would scarcely have accommodated all who wanted to see the game. G. P S.

BRADFORD CITY'S LOSS

The Wednesday Succeed in Securing Transfer of Tom Walker

After prolonged negotiations The Wednesday and Bradford City have come to terms for the transfer of Tom Walker, the Bradford City back.

Walker came from a Scottish junior club to Bradford City in 1924.

FOOTBALL IN BRIEF

SCOTTISH CUP.—**Replay**—St. Johnstone 0 Aberdeen 0 (after extra time).

SCOTTISH LEAGUE.—Dundee United 2, Hearts 3; Morton 5, Hamilton Acads. 2, Airdrieonians [illegible], Raith Rovers 0; Falkirk 1, Glasgow Rangers 1.

DIVISION III. (N.).—Chesterfield 4, Wigan Borough 0.

ASSOCIATION MATCHES.—Essex 7, Suffolk 1. Hants County 10, Royal Navy (Portsmouth) 0.

RUGBY UNION.—Cambridge University 1[illegible] pts., Royal Navy 12 Civil Service 14, Army 9.

C Rennox, Manchester United's inside left, who played a fine game against Sunderland in the Cup replay

Kid Berg, who will meet Andre Routis in the big boxing tournament at Albert Hall on March 18.

MANCHESTER'S WIN

United Forwards in Brilliant Form Against Sunderland

Sterling work by the United forwards in the first half won them the game against Sunderland at Manchester.

At the very outset McInroy was called upon to clear a shot by Spence, and the latter gave McPherson a good chance, which the centre missed.

Rennox was also prominent with a great drive that struck the bar before McPherson opened the score after eight minutes

Almost immediately McInroy was called upon to stop a fine shot by Smith, who eventually put the United two up ten minutes from the interval.

Sunderland did much better in the second half and brilliant footwork by Kelly led to a beautiful goal by Halliday.

This success came within seven minutes of the restart. Ten minutes later Sunderland again found the Manchester goal with a shot from Prior, but an appeal by the United for handling by Halliday was successful.

Halliday and Kelly gave Mew a very hot time afterwards, but the United custodian proved a very sound defender

The attendance was 58,661 and the receipts £4,823.

SIXTH-ROUND DRAW

The last eight for the English Cup are now paired as follows:—

Clapton Orient v. Manchester City.
Nottingham Forest v. Bolton Wanderers.
Swansea v. Arsenal.
Fulham v. Manchester United.

Matches to be played on the ground of the first-named clubs on March 6.

BILLIARDS CHALLENGE

Smith Replies to Lindrum's £20,000 Offer for Game of 32,000 Up

Smith has replied to the cablegram received yesterday from Walter Lindrum, the Australian professional billiards champion, stating that he is prepared to meet Smith or any other English player in a straight-out game of 32,000 up for £20,000.

The English player states that he is willing to play Lindrum for that sum either on the terms that he (Smith) previously suggested, that is, half the game with ivory balls and half with composition balls, or the whole game with ivory balls.

MORE POINTS FOR BURY

Bullock Gets a Brace in Match with West Bromwich

On their own ground, Bury defeated West Bromwich Albion by two goals to nought. The margin in their favour rather flattered the winners, for West Bromwich Albion had quite a large share of the attacking movements, and were often dangerous.

Bullock put Bury in front after sixteen minutes, after a period of strong pressure by the Albion had failed to produce a goal.

Bury had the best of matters for some little time following change of ends, but the Albion gradually forced them back, and Richardson was called upon to save from Carter and Magee.

Before the close, however, a corner kick was headed in by Bullock for Bury. There were 10,000 spectators.

FIVE MINUTES SHORT

Teams Recalled After "Final" Whistle at Boscombe

After the referee had whistled for time in the Third League match at Boscombe yesterday, and the Brighton team and several of the Boscombe players had returned to the dressing-room, it was found that five minutes short had been played.

The players were sent out again and the full-time completed

The match was a triumph for the Brighton forward, Nightingale, who scored all three goals for the visitors. Boscombe failed to find the net.

CANTABS' FINE WORK

Large Crowd Witness Satisfactory Trial at Henley

Cambridge continue to show improved form. They had two outings at Henley yesterday.

A large crowd watched the crew during the afternoon. Starting to row from Henley Bridge the Light Blues reached Hambledon Lock, a distance of two and a half miles, in 11m. 17s. It was a satisfactory trial.

Oxford had their last row on the home waters yesterday. They had a straightaway pull for about three and a half miles. The boats will be sent to Bourne End this morning.

OXFORD'S GOLF DEFEAT

Fine Play by Geoffrey MacCallum for Sonning Side

A weak Oxford golf team was badly beaten at Sonning yesterday the Sonning club winning on singles and foursomes by eleven matches to two.

A feature of the match was the excellent play of Geoffrey MacCallum, who led the Sonning side. He is one of the nominated players in connection with the Walker Cup match, and in the top singles match beat J H Taylor, jun., by the big margin of 7 and 5. MacCallum's score for the thirteen holes equalled one over fours.

Geoffrey MacCallum played with his brother, W MacCallum, in the first foursomes, and they beat J A. Mackintosh and C F Penruddock by 3 and 1.

ARMY RACKETS FINAL WINNERS

The Coldstream Guards (Lieutenant G. N. Scott-Chad and Lieutenant J R Duckworth-King) retained the Army doubles championship, at Prince's Club, Knightsbridge, yesterday, beating, in the final, the King's Royal Rifle Corps (Lieutenant J. N. Cheney and Lieutenant C. J Wilson).

NEWBURY PROGRAMME AND YESTERDAY'S RACING RETURNS

2.0—READING (S.) 'CHASE, 150 sovs; 2m. 50y.

Irish Cheer	Poole	12	3	Com'der Smith	St'bs	11	10
Prosperitz	E.Piggott	12	0	Flushed	R.Payne	11	10
Cindrally	E.Doyle	11	13	Bachelor's Lady	Wa'd	11	9
Charabanc	F.Morgan	11	9	Craganock	H.Brown	11	6
Grevisk	Woodland	10	13	Vive-la	E.Piggott	11	6
Ringles Cross	Wood'n	10	9	G.R.	H.A.Brown	11	3
Above arrived.				Cashlie	DeWinton	11	3
Hackdaile	Whitelaw	12	7	Belem	Gubbins	11	1
Broken Wand	White'w	12	2	Merry Chap	Laye	10	13
Tim	Stanley	12	2	Ill Fame	H.Brown	10	9
Heathencote	R.Payne	12	1	Valentine Vox	Hulme	10	4
Silken Prince	Martin	11	11	Humming Bee	Read	10	3

2.30—LAMBOURN (S.) HURDLE, 150 sovs; 2m.

3.0—SPRING 'CHASE, 500 sovs; 2m. 50y.

Preface	D.Harrison	12	5	St. Caradoc	Phillips	11	7
Drumhirk	R.Payne	12	3	Blackbeen	Philip	11	7
Golden Ashe	Hastings	12	3	Miss Balscadden	L'say	11	7
Emphatic	Hatt	11	12	Agincourt	F.A.Brown	11	7
Gold Flare	Fergusson	11	7	Longhaul	Whitaker	11	7
The Big Three	Cund'll	11	7	Horse Ma'ne	E.Piggott	11	7
Mountain Blue	H't'gs	10	5	Wandoo	Poole	11	7
East Africa	Powell	10	5	Slieve Rue	Hastings	11	5
Rouleau	Barrett	10	0	H'b't's Choice	F.A.B'n	11	5
Irna	Woodland	10	0	Dromore	Whitaker	11	0
Above arrived.				Witness	Larkin	11	0
Low Tide	Coulthwaite	11	12	Royal Arch II.	W'ker	11	0
British W'rm	Edwards	11	12	Tall Story	Alexander	11	0
Beyrob	Powell	11	12	Fortissimo	W.Payne	11	0
Argo	H.A.Brown	11	12	Paxford	Blair	11	0
Noble Rowland	Bl'tsoe	11	7	Count Spaghetti	W'w	10	5
Zain	Whitaker	11	7	Wild Buck	Powell	10	0

3.30—GREENHAM HURDLE, 400 sovs; 2m.

First Magic	Poole	12	1	Spanish T'rn	MacColl	11	0
Lenglen	Newey	11	11	Firing Line	E.Piggott	10	13
Nane Snugger	East	11	4	**Above arrived.**			
Glen Andred	Cundell	11	4	Halberdier	R.Payne	13	0
Royal Archer	East	11	2	Despote	Poole	12	7
Signet	Poole	11	1	Inverveigh	W.N'ht'gall	12	3
				Carryduff	H.Turner	11	0

4.0—UNITED SERVICES HUNTERS' CHALLENGE CUP, 100 sovs.; 3½m.

Croft House	F.-S'nkey	12	7	Terebene	Pte.	11	0
Stonevale	Bletsoe	11	0	Foxie II.	Bletsoe	11	0
Ulster Vale	Bletsoe	11	0	French Ace	Lindsay	11	0
Above arrived.				Coris	Laye	11	0
Far Flight	H Brown	12	7	The Clipper	Woodl'nd	11	0
Eamon Mor	Bletsoe	12	7	One Star	Lindsay	11	0
Myriad	Turner	12	0	Highball	S.Bennet	11	0
Penguin	Pease	12	0	Meva	Bletsoe	11	0
Jolly Glad	Forwood	12	0	Uppergrange	Pease	11	0
				Lock All	Westm'rland	11	0

4.30—MODERATE HURDLE, 200 sovs; 2m.

The Carpenter	Rayson	12	4	Zarope	Hastings	11	13
Up Garryowen	Ant'y	12	3	Mirathorn	Cramsie	11	12
Windover	MacColl	12	3	Wellwisher	J.Ward	11	10
Canova	Savill	12	2	Kirkloisk	F.Morgan	11	10
Hideaway	Poole	12	2	Lackey	Pte	11	9
Illyrian	Poole	11	12	Sound Asleep	DeWi'n	11	9
Pinnace	Barrett	11	11	Burnt Heather	H.H'n	11	8
Perusia	McDougal	11	10	Wild Almond	Gwilt	11	7
Tiny Town	Hastings	11	8	Wharekoa	A.Escott	11	5
Alfred the Gr't	Allden	11	5	Azimuth	Laye	11	5
Oh! Dick	C.Stevens	10	13	Ballast	T.Leader	11	2
Above arrived.				Any Excuse	Grey	11	2
Nightshift	Bletsoe	12	7	North Ham	Bradford	11	1
Loyal Scot	F.Hartigan	12	7	Maltoi	Powell	10	13
Real Royal	F.Brown	12	5	Samos	W.Nightingall	10	12
Dash o' White	Goby	12	4	Survivor	W.Payne	10	12
Consonant	G.Bennett	12	3	Kroon Belle	Willmot	10	11
Knock Brack	Tho'son	12	1	St. Cormac	Whitaker	10	11
Jamnagar	Martin	12	0	Blue Paper	J.Scott	10	9
Verneuil II.	Newey	11	13	Llangeria	Blair	10	9

NEWBURY RETURNS

2.0.—BERKSHIRE (S.) HURDLE. 2m.—ALFRED THE GREAT (7-2, T. Morgan), 1; LANDMAN (10-1), 2; GREEN WHEAT (7-1), 3. Also ran: Kissing Song (7-2), Yarnton (9-2) Stargazer, Royal Heron, Tregenwell, Polisson, Optimus and Ligan (10-1) Six; bad. (Allden.)

2.30.—SWINDON (S.) CHASE. 2m. 50yds.—TIME ENOUGH (5-2, Mr. F. Usher), 1; BOOMERANG (5-4), 2; LONG TUNE (100-7), 3. Also ran. Broadway (7-1), The Heir (8-1), Educated Evans, Square Dance, Cross Paddy and Leap Year (100-7). Eight bad. (Smyth.)

3.0.—FEBRUARY HURDLE. 2m.—HIDENNIS (2-5, T. Leader), 1; BLACK SHEEP (8-1), 2; STARDUST (100-8), 3. Also ran: Solitary (100-8), Mizzen Mast (100-7), Donegal, Royal Defence, Goldbound, Mat McGlue and Set Fast (20-1). Ten. two. (H. Leader.)

3.30.—NEWBURY 'CHASE. 3m. — MASTER BILLIE (9-2, E. Foster), 1, TOP LIGHT (2-1), 2; SPRIG (7-1), 3. Also ran. Postino (9-2), Cash Box and Turkey Buzzard (10-1), Vive, Manser's Pride and Pencoed (100-7). Four: three. (Whitaker.)

4.0.—AMATEURS' HURDLE. 2m. — TRUTHFUL JAMES (9-2, Mr. R. Bennett), 1, GREENHORN (2-1), 2; NOCTIFER (9-2), 3. Also ran: Phantom Willie (6-1), Waterford Glass II. (10-1), Trusty, Swift Rowland, Newtown Park, Reading, White Heat and Tons of Money (100-7) Three: four. (Powell.)

4.30.—WEYHILL 'CHASE. 2m. 50yds.—HYMIR (3-1, J. Hogan), 1. COLESTOWN (10-1), 2; TEST MATCH (4-1), 3. Also ran. Charlie Wise (4-1), Gris De Lin (7-1), Holdcroft, Mitchells, Tully, Guidance and Rocking Horse (10-1). Four one. (C Piggott.)

"SUNDAY PICTORIAL" NAP

ESPSCZBSCF.

NEWBURY WIN FOR MASTER BILLIE

Hidennis Gives Black Sheep a Lesson in Hurdling

HINTS FOR TO-DAY

By BOUVERIE

Racing at Newbury yesterday was on a much higher plane than anything we have seen in the south for some time, and that in spite of the fact that Old Tay Bridge did not put in an appearance for the chief 'chase.

Top Light, as generally anticipated, started a good favourite, and the fact that he was beaten by Silvo's stable companion, Master Billie, opens up nice possibilities for Aintree.

Even before Silvo went under a cloud there were whispers that Captain Whitaker had a very useful second string to his bow and judging by yesterday's display, rumour was right—for once.

NEWBURY SELECTIONS

2. 0.—SILKEN PRINCE.
2.30.—CLARKIA, if ab. ANNAM.
3. 0.—PREFACE.
3.30.—FIRING LINE.
4. 0.—FAR FLIGHT.
4.30.—ILLYRIAN.

DOUBLE EVENT FOR TO-DAY
SILKEN PRINCE and FIRING LINE.*

Master Billie was meeting Sprig on exactly the same terms as they will be opposed at Liverpool, and the chief question between the pair is will yesterday's winner stay so well as the Newmarket horse?

Sprig was always among the leaders on this occasion, his jumping as usual left nothing to be desired and there will be few sounder horses facing the tapes on National day.

M. Tighe.

Black Sheep made his first appearance in the February Hurdle and got a nice lesson on how hurdle races are won from Hidennis.

Set Fast put up a good show until weakening two hurdles out. Tighe on Black Sheep made a clever recovery when his mount stumbled on landing over the last hurdle, but Hidennis had gone clear away to win by ten lengths.

Preface appears well placed for another victory in the Spring 'Chase this afternoon, albeit I hear that Slieve Rue is expected to give a very good account of himself.

Firing Line—a winner over the course—ran well enough at Hurst Park last week to justify following in the Greenham Hurdle, and Illyrian looks very nicely treated in the Moderate Hurdle.

ALBERT HALL'S BIG NIGHT

Kid Berg and Young Johnny Brown in Bouts on March 18

Will Frank Goddard or Phil Scott win the heavy-weight championship of Great Britain?

That is the chief topic in boxing circles just now, and the answer will be forthcoming at the Albert Hall on Thursday, March 18.

There are other excellent items in the programme. Teddy Baldock, the undefeated fly-weight, is hoping to gain further honours against A. O. Barber.

Kid Berg, of Stepney, who was defeated by Harry Corbett a fortnight ago, opposes Andre Routis over fifteen rounds, and Young Johnny Brown and Antoine Merlo are another pair that should put up a thrilling battle.

Exclusive pictures of these contests will appear in *The Daily Mirror* and in no other daily picture paper.

OTHER SPORT IN BRIEF

Interesting Items on Men and Matters of the Moment

Middlesex Golf Championship.—The Middlesex Club championship was won at Northwood yesterday by Fulwell.

Billiards.—Davis 9,001, Smith 5,656; Carpenter 6,129, Inman 4,000. Amateur championship Stroud 1,000, F. H. Cooke 750.

Jockey Fined.—V Piggott was fined £10 at Newbury yesterday for failing to weigh in after finishing third on Broadway in the Swindon Steeplechase.

Irish Rugby Change.—J. H. Gage (Queen's) will take the place of F. Hewitt (Instonians) in the Irish Rugby team to meet Scotland, it was announced last night.

Yesterday's Hockey.—Tulse Hill 1, Cambridge University 0; Royal Air Force 3, Middlesex 4; Bucks 3, Herts 2. Bedford 2, Oxford 2; R.M.C. (Sandhurst) 1. The Army 4

Roller-Skating Title.—The one mile British amateur roller-skating championship was won at Kingston Rink (Surrey), last night by R. A. Symondson (Cricklewood) in 5m. 2s.

To-night's Boxing.—At the Ring Alf Simmons (Hackney) and Rene Kelly (France) meet over fifteen rounds. At Premierland Harry Leach (Doncaster) and Kid Lewis (Manchester) meet in a return contest over fifteen rounds.

Last Night's Boxing.—Harry Corbett (Bethnal Green) beat Mick Hill (Tooting) on points over fifteen rounds at Hoxton Baths. Billy Bird (Chelsea) defeated Battling Van Damm (Holland) at Fulham Baths, the referee stopping the contest in the second round.

Scottish Cup Draw.—The draw for the fourth round of the Scottish Cup yesterday resulted: Morton v. Rangers, St. Mirren v. Airdrieonians, Third Lanark v. Aberdeen or St. Johnstone, Celtic v. Dumbarton. To be played on March 6. Kick-off 3.30, replays 3.15.

To-day's Football.—Swansea v. Blackpool (Division II.). Charlton v. Watford, Queen's Park Rangers v Aberdare, Newport County v. Millwall (Division III. S.). Grimsby v. Barrow (Division III., N.). Clapton Orient v. Oxford University (Hospital Fund match). Arsenal v. Cambridge University, West Ham v. R.A.F. (Association matches). Notts County v. New Brighton (Midland Combination) Fulham v. Palace (London Combination).

Ferdy v. Peter: See page 13

The Daily Mirror

THE DAILY PICTURE PAPER WITH THE LARGEST NET SALE

ARSENAL'S GREAT WIN IN CUP REPLAY—THOUSANDS LOCKED OUT OF GROUND

Brain, the Arsenal centre forward, about to shoot his side's second goal fifteen minutes after the start.

Spiers fails to stop the fast shot from Dr Paterson that scored the first goal for Arsenal

Spiers punches away, though closely beset by Arsenal forwards.

Harper the Arsenal goalkeeper gets clear

Some of the crowd of 20,000 who were unable to gain admittance.

Police rescuing a woman spectator from the crush.

The Arsenal yesterday gained the greatest Cup triumph in their history when, in the replayed tie on their own ground at Highbury, they beat Aston Villa by two goals to nil. | A crowd of 55,400 watched the game and nearly half as many would-be spectators were unable to gain admittance.—(Daily Mirror photographs.)

Printed and Published by THE DAILY MIRROR NEWSPAPERS, LTD., at 23-29, Bouverie-street, London, E.C.4.—Thursday, February 25, 1926.   Telephone Central 3440.

WINNERS OF EMPIRE HAMPERS

Consolation Prizes of Empire Hampers have been awarded to the following 15 Competitors in our "Book Titles" Picture Puzzle, whose efforts proved to be next best to those of the winners:—

Allen, Mr. John, 4, Newton-av., Longsight, Manchester; Atkins, Mrs J. E., 22, Park-av. North, Hornsey; August, O., Crown Hotel, Scarborough; Yorkshire; Avery, A. M., Rosemary, Waghorn-rd., Snodland; Aylott, Mrs., 32, Bank-st., Braintree.

Bailey, F., 42, Station-rd., Wealdstone; Ball, Mrs. L., 72, St. John's-lane, Totterdown, Bristol; Barker, Mr. W., 2, Spring-terr., Waterloo-st., Hull; Barrow, C. H, Mollaine, Monger-rd., Clacton-on-Sea; Bealey, B. C., 33, Paris-st., Exeter; Bentley, Miss F., 81, Featherstall-rd., North Oldham; Benton, Mrs. M., 17, Powis-terr., Aberdeen; Blanchard, C., Saxilby, Lincoln; Blunden, Mr J., 51, Pond-rd., West Ham; Boddy, Mr. G. F., The Anchor, Lavender-st., Brighton; Bonaker, Mrs., 19, Corinne-rd., Tufnell Park; Boulton, Mrs. M. 2, Earl-st., New Ferry, Cheshire; Branson, Miss, 160, Otley-rd. Leeds; Briggs, Mrs. M 5, Palatine-av., Lancaster; Bromfield, Miss K., 2, Hunton-cottages Common-rd., Stanmore; Buckley, Mrs. M. E., 5, Whitehouse-lane, Sheffield; Burge, G., Ivanhoe, Sandbanks-rd, Parkstone.

Campbell, Mrs. A., 12, The Crays, Forest, Melksham; Campbell, Adam V., 7, Normanton-st., Brighton; Cartwright, J. C., 60, Knightsbridge; Challoner, W., 36, Sandy-lane, Lymm. Christie, J., 10, Harringford-rd., Aigburth, Liverpool; Christopher, S., 29, High-st., Strood; Clapham, Mr. R., 52, Avondale-rd., Lancaster; Clark, E. L., Lenaways, Ospringe, Faversham; Codman, Mr. E., Wighton S.O. Norfolk; Crittenden, S., 44, Grecian-st., Maidstone; Cubby, Miss E., 175, New England, Peterborough.

Darke, F. I., 23, Hagley-st., Halesowen, Birmingham; Davies, Mr. K. I., 18, Kings-ter., Nantyffyllon, Dove, John, 40, King's-rd., Brentwood; Downing, Mr. C. F., 1, Chesney-st., Battersea; Dunn, Jesse, 8, The Crescent, Blackheath, Birmingham; Ellis, H. H., 177, Harvist-rd., Kensal Rise; English, Louisa, 43, Dale-st., Ossett; Finney, R., sen., 28, York-ave., Egerton-rd., Whalley Range, Manchester; Gilbert, Mrs. C., 22, Hemdean-rd., Caversham, Reading; Goldsmith, Bert, Shadoxhurst, Ashford; Goodson, Mrs., 23, Cromwell-rd., Melton Mowbray; Grierson, James, 8, Allars crescent, Hawick; Groves, James, West-st., Harrietsham; Guscott, Mrs., 15, Glendower-rd, Peverell, Plymouth.

Hall, George, 23, Elton-st., Stretford, Manchester; Hansen, G., 20, Hack-rd., Tidal Basin; Harper, Robert, 6, Church-st., Harwich; Hart, Albert, Council Cottage, Margaretting; Haughton, R., 23, Daleview, Ballybrack, Co. Dublin; Headland, Mr. G., Halford-st., Thrapston, Kettering; Henderson, Mrs. E., 23, Gairloch-rd., Camberwell; Hindmarch, D., 65, Ruby-st., Saltburn-by-Sea; Hitchcock, Mr. H. J., 5, Tuckers-row, Mile End, Swansea; Holmes, J., 25, Industry-rd., Darnall, Sheffield; Holway, Mr. A. E., 7, St. James's-pl., Mangotsfield, Hughes, Mr. C., Torksey, Lincoln; Humphreys, J., 10, Princess-st., Nelson; Huxtable, F. W., "Carey," Cory-st., Sketty, Swansea; Jakeman Mrs., 12, Woodhead-rd., Holmbridge, Yorks.

James, A. E., 27, Stanley-rd., Carshalton; Jenkins, Mrs., 70, Weymouth-ter., Hackney-rd. Jennings, A. E., 70, Ackroyd-st., Morley; Jones, Mrs. R. V., 21, Bonvilston-rd., Pontypridd; Jones, W. D., 46, Parcmaen-st., Carmarthen; Kalabza, W., 5, Culver-rd., St. Albans; Kennett, M., 49, St. James's-st., Doncaster; Kieboonis, J., 66, Wimbledon Park-rd., Southfields; Kimble, Mrs. M., St. Paul's-rd., Chichester; King, C. A., 134, Rushley Mead, Letchworth; Kirk, J. H., 1, Piercefield-st., Kentish Town.

Langley, A., 20, Petley-rd., Hammersmith; Lawrence, Hugh, Elmdale, Lowestoft; Lawrence, Mr. S. G., 28, Pitt-cres., Durnsford-rd., Wimbledon; Leaney, W., 65, Penberth-rd., Catford; Leask, L., 5a, Bluecoat-st., Nottingham; Linford, Mrs. I. E., Poplar Farm, Scarning, East Dereham; Liptrott, L., 3, Radford-rd. Nottingham; Lowman, A. H., Post Office, Lt. Glemham; Lucas, Mrs. L., 32, Woodchurch-rd., Birkenhead; Lynham, J. L., 8, Nador-st., Bradford-rd., Manchester.

Maitland, E., 9, Thornlea-gdns., Low Fell, Gateshead; Martin, S., 14, Hainault-rd., Leytonstone; Masterton, Lewis Hawthorn-pl., Upnall; Metcalf, Fred S., 20, Farlington-rd., North End Portsmouth; Minter, W. G., Ickham, Canterbury; Mitchell, Miss F., 61, Primrose-rd Norwich; Moody, G. H., 8, Manor-drive, Halifax; Moody, Mrs. R., 25, Bell-rd., East Molesey; Morris, A. B., 3, Rigby-rd., Southampton; McCarron, Mrs., 61, McDuff-st., New Bank, Glasgow; Mustad, Mr. S., 431, Wellington-st., Grimsby.

Neale, Mrs. T., 31, Islip-road, Sunnymead Oxford; Newman, Mr. D., Handcross, Sussex; Newman, H. K., Rosemount, South Benfleet; Neakes, Miss E., 119, Queen's-rd., Buckhurst Hill; Nunn, Mr. B., 4, The Green, Feltham; Oakes, D. M., 13, The Broadway, Worthing; Owen, Mrs., 39, Westgate-end, Wakefield; Parr, Percy, 15, Essex-st., Old Trafford, Manchester; Patten, W. H., 71, Sand-st., Woolwich; Petherbridge, W., Bucker Lea, Pantbach-rd., Whitchurch; Pollard, D., 92, Parrin-lane, Monton, Manchester; Pulling, F. A. 29, Ruskin-rd, Hove; Pyle Mrs. T., Park House, Homefield-rd., Worthing.

Ramsay, W. J., 18, Leamore-st., King-st., Hammersmith; Rance, Mrs. R., 18, Prebend st., Bedford; Richards, W. J., 64, Elgin-cres., London, W.11; Robinson, Winnie, 66, Lordship-rd., Stoke Newington; Rodgers, Mrs., 28, Holmfield-rd., Blackpool; Rowles, Mrs. W. H., 62, High-st., Pontardawe; Russell, G. H., 4, Salisbury-st., Chester; Ryan, Miss M., Cavendish Hotel, Eastbourne.

Sangster, C., 38, Orchard-place, Blackwall; Sear, Mrs., 68, Haslemere-rd., Thornton Heath; Sell, Robert, 33, Coleys-lane, Northfield, Birmingham; Shortt, D., 25, Marguerite-rd., Dublin; Shone, B., 63, Albert-rd., Oswestry; Simm, William, 23, Spring-gardens, Farington, Lancs.; Souter, Gwen, 19, Stour-st., Canterbury; Southon, Mr. D., 24, East-st., Farnham; Stewart, H. A., 160, Coombe-rd, Brighton; Stimpson, T. W., 18, Lawson-st., North Shields; Sweetman, W., 6, Alexandra-ter., Barnsley-st., Hull; Smith, Mrs. E. I., 33, Audley-gardens, Seven Kings.

Taylor, B., 17, Wellwinch-rd., Milton Regis; Taylor, E. A., 15, Patteson-rd., Aylsham-rd., Norwich; Terry, A., 27, Pontygwindy-rd. Caerphilly; Thomas, L., 6, Union-st., Aberystwyth; Thomas, Rosa C., Bank House, Uckfield; Trahan, Frank, Fir Tree, Harperley Station; Vaughan, T. A., 31, Grosvenor-rd., Forest Gate.

Wallwork, M., Queen's Hotel, Llanfairfechan; Watts, M. F., 19, Fordmill-rd., Catford; Westgate, C. A., Hempstead-lane, Hailsham; Williams, Mrs. A., Awelfryn, Latimer-rd., Llandilo; Williams, F., 290, Midland-rd., Royston, Yorks; Williams, E. T., Assheton House, Caernarvon; Wilson, Mrs. F., 7, Scudamore-lane, Kingsbury; Wilson, F., 5, Marylebone-st., London, W.1; Wilson, G. E., 37, Aylesbury-st., Bletchley; Winter, Mrs., 17, Primrose-pl., near Godalming; Wisker, H., 71, Church-path, Acton Green, Chiswick; Woodhouse, T., 31, Dale-st., Leamington Spa; Woods, Mr. S., 22, Ophir-gardens, Chichester Park, Belfast; Worsnop, John, 23, New Works-rd., Low Moor, Bradford, Wright, Harry, 29, Bertha-st., The Broom, Ferryhill, Durham; Yeo, George, 11, Burn-view, Bude.

CLUBS THAT HAVE MADE SOCCER

Arsenal's Pioneer Work in the South—Memories of Players Who Have Made the Gunners Famous

By P. J. MOSS

Is this to be the Arsenal's year for the Cup? If it is to come to London it would be fitting for the oldest of London's professional clubs to capture it. Their victory over Birmingham during last week certainly leaves the road more or less open.

I remember the Royal Arsenal playing a match on Tottenham Marshes, I think, against the Spurs, in the early eighties, when the majority of their team turned up in uniform, but it was not until 1886 that the club was really instituted.

Mr. F. Beardsley, who came from Nottingham to work in the Arsenal workshops, was a prime mover, and Mr. John Humble, for some forty years a committeeman and director, and Mr. A. Brown, were others who started and kept the club going in its earliest days.

Beardsley was the team's first goalkeeper; Danskin, a footballing Scot from Kirkcaldy, was a back; Peter Connolly, another Kirkcaldy man; Julian, a Lincolnshire boy; and two Crichton brothers, I think from Wolverhampton, were other early players.

The club had many troubles, particularly with regard to their ground. The Invicta ground was practically ruled out of the question by the landlord's demands, and in 1888-89 the club moved to the Manor Field. In 1890 the club were back at the Invicta ground, and then in 1893 the Manor Field was bought, and there the Arsenal remained until the club moved to Highbury in 1913.

The first momentous happening of the club came in 1892, when Mr. Humble, then chairman, moved that they embrace professionalism.

Before that the Arsenal had won many amateur trophies, including the London Senior Cup, and it is on record that in 1890-1 Derby County beat them in the first round proper of the English Cup by 1 goal to 0. Mr Gunning, the hon. secretary of the L.F.A., was referee, and the goal was hotly protested against at the time.

SOUTHERN OUTCASTS

After professionalism was adopted the Arsenal were the outcasts of the South. They could get few fixtures with their old opponents, and matches had to be arranged with Northern and Midland clubs. But happier days were in store, and in 1893-4 they were admitted to membership of the Second League, and all was plain sailing.

Generally holding a position somewhere in the middle of the League table, the Arsenal strove hard for ten years to bring First Division football to London, but it was not until 1903-4 that they won promotion by finishing second to Preston.

The Arsenal maintained their position in the premier division until 1912-13, and were re-elected after the war when the League was increased from twenty to twenty-two clubs. That was a sore point with my friends at Tottenham.

Mr. John Humble, Mr. W. H. Leavey, Sir Harry Norris, and in the last few years Sir Samuel Hill-Wood have worked hard to keep the Arsenal in the first flight of the League. The cause celebre in which Sir Harry and the F.A. were concerned was an unfortunate business in all respects, and the less said about it the better.

Noteworthy men in the managerial side of football have held office at Woolwich and Highbury. The first I can remember was the late Harry Bradshaw, afterwards secretary of the Southern League.

He was followed by Phil Kelso, one of the best judges of a player I have ever met, who subsequently piloted the Fulham club for many years.

GREAT GOALKEEPERS

Leslie Knighton, now manager at Birmingham, had a turn, and he was followed by Herbert Chapman, the present chief who hopes this season to follow up his triumphs with Huddersfield by seeing the Arsenal land the English Cup.

So much for the bare outline of the club. My recollections of players are very pleasing. In their time the Arsenal have numbered some fine players in their ranks, but few have done them better service than Jimmy Ashcroft, a great goalkeeper, who subsequently went to Blackburn.

In 1906 Ashcroft played in all three internationals for England. He kept a clean sheet against Wales and Ireland, but the Scots put two past him and won 2—1 at Hampden. Ashcroft was a Kentish product and joined the Arsenal from Sheppey.

Another international goalkeeper who played for the Arsenal was W. Harper, who came south from the Hibs. He had a string of eleven caps for Scotland and finished up after the 1926 season with a dispute with the club and went to America.

At the moment the Arsenal are well served by David Lewis, a Welshman who had a brief spell with the Orient before joining the Arsenal. J. Preedy is his understudy.

Leigh Richmond Roose was another Welsh international goalkeeper who played for the Arsenal. He had no fewer than twenty-four caps for Wales.

Roose was one of the most brilliant, if the most unorthodox, keepers the game has known, but was more closely identified with Sunderland and Everton than the Arsenal.

A. Lievesley, the famous Sheffield United goalkeeper, had a spell with the Arsenal, and others whom I remember are E. Bateup and J. H. Caldwell of Everton.

The Arsenal have always had good backs. Joe Powell, one of the very early ones, was one of the best. This ex-soldier was injured while playing at Kettering and died as the result of the accident. Jock Calder was another old-time stalwart.

Jimmy Sharp was another great Arsenal back who played for Scotland against England twice, earned several other caps, and later on went to Fulham. One of the soundest backs who ever kicked a ball. Jimmy was, and I believe still is, a very fine golfer. He might have secured a professional's billet in the little ball game, but his heart has always been in football.

When J. Cross partnered Sharp at back, with Jimmy Ashcroft in goal, there were not many better defences in the country than the Arsenal possessed. Cross got his cap against Ireland for Scotland when with Third Lanark in 1903.

The Arsenal's great team of 1906: Top Row—R. Dunmore (trainer), J. Sharp, J. Ashcroft, P. R. Sands, A. Cross, P. Kelso (manager). Second Row—A. Gray, R. Templeton, A. Ducat, T. T. Fitchie, R. McEachrane. Bottom Row—J. Bellamy, J. Dick, J Blair.

But perhaps the back who intrigued me the most was John Jackson, a fine upstanding, fair, curly-haired Scot. He was one of the most fearless backs I ever saw, and because of his very daring was rarely hurt. Jackson could kick like a mule with both feet, and if his placing was not always too sound his defence was always beyond criticism.

He is the father of the Rev. John Jackson, the Liverpool full-back. When I saw the reverend gentleman come on to the field for the first time my mind was carried back to many a stirring game at Plumstead.

SON OF HIS FATHER

He is his father over again—the same fearless, dashing player, the same fair hair, the same athletic poise of body with a touch of swagger in his walk. It was a veritable page from the past.

J. Shaw was another fine full-back who wore the Arsenal colours for a good many years.

Since the war the Arsenal have not—perhaps with the notable exception of T. Parker—had quite such distinctive backs, although they have always been good. J. A. Mackie, A. L. Kennedy, and now a young back who is improving every match in E. Hapgood, have played well in the Arsenal defence.

Parker is now something of a veteran with the Arsenal, but I am sure that the old Southampton man will in the future be reckoned one of the best the club has had.

Great half backs, too have worn the Woolwich red. First and foremost of all I should place John Dick, who came to Plumstead somewhere about 1897. As a centre-half, captain, and gentleman, on and off the field, he was never beaten. He dropped out after the season 1909-10.

Andy Ducat was another Arsenal half-back who has made history on both the football and cricket field. He went to the Villa, sustained a broken leg in his first match, and subsequently won an English Cup medal with the Villa before he went to Fulham as player-manager.

BANK OF ENGLAND TEAM

Roddy McEachrane was, perhaps, the cleverest half-back who ever played for the Arsenal, and Percy Sands, their amateur half-back, was another popular favourite at the Manor Field.

Since then Billy Blyth, who also played in the front rank, J. D. Butler, R. F. John, who always reminds me of John Dick, and A. Baker have all rendered splendid service, and in H. Roberts and W. Seddon the Reds have to-day a couple of half-backs who should go a long way with experience.

The present Arsenal team has been dubbed the Bank of England team because of the money the forward line has cost in transfer fees, but the club has not always had the money to pay such big prices. Indeed, it was the Arsenal that once tried to put a limit on transfer fees.

But I can remember some forwards as good as any in the team to-day. One in particular was Bobby Templeton.

He was a veritable dancing master among footballers, and during the time that he and Tom Fitchie, who made fame as a schoolboy footballer when he scored over 100 goals in a season, were playing as a left wing there was none better in the country.

It was said of Templeton that he could dribble a football round a sixpence. He gave a great display of fancy work against England at Hampden Park in 1910, and was criticised in some quarters for so doing. But Scotland won, and Templeton was a rare handful to Bob Crompton on that day.

Andy Ducat was originally seen in the forward line for the Arsenal, but in the old days, perhaps, the best they had was Tim Coleman, who joined

(Continued in column 4)

POPULAR NATIONAL

Easter Hero Already at Short Odds for Liverpool

By STONEHENGE

The first acceptance stage of the Grand National Steeplechase is responsible for the withdrawal of only twelve of the original eighty-four entries. Thus early it is apparent there will be another unwieldly field on March 28.

On the day we shall probably be searching for the likely winner from among those who have stood up in previous seasons. Many would sooner have a horse who has survived the National trip than a newcomer with a brilliant "Park" certificate.

Easter Hero is favourite for the race, and I can see no prospect of backers getting better odds than 8 to 1, providing he keeps well. Last year he was favourite at 9 to 1. In the event of a well-backed animal winning the Lincolnshire, Mr. J. H. Whitney's 'chaser will be at an absurdly short price on March 28.

There is no doubt from his appearance that Easter Hero is thriving on the preparation planned by Jack Anthony. He is to run, all being well, for the Cheltenham Gold Cup at the National Hunt meeting on March 11.

There are knowledgeable folk of my acquaintance who have impressed upon me the taking appearance of May King. He has proved his ability to jump and stay the Liverpool country, and 40 to 1 is a nice price about a horse of this type.

In a list of quotations I have received, Gregalach, Great Span, Donzelon, Shaun Goilin, Grakle, K.C.B. and Sandy Hook are 20 to 1 chances. Those who bet at this stage on any of these take an exceptional risk.

Bovril III, Master Billie, Delarue, Drinmond and Melleray's Belle have all proved equal to the Liverpool fences, and that in itself is an asset. It will be soon enough to take an active interest when an official market has been formed.

STONEHENGE'S CODE

Stonehenge's best thing of the day is indicated in the *Daily Mirror* by means of the following code:—

M	N	O	P	Q	R	S	T	U	V	X	Y	Z
W	D	C	B	I	F	G	H	K	J	A	L	E

Thus ZYOTC would indicate ELCHO.

List men are obliging casual backers with quotations on the Lincolnshire. Le Phare, Square Rock and Arctic Light are quoted at 20's. Acceptances will be made known during the week, and one can then go into the race in detail.

I have already mentioned that Cecil Ray has been engaged by Captain Cohn. There has been a big tip for Slipper for some time, but one must remember that Vatout has a forward display in the Cambridgeshire to recommend him.

This week we can lose our money at Warwick, Gatwick and Lingfield. If the majority of the Liverpool horses engaged turn out some of the longer distance steeplechases will be well worth seeing.

HINTS FOR THE WEEK

WARWICK.—Monday.—1.30, Le Mont d'Here or Assignee; 2.0, Sans Blague or Cloringo; 2.30, Family Hope; 3.0, Bicester or Mountain Slip; 3.30, Byron or Kelalia; 4.0, Corduroy or Porporino.

Tuesday.—1.30, Letham; 2.0, Tarsus or Robbers' March; 2.30, Fog Horn; 3.0, Sanpere; 3.30, Martyr or Pamperer; 4.0, Corduroy or Melanippe.

GATWICK.—Wednesday.—1.30, Court Scandal II or Nautical Swell; 2.0, John Haig or Duc de Guise; 2.30, Ballyhanwood or Delarue; 3.0, Master Orange or Sidi Gaba; 3.30, The Druce Machine or Colliery Band; 4.0, Ivory or Michaelmas Day.

Thursday.—1.30, Pine Bluff or Newtown Wonder; 2.0, Colenso or John Haig; 2.30, Castletown; 3.0, Golden Rain or The Torch; 3.30, Gainsharp or Royal Tango; 4.0, Strong One

LINGFIELD.—Friday.—1.50, Prince Regent or Endwell; 2.20, Clear Cash; 2.50, Glangesia or Æsop; 3.20, Montpelia or Repaid; 3.50, Swift Rowland; 4.20, Near East or Llandreamer.

Saturday.—1.50, Byron or Marauder; 2.20, Gib; 2.50, Master Orange or Beau de Ghent; 3.20, Roman Road or Camp Bed; 3.50, Safe in Bed or Island; 4.20, Yearly or Ivory.

STONEHENGE.

(Continued from column 3)

the club from Northampton and was for years the most popular man in the team, alike with players and spectators. He was a veritable box of tricks.

Charlie Satterthwaite was a dashing inside-left for the Arsenal. When he got going with the ball he took some stopping. He scaled nearly 13st.

No mention of the Arsenal club would be complete without reference to Gordon Hoare, another famous amateur inside left. A player of many amateur caps, he was in the England side that won the Olympic Games trophy at Stockholm in 1912.

H. T. W. Hardinge, the Kent cricketer, was for a long time an Arsenal forward. He got his cap in 1910, when with Sheffield United.

Jock Rutherford in later years has been the most famous forward in the club, and another Scottish winger who has delighted the crowd at Highbury was Dr. Paterson, who made his early fame with the Glasgow Rangers. He was, however, of English birth, and it is within my recollection that he once played as a mystery forward for the Arsenal in 1925-6, after it had been given out that he had retired. He figured on the programme as A. N. Other and helped the Gunners to beat Aston Villa in the fifth round of the Cup.

CAPPED FORWARDS

In recent years the Arsenal have had many internationals in their forward line. Joe Hulme has been capped several times for England. Roger Boreham has had amateur caps for England. David Jack, their present star forward, has also played for England, C. Jones is about the best forward Wales can call on, and Alec James is a Scottish star.

These men cost the Arsenal a mint of money, and they have, in addition, such fine players as J. Brain, J. Lambert and Dave Halliday among their centre-forwards. The Arsenal with their present team should soon make history in League or Cup.

That they have never won either is surprising. The nearest the Gunners have ever come to winning the F.A. trophy was in 1926-7 at Wembley when they were beaten by Cardiff City in the Final by a goal to nothing, and the Cup went out of the country for the first time.

That match was something of a tragedy, for Lewis, the goalkeeper, who saved a low shot from Ferguson, the Cardiff centre-forward, turned to rise from the ground and dropped the ball behind him over the line. It was the only goal of a match the Arsenal should have won, for they had the best of the exchanges, but their forwards missed many chances through bad finishing.

So we are hoping in London for good luck for the Gunners in this season's campaign.

NEXT WEEK: DERBY COUNTY

ARSENAL BRING ENGLISH CUP BACK TO THE SOUTH

Dunne (left), who netted one of Sheffield United's goals against Everton yesterday. Bruce, whose goal made Middlesbrough practically safe from relegation.

EVERTON MAKING GREAT FIGHT FOR SAFETY

Sheffield United Lose by the Odd Goal

The big question of relegation from the First Division is still in abeyance as Everton won their game and Newcastle, Sheffield United and Grimsby all lost.

Everton did themselves a doubly good turn by beating the Blades 3—2 at Goodison Park.

The winners were fortunate in the second half when the Sheffielders had most of the game. Everton, however, had established a goal lead in the first half, White netting twice to one successful scoring effort by Gillespie for the United. However, Dunne made the scores level within a few minutes of the restart.

Martin eventually restored Everton's lead, and, although Sheffield made vigorous efforts to draw level again, they were foiled.

NOT YET SAFE

Grimsby Lose by a Goal Against the Wednesday

Grimsby Town had the hardest match of the safety-seekers in visiting Wednesday's ground. The Fishermen put up a gallant battle but retired beaten by a goal to nil.

It was level pegging in the first half. The all-important goal came when Jacobson had the misfortune to put through his own goal.

Middlesbrough, who are not safe yet, got a valuable point at Fratton Park, where Portsmouth could only draw 1—1.

Both the goals came in the second half, Bruce giving the Borough the lead and Easson equalising. Portsmouth missed a fine chance of winning, as right on time Weddle missed an open goal.

There was a thunderstorm at Derby, where Newcastle were beaten 3—1. The flooded pitch made play difficult. Newcastle were outplayed.

VILLA SURPRISED

Vic Watson Scores Hat Trick for West Ham

West Ham look like finishing in the first half-dozen. They surprised the Villa at Birmingham yesterday, winning by the odd goal in five.

The Villa started well, but the Hammers scored first through Watson. Brown equalised from a penalty only for Watson to score again and Houghton to equalise once more.

Clever work by Ruffell enabled Watson to get the winning goal later and register the hat trick.

It is just as well Manchester United are safe, as they went down 3—1 at Leeds.

SHOCK FOR BLACKPOOL

Prolific Goal-Scoring in Second League Games

Blackpool, who have the divisional championship within their grasp, met with something of a shock at Swansea in being beaten by 3 goals to 0 in a fast and exciting game. Thomas got the first goal and R. Williams the second before the interval. Although Blackpool improved, Swansea were equal to all demands on their defence. Just before the end Easton got Swansea's third goal from a free kick.

Eight goals were scored at Wolverhampton, where the Wanderers shared the honours with Bradford.

After a goalless first half West Bromwich Albion defeated Stoke City by 3 goals to 0 at Stoke.

Cardiff City defeated Bury by 5 goals to 1 at Cardiff.

Charlton Athletic defeated Southampton at the Valley by 4 goals to 1, all the goals being scored in the second half. Wyper and Rankin scored good goals, and Haines reduced the lead. Charlton replied with goals by Astley and Whitlow.

NAP HAND BY MORRIS

Hat Tricks for Bournemouth, Exeter and Watford

Morris was in brilliant form for Swindon against Norwich City. He scored twice in the first half, and came along with three more after the interval. Anderson netted for Norwich with the last kick of the match.

Eyre did the hat trick for Bournemouth against Clapton Orient. Martin accomplished a similar performance for Newport County at Exeter, and James scored all of Watford's three at Southend. Hammond also scored three for Fulham against Brighton. Haley and Price also netted for the Cottagers.

Plymouth, who have secured promotion, were beaten at Selhurst. Clarke headed a goal for the Palace, and brilliant play by Simpson produced two more goals.

Huddersfield Beaten by Two Clear Goals After a Fine Game at Wembley

JAMES, THE SCHEMER, INSPIRES LONDONERS

For the third time since Blackburn Olympic captured the trophy for the North in 1883, the English Cup has been brought to the South of England. Arsenal beat Huddersfield at Wembley yesterday by two goals.

For the most part it was a very fine match, and although there was a long period in the second half when Huddersfield kept the Londoners defending, the superior finishing power of the Arsenal forwards decided the issue.

The problems of relegation from the First Division will not be settled for another week. There is still a slender chance of Everton escaping, but they, Sheffield United, Burnley and Grimsby are all in a dangerous position.

If Chelsea can avert defeat in their last match, against Bury, they will accompany Blackpool into the First Division. One more point will assure Port Vale of a return to the Second Division.

GREAT PLAY IN WEMBLEY'S FINEST GAME

Royal Spectators of a Titanic Struggle

By P. J. MOSS

Was it an augury that the King, who was greeted with tremendous cheering, shook hands first with Tom Parker, of the Arsenal, when the teams lined up to be presented to his Majesty? The crowd took it as such, and the Arsenal won a good, hard game by 2 goals to 0.

They were both good goals, and Lambert, when he clinched matters late in the second half, scored a characteristic goal.

The game was a fluctuating one. In the first half it was nearly all Arsenal. In the second it was nearly all Huddersfield. Arsenal took two of their scoring chances, Huddersfield did not, and so the spoils went to the more deserving.

Some reputations were enhanced in the match. Goodall, the Huddersfield right-back, never put a foot wrong in the game, but James, of the Arsenal, was the outstanding figure in the match.

Little less noticeable was John, Arsenal's left half-back. He surely played the game of his life. It was no light task to be up against Jackson and Kelly, but still he not only did that but played to his own forwards, particularly in the first half.

PARKER'S GREAT GAME

Tom Parker, the Arsenal captain, was in his best form at right-back. I think he was twice very wrongly penalised for bringing Smith, the Huddersfield left winger, down. Admitted they were heavy charges, he played the ball each time. In the first half it nearly cost the Arsenal a goal, as Preedy, in saving from the free kick, fell on the ball and was surrounded by a crowd of players and was lucky to be able to throw the ball over the line.

Arsenal won because they had more punch in the centre, and because their supposedly weak link, the half-back line, rose to a great occasion. Huddersfield's three inside forwards, Kelly, Davies and Raw, were hardly in the picture against Seddon, John and Baker.

Hapgood at times gave the Arsenal partisans in the crowd palpitations. He gave Jackson too much rope, and ran by the side of the flying winger instead of bundling into him. Two or three times it was nearly fatal.

Once in the first half Jackson doubled back and drove in a fast, curling, spinning ball, which went inches wide, and on another occasion he put the ball at Davies's toes in front of goal.

Jackson did not give one of his scintillating displays. He seemed rather subdued to me, and played as if he were expecting the man to charge him. In fact, he seemed to be drawing the man, and the fact that he was not charged seemed to surprise him.

SMITH HUDDERSFIELD'S STAR

It was Smith, on the left wing, who made the most of the chances he got. He was always the life and soul of the Huddersfield attack, and his duels with Parker were one of the features of the match.

Many times he got across centres which would in an ordinary game have spelt goals. From one of them Jackson headed inches wide, but most of them were wasted.

The Arsenal wingers, Hulme and Bastin, were well held by the Huddersfield defence throughout, and Jack, who got a nasty knock early on, was never quite in his best form.

Lambert played his usual light-hearted, rollicking game. Always ready for a tilt with either of the backs, always on the qui vive for a chance to slip through, he gave the Huddersfield defence a lot to think about.

He missed one easy chance in the first half when he tried to lob the ball over Turner, who had come out to meet him, and sent it wide of the post. He was through on another occasion and Turner literally took the ball off his toes as he was in the act of shooting.

Hulme, too, made a bad miss at a sitter from a lovely pass by Bastin.

Arsenal's first goal came after fifteen minutes' play. A free kick was given for a very doubtful foul on James. As the whistle went James picked up the ball, placed it on the ground and, quick as a flash, sent it along the ground to Bastin.

All this happened before the Huddersfield defence had positioned itself. James dashed to the centre for the return pass, and in a trice the ball was in the net and the Arsenal on the way to their first Cup triumph.

Up to the interval Arsenal played the more dashing game, and Huddersfield the prettier football. From their tap tapping and mid-field passing one would have imagined that they were so certain of victory that they could afford to wait for the goals that were certain to come. And so the Arsenal led at the breather.

SECOND HALF CHANGE

When the second half opened the Londoners were practically penned in their lines for long periods. It was then that the footballing genius of James, who was now the prime mover in defence as he had been the inspiration of attack in the first half, was seen at its best.

Always trying to get the other forwards away, he also proved a rare stumbling block to the Huddersfield men.

Preedy's audacity in running out to the ball, and running with it when he had got it and bouncing it when he might have cleared, must have given the Arsenal's supporters heart disease at times. Once he ran round two men quite ten steps without bouncing the ball and got away with it.

Referees nowadays honour the rule of carrying the ball more in the breach than the observance. Still Preedy, if daring, was lucky, and in this period of durance Parker and Hapgood, the Arsenal backs, never faltered.

Then came the deciding goal. Preedy cleared rather luckily from a combined onslaught on his goal. His clearance went to James, who with a long kick, dropped the ball into the middle of the field, well over Wilson's head and close to Lambert.

The Arsenal centre-forward went on with the ball. Turner came out, in this case I thought too far and too soon, because Goodall was coming up top speed to challenge Lambert.

LAMBERT'S CLINCHING GOAL

Quite coolly Lambert waited until the goal was open, and with a gentle tap he sent the ball slowly along the ground over the line and into the net.

The goal settled it, but Huddersfield lost none of their excellent form in all save goal-scoring.

I had forgotten to mention that the Zeppelin sailed over the ground during the second half.

It went over just as Preedy was taking a goal kick. He glanced up at it and paused, but the referee waved to him to get on with the game. The Zepp passed and we forgot it in the thrilling struggle before us.

The final whistle came. James was in command of the ball at the moment, and he captured it and brought it off the field. If a player is allowed to keep it as a trophy none deserved it more than the little Scot, who certainly was the hero of the game.

And then, to more and more cheering from the crowd, delighted that the Cup has come to London again, the King presented the trophy and the medals, and the great football campaign, so far as the Cup is concerned, was over until next September.

The official attendance was given as 92,488, and the receipts were £23,265 13s. 6d.

WHO WILL JOIN MERTHYR?

Gillingham at Present in the Worst Position

Which club will have to seek re-election, along with Merthyr, in the Southern section?

Gillingham, who defeated Merthyr by six clear goals, all scored by Cheesmur, must win their remaining game if they are to escape.

Torquay, who gained a point at Northampton in a 2—2 draw, are a point ahead of Gillingham.

Bristol Rovers are, at present, a point behind Gillingham, but they have a match in hand.

Walsall are now out of the danger zone, but they found Brentford too good for them.

LONDON WELSH TRIUMPH

Blackheath Beaten in Final of Seven-a-Sides

London Welsh won the final of the Middlesex seven-a-side tournament at Twickenham yesterday, defeating the Blackheath second string in the final by six clear points.

W. C. Powell opened the scoring by nipping round from a scrum, going over with a try.

Soon afterwards A. H. Jones got another try for the Welsh, and that ended the scoring.

In the semi-final the Welsh beat the Harlequins, winners for the last four years, and Blackheath beat Bart's Hospital.

Cheesmur (left), of Gillingham, who scored his club's six goals against Merthyr. Pynegar, the Port Vale forward, who netted twice at Tranmere.

WHO GOES OUT OF THE SECOND DIVISION?

Reading and Notts County in Great Danger

The relegation problem in the Second Division is still without solution. At the moment things look blackest for Reading and Notts County, both of whom have now concluded their programmes.

Hull City and Bristol City, however, have not yet got clear of the two bottom positions, though both gained good wins yesterday.

Hull beat the Spurs at Hull by two clear goals, and deserved their success because they made the better use of their chances. Tottenham had a big share of the game in midfield, but failed to finish off their attacks. Mills and Alexander netted Hull's goals.

Bristol City's display in beating Nottingham Forest 4—1 was worthy of a club of much higher standing. They were superior at all points of the game. Williams (3) and Dickie got Bristol's goals, and Dent was the Forest's scorer.

READING'S MISTAKE

Millwall Net Only Goal When Defence Stands Still

Fellow-unfortunates in Bradford City and Barnsley were brought together at Bradford, where Barnsley claimed the only goal, thus considerably improving their position.

Had the Bradford forwards been able to shoot accurately, the result might have been the other way about, for they had all the game in the second half, but could not discount Curran's first-half goal for Barnsley.

Both these clubs, however, may yet finish above Reading, for each is one point behind the Biscuitmen with a game in hand.

Reading were beaten at home by Millwall, for whom Cock netted the only goal while the home defenders stopped playing to appeal for offside. This mistake may send the Biscuitmen down.

If Notts County had won their home game against Oldham Athletic, not only would it have relieved the County of a good deal of anxiety concerning their position, but also simplified the promotion problem in the Second Division.

Notts were one goal up at half time, this being scored by Mills from a free kick just before the interval. After a heavy thunderstorm the game was resumed on a swamped ground. It ran mostly in favour of Notts, but in the later stages the superior combination of Oldham resulted in Taylor scoring the equaliser.

Failure to beat Oldham means that Notts are now in desperate straits. With their programme finished they have compiled no more points than Hull.

FROGLEY'S NEW RECORD

Harringay Beat Crystal Palace in the League

Harringay beat Crystal Palace by 31 points to 22 in the inter-league match at Harringay yesterday. Roger Frogley, who was twice successful for Crystal Palace, established a new flying start record of 75 1-5s. Vic Huxley beat Roger Frogley in a challenge race by two events to one.

Huxley also won the Big Six match at High Beech, beating George Greenwood (Wembley) in the final in easy style. Huxley also beat Jack Barnett in a scratch race.

Billy Dallison beat Len Parker by fifteen lengths in the final of the Big Four contest at Stamford Bridge. Frank Arthur won the Bridge scratch race easily.

Winning both heats, a team of three Wembley riders beat a Lea Bridge team at Lea Bridge. Harry Whitfield beat Buster Frogley in the final of the match race, and also carried off the Lea Bridge handicap.

In a challenge match at the Crystal Palace the home riders beat West Ham by 33 points to 20.

FOR THE EMPIRE GAMES

The following team in order of weights, from fly upwards, has been selected to represent the Amateur Boxing Association in the Empire Games at Toronto:—T. Pardoe, H. Mizler, J. W. Duffield, J. Waples, F. Brooman, F. Mallia, J. W. Goyder and Signaller Stuart.

SURREY AT PRACTICE

Much bright cricket was seen at the Oval in the Surrey trial game between sides captained by E. G. Hayes and Major Luther.

R. Felton was the outstanding player, performing well both as batsman and bowler. Scores:

Hayes's Side: 312 for 8 dec. and 190 for 6 dec. (Mobey 30, R. Felton 52 (ret.), D. B. Desai not 20).

Major Luther's Side: 248 for 10 dec. (E. G. Stroud 44, Smith (E. C.) 41, J. G. Merrall not 31, Major Luther not 19). Bowling: Felton 3 for 17, Spence 2 for 45. Second Innings: 126 for 4 (J. E. Merrall 45, E. G. Stroud 29, F. Gurchow not 30). Match drawn.

£750 PUZZLE CONTEST—P. 25

SUNDAY PICTORIAL

THE GREAT SUNDAY PICTURE NEWSPAPER

THE KING SEES ARSENAL BEAT HUDDERSFIELD IN MEMORABLE CUP FINAL

THE KING handing the F.A. Cup to Parker, captain of the victorious Arsenal team.

A CROSS SHOT proves too fast for Preedy to intercept.

ARSENAL defenders busy in the goal area.

PREEDY, the Arsenal's goalkeeper, injured in a scrimmage in front of his goal.

Arsenal missed several excellent chances of scoring in the first half of the Cup Final at Wembley yesterday. Their second goal was scored a few minutes before the end. The

JACK, Arsenal's inside-right, heading in front of Huddersfield's goal.

veteran, Smith, was Huddersfield's most dangerous forward. In the second half Huddersfield had the better of the play, but Wilson, their captain, twice failed to score.

Printed and Published by SUNDAY PICTORIAL NEWSPAPERS (1920), Ltd., Geraldine House, Rolls Buildings, Fetter-lane, London, E.C.4.—Sunday, April 27, 1930. Tel. Holborn 4321.

ARSENAL WIN THE LEAGUE BANNER FOR THE SOUTH

Tom Parker (left), captain of the new League champions, Arsenal, and Bowden, of Plymouth, who is to travel to Canada as a member of the F.A. team.

HIGHBURY TRIUMPH

Arsenal Bring the League Flag South at Last

LIVERPOOL LOSE FINE GAME

The Arsenal have at last won the League. They beat Liverpool at Highbury yesterday 3—1, and that landed them high and dry above the possibilities of any other club.

The championship has never come south of Birmingham since it was instituted in 1888-9. Bristol City were second in 1906-7, the Spurs second in 1921-22, Cardiff second in 1923-24 and the Arsenal second in 1925-26.

That was the first record put up by the Arsenal. The second is that they have already scored more points than any other side winning the title. West Bromwich had 60 in 1919-20 and Liverpool 60 in 1922-23. The Arsenal's in whas been the result of consistency.

Yesterday's match with Liverpool was a splendid exhibition. Both teams played fast, skilful football. Liverpool were best at the start, the Arsenal outstayed them, and in the end were good winners.

NO MAD STAMPEDE

There was plenty of cheering from the 45,000 spectators at the finish, but there was no mad stampede across the pitch. The Arsenal railings are not too easy to climb, but I thought the crowd took the success quite calmly.

Liverpool, as I have said, started with great dash. They had a strong wind behind them and for a time nearly all the play was in the Arsenal lines.

Liverpool were in front after three minutes. After several raids on the Arsenal goal, Barton, the outside right, flashed in a fine low centre bang at the Arsenal goal. Roberts tried to kick it out but the ball hit him on the leg and screwed off wide of Harper's left hand.

He had positioned himself to take the shot and had no chance after it struck Roberts. One could not blame the Arsenal pivot. He had to take a very awkward kick at a very fast ball, and it beat him.

For a time the Arsenal were outplayed, although Lambert had one fine chance of equalising. Then Barton brought off a similar effort, but this time Parker cleared, and Hodgson missed at close range from a nice pass by Gunson.

Arsenal gradually found their game. Bastin hit the underpart of the crossbar with a rasping shot, and Lambert shaved the bar with another.

Half-way through, from a corner kick well taken by Bastin, Jones dropped the ball into the goal mouth and Jack equalised.

BRILLIANT ATTACK AND DEFENCE

Hulme and James played some brilliant football up to the interval, but there was no more scoring, the back play on both sides being splendid, Parker and Jackson standing out from their respective sides.

It was the Arsenal's game in the second half, although Liverpool were always dangerous in their raids.

Bastin put them in front after twenty minutes. Lucas handled and, following the free kick, James flicked the ball to Bastin, who cut in and scored cleverly.

Some clever work by Lambert gave Hulme a chance to send in a perfect centre. Lambert was there to take the return pass and score a copybook goal.

The Liverpool defence tired under the pressure towards the close, but it held out and, indeed, Liverpool nearly scored in the last minute. With Harper out of his goal the ball bobbed about in the goalmouth, but the back scrambled it away.

It was as good a game as I have seen at Highbury this year, and there was real Cup-tie excitement as thrill followed thrill in the exciting exchanges.

P. J. M.

HAMMERING IT HOME

West Ham Thoroughly Earn Point Against Manchester City

West Ham gave a polished display at Manchester and thoroughly deserved the point they gained in a 1—1 draw with the City.

West Ham crossed over a goal in arrears, but this was not surprising, as they were playing against a very troublesome wind.

Manchester's goal had many thrilling escapes, and Yews, Ruffell and Gibbins tested Langford severely before Cowan scored for the City.

West Ham launched attack upon attack in the second half, and it looked as if Manchester were going to take both points against the run of the play, when Gibbins levelled the scores.

INDIFFERENT FINISHING

Neither Charlton nor Oldham seemed unduly anxious to exert themselves at the Valley, and after a moderate game the sides were level with one goal each.

Indifferent finishing by the forwards of both sides spoilt a number of raids. Johnstone gave Oldham the lead, and before the interval Pugsley, the Charlton half-back, equalised.

Oldham, helped by the wind, enjoyed the better of matters in the second half, but their forwards lacked punch.

Liverpool Yield the Points at Highbury—Leeds Almost Booked for Division II—Albion's Promotion Chance

BIRMINGHAM ENSURE LEAGUE POSITION

Nearly all the problems of the League have been solved. Of those that remain only two are of great consequence. They are: Who will accompany Everton into the First Division, and which of three clubs, Lincoln, Tranmere or Chesterfield, will gain promotion to the Second Division?

Arsenal made sure of the championship yesterday, which, for the first time in history, comes South, and the chance of Leeds escaping relegation has been reduced almost to vanishing point.

West Bromwich Albion strengthened their promotion chance by taking a point from Bradford, while their rivals, the Spurs, were undergoing defeat by the City at Bristol. Albion are strong favourites for the double—Cup and promotion.

Plymouth Argyle's defeat of Reading makes it almost certain that the Biscuitmen will go down. They are a point behind Swansea and only one game left to play, while Swansea have two. Lincoln City's home defeat greatly prejudiced their chance of going up.

BIRMINGHAM'S RELIEF

Victory Over the Wednesday Brings League Security

By defeating Sheffield Wednesday at St. Andrews by two clear goals, Birmingham are able to approach the Cup Final without a care as to their League position, the points thus obtained sufficing to take them clear of the danger area.

Although the second half was well advanced before Birmingham were able to claim any material advantage, they were always the better side.

They hammered away at the Wednesday defence for long periods at a stretch, and had their finishing been on a level with their midfield work they might have won by a wider margin.

Although doing well in other respects, Curtis and Fillingham, the latter of whom led the attack in place of Bradford, each missed chances.

Nevertheless, Brown must be given credit for an able display in the Wednesday goal. He made many fine saves before he was eventually beaten by Gregg and Curtis near the end.

GOOD GAME SPOILT

Referee Cautions Sunderland and Chelsea for Rough Play

What promised to be a very interesting game was spoiled by rough play in the second half at Roker Park, where Sunderland defeated Chelsea by two clear goals.

Sunderland played Keeton and Robinson on the right wing and within three minutes' play Gurney gave the Rokermen the lead.

McDougall was a splendid defender for Sunderland, and the Chelsea right wing was very clever, but Robinson increased the score before the interval and the second half was blank.

Irving, the Chelsea half-back, was injured before the break, and when McDougall had to retire the referee found it necessary to caution the sides.

PLYMOUTH WORRIES END

And How Reading May Avoid Relegation to Division III

Plymouth Argyle now have no relegation troubles. Their defeat of Reading at Home Park by three goals to one puts them in a safe position.

Reading, on the other hand, are deeper into the mire. For them to escape relegation Swansea must lose their remaining games, and the Biscuitmen must win their last fixture—and then goal average will decide!

In the opening half it was a case of the Plymouth attack versus the Reading defence, and resloutely as the visitors' rearguard played, they conceded two goals to Roberts and Leslie.

The second half was full of incident. Mantle was prominent in the Argyle raids and netted his side's third goal before McNeil scored for Reading following a free kick.

SPURS' HOPES FADE

Defeat at Bristol That Makes Promotion Unlikely

Defeat at Bristol has probably deprived the Spurs of all real hope of gaining promotion to the First Division. They played a very moderate game against Bristol City, who won on their merits by the odd goal of three.

There was no score in the first half, during which the home side had much the better of the game without being able to beat the stern defence offered by Lyons and Hodgkinson and the fine goalkeeping of Spiers.

In the second half Homer scored for Bristol from a pass by Elliott. Ten minutes later Hunt, who had changed places with Rowley, equalised with a long shot.

For a time there seemed some hopes of the Spurs pulling off a victory, but Bristol rallied and, following good work by Robson, Craig recovered the lead for the Westerners.

The Spurs' forwards were altogether lacking in combination for the greater part of the match and never produced the right tactics against a determined side that cut out all the frills and always went straight for goal.

This is the sixth successive match the Spurs have played without victory.

BAD FOR LEEDS UNITED

Desperate Struggle Against Aston Villa Unavailing

Leeds United fought desperately to secure the points in their vital game with Aston Villa at Elland-road, but were defeated by 2 goals to 0.

Leeds dominated play early on, and the Villa's goal was often in danger, but R. Miles was in great form.

The Villa defence held out, and at the end of forty minutes Waring opened the scoring.

Five minutes after the resumption of play Chester scored the Villa's second goal, and from this point the visitors held the upper hand.

The home team played wildly at times, and an injury to Hart further weakened them.

NOT CLEAR YET

Thames Defeated at Home by Bristol Rovers

It was not a good game at the West Ham Stadium, where Thames were beaten by their visitors, Bristol Rovers, by the odd goal of three.

Thames, who require one point to make sure of retaining their position in Division III, had the best of matters in a scrappy opening half, but crossed over all square

It was only in attack that the Rovers held an advantage, and whenever they were in shooting distance they were dangerous. Attwood netted twice for Bristol, and Donnelly reduced arrears from a spot kick after the interval.

POINTS FROM YESTERDAY'S LEAGUE AND OTHER MATCHES

The Potteries Derby between Port Vale and Stoke was mainly a defensive affair, neither side scoring in a hard game.

Paignton Rugby Club at Teignmouth won the Devon Senior Cup against Sidmouth by a penalty goal and a try to nil.

Allen, the Coventry goalkeeper, saved his side a point by his splendid keeping in a goalless draw against Brighton.

Leicester's inside right, Hine, took a benefit against Newcastle, and celebrated it by playing a big share in his side's comfortable victory.

Holland, Watford's goalkeeper, dislocated a thumb against Crystal Palace and went to outside-left. Davison took his place in goal and performed creditably.

Great goalkeeping by Jones saved Bolton from a heavy defeat at Portsmouth. The Seasiders maintained a continuous bombardment, but Jones was only once beaten.

Luckless Manchester United made a better fight against the County at Derby than the score of 6—1 credits them for, but the County forwards were in irresistible mood. Hence the result.

Judging by the keen way in which Q.P. Rangers and Gillingham contested their game at Loftus-road, one would have thought that promotion hung at the end of the result.

Bowen, of Northampton, retired injured midway through the second half at Swindon, but the home team had already established a comfortable lead. Morris did the hat-trick for the Railmen in the second half.

A penalty goal in the last half-minute of extra time enabled Sutton United to beat Dorking by the odd goal in nine in the final of the Surrey Charity Shield. A Sutton player was ordered off midway through the game.

Cambridge Town beat St. Albans in the A.F.A. Cup Final at Ipswich by the only goal scored, and thus landed the A.F.A. double event, for they are already assured of the championship of the Southern Amateur League. The double has been brought off only twice previously.

After Houghton had given Exeter the lead at Walsall, W. Bradford netted twice for the home club before half-time.

Smarter in attack, Sheffield United defeated Grimsby at Bramall-lane with greater ease than the score of 2—1 suggests.

Despite the fact that Nottingham Forest were beaten at Barnsley, they are saved from relegation by Reading meeting with defeat at Plymouth.

Poor football was served up at Cardiff, where neither the City nor Preston was able to score. Preston were the cleverer side, but lacked finish.

Badly in need of points, Blackpool hammered desperately at the Huddersfield defence, but they failed in front of goal and could only divide the spoils.

No goals were scored at Valley Parade, where Bradford City and Millwall were engaged. Neither side deserved to, as opportunities were missed in galore.

With a little luck in finishing, Bury's superiority over Southampton would have been expressed by more than a single goal. J. R. Smith twice hit an upright before scoring.

Injuring his head in a collision, McLean, of Blackburn, had to have stitches inserted in the wound against Middlesbrough, for whom Camsell scored his two hundredth League goal.

Tunbridge Wells Rangers, with five matches still to play, require one more goal to establish a record for the Kent League. Sixty of the 149 goals scored have been by Richards, the centre forward.

Newport are doomed to seek re-election to the Southern Section of Division III. Yesterday Norwich, who are not much better placed, but have a slight chance of escaping, beat their rivals for the wooden spoon by 4—1.

Chesterfield have a bright opportunity of "pipping" Lincoln and Tranmere, who show signs of cracking in the race for promotion. Lincoln, the leaders, visit Chesterfield on Wednesday, and in any case the latter club will have a large say in the matter of "who goes up."

Spiers (left), the Spurs' goalkeeper, who played a fine game against Bristol City yesterday, and Carter, the West Bromwich inside-right, who helped his side to share points with Bradford.

BRADFORD DO WELL

Narrow Escape for Albion at the Hawthorns

TOO-ANXIOUS FORWARDS

West Bromwich Albion, the Cup-finalists and favourites for promotion, were given a tremendous tussle at the Hawthorns by Bradford, who held them to a 1—1 draw.

Albion's goal had a marvellous escape soon after the commencement, when a clearance by Pearson rebounded from McMillan towards the net, for the goalkeeper to make a lightning-like save.

Both sides were keyed up and played tremendously hard and fast football.

Bradford were a good team, and slightly superior in the first half, when both goals were scored. Shaw got the Albion's goal from a penalty, and almost immediately afterwards McMillan got the equaliser.

The Bradford forwards were very active in the second half, and, as their defenders were equal to the best efforts of the Albion attackers, they were indeed a good side.

Through their over-anxiety to get the decider the West Bromwich forwards did not play their usual game. They stormed the opposing goal towards the end, but failed to score. Bradford had a goal disallowed for offside.

EVERTON'S FAREWELL

Last Home Game in the Second Division Well Won

Everton's last home appearance in the Second Division coincided with a narrow victory over Burnley by the odd goal of five.

All three of Everton's goals came in the first half. Johnson got the first after only four minutes' play, and within two minutes Critchley put on the second. Beel reduced Burnley's arrears, but Wood put through his own goal to give the Toffeemen a 3—1 interval lead.

Everton played in a leisurely way in the second half, during which Prest scored Burnley's other goal.

SWANS STILL NOT SAFE

Forward Failings Cause Loss of Needed Point

Swansea Town still need a point to ensure their place in the Second Division, for, although having the better of play throughout, they had to be content to share spoils on their own ground with Wolverhampton, each side scoring once.

After the Wolves had had a goal by Hartill disallowed for off-side, Williams gave Swansea the lead five minutes from the interval. They kept in front until midway through the second half, when Hartill netted for the Wolves following a breakaway.

ON THE SPEEDWAY

Crystal Palace Win League Match Against Southampton

Despite some brilliant riding by Jack Parker, their captain, Southampton were beaten in their Southern League match with Crystal Palace on the Londoner's track yesterday, the Palace winning by 30 points to 24. Parker won each of his three races for the visitors.

In the final of the senior scratch race Ron Johnson beat Buster Frogley at a speed of 43 m.p.h.

High Beech, on their own track, won their League match against Harringay by 29 points to 24.

In the Big Four match rain interfered. Phil Bishop and Syd Bishop qualified for the final. Bishop beat Clem Cort at 42.04 m.p.h., and Edmunds defeated Vic Huxley, who retired in the second lap through engine trouble.

In a friendly match at Lea Bridge, West Ham beat Southampton by 32 points to 19.

GREYHOUND WINNERS

White City.—8.0, Blow Away (3-1); 8.15, Hectorena (3-1); 8.30, Talbot Six (5-2); 8.45, Leg Before (2-1); 9.0, Melksham Gargoyle (6-1); 9.15, Clean Light (4-1); 9.30, Nom de Guerre (3-1).

Wembley.—8.0, Naughty Jack Horner (10-11); 8.15, Rory of the Hill (2-1) 8.30, Pass the Mint (7-2); 8.45, Dhoukobor (9-4); 9.0, East Bromley (4-6); 9.15, Tolgus (7-4); 9.30, Merriron ([illegible]-1).

Wimbledon.—8.0, Hand Away (6-1); 8.15, Little Speed (6-1); 8.30, St. Asaph (2-1); 8.45, White Wave (13-8); 9.0, Harsac (5-1); 9.15, Island Rock (evens); 9.30, Rockfleet Boy (2-1).

Clapton.—8.0, Fine Slip (7-1); 8.15, Simile (2-1); 8.30, Call Around (8-11); 8.45, Lighted Match (8-1); 9.0, Gleann a Cruim (3-1); 9.15, Michael Boy (evens); 9.30, Noted Solicitor (7-2).

West Ham.—8.0, Cloister Bell (5-1); 8.15, Seldom Led (5-4); 8.30, Gedney Prior (3-1); 8.45, Passing Fair (5-4); 9.0, Winsome and Willing (4-1); 9.15, Karl's Hopeful (4-1); 9.30, Guiding Pal (7-4).

ARSENAL MAKE SURE: SPURS NEARLY UP

JACK'S THE BOY, BUT NOT FOR CHELSEA

Hulme's Deputy Scores First and Makes the Second

VITAL SLIP BY BACK

It is doubtful whether a greater struggle has been seen at Stamford Bridge than that when the Arsenal scored a 3—1 victory over Chelsea, made certain of regaining the League championship, and plunged their rivals once again into the thick of the relegation fight before a crowd of 74,141 people.

Arsenal's success was thoroughly well deserved, for although Chelsea had a big share of the game, they lacked the thrust of their visitors.

That was accounted for largely by the fact that Roberts marked Gallacher so closely that the Chelsea centre forward received the ball when unhampered only on rare occasions.

Even so, Gallacher might have done better had his colleagues plied him with passes along the ground instead of lifting the ball in the air.

Both defences played well, Russell, at right half, doing good work against the tricky James, but the forwards frequently failed to take advantage of the helpful passes provided by their halves.

Hulme was a last minute absentee, but, with due respect to the flying right-winger, he was not really missed.

David Jack took his place, and in the twenty-second minute he cut in in the real Hulme style and put the Arsenal ahead.

The next few minutes really decided Chelsea's fate, and a dramatic slip by McAulay deputising for Law, at back, proved fatal.

He attempted to pass the ball back to Woodley, and, in doing so, sent behind. Jack took

David Jack, who deputised for Hulme at outside right and put Arsenal on the winning path by scoring the first goal and helping in the second.

the corner kick and Bastin shot through to put the Arsenal two up.

Chelsea tried hard afterwards to reduce the leeway, but their attack lacked finishing power, although Gallacher and Gibson made creditable efforts.

Gallacher practically started the second half by netting, but the referee disallowed the point because the centre forward was said to have handled the ball.

That temporarily seemed to knock the steam out of Chelsea, and Bowden eventually led up to the Arsenal's third goal. After his great dribble Bastin came in possession and the left-winger made no mistake with his shot.

Then Chelsea hit back, but too late. Mills hit the bar with a penalty for hands against Roberts, Gallacher reduced arrears, nearly scored again, and then Moss cleared well from a hot shot by Mills.

WOLVES NEARER SAFETY

Lively Forward Line Finds Loopholes in the Derby Defence

Wolverhampton Wanderers materially improved their chance of remaining in the First Division by beating Derby at Wolverhampton by 3 goals to 1.

Although it was not until the second half that they could claim any material advantage, Wolverhampton always impressed as the better side.

Ably led by Hartill, the Wolverhampton forwards were a lively line, and but for the agility of Kirby in the Derby goal the Wanderers would have won by a much wider margin.

The first half was goalless, but it would not have been so had not Deacon headed across the face of the Derby goal with Kirby out of position, and later Kirby just managed to intercept a hard drive from Hartill that was going straight for the net.

The second half was only a minute old when Hartill put the Wolves ahead with a great shot, and Hetherington increased their lead when he headed through from a corner kick taken by Phillips.

Wolverhampton were clearly on top, and they further consolidated their position when Rhodes scored. Duncan reduced Derby's arrears a minute later, but the County, though fighting hard, were never able to shake Wolverhampton's grip.

GOOD FOR LEICESTER

Win Over Sunderland Improves Chance of Escaping Relegation

Leicester did themselves a good turn in their struggle to escape relegation by beating Sunderland at Filbert-street by four goals to two.

Davis should have scored for Sunderland when close in, but McLaren got the ball away, and after thirty-six minutes Maw put Leicester in front. Two minutes later Lochhead added a second goal following a scrimmage in the goal mouth.

Leicester increased their lead in surprising fashion immediately on resuming. Black, their right back, scoring from a free kick from inside his own half.

Sunderland's rearguard was badly at fault and blundered again a few minutes later when Maw added a fourth goal.

Gallacher reduced Sunderland's arrears with a fierce drive, and Gurney added a second goal when the Leicester defence was at fault.

Ambulance men attending to spectators who collapsed in the great crush at yesterday's match between Chelsea and Arsenal at Stamford Bridge.

KINGSTONIAN'S AMATEUR CUP

Stockton Leading When Player Breaks a Leg

Stockton had all the bad luck that was going in the replayed Amateur Cup final at Darlington yesterday. They were leading by a goal when Thompson broke a leg and Kingstonian won by four goals to one.

The ground record was broken by the presence of 20,000 spectators. N. Pass and W. Stirling, for Butler and Prest, were the Stockton changes.

A cracking pace was set up right from the start, and at the end of three minutes Coulthard scored for Stockton after receiving close in from Stirling.

Kingstonian did not get the pace of the ground quite so quickly as the northerners, but they were impressive once they settled down, and Gibson came very close with a fine shot after a concerted raid by the southern forwards.

Two corners were forced, and Newton, in the Stockton goal, did well to get the flag kicks away.

Thompson, the Stockton right back, was injured after about a quarter of an hour and left the field. It transpired that he had broken a leg.

Meantime Kingstonian were pressing hotly, and Macey had hard luck when a fine shot from his foot struck Little and was deflected. The absence of Thompson was a great handicap to Stockton, and, with Whitehead, Gibson and McCarthy doing well for Kingstonian, the equaliser always seemed likely to come.

Newton, however, was in brilliant form and saved all kinds of shots.

Three dangerous free-kicks against Kingstonian were unproductive, but Anderson nearly scored on the third occasion.

Though depleted Stockton were plucky, but Kingstonian were always the cleverer side. Okin made many brilliant advances, and from one of his passes Gibson headed the equalising goal.

Play continued fast. Brodrick was rarely troubled, but Newton was many times in action.

Shortly after the resumption Urpeth put Kingstonian ahead from a penalty for hands. The depleted Stockton side were rarely in the picture, and after twenty-two minutes Whitehead scored a third goal for the visitors. Subsequently both Whitehead and Gibson hit the post.

Thirty-eight minutes after the resumption Whitehead, with the Stockton defence spreadeagled, put Kingstonian further ahead. Stockton made a last rally, but were well held by a good defence.

After the match Sir Charles Clegg, president of the Football Association, presented the Cup to Macey, the Kingstonian captain.

BRENTFORD MAKING SURE

Holliday Plays Big Part in Defeat of Brighton

By winning at Brighton yesterday by the odd goal in three, Brentford established themselves in an almost impregnable position at the head of the Southern Third Division, and with four more matches to play—three of them at home—they now need but three further points to make certain of promotion.

Playing fast and skilful football, Brighton forced the leaders to give of their best, but Brentford had an answer to all the wiles of the Albion, and they finished worthy winners.

They owed much to Holliday, the former Middlesbrough centre forward, who returned to lead the attack after missing two games through injury.

Keeping his wings well together, he was always on the look-out for a chance to break through on his own, and his spirited tactics caused the Brighton defenders to become flurried and uncertain.

He found a ready supporter in Hopkins at outside right, and Robson, who came into the side in the absence of Scott, also played his part manfully in Brentford's plan of attack.

Brighton, too, had a clever leader in Attwood, but the Brentford half-backs covered their lines so well that Baker, in the leaders' goal, was never so hotly beset as was Webb at the other end. At the same time he had by no means an easy afternoon.

The game was forty minutes old when Holliday broke through to give Brentford the lead with a brilliant header, and though Attwood equalised after a series of mass attacks, Hopkins ensured a Brentford victory with a sparkling goal ten minutes from the end.

ALDERSHOT MARKSMEN

Failure to Accept Chances Costs Exeter Valuable Points

Exeter badly jeopardised their chance of overhauling the leaders in losing at Aldershot by four goals to one.

Webb was the only member of the City team who showed much ability as a marksman, but even he could not compare with Smithson and Lane, of Aldershot.

It was not until five minutes from the interval that Aldershot went ahead through Proud, but three minutes later Smithson strengthened their position with a second goal.

Exeter pressed strongly for long periods in the second half, but weakness in finishing nullified good midfield work, and Aldershot added two further goals through Lane and Smithson within as many minutes. Exeter's only success was from a penalty taken by Child five minutes from the end.

NORWICH IN CONTROL

Norwich might have beaten Coventry by a much wider margin than the odd goal in three had they made the fullest use of their chances.

They controlled the game for long periods, but lack of steadiness in front of goal, coupled with some great defensive work by Morgan, Perry and Wilmot, kept their tally down.

All the scoring took place in the first half, Lake giving Coventry the lead for Scott and Murphy to reply for Norwich.

CHARLTON'S DEATH KNELL?

Home Defeat by Bury Dims Hope of Avoiding Relegation

Charlton may long remember Bury's visit to them at the Valley yesterday. The Athletic suffered a 3—1 defeat—a result that seriously injures their chances of escaping relegation.

Charlton gave a most disappointing exhibition, despite the fact that they scored first after six minutes through Hobbis, who shot low through a crowd of players when Harrison was unsighted.

Bury equalised six minutes later through Vernon, and after that there was never any doubt as to the result.

Bury were quicker on the ball, more resolute and more skilful in all they did. Had it not been for the good work of Ivill and Oakes, Charlton's full backs, and Pugsley, in defence, the defeat would have been even heavier.

Amos and Robbie, the Bury wingers, proved a constant source of danger to the Charlton defence and Vernon was well supported by Chalmers and Whitfield.

It was Robbie who got Bury's second goal twenty-seven minutes after the start.

Though the visitors concentrated on defence in the second half they put on another goal through Robbie, who was easily one of the best forwards on the field.

HIGHEST SCORES	
OLDHAM	6
CARDIFF	6
ROCHDALE	6
BEST AGGREGATE	
ROCHDALE 6, HARTLEPOOLS 2	8

THE REAL CARDIFF

Northampton Thrashed 6—0 at Ninian Park—Henderson's Proud Feat

Nearly every follower of football has a soft spot in his heart for gallant Cardiff, who yesterday thrashed Northampton 6—0 at Ninian Park, and slightly relieved their anxieties about applying for re-election.

The game was a personal triumph for Henderson, their centre forward, who scored five goals, which is the best individual performance for Cardiff since their First Division days. Cribb netted the other point after Henderson's first.

Northampton were weak in defence, badly beaten for pace, and their forwards, although neat in ball control, had few chances.

POINT FOR THE ORIENT

Weak finishing by the Clapton Orient attack and some brilliant goalkeeping by Slater enabled Watford to retain one point in their home game, which ended 1—1.

The Orient were continually attacking in the opening half, and it was evident that Watford were suffering from that end-of-the-season feeling.

Fletcher netted for the Orient in the second half, and after one or two missed chances Watford levelled matters near the end through Barnes.

FULHAM IN A ROUGH AND TUMBLE

No Goals, No Good Football but Thrills in Plenty

HOWE BADLY HURT

Two sound defences were seen at Tottenham yesterday, where the Spurs and Fulham played a goalless draw, and the forwards on both sides were almost blotted out. Tottenham now want only two points to make certain of promotion and have three games to play.

Of constructive football there was none. It was a game of spoiling. The burly Fulham defence incontinently knocked the Tottenham forwards off the ball, and the smaller Spurs' backs and half-backs tackled so keenly that all the plans of the Fulham inside forwards came to nothing.

Fulham had two good wingers in Arnold and Finch. Both frequently threatened danger, and Evans was always foraging for Tottenham.

Hunt was held in check by Gibbons throughout. He never had a real pass in the match, and he was unable to make openings for himself. Howe was hurt in a collision with Tootill after nine minutes, when he headed just over the bar, the nearest thing to a score in the match.

A few minutes afterwards he was hurt again in a tackle by Barrett and thereafter limped about at outside right, and as luck would have it practically all the scoring chances went to him.

So it became a matter of watching the defences. There were always two men against any forward who had the ball at his toes. Hard

Mr. P. J. Moss, a member of the original Tottenham Hotspur team, who will describe next Saturday's English Cup Final in the "Sunday Pictorial."

knocks were given and taken, and in this respect the heavier team scored heavily.

Perhaps the best player on the field was Rowe, the Tottenham centre half. He covered both his backs with almost uncanny certainty, and almost with the last kick of the match saved what looked like a certain goal by kicking out from under the bar from Woods with Taylor out of his place.

Gibbons, the Fulham centre, never left Hunt, and nearly double his size, always got the ball when it was in the air, as it mostly was. He tried heroically to set his forwards in motion, and when he found that Rowe was holding the middle so strongly he passed out to Finch or Arnold time and again.

T. Evans had a big hand in stopping Arnold, and Felton and Whatley have not played better at back this season.

Keeping was in great form for Fulham; Hindson played well but gave away too many free kicks, and Barrett entered into the rough and tumble so wholeheartedly that he aroused the ire of the crowd. P. J. M.

BACK WITH THE BEST

Stoke Regain Their Place in First Division with an Easy Win

Members of the Football League when the competition was founded in 1888, Stoke City return once more to the First Division next season.

They gained an easy victory by 5 goals to 2 over Lincoln City on their own ground yesterday. Even if they lose their remaining matches Fulham cannot match their goal average.

There was a sensational opening to the game when Liddle headed through almost from the kick-off.

After eighteen minutes the ball appeared to cross the goal-line when Ware shot, but Stoke's appeal for a goal was disallowed.

Sale added a second goal five minutes later, and with the home side continuing to have the better of matters, Palethorpe got a third goal two minutes before the interval.

Lincoln attacked dangerously on the resumption, and after Wilkinson and Hall had missed easy chances, Hall eventually reduced the arrears. Half an hour after change of ends Horne reduced Stoke's lead to 3—2.

The home side, however, finished strongly, and Palethorpe and Sale added further goals before the end.

HAMMERS HIT REALLY HARD

Bold Play Earns First Away Success with Win Over Manchester United

Judging by the confident way West Ham played against the United at Manchester yesterday one could scarcely believe that they were a team in deadly fear of relegation and, until this 3—1 success, without a single victory on foreign soil.

Play jogged along leisurely and Brown should have scored early on for Manchester, but he hit the side netting.

Both sides missed easy chances, but in the thirty-fifth minute West Ham went ahead, Morton putting the ball past Moody as the goalkeeper went out to meet him.

West Ham put in some brisk work in the second half and deservedly went further ahead when a shot by Wilson found the net.

Manchester's play all round was unsteady, but Dewar reduced the lead with the visitors appealing for offside.

ARSENAL'S LEAGUE "DOUBLE" IN SIGHT!

ANOTHER SLIP BY HUDDERSFIELD

Chelsea Fall Back in the Danger Zone

BRENTFORD OUT?

Arsenal are within sight of winning the League championship for the second successive season, as Huddersfield made their task of overhauling the Londoners almost an impossibility through losing at Middlesbrough.

Birmingham steered a bit clearer of relegation with a win over the Spurs, but Chelsea fell back to the last but one place.

In the Second Division, Brentford failed at New Cross and are a point behind Bolton and Preston, who now have the best chances of joining Grimsby to Division I.

Chesterfield have come back to the others in the Northern Section of Division III. It is level pegging with them, Barnsley and Stockport as to who accompanies Norwich to the Second Division.

'NO LUCK' SUNDERLAND

Chapter of Misfortunes in Keen Game at Highbury

By P. J. MOSS

Arsenal 2, Sunderland 1

Sunderland must surely be reckoned the unluckiest side that have lost a League match at Highbury this year. They had the greater part of the play and were beaten.

The Sunderland forwards at times played great football, and only the exceptional defence of the Arsenal kept them out. They had the ball in the net twice, and once Male kicked clear from under the bar with Moss well beaten.

There were times in the game when the Sunderland forwards gave the Highbury spectators glimpses of the forward play traditional from the "team of all the talents." They were five attacking forwards leaving the feeding to the half-backs. And how that line did play!

The game was fought at a terrific pace from start to finish. Quite early in the game Sunderland had their first bit of bad luck when Connor hit the post with a fast, low shot, and a minute later he skimmed the bar with another whizzer.

DRAKE'S GREAT GOAL

Connor, on the Sunderland left wing, led up to most of the determined attacks on the Arsenal goal, and in these opening moments Male and Hapgood tackled and kicked admirably.

Sunderland's second piece of bad luck came when, from a bout of heading in the goal area after Moss had saved twice, Connor or Gallacher beat Moss from close range, only to have the point disallowed.

The game was twenty-four minutes old when Ives miskicked. Drake got the ball and bullocked his way between the backs. Middleton came out to check him, but was seconds late, and the ball was scrambled through.

Beasley, after a delightfully tricky run, beat the defence. While they were waiting for him to pass back to Drake he held on to the ball and scored a great goal.

Drake was sandwiched close in just afterwards by the backs, and brought down heavily. Bastin took the penalty kick, and was many yards wide of the mark with the shot.

For a time after this the Arsenal were all over their opponents, but just on half-time, from a dropping centre by Connor, Moss was beaten, but Male kicked out literally from under the bar. Bad luck No. 3.

Connor, playing great stuff, frequently beat Male and Parkin, and from one of his efforts Carter, after fifteen minutes, beat Moss.

Try as they would they could not break through again, and towards the close the Arsenal had a bigger share of the play, Beasley again being prominent with good shots which tested Middleton, and Bastin shooting wide with Middleton out of his goal.

ENGLAND BOYS WIN

Wales 0, England 2

Although doing most of the attacking, Wales were beaten by a cooller and more resourceful side in the boys international at Cardiff.

There was plenty of fire about the Welsh attack, and several of their forwards were brilliant individualists, but they failed because they did not combine effectively.

The English lads were much more methodical and undoubtedly deserved their win. England had a decided advantage at half-back, where Cattell and Wheeler were particularly prominent.

Both, however, were overshadowed by Pugh, the Welsh centre-half.

Much credit for England's victory is due to N Fowler, their captain, who was undoubtedly the best defender on view.

England's first goal came a few minutes before the interval, when following a well-conceived movement, Butler created a splendid opening for Booth to score. Subsequently it was nearly all Wales, and once they actually did get the ball into the net, only to be ruled offside. In the last five minutes they fell away, and Johnston scored England's second goal.

Middleton, Sunderland goalkeeper, saving against Arsenal at Highbury.

NORWICH THERE

Promotion Points Secured from Coventry in Fine Fight

Norwich City 3, Coventry City 1

It was fitting that one of the best games seen at the Nest this season should give Norwich the final points necessary for promotion.

Coventry, their League rivals, always playing well, strove stubbornly, but had to acknowledge the better team.

Department for department, the sides were well matched, but the home side possessed just that little extra thrust that made the difference.

Norwich took the lead through Bell after ten minutes, but the triumph was short lived, for an equaliser was scored by Jones five minutes later.

With the last kick of the first half Burditt put Norwich ahead again, and the Canaries continued their superiority into the second half. They resumed at once in irresistible style, and the Coventry goal was bombarded.

Vinall made the issue safe with a third goal midway through this period, and although Coventry rallied gamely they were held out by a rigid defence.

The struggle was marred towards the end by a little ill-feeling which crept into the play—the only blot on an otherwise sporting match.

HIGHEST SCORE

BRIGHTON	6

BEST AGGREGATES

MANCHESTER CITY 4, CHELSEA 2	6
NEWCASTLE 5, WOLVES 1	6
SOUTHAMPTON 4, GRIMSBY 2	6
BRIGHTON 6, BOURNEMOUTH 0	6
DONCASTER 5, ACCRINGTON 1	6

HAMMERS OVERHAULED

Two Goals Lead Clipped Back by Bradford City

Bradford City 2, West Ham 2

After leading by two clear goals in this match at Valley Parade, West Ham were practically run off their feet by Bradford City, and the final whistle saved them from defeat.

In an amazing opening ten minutes the Hammers scored twice. The first, from Fenton's foot, followed a perfect centre by Ruffell. The second resulted from a blunder by Bradford's goalkeeper, who misjudged a high kick by Chalkley, which Ruffell headed through.

The City improved eventually, and Spence scored for them with a great shot. Play was even after that until the interval, just prior to which Goulden missed a good chance for the Hammers.

Soon after the restart Spence fired hard against the cross-bar, and Bradford's fierce pressure was rewarded when Hallows shot into the net through a crowd of players.

Warhurst saved under the bar from Fenton, but Bradford were definitely on top through this half, and the visitors' goal was having some narrow escapes when the end came.

SAINTS TUMBLE GRIMSBY

Southampton 4, Grimsby 2

Southampton's win against the Second Division champions, Grimsby, at the Dell was a noteworthy performance and a triumph of thrustful forwards and sound defence.

It was the more creditable because the visitors took the lead after only four minutes' play, Jennings scoring a fine goal from a difficult angle.

Southampton, however, played extremely well, and Brewis converted from a centre by Neil, taking the goalkeeper unawares with a first-time shot.

McIlwaine afterwards put Southampton ahead, but two minutes from the interval Jennings got through to level the scores.

After the interval Lewis struck the Southampton cross-bar with a hard drive; the ball fell in front of goal, where Adams, the best back on the field, kicked away.

Southampton were handicapped by an injury to McIlwaine, which made him a passenger, but went ahead through Holt, who took McIlwaine's place at centre forward.

Adams scored Southampton's fourth goal from a penalty for hands.

CHELSEA MISFIRE

Cup Finalists Put Them Out of Their Stride

TILSON'S HAT TRICK

"SUNDAY PICTORIAL" SPECIAL

Manchester City 4, Chelsea 2

Chelsea, with the exception of a determined rally in the second half, gave an amazingly lethargic display against Manchester City at Maine-road, and therefore cannot grumble at the loss of two valuable points.

It was by no means a brilliant game, for the Cup Finalists were obviously taking no risks that might have brought injury.

The opening stages were more reminiscent of a friendly encounter than a League struggle. Manchester showed splendid opportunism, thanks to Tilson, who scored a hat-trick.

The Pensioners began in lively fashion, Gibson and Horton being especially clever, but Mills spoiled a good movement by remaining offside.

SWIFT QUITE SAFE

After Craig had smartly stopped Toseland, Swift had to save from Russell. The Manchester goalkeeper was always very safe, and both of the goals that beat him left him no real chance.

The first goal came after seventeen minutes, when Tilson scrambled through Brooks's centre. Chelsea equalised before the interval, but it was a fortunate point that Mills obtained.

On the resumption came some real thrills. Tilson added two great goals with efforts which left Woodley hopeless, and Gibson scored Chelsea's second point.

The Chelsea inside left took advantage of some hesitation on the part of the City defence to get this latter goal, which he netted with a hard, low shot that completely deceived Swift.

After the lively Brook had hit the post and Swift had saved well from Russell, Tilson was brought down in the penalty area. Herd struck the upright from the spot kick, then Toseland again put the home side two goals ahead.

The Cup finalists, who wore the maroon shirts they will wear at Wembley, were fortunate in that Chelsea never appeared to get properly in their stride—even during the hectic last ten minutes.

SPURS TOO SHARP

Forceful Methods Pay Birmingham—Whatley's Misfortune

Birmingham 2, Spurs 0

Tottenham showed their best form in the early part of this game at St. Andrews, but after Whatley had put through his own goal to give Birmingham the lead they tried to be too skilful, and against such robust rivals the tactics, naturally, did not pay.

Hibbs only just managed to tip a header from Evans (W.) over the bar, while Moffet failed hopelessly for Birmingham when their attack had its first chance, but luck was with them, for soon afterwards Whatley headed past his own goalkeeper, Nicholls.

Birmingham lost their leader, Fillingham, with a cut eye, and with this player absent Meads missed a great chance of levelling the scores. At full strength again Birmingham became more aggressive, and a shot from Guest skimmed the bar.

There was not much polish about Birmingham's play, but Tottenham, on the other hand, often failed through over-elaborateness.

There was an unusual incident just before half-time, when Birmingham were awarded a free kick. Bradford shot straight into the net, but just before he kicked the ball the referee whistled for half-time, and the goal was disallowed.

Birmingham were definitely on top in the second half, and after several shots had been scrambled away by the Tottenham defenders Calladine headed through.

Nicholls saved shots from all angles, while Hibbs was rarely troubled on his return to the Birmingham goal.

BEES' HOPES SADLY CHECKED

Millwall Half-Backs Turn the Scales

STRAIN TELLING

By TOMMY CLAY (England and Spurs)

Millwall 2, Brentford 0

Millwall were right on their toes in this match, and the result does not flatter them in the least. The whole team worked with a purpose; the half-backs were in tip-top form and Brentford had their promotion hopes sadly checked.

The New Cross side seemed to sense that Holliday was the Bees' most dangerous man. Accordingly, Turnbull, with admirable assistance from Forsyth, gave the centre-forward very little scope.

Turnbull.

Altogether the Brentford attack was not seen in a particularly good light. Their shooting lacked its usual fire and the display gave me the impression that they were feeling the strain of a long season.

I must point out, however, that Brentford's forwards did not receive support from their middle-line trio to the same extent as did the Millwall attackers.

Only the amateur, J. C. Burns, played up to standard. In fact, he was opposed to the best flank of the Millwall forward line—McCartney and Alexander—and his work commands nothing but praise I cannot really hand out bouquets to any other man in the Brentford ranks, although one must not lay blame for this reverse at the goalkeeper's door.

Clough had a couple of none-too-certain backs, Bateman and Astley, in front of him, and that first goal which he let in—a free kick from Hancock for hands—was pardonable, as he was hampered by Yardley, the Millwall leader, besides having the sun in his eyes. It was a dropping kick, too!

This goal knocked a lot of steam out of Brentford. A little later McCartney forced Bateman to concede a corner and from the kick Forsyth headed number two.

Brentford did not promise to make any sort of fight early in the second half. However, they woke up only to find that Yuill, the Millwall goalkeeper, is hot stuff when he has his eye in. We saw Scott and Hopkins show flashes of neat combination; Walsh positioned himself admirably in the home defence and James, the Bees' centre half, was spoken to by the referee after Fishlock had been fouled.

FULHAM OUTSHONE

Superior Combination Gives Bradford a Well-Earned Victory

Fulham 0, Bradford 2

Bradford maintained their interest in the struggle for promotion by gaining a well-deserved victory over Fulham at Craven Cottage.

They scored in practically the last minute of each half. A smart breakaway by Blackmore on the left wing enabled Lewis to give them the lead, while Suggett provided the centre from which Robertson headed the second goal. In both instances the movements were capitally worked out from midfield.

At no stage in the game did Fulham combine so effectively, chiefly because the halves and Price were slow in taking up position.

The quick raids of Lewis and Suggett on the wings gave Bradford a big advantage, and they were also indebted greatly to Crayston, who showed exceptional skill at right half.

SNAPSHOTS FROM THE TOUCHLINES

For the third time in Blackburn's history they finish their home fixtures with an unbeaten record. They are the only side in the First Division this season with such a distinction.

* * *

Huddersfield could make nothing of the Boro's rearranged attack with Camsell at outside right.

* * *

After the Sheffield Wednesday-Liverpool match, Mrs. Blenkinsop, the wife of the England back now with the Anfielders, was presented with a silver coffee service by the Supporters' Club as a mark of appreciation of her husband's services when with the Wednesday.

* * *

It is alleged that spectators threw cushions in the direction of the referee of the Hull-Preston match as he was leaving the field.

* * *

One hundred thousand people saw Glasgow Rangers beat St. Mirren in the Scottish Cup final by 5—0 and regain the trophy they last held in 1931-32.

* * *

Portsmouth wore their Wembley colours against Everton at Goodison Park in a game that was not too interesting.

* * *

The biggest Barrow crowd of the season—8,096—saw the home side put Chesterfield in the cart.

* * *

Marsh, the Q.P.R. half-back, obtained his side's only goal against Bristol Rovers, a few minutes from time.

Bamford has scored forty goals for Wrexham this season.

* * *

Imrie, the half-back, whom Newcastle recently obtained from Blackburn, scored three goals against Wolves.

* * *

Our correspondent wires that the busiest man of the Swindon-Charlton match was Wright, the Londoners' goalkeeper. After reading this you'll be shocked at the result.

* * *

The same applies to Cardiff. Yet they won 3—1 at Aldershot.

* * *

Mitcheson, the Port Vale player, scored thrice in three minutes. That put another Oh! in Plymouth.

* * *

A fellow with the name of Ivory ought to know how to pot them. Apologies to the York player who scored again yesterday.

* * *

Crystal Palace made a dogged fight of it at Torquay, but they were beaten for pace.

* * *

Two backs at Lea Bridge—Robinson (Orient) and Ewington (Watford)—made their first appearances in League football. Watford's winner was scored two minutes from time.

ARSENAL SMASHING WAY TO RECORD?

R. John.

Dynamic Attack and Team-Work Crush Spurs

AMAZING 5—1 SUCCESS

By TOMMY CLAY

the former England and Tottenham Hotspur right back

Arsenal are smashing their way towards equalling Huddersfield's record of winning three League championships off the reel. A week ago they humbled the then leaders, Manchester City. Yesterday they trounced the Spurs. And on each occasion their dynamic attack alone made the result possible. Tottenham are probably still wondering how they came to lose by such a staggering margin at Highbury. I cannot sympatnise with them because of their rivals' better team-work, and had their forwards had more punch the score would certainly not have been 5—1.

Other factors which ultimately led to the Spurs' downfall were that in the space of fifteen minutes early in the game Willie Evans, Rowe and Meads each had to visit the touchline on account of injuries, and that Tottenham made two team changes where one ought to have been necessary

Evans had to have his face attended to. Rowe suffered an injury to his back—it is a matter of conjecture as to whether his mishap had any effect on the result—and Meads apparently strained his leg.

Whatley was unable to take the left back position, and to remedy this blow T. Evans was taken from right half and moved to the vacant position and Colquhoun reinstated in the middle line.

This move was not a success, as from the start Beasley, the Arsenal outside right, played a brilliant game, reminding me of Hulme at his best, and netted the very first goal with a right foot shot which gave Nicholls no earthly chance of saving.

After the interval Tommy Meads changed places with T. Evans, kept Beasley quiet and played one of the best defensive games I have ever seen him play.

The match must now convince the Spurs that they want new wing halves and that the positional play of their forwards, for the present, is all wrong!

ARSENAL STARS

The stars of the Arsenal were John, who came in for Copping at left half, James—who, comparatively speaking, did little but plenty of good—Crayston and Hapgood. Beasley, as I have said, was a star on his own in the first half only.

Nothing seemed to go right for Tommy Evans. It was his punt back to Nicholls which made the goalkeeper put through his own goal to give Arsenal a 2—0 lead.

That knocked some sting out of the Lilywhites, and James was not slow to sum up the situation. His deft footwork left Drake in a position in which he could scarcely have missed a goal even had he so desired! 3—0—and that was all until the interval.

For a few brief minutes after half-time it looked as if we were to see a Spurs revival, but Bob John eventually broke up their raids and gave Drake another goal.

Arsenal slightly eased up at this stage and gave the crowd of 70,000 an exhibition of how football should be played. Some criticised this action, but they could afford to play pretty with such a commanding lead.

Still, Tottenham were serious, and several attempts just went astray before Drake completed his hat trick and Hunt netted the only point for the visitors.

BRUM UPROAR

Gallacher's Last-Minute Goal Gives Chelsea First Away Win

"SUNDAY PICTORIAL" SPECIAL

Birmingham 0, Chelsea 1

Following a drab game at Birmingham there was a remarkable scene in the crowd. With only a minute to go, Gallacher beat Hibbs, Birmingham's international goalkeeper, to get the only goal of the game. A spectator, it is understood, passed an "uncomplimentary remark" to Hibbs. At the end of the game the latter turned towards the crowd for a moment, and then left the field.

This was a signal for a general altercation to break out among the crowd behind the goalmouth, who were joined by others from different parts of the ground. It is alleged that some blows were struck and several people received minor injuries before the police could intervene and disperse the crowd. One of the barriers was broken down during the scene.

A goalless draw would have been a more fitting result to a game in which the attacking work on both sides was unworthy of two First Division teams. On the whole, Birmingham had more of the play but had they scored it would have been flattering to the finishing power of their forwards. The passing of both sides was poor and combination, except for short periods, was entirely lacking.

YOUNG PIVOT'S GOOD MATCH

Gallacher was well held by Crawshaw until that last fatal minute. Crawshaw, a young pivot, who was obtained from Accrington Stanley last season, was making his debut as deputy for Morrall, who was unfit. Mangnall, Birmingham's leader, was often tricky, but he seemed to have lost the thrust which gave him a hat-trick at Liverpool a week ago.

Chelsea's new winger, Spence, had little of the ball, but on occasions he showed that with better support he would probably become a force in the team. Horton, on the other flank, also showed a good turn of speed, and put in a few good shots, but Gregg and Mills seemed to forget they had men on the flanks. When they did decide to swing out a pass it was generally a poor one.

Grosvenor worked hard at inside right in the Birmingham side, but his industry was generally unavailing. Birmingham's most thrustful attacker was the right half, Stoker, who twice gave Woodley difficult shots to deal with. The defences were sound, but they would have been poor indeed had they been otherwise against feeble attacks.

It was Chelsea's first away success of the season.

CHARLTON'S SAD DAY

Coventry Give Them a Severe Drubbing and Take Over the Leadership

"SUNDAY PICTORIAL" SPECIAL

Coventry 4, Charlton Athletic 0

The meeting between promotion rivals at Coventry ended disastrously for Charlton, who were defeated by four clear goals.

The Londoners will probably reflect upon the two glaring mistakes made by Price in the first half as the beginning of their downfall, for had they scored on either occasion the run of the play would have been altered completely.

Coventry, gingered up by these mistakes, settled down to play fast and effective football which produced a goal from Birtley at the end of half an hour's play, and it was by this goal that the home team led at the interval.

Charlton's defence fell to pieces in face of the terrific onslaughts of the Coventry forwards in the second half. Jones, the home inside right, started the rout by scoring from forty yards three minutes after resumption, and from then onwards there was only one team in it.

Birtley obliged Bourton with a centre from which the home player headed a goal, and shortly afterwards Bourton returned the compliment for Birtley to bring the total to four.

But for the valiant work of N. Smith, the only Charlton defender to shine, Coventry would have at least brought their total to the five goals which their own supporters seemed to regard as their right.

It was a great day for Coventry, who, as the result of this victory, take over the leadership from Charlton.

The winners were brilliantly served by their full backs, Brown and Bisby. Brown was chiefly instrumental in preventing Hobbis, the Charlton match-winner, from functioning as well as usual on the left wing.

Jobling contrived to keep Bourton, Coventry's star goal-scoring leader, in check for the first half of the game, but afterwards the home centre got the better of the argument and played a lively part in completing Charlton's fall from grace.

HIGHEST AGGREGATES

Carlisle 5, Gateshead 4	9
Falkirk 8, Ayr 1	9

HIGHEST SCORE

Falkirk	8

VILLA FADE OUT

Flashy Brilliance of No Avail Against Goal-Minded Stoke

"SUNDAY PICTORIAL" SPECIAL

Stoke 4, Aston Villa 1

Stoke set a terrific pace, and their speed did not seem to affect the accuracy of their passing.

The Villa often showed flashes of brilliance, but were inconsistent, and there were periods when their work was crude and unconvincing.

Liddle.

Talbot, who deputised for the injured Allen, did not have a good match, and was handicapped in the second half by an eye injury.

Gardner was also injured, but despite being lame he was the Villa's best half back.

Stoke, however, were irresistible. They revealed great power in attack, exploiting both Matthews and Johnson on the wing to the best advantage.

There was no scoring in the first half, but it was only by desperate concentration on defensive tactics, and as the result of some superb goalkeeping by Morton, that the Villa crossed over on level terms.

With the handicap of Talbot's injury the Villa were unable to stem the tide against them afterwards. Liddle shot the first goal four minutes after the resumption, and fifteen minutes later Johnson increased the lead.

The Villa's attack for a spell flickered into life, Waring reduced the arrears, but Stoke's sweeping attack was rewarded when Sale and Liddle added further goals before the end.

Victor Watson, of West Ham, heading the ball towards the Swansea goal

NOT ALL HONEY!

Bees Get Goals but Notts Give Them Trouble

By TED HUFTON, England and W. Ham

Brentford 4, Notts County 1

Brentford's victory over Notts County, coming after a run of failure, or, at the most, only partial success, doubtless put their supporters in good heart, but to the critical mind it was anything but a convincing performance.

Without going so far as to describe them as lucky winners, I cannot concede that they were ever three goals better than their opponents.

In many respects, indeed, I would rank the County, on yesterday's display, as the more skilful side. They were quicker on the ball and developed their movements with much greater facility than did Brentford.

Their fault was that they lacked a controlling influence at the vital moment. Too often their finishing efforts were made hurriedly or from too wide a range.

If only this could be remedied they would soon begin to climb the table. Their midfield work was worthy of a team in the running for promotion.

I wish I could have said the same of Brentford, but truth forbids me. Frankly, I have not seen the Griffin Park side play so poorly for a long time. They were only a shadow of their early-season selves.

BRILLIANT McKENZIE

Though he scored two goals, the inclusion of J. C. Burns at inside left was not a success. He seemed a trifle cumbersome for an inside forward and was out of touch with the men on either side of him.

But McKenzie, who filled the left half vacancy, was decidedly a success. He is a born footballer, a sound defender and a brilliant constructive player, and I fail to understand how he does not command a regular place.

James, at centre half, was another strong defender, subduing McCartney, just as completely as Walker, his opposite number, did Holliday.

If Brentford had an advantage worth calling such, it was at full back, where Bateman and Poyser always inspired more confidence than did Mills and Feebery, who were inclined to falter under pressure.

Errors by the County defence gave Brentford their first two goals. A miskick by Mills allowed Burns to score in the first minute, and a second goal came when Mills put into his own net after Poskett had failed to clear a centre from Holliday.

Burns scored Brentford's third goal in the first half and later, after Higgins had reduced arrears with the best shot of the match, Fletcher put on a fourth.

Curiously enough, both sides missed a penalty, Mills failing for the County and Holliday for Brentford.

QUICK-FIRE FULHAM

Fulham 3, Bradford City 1

Fulham maintained their improvement in form by administering a sound defeat to Bradford City at Craven Cottage before a crowd of 21,000.

They were cooler and quicker in attack, making most of their opportunities. In the forward line, with Hammond as the prime schemer, they passed the ball to and fro with bewildering accuracy.

Fulham took the lead in the first thirty seconds before a City player had even touched the ball.

Bradford City were more direct in their methods and gave the Fulham defence some anxious moments through quick, first-time passing.

Moore, Peachey and Burnicle, the City half-backs, tackled with resolution, while Wallbanks, left back, was another outstanding player on the losing side.

Fulham scored the only goal prior to the interval through Price. Following the change of ends, Arnold increased Fulham's lead, and after Peel had headed a goal for the City Newton closed the scoring by heading a centre from Arnold into the net.

Smith Beats Newman.—In their series of twenty-four billiards matches, which ended at Thurston's last night, Willie Smith beat Newman 13—11. Closing scores in yesterday's game were: Smith 800, Newman 603; Smith 800, Newman 600.

Hockey.—Cambridge Univ. 3, Beckenham 3; Southgate 3, Oxford Univ. 2; Wimbledon 2, Bromley 0; Tulse Hill 2, United Services 1; Richmond 4, Spencer 3; Hampstead 1, Mid-Surrey 0; Staines 1, H.A.C. 1; Dulwich 4, Brondesbury 0; R.E. 2, Teddington 0; Staff College 4, Epsom 2.

RAMS OVERTURN CUPHOLDERS

One Goal Decides — Claims of Barkas as England Back

DEFENDERS' DAY

By BILLY MEREDITH

Manchester City 0, Derby County 1

Tom Cooper, England's international captain, took a big hand in this game of missed chances at Maine-road, when the Cup-holders sustained their first home defeat of the season.

One conclusion I carried away from the match was that Cooper and Barkas would make a sterling pair of backs for England.

Barkas was a tower of strength in defence and his passes to colleagues were a joy to see.

The City were forced to change Barnett for Dale, who was down with lumbago. The Duke of York was introduced to both teams.

Derby's charge nearly fell in the first minute when Crooks went away to the other end only to see Groves drive wildly over—as he did on two other occasions.

Swift was frequently in action in the home goal, but did nothing serious except to save superbly from the feet of Duncan.

The pace of the game was terrific, and we had a brilliant display of approach work by Derby, although their finishing was bad. It was remarkable how frequently Groves drove wide.

The City, however, were frequently in the picture, and Brook was beaten by the pace of a centre from Tilson when only two yards from Kirby.

GLORIOUS TACKLE

Once Barkas checked Stockill with a glorious tackle right in front of Swift. Bray and Barkas were stars of the game, but Derby's defence was likewise, not allowing the opposing fast-moving attack any latitude.

The first thrill after the interval came when Marshall dribbled clean through, but Tilson topped his shot. Then Duncan put the ball away very wide when a goal seemed certain.

From great work on the right Tilson at last eluded his attendant defender and his shot, taken from an awkward angle, hit the upright. It was hard lines.

Swift was only once tried during a long spell of pressure by the Citizens. But what a rare set of defenders Derby were!

Both sides were straining every nerve at this period. Duncan missed scoring by a miracle, then Crooks missed a sitter. Nicholas came through to test Swift with a nasty one.

Then, after thirty-six minutes, Barnett let in Stockill, whose shot hit the bar for Crooks to net the rebound. A good goal, but against the run of play.

A draw would have more fairly recorded the game, although Derby cannot be grudged the only goal scored.

HAT-TRICK FOR WEDDLE

Preston Fail Badly Against Intensive Attacks of Portsmouth Forward Line

Portsmouth 4, Preston North End 0

Portsmouth, playing without Mackie, the Irish international, pressed the North End defence to such good purpose that they practically walked away with both points.

Such a result was rather unexpected, for in many quarters Preston were fancied. Portsmouth, however, were dominant in both forward and half-back lines.

After shots at the Portsmouth goal by Critchley and Pears had been cleared, Worrall scored from a scrimmage in front of the Preston goal.

Ten minutes later Portsmouth went further ahead with a fine goal headed in by Weddle from Worrall's centre. Gilfillan saved in good style from Pears, and Holdcroft from Worrall and Jack Smith.

Running cleverly through on the left wing, Rutherford centred to Worrall, and he headed to Weddle, who nodded the ball over the bar. A narrow escape.

After twenty-four minutes Weddle put in a very fine solo effort, and scored with a low, hard drive. Pears, from a free-kick, struck the crossbar with Gilfillan well beaten, Weddle heading in from Worrall's centre after thirty-five minutes, thus completing his hat trick.

PALACE ADMIT DEFEAT

Clapton Orient 2, Crystal Palace 0

The Palace showed up well in the goalless first half of their game with the Orient at Lea Bridge. This early promise, however, was not maintained, and Clapton had things their own way.

Mayson figured prominently as the leader of the Orient's raids, and Fellowes, at centre half, also put in some sound work.

After losing Ware, Clapton scored twice in the last quarter of an hour, following some brilliant quick-passing movements.

Haynes and Heinemann, the Palace wing halves, were outstanding for their fine play in midfield.

Fifteen minutes from the finish Mayson provided the centre from which Crawford scored when Owens failed to effect a clearance.

This was Owens's only mistake. With Rossiter, his partner, several times missing his kicks, Owens had a rather thankless task.

The best effort for the Palace came from Crompton, who struck the far post. Dunn erred in clearing and gave Foster a simple chance to add the second goal.

LONDON COMBINATION.—Brighton 2, Northampton 1; Palace 3, Bristol City 1; Charlton 0, Portsmouth 2; Luton 1, Arsenal 2; Leicester 0, Brentford 1; Q.P.R. 2, Coventry 0; Swansea 3, Reading 1; Southampton 2, Watford 1; Southend 1, West Ham 3; Tottenham 1, Bournemouth 2; Chelsea 2, Millwall 2.

ATHENIAN LEAGUE.—Barnet 2, Romford 1; Golders Green 7, Sutton United 1; Leyton 2, Walthamstow Avenue 1; Enfield 6, Southall 0.

ENGLISH SCHOOLS SHIELD.—Brighton 5, Worthing 0; Cambridge 4, King's Lynn 0; Grays 5, Chelmsford 2; South London 4, Lambeth 0; Luton 6, Hertford 0.

KIRCHEN MAKES 2-GOAL DEBUT

NEW WINGER
A BRAINY PLAYER

Off-Side Tactics Help Tottenham Rout

FROM OUR OWN CORRESPONDENT

There's no need to ask around Tottenham way who are cocks o' the south now. That 6—0 defeat by Arsenal at White Hart-lane yesterday will take some considerable time to erase from memory.

So much depended on the result. Victory for Arsenal just meant another step towards the championship, which they have already won twice in succession.

To Tottenham something even more valuable than that was at stake. Recent events have sadly affected their morale. Relegation is around the corner, and local pride had to be upheld. The match has left them in a sad state.

And Tottenham have only themselves to blame. They tried to check the faster Arsenal side with an offside trap, and in so doing piled more weight on their already over-burdened shoulders.

It would not have been so bad had the Spurs the skill to exploit this trick—but they had not. They succeeded up to a point; then fell a goal behind to Drake and could not get out of the dreadful hole.

Added to this Channell and Whatley were not prepared for the unexpected—the one thing

they ought to have been, especially with Arsenal as their opponents.

It would not help matters to describe each and every Arsenal goal. After Drake started the Tottenham rout Dougall and Kirchen made it three before the interval.

Drake and Kirchen got through again afterwards and a pitiful Spurs' exhibition was complete when they gave away a penalty, which Bastin converted.

Tottenham cannot seriously advance excuses because they had to introduce Burgon and D. Hunt (left wing) and Phypers (right half) into their side.

KIRCHEN'S SUCCESS

Arsenal had to make more changes in fact in playing Dougall (inside left), Kirchen (outside right), Sidey (pivot) and Compton (left back)

Kirchen, the former Norwich youth, fitted into the attack remarkably well besides showing that he possesses a football brain. It was ironic that this youth, whom Tottenham were so anxious to secure, should play such a big part in their downfall.

Compton did well as Hapgood's deputy. In fact that was the striking difference between the sides. Arsenal were a team in the fullest sense of the word. Tottenham were a collection of individuals.

Spurs could do with an "old head" to calm and restrain these youths.

I was told that one must go back to the 1914-15 season before a six-goal home reverse can be found against Tottenham.

TWO NEW LONDON R.L. CLUBS

The Rugby League Management Committee, at their meeting in Leeds yesterday, heard applications by Mr. S. E. Parkes and Major T. V. O'Neil Joyce for admission to the League of two London clubs, Streatham and Mitcham and Acton and Willesden.

A special general meeting in Manchester on March 21 will consider the applications.

Kirchen (dark shirt, on ground), Arsenal's new player from Norwich, who was making his first appearance in the side, scoring Arsenal's second goal yesterday.

Teach Young Idea How to Shout!

ALBERT HALL MYSTERY—HIGHER FEES

By THE CLUBMAN

THERE was an amusing sidelight on the Albert Hall riot of boys' boxing, arranged by the working boys' club organisation this week.

The fact that the show produced some grand "mills" is pretty well known by now, as is the fact that one or two onlookers said that the finals beat everything except the police tournament for that perfect mixture of good boxing and good sportsmanship.

What has escaped attention is the attitude of the authorities to the 3,000 or 4,000 youngsters on the slack side of the ropes.

* * *

They made it their business to stop cheering, counter-cheering and the other accepted manifestations of high spirits during the actual progress of the rounds.

The theory, apparently, was that the boy enthusiasts only make joyous noises when some-one is being hit! Seemingly, such an attitude by the spectators was not considered to be truly sportsmanlike.

Well . . . And, as you might add, well, well, well!

It possibly escaped the knowledge of the said officials that boxing crowds simply insist on letting off more hot air than any other sporting fellowship in the country.

Outstanding Lads

A FOOTBALL crowd, telling the referee a few home truths about his family life, is mild compared with your fight fans when they disagree with a decision.

As for the suggestion of bad sportsmanship, I can only infer that when a working-class boy is at the Albert Hall he can be excused for having left his old school tie at home!

Really, this federation of boxing clubs for boys is a grand idea. It has produced many outstanding lads. But don't let it start breeding the wrong sort of spectator.

* * *

I don't profess to know whether this year's Oxford crew is capable of breaking records.

One or two rowing men of my acquaintance seem to think that they have less than an even chance of breaking the recent Cambridge run of victories.

But that is holy territory on which we Regent's Park oarsmen dare not paddle.

In the matter of breaking oars, though, they seem to be better equipped than most crews.

I do suggest that they had better break their allotted quota before the actual Boat Race. The spectacle of Oxford drifting Southend-wards on the running tide, with a sheet hoisted in distress, would be just too funny—for everyone but the crew.

Arsenal Blamed

RATHER a lot of unfair comment of late, particularly in the north, against that happy band of pilgrims known as the Arsenal.

One or two authorities, annoyed that their own particular team cannot buy the best centre

forward breathing for the price of a holiday at Brighton, are blaming the present record inflation of transfer fees on the Highbury directors. This, of course, is sheer nonsense.

Consider the situation. The record high price for a transfer was generally agreed to have been paid by Aston Villa for Allen, of Portsmouth, and Chelsea, during the pre-Jackson days, at least equalled Arsenal in the matter of buying expensive players.

James is the only remaining man in the Arsenal team to cost anything like £10,000.

* * *

The fact that Kirchen cost about £5,000 does not mean that the Arsenal are putting up prices; it proves that so many clubs are hoisting the danger signal that the prosperous teams have to pay inflated money for their new men.

If the Spurs suddenly come out in a last-minute rush of buying, and it is high time they did, they will find themselves paying £6,000 for quite ordinary propositions.

Matter of Showmanship

GOOD news that Walter Hagen, the American golfer, is to come over here once more and try his luck at the Open.

Hagen is one of the greatest players in the history of the game, and it is rather tough luck on him that the incredible exploits of Bobby Jones robbed him of so much kudos during some of his best years.

He is actually more than that. He is one of the game's greatest personalities.

His appearance in the Open at Muirfield this year will guarantee his partner the biggest gallery of the day, not even excluding Henry Cotton, for Hagen has that curious instinct for showmanship peculiar to American golfers.

Some of our own men would be so much better off if they possessed a little of it themselves.

TOO MANY MATCHES!

They Don't Know What to Do—Amateur Club Has to Quit League

Harwich and Parkeston, the all-conquering East Anglians—they have scored 139 goals this season—are so hopelessly in arrears with their Southern Amateur fixtures, that they have resigned from that league.

They will endeavour to finish the present campaign, but it is a moot point whether they can do so, as already they are semi-finalists in five cup competitions.

WITH THE GREYHOUNDS

The Hurdler's selections for to-day are:—

White City.—8.0, Macsboley Buckle; 8.15, Melksham Ivan; 8.30, Glittering Sparks; 8.45, Gallant Ranker; 9.0, Top Pace; 9.15, Tubberona Prince; 9.30, Jooney.
Stamford Bridge.—Afternoon—3.15, Bill's Fine Form; 3.30, Captain Digby; 3.45, Wax Model; 4.0, Grahamsvaun; 4.15, Lord Horner; 4.30, Glib Retort; 4.45, Dick the Villain II.
Clapton.—8.15, Gem; 8.30, King Cup; 8.45, Warwick Baron; 9.0, Achilles; 9.15, Deemster's Heir; 9.30, Gilted Rival; 9.45, White Cottage.
Catford.—8.15, Ashleaf Lad; 8.30, One Way Fashion; 8.45, Wedgewood Crockery; 9.0, Mick the Mopcher; 9.10, Bench and Bar; 9.25, Eastry Girl; 9.40, Blacklion Hero; 9.55, Darling Descent.
Wandsworth.—Afternoon—3.15, Indiarubber; 3.30, York-field; 3.45, Horace Horsecollar; 4.0, Jazzing Coon; 4.15, Brilliant Pop; 4.30, Bargy Boy; 4.45, Alabbar Star. **Evening**—8.15, Red Sunrise; 8.30, Hearty Barney; 8.45, Wise Fanny; 9.0, King of the Fianna; 9.15, Come Right; 9.30, Pete's Fancy; 9.45, Miss Jordan.
Double—Melksham Ivan and Tubberona Prince at White City.

LAST NIGHT'S WINNERS

Wembley—8.0, Fairy Dinkie (T.5) (3-1); 8.15, Honey Buzzard (T.2) (9-2); 8.30, Mick's Revenge (T.4) (2-1); 8.45, Arab Swallow (T.1) (7-4); 9.0, Grubby Fingers (T.6) (5-1); 9.15, Micky the Mule, (T.1) (2-1); 9.30, Jack's the Boy (T.4) (7-2).
Harringay—8.0, Gnide Rope (T.6) (7-1); 8.15, Rubber Band (T.3) (13-8); 8.30, Foregate House (T.3) (9-2); 8.45, Kunla (T.2) (3-1); 9.0, Gladsome Rose (T.3) (9-4); 9.15, Garland Rose (T.4) (9-2); 9.30, Cross Green (T.2) (5-2).
Wimbledon—8.0, Essential (T.1) (5-1); 8.15, Tetraville (T.2) (6-4); 8.30, Mauna Loa (T.6) (2-1); 8.45, Candy's Special (T.5) (5-2); 9.0, Denham Peter (T.3) (7-4); 9.15, Highland Fashion (T.1) (9-4); 9.30, Good Choice (T.3) (7-2).
West Ham—8.15, Calcarr Lion Heart (T.2) (6-4); 8.30, Allen's Road (T.6) (4-1); 8.45, Happy System (T.3) (2-1); 9.0, Betty Macona (T.3) (11-8); 9.15, Double Devoted (T.4) (8-1); 9.30, Hers (T.5) (7-4); 9.45, Loud Laughter (T.6) (9-4).

MISS ENID WILSON BEATEN

Women Golfers Suffer Heavy Defeat by Oxford University Team

Conceding six strokes in each game, Oxford University golfers defeated a team of women players at Beaconsfield, yesterday, by ten games to two, after winning all the foursomes.

The women's team included several players who lost to Cambridge at the week-end by twelve games to two, and was strengthened by the inclusion of Miss Enid Wilson, the ex-champion.

Miss Wilson, however, played her iron shots indifferently and she was beaten 5 and 3 by J. J. F. Pennink, the Oxford captain.

CANTABS' GOLF RESERVES

K. C. Fyfe, the Scottish international Rugby football player, and P. A. Carter have been chosen as Cambridge reserves in the golf team to meet Oxford in the inter-Varsity match at Burnham (Somerset) on March 26 and 27.

TITLE-WINNING IS AS SIMPLE AS ABC!

Otherwise—Arsenal, Bees, Charlton

Robson.

LONDON SET FOR TREBLE

Spurs Almost K.O. Now —Leicester Move Up

DIVISION II POSER

O'Callaghan.

ARSENAL four up and three to play. The League title looks good for Highbury now—for the third year in succession. Sunderland, their only rivals, yesterday dropped a point to struggling Birmingham.

* * *

Tottenham are still in the same division—but not for very much longer. The usual story yesterday. Beaten 4—1 at Stoke. Their only hope of avoiding relegation now lies in the possibility that neither Leicester nor Middlesbrough will win another match. Even then the Spurs would have to win all theirs!

* * *

It must be galling for Tottenham to see the improvement that Leicester have made since O'Callaghan joined them.

* * *

The old Spur shot the goal that won his side a point from Sheffield Wednesday yesterday, with the result that the City's hopes of avoiding "a drop" are brighter than ever.

* * *

Middlesbrough, beaten at home by Grimsby—the after effects of that Good Friday affair at Highbury, perhaps—are now twenty-first in the table—and far from being pleased about it.

* * *

A smashing win at Portsmouth helped the Wolves nearer safety, and Leeds did themselves a good turn in holding the Villa to a draw.

* * *

Brentford, in full sail for promotion, are leaving nothing to chance. Beat Port Vale 8—0 yesterday. Holliday and Robson each scored three. Another three points and the Bees must be champions.

* * *

Blackpool, West Ham and Bolton all won, but the former two gave their supporters a few cold shivers before making sure. They were both behind at half time to lowly clubs.

* * *

Back to their best form—as witness their 3—1 win at Newcastle—Bolton with a match in hand over the other two, seem likely to go up after all.

* * *

Relegation now virtually assured for Notts County and Oldham. County are five points behind Bradford City with three matches to go. Oldham are only one degree better off!

* * *

Charlton, winning at Newport, while Reading lost a home point to Brighton, look like completing a great championship treble for the Metropolis. Three more points will make them sure of promotion whatever happens.

* * *

Newport are almost certain to have to apply for re-election. Southend look like accompanying them on the carpet at the League annual meeting.

* * *

Doncaster beating Tranmere for a second time, won back to the top of the Northern Section with two matches in hand of Chester, their only possible challengers now.

NEWPORT'S HERO

Reserve Keeper's Great Display Fails to Hold Up Charlton

Newport 0, Charlton 2

Charlton made numerous changes for this game, but it did not affect the rhythm of the side, for they took another step towards Division II at the expense of the sectional wooden spoonists.

Paget and Haycox early tested Wright, the Charlton goalkeeper, while Oakes headed away in the goalmouth from a dangerous lob by Clarke.

Charlton, who had an excellent half back line, made generous use of widely flung passes on a heavy ground, and their wingers, Hobbis and Wilkinson, were constantly in the picture.

Williamson, Newport's reserve goalkeeper, played magnificently in stopping a barrage of shots from Charlton's lively forward line and deservedly was given a tremendous ovation.

FOR TOTTENHAM?

Charlton's steady methods and machine-like co-operation between the half backs and forwards told its tale against a weary Newport defence in the second half, and Turner and Smith scored.

Smith, the right full back, had to go to the right wing position because of an injury when he netted.

Charlton made skilful use of their wings, and Newport's defence was often in great trouble, and only Williamson's goalkeeping prevented a heavier score.

Mr. Morton Cadman, of the Spurs, watched the Newport goalkeeper's display. Will he be seen at Tottenham soon?

FULHAM FIGHT TO WIN

Manchester United Get Early Goal, but Then Concede Three in Great Game

Fulham 3, Manchester United 1

If Manchester United still thought they had an outside chance of getting back to Division I it disappeared at Fulham, although they scored a glorious shock goal at the start of the game and showed good all-round strength.

Robertson repelled a raid on the Fulham left, passed up to Bryant who dashed away and turned the ball inwards.

Bamford took it in his stride, swept between the backs, and put in a powerful cross shot which Tootill could not get near.

The crowd then saw Fulham waste a penalty kick. Hammond's first attempt was saved, but the referee judged that Langford came out of goal. So Hammond had another chance, and Langford put a hot shot over the bar.

Consequently Fulham had to fight for more than twenty minutes before they equalised. Then Finch put across a centre which Perry glanced into the net. Just before the interval Warburton centred, and the ball curled inside the far post.

Holding a narrow lead, Fulham withstood strong pressure on resuming. Then they had a full share of the play, and midway through the second half made themselves practically sure of victory.

Barrett joined in a left-flank raid, and from his pass Hammond scored. That completed the scoring, but daring raids on each goal kept the game full of life.

HIGHEST SCORE	
Brentford	8
BEST AGGREGATES	
Brentford 8, Port Vale 0	8
Blackburn 6, Everton 2	8
Reading 4, Brighton 4	8

ONLY ONE HOPE

And That a Remote One for Spurs—Drastic Changes

Stoke 4, Spurs 1

Whatever the Spurs may do now, they can only escape relegation if all the others in the hunt fail to win a single match. As they played against Stoke yesterday they are a team resigned to their fate.

The Spurs made drastic changes, every forward position being altered, but on a treacherous rain-soaked ground they were badly outplayed in the first half, and in twenty-two minutes were three goals down.

Sale scored after seven minutes, Hooper, the Spurs goalkeeper, appearing to drop the ball. Sale headed the second goal from Matthews's centre seven minutes later.

After twenty-two minutes Liddle headed a third goal.

STOKE ALWAYS MASTERS

Liddle, the City inside right, was injured, and changed positions with Matthews, but Stoke were always masters.

Four minutes after the interval D. Hunt reduced the Spurs' arrears.

Stoke's play deteriorated and the defence was not convincing, but the Tottenham forwards could make little headway. Stoke were handicapped by an injury to Turner.

George Hunt made repeated efforts to set the Tottenham attackers working smoothly, but Bolan and Burgon were disappointing on the wings and Sale increased Stoke's lead.

READING HELD TO A DRAW

Free-Scoring Game with Brighton, Who Deserve Their Share of the Spoils

Reading 4, Brighton and Hove Albion 4

A level, but none the less gruelling, game, with plenty of thrills for the 5,000 spectators. At half-time each side had scored two goals, and at the finish the score was 4—4. The result did justice to both teams.

Brighton played the more attractive football in the early stages, when they had the advantage of the wind. Within twenty-five minutes they were two goals up through Short and Brown.

Reading recovered well and got on level terms with goals by Chandler and McGough.

After repelling a number of fierce Reading raids, Brighton broke through the home defence, and within three minutes of resuming, had scored two goals more through Short and Wilson.

Reading hit back, and quickly were on level terms again, Hayhurst and Fielding scoring good goals.

Dons Had Their Chances but—

BISHOPS WON AMATEUR CUP REPLAY

By TED HUFTON (England and W. Ham)

Wimbledon 1, Bishop Auckland 2

Stamina and opportunism beat Wimbledon at Stamford Bridge yesterday in the Amateur Cup Final replay.

With due allowance for the handicap Wimbledon sustained when Barnes, their schemer in chief, was badly shaken up in the first half, I made the Auckland worthy winners.

They lacked the frills and subtleties of the Dons, it is true. Copy-book football meant nothing to these hard-fighting, hard-hitting Northerners.

But the Bishops had the staying power, the courage—and infinitely the greater thrust.

In these respects they were the ideal Cup-fighting team.

To an extent, I believe Wimbledon contributed to their own downfall. They had more chances in the first half than fell to their opponents during the whole of the game. All save one went untaken.

Had Wimbledon continued as they began all might have been well with them. Their short, stabbing passes, deft footwork and skilful positioning at first threatened to outwit a defence that took its time to settle down.

FATAL HESITATION

When Dowden gave them the lead after five minutes the Dons seemed set for their first Final victory.

But it was not to be. Hesitation in front of goal, falling off in the power of the half backs and the Auckland's heroic defence all helped in turning the tide.

Shortly before the interval Wilson levelled the scores. Then came the Auckland's second goal from Bryan and the match was won and lost.

Not even a do-or-die late rally inspired by Dowden and Barnes could shake the Auckland once they had forged ahead.

Hopps, cool and capable, kept a great goal for the winners, and Shield, Mitton and Bryan were others who played a leading part in securing the trophy for the northerners for a sixth time—a record for the competition.

On the Wimbledon side, I was most impressed by Dowden, Barnes and Smith, all of whom did magnificently throughout.

Zenthon did one or two good things, and the half backs, Wright, Bridge and Reeves, took the eye until they shared in the second half fade-out of most of their colleagues.

BOOMERANG RESULT

Exeter Remind Palace That They Live in a Glass House!

Crystal Palace 0, Exeter City 1

The vagaries of holiday form were never more apparent than at Selhurst Park, where Crystal Palace, after scoring thirteen goals in two games, were beaten by Exeter.

Earlier in the season the Palace won 6—0 on Exeter's ground!

The City owed their success almost solely to their defence. Chesters, the goalkeeper, gave a brilliant display, and received capital support from his full backs, Miller and Gray. Webb, at centre half, gave Rooke no scope.

In the first half the Palace, with Manders and Carson combining smartly on the right wing, played excellent football, and Exeter were fortunate when, in a breakaway, Poulter got in a cross shot which Owens tried to clear, but only helped into the net.

This success acted like a tonic to the visitors. The whole team rose to the occasion, and by quick and sure tackling they completely upset the Palace combination.

Later in the game Dunn, the Palace goalkeeper, twice ran out and smothered shots from Poulter, who refused to be dominated by Wilde.

REAL SOCCER AT HIGHBURY

Reds and Huddersfield in Great Game

BEASLEY'S WINNER

By TOMMY CLAY, England and Spurs

Arsenal 1, Huddersfield 0

All the ingredients for a "best-of-the-season" game were there for this match at Highbury. Huddersfield, the only club to win three League championships in succession, were facing Arsenal, who needed both points to further their chances of equalling this great record.

The crowd were not disappointed. Only one goal was scored—that after a melee—and the issue was really open right until the final whistle. It was real football all the way through, the like of which it is not often my good fortune to witness.

Davidson and Dougall took the places of Bastin and James in the Arsenal team, while Luke was fielded instead of Lang as Huddersfield's outside left. The changes made little difference.

At one period this season Huddersfield were at the foot of Division I, but now they possess a side which must be noted for honours in the next campaign.

They have a great defence, in which the pivot, Young, and Willingham, right half, are the dominating men, while their forwards are benefiting by the advice and guidance of their manager, Mr. Clem Stephenson.

BRAINY LEADER

In Lythgoe, at centre forward, they have a leader who, if not a star of the highest order, certainly knows how to use his brains, while the other men interchange positions in a style reminiscent of Huddersfield's championship hat-trick days.

Little wonder, then, that the Arsenal were held to one goal. It was also in defence that the Londoners shone, and Crayston, before any other player in red, deserves praise. In all-round ability he got full marks, and it may truthfully be said he never put a foot wrong.

Hill, on the other flank, also did well, but it would be like painting a lily if I showered praise on other members of the rearguard.

It seems that they cannot make mistakes. They are too well drilled and above all are faithful pupils to the lessons they were taught by the late Herbert Chapman, who had hands in both Arsenal and Huddersfield.

The Arsenal forward line was admirably led by Drake, although he was shadowed effectively by Young.

Rogers shapes as if he will fit into the side with more experience of these games. Beasley got the all-important goal.

RIGBY THE STAR

Orient's Best Player Against Aldershot—Yet They Are Not Keeping Him!

Clapton Orient 3, Aldershot 1

A fine first half display gave Clapton Orient such a mastery over Aldershot at Lea Bridge that the result was never really in doubt.

The man of the match was undoubtedly Rigby, Orient's left winger. Besides scoring twice he made numerous openings for his colleagues, while his combination with Crawford proved the best thing of the match. Yet he is one of the men Orient are not retaining!

Aldershot were seldom other than on the defensive, and they owed a great deal to the fine work of Robb, in goal, for escaping so lightly.

Sheppard, the left half, and Middleton backed up their goalkeeper in capital style, but in attack Aldershot were very weakly served.

Orient went in front after twelve minutes, through Halliday. Oakes equalised ten minutes later, but almost immediately Rigby restored Orient's advantage and in the second half put on a third goal.

Hammers Show Promotion Form

BUT SAINTS FIGHT ALL THE WAY

West Ham United 2, Southampton 1

BY their defeat of Southampton at Upton Park yesterday, West Ham are still well in the running for promotion.

The 31,000 spectators enjoyed a hard, keenly fought game, for the Saints gave the Hammers a good tussle and acquitted themselves valiantly.

The fact that they lost by the odd goal in three throws no discredit on the type of football they served up.

George Watson kept goal for West Ham in place of Conway, and proved a sound deputy.

Certainly West Ham did the larger share of the attacking, and might well have scored more often, but on the whole Southampton's defence, with Roberts, left back, Woodhouse, right half, and Light, in goal, outstanding, worked well. The forwards were always dangerous in breakaway, particularly Fishlock and Tully, the wingers.

Chalkley, at right back for West Ham, was none too certain, and it was through a blunder on his part that Southampton got their goal. Fortunately Watson played confidently in goal, and all the halves tackled with resolution.

Morton, Goulden and Ruffell were the best members of the home front line, and set in motion many good movements.

West Ham forward trying to beat Light, Southampton goalkeeper.

A long pass by Marshall led to West Ham's first goal in twenty-four minutes, Ruffell going on to score with Southampton appealing for offside.

Fishlock equalised shortly before half-time, but Fenton headed the winning goal from Ruffell's corner midway through the second half.

Morton hit the inside of a post when it seemed that he must score. Dangerous raids by the Saints caused Watson anxious moments, and twice he saved well from Tully.

PLAIN MR. DRAKE'S ARMADA ACT

Goal Down Was Spurs' Tonic

CHANGE OF TACTICS BRINGS SUCCESS

By TOMMY CLAY, England and Spurs

Spurs 2, Norwich 1

THERE was an Arsenal touch about much of Norwich's play at White Hart-lane and their effective covering gave Tottenham quite a lot of trouble, particularly in the very early stages, when the Spurs adopted a dainty try-to-be-Division I style.

But a goal against is invariably more of a tonic to a team than a goal for. It was for Tottenham when Goffey converted a centre from Russell following a mistake by Channell, for it rammed home to them the error of their ways.

They cut out that semi-W formation, followed Norwich's five-man attack, forced an equaliser through McCormick, and then got on top without ever causing their rivals to panic.

Indeed, so good was the work of Norwich's halves—Burke (pivot) and Robinson on his right—and Goffey at inside right, that one or two gilt-edged chances were there to be taken.

For example, just before the end, when it got so dark for us to see what was really going on, a clearance by Bowen to Robinson and pass from the latter to Russell led up to a melee in front of Taylor, the Spurs goalie.

Taylor was out of position and Russell realised it. He tried to calmly trap the ball, and place it out of the reach of Taylor. Three yards away from the goalmouth. Could Russell miss? He did—but don't ask me why or how!

NORWICH'S TROUBLE

That was the trouble with Norwich. They could work the ball well but could not seem to get the necessary direction and punch in the final shots

Both Tottenham's goals were well worked out, particularly the first, when Channell robbed Manders, of Norwich, took the ball through to Alsford, his right half, who in turn gave it to Howe.

At that precise moment Howe saw that McCormick (who should have been at ouside right) was out of position, so he made his way out to the wing and then transferred inside to McCormick, who netted a clever equaliser.

The game now developed into a battle of brains with Tottenham's right wing a dominant force. Corner after corner went to the Spurs in the second half, and then young Edrich (for the most part eclipsed by Robinson) centred accurately a McCormick header, and a final touch by Morrison brought the goal which put the home side on top of Division II again.

Morrison did not have a good match. He over-ran the ball several times when he ought to have turned it to good account.

Norwich are certainly building a sound side. The Spurs, however, had no particular stars apart from the McCormick-Howe wing.

West Ham boys beat East Ham rivals in annual charity match, and won cup presented by directors of West Ham United.

STUNG ONCE AGAIN

Brentford Become First Side to Lose Home Points to Liverpool

Brentford 1, Liverpool 2

It has taken Liverpool almost four months to record their first away win. And they accomplished it at Griffin Park with ten men.

Only seven minutes had elapsed when Hanson, the Liverpool outside left, was carried off the field with a leg injury, and he took no further part in the game.

Actually the match was remarkable for the great number of stoppages for minor injuries. Yet the football from the beginning to end was fought out in a most sportsmanlike spirit.

Brentford had more than a full share of the game, but while they revealed some high-class midfield play, the inside forwards, Holliday, McCulloch and Robson could make no impression on the rock-like defence of Bradshaw, Cooper and Blenkinsop.

The Liverpool internationals had to stand up to many harassing attacks by the home forwards, but though Bradshaw was handicapped with a gashed face, he never shirked heading the ball.

Glassey gave Liverpool the lead in the first two minutes. Wright added the second goal after sixty-two minutes, and in a failing light Robson obtained Brentford's goal.

Wembley Lions suffered their first defeat by 3—1 by Richmond Hawks in the London-Paris inter-club ice hockey tournament at Wembley last night. During the match D. Smith (Lions) came into violent collision with an opponent and sustained a fractured jaw.

Palethorpe.

SEVEN SHOT GUNNER SINKS VILLA

Cruising Role Holds Off the "Stopper"

Massie.

"SUNDAY PICTORIAL" SPECIAL

Aston Villa 1, Arsenal 7

IN the days of good Queen Bess a certain man named Drake—Sir Francis of that ilk—smashed up the luxury Spanish Armada. Yesterday at Villa Park plain Mr. Drake—Ted this time—smashed the Villa's team of stars on which something like £30,000 has been spent in the last month or so.

Morton, the home goalkeeper, must have thought the spheres which flashed past him with monotonous regularity were cannon balls, with such force and accuracy were they directed.

Drake broke all records by scoring the whole of his side's seven goals, and the way he played it would not have been surprising if he had reached double figures, though it must be admitted that at times he was smiled on by Dame Fortune.

Faced with Griffiths, captain of Wales and regarded as a fine stopper, Drake did not keep to the middle of the field, but wandered right out on to the wings.

Time after time he would bear down on the home goal with the defence wondering just where he had come from. His shooting was remarkable, and he had really few likely openings except for the seven which he converted.

It was not a one-man victory, for Arsenal played as a team, showing combination in general and covering in defence that were sadly lacking about the Villa.

Remarkable as it may seem, play was fairly even from a territorial point of view. But Villa's attack was shipwrecked on the rock-like defence of the champions.

Wilson did not have an idle time in goal, but most of the shots with which he had to deal were of a hopeless variety. He was covered so well by the rest of the defence and the Villa were such poor finishers that one goal for the home side was about their due.

There was one weak link in the Arsenal attack, Bowden, playing a singularly in-and-out game. He would make a brilliant move and then muff the next hopelessly, while his shooting was wretched.

Drake scored a hat-trick in the first half, but on one occasion he appeared to be off-side when the ball was deflected to him by a Villa defender.

In the first five minutes of the second half he added another two, and had scored a sixth when Palethorpe headed in Villa's solitary one. Late in the game the Arsenal centre forward headed number seven.

Palethorpe deserved a goal for his whole-hearted work in face of a most difficult task, for he got little support from the other members of the line with the exception of Astley.

Massie, the Scottish international, made his debut at Villa Park, but he, too, had a most difficult job. His defence did not impress, but he did show some nice touches constructively.

FULHAM FALTER

Goal Packing Causes Cottagers' Downfall

By P. J. MOSS

Fulham 1, Doncaster Rovers 3

Doncaster Rovers outplayed and outpaced Fulham, and but for playing for keeps and packing their goal when three up with nearly half an hour ago, they probably would have made victory more decisive.

Reminiscent of the old-style Corinthians, they out-played Fulham in the first half. They were tremendously fast, and had none of the ideas that a player's first duty is to get rid of the ball.

The five forwards, moving as a line, chased the ball all the time. Beaten for it, they went after it. Consequently the half backs were able to assist in attack, and there were no gaps. It seemed as if there were always two Doncaster men on the ball to one Fulham player.

The veteran Jacobson, the old Grimsby stalwart, at left back, was another deserving particular mention. Like good wine this veteran improves with age. He is one of the inspirations of the side.

OFF DAY FOR PERRY

It must not be inferred that Fulham played badly. Some of their moves were delightful to watch, Worsley and Smith, on the right wing, giving Perry several fine chances. Perry, however, had a bad day. Twice he missed open goals, and once hit the post.

In the first half Doncaster forced no fewer than eleven corners, but scored from none. The only goal of this period was headed by Baines from a nice centre by Turner.

Baines got his second goal after Keeping and Hindson, the Fulham backs, had both failed to tackle Burton, and the third came from a long dropping centre by Emery. Baines brought the ball down, and when tackled, passed to Burton, who scored.

Then came the goal packing, and in the congestion Finch was fouled just outside the penalty area. Finch placed the kick well, and Hammond headed past Imrie.

SAINTS LACK FINAL SNAP

Poor Finishing Again Deprives Them of Good Approach Work's Reward

Newcastle United 4, Southampton 1

Southampton often played the better football, but their old fault—ineffective finishing—prevented them establishing a deserved lead.

It was all square at half time, Smith having scored for Newcastle and Brewis for Southampton. Probably Newcastle would not have got on top but for Imrie, a half back, setting an example to forwards who finished no better than Southampton's by giving them the lead.

This proved a tonic goal, for in seven minutes Smith and Pearson made the Newcastle total four.

Southampton, who were without Brewis (injured) in the closing stages, had hard-working attackers in Fishlock and Watson.

VICTORY—AND RECORD

Oxford beat Cambridge by one point, and A. A. Robertson, first home for the winners, lowered the course record by 30 3-5s. in the inter-Varsity cross-country race yesterday. Robertson's time for the seven and a half miles was 41m. 56 2-5s.

HIGHEST SCORES

Southall	8
Arsenal	7

HIGHEST AGGREGATES

Aston Villa 1, Arsenal 7	8
Motherwell 5, Partick 3	8
Southall 8, Newport (I.O.W.) 0	8
Tranmere 6, Scunthorpe 2	8

IDEAS LIMITED

But Chelsea's Company Had Not Punch to Ram Them Home

"SUNDAY PICTORIAL" SPECIAL

Preston 2, Chelsea 0

There seems to be no holding P.N.E. on their own ground. They have won their last five matches by a total score of 13 goals to 1.

Chelsea were no match for them from the start. They had good constructive ideas, but they were too slow in developing them, while they also lacked thrust in the vicinity of goal.

They found the barrier in front of Holdcroft so unyielding that the home goalkeeper had little to do beyond cutting out centres and close shots, which he did with characteristic polish.

Cheyne rambled and schemed, but to no advantage, and Gibson, whose footwork on the hard ground was a delight, tried to do too much. Craig was Chelsea's man of iron. He had a steel-like hold on Maxwell—a lively raider, who led him astray sometimes, but seldom beat him.

WOODLEY SHAKY

Law's composure and clean kicking were ever factors in Chelsea's determined resistance to the heavy pressure Preston exerted. Even so Woodley was kept comfortably occupied in goal, and he rarely erred in his timing of shots and centres.

But for all that he was well beaten when after eighteen minutes Dougal deceived the defence by slipping into the middle to score with a surprise shot following a free kick for hands against Craig.

Just on the interval Woodley misjudged a swerving centre from Dougal which went off the crossbar to H. O'Donnell, who showed a dazzling glimpse of footwork in manœuvring an opening to score a brilliant goal which brought the crowd to its feet.

"OWN GOAL" SUCCESS

Luton Town 1, Bristol City 0

Luton, in their promotion effort, will not meet with a harder game than Bristol put up, and they may not meet with such good fortune again for many a day.

Only one goal separated the teams at the end, and that goal was scored by Roberts, who put through his own goal after fourteen minutes.

Pearce gave a glorious display at centre half for Bristol, keeping the burly Thayne in subjection, especially in the first half, when Luton's attack was almost desperate in their efforts to increase the score.

Thayne is forceful without being clever, but Pearce withstood a terrific buffeting.

Luton twice claimed they had scored, but the goals were disallowed, while Bristol suffered similarly when Coen was forced over his line.

The forwards on both sides were apt to be slovenly in their final passing, and a good illustration of inaccurate shooting was when White and McGurk both failed to score with Coen on the ground.

Turner, in final minutes, also failed when an open goal yawned in front of him.

Spots Without Bother

PENALTY KICK DAY AT CHARLTON

By TED HUFTON, England and W. Ham

Charlton Athletic 2, West Ham 2

WHEN you talk about a "local Derby" such as this and three penalties in the same breath, you are liable to give the impression of frayed tempers and too-vigorous football.

There were three penalties in this match—all in seven minutes, and all for "hands." I have never experienced such a thing before.

But no "feeling" crept into the game. In fact, two of the offences for which penalties were given were accidental, and there was not one serious foul throughout.

The result was fair, even when you consider the chances Charlton missed early on. Over-keenness caused these misses, and Boulter and Allen were the chief offenders.

Afterwards West Ham played so well that I really thought they were going to end Charlton's long run of home successes.

If ever a match ought to be dedicated to half backs it is this one.

Half-back-in-chief was Barrett. He did the work of a man and a half, and so bottled up Allen that I doubt if Charlton's centre will ever have a match in which he is so impotent. Barrett also found time to give his attack some assistance, and in this respect his play contrasted strongly with that of Rist, the Charlton pivot, who played a purely defensive game to the exclusion of Mangnall.

CONWAY'S FREAK SAVE

The other men who stood out in this game were Walker (A.), West Ham's left back, who practically blotted out Wilkinson, and Charlton's left wing triangle, Hobbis, Boulter and Welsh.

The way Hobbis controlled the ball while flashing down the wing gave Fenton (E.) and Chalkley, on the right flank of the Hammers' defence, as hard a job as they are likely to have for a long time.

We also saw some good goalkeeping at both ends. In this connection I must mention a freak effort of Conway's. In dealing with a free kick by Wilkinson he clung to the cross-bar with one hand and twisted the ball from under to over the bar with the other to save at the expense of a corner.

Goulden gave West Ham a half-time lead with a swerving shot after receiving a back pass from Mangnall. Then followed those three penalties in the third, sixth and tenth minutes of the second half

From the first Smith equalised for Charlton; from the second Barrett put the Hammers ahead again; and from the third Smith saved, as it turned out, a point for his side.

To sum up, two hard-fighting sides kept it up for ninety minutes, and either might have landed in a winning goal in the last quarter of an hour's darkness.

FORWARDS' DAY OUT

Pompey's — and Blackburn's — Give the Crowd Plenty of Thrills

Portsmouth 3, Blackburn Rovers 1

What a game! Shot after shot, magnificent saves by both 'keepers and each defence at full stretch.

Vause, of Blackburn, started the fireworks with two great shots which Gilfillan pushed away. Then Easson centred to Parker, who easily beat Binns at the other end.

Binns thrilled the crowd with a magnificent save off a shot from Worrall, while a few minutes later Gilfillan saved in great style from Bruton.

The Rovers continued to press, and Thompson scored. Not to be outdone, Parker headed Pompey's second goal a few minutes later.

Binns brought off another fine save from McCarthy and Thompson fumbled a great chance to put Blackburn level by erratic shooting.

Just to bring the game to a satisfactory end, two minutes from the finish Worrall scored a wonderful goal to put Pompey further ahead. It was a game keenly contested and full of thrills from start to finish.

Tough guy in Guy's Rugger team falls on ball and checks a Liverpool movement.

HOCKEY IN BRIEF

Cheshire 0, Yorkshire 0; Durham 3, Northumberland 2; Southgate 2, Beckenham 1; Richmond and Kingston Hill 6, Staines 0; Tulse Hill 8, Hampstead 0; Mid-Surrey 4, Bromley 0; Wimbledon 8, Dulwich 0; H.A.C. 5, East Grinstead 0; Teddington 2, Surbiton 2; Spencer 7, Bank of England 0; Nat. Prov. Bank 7, Barclays Bank 0; Purley 2, Blackheath 2; Civil Service 3, Westminster Bank 2; Staff College 1, R. E. Aldershot 1; Polytechnic 3, Lloyds Bank 1.

ARSENAL JOY

FOR THE CUP IS THEIRS!

The Cup comes south ! Alex James, captain of Arsenal, holds aloft the trophy while he himself is held aloft by team-mates. The final was a match of one goal—that scored by Drake late in the second half. Sheffield almost equalised immediately, but, beyond that, they made no rally.

"MAKING IT UP" WITH HUSBAND

Margot Grahame, English-born film actress, says she is arranging a reconciliation with her husband, Francis Lister, the actor (top picture), from whom she separated last summer. She is sailing for London within a few days.

CRICKET AGAIN, and Barling hits out in a way that Surrey supporters will hope to see repeated often this season. He was playing for a team captained by E. R. T. Holmes against Oxted and Limpsfield.

Goal - scorer Drake heads the ball away from Johnson (stripes), Sheffield United's centre half. Drake was a doubtful starter until a few days before the match.

ARRESTED at Ventimiglia with his schoolmaster, Martin Privett has returned home to Fareham. They accidentally crossed the Italian frontier without passports and were held under arrest for five days.

DRAKE MAKES IT ARSENAL'S CUP

Prior

Oakes

ALL BUT IN DIVISION I

Only One Danger to Charlton

Charlton Athletic 3, Bradford 1

From Division III to Division I in a couple of seasons is the record Charlton all but made their own by a well-merited victory over Bradford yesterday.

It's long odds against them being pipped. West Ham can just do it, but our money's on Charlton.

Showing smart combination, Charlton called the tune all the time against Bradford. But in view of the strenuous time they had against a relentless attack the Bradford defenders must be given full marks.

Farr effected some fine saves, and the full backs, Lloyd in particular, showed resolution. Danskin did well at centre half, although opposed to a clever centre forward in Prior. The last-named led the Charlton attacks skilfully and scored two fine goals.

REDUCED TO TEN MEN

Bradford's forwards moved quite well when they did get going, Nolan being a thrustful centre. The Charlton defence played splendidly, Joan Oakes, at centre half, again being outstanding, with Welsh a fine attacking half back.

Charlton gained the lead in the first minute, Wilkinson scoring from a centre by Hobbis. Bradford immediately levelled the scores through Nolan following a corner on the left.

Prior regained the advantage for Charlton, and fifteen minutes later scored again.

Bradford fought gamely throughout, particularly in the second half, when they were without Barrett (injured)

MEEK AGAIN AMONG TOTTENHAM GOALS

Tottenham Hotspur 3, Doncaster Rovers 1

Spurs must have pleased their supporters with their 3—1 win, but they scarcely deserved their two-goal victory.

Over-elaboration spoiled their chances in the first half. The forwards kept the ball too close, and though they were well supported by their halves they lost opportunities which ended in dilly-dallying over shooting.

For twenty minutes or so following change of ends, however, Doncaster were well on top. The well conceived and rapid movements of their forwards proved too much for the home half backs, and it was fortunate for Tottenham that Whatley and Buckingham were at their best in defence.

A leg injury then rendered Turner (A.), the visitors' outside left, practically ineffective, and Tottenham pressed strongly.

The home team made a fine start by gaining the lead, Meek scoring after Imrie had saved from Edrich. Doncaster, keeping play well open, equalised twelve minutes later through Baines, who headed past Cooper from an opening made by Turner (A.)

A smart movement between Edrich and Meek ended in Duncan regaining Tottenham's lead ten minutes before the interval. Ten minutes from the close Meek completed the scoring.

"LAST KICK" GOAL STOPS CHELSEA WIN

Wolverhampton 3, Chelsea 3

Of the six goals scored in this match four came in the last eight minutes.

Wolverhampton took the lead in ninety seconds from a penalty successfully taken by Shaw.

Chelsea drew level in the twenty-second minute, Oakton getting over a good square centre, from which Burgess drove into the goal.

Wolverhampton had further scoring chances, but splendid goalkeeping by Woodley, who three times saved well from Martin, and splendid defensive work by Law and Barber kept the home forwards out.

For thirty-five minutes of the second half Wolverhampton monopolised the play, but could not get past the Chelsea defence until the eightieth minute, when Martin gave Wolverhampton the lead again after Ashall had done all the work.

Three minutes later Mills put his side on level terms with a fine header following a centre from Spence. Mills gave his side the lead in another three minutes — Wolverhampton keenly disputed this goal—and with two minutes to go Martin, showing wonderful enterprise, put Wolverhampton level

No Real Rally by Blades in "Missed Chance" Final

HOOPER'S VITAL ERROR

By TOMMY CLAY, England and Spurs

Arsenal 1 (Drake), Sheffield United 0

A GOAL by Drake fifteen minutes from the end enabled the Arsenal to bring the Cup to London for the second time and thus equal a record held by the Spurs, who have also won two finals.

If there are still people who doubt the Arsenal's wisdom in playing Drake, then this vital goal must silence them. It was the only real chance the centre forward had in the whole game, and the way he brought the ball under control and then drove in a hard, true, left-foot shot—the leg which was operated on, mark you —was masterly.

It was hard luck on Sheffield, though. Their captain and right back, Hooper, made one mistake. That error let in Bastin, who squared the ball for Drake to do the rest and prevent the trophy from going to Sheffield for the second year in succession.

After this vital shot had been sent in and the ball returned to the centre Sheffield nearly equalised when Barton got a clear run on the right wing.

The Arsenal defence was caught napping. An equaliser seemed certain, but with Wilson, the goalkeeper out of position, Dodds's header hit the cross-bar to bounce back clear of danger.

GREAT DEFENCE

It was the Arsenal defence which saved the day. Male simply could not—perhaps would not is better—put a foot wrong, and, despite the constant inter-changing of positions by the Sheffield forwards he was not to be caught unawares.

If anyone in the Arsenal could be accused of being "sold the dummy," it was Hapgood, who nearly allowed Barton to level matters near the end.

Roberts played quite a normal game at centre half, but it must be admitted that Dodds, the strong and speedy Sheffield leader, gave him more to think about than many other centres have done in the past.

Dodds was exceptionally strong in veering out to the right wing, and although he made several chances after giving Roberts the slip nothing ever came of them. When cutting out to the left wing Dodds was sadly lacking in ideas, and time and again allowed the ball to be taken off his toe.

There was one glaring fault in the Sheffield attack. They had evidently planned to interchange positions, but in doing so they often perplexed themselves more than their opponents.

PICKERING'S BIG PART

Frequently a player was left with the ball and hesitated—thus wasting valuable time—in order to discover if there was anyone in the right place for the right pass.

Nobody was more puzzled about this than Williams, the dandy little outside left, who came in for the injured Bird. Williams had some nice touches, but seemed nervous about using them in case nobody was up to take his passes

But for sheer combination and skill Sheffield have to be congratulated. The way Pickering welded the half back line and attack together was, next to Male's great full back display, the best thing in the match. Johnson, at centre half for the United, was great, clean, strong kicking being a feature of his play.

That Sheffield failed to profit by his work was because Barclay, apart from one or two early touches, had an off day and that Dodds could never find a way through.

Sheffield had the chances to make goals, but they could not get in telling shots, while Arsenal, with not so many opportunities, could have won the match by a wider margin. Hulme spoilt many movements by holding the ball too long.

It was at left half that Sheffield had a decided weakness. McPherson was not fast enough to hold Hulme, who played as if he were his side's match winner until it came to giving somebody else the ball to put in the final shot.

The only occasions the Sheffield goal was really in trouble was when Crayston cut through directly after the kick-off at half time and when Bowden and James sent in a header and a shot respectively in quick succession.

SHEFFIELD'S GILT-EDGED CHANCE

Bowden's header was only just collected by Smith, the Sheffield goalie, and as he scrambled it away along the line Drake tried desperately hard to force him over. He was unlucky, though. James's shot was unexpected, and the way Smith saved showed his class.

Just before the Bowden incident Dodds missed a gilt-edged chance of opening the score. The whole attack simply had the Arsenal defence bewildered, but when Barclay sent over an unexpected centre Dodds was caught sadly unawares, and then made a do-or-die effort which only made the miss look worse than it really was.

It was at wing half where the superiority of the Arsenal lay. In Crayston they had a man ever ready to go up and attack. Copping did not seem so eager in this respect, because he had a very clever winger in Barton to subdue.

WELL-DRILLED ARSENAL

Once or twice when Barclay and Barton criss-crossed from outside left to inside left and back again, Copping was guilty of some charging which was not quite according to the book of rules. Only once did the referee pull him up.

Considering the pace at which the game was played and the ding-dong encounters that took place, tempers were kept remarkably well.

To sum up the affair in a few words, gallant Sheffield were beaten by a well-drilled team who stuck thick and thin to plans that have carried them so successfully to the top of the tree.

By no stretch of imagination could it be said Arsenal were the more clever side. They were not. They knew how to take chances, and that decided a game which might have ended all square but for one unfortunate slip. Just to show how Cups are won and lost Sheffield had a similar chance to that which brought Arsenal's goal, in the very opening minute, but the ball struck Wilson and went for a corner.

Arsenal forwards give Smith, Sheffield United goalie an anxious moment.

HAMMERS THERE—IN CASE OF ACCIDENT

"SUNDAY PICTORIAL" SPECIAL

Port Vale 2, West Ham 3

West Ham wanted the points to retain a chance of going up. Port Vale needed them just as badly to keep alive their hopes of staying in. West Ham got them—so they're still near enough to pop up if either Charlton or Manchester United slip.

But Port Vale were decidedly unfortunate not to force a draw. They were the better side in the first half. After the interval, though West Ham were more polished and less hurried in their work, the home side had a good deal more of the play territorially.

There were periods when the Vale's forwards had the West Ham defenders in difficulties. The visitors were by no means impressive in defence. Conway made some spectacular saves, but he took risks and often left his goal unguarded.

He was out of his goal on two occasions when Shenton and Jones struck the crossbar in the first half.

Roberts gave Port Vale the tonic of an early goal when he dribbled past Conway in seven minutes, but six minutes later Foxall equalised and five minutes before the interval Mangnall, from Doc. Marshall's clever pass, put West Ham in front against the run of the play.

In the second half two goals followed in the breath-taking spell of a minute. First Caldwell headed past the advancing Conway to put Port Vale on level terms, but immediately the game had been restarted Mangnall scrambled the ball through in a goal-mouth struggle.

Port Vale did not deserve to lose and merit sympathy for putting up a great fight. They lost many chances through their desperate anxiety to make sure of winning.

Steve for Mahmoud.—S. Donoghue has been engaged to ride Mahmoud in the Two Thousand Guineas on Wednesday.

Surrey Golf Champions.—Represented by F. Francis, E. F. Storey, W. L. Hartley and P. W. L. Risdon, Surrey won the English county golf championship at Deal yesterday with 624. Kent, 627, were second, and Lancs, 633, third

FULHAM LEADER IN THE WARS

Fulham 0, Swansea 1

An indifferent display by the Fulham attack in front of goal was partly responsible for the poor game seen at Craven Cottage. The match was set aside to provide benefits for Barrett, Gibbons and Finch.

Apart from Gibbons, who figured prominently at centre half, and Clarke and Tomkins, the wing half backs, Fulham appeared to lack enthusiasm, and throughout the second half, with Woodward, the leader, a passenger with a dislocated shoulder, on the right wing, the Fulham forwards were even less effective.

Brain, the Swansea centre forward, gave Gibbons much trouble and although he was ruled off-side a number of times, he was a capable leader and collaborated well with Bussey and Olsen, the inside forwards.

Lawrence, the Swansea right back, who scored the winning goal from a penalty kick twenty minutes after the interval, defended stubbornly and prevented the Arnold-Hammond wing from being at all dangerous.

Lions Take the Lead.—Wembley Lions went to the head of the National Ice Hockey League by defeating Wembley Canadians 5—2 last night

The most interested spectators at the Cup Final were four players of the rival teams who were not taking part. They were Stacey (Sheffield), Bird (Arsenal), Beasley (Arsenal's twelfth man) and Cox (Sheffield's twelfth man).

VILLA SOUND LAST POST

Farewell to Division I

"SUNDAY PICTORIAL" SPECIAL

Aston Villa 2, Blackburn Rovers 4

Famous Aston Villa ended an inglorious season in inglorious fashion in being soundly beaten before their own supporters by Blackburn Rovers, whom they now accompany into the Second Division.

On their display in this match, Villa deserve the last place rather than the Lancastrians, who were easily the more impressive side, except for one short spell in the second half.

Villa's lack of combination throughout the season was as glaring as, if not more glaring than, ever, and there was a touch of luck about both their goals.

Callaghan, who was on the injured list, was sadly missed at centre half. Allen, who deputised, seemed ill at ease. Cummings, too, was below form, and often found Bruton, the Rovers' international right winger, too much for him.

As a matter of fact, it was Bruton's trickiness that directly led to three of the Blackburn goals —the first, the second and the fourth. Sale scored two of them, and the ex-Stoke man, who was the outstanding inside forward on the field, thoroughly deserved this reward for his hard work.

GOALKEEPER'S ORDEAL

The first goal came after five minutes, Sale nodding through. Five minutes later Halsall got number two, and after twenty minutes Thompson added the third.

Villa's only reply to these three goals was one by Broome, whose shot Pratt (J.), Blackburn's amateur goalkeeper, let slip through his fingers. But bar this mistake he came through the ordeal of his League debut with flying colours.

Early in the second half Gorman, the Rovers' right back, handled in the area when a goal did not seem imminent, and Houghton shot in from the spot.

Playing with desperation, Villa extended the Rovers' defence for a quarter of an hour after this. But Blackburn came again and Sale shot in another Bruton centre to settle the issue.

BEES DAZZLED BY THIS LIGHT!

Brentford 2, West Bromwich Albion 2

Light, the former Southampton 'keeper, dazzled the Bees' forwards yesterday with some of his saves.

For although this clever young goalie had a trying afternoon he emerged with flying colours. His coolness and courage, combined with clever anticipation baulked Brentford's nippy forwards time and again, and Albion owed a big debt to him

Brentford really deserved to win a thrilling encounter, for they were stronger and better balanced in every phase of the game, except shooting. Once the defence had recovered from a goal by Richardson (W. G.) in four minutes, Mathieson, Wilson, Bateman and the halves never looked like giving way.

McCulloch led the home forwards strongly, and Scott and Holliday, his immediate colleagues, worked untiringly from start to finish.

It was Scott who equalised after thirteen minutes, and Reid headed through for Brentford shortly before half-time. Albion, however, never gave up trying, and Wood saved them a point with a rather lucky goal just on time

GUEST SIDE TAKES RUGGER "SEVENS"

Sale, the "guest" team, won the seven-a-side tournament at Twickenham yesterday—the first occasion on which they had entered—after a most enjoyable afternoon's sport. They beat Blackheath in the final, 18—6, writes Line-Out.

The Northerners, with Claude Davey and Wooller in smashing form, were just a bit too fast for all their opponents and looked likely winners from their first match, when they made short work of Rosslyn Park and the dreaded Obolensky.

But the team which made the greatest impression was the comparatively unknown Metropolitan Police, who lost to Blackheath in the semi-final after extra time.

The Police showed fine snap and decision, and in A. C. Jones had the "find" of the day. Much more will be heard of Jones next season.

Old Haberdashers, another "unknown," also put up a good performance, and their game with the Police in the eighth round was perhaps the titbit of the day

★ John Thompson's Monday Soccer Chat

WAR-BLINDED MAN 'SEES' HIS FIRST MATCH

Fortunately for Hubbick, Bremner, Arsenal's new inside right, missed—Hubbick, not the ball—when Bolton's left back slipped and fell when tackling the Arsenal player as he was taking a shot at Highbury.

FOOTBALL curtain comes down with a grand flourish after one of the most dramatic finishes the game has ever known.

It's been a great and memorable season, with the quality of football consistently high and with a spirit of fair play generally dominating the doubtful methods which have marred some previous years.

And so at last we know who triumphs and who fails in the almost frightening desperation of the final struggle for points.

Gloom in several camps this morning as managers of relegated sides keep thinking "if only . . ." Joy in others where success has smiled on the promoted ones.

Ambition rewarded at Millwall and Tranmere, ambition made even keener by this encouragement, a feeling that "nothing can stop us now, First Division for us next."

Pity that goal average should make two decisions—who should rise with Aston Villa and who should fall with Stockport.

Bad luck on Sheffield United, who had finished their programme and so had to sit back and await the results of the Manchester United and Coventry games Coventry could only draw, but United beat Bury to damn Sheffield's hopes.

Spare sympathy, too, for Barnsley. They drew with Notts Forest, went down because of .002 of a goal

✦ ✦ ✦

NOW for the champions of them all the mighty Arsenal, at the top for the fifth time in eight seasons.

Congratulations, Mr. Allison, on turning the tables on the know-alls who were too soon mourning what they called the departed greatness of the Arsenal.

Wolves failed at Sunderland, so Major Buckley's biggest ambition was not fulfilled

Nonsense, though, to say that gland treatment has failed . . . running-up in the First Division can hardly be called "failure."

✦ ✦ ✦

WHAT will the Leagues look like next season; will Ipswich get in, and, if so, who'll drop out?

Those are the big queries to-day. Here's what I think: With both Barnsley and Stockport in the Third Division North, Barrow (that town's a Rugby League stronghold) may drop out, and Ipswich may fill the vacancy in the Southern Section

✦ ✦ ✦

OF the many touching and human little incidents I have witnessed behind the Soccer scene this season none will stand out in my memory more than one which took place at Charlton on Saturday.

Through the kindness of his friend, manager Jimmy Seed, a war-blinded man was able to follow every movement of the game and spend the most enjoyable afternoon of his life.

Our story began a few weeks ago. It was then that Jimmy met Bill Dykes, with whom he played football before and during the war

Jimmy went to see Bill in hospital and invited him to "see" Charlton play Preston—the first match Bill had been to since he was blinded. After the game there was a reunion celebration in the boardroom.

They sat together during the game, Jimmy describing every shot and every save so graphically that Bill became excited, knocked another spectator's stick to the floor as he half-rose to cheer on his pal's team.

He was thrilled, too, when he held for a moment the cup which Preston had brought with them. "It makes me very proud to touch this," he said.

Later he praised Jimmy's ability as a commentator. He smiled. "I couldn't have enjoyed the game more if I'd been able to see it," he said.

"Myself and Mr. Dean, who's come with me, are the two most envied men in the hospital. I enjoyed every move in the game, and I'll be able to describe it all to them when we get back to-night.

"I've been looking forward to this day tremendously and it's been just what I expected . . the most wonderful day of my life.

"It's been something I shall remember always. Jimmy's a grand sport to have done all this for me."

And while the crowd clamoured for him to go out and make a speech, Jimmy came down to the board-room to look after his friend

✦ ✦ ✦

LATER the Villa team left Birmingham on the first stage of their German tour.

Yesterday officials and players and their wives joined the liner Europa at Southampton on their way to Bremerhaven.

During the trip to the Continent, Mr. F. H. Normansell, chairman of the club, presented to the captain of the Europa's football team, one of the best ship teams on the North Atlantic, the ball used in the Norwich game.

Villa will play three matches against German teams and will be guests of the German Football Association at the international match between Germany and Britain at Berlin on May 13

✦ ✦ ✦

Swansea and West Ham both won away from home for the first time in the season.

Wolves who are already getting ready for "the next time," are reported to have paid £1,000 for Tagg, twenty-year-old inside forward from Crewe.

✦ ✦ ✦

NO holidays for the Sunderland players—not yet, anyway.

Sunderland are entered for the Empire tournament at Glasgow, and manager Cochrane believes that if they are to win the players must be thoroughly fit.

So, although it may not be so exacting, training must go on as usual.

First round is due on May 25.

I think this will take some beating for an example of end-of-the-season irony.

Newcastle United, only saved from a drop on goal average, transferred Jack Smith to Manchester United and Jimmy Richardson to Millwall. These players helped their new clubs to promotion.

Their old rivals at Sunderland, always safe in the First Division, sold McNab and McDowell for £14,500, and the clubs who bought them, West Bromwich and Manchester City, were relegated.

✦ ✦ ✦

LEAGUE champions last season and top-scorers this year, Manchester City, one of the relegated First Divison clubs, are down . . . but not out.

They have one big slogan in mind for next year . . . "Back to the top-liners" . . . and they mean to make the grade.

Manager Wild, of the City, said yesterday, "Naturally we're sorry to go down, but we were the first to congratulate our neighbours, Manchester United, on their re-entry to Division I.

✦ ✦ ✦

HERE'S Pat Collins to describe Arsenal's moment of triumph :—

Picture the Highbury enclosure at a minute to five o'clock on Saturday. Arsenal had the game won, the Wolves were losing at Sunderland. Any minute the result of their rivals' game would come through. A win for Wolverhampton meant no championship for North London.

The men out there were forgotten for the moment, every eye was turned towards the score-board where the result would appear. Suddenly a great burst of cheering from those nearest the board. The Wolves had lost. . . .

The cheers swept round the ground until they became one mighty roar.

Then the final whistle. Arsenal had finished like champions with a five-goal victory.

There was no holding the crowd. From every side they poured on to the pitch. The players rushed for the safety of the dressing-rooms.

All except Eddie Hapgood. In a moment he was swept up, found himself being tossed about on a mass of heads as the crowd shouldered him.

✦ ✦ ✦

Then the crowd clustered at the foot of the stands, yelling: "We want Carr. We want Carr." It was a fitting tribute in view of the great game the Arsenal youngster had played.

Police were powerless to stop the onward surge of the crowd, which became bigger every moment. Then came the best move of the afternoon, better even than the best Arsenal move of the game.

The Arsenal band leader had struck up "Auld Lang Syne," the crowd sang it, but they still went on jostling. Came that brilliant move. The strains of the National Anthem rang out over that pushing, shouting stream of humanity.

Instantly the shouting died, the pushing ceased and hats were whipped off. The invaders stopped in their tracks, and as one great choir they all took up the song.

That was the greatest thrill of the afternoon. The game that went before was suddenly a dim memory, even though it had meant so much.

£1,760 Goes to Players

Players talent money amounting to £1,760 will be distributed among the winners and runners-up of the League's four Divisions, under a new Soccer ruling. This is in addition to £2 win and £1 draw bonuses paid during season. Here's where the money goes :—

DIVISION I. — Champions, Arsenal; talent money, £275. Runners-up, Wolverhampton, £220. Relegated, Manchester City and West Bromwich Albion.

DIVISION II.—Champions (promoted), Aston Villa, £275. Runners-up (promoted), Manchester United, £220. Relegated, Stockport County and Barnsley.

DIVISION III (S.).—Champions (promoted), Millwall, £220. Runners-up, Bristol City, £165. To seek re-election, Walsall and Gillingham.

DIVISION III (N.).—Champions (promoted), Tranmere Rovers, £220. Runners-up, Doncaster Rovers, £165. To seek re-election, Accrington Stanley and Barrow.

Honours winners in the leading amateur leagues were:—

ATHENIAN. — Champions, Walthamstow Avenue. Runners-up, Barnet.

ISTHMIAN.—Champions, Leytonstone. Runners-up, Ilford.

EASTERN COUNTIES. — Champions, Lowestoft Town. Runners-up, Bury Town.

ESSEX COUNTY.—Champions, Harwich and Parkeston. Runners-up, Crittall Athletic.

LONDON. — Champions, Eton Manor. Runners-up, Epsom.

SPARTAN. — Champions, Waterlows (Dunstable). Runners-up, Windsor and Eton.

★

It's nice to be popular, but we think we should run if we saw a huge crowd rushing at us even if their intentions were friendly. This is only part of the crowd which invaded the pitch to cheer and chair their heroes — the Arsenal players— after they had beaten Bolton and won the championship.

HOW THEY FINISHED

DIVISION I

Arsenal	5	Bolton	0
Charlton	0	Preston	0
Everton	1	Derby	1
Grimsby	2	Chelsea	0
Huddersfield	1	Manchester City	0
Leicester	1	Birmingham	4
Middlesbrough	4	West Brom. Albion	1
Portsmouth	4	Leeds	0
Stoke	2	Liverpool	0
Sunderland	1	Wolverhampton	0

	P.	W.	D.	Pts.		P.	W.	D.	Pts.
Arsenal	42	21	10	52	Blackpool	42	16	8	40
Wolves	42	20	11	51	Derby	42	15	10	40
Preston	42	16	17	49	Everton	42	16	7	39
Charlton	42	16	14	46	Hud'ersfield	42	17	5	39
Middlesbro'	42	19	8	46	Leicester	42	14	11	39
Brentford	42	18	9	45	Stoke	42	13	12	38
Bolton	42	15	15	45	Birm'gham	42	10	18	38
Sunderland	42	14	16	44	Portsmouth	42	13	12	38
Leeds	42	14	15	43	Grimsby	42	13	12	38
Chelsea	42	14	13	41	Man. City	42	14	8	36
Liverpool	42	15	11	41	W.B.A.	42	14	8	36

DIVISION II

Aston Villa	2	Norwich	0
Barnsley	2	Notts Forest	2
Bradford	0	Swansea	1
Chesterfield	0	West Ham	1
Fulham	3	Blackburn	1
Luton	4	Newcastle	1
Man. Utd.	2	Bury	0
Plymouth	4	Southampton	0
Stockport	1	Coventry	1
Tottenham	1	Sheffield Wed.	2

	P.	W.	D.	Pts.		P.	W.	D.	Pts.
Villa	42	25	7	57	Luton	42	15	10	40
Man. U.	42	22	9	53	Plymouth	42	14	12	40
Sheff. U.	42	22	9	53	Norwich	42	14	11	39
Coventry	42	20	12	52	South'pton	42	15	9	39
Spurs	42	19	6	44	Blackburn	42	14	10	38
Burnley	42	17	10	44	Sheff. W.	42	14	10	38
Bradford	42	17	9	43	Swansea	42	13	12	38
Fulham	42	16	11	43	Newcastle	42	14	8	36
West Ham	42	14	14	42	Notts F.	42	14	8	36
Bury	42	18	5	41	Barnsley	42	11	14	36
Chesterfield	42	16	9	41	Stockport	42	11	9	31

DIVISION III (S.)

Aldershot	1	Swindon	1
Bournemouth	1	Bristol R.	3
Bristol C.	3	Notts Co.	1
Clapton Orient.	1	Southend	1
Exeter	1	Millwall	5
Mansfield	1	Brighton	1
Newport	1	Walsall	2
Northampton	0	Cardiff	0
Q.P.R.	6	Torquay	3
Reading	2	Gillingham	0
Watford	1	Palace	2

	P.	W.	D.	Pts.		P.	W.	D.	Pts.
Millwall	42	23	10	56	Southend	42	15	10	40
Bristol C.	42	21	13	55	Bournem'th	42	14	12	40
Q.P.R.	42	22	9	53	Mansfield	42	15	9	39
Watford	42	21	11	53	Bristol R.	42	13	13	39
Brighton	42	21	9	51	Newport	42	11	16	38
Reading	42	20	11	51	Exeter	42	13	12	38
Palace	42	18	12	48	Aldershot	42	15	5	35
Swindon	42	17	10	44	Orient	42	13	7	33
North'pton	42	17	9	43	Torquay	42	9	12	30
Cardiff	42	15	12	41	Walsall	42	11	7	29
Notts Co.	42	16	9	41	Gillingham	42	10	6	26

IRISH LEAGUE (Cup Final Replay).—Belfast Celtic 2, Bangor 0

DIVISION III (N.)

Barrow	4	Lincoln	1
Carlisle	6	Rotherham	1
Chester	3	Accrington	1
Doncaster	1	Tranmere	1
Gateshead	5	Darlington	2
Hartlepools	2	Wrexham	0
Hull City	1	Crewe	1
New Brighton	1	Port Vale	1
Oldham	1	Bradford	2
Rochdale	1	Halifax	1
York City	1	Southport	2

	P.	W.	D.	Pts.		P.	W.	D.	Pts.
Tranmere	42	23	10	56	Carlisle	42	15	9	39
Doncaster	42	21	12	54	N. Brighton	42	15	8	38
Hull	42	20	13	53	Bradford C.	42	14	10	38
Oldham	42	19	13	51	Port Vale	42	12	14	38
Gateshead	42	20	11	51	Southport	42	12	14	38
Rotherham	42	20	10	50	Rochdale	42	13	11	37
Lincoln	42	19	8	46	Halifax	42	12	12	36
Crewe	42	18	9	45	Darlington	42	11	10	32
Chester	42	16	12	44	Hartlepools	42	10	12	32
Wrexham	42	16	11	43	Barrow	42	11	10	32
York	42	16	10	42	Accrington	42	11	7	29

RUGBY LEAGUE.—Cup Final—Barrow 4 pts. Salford 7.

PICTORIAL

HIGHLIGHTS FROM YESTERDAY'S SOCCER

2 PROMOTION GOALS COST A BROKEN ARM

FIVE of the championship, promotion, relegation and re-election issues have been settled. Arsenal are League champions, Birmingham return to the sphere they vacated nine years ago, Grimsby Town step down to Division II, Doncaster, after but one term in that Division, and Millwall are relegated to the Northern and Southern sections, while Halifax Town and New Brighton must apply for re-election.

DRAMA of the day was enacted at Newcastle where, three minutes from time, the United and Sheffield Wednesday were sharing two goals apiece before a capacity crowd of 66,480.

Then, before the eyes of his parents, watching him for the first time in big-time Soccer, young winger Houghton sprang to life, slammed a couple of goals into the Wednesday net, and almost put Newcastle back where they belong after fourteen years in Division II.

The cost? Houghton's removal to hospital with a broken arm and a leg wound which necessitated stitching

✦

ARSENAL sat for their championship photograph, then took the lead through Don Roper. But that was as long as they were "in the picture."

Thereafter goals by Johnny Stamps and Billy Steel enabled Derby County to complete the double over them—a feat no other club has accomplished this season.

✦

STAN PEARSON, the man whose hat-trick gained Manchester United their Cup Final ticket, was responsible for Chelsea's downfall at Old Trafford.

The visitors were never five goals inferior, yet United's loss of Rowley (injured) may prove the greater upset.

✦

MILLWALL may well feel that everything has been against them throughout the season. The goal which sealed their fate at Fulham was "made" for Thomas (R.) by full back Bacuzzi.

With Woodward carried off concussed, and Jones suffering from a knee injury, Spurs accomplished a praiseworthy performance by drawing at Coventry, where Barratt (own goal) gave them an interval lead.

✦

BRENTFORD and West Ham are the width of London apart but had much in common. Both engaged in goal-rushes. The Hammers got three in five minutes (Hall, Woodgate and Wade) at Leicester, and Brentford three in seven minutes (Blakeman, Gibbons and Buchanan) against Bury. Dawson later scored a fourth.

Southampton have fallen out of the promotion race and Queen's Park Rangers' form at Exeter hardly encourages Bournemouth to think Rangers will crack now.

It looks like a case of "so near and yet so far" for the county of Hampshire.

✦

THE loss of Tommy Lawton and two home defeats within the space of a few days have been Notts County's lot.

Recovering from concussion, Lawton was a spectator of Norwich City's win at Meadow Lane yesterday.

✦

NOTTS FOREST paid Luton Town £9,000 for the transfer of centre half Horace Gager.

They probably consider the fee a bargain basement expenditure — Gager's penalty goal and dour defence ensured retention of their Second Division status.

✦

CRYSTAL PALACE failed to reproduce their Bristol Cup-tie win, but Graham enhanced his goalkeeping reputation

The goal which former Brentford favourite, Len Townsend, scored against them was his 32nd of the season.

✦

SNAPSHOTS: Swansea, last of the clubs to do so, surrendered their unbeaten-at-home record.

Morton and Rangers failed to decide their Scottish Cup Final and replay at Hampden Park on Wednesday.

Ironical fate. That New Brighton should produce stars Denis Westcott (Wolves) and Johnny Stamps (Derby County) and now seek re-election.

AMATEUR CUP FINAL

Leytonstone's double

Leytonstone 1, Barnet 0

"I SHALL never forgive myself." So said Ronnie Phipps after the game. He was referring to his amazing miss in the first half, which probably lost Barnet the Cup

Unmarked three yards from goal, he ballooned Kelleher's pass over the bar. Up to then Barnet had looked the more likely scorers. But after, Leytonstone got well on top and were worthy winners of an exciting game.

Bunny Groves, who passed a last-minute fitness test, got the goal that mattered in the sixty-eighth minute.

For once, he found himself unattended by schoolmaster Tommy Leek, who had been playing the game of his life. Groves made no mistake in slamming home Smith's header.

Leytonstone thus join the select band who have won the Cup twice running. Their forwards were the match winners. Groves, Joseph and Smith gave the Barnet wing halves so much to do that they could not feed their forwards.

Lester Finch got few chances to show his match winning qualities. Dennis Kelleher worked like a trojan and was the only Barnet forward who looked likely to pull the game out of the fire.

Jim Paviour produced his best club form for the occasion, giving Phipps only one chance to score

With the rest of the Stone's defence playing at the top of their form it was easy to see how they have conceded only one goal throughout the competition

McDonald Bailey not through yet

McDONALD BAILEY, the British sprint hope for the Olympic Games, who has been suffering from hip trouble, yesterday saw Sir Adolphe Abrahams, the specialist.

Sir Adolphe expressed the opinion that Bailey would not be exactly 100 per cent. fit for the Olympics, but the sprinter, with his usual optimism, was not dismayed, and stated afterwards:—

"I am not willing to give up track racing until every conceivable thing has been done to get me absolutely fit." he said.

OLYMPIC PROFILE

OLNEY WORKS FOR SUCCESS

IN October, 1946, Alex Olney joined his first athletics club Thames Valley Harriers. Today this protege of Sydney Wooderson is regarded as Britain's No. 1 for the Olympic 5,000 metres.

Alex has always been interested in sport generally, and before the war took his cricket very seriously. He competed in athletics at school, but not until he was serving with the paratroopers in Italy were the potentialities of his track form revealed.

His work as a sales engineer with a fire-extinguisher firm curtails his training hours, but the Middlesex three-mile champion manages to spend four evenings a week at Paddington Recreation Ground and other tracks within reach of his Richmond home.

Alex has the great benefit of having Wooderson as his guide and mentor, and between them they are busily working out suitable schedules. Alec White, Thames Valley secretary and former Scottish international half miler, also takes a great interest in his progress.

During the winter months Alex, like most athletes of the middle-distance calibre, keeps fit by cross-country running, at which he has had considerable success—including international honours. D. F.

JON'S SPORT PARADE

My autographed drawing today is of Ray Lindwall, Australia's speed merchant, reputed to be the fastest bowler in the world.

With the bat he is no mean performer, having scored a century in a Test against England. He is also a reliable fielder near the wicket.

Out of season Lindwall is a top-grade Rugby League player.

Cup Final spy wasted his time at Charlton

By Stanley Halsey

Charlton 2, Blackpool 0

FORTY-FIVE thousand fans and a Manchester United Soccer spy, who caught a pre-Cup glimpse of Blackpool at The Valley, will back Manchester United to win the Cup.

But not Stanley Matthews. Stan, the world's wizard winger and the only Blackpool player to provide a few streaks of Soccer skill and entertainment yesterday, gave Blackpool as his private tip in the chatter of the dressing room

Practically every prized Soccer trophy decorates his private den. One is missing—a Cup winner's medal. Matthews longs for that beyond all the riches of his successful career.

Stan's Hope

I hope he gets it. Certainly if Blackpool serve up the plotless, mediocre Soccer seen yesterday, Manchester United must command the Final by the biggest goal margin recorded since Bury beat Derby 6—0 in 1903. But of course, they won't.

Nutshell sum-up of the Valley situation was that both teams were playing for safety. Charlton for safety in the zero zone which they have practically obtained, Blackpool for the kind of safety that would avoid reckless injuries to their Cup key men.

To nominate the personality of this game one must turn to Charlton centre forward Vaughan, much more confident these days.

A quick snap pass from Vaughan to Hurst created the opening that brought Charlton's first goal through McCrae.

Vaughan's second-half goal was worth the match. His taking of the ball, his turn and precision placing of his shot made it one of the best I've seen this season.

Charlton could have had a third goal from a twice taken penalty. Revell hit the first shot cleanly. The referee ruled that the goalkeeper was not on his line when the hurried kick was taken. The second shot was tame, and saved.

CLIFF BASTIN says: Charlton without showing anything outstanding won easily. Vaughan was the star.

Blackpool were far below form. Matthews shone only occasionally. Mortensen was right out of the picture.

Snooker.—Joe Davis beat John Barrie 37 frames to 36 at Leicester-square Hall last night. Final session scores (Davis first): 83—70, 89—42, 53—93, 75—72, 55—97, 81—77, 83—56.

DON AS GUEST OF UMPIRES

DON BRADMAN came along to the committee room as an invited guest at a meeting of English first-class umpires at Lord's yesterday, writes FRED ROOT.

When leaving, Colonel R. S. Rait-Kerr gave Don copies of the amended M.C.C. laws of cricket. The Colonel said he was broadcasting the main items of alteration on Tuesday.

Bradman noted there were only sixteen copies, and jocularly informed the Colonel that for fear of his making a faux pas in the broadcast there were seventeen Aussie players making the trip.

He himself, Bradman, knew all the catches in the rules, so he presumed the Colonel thought there was no need for him to have a copy.

Race results and prices at 3 meetings

LINGFIELD

2.0 (5f.).—**Annie Besant** (1-4 f, G. Richards) 1, Double Deal (7-1) 2, Woodborough (8-1) 3. Also ran: 33 Amber Rose, Pink Rose, Silver Princess, Royal Bow (Fk. Butters.) ½ lgth, 4.

2.30 (5f.).—**Entrancer** (13-2, K. Gethin) 1, Roman Circuit (4-9 f) 2, Bold Sight (20-1) 3. Also ran: 1 Adanom. (P. Thrale.) ½ lgth, 3.

3.0 (1m.).—**Minster Lovell** (2-1 f, T. Burn) 1, Lady Rosa (100-9) 2, Winter Wheat (20-1) 3. Also ran: 9-2 Kishore, Bramhall Kid, 10 Northumbria, Fairstream, 100-6 Birijik, Sixteen Bells, 20 Supersonic, Mariner's Call (W. Smyth.) 6 lgth, nk.

3.30 (6f.).—**Pando** (2-1 f, W. Rickaby) 1, Top Walk (3-1) 2, Elysium (11-4) 3. Also ran: 9-2 Foxendown, 20 Marygreen. (J. Wood.) 3 lgth, 1½.

4.0 (2m.). — **National Spirit** (6-4, G. Richards) 1, Kingsmead (11-8 f) 2, Cesar (100-9) 3. Also ran: 100-9 Filius, 100-8 Hollywood Model, 33 Compact, Useful. (V. Smyth.) Sh hd, 8 lgth.

4.30 (1½m.)—**Twelve Club** (13-8 f, E. Smith) 1, Quags (20-1) 2, Lady Victoria (100-8) 3. Also ran: 4 Bruce Lowe, 5 Ishkan, 100-8 Suresh, 100-7 Noble Mead, 20 Rosscar, Chiffchaff, Ravenswood, Coup de Vent, Antrim Castle, Henry the Third, Argine, Windrow. (R. Jarvis.) 3 lgth, nk.

BEVERLEY

2.30 (1m.).—**Blue Light** (11-4 f, P. Maher) 1, Gallivant (100-7) 2, The Reel (8-1) 3. Also ran: 11-2 Statute Book, 8 Pink Blossom, Jim's Cherry, Ocean Calm, 100-7 Guisbro Lass, Golden Crag, 20 Sunny Dulce, Gay Gordon, Game Licence, Scarpin, Truanna. (Moulton.) 1 lgth, 2.

3.0 (5f.).—**Refund** (5-2 f, G. Younger) 1, Royal Mirari (5-1) 2, Arctic Lord (3-1) 3. Also ran: 4 Ice Cap, 100-8 Donate, Westerly Wind, Strand Varnish, 25 Freddy M., Mikado II, Wintersun, Pampas Choice, Satlight, Maureen Bay, L'Aube (R. A. Jones.) Hd, 2 lgth.

3.30 (1m. 5f.). — **Crusader's Horn** (11-4, W. Evans) 1, John Moore (5-2 f) 2, Navigate (7-2) 3. Also ran: 8 Bosnia, 10 Master Builder, 100-8 Scottish Welcome, 100-6 Exhibitioner, 20 Arch Design, Convalescent, Leighdale, Whitley Light, The Quin. (Elsey.) Nk, 3 lgth.

4.0 (5f.).—**Brelades Bay** (20-1, J. Walker) 1, Mira Flores (8-1) 2, William the Fourth (8-11 f) 3. Also ran: 6 Captain Tim, 13-2 Deemster, 10 Just Double, 20 Eric B., Terrier, Here's Cherry. (Storie.) ½ lgth, ½.

4.30 (5f.). — **Ballyrogue** (20-1, W. Carr) 1, Tudor Emblem (4-5 f) 2, Solenda (20-1) 3. Also ran; 7-4 Royal Lion, 100-6 Angels Path, 20 Grantown, 33 Sunhaven, Jim Dandy, Wavegem, Village Victor, Royal Cause, Epic Star, Fairfree, Arbella, Java Star. (Hammett.) 5 lgth, 4.

5.0 (1½m.).—**Haberdasher** (6-4, W. Evans) 1, Reed Mace (5-4 f) 2, Le Hose (20-1) 3. Also ran: 100-8 Fairdonian, 20 Prince Marco, Annagain, Golden Surprise, Benula, Broadmoor, Five Minutes More, Stellus, Euphegenia, Sally M., Colbert, Fair Dell (Elsey.) 1½ lgth, 3.

BOGSIDE

2.15 (2m.).—**Irish Lizard** (6-4 f, H. Nicholson) 1, Edgewood (7-1) 2, Shining Gold (2-1) 3. 16 ran.

2.45 (5f.).—**Linkabo** (7-2, J. Caldwell) 1, Spoilt Child (20-1) 2 Bettsann (1-3 f) 3. 5 ran.

3.15.—**Scottish Grand National** (about 3m. 7f.).—**Magnetic Fin** (100-8, L. Vick) 1, Bruno II (7-1) 2, Ulster Monarch (10-1) 3. Also ran: 5 Gallery, 11-2 Caddie II, 6 Bandra, 8 Drunken Monk, 10 Knockirr, 100-8 Bricett, 20 Closure, Copper Twist, Fighting Line. (W. Hall.) Hd, 8 lgth

3.45 (1m.): — **Tower Knowe** (8-1, C. Spares) 1, Troonbay (6-1) 2, Mountshannon (100-8) 3. 6 ran.

4.15 (1m. 4f.). **Red Salute** (5-4 f, N. Stirk) 1, Stiletto (100-8) 2, Autumn Mist (17-2) 3. 6 ran.

4.45 (3m.).—**Dynevi** (4-1, Capt. J. Smith) 1, Gallochmore (11-8 f) 2, Cat Burglar (100-8) 3. 8 ran.

REPORT TO THE NATION No. 14

BRITAIN'S BUDGET

What we get for our money

What happens to the money we pay in taxation? Some of it is spent for us, on things we need and can't buy for ourselves—like roads, schools and a navy. Some of it is given straight back, as money, to the people whom we have all decided to help—the old, the sick, the mothers and the unemployed—and as interest on money the Government has borrowed in time of need. See how each £1 of our money is divided.

£1

DEFENCE. This includes the Navy, Army and Air Force pay, food, clothing, arms and equipment. **4/8**

FOOD SERVICES. This includes part, but not all, of the subsidies which help to keep down prices of essential foods. **2/2**

EDUCATION, HEALTH & HOUSING. Schools, hospitals, homes—the things that mean so much to our children's futures. Partly met by local rates, Government's contribution is **3/3**

CASH BENEFITS. These include old age pensions and family allowances, as well as the Government's contribution to the National Insurance Scheme. **2/5**

INTEREST ON LOANS. This is the interest the Government pays on all the money lent to it, including Savings Certificates, Defence Bonds, etc. **3/4**

THE REST OF OUR £1. Police, roads, farm services, civil aviation, colonial development, occupation of Germany, etc. **4/2**

These benefits and services can only come out of our National output. If output falls, they will have to be cut. When output rises, we shall be better able to afford them.

It all adds up to—

Credit Column

MESSRS. SMITH, BROWN, JONES AND ROBINSON of here, there and everywhere have again done a year's hard work and paid their taxes with no more than the usual amount of grousing.

MORE AND MORE PRODUCTION

Issued by His Majesty's Government

Daily Mirror | TUES., APL. 19 | FORWARD WITH THE PEOPLE

Geraldine House, Fetter-lane, E.C.4. Holborn 4321. And at 42-48, Hardman-st., Manchester, 3. Blackfriars 2313.

The man with the magic touch is crowd's delight

THE man with the magic hands and feet—Denis Compton, England cricketer and Arsenal footballer—at Highbury yesterday gave 47,000 of Soccer's millions of fans all the thrills they travel miles every week to see but seldom do.

It was magic in his left foot which made two goals that sent Blackpool away goalless and pointless. And his first kick of the match gave Arsenal their first victory in eight matches.

This, a lob into the goalmouth, enabled Lishman to crack the ball past the Blackpool goalkeeper.

The game was only fifty seconds old. Then, after thirty-seven minutes, Denis sent a neat pass to McPherson, whose tap was headed in—Lishman again.

It was the real old Denis though perhaps a little slower, with the fans applauding his every touch. Mortensen missed two golden opportunities for Blackpool, who felt the absence of Matthews.

But Denis sent the crowd away enthused about a match they will talk about for years to come.

Rumour has it that Compton will retire from Soccer at the end of the season. But how could anyone wishing to give up the game play such a blinder as this?

And if he did wish to give up the game how could the crowd let him go?

The 'Wizard' Who Could Not Save Them

And here is the story of a Soccer wizard who did not come off—red-haired Peter Doherty, Huddersfield's Irish international with the twinkling feet.

Twice Peter has saved his side from relegation in successive seasons, but, back in the team against Liverpool, all his efforts could not prevent them being beaten by four clear goals.

Doherty worked like a Trojan, spoon-feeding his younger colleagues, but their habit of trying one more too many proved their downfall.

Hero of Charlton's 1—1 draw at Everton was goalkeeper Sam Bartram. Charlton looked booked for a heavy defeat as the Everton forwards swarmed round goal, but Bartram defied all scoring efforts, apart from that by Eglinton in the second half.

The magic left-foot in action. . . . Denis Compton takes a corner in the game at Highbury. Every move he made was cheered by the crowd.

WAYMAN'S RETURN WAS NOT ENOUGH

SOUTHAMPTON have hit the "goaldrums." Not even the inspiration of Charlie Wayman, who came back at centre forward against Grimsby yesterday, could get the attack into proper form.

They had three parts of the play, but, after taking the ball to the penalty area, they seemed to lose their ideas—and a point in this goalless draw.

Bates might have won the match in the second half, when he had the ball yards inside the penalty area, unmarked, but shot wide.

The forward line was sluggish, particularly on the wings. Day, at outside right, had one of his poorest games of the season.

Defence Sound

The defence was sound enough, although they had to keep a close watch on tall, long-striding Briggs, who more than once threatened to go through in lone raids for Grimsby.

Chisholm, in the Grimsby goal, made a great save from Wayman from close range, when the centre forward was given the ball by Scott—once again the most active forward in the line.

Crowd roared—and Jack got the winning goal

FIVE minutes to go at the Hawthorns and forty thousand West Bromwich supporters waited for two things—for Albion's forwards to get a goal and for the half-time score of promotion rivals, Fulham.

The board went up: Fulham lead 2—1. The crowd roared and almost immediately Jack Haines bent almost double to send in the low header which kept Albion in the First Division running.

Tough luck on Coventry, whose scratch team, upset by holiday injuries, gave a grand display.

But good luck for Jack Haines, who otherwise had a bad day.

WON ALL THREE

The Barbarians won the third match of their Welsh tour yesterday when they beat Swansea by two goals to a try.

ONE CLUB'S REVIVAL HITS A RIVAL'S TITLE HOPES

VICTORY for Middlesbrough over the mighty Newcastle . . . defeat for Huddersfield and Preston. But it is still anybody's guess who will go down into the Second Division.

At the top of the table, Portsmouth slipped with defeat at Birmingham, but they still have a strong grip on the leadership.

Southampton, clinging to the lead of Division II, are in danger of having the championship snatched from them.

Loss of a point at home—even though centre-forward Charlie Wayman was back, leaves them only two points ahead of Fulham and three in front of West Bromwich Albion, who both won.

But the Midland club has three games in hand, the Londoners one.

It is as you were at the top of Division III (N.). Both Hull and Rotherham won, but although still level on points, Hull have two games in hand.

Swansea strengthened their position at the head of Division III (S.) with their defeat of Newport.

Manchester United, Swansea and Hull were the only sides to gain full points for the three holiday games, although West Bromwich have a chance to do the same today at Coventry.

Highlight of the day was Middlesbrough's grand win.

Two second half penalty kicks by Hardwick, after Newcastle were leading 2—1, gave them the points that may keep them in Division I.

HOLDEN WINS

The Doncaster - Sheffield marathon race yesterday was won by Jack Holden (Tipton Harriers) in 2h. 41m. 55s., two minutes ahead of B. L. Hensley (Gosforth).

'CHASING HINTS

CHEPSTOW.—2.0, Tredilion; 2.30, Golden Horus; 3.0, Royal Fusilier; 3.45, Cromwell.

WETHERBY.—2.15, Memmerkirk; 2.50, Martin J.; 3.55, Dancing Flame.

Three race cards and Bouverie's Best on Page 7.

LEAGUE RESULTS AND TABLES

DIVISION I

Arsenal .... 2 **Blackpool** .. 0
Lishman 2

Birmingham 3 **Portsmouth** .. 0
Stewart, Badham, Hindmarsh (og)

Chelsea .... 1 **Man. City** .. 1
Campbell — Munro

Derby ...... 2 **Burnley** 0
Stamps, Steel

Everton .... 1 **Charlton** 1
Eglinton — Vaughan

Huddersfield 0 **Liverpool** .. 4
Balmer 2, Barron, Liddell

Man. Utd. .. 3 **Bolton** 0
Rowley 2, Mitten

Middlesbro .. 3 **Newcastle** .. 2
McCrae, Hardwick 2 — Milburn, Mitchell

Sheffield U. .. 1 **Wolves** 1
Whitelum — Mullen

Stoke ...... 2 **Preston** 0
Peppitt, Steele

	P.	W.	D.	L.	Goals F.	Goals A.	Pts
P'tsm'th	38	23	8	7	76	35	54
N'castle	39	20	10	9	69	54	50
Man. U.	35	17	10	8	66	34	44
Derby ..	37	18	8	11	59	51	44
M'ter C.	39	15	14	10	46	46	44
Arsenal	38	15	13	10	65	40	43
Charlt'n	39	15	12	12	62	59	42
Wolves..	36	15	10	11	69	58	40
Stoke ..	38	15	8	15	60	59	38
Liverp'l	38	12	13	13	50	37	37
B'ham C	39	11	14	14	35	35	36
Burnley	39	12	12	15	42	47	36
Blackp'l	39	11	14	14	50	62	36
Sund'l'd	37	10	15	12	43	55	35
Villa ..	37	14	7	16	53	71	35
Chelsea	38	11	12	15	65	64	34
Bolton ..	38	13	8	17	55	64	34
Evert'n	38	11	10	17	37	61	32
Sheff. U.	37	11	9	17	54	66	31
Preston	38	10	9	19	56	70	29
Mid'bro	37	10	9	18	40	52	29
H'd'f'ld	38	10	9	19	34	66	29

RUGBY UNION.—Manchester 13 pts., North of Ireland 3; Cardiff 12, Harlequins 0; Newport 8, London Welsh 3; Swansea 0, Barbarians 5; Bath 27, O.M.T.S. 6; Blackheath 17, West of Scotland 13; Exeter 16, Moseley 5; Bedford 26, Wakefield 8; Redruth 6, Wasps 6.

DIVISION II

Barnsley .... 2 **Lincoln** 0
Richardson 2

Bradford .... 1 **Notts F.** 2
Donaldson — Scott, Ashman

Brentford .. 1 **Spurs** 1
Dare — Walters

Bury .... 3 **Leeds** 1
Whitworth 2, Massart — McMorran

Cardiff ...... 1 **Blackburn** .. 0
Lever

Leicester .... 1 **West Ham** .. 1
Lee — Robinson

Luton ...... 1 **Fulham** 3
Brennan — Rowley, McDonald, Thomas

Plymouth .. 3 **Q.P.R.** 1
Strauss 2, Tadman — Addinall

Southampton 0 **Grimsby** 0

W.B.A. ...... 1 **Coventry** 0
Haines

	P.	W.	D.	L.	Goals F.	Goals A.	Pts
So'pton	40	23	8	9	68	34	54
Fulham	39	22	8	9	72	35	52
W Brom	37	22	7	8	63	36	51
Cardiff .	39	18	11	10	58	46	47
Spurs ..	39	16	14	9	64	41	46
W. Ham	38	18	9	11	55	47	45
Ch'field	38	13	15	10	48	44	41
Shef. W	38	14	10	14	59	54	38
Barnsley	39	13	12	14	59	56	38
Bury ..	37	16	5	16	58	68	37
Q.P.R...	39	13	10	16	40	58	36
Leeds..	39	12	11	16	55	61	35
Bradf'd	39	13	9	17	63	73	35
Blackb'n	39	14	7	18	50	59	35
Luton ..	38	12	11	15	46	55	35
Grimsby	38	12	10	16	65	70	34
Cov'try	38	14	6	18	53	58	34
Brentf'd	38	11	12	15	37	46	34
Plym'th	38	12	9	17	45	55	33
Not'm F	39	12	6	21	42	52	30
Leic'ter	37	8	14	15	55	72	30
Lincoln .	40	7	12	21	50	85	26

SCOTTISH LEAGUE.—Division A—Celtic 2, Clyde 1; Rangers 3, Albion 1.

DIVISION III (S.)

Bristol City .. 1 **Port Vale** .. 1
Stone — Polk

C. Palace .. 0 **Torquay** 1
Lewis

Exeter ...... 3 **Millwall** 0
Clark, Smart, Rew

Ipswich .... 1 **Southend** 3
Jennings — Dudley 2, Lawler

Northampton 1 **Brighton** 1
King — McCurey

Norwich .... 0 **Aldershot** .. 0

Notts Co. .. 2 **Bournemouth** 3
Evans, Lawton — McGibbon 2, Blakeman

Reading .... 1 **Bristol R.** .. 0
Blackman

Swansea .... 2 **Newport** 1
Scrine, Richards — Parker

Swindon .... 1 **L. Orient** .. 1
Owen — Brinton

Walsall .... 0 **Watford** 1
Thomas

	P.	W.	D.	L.	Goals F.	Goals A.	Pts
Swansea	38	25	7	6	83	33	57
Reading	38	23	3	12	74	49	49
B'mouth	39	20	7	12	64	46	47
B'stol R	39	19	8	12	57	46	46
Swindon	39	16	14	9	60	56	46
Brighton	39	14	17	8	48	51	45
Ipswich	39	17	9	13	73	68	43
Millwall	39	17	9	13	60	59	43
Notts C.	39	19	4	16	99	61	42
Norwich	39	16	10	13	65	46	42
Torquay	38	15	10	13	59	67	40
P. Vale	39	13	10	16	47	51	36
Exeter	38	13	10	15	56	70	36
Walsall	38	14	7	17	51	57	35
Newport	37	12	8	17	63	85	32
B'stol C	38	10	12	16	41	59	32
N'th'ton	39	11	9	19	48	55	31
Orient .	38	10	11	17	53	74	31
Ald'shot	38	10	10	18	44	53	30
Watford	39	8	14	17	36	51	30
S'thend	38	7	15	16	34	42	29
C. P'lace	38	7	10	21	34	70	24

DIVISION III (N.)

Accrington .. 6 **Bradford C.** 0
Keeley 2, Butler 2, Travis 2

Carlisle .... 0 **Hartlepools** ... 0

Gateshead .. 0 **Hull** 2
Moore, Harrison

Halifax .... 3 **Oldham** 1
Murphy, Crossley, Whittingham — Haddington

Mansfield .. 2 **Barrow** 0
McCarter 2

New Brighton 2 **Crewe** 1
Roberts, Eaves — Meaney

Rochdale .... 2 **York** 0
Connor, Birch

Rotherham .. 2 **Doncaster** .. 0
Guest, Shaw

Southport .. 2 **Chester** 1
Wyles, Maddison — Davies

Stockport .. 2 **Darlington** .. 0
Brown 2

Wrexham .. 0 **Tranmere** .. 0

	P.	W.	D.	L.	Goals F.	Goals A.	Pts
Hull ..	37	25	9	3	82	23	59
R'th'h'm	39	27	5	7	86	42	59
Donc'ter	38	18	9	11	50	35	45
Darl'gt'n	39	19	6	14	79	69	44
Wr'xh'm	39	17	8	14	55	56	42
Stockp't	38	15	11	12	55	47	41
Oldham	38	17	7	14	66	61	41
R'dale	38	16	8	14	50	50	40
Gatesh'd	38	14	11	13	60	51	39
York ..	39	15	9	15	73	68	39
Barrow	38	13	12	13	37	37	38
T'nmere	38	12	14	12	42	50	38
Mansf'ld	39	12	13	14	47	46	37
H'pools	40	13	10	17	41	53	36
Carlisle	39	13	9	17	54	74	35
Crewe ..	38	14	7	17	48	72	35
Chester	39	10	12	17	52	53	32
Acc'ton	38	12	8	18	51	56	32
N. Brig'n	38	12	7	19	38	53	31
Halifax	38	10	10	18	41	59	30
B'f'd C.	37	9	8	20	41	69	26
Southp't	37	7	9	21	36	60	23

RUGBY LEAGUE: Bramley 25 pts, Featherstone R. 6; Halifax 19, Belle Vue R. 7; Hull 7, Hunslet 9; Salford 9, Wigan 9; Leeds 30, Castleford 4; Leigh 5, Warrington 2; Barrow 15, Oldham 3; St. Helens 2, Keighley 4; Wakefield T. 5, Huddersfield 10; Dewsbury 14, Batley 2; Rochdale H. 2, Workington 20; Whitehaven 0, Bradford N. 7; Widnes 14, Swinton 2; York 9, Hull K.R. 13.

FIXTURES FOR TODAY

DIVISION I
3. 0 Villa v. Sunderland
3. 0 Wolves v Sheff. U.

DIVISION II
3. 0 Coventry v. West Brom.
3. 0 Sheff. W. v. Chesterfield

DIVISION III (S.)
6. 0 Torquay v. Palace

DIVISION III (N.)
3.15 Bradford C. v. Accrington

SCOTTISH LEAGUE—A
Third Lanark v. Hibs.

SCOTTISH LEAGUE—B
6.30 Arbroath v. Hamilton Ac. (at Celtic Park)

THEY NEVER LOOKED LIKE CHAMPIONS

PORTSMOUTH, beaten 3—0 at Birmingham, gave little indication that they were likely to win the League championship.

And Birmingham scored three times in a game for the first time this year, without producing anything extraordinary.

Portsmouth's attack made little impression on the sound Birmingham defence, and their own defence was inclined to be shaky under pressure.

The League leaders were unfortunate in losing Dickenson with a cut head, shortly before the interval, and when he returned he played in the forward line, with Phillips dropping back to wing half.

But even with a full team they seldom looked like saving a point.

FIVE FOR TODAY BY JEAN STUART

EPSOM
2.35—Soraniyeh
3.15—Fedor II (e.w.)

BIRMINGHAM
3. 0—River Tay

NEWCASTLE
2.30—Panair
3. 0—Kishma

The Flutters

LOOK HERE! I'M NOT LETTING A POSH LUNCH GO TO WASTE. WHY DON'T YOU BOYS COME ALONG AND HELP ME EAT IT?
I HAVEN'T HAD A MEAL LIKE THAT FOR MONTHS! VERY HANDSOME OF YOU MR. - ER - UM...
TOM KETCHUP'S THE NAME...
OH! CONFOUND IT! LOOK AT THE TIME — I'VE MISSED IT...
ANYTHING WRONG?
IT'S NOTHING... ONLY I PARTICULARLY WANTED TO BACK A HORSE IN THE TWO O'CLOCK RACE. NOW I SEE IT'S GONE TWO!
OH.. HM
H92

WEATHER
Mainly fair, but a lot of cloud.
OUTLOOK: Similar.

Printed and Published by the DAILY MIRROR NEWSPAPERS, Ltd., at Geraldine House, Rolls Bldgs., Fetter-lane, London, E.C.4.—Tuesday, April 19, 1949. Tel. Holborn 4321.

THE BOYS WHO BAGGED THE CUP

Sprawling on the shoulders of goalkeeper Swindin and his right back Scott, Arsenal's captain, Johnny Mercer clutches the Cup that eleven good men and true had won for the South again after their battle with Liverpool at Wembley Stadium yesterday. From the extreme left are Lewis, the goals scorer, Cox, Goring, Barnes and Denis Compton. From the right, Logie (front), Leslie Compton and Forbes.

ONE-LEGGED GOOSE GETS A RUN-AROUND

Barney is a goose who was born with only one leg, and for eight years in his life he has had to hop and hope. But he has been the friend of Mrs. Morcy, in Missouri, since she petted him four hours after he was hatched. When his mistress told of Barney's plight on the radio the owner of an artificial limb factory decided to make Barney this wagon, which he calls a goosemobile. Barney "walks" on his leg through a hole in the bottom

SPORT PICTORIAL

Fight managers can be humane

By PETER WILSON

IN the main I don't care a lot for fight managers. They've been described as "licensed pickpockets" and I wouldn't care to dispute that description in some case

So I'm extremely happy to pay tribute to a manager who has allowed humanity to outweigh cash — even though there's no percentage on humanity.

The manager concerned is one whom I've often criticised—Benny Huntman—and the humane and wise thing he's done is to pull Danny O'Sullivan, bantam-weight champion of Great Britain, out of his next engagement in which he was scheduled to meet Ray Fitton at Manchester, on May 19.

At Harringay, O'Sullivan with Spain's Luis Romero figured in about the greatest fight between little men I've seen since the first Benny Lynch-Peter Kane battle nearly thirteen years ago. Oddly enough, both scraps ended in the thirteenth round

✦ ✦ ✦

CRITICS were united in hailing Danny boy's defeat as more memorable than many victories.

"One of the games. shows ever by a British boxer" (Norman Hurst "Daily Graphic"), "We can only praise O'Sullivan for his wonderful pluck" (Clifford Webb, "Daily Herald"). "The bravest boxer who ever stepped into a ring" (Desmond Hackett "Daily Express")

I agreed with every letter they wrote. Then, to my dismay and disgust. I read that O'Sullivan was being tossed back into the pit of punishment just over three weeks after Romero had slammed him to the canvas eleven times in less than forty minutes.

They weren't putting him in with a mug. They'd matched him with Ray Fitton, the Manchester feather-weight who had twice gone the distance with Romero, drawing with him the second time.

That, in my opinion, isn't boxing—it's butchery! I spoke to Benny Huntman and he told me he'd had O'Sullivan examined by a specialist who could find no ill-effects from the Romero fight

With every deference to the doctor, I don't think he or any other medical expert can gauge the reaction which a fighter suffers after a merciless beating!

Huntman insisted that neither he nor O'Sullivan wanted the money. But pro fighters—and managers—are in the game for what they can make Otherwise they'd be amateurs.

For once, though, someone has taken the long view—that O'Sullivan will live to fight another day if he's given a few weeks right away from the ring, without the grind of training without the climaxing ordeal of a tough fight.

O'Sullivan deserves that. A fight manager has done the right thing

✦ ✦ ✦

I WANT to smash a dirty rumour. Since Albert Finch became Britain's new middle-weight champion at Nottingham I've received letters, phone calls and whispered suggestions, behind cupped hands, that Dick Turpin was robbed of the decision because of a recurrence of the old colour bar.

My answers to these are: Gibberish, balderdash and downright lies.

FINCH WON THE TITLE BECAUSE, IN MY OPINION, HE SCORED MORE POINTS ACCORDING TO THE LAWS OF BOXING THAN TURPIN DID.

No one campaigned longer —or more successfully— against the colour bar than I did. No one has defended Turpin more vehemently when the weight of critical opinion was arrayed against him.

BUT, THIS TIME, HE THREW HIS TITLE AWAY. Certainly in the seventh, eighth and ninth rounds it seemed as though it were merely a question of which punch Turpin was going to use to finish off the affair.

But from the tenth to the fifteenth round — FORTY PER CENT. OF THE FIGHT —I didn't give Turpin a round. Three were even and three went to Finch.

The referee, Peter Muir, of Scotland, handled the fight admirably. And the suggestions that the Board of Control were determined not to give a Lonsdale Belt to a coloured man are so ridiculous that they wouldn't be worth denying if they weren't so widespread.

BETWEEN THE ROUNDS

● *There should be two first-class top-liners at Empress Hall tomorrow night. Bill Jackson, Jamaican middle-weight, meets Luc Van Dam, the Dutchman with a decision over our middle-weight champion Albert Finch, and Bobby Boland, Dundee, swaps leather with Hadi Tijani, of Tunisia.*

● *Tijani is a tap dancer in cabaret 'way back in Tunis—and his record includes wins over Theo Medina, Tino Cardinale and Alvaro Nuvoloni. But remembering Boland's fine win over Fernando Gagnon, I'll take the Scot.*

1945!

★ *Joe Mercer as he was at the end of 1945 bringing home the bacon in his father-in-law's grocery shop.*

1950

★ *Joe Mercer as he was yesterday at Wembley "bringing home the bacon" again — the F.A. Cup—for Arsenal*

HE BROUGHT HOME THE BACON FOR ARSENAL!

By GEORGE CASEY, Sports Editor

IF there is a happier man in Britain this morning than spindle-legged Joe Mercer, captain of the Arsenal football team and voted "Footballer of the Year" by football writers, then I'd sure like to meet him.

Arsenal won the F.A. Cup by defeating Liverpool 2—0 in the Final yesterday and joined Bolton Wanderers as the only clubs to record three F.A. Cup victories at Wembley.

✦ ✦ ✦

BUT these facts alone are not enough to make Joe Mercer the happiest man in Britain. The real story of his triumph dates back to 1945 after his demob from the Services in the Second World War.

Joe was an England international, and his club was Everton. But he wasn't exactly happy the following year. He was asked on one occasion to play on the wing AS AN EXPERIMENT. That didn't seem right to Joe. A man of his thirty years can't remodel his game at that time of life.

So in November, 1946, Joe moved south to Arsenal

✦ ✦ ✦

AT Arsenal he found a spirit which isn't all-too-plentiful among big clubs. In Joe's own words it's "All for one and one for all" at Highbury. Joe became happy.

He was even allowed to train in the North—on Liverpool's ground, too!—and continue learning the grocers business of his father-in-law. Joe has told the world all the Arsenal manager Tom Whittaker did for him and how the fact that he was free from worry about his future after his footballing days, made him a new man.

Joe, the master of attacking half-back play had to settle down to modify his game to suit Arsenal's style. He was happy. He did it—and in 1948 Arsenal won the League Championship.

About this time there came more rumours that Joe would retire. Close friends and relatives more or less gave advice that it was wise to go out on top.

✦ ✦ ✦

JOE MERCER said, "Just one more season"—and on he went again in that dour and sportsmanlike way of his. He'd made a success as a business man "bringing home the bacon" in the grocer's shop.

Now, in 1950, he's "brought home the bacon" again —the F.A Cup—for the Arsenal.

Lewis beats Sidlow to score his first Cup goal.

ARSENAL DIDN'T NEED ANY LUCK

By STAN HALSEY

WE on our Press box perch were just commenting on the leisurely, almost cocky way the Liverpool defence was coping with Arsenal's sporadic raids, when suddenly it happened. In the fifteenth minute a dramatic, telling goal eased Arsenal's Wembley nerves and set them on the way to Cup conquest.

And the old worn tag "Lucky Arsenal," could not be applied to this exciting effort which raised the one real resounding Cockney roar, set rattles whirling, while rosettes were flung in the air like confetti in delirious delight. Otherwise it was the quietest Cup Final crowd I have heard.

The goal came from a sound if spectacular move, launched by fiery-headed right half Forbes, whose red-headed temperament—eager, ever ready—seemed transferred into his play. He gave the little, scheming inside right Logie, lover of the short crisp pass, just the ball that mattered. Logie bamboozled the defence completely.

He noted this time, as Cox did later, the sly way Lewis, two-goal scorer in this triumphant match, eluded almost Scotland Yard marking by slipping from inside right to inside left. Logie put the ball into a perfect, goal-for-the-kicking open space.

A Great Goal

Lewis scored, then disappeared in a mob of back-slapping, crazily congratulating colleagues who relaxed the dignified drill of their hand shakes only at Highbury—in the excitement of the moment.

Certainly that was the most stirring incident of the first half. Matched in Cup thrill only by Liverpool's lively, almost lung-bursting finish—when rwo goals down they sought to save a lost cause in the last ten tremendous minutes.

I shall not forget the courage of right half skipper Taylor, in that crescendo spell. It was indelible in one's memory. Badly knocked up in a tackle, off five minutes for patching-up treatment, Taylor insisted on returning to launch one of the finest last-ditch efforts I've seen in football.

Forget the injury seemed Taylor's attitude. His plucky pass gave Stubbins a wonderful scoring chance, but it was lost. A goal there might have roused Liverpool to game-saving heights at that tense, turbulent time.

Again from Taylor's desperate inspiration Fagan got the ball but hit the crossbar. Then Swindin in a glorious moment that ranked him as the greatest uncapped goalkeeper in the kingdom, made the kind of save that was reckless and brilliant.

Splendid Save

A great save from Stubbins, it made a fine curtain fall to the final—though just to rub in their triumph, when the Liverpool last throw lapsed, Arsenal right winger Cox hit an upright a minute from the end.

Arsenal, however, were absolute winners. They sank that slanderous "Lucky Arsenal" label for ever by playing far more intelligent and better organised football than Liverpool, who fell sadly away after the sting of that early Lewis goal.

Arsenal kept the rain-heavy ball low, and despite the slowing conditions of the wet, lush Wembley turf, contrived to link their attack with many fine, fast, player-finding passes. Liverpool had some good scoring chances, but always their finishing was their finish

Those Half-Backs!

Arsenal wing-halves were the team's technical triumph. Forbes (how glad Tom Whittaker must be he played him at the expense of loyal Archie Macaulay's feelings) emerged as a great storming character dominating the match.

The tireless eagerness which carried him from challenging forward forays into deep defence at critical moments made him even more outstanding than the mop of red hair that crowned his every effort.

Joe Mercer, often dubbed "Grable Legs" in friendly burlesque of the spindle shanks that carried him to footer fame, earned himself the great climax to his glittering career when he took the most precious bauble in world sport from the hands of the King.

Forbes held Liddell, the great Liverpool menace, who switched to the right wing in an effort to save Liverpool with skill not usually associated with such a rip-snorting type of player

Forbes showed his guts too by forgetting the ache of the football-sized bruise he received in a tackle early in the game

In fact, the whole key to this result is that Arsenal blotted out the Liverpool inside forwards so completely that their attack spluttered like a faulty plug.

After seventeen minutes in the second half, however, Arsenal scored the goal that clinched the game even though it roused Liverpool to that last warring rally like a bee sting.

An immaculate Mercer pass found little Cox determined he would have a foot in the final as he did in the semi-final success.

It was almost an encore of Arsenal's first goal.

Lewis foxily evaded close defensive marking. Cox passed and Lewis, again exploiting the clever but scarcely noticeable Arsenal inter-change plan, scored a decisive goal.

Still, Liverpool had their scoring chances. Three at least in the first half when they opened attack as stormily as they finished. Once, Liddell crossed the ball, Stubbins launched himself to head but merely disturbed the parting in his hair. The ball went to Payne who should have scored.

Oh, Scott!

It was during this point of Liverpool pressure that I saw Scott, Arsenal right back, harassed by Liddell throughout, do a thing I have never seen him do before. He perpetrated a very obvious foul in order to check Liddell. Get back your quickness on the turn, Laurie!

Leslie Compton was splendid at this time—one magnificent header diverting what might have been a grand goal.

Cliff Bastin says

● So my old club has again won the F.A. Cup. There was no question about who were the better side. It was Arsenal nearly all the way. True, Liverpool did miss some easy scoring chances, particularly Stubbins and Fagan, but for all-round football it was Arsenal that were the tops.

● In Jimmy Logie, Arsenal had the best forward on the field. Young Goring, at centre forward, also had a great match. In fact the whole Arsenal forward line were much superior to Liverpool's attacks.

Liverpool, I thought, made a great mistake in leaving Logie with so much room in which to work. The marking of the Liverpool wing halves was greatly at fault, and was one of the failings of their team.

● Liverpool's forwards just did not have that necessary craft to split the close-covering Arsenal defence. Alec Forbes, at right half, was outstanding. He was always using the ball well and his tackling was superb.

● Leslie Compton was his usual stonewall self and his head came to the rescue of Arsenal many times, while Scott and Barnes improved as the game went on. Swindin, however, had a venturesome, but successful, afternoon.

Only Liddell shone in the Liverpool side.

Printed and Published by SUNDAY PICTORIAL NEWSPAPERS (1920) Ltd. Geraldine House Rolls Buildings Fetter-lane. London E.C.4—Sunday April 30, 1950. Tel Holborn 4321

DEREK DOOLEY

*D*EREK DOOLEY, famous Sheffield Wednesday centre forward whose career was ended by an accident on the playing field, will be at Wembley today.

He will be there for the 'Daily Mirror' to watch the all-Lancashire Cup Final between Blackpool and Bolton Wanderers.

His comments—the match as seen by a great footballer—will appear in Monday's 'Daily Mirror.'

AGAIN!

STANLEY MATTHEWS REACHES CUP FINAL

IN C·W·S FOOTBALL BOOTS!

It's a tough, testing road to Wembley but Stanley Matthews, most brilliant player of the age, has travelled it triumphantly again—in C.W.S Football Boots!

Nearly a quarter of a million wearers of these famous boots will be wishing him well when the Maestro steps out on to the Wembley turf to-day—wearing his

C·W·S

STANLEY MATTHEWS FOOTBALL BOOTS

You can buy these famous boots at your

CO-OPERATIVE SHOE SHOP

Langton Hassall Lofthouse Holden Bell Barrass Wheeler Banks, R. Ball Hanson

ONE MAN CAN MAKE IT GREATEST FINAL

WE all have little passions in life, and there is no limit to them.

They range from spring in the Green Park to Brighton beach and drifted snow on a Yorkshire moor.

The Master

They may include Gracie Fields and the memory of Garbo, the taste of fried onions, and the call of a seagull and the vision of a country pub in sunshine.

One of my passions is Stanley Matthews, the very name itself, the spectacle of a man standing still with a football stationary at his feet and a cluster of defenders scurrying into haphazard and hopeless position to check him.

This, as it has been these twenty years, is the most astonishing single sight in football.

And this, no matter what else happens on the Wembley field, will make the Blackpool-Bolton Wanderers match today probably the most extraordinary Cup Final of them all.

From 100,000 people the

BOB FERRIER sums up—and takes Blackpool to win

partisans included, will come a wave of sympathy for Matthews, in his third Cup Final in five years, such as football or any other sport has never known. It will be almost tangible.

Over the dog-track, over the dirt-track, over the touchline, as it does across the floodlights in the odd magical moments in the theatre, will flow and counter-flow a flood of emotional compassion from the crowd to the players and to Stanley Matthews.

"It may seem to you to be outling a football match and a football player on rather a high plane, but this match will offer the greatest unspoken tribute on the sport's greatest occasion to a man who has graced and dignified football for two decades.

He is a legend in his own lifetime—and Bolton will have to find the answer to him if they hope to win the Cup.

His ball control, speed, balance, personal physical fitness, all the outcome of original talent, practice and the thing you cannot buy, experience, are merely parts of the pattern.

His greatest asset, to me, is his perception of the balance of his opponent. Matthews will sway his body over the ball to make the full back move. In that one fleeting moment when the back is moving from one foot to the other, Matthews moves the ball quickly and follows it in a flounce of billowing shirt and shorts.

This is the man who can win for Blackpool just as Nat Lofthouse could for Bolton.

Greatest Strength

All my romanticism calls for a Blackpool victory. All rational thoughts, too, plumps for a Blackpool victory.

The greatest strength of the Bolton side is the inside forward trio Bill Moir, Nat Lofthouse and Harold Hassall.

Yet, somehow, I have a strange feeling that this might be a draw, even after extra time. Just one of those things.

But I go for a Blackpool victory. And I have another feeling—that if it happens, Harry Johnston, that great Blackpool captain, might just send 'Stan' up the steps first, to claim the Cup.

One long shout —that did it

By GEORGE HARLEY

THERE were only 5,628 spectators at Selhurst Park last night, but their non-stop roars of encouragement inspired 'Crystal Palace to beat Bristol Rovers, champions of their section, by the only goal.

And the enthusiasm at the finish suggested that Palace had won promotion, the F.A. Cup—and the world's skating championship on this muddy mess of a pitch.

The match was exciting as a 3-D thriller.

Rovers fought as if promotion still depended on their efforts, and they were indeed unlucky to lose.

They dominated the second half and the Palace goal had escapes which not even Houdini could have dreamed up.

Yet Palace deserved to be leading at half-time by a goal cleverly headed by Thomas from an Andrews pass.

The match proved that they have made a bright discovery in Ron Downs, a young outside left.

HIS LAST GAME

After leading his team to the top of the League last night, Arsenal captain Joe Mercer announced that he is retiring from football.

ARSENAL THERE AGAIN

ARSENAL are champions of the Football League—on goal average over Preston North End—for a record seventh time, writes BOB FERRIER.

A 3—2 win over Burnley at Highbury last night gave them yet another title, and mighty thankful Gunners they were to get off the Highbury mud.

Burnley made it a glorious end to the season. After scoring in the first few minutes, through outside right Stephenson, they reeled under a fantastic forward blitz which brought Arsenal three goals in less than fifteen minutes, yet fought back magnificently in the second half. Then the whole stadium was alive and alight. Fifty-one thousand made as much noise as I've ever heard on a football ground. Every Arsenal clearance was greeted like a Cup-winning goal.

And somehow, until the weary end, Arsenal held out and won.

Forbes equalised the Stephenson goal. Next we had Logie ducking under a Roper corner kick and Lishman scoring on the volley.

Then Within a Goal

To round the thing off, Marden nodded back a Roper cross, Goring let it pass him, and Logie flicked in the goal.

After half an hour of the second half Elliott met a McIlroy cross full tilt to put Burnley within a goal of Arsenal.

Here was a great show from all the lads. Well done, Arsenal.

ARSENAL'S AMAZING 21 DAYS

WRIGHT BOYS DEVASTATING

ARSENAL have gone from diabolical (manager Billy Wright's description) to devastating (mine) in twenty-one days. The season's top attendance, 56,757, saw League champions Manchester United destroyed.

"After Chelsea beat us 3—1 at home three weeks ago we tore ourselves apart," said a jubilant Wright.

"We had to learn to destroy the opposition, not to let them play football; to shut them in their own half, not ours."

This was the simple but successful recipe Arsenal used against Bobby Charlton, Denis Law and the star-studded Manchester men.

In typical Highbury fashion, the Gunners gave the champs a goal start, roared back to a 3—1 lead then put United into the match again when goalkeeper Jim Furnell chucked the ball into the back of his net.

Great entertainment. And no single player deserves prouder mention than David Court, the 20-year-old wing half who conquered the man who mesmerised him in this fixture last season—£115,000 Denis Law.

Court stuck patiently and skilfully to the task of subduing Law.

Apart from one amazing header by the spring-heeled Scot (cleverly steered off his own goal by Don Howe) Court was the boss.

Power Line

It was the power of the Arsenal half-back line which made Wright so happy and the Manchester forwards so frustrated.

At last Frank McLintock looked his old Leicester self and that £80,000 transfer fee seemed justified.

Centre half Terry Neill was easily the most outstanding of the five currently selected internationals on view.

The weakest was England's right half Nobby Stiles.

True, both his role and position were different in this game to the one he will employ against Wales on Saturday.

But he erred at the time of the first and second Arsenal goals.

A spectacular Charlton header brought United the opening goal direct from a John Connelly corner—"My first League goal with my

Arsenal 4
Man. Utd. 2

By SAM LEITCH

head for two years," said Charlton.

Then Joe Baker's sharp football got the equaliser.

What a brilliantly busy centre forward he is these days.

Arsenal, somewhat luckily I thought, took an interval lead when John Radford's persistence struck home goal Number 2 three minutes before half-time.

Arsenal cut out the close stuff after the interval and looked so much better for it.

Tired Team

They seemed fitter and stronger than Manchester United, who were no doubt tired by that midweek travelling to Helsinki on European Cup duty.

When that bundle of right-wing effervescence, George Armstrong, volleyed an eye-popping Arsenal third goal, United were all in.

But a goalkeeping boob by Furnell allowed United's spritely left winger teenager John Aston to put the Manchester men right in the mood again at 2—3 down.

Finally, a headed goal by George Eastham—almost as rare a footballing occurrence as a headed goal by Charlton—clinched a courageous and skilful win for Arsenal ten minutes from the end.

The last time Arsenal managed to hit a Manchester United side for four goals was in the last thrilling match Matt Busby's men played before the tragic Munich crash in 1958.

It would be wrong to imagine that all the Arsenal problems are solved because of this win.

But to be fair to manager Wright, on the day he has no more irritations than manager Busby.

A little more "destroyer" tactics from the champs would not hurt.

Pretty light-hearted effort, this pushing and shoving by Denis Law and Don Howe. Both seem to be amused. But as things turned out Howe had the last laugh.

HAYNES SHINES

Sunderland 2, Fulham 2

★ There's long been a cry for a striker in this highly expensive Sunderland team, writes **VINCE WILSON**. But Fulham, London's great unpredictables, proved so convincingly that the Roker men are not alone.

★ John Key and Brian O'Connell had golden chances for Fulham inside the first ten minutes.

★ The two captains, Jim Baxter and Johnny Haynes, provided all the brilliance in this frustrating game. But it was a Baxter blunder after a wonder second half, that led to Fulham's shock equaliser only seconds from time.

★ He tried to find McNab, floated his pass too high and John Key took possession. The ball went on to Haynes and while defenders anticipated a shot, he pulled back an inch-perfect pass for Bobby Robson to score.

★ Only five minutes earlier Baxter glided a penalty wide of Tony Macedo when George Cohen brought down Mulhall.

★ And between those exciting late goals Graham Leggat broke through on the left for Fulham but shot wide.

★ Fulham's best football came in the first half. Terry Dyson created havoc all along the line and twice just failed by inches to convert Haynes's passes.

★ Sharkey caught Macedo napping in the seventh minute when he shaped to pass but hit the roof of the net. Fulham equalised soon afterwards when O'Connell met Dyson's centre with a strong header. Then came those late, sensational goals.

SUBS ON PARADE

Charlton 0, Huddersfield 2

FACED with their most formidable task yet, Charlton failed to check promotion-hunting Huddersfield. The Huddersfield defence proved too tough a nut for Charlton's attack, writes **PETER KINLAN**.

Workmanlike Huddersfield disturbed the Charlton rhythm with an eighth minute goal.

Right winger Kevin McHale prodded John Quigley's cross to Massie who promptly hammered beyond goalkeeper Jones from ten yards.

The second half brought into action two substitutes for right backs.

Keith Peacock came into Charlton for Billy Bonds and Huddersfield right back Dennis Atkins was replaced by Stephen Smith.

Substitute Peacock failed to snap up an equalising chance within thirty seconds of the restart.

Charlton's hope of remaining unbeaten for seven successive games receded in the sixty-first minute when one of the Huddersfield dangerous raids produced their second goal.

Centre forward Tony Leighton neatly back-headed a ball to the feet of left winger Mike O'Grady who accepted the close range chance.

Portsmouth . . . 4
Leyton O 1

● This defeat puts Orient in real trouble, although the club's policy is still to try and keep struggling along without buying new players.

● What is really lacking is confidence, for only occasionally were there flashes of fiery spirit which could have been dangerous to Portsmouth.

● But there were some bright features for Orient, particularly the performance of centre half David Webb. It was not until near the end that Pompey leader Ray Hiron got the better of him.

● Orient could have exploited gaps in the Pompey defence, but only flashes by right winger Jimmy McGeorge showed promise.

● Edwards headed Portsmouth's first goal after fourteen minutes and cracked the second in the fifty-second.

● Colin Flatt, the Orient leader, neatly headed their only goal two minutes later, but Hiron settled things for Portsmouth with two goals in the last quarter-hour.

Preston 2
Palace 0

● Crystal Palace decided early that the only way to keep Preston at bay was by close marking and rugged tackling.

● But it cost them a goal, reduced them to ten men, put the names of two of their players in the referee's notebook and ruined the match.

● Palace paid the first instalment of this price in the 36th minute when, after a foul on the edge of the penalty area, Preston skipper Nobby Lawton tapped the free kick left and Howard Kendall hit a fifteen yard shot into the net.

● Then, just before the interval Palace full back Terry Long was booked and after the interval wing half David Payne had his name taken, both after fouls.

● The toll continued and in the 58th minute Payne was ordered off by the referee after Preston's Brian Godfrey had been fouled.

● Alex Dawson hit Preston's second goal five minutes later, but though they dominated the game, their finishing was poor.

HAMMER BLOWS LACKED WEIGHT

W Ham 1, Blackpool 1: By VIC SELWYN

IN the closing seconds West Ham's inside forward Martin Peters retrieved a hopeless-looking ball from the line and crossed it to centre forward Johnny Byrne.

The centre forward's shot was miraculously saved by goalkeeper Tony Waiters, only for the ball to bounce out to Geoff Hurst to score.

West Ham had snatched a point.

Nine minutes earlier, centre forward Ray Charnley had scored for Blackpool, his shot recoiling off the inside of the post.

Blackpool's man of the match, Alan Ball, the best inside forward of the day, laid on that goal with one of his simple attacking moves that contrasted with West Ham's endless tip-tap.

One point seemed sufficient reward for either side.

A fair part of the match was as inspiring as last month's cold rice pudding.

Only for a fifteen-minute spell in the second half did West Ham click.

In that spell, Byrne put in two fine shots. Waiters stopped them both — the second a brilliant punch from a fierce long shot.

But West Ham could not take advantage of their opportunities even when Waiters was out of goal. Winger Sissons crossed the ball continuously but no one connected.

For Blackpool, Alan Ball was a one-man attack. West Ham gave him room to work in and he used it. But his colleagues could not score either.

Most of the game West Ham played a 5-1-4 formation with Eddie Bovington as link man. But the side lacked any midfield build-up.

Blackpool captain Jimmy Armfield pulled out of the match because of stomach trouble. Tommy Thompson, replacing him knew exactly what to do. There was not a move to beat him.

Langley winner

QPR 2, Peterborough 1

WILLIE DUFF, Peterborough goalkeeper was in brilliant form. With a plum performance he held on to a point until almost the last kick of the match.

And it took a penalty to beat him. Duff deserved a point, even if the rest of his side could hardly grumble at the result.

Peterborough snatched a surprise lead in the 13th minute in a defensive mix up. Beesley punted a long shot down the middle and with Springett in a tangle with his two backs Watson deflected the ball in.

Until then it was all Rangers. And they were well on top when Collins got the equaliser.

Les Allen was brought down just outside the penalty box. Ian Watson took the kick and Allen pushed the ball on for John Collins to slam home after 28 minutes.

Rangers continued to dominate in the second half, but Duff held out until Allen was brought down by Wright inside the box. Full back Jim Langley scored his first goal for Rangers with his carefully placed kick.

Brighton 2, Millwall 2

CHARLIE LIVESEY, playing his first home match for Brighton since joining the club from Northampton scored a dramatic goal in the last minute to salvage a point.

He swung a shot into the far corner of the net after a right wing raid to end a thriller, a little too tough and ill tempered at times, played in pouring rain.

Brighton were first to settle down, taking the lead when Wally Gould netted from close range after Alex Stepney had dropped a corner from the left.

But within three minutes Hugh Curran had equalised, heading down and into the net when Bill Neil crossed accurately from the left.

When Barry Rowan put Millwall 2—1 in the lead with 23 minutes remaining, it looked as though Brighton were beaten. They were making their chances but squandering them, either through over-elaboration or hasty shooting.

Mel Hopkins was injured just before Millwall's second goal, and Neil raced past him to give Rowan his chance.

SPURS OUT OF TOUCH

Aston Villa 3, Spurs 2

NEVER was there an indication that four Tottenham men will be playing international next Saturday. Dave Mackay certainly started with his usual verve though faded as if he tired on a waterlogged pitch, writes **ARCHIE QUICK**.

But Spurs' other three, Alan Gilzean, Bill Brown and Jimmy Greaves, were never in touch with a greasy, skidding ball.

Brown did not like it for one and he dropped a shot from full back Charlie Aitken smack at Phil Woosnam's feet for the Welshman to drag in Villa's number two at the second attempt.

Gilzean could have changed the tenor of the game in the first two minutes if he had netted instead of hitting an upright.

Villa were without centre forward Tony Hateley for seventy-eight minutes. He was stretchered off with a groin injury. Graham Parker substituted, but Woosnam never allowed his attack to become disorganised.

Before the game had hardly started Gilzean and Greaves should have had goals; instead Bobby Park without fuss popped Villa into the lead after 12 minutes.

Next came Bill Brown's boob ten minutes later and Villa made it 3—0 again without frills when Willie Hamilton ripped in a 20 yarder.

In contrast to Villa's clean cut affairs, Spurs' two goals were ragged.

Maurice Norman who had gone up for an earlier corner got Spurs' first after 53 minues. He drove it through a crowd of players.

Robertson switched to the right, got the second with five minutes to go.

THREE ACES

IN Norwegian champion Sverre Harrfeldt, team captain Ken McKinlay and Norman Hunter, West Ham had a speedway trio who were unbeaten by any of the home team at Belle Vue last night.

Belle Vue's troubles began before the match. Cyril Maidment had not recovered from a track crash at Wimbledon and Sandor Leval failed to pass a fitness test.

BRITISH LEAGUE.—Belle Vue 30 (Fisher, Nevitt 7), West Ham 47 (Harrfeldt, Hunter 12).

FOUR TEAM TOURNEY (at King's Lynn).—Sheffield 29 pts., Exeter 26; Kings Lynn 22, Long Eaton 19.

So near . .

Walsall 1, Brentford 1

BRENTFORD looked well on the way to their first away win of the season when they took the lead after the interval. But a lucky Walsall goal by Sissons, who fired through a crowded goalmouth, put paid to their hopes twenty minutes later.

Brentford went ahead through inside left Billy Cobb. As the home defence hesitated he dashed in to head a lob from Holley past Carling.

But the goals apart, there was little to enthuse over. A rain-soaked pitch upset both sides.

The first half was atrocious with Brentford apparently fearing Walsall's reputation. But things were different when the Londoners snatched the lead.

Walsall were stung into action by this reverse and crowded on the pressure. But once Walsall had equalised with their surprise goal, Brentford again took command.

They were unlucky not to regain the lead ten minutes from the end when Lazarus hit the inside of the post and the ball rebounded to safety.

Watford 4
Oldham 0

CLIFF HOLTON whose power-shooting has lifted Northampton and Crystal Palace to higher spheres, helped Watford into third place in the Third Division with another snap shooting display.

Burly Holton grabbed a third minute goal to stun Oldham, who are still awaiting their first away goal and point.

Watford's overnight signing from Plymouth, right winger Stewart Brace, outpaced the Oldham defence with a 40 yard run, Holton was on the spot to sidefoot the ball home.

Holton snapped his second goal in the twenty-sixth minute after 'keeper Bollands had failed to hold a sizzling drive from Brian Owen, a young inside forward with the golden touch.

It was from a Holton nod midway in the second half that Owen roared in to snatch the fourth goal.

A torrential downpour made conditions difficult for the pocket-sized Watford forwards, other than big Holton, but they tossed away at least four easy scoring chances.

Harris got Watford's third goal after Owen had teased bemused defenders into a blunder.

GRATEFUL GRACE

Scunthorpe 0, Gillingham 1

ALTHOUGH Gillingham deserved their win this display was not far removed from mediocrity. But they did produce better team work and created slightly more scoring chances.

The only goal came in the fifty-first minute when left winger John Meredith crossed a high ball and Hemstead missed his clearance.

Sidebottom ran out of goal to cover but right winger Gordon Pulley collected the ball first and crossed it to Grace, who gratefully netted into an empty goal.

It was hard luck on Derek Hemstead who had regained his place in the Scunthorpe side and otherwise played a sound game.

Try as they would Scunthorpe could not pull themselves together and that left Gillingham in control for almost the rest of the second half

BEST DOG BETS

HARRINGAY.—8.17, June Star II; 8.34 Rubion Rusty; 8.51, April Dream; 9.9, Granite Brindled; 9.27, Tykela; 9.45, Amazon Queen.

WEMBLEY.—8.19, High Drifter; 8.35, Fawn Buffalo; 8.51, Arvada; 9.7, Link Bird; 9.21, What About This; 9.39, Just Cruising.

Arsenal boost bid for Europe

AND THEY'RE SET FOR LONDON'S No 1 SPOT

ARSENAL beat off a bright Wolves challenge for the victory that must surely send them into Europe next season.

Chelsea and West Ham can now write off what was previously only a slender chance of catching them on the run-in for London's top-team title.

And as Arsenal head for the Fairs Cup it is not without significance that they have now taken nine points in an unbeaten run of six First Division games since the Wembley disaster against Swindon.

But Wolves were not easily mastered. A side minus four injured first-teamers were tight and well organised.

By HARRY MILLER

| Arsenal | . . . . . | 3 |
| Wolves | . . . . . | 1 |

Clever

Two of the youngsters drafted in by manager Bill McGarry — Scottish defender John McAllie and winger John Farrington — were particularly impressive.

Wolves' biggest failing was their inability to get anyone running on to the clever head flicks of skipper Derek Dougan, who thoroughly mastered Ian Ure in the air.

Arsenal's first goal came after twenty-seven minutes when David Court glanced a George Armstrong cross in front of goal and Jimmy Robertson drove in.

Wolves fell further behind a minute from half-time. Gerry Taylor failed to intercept a Bobby Gould forward pass and Armstrong shot past Phil Parkes.

Parkes saved a fifty-sixth-minute Jon Sammels penalty before Les Wilson hit the goal four minutes later that put Wolves back in the game.

But in another three minutes it was all over. George Graham, rapidly establishing himself as the new midfield master of Highbury, was allowed to move unchallenged on to a Gould cross and score with a spectacular scissors shot.

Graham's goal also made it the first time Arsenal have scored more than twice at home this year.

Derek Dougan, Wolves skipper, takes the law—and Arsenal's Bobby Gould—into his own hands. David Smith, the official referee, is on his way and Gould just hopes he hurries.   *Picture: MONTE FRESCO*

SPURS RIDING HIGH TILL ASTLE STRIKES

West Bromwich Albion 4, Spurs 3

THREE second-half goals in nineteen minutes—two of them from centre forward Jeff Astle—swept Albion to a sensational victory over a side who were leading 3—1 in the 47th minute.

For Astle—he hit the winner in the 69th minute—it meant the end of a hoodoo. For so long unable to score League goals he has now hit three in two home games.

Spurs, after reeling under the savagery of Albion's opening assault, shocked them with a goal in ten minutes. Full back Cyril Knowles hammered the ball past John Osborne from 25 yards.

Albion, quickly level with a goal by Bobby Hope, slipped again when Jimmy Greaves soft-footed a penalty kick past Osborne.

Two minutes after the interval Greaves struck again with a brilliant shot that ended a solo break.

Sweep

It looked all over for Albion. But, mounting attack after attack, they pulled a goal back in the fiftieth minute with a close-range shot by Astle.

Nine minutes later Astle headed the ball down for Tony Brown to sweep it in off the underside of the bar.

Astle's winner came when he ran on to a ball from Dick Krzywicki which Phil Beal should have cleared.

One minute from time, Neil Johnson thought he had equalised for Spurs but another player was offside.

Morgan muffs chance to break ice . .

Sunderland 0, QPR 0

ONE consolation for Rangers when they re-appear in the Second Division next season is the thought of others equally deserving the humiliation.

This is the level to which once proud Sunderland have sunk.

Rangers plainly bore the trademark of a rough season — a desperate inclination to fall back on offside tactics.

They had no need to worry—Sunderland are completely unadventurous.

Rangers did not seem to realise that they had a chance of scoring their first away win of the season.

Ian Morgan, with a splendid chance in the thirteenth minute, shot outside, and Alan Wilks hooked the ball over the Sunderland bar from a free kick by Ian Watson.

TWO-GOAL GLORY FOR NEW SAINT

Southampton 5, Burnley 1

SOUTHAMPTON have produced another young forward of tremendous potential. Bobby Stokes, 18, already an England youth international, celebrated his League debut by scoring two goals in a win that lifted Saints into sixth place in the First Division.

And no one was happier than his Welsh international team-mate, centre forward Ron Davies. "What a fantastic start," said Davies. "He took his goals well and did a lot of good work."

Stokes said: "I was delighted but I just happened to be in the right place at the right time. It all takes some believing."

Southampton's other scorers were Mick Judd Davies (penalty) and Terry Paine. Colin Blant got Burnley's goal.

Fulham's sad farewell . .

Hull 4, Fulham 0

FULHAM, on the day they learned they will be relegated for the second season running made a sad farewell to the Second Division.

For twenty-five minutes it looked as though Fulham would fight every inch of the way to maintain their faint hope of survival.

But once Ken Wagstaff had pierced them with a well-taken goal they seemed to abandon all hope.

From then on it was all Hull and they coasted to victory.

Wagstaff whipped in a second goal five minutes later and Malcolm Lord made it three at the interval with a neat header from a corner. Within three minutes of the restart Wagstaff completed his second hat trick of the season.

It is difficult to reconcile the fact that only last season Fulham were in the First Division.

The rare flashes of spirit and determination they showed came from Brian Dear, Steve Earle and Les Barrett.

But when they reached striking distance they were slow to finish and Ian McKechnie in the Hull goal was only seriously troubled by a low shot from Dear and a header by Earle.

Despite the recall of hard-working Johnny Byrne, Fulham had no one to compare in midfield with Chris Simpkin.

TAKE A REST, SAYS RAY

Reading 3, Crewe 1

RAY HENDERSON, caretaker manager of Reading, gave his lads two days off after this win—their fifth Easter point in three games.

"I am really proud of them. They have responded magnificently and worked very hard on the field. Now we are getting results," said Henderson.

The extra training sessions he has ordered—he even brought the players in on Sunday—has certainly sharpened them.

Ernie Yard gave Reading a half-time lead and Peter Silvester slammed two more after the interval. Alan Tarbuck scored for Crewe.

OXFORD CRASH AS REF TAKES BOLD DECISION

By DAVE HORRIDGE

Blackpool 1, Oxford United 0

BLACKPOOL fans left Bloomfield-road yesterday scratching referee George McCabe the best they have seen this season.

With only four minutes left, he took a referee's most controversial gamble by playing the advantage rule—and let Alan Suddick score the goal that beat United.

Oxford left back Cyril Beavon used a hand to cut out a pass from inside right Ron Brown. But he only took the pace off the ball and was left trailing as Tom Hutchinson reacted to the referee's "play on" signal by racing along the touchline.

Fight

Hutchinson rolled the ball back for Suddick to crash it in.

The goal deprived United of what would have been their fifth Easter point.

Yet Oxford could have won the match in the first half-hour.

Three times outside right Dave Sloan might have scored. Centre forward Ken Skeen hammered another chance against goalkeeper Alan Taylor and Blackpool left back Bill Bentley belted the ball away with Taylor beaten.

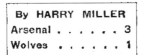

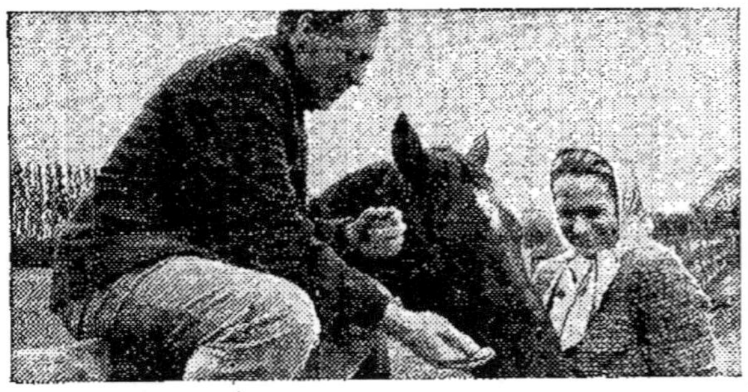

The Hardings are always so full of beans.

Do you envy people like the Hardings who always seem to enjoy really positive health? People who are always on the go, full of life.

Stop envying them right now. And start enjoying life yourself. How? If your tiredness is just the simple matter of vitamin and iron deficiency (and it so often is), then what you need is to take a little extra vitamins and iron every day.

The simplest way to get the vitamins and iron you lack is with Sanatogen Selected Multivitamins Plus Iron.

Just one pleasant-tasting tablet each day provides you with the seven vitamins and all the iron you need—the iron that is essential if you are ever going to enjoy the positive health that can bring you a full and active life.

BANK HOLIDAY SPORTS SUMMARY

MOTOR RACING

BRANDS HATCH. — Formula Ford: I. Ashley (Alexis). 88.01 m.p.h. **Formula 5,000** (Guards Championship): P. Gethin (McLaren Chevrolet). 100.94 m.p.h. **Production Sports Cars:** J. Quick (Jaguar E). 88.07 m.p.h. **Historic Racing Cars—Pre-war:** P. Waller (E R H). 77.94 m.p.h.! Post-war: M. Fraser (Lotus Climax). 87.54 m.p.h. **Saloon Cars:** K. Cawes (Ford Anglia). 83.96 m.p.h.

MALLORY PARK. — Formula Ford: D. Barker (Lotus). 99.15 m.p.h. **Clubman's Sports Cars:** R. Cochran (Blaydon). 86.45 m.p.h. **Grand Touring Cars:** J. Baldes (Chevron). 92.34 m.p.h. **Formula Three:** A. Rollinson (Brabham). 97.75 m.p.h. **Saloon Cars:** R. Williamson (Ford Anglia). 83.61 m.p.h.

THRUXTON. — Wills Trophy (Formula II): J. Rindt (Lotus). 113.46 m.p.h. **Wills Embassy Race** (Sports cars): B. Redman (Lola). 107.34 m.p.h. **Wills Three Castle Trophy** (Saloon cars): R. Pierpoint (Ford Falcon). 93.72 m.p.h.

MOTOR CYCLING

INTERNATIONAL—500cc. RACE (Imola, Italy): MV Agusta's 43m. 61.7s.: 1. G. Agostini (Australia). 2. B. Carruthers (Australia, Aermacchi): 3. J. Cooper (G.B, Seeley): 4. B. Smith (G.B, Paton): 5. B. Nelson (G.B, Paton).

CRYSTAL PALACE.—125 c.c.: J. Ringwood (125 M Z). 70.65 m.p.h.

350 c.c. (non-experts): B. Lee (344 Aermacchi). 72.55 m.p.h. 1.000 c.c. (non-experts): R. Francis (Monard). 75.53 m.p.h. 1,000 c.c. **Sidecar:** C. Vincent (B S A). 73.41 m.p.h. (track record). **250 c.c.:** J. Ringwood (Yamaha). 74.03 m.p.h (track record). **350 c.c.:** M. Andrew (Seeley). 75.0 m.p.h. 1,000 c.c.: R. Pickrell (Dunstall). 78.38 m.p.h.

OULTON PARK. — Ultra Lightweight: S. Graham (Suzuki). 83.40 m.p.h. **Junior Race** (350 c.c.): R. Gould (Yamaha). 87.20 m.p.h. **Lightweight:** Gould (Yamaha). 85.66 m.p.h. **Sidecars:** H. Fath (U R S). 81.17 m.p.h. 500 c.c.: D. Woodman (Seeley). 87.92 m.p.h. 750 c.c.: R. Kemp (Curley Norton). 87.45 m.p.h.

SNETTERTON. — Senior: P. Elmore (Matchless). 84.90 m.p.h. **Junior:** M. Collins (Seeley). 83.69 m.p.h. **Open solo:** O. Judge (RGM Metise). 84.48 m.p.h. **Lightweight:** P. Parfitt (Yamaha). 79.32 m.p.h. **Ultra lightweight:** D. Kershaw (Insley Bultaco). 74.19 m.p.h. **Side-car** (1.000 cc first race): P. Wright (Triumph). 77.26 m.p.h. **Second race:** P. Williams (NSU). 78.67 m.p.h

CYCLING

MACKESON ISLE OF WIGHT TOUR.— Stage Four (65 miles): 1. R. Barnett (Holdsworth) 2h. 57m. 16s. 2. T. Gowland (Carlton) 2-57-16. 3. B. Lawrie (Falcon) 2-57-16. **Overall Result:** 1. L. West (Holdsworth) 11-35-12. 2. D. Bonner (Mackeson) 11-32-2. 3 (equal). C. Lewis (Mackeson). W. Mason (Carlton) 11-39-4. **King of the Downs:** P. Gordon (Broadhurst) 63 pts.

CHILTERN FOUR-DAY. — Last stage (93 miles): J. Winstanley (Finsbury Park). 3-13-31. **Overall classification** (304 miles): G. Wiles (Medway R.C) 13-10-32. **COVENTRY.—500 metres international sprint:** N. Fredborg (Denmark) 12.5s. **individual pursuit,** 4,000 metres: G. Thomas (Birmingham R.C.C) 5m. 17.6s. **Grand Prix:** H. Jackson (Portsmouth). 15m. 57.1s. **5-mile Point-to-point:** M. Bennett (Solihull) 30pts. 18m. 41.4s

GOLF

GREENSBORO OPEN (N. Carolina).—Final scores (with last round): 274—G. Littler (US 69, 69. 67. 69): 277. J. Boros (US 67. 70. 67. 73); 278. Littler won "sudden death" play-off. 275—G. Player (S. Africa) 70: 276—R. Cole (S Africa) 68: J. Rodriguez (Puerto Rico) 70. Other scores included: 283—M. Gregson (GB) 75: 289—B Huggett (GB) 72

SPEEDWAY

BRITISH LEAGUE. — West Ham 41 (T. Clarke 11, O. Byrren 11. K. McKinlay 9). Leicester 37 (J. Boulger, R. Wilson 12).
King's Lynn 44 (Simmons 11, Betts 10, Featherby 8), Swindon 34 (Briggs 16).
EASTER TROPHY—2nd Leg: Exeter 43 (J. Squibb 3, M. Ashby 11), Poole 35 (O. Fossener A. Haley 8). Poole won on aggregate 79—77.
CHALLENGE MATCH.—Newport 42 (Strachan 10 Ashb 8), Wolverhampton 36 (N. Boneock 15).

LAWN TENNIS

CARIBE HILTON TOURNAMENT (San Juan, Puerto Rico).—**Men's doubles final:** P. Dent, J. Alexander bt F. Cunlis, M. Cox (G B) 8—6. 6—3.
NORTH OF ENGLAND TOURNAMENT (Southport).—**Men's singles semi-finals:** R. Clark (New Zealand) bt J. McBrien 6—2. 6—1: C. Chu bt G. Stubbs 6—2. 6—3. **Women's singles semi-finals:** Mrs. S. Brasher bt M. Love 6—1. 6—1. J. Townsend bt O. Fleming (New Zealand) 6—3. 6—3.

TABLE TENNIS

J. M. ROSE BOWL.—National semi-final: Birmingham 5 Northumberland 5.

FENCING

INTERNATIONAL (Bloemfontein).—Britain bt South Africa 13—4.

ATHLETICS

SOUTH AFRICAN CHAMPIONSHIPS (Port Elizabeth).— **Hammer:** R. Payne (GB) 213ft. 11in (S. African all-comers record). **Men's 1500 metres:** 1. S. van Zil (S A) 3m. 48.1: 2. J. Whetton (GB) 3m. 48.4s.

Highbury goes wild as Mee's men crush Belgians

ARSENAL—FAIRS CUP CHAMPIONS!

By HARRY MILLER

Arsenal 3, Anderlecht 0 (agg.: 4—3)

ARSENAL wiped away seventeen years of looking on as others lifted the trophies by winning the European Fairs Cup at Highbury last night.

Beaten 3—1 away in the first leg of the final, Bertie Mee's heroes finally destroyed Anderlecht with a supercharged display of attacking Soccer to mark up their first major success since winning the First Division championship in 1953.

Now Europe must be wondering if England will claim the Fairs Cup as exclusive property with Arsenal following Newcastle and Leeds in winning the competition in successive seasons.

Arsenal were backed in their glory bid by a barrage of sound that must have been heard all the way across north London.

They were bolstered, too, by a decision earlier in the day that away goals in the normal ninety minutes count double. It gave obvious added value to Ray Kennedy's late goal in Brussels last week.

But Arsenal early on found it a struggle to hit their stride as pass after pass went astray.

Suspect

The pressure that should have been put on Anderlecht's suspect back four from the first muddy moments took time to gather momentum.

It needed full back Bob McNab to move through and make Jean Trappeniers' fingers tingle with a fierce 25-yarder before Arsenal got the

It's the end of 17 years in waiting

"attack-attack" message.

As their build-up began to take a more cohesive shape, George Armstrong raided down the right and centred for George Graham to force Trappeniers into a flying save at the post from his forceful header.

Anderlecht's defenders looked decidedly unhappy whenever the ball was hit high and deep into their penalty box.

Eddie Kelly might have done better than blaze high over the bar when the ball came to him just outside the area.

But in the 26th minute Kelly, from an identical position, drove Arsenal in front. And the goal could hardly have come at a better time.

An Armstrong corner on the right was played back out of the penalty area by Frank McLintock to Kelly. The young Scot, twenty yards out, switched the ball to his right foot and as Anderlecht's defenders hesitated, shot firmly into the far corner of the net.

Tight

Dutch international striker Jan Mulder, the Anderlecht ace in Brussels, found Arsenal's marking tighter and the going a lot tougher this time.

Anderlecht wisely decided against a second-half policy of pulling every player back.

Wilfried Puis raced down the left, evaded a flying Armstrong challenge and centred to the near post. Thomas Nordahl met the ball with a shot that rebounded from the upright. But Mulder's drive was turned for a corner by Wilson.

Arsenal pushed on. So did the precious minutes. The break Arsenal had been hammering and hoping for came dramatically after 73 minutes.

John Radford scored to make it 2—0 to Arsenal. Sixty seconds later Jon Sammels scored another.

The Radford goal was a header following a centre from McNab. It made the aggregate score 3—3 but put Arsenal in front on the away goals counting double rule.

But that rule was made as good as obsolete when Sammels raced in from the right to score with a shot that glanced into the net off the far post.

ARSENAL: Wilson; Storey, McNab, Kelly, McLintock, Simpson, Armstrong, Sammels, Radford, George, Graham.

ANDERLECHT: Trappeniers; Heylens, Martens; Nordahl, Velkeneers, Kialunda, Desenghere, Devrindt, Mulder, Van Himst, Puis.

Anderlecht goalkeeper Jean Trappeniers punches clear as George Graham leaps dangerously close for Arsenal at Highbury last night.

Spurs boy sent off at Coventry

By PETER INGALL: Coventry 2, Spurs 2

(after extra time)

GRAEME SOUNESS, 16, Spurs' hard-tackling Scottish left half, was sent off in the 64th minute of this dramatic F A Youth Cup final replay at Highfield-road last night after allegedly kicking Coventry's Dennis Mortimer.

Souness, who also was booked in the second leg last week, was making his way to the dressing room as Coventry scored for the second time but Spurs hit back to take the game into extra time.

Steve Perryman scored for Spurs with a 25-yard shot in the ninth minute, but Coventry equalised from the kick-off through Alan Green.

From the kick awarded against Souness Johnny Stevenson put Coventry ahead.

Spurs stormed back and John Oliver equalised in the eighty-third minute. Spurs right-half Mick Dillon was booked for kicking the ball away.

They will replay again at White Hart Lane on Friday.

RESULTS

FAIRS CUP FINAL
Second leg

Arsenal .... 3 **Anderlecht** 0
Kelly, Radford, Sammels — H-T: 1—0 — 51,612
(Agg.: Arsenal win 4—3)

FOURTH DIVISION

Grimsby .... 5 **Colchester** 3
Hickman 3, Oates 2 — Light 2, Hibbs
H-T: 2—1 — 2,074

FA YOUTH CUP FINAL
Play-off

Coventry .... 2 **Tottenham** 2
Green, Stevenson — Perryman, Oliver
H T: 1—1
(After extra-time. Score at 90m. 2—2).

SCOTTISH LEAGUE.—Div. II: Alloa 1, Falkirk 1; Brechin 2, Berwick 0; E. Stirling 2, Dumbarton 1; Queen's Park 0, Montrose 2.

FOOTBALL COMBINATION. — Swindon 0, Bournemouth 3.

SOUTHERN LEAGUE.—Premier Div.: Brentwood 1, Worcester 0. **Div. I:** Ramsgate 0, Dartford 1; Trowbridge 1, Corby 1.

MIDLAND LEAGUE.—Long Eaton 2, Lonckheed 2; Sutton 3, Barton 1; Worksop 1, Warley 2.

DEVON PROFESSIONAL CHALLENGE BOWL: Torquay 1 (Mitchinson), Exeter 0. Att.: 3,052.

WEST MIDLANDS LEAGUE.—Brierley Hill 0, Bilston 1; Redditch 0, Bromsgrove 5; Stratford 0, Tamworth 5; Lye 1, Baddesley 4; Warley 4, Halesowen 1.

MIDLAND COMBINATION: Smethwick 3, Malvern 0.

£60,000 STRIKER FOR LIVERPOOL

LIVERPOOL yesterday paid £60,000 to Sheffield Wednesday for 23-year-old top scorer Jack Whitham.

After the deal had been completed at Anfield, Wednesday team chief Danny Williams said the club were in the market for players. "I have got my eye on one or two players, and there could be quick developments," he added.

Whitham, who was born in Burnley, joined Wednesday's junior staff in 1964 and made his League debut three years later.

Last season, he was the club's top scorer with eleven League and Cup goals.

TITLE-CHASER McCLUSKEY TO FIGHT AUSSIE

By RON WILLS

JOHN McCLUSKEY, British flyweight champion, flies to Sydney next month to launch Australia's first wine-and-dine boxing club.

He fights Australia's unbeaten champion, aborigine Harry Hayes, cousin of former world bantamweight champion Lionel Rose, for the vacant Commonwealth title on June 16.

The top-of-the-bill contest will be watched by 1,000 dinner-jacketed members, paying from £8 to £14, at Sydney's Chevron Hotel.

Challenge

McCluskey, currently honeymooning in Spain, leaves for Australia on May 26 with trainer Danny Vary.

And if he beats Hayes, Scot McCluskey will challenge Alan Rudkin for the British and Commonwealth bantamweight titles.

But that fight may have to wait. Yesterday, Rudkin rejected a bout with World Boxing Association flyweight champion Berkrerk Chartvanchai of Thailand and seems certain to fight world bantamweight champion Ruben Olivares again in September.

PETER WILSON at the British Hard Court Tennis

KO for Roche—the frozen shadow

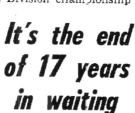

HEAVEN knows what it's like to PLAY in the Rothman-sponsored British Hard Court Lawn Tennis championships at Bournemouth.

All I can say, from personal experience, is that it's almost impossible to WATCH a match for longer than a set without congealing in the paralysing cold, or seriously to evaluate the merits of winners or losers in conditions suitable only for stalagtites and stalagmites.

The cold was at least partly responsible for the major upset of yesterday when the No. 1 seed here and the man generally regarded No. 2 in the world, Australia's Tony Roche, was beaten 6—3, 6—2, 3—6, 7—9, 6—1 by Georges Goven, of France, who thus scored the best win of his career.

But to be fair to Roche—without being unfair to the Frenchman—the left-hander was a sad shadow of his greater days.

Three years ago, in the Welsh championships, he injured his playing shoulder and since then he has been plagued, off and on, with shoulder and elbow trouble.

Last week he made a comeback to competitive lawn tennis after a two months' lay-off and yesterday, before going on court, he soaked his arm in hot water for an hour, while his first action after getting back to the dressing room was to warm it again in front of a gas fire.

Already there has been talk of Roche taking a year off from the game to give the muscles a chance to heal.

Exceptional

But, asked following his defeat whether he now intended to retire temporarily, he said that the cold was so exceptional in Bournemouth that he would have to give it a go somewhere else before making up his mind.

Goven, although at times looking almost too nervous to accept this gift the gods were offering him, pursued the right tactics by staying at the bask of the court. And with Roche unable to flog his stretched sinews into playing his normal muscular game, there were long periods when the encounter resembled an old-fashioned women's singles, with baseline play dominating the exchanges.

It's a frightening prospect for Roche, a fine player and a good sportsman, that with his 25th birthday still a month off his whole career could be in jeopardy.

The last eight in the men's singles are made up of two Frenchmen—Goven and Francois Jauffret, who had to play more than seven sets of singles in first concluding his held-over match against Australia's Bill Bowrey and then defeating his fellow countryman Daniel Contet.

Controversial

Then there is the Egyptian Ishmael El Shafei, who completely outvolleyed and generally outgunned British contract professional Graham Stilwell and Bob Hewitt, the controversial Australian transplanted to South Africa, who eliminated another South African Frew McMillan.

Nikki Pilic, of Yugoslavia, disposed of yet another South African, Keith Diepraam, after five somewhat tedious sets and Tom Okker, the Dutchman of the winged feet, lost only three games in the three sets he won against 39-year-old John Barrett, yet surrendered the third set in which he took only two games.

That leaves two Britons Gerald Battrick and Mark Cox.

Cox had little trouble against that cheerful dusky player "Bill" N'Godrella, but Battrick, the one remaining Davis Cup hope, had a most peculiar encounter with Pierre Barthes, the French contract professional.

The Welshman had to save five set points at 4—5 in the second set and did so brilliantly.

But whether winning or losing points, Battrick gesticulates and appeals passionately in the well known police court phrase to a person or persons unknown.

All I can say is that he doesn't appeal to me.

Outbursts

You can excuse, if not admire, temperamental outbursts from a genius. Battrick has yet to prove himself in that category.

In the meantime, if I am going to watch Welsh histrionics I'll take Richard Burton rather than Gerald Battrick.

In the women's singles, young Evonne Goolagong, who must be wondering what made her leave the balmy breezes of her native Australia for this ice palace, nevertheless played, according to her coach Vic Edwards, better than ever before to beat Nell Truman, younger sister of Christine, with the loss of only two games in the first set and none in the second.

It will be interesting to watch the engaging Miss Goolagong in the next round against that wayward genius Rosemary Casals.

Virginia Wade and Billie Jean King, making their first appearances, got through in comfortable style. Miss Wade crushed Cecilia Martinez, of the U S A, with the loss of one game and Mrs. King beat her compatriot Pam Teeguarden 6—4, 6—1.

SPORTS SUMMARY

GOLF

PENFOLD PROFESSIONAL TOURNAMENT. — Leading Qualifiers for tournament proper— Ham Manor: 70—D. Small (Dunnikier Pk), R. Livingstone (Churchill and Blakedown). 71—A. Fleck (Northwood), K. Warren (Bedford). 72—C. Green (Milltown), J. Cook (Brickendon Grange), R. M. Anderson (Ryl Jersey), A. Moore (Finchley), A. Brooks (Lanark), A. Thompson (Runcorn). 73—A. Sadler (Whittington Bks), B. Allen (Stockport), S. Levermore (Hadley Wood).

Hill Barn: 69—B. Tupling (Tankerley Park). 70—P. McGuick (County Louth), J. Dauthies (Vale of Leven), G. Smith (Royal Guernsey), G. Parton (Chester). 71—J. Little (Hindhead), J. Frew (Bury St. Edmunds), L. Evans (S Afr), S. Brown (Hallamshire), D. Jones (Shandon Park).

LAWN TENNIS

BRITISH HARD COURTS CHAMPIONSHIPS (Bournemouth). **—Men's singles, first round:** ✱A. Roche (Australia) bt R. Case (Australia 6—2, 9—7, 1—6, 6—1; F. Jauffret (France) bt ✱W. Bowrey (Australia) 7—5, 1—6, 4—6, 7—5, 9—7. **Second round:** ✱R. Hewitt (S Afr) bt F. McMillan (S Afr) 6—2, 6—2, 6—2; ✱N. Pilic (Yugo) bt K. Diepraan (S Afr) 9—7, 3—6, 3—6, 6—4, 6—2; G. Battrick (G B) bt ✱P. Barthes (France) 6—4, 8—6, 7—5; G. Goven (France) bt ✱A Roche (Australia) 6—3, 6—2, 3—6, 7—9, 6—1.

✱ I El Shafei (U A R) bt G. Stillwell (G B) 6—0, 6—3, 9—11, 6—1; ✱M. Cox (G B) bt W. N'Godrella (France) 7—5, 6—3, 6—1; U. Jauffret (France) bt D. Contet (France) 6—1, 6—3, 10—8; ✱T. Okker (Holland) bt J. Barrett (G B) 6—1, 6—0, 2—6, 6—1.

Women's singles, first round: ✱R. Casals (U S) bt P. Cody (U S) 6—3, 6—0. **Second round:** E. Goolagong (Australia) bt F. Truman (G B) 6—2, 6—0; ✱V. Wade (G B) bt C. Martinez (U S) 6—0, 6—1; ✱K. Melville (Australia) bt J. Townsend (G B) 6—3, 6—4; ✱Mrs. B. King (U S) bt P. Teeguarden (U S) 6—4, 6—1; ✱R. Casals (U S) bt Mrs. J. Chanfreau (France) 6—3, 2—6, 6—1.

RUGBY UNION

CLUB MATCHES: Exeter 9 pts, Gloucester 11; Pontypridd 9, Llanelli 11; Tredegar 9, Glamorgan Wands 3.

Northampton 12, Bedford 8.

Tourists riding for a fall as Headley piles on the agony

By PETER LAKER

INTIKHAB ALAM'S Pakistanis proved themselves brave, brilliant and brittle in an eventful day's cricket at Worcester—and the sequel today may well be defeat.

By the close last night, their first-innings collapse from 211 for 3 to 241 all out had been aggravated by a masterly unbeaten 96 from Jamaican Ron Headley, and Worcestershire now hold a mountainous lead of 227 with all their wickets in hand.

Yet, earlier in the day, Zahir Abbas, a lithe, bespectacled 24-year-old who collected five centuries at home last winter, had charged to another—with an arrogance that reduced Worcestershire's attack to mediocrity.

Sadiq Mohammad, left-handed brother of the illustrious Hanif and Mushtaq, offered firm support with a 26th-birthday half-century.

At 151 for 2, Pakistan were on the crest of a wave, with a sporting chance of overtaking the county's first-innings' 305 for 5 declared.

Then Sadiq pushed wide of his legs at the off-spin of Basil d'Oliveira and was caught by Alan Ormrod at slip.

Zahir continued to command the field with fierce on-side clips and a deadly, unorthodox front-footed cut that is certain to win him many admirers this summer.

The completion of his century captured the essence of his entire innings. After a full-blooded cover-drive for four off d'Oliveira, he reached the 100 with a disdainful flick square for four and two twos in the same vicinity off the pace of Van Holder.

The tragedy for the tourists was the enforced retirement of Azmat Rana, with a fever, at 194 for three.

The collapse was under way 17 runs later, when Zahir was run out.

Trouble

Asif's dismissal, at 229, was the ultimate in recklessness—an extravagant head-up thrash at Gifford, which left his leg-stump wide open.

Apart from a few brisk blows by Shafqat, who remained unbeaten with 19, the innings was over.

In the closing 140 minutes, Headley and Ginn Turner had an opening partnership of 163 which spells all sorts of trouble for the Pakistanis today.

GLOUCESTER HOPES ARE CRUSHED BY WOOD AND LEVER

By CHRIS LANDER

BARRY WOOD, a twenty-eight-year-old Yorkshireman, put Lancashire in sight of victory at Bristol yesterday with an undefeated 165—the highest score of his career.

His patience, application and sound stroke-play made it a day of misery for Gloucester as Lancashire hammered close on 400 runs on a perfect pitch.

Lancashire indulged themselves in a dozen bonus points, a massive lead of 226, and then paceman Peter Lever obliged with two quick wickets.

Big Hit

Gloucester, totally outplayed so far, finished on a wavering 54 for two, and still need 172 to make the Lancastrians bat again.

Wood was Lancashire's prop and he shared in century partnerships with Harry Pilling (53) and Clive Lloyd (58).

Lloyd, shaking off a bout of influenza, played all his typical flamboyant strokes, including one incredible pull for six off Roger Knight.

Lancashire pushed on for seven batting bonus points and could easily turn this into a total haul of twenty-two today. Skipper Jack Bond declared on 394 for six at just the right moment.

Lever, bowling with all the fire and energy that he gave to England's attack in Australia, had John Sullivan caught trying to hook too soon and Mike Bissex snapped up behind the wicket.

Ron Nicholls and David Shepherd survived a later onslaught from Ken Shuttleworth and from the dodgy start of 28 for two, gave Gloucester faint hopes of saving the match.

Close cracks a ton as Yorkshire slip again

BRIAN CLOSE slammed a century in his first county championship innings for Somerset yesterday—as Yorkshire, the county who fired him, slid towards defeat against Kent.

The incredible Close, now forty-years-old, scored an unbeaten 104, which included fifteen fours, as Somerset scorched to 350 for three, still thirty-one behind at Leicester.

There was no lack of support, reliable opener Roy Virgin slamming 120 and Graham Clarkson an unbeaten sixty-nine.

How once-great Yorkshire must have itched for a dash of that Close magic as they tottered on the verge of defeat against Kent at Bradford.

Bowled out in the first innings for 93, they trailed by 214 as Colin Cowdrey scored eighty-three and Stuart Leary seventy-four in Kent's 307.

Then Yorkshire tumbled to 98 for five in their second innings.

PLAYBOY!

"I'm getting suspicious about our opening bat—he's always out first ball when United are at home!"

—ARSENAL'S

Moment of danger for Arsenal last night as Steve Perryman (left) and Martin Peters go bounding in as goalkeeper Bob Wilson jumps to save.

CRICKET SCOREBOARDS

Worcs v Pakistanis

WORCESTER. — Worcs., all second innings wickets standing, lead by 227.
WORCESTER. — First Innings 305-5 dec. (Turner 179). **Second Innings** 163-0 (Headley 96 not. Turner 62 not).
PAKISTAN—First Innings (Saturday: 35-2.)
Sadiq, c Ormrod, b D'Oliveira 59
Zahir, run out ... 110
Saeed, c Ormrod, b Slade ... 9
Asif Iqbal, b Gifford ... 8
Shafqat, not out ... 19
Intikhab, c Turner, b Slade ... 0
Sarfraz, b Slade ... 0
Asif Masood, run out ... 0
Azmat, ret. ill ... 4
Extras ... 14
Total ... 241
Fall of wickets (cont.): 3-151, 4-211, 5-214, 6-229, 7-237, 8-237, 9-241.
Bowling: Holder 13-1-67-2; Carter 8-1-36-0; Gifford 23-6-41-1; Slade 17-6-54-3; D'Oliveira 11-1-29-1.
Today: 11.0-5.30 or 6

Yorks v Kent

BRADFORD. — Yorks., 5 second innings wickets standing, need 116 to avoid innings defeat. Bonus pts.: Yorks 2, Kent 7.
YORKSHIRE. — First Innings 93 (Underwood 7-28).
Second Innings
Sharpe, run out ... 0
Woodford, c Cowdrey, b Shepherd ... 23
Padgett, lbw, b Shepherd ... 48
Hampshire, c Knott, b Shepherd 0
Dalton, st Knott, b Underwood 0
Hutton, not out ... 12
Old, not out ... 13
Extras ... 2
Total (5 wkts) ... 98
KENT.—First Innings: 307 (85 overs: 200-5; Cowdrey 83, Leary 74, Luckhurst 66).
Today: 11.0-5.30 or 6.0.

Surrey v Essex

OVAL. — Surrey, 8 second inns wkts standing, lead by 101. Bonus pts: Surrey, 6, Essex 5.
SURREY. — First Innings 242 (Roope 75, Storey 70; Boyce 4-26).
Second Innings
Edrich, c East, b Acfield ... 38
Edwards, run out ... 46
Stewart, not out ... 6
Pocock, not out ... 10
Extras ... 4
Total (2 wkts) ... 104
Fall of wickets: 1-84, 2-88.
ESSEX.—First Innings (Saturday: 48-1)
Ward, c Long, b Pocock ... 63
Saville, c Edrich, b Willis ... 22
Fletcher, b Waller ... 24
Francis, lbw, b Pocock ... 7
Boyce, c Roope, b Willis ... 8
Turner, c Roope, b Waller ... 0
Hobbs, c Roope, b Uocock ... 71
East, c Lowe, b Jackman ... 19
Lever, run out ... 6
Acfield, not out ... 8
Extras ... 11
Total ... 245
85 overs: 166-7.
Fall of wickets (contd): 1-8, 2-57, 3-105, 4-112, 5-129, 6-139, 7-143, 8-179, 9-214.)
Bowling: Jackman 24-9-52-2; Willis 26-7-62-2; Pocock 32-12-73-3; Storey 11-3-20-0; Waller 12-7-27-2.
Today: 11-5.30 or 6.

Hants v N'hants

SOUTHAMPTON. — Hants, 7 second inns wkts standing, lead by 71. Bonus pts: Hants 5, Northants 4.
HAMPSHIRE. — First Innings 286-5 dec. (Sainsbury 62).
Second Innings
Richards, b Bailey ... 19
Greenidge, lbw, b Steele ... 20
Gillat, b Bailey ... 0
Marshall, not out ... 15
Livingstone, not out ... 0
Extras ... 11
(7 wkts dec) ... 270
Total (3 wkts) ... 55
Fall of wickets: 1-21, 2-21, 3-51.
NORTHANTS.—First Innings (Saturday: 56-0)
Osman, lbw, b Cottam ... 25
Willey, c Livingstone, b Rice ... 133
Mushtaq, lbw, b Cottam ... 53
Watts, b Sainsbury ... 4
Steele, b Cottam ... 0
Crump, not out ... 32
Sharp, b Jesty ... 0
Breakwell, c Richards, b Castell 2
Bailey, not out ... 10
Extras (7 wkts dec) ... 270
(85 overs: 208-4).
Fall of wickets: 1-59, 2-164, 3-199, 4-200, 5-243, 6-244, 7-250.
Bowling: Cottam 29-9-58-3; Castell 24-6-62-1; Rice 20-2-58-1; Sainsbury 21-9-31-1; Richards 7-3-14-0; Jesty 20-6-36-1.
Today: 11-4.30 or 5.

Gloucs v Lancs

BRISTOL.—Gloucs, 8 second innings wickets standing, need 172 to avoid innings defeat. Bonus points: Gloucs. Lancs 12.
GLOUCS.—First Innings 168 (Shuttleworth 6-47). **Second Innings** 54-2 (Nicholls 18 not, Shepherd 16 not).
LANCASHIRE—First Innings (Saturday: 117-1)
Wood, not out ... 165
Pilling, b Bissex ... 53
Lloyd (C.), c Westley, b Knight 58
Engineer, c Brown, b Allen ... 14
Hayes, c Brown, b Knight ... 14
Bond, c Westley, b Proctor ... 23
Extras ... 13
Total (6 wkts. dec.) ... 394
(85 overs, 330-3)
Fall of wickets: 1-89, 2-194, 3-298, 4-331, 5-354, 6-394.
Bowling: Proctor 22-2-5-75-1; Davey 11-0-37-0; Brown 6-1-16-0; Allen 23-1-105-2; Mortimore 13-3-30-0; Bissex 7-0-29-1; Knight 17-2-89-2
Today: 11-5.30 or 6.

Sussex v Warwick

HOVE.—Sussex, 5 second innings wickets standing, lead by 63. Bonus points: Sussex 4, Warwicks 7.
SUSSEX.—First Innings 207 (Greig 64).
Second Innings
Buss (M.), b Brown ... 14
Greenidge, b Gibbs ... 40
Prideaux, lbw, b Brown ... 1
Parks, b Brown ... 5
Greig, c Smith (M.), b Ibadulla 30
Graves, not out ... 2
Total (5 wkts) ... 92
Fall of wickets: 1-26, 2-32, 3-46, 4-74, 5-92.
WARWICKSHIRE.—First Innings 236-9 dec. (85 overs; 200-5; Abberley 65, M. Smith 65).
Today: 11-5.30 or 6.

Notts v Glam

NOTTINGHAM. — Notts, all second innings wkts standing, need 362 to win. Bonus pts: Notts 4, Glam. 7.
GLAMORGAN. — First Innings 236 (Fredericks 66, Shepherd 53 not).
Second Innings
A. Jones, b Sobers ... 34
Fredericks, not out ... 145
A. Lewis, c Taylor, b White ... 20
Davis (R.), c and b White ... 26
Cordle, c Stead, b White ... 0
Lyons, run out ... 6
Extras ... 13
Total (5 wkts dec.) 244
Bowling: Stead 16-3-52-0, W. Taylor 12-0-46-0, Sobers 11-3-35-1, M. Taylor 8-3-2-37-1, White 15-1-49-3, Harris 1-0-1?-0.
NOTTS. — First Innings (Saturday: 26-3)
Smedley, b Nash ... 10
Sobers, b Nash ... 26
White, c Lyons, b Nash ... 15
Bielby, c (E.) Jones, b Fredericks ... 28
M. Taylor, c Walker, b Williams 11
Pullan, c (E.) Jones, b Fredericks ... 3
Stead, not out ... 0
W. Taylor, c Fredericks, b Williams ... 0
Extras ... 7
Total (46 overs) ... 115
Bowling: Nash 20-7-3?-5, Williams 16-3-41-3, Cordle 3-0-15-0, Shepherd 5-2-12-0, Fredericks 3-2-1-2.
Second Innings: 4-0.
Today: 11.0-5.30 or 6.

Derby v Middx

DERBY. — Middx., all second innings wickets standing, lead by 48. Bonus pts: Derby 6, Middx. 6.
MIDDLESEX. — First Innings: 303-8 dec. (Parfitt 103, Brearley 62). **Second Innings;** 3?-0 (Russell 17 not, Smith 13 not).
DERBYSHIRE.—First Innings (Saturday: 13-0)
Gibbs, b Latchman ... 57
Hall, c Murray, b Jones ... 39
Swarbrook, b Jones ... 37
Wilkins, lbw, b Jones ... 25
Harvey, c Russell, b Latchman 47
Buxton, st. Murray, b Latchman 8
Taylor, st. Murray, b Latchman 4
Eyre, not out ... 30
Russell, lbw, b Titmus ... 4
Smith, not out ... 15
Extras ... 19
Total (8 wkts dec.) 285
(85 overs: 237-?)
Bowling: Price 17-4-4?-0, Herman 6-0-25-0, Latchman 34-8-82-4 Jones 27-9-68-3, Titmus 19-5-48-1.
Today: 11.0-5.30 or 6.0.

Leics v Somerset

LEICESTER. — Somerset, 7 first inns wkts standing, need 32 for lead. Bonus pts: Leics 7, Somerset 4.
LEICESTERSHIRE. — First Innings: 381-5 dec (Inman 1?5, Dudleston 67, Illingworth 56 not).
SOMERSET.—First Innings. (Saturday: 15-0)
Virgin, b Illingworth ... 120
Kitchen, c Tolchard, b Booth ... 47
Robinson, c Birkenshaw, b Booth 0
Close, not out ... 104
Clarkson, not out ... 69
Extras ... 10
Total (for 3 wkts) ... 350
(85 overs: 218-3)
Today: 11-5.30 or 6.

Keegan moves to Liverpool for £35,000

BILL SHANKLY switched his attention from Cup Final opponents Arsenal to lowly Scunthorpe yesterday and bought the Fourth Division club's midfield player, Kevin Keegan, for £35,000.

Keegan, 20, has been the target for a lot of clubs and Shankly said: "We have had him watched for nine months by the same man who watched John Toshack. He is our type of player. He tries without being told to."

Four years ago Shankly bought goalkeeper Ray Clemence from Scunthorpe.

Injured

Brian Kidd, Manchester United's England striker, withdrew his transfer request yesterday after a long talk with manager Sir Matt Busby.

Rangers have hit injury trouble for their Scottish Cup Final clash with Celtic at Hampden Park on Saturday.

Midfield star Alfie Conn will miss the game with a damaged cartilage and three more, Willie Mathieson, Colin Jackson and Willie Henderson are undergoing treatment.

Tomorrow: SUMMER POOLS By LONGSIGHT

GLORY, GLORY NIGHT!

Two minutes left as Kennedy goal lands the title

Tottenham 0, Arsenal 1

ARSENAL won the League championship in glorious style last night, beating Spurs in their final match to settle an incredibly close race with Leeds.

It was impossible to contain thousands of their supporters when referee Kevin Howley, in the last match of his career, blew the whistle which signalled Arsenal's triumph by one point. And no one could deny Arsenal their reward.

They played better than they have for months, keeping their heads, but with their hearts blazing throughout the contest.

With the gates locked and thousands of supporters left in the streets outside, Arsenal settled down quickly to reveal the mood they had managed to whip up for another great effort.

KEN JONES at the big match

Battle

There was no question of any Arsenal player labouring with Wembley on his mind, and three fouls by Arsenal in the opening two minutes showed Spurs that they had a real battle on their hands.

It was Arsenal who nearly went in front in the sixth minute. Charlie George turned on a pass from full back Pat Rice to hit a marvellous shot that nearly caught Spurs' goalkeeper Pat Jennings by surprise.

George leapt excitedly, believing he had scored, but Jennings deflected the ball into the massed ranks of supporters behind his goal.

Playing with great determination and showing the more positive approach, Arsenal continued to take the game forward.

But they were thrown back at last when a move by Spurs gave Steve Perryman the chance to strike a fearsome volley which might have beaten Bob Wilson if it had not struck a defender.

Then, when Alan Gilzean centred cleverly, Wilson and Martin Peters were hurt as they challenged for the ball.

When Spurs were caught offside for the fifth time in quick succession, it brought the slow-handclap from the crowd.

Although this Arsenal tactic was clearly irritating, it served to inhibit their opponents.

It forced Spurs to lengthen their passes in an attempt to play over the top of Arsenal's defence, but it took the rhythm out of their play.

An untidy volley from George Graham, which sent the ball high in the air, was Arsenal's next threatening gesture. But they were under pressure themselves when Jennings boomed an enormous free-kick into Arsenal's penalty area.

'Needle'

A bad foul by Peter Simpson on Martin Chivers revealed the "needle" which began to creep into the match.

It was then that Peters produced a stroke of genius to come close to scoring a great goal. Chivers laid the ball back to him and, with Arsenal expecting Peters to pass, he took it on the volley. It completely beat Wilson—only to rebound from the stanchion behind the crossbar.

Arsenal went forward again and Frank McLintock, up in support for a corner, had a point-blank shot blocked two yards from goal by Phil Beal's urgent challenge.

At that stage, Arsenal were in almost complete command—forcing four corners in succession before Spurs managed to work the ball clear.

Yet Peters again—this time with a shot on the turn—nearly took a goal. Wilson, alert to the danger, got his fingertips to the ball and turned it away for a corner.

As the second half opened, it was clear that there was even more tension in what was surely the most momentous match ever staged at White Hart-lane.

Goalkeeper Bob Wilson was hurt as he came out bravely to fall at Kinnear's feet, and then Arsenal had their greatest let-off of the night when Gilzean missed from two yards after a low cross from Knowles had scythed through the penalty area.

Charlie George, a strange mixture of adult temperament and childish petulance, came into the game with sensible passes and Arsenal settled down to play their best fotball of the night.

They took control, and then gloriously — with just two minutes left—Ray Kennedy, who began this season as a reserve, scored the goal which gave Arsenal the title.

Freedom

A scramble in the Spurs' goalmouth led to a centre, and Kennedy, at last finding some freedom in the air, headed the ball in off the underside of the bar.

There was one last despairing Spurs attack, but Arsenal survived—to be swamped by an hysterical, chanting crowd at full time.

Alan Gilzean (left) is back to help as Spurs' defence gets in a tangle, with goalkeeper Pat Jennings playing it close with Phil Beal.

Pictures: MONTE FRESCO

TOP POSITIONS

	P	W	D	L	F	A	Pts
Arsenal	42	29	7	6	71	29	65
Leeds	42	27	10	5	72	30	64
Wolves	42	22	8	12	64	54	52
Liverpool	42	17	17	8	42	24	51
Chelsea	42	18	15	9	52	42	51
Spurs	41	18	14	9	53	33	50

SUMMARY

FIRST DIVISION
Tottenham .... 0 Arsenal 1
H T: 0—0 Kennedy
51,992

TEXACO CUP FINAL
Second Leg
Wolves .... 0 Hearts 1
H T: 0—1 Fleming
28,462
(Agg: Wolves Win 3—2.)

FOURTH DIVISION
Southend .... 1 Lincoln 1
Best Svarc
H-T: 0—0 4,523

SOUTHERN LEAGUE. — Premier Div.: Telford Utd. 4, Dover 1; Chelmsford 3, Yeovil 1.

SPEEDWAY
BRITISH LEAGUE. — Div. 1: Reading 42 (Michanek 10), Lovaars 9, Curtis 8); Cradley Heath 36 (Persson 1x, Andrews 11); Exeter 49 (Olmes 12, Ingram 7); Newport 38 (Lovat 12, Stangeland, Andrew 9).
Div. II: Crewe 50 (Jackson 11, Meeks 10); Peterborough 22 (Ross 8, Greer, Carter 5).

GREYHOUNDS
HENDON.—2.30: Breck Ranger 6-1 (3-1, £2·20). 2.45: Night Dancer 4-1 (5-6, £1·71). 3.5: Glor Na Mara 7-2 (2-3, £4·14). 3.22: Joyful Punch 11-4 (5-2, £1·32). 3.39: Orange Duke 10-11 f (6-2, 75p). 3.56: Barnoch 7-2 (1-3, £2·39). 4.14: Ponso Painter 6-1 (6-1, £1·72). 4.35: Sunset Rambler 16-1 (3-5, £6·72).
Quinella: £1·25·63.

Mahoney axed —Wales bring back Reece

STOKE forward John Mahoney has been dropped by Wales for the home international championship, which they start with a match against Scotland at Cardiff on May 15.

Cardiff-born Mahoney played against Czechoslovakia in the Nations Cup at Swansea less than a fortnight ago, but was replaced at half-time by Arfon Griffiths of Wrexham.

Now Mahoney, 23, holder of three full caps, is not even in the Welsh championship squad of sixteen.

But Gilbert Reece, Sheffield United's left-winger with the lethal shot, is back in favour.

Brilliant

Reece, 28, was not considered for the Czechoslovakia match because he walked out on Wales the night before they met Rumania last November.

He said at the time he was tired of being continually called into the national squad without getting a game.

Some Welsh selectors felt Reece should never again be chosen for his country. But his brilliant form for United and a shortage of top-class wingers have forced them to change their minds.

Reece, whose two goals on Saturday put Sheffield

By TOM LYONS

United back in the First Division, said last night: "It's nice to know I am not being ignored in view of what happened a few months ago.

"I feel in great shape, following our promotion success and I hope Wales will use me in the championship."

Wales are strengthened by the inclusion of Leeds pair Gary Sprake and Terry Yorath. Both missed the Czech match because their club would not release them. Squad:

Sprake (Leeds), **Millington** (Swansea); **Rodrigues** (Sheff.), **Weir, Thomas** (Swindon); **James** (Blackpool), **Roberts** (Arsenal), **Walley** (Watford); **Yorath** (Leeds), **Durban** (Derby), **Phillips** (Cardiff), **Griffiths** (Wrexham), **Davies** (Southampton), **Toshack** (Liverpool), **Davies** (Newcastle), **Rees** (Forest), **Reece** (Sheffield United).

TRIUMPH FOR WOLVES AFTER SHOCK

Wolves 0, Hearts 1 (agg 3-2)

WOLVES became the first English club to win the Texaco Cup last night —despite losing this second leg of the final at Molineux.

In fact, they have to thank the two-goal lead they gained in Scotland three weeks ago to win them the trophy on a 3—2 aggregate.

Wolves' success gave the Midlands a unique hat-trick. Aston Villa were the first to win the League Cup and Derby first to win the Watney Cup when these tournaments were started.

Wolves almost increased their first leg lead in the opening minutes.

Mike Bailey put over a swerving corner, and Jim McCalliog produced a

By PETER INGALL

header which Hearts defender Ian Sneddon hooked off the line.

Wolves had command without really pressing home their advantage. They weer also inclined to be casual, a product of their clear first leg lead.

In the twentieth minute, Bailey again split the Hearts defence with a fine pass—this time finding Ken Hibbitt.

But the young Wolves forward, given a clear opening, chose to try to beat two defenders, instead of going forward, and his final shot went over the bar.

Hearts gave the game the livener it needed with a twenty-fifth minute goal.

Jim Townsend hit a long ball deep into the Wolves penalty area, John McAlle mistimed his attempted clearance

and George Fleming went bursting in to blast the ball into the net.

Wolves became a little desperate and decided to send on Mike O'Grady for Hibbitt. O'Grady quickly hit a shot wide and was just wide with another effort.

O'Grady was booked for a tackle on Mike O'Grady before Derek Dougan forced Hearts goalkeeper Cruickshank into a great save from a header.

TONIGHT'S FOOTBALL

(Kick-off 7.30 p.m. unless stated)

FIRST DIVISION
Southampton v. C. Palace ....

SECOND DIVISION
Luton v. Cardiff ....

THIRD DIVISION
Preston v. Rotherham ....
Swansea v. Halifax ....
Aston Villa v. Reading ....

FOURTH DIVISION
Grimsby v. Crewe ....

Walsall bank on Villa

ASTON VILLA can do neighbours Walsall a good turn by beating Reading at Villa Park tonight, writes Peter Ingall.

If Villa win, Reading will be relegated to the Fourth Division for the first time and Walsall will be saved. Any other result will put Walsall down.

But Villa manager Vic Crowe is only concerned with his own club. He said: "My players are bound to be aware that the result means relegation for either Reading or Walsall, but they have a duty to do well for Villa.

"I shall impress on them that we want to finish as high as we can into fourth place."

Walsall boss Bill Moore will be watching anxiously from the stands.

SVARC KEEPS LINCOLN IN WATNEY CUP BID

Southend 1, Lincoln 1

LINCOLN KEPT their fading hopes of qualifying for the Watney Cup alive with a goal near the end at Southend last night.

But the Cup, competed for by the highest scoring teams in the four divisions, looked further from Lincoln's mind as they failed to push enough men forward.

Lincoln have now netted 70 goals, the same as Peterborough, but Colchester, with 69, still have a game to play.

Lincoln's hopes faded when star left-winger Dave

Smith limped off in the fifty-ninth minute, after a series of tough tackles.

Smith had a field day before going off. He beat the Southend defence almost at will, but Lincoln never had enough men up in support to take advantage of his well-flighted crosses.

Southend scored after seventy-four minutes when Billy Best headed in a fine goal.

Then four minutes from time Bob Svarc netted as the Southend defence stood and watched.

7 SPORT MIRROR

TUDOR JAMES is on his way to Australia and New Zealand for the British Lions' Rugby Tour. Can the Lions beat the World Champions? Tudor thinks so. See page 36.

TED DEXTER reckons the man who utters words of truth in cricket is brave or even rash. West Indies and Notts skipper Gary Sobers spoke the truth. So what? Turn to page 37.

KEN MONTGOMERY tells a great story of the Soccer player who was ten minutes away from death three weeks ago. Yet despite his terrible accident he'll play next season. See page 38.

JOHN TRICKETT is a classic writer on racing. He describes facts, fancies and fortunes as few other journalists can. You'll believe this. Read his tongue-in-cheek Derby piece on page 39.

EDDIE WARING is the No. 1 expert on Rugby League. He has lively views on Saturday's R.L. Cup Final at Wembley. He writes of the personality of the game on page 40.

FRANK McGHEE knows the date USA wish Cassius Clay to fight our heavyweight champion Joe Bugner. Will the bout take place? Read Frank McGhee on page 41.

GRAHAM AND GEORGE A

Neat footwork from Arsenal's George Graham (left) as he beats John Toshack to the ball.

Arsenal skipper Frank McLintock gets down to the job of beating Toshack and Evans.

IT'S TONS OF TROUBLE BY SMITH AND AMISS

TWO double century partnerships dominated yesterday's county cricket.

At Middlesbrough Warwickshire's 37-year-old former international skipper Mike Smith teamed up with another England man Denis Amiss to knock up 225 between them against Yorkshire.

Smith, whose early form suggests he could be recalled to Test cricket, scored 113 in 4¼ hours. Then he played on to his wicket.

Amiss went in the next over for 112—caught by Wilson off Nicholson.

Yorkshire injury crisis gave their new skipper Geoff Boycott no alternative but to turn out in his first senior game since breaking an arm on the recent Australian tour.

At first it seemed well worth the gamble with two Warwickshire men going for 12, but Rouan Kanhai scored an aggressive 38 to blast the attack before Amiss and Smith's fourth wicket stand.

The second "double" act was at Dartford where Colin Cowdrey and Alan Ealham rescued champions Kent from trouble in their first home match.

Cowdrey's century was the 96th of his career while Ealham's was his first.

They came together after Mike Denness and Brian Luckhurst went for 16 against Leicestershire.

Australian spinner Kerry O'Keefe had a great debut for Somerset — snatching five for 41 in 25 overs—to shoot out Sussex for 127 at Taunton.

The bare, dry pitch gave him some movement with the ball when he came on at 35 for one and he swept away Prideaux, Parks and Greig in twenty-eight balls for five runs.

Pakistan left out Mushtaq for their match at Northampton so he played for Northants, wrecking their middle order of Shafqat, Intikhab and Saeed for three runs off nineteen balls.

But a tail-end blitz hoisted their score to 262 all out.

The Essex spin attack of Robin Hobbs and Ray East tore the heart out of Glamorgan who crashed to 202 all out after a bright start.

West Indian Test star Roy Fredericks gave the Welsh high hopes early on. He lasted 36 out of 54, including a huge six off East

WRECKER LATCHMAN

ON the odd occasion when Gary Sobers loses his wicket to a leg-spin bowler as he did to little Harry Latchman at Lords yesterday, there is a tendency to jump to conclusions writes TED DEXTER.

His Achilles Heel has at last been exposed. He cannot control himself when tempted by the seductive curve of a flighted ball.

These are the kind of thoughts expressed. It certainly looked that way when the great man lashed wildly to leg in the fourth over after lunch, and heard his stumps rattle behind him with the score only six

However, research on his performances last year in two matches against the leg-spinners Intikhab of Surrey and Mushtaq of Northants, reveals a total of 399 runs for only once out

So leg-spin may not be the whole answer after all.

From first to last there was enough swing and turn in the warm conditions to keep the four Middlesex bowlers interested and Nottinghamshire's batsmen on the hop.

It was not until late in the day that a spirited, if unorthodox, stand between Taylor and Pullan—which put on 57 for the eighth wicket—broke the Middlesex grip.

The new Middlesex skipper Mike Brearley bravely asked Notts to bat and his gamble looked good from the start.

Harris was caught behind off Jones for five; and basher Hassan could not resist a big swing at Titmus despite the waiting fielders in the deep Featherstone took the howitzer catch.

Much responsibility now rested on Bolus, and he used every trick to keep the threat of Titmus at bay, but was finally out for a cautious fifty-four.

Latchman, who finished the innings with splendid figures of 6 for 57, took a while to find the right line while bowling wide of the off-stump.

Bolus was one of Latchman's victims, holing out to Smith at square-leg off a full toss.

At the 85-over mark Middx had earned three points, while the 153 runs which Notts had put together so laboriously left them without any bonus.

A quick flurry from this point saw both runs and wickets come quickly, and the teatime score of 129 for 7 became 179 all out.

See TED DEXTER, Page 37

STRIKES ROB RUGBY LIONS OF SLEEP

TRAVEL weariness, the scourge of the 1969 Welsh tour of New Zealand, has hit the 1971 British Lions Rugby Union side, writes TUDOR JAMES.

They arrived at Hong Kong yesterday after a strength-sapping twenty-four hours on their aircraft since leaving Heathrow on Friday morning.

They were five hours late after a spate of strikes which kept the Lions on their aircraft during refuelling stops.

Manager Doug Smith dismissed ideas that it is a shadow side and said "All the players are Lions. My aim is to give every player a game in the two matches in Australia."

The Welsh half back pair Gareth Edwards and Barry John are rested

Hiller gets the controversial full back spot although John Williams looked among the fittest of the party.

It seems madness to pit the strong New South Wales team only a week after arriving. It's virtually an Australian national side

FATIGUE

Many players complained of acute fatigue.

There was a series of announcements that the Lions would not be able to leave the plane because of industrial disputes at the airports.

The British squad sweated it out at Frankfurt for almost three hours and it was the same story at Rome.

The players spent the time signing more than 500 sheets of autographs which will be distributed in New Zealand.

The Lions spent Saturday night in the posh Hilton Hotel in Hong Kong, this greatest of all trading centres in the East.

Said coach Carwyn James, "The players will have a few extra hours sleep before practice at the home hard ground nearby and then a shopping expedition."

James has honed the side to razor sharpness during the five days special training at Eastbourne and was optimistic about the players soon regaining peak fitness

DENIAL

The team fly to Brisbane today for the game against Queensland on Wednesday.

the final round and after five holes, was one stroke in front of Brown and two ahead of Shade.

Coles opened with two birdies and was four under par overall at the fifth. But by the ninth Shade had drawn level again

Coles kept up the pressure and, with six holes to play, was four under par.

Coles came home in 34 for a 70 and 284, looking the likely winner while Shade took a six at the 13th to be two under par

A LAST round charge by Neil Coles (Coombe Hill) clinched the £1,500 top prize in the tenfold £8,000 golf tournament at Queens Park, Bournemouth.

He turned in a 70 for his winning 284 aggregate as his nearest challengers Ronnie Shade (Duddingston) and Stuart Brown (Haltemshire) could not stand the pace on the run in

Shade on 138, the overnight leader at the 36-hole halfway stage, had worked hard to maintain his three strokes lead over the international field after nine holes of the third round.

Despite a magnificent effort by Malcolm Gregson (West Sussex) who opened with birdies three and two holing putts of five yards, Shade managed to keep his nose in front.

A hooked shot cost Shade a two over par six and he reached the turn in a one over par 38. Gregson also turned in 38.

Shade played the first three holes of the homeward journey in par figures and remained three strokes ahead of Gregson and Brown.

Shade, three putting at the short 14th and underclubbing at the 15th, lost two strokes and came home in 37 for a 54 holes total of 213.

This left him sharing the lead with Brown who had a 71. Gregson drifted for a 78 on 219

Coles then loomed as the dangerman when with four birdies he finished in 69 for a 214 total, one stroke behind the leaders with 18 holes to play.

Coles charged ahead in

284—N. Coles 71, 74, 69, 70.
285—W. Cunningham 73, 71, 71; D. Sewell 71, 73, 71, 70; S. Brown 71, 71 71 75; R. Shade 69, 69, 76.
289—P. Oosterhuis 74, 72, 71 72.
290—V. Hood 71, 72, 67, 74.
291—H. Hitchcock 74, 70, 74, 73.
292—H. Boyle 75, 66, 74, 73; W. Stawe 73, 76, 70, 73.
293—T. Harlen 71, 74 75, 73.

Mike Bonallack, the British Walker Cup captain, spreadeagled the field to win the Golf Illustrated Gold Vase for the fifth time at Sunningdale, Berks, with a record aggregate of 137 (68, 69)—three under par for the 36 holes. Second was Roddy Carr, 143, with G. Dixon, I. Mosey, P. Benka, B. Critchley on 145

Ginny tonic

VIRGINIA WADE gave Britain's fading tennis fortunes a fillip in Rome when she slammed her way to the final of the Italian championships with a 6—4, 6—3 win over West German Helga Hosl Schultze.

"Everything was going for me today," she said and proved it by partnering Helga Niessen, whom she faces in the tomorrow's final, to a 6—3, 6—2 doubles semi-final win over Brenda Kirk and Laura Rossovw, of South Africa.

The men's semi-finals will be between Arthur Ashe, who beat Roy Emerson 6—4, 6—4, and Rod Laver, and Tom Okker and unseeded Czech Jan Kodes, who shocked favourite John Newcombe 2—6, 6—1, 7—5

ARSENAL
Wilson; Rice, McNab, Storey, McLintock (capt.), Simpson, Armstrong, Graham, Radford, Kennedy, George. Sub: Kelly.
Referee: Norman Burtenshaw (Great Yarmouth)

LIVERPOOL
Clemence; Lawler, Lindsay, Smith (capt.), Lloyd, Hughes, Callaghan, Evans, Heighway, Toshack, Hall. Sub.: Thompson.
Linesmen: G. C. Kew (Leeds) and J. Bell (Newcastle).

ROAD TO WEMBLEY

ARSENAL.—Round 3: Yeovil 3—0. Round 4: Portsmouth 3—2 (after 1—1 draw). Round 5: Manchester C. 2—1. Round 6: Leicester 1—0 (after 0—0 draw). Semi-final: Stoke 2—0 (after 2—2 draw)
LIVERPOOL.—Round 3: Aldershot 4—0. Round 4: Swansea 3—0. Round 5: Southampton 1—0. Round 6: Spurs 1—0 (after 0—0 draw). Semi-final: Everton 2—1.

LETHAL DOUBLE ACT

ARSENAL ROAR TO CUP TRIUMPH

WITH EXTRA TIME GOALS

ARSENAL 2   LIVERPOOL 1
Graham, George   Heighway
After extra time—90 mins 0—0

By FRANK McGHEE

Charlie George is still top man in this tussle with Liverpool's Steve Heighway.

THE half-hour that saw Arsenal's dream of the double achieved must still seem barely believable — even to them.

It all happened in extra time at Wembley: thirty minutes of ordeal by exhaustion, into which were crammed the emotions of a lifetime.

It was climaxed by the great goal which won it, slammed from more than twenty yards by young Charlie George, who then flung himself on to his back where he lay quivering with joy.

But the drama has to start with the moment twenty minutes earlier when any exultation in the air was strictly reserved for Liverpool and their fans.

In the very first minute of extra time Liverpool had at last gone ahead in a game that had seemed certain to be settled by the first goal.

To add to its drama, the goal was created by Peter Thompson the man they had brought on as substitute to bring some ideas and initiative into the Liverpool attack

DESPONDENT

No side could have been deeper in despondency than Arsenal. Yet, ten minutes later, they were level.

Centre-forward John Radford, standing with his back to goal, played a ball blindly over his head.

Eddie Kelly who, to add to the ironies of the match, had also come on as a substitute for Peter Storey, seemed to have little chance of winning the ball

Two of the great tacklers of the game, Emlyn Hughes and Tommy Smith were converging on him; and Liverpool keeper Ray Clemence was also coming fast from his line.

But Kelly managed to steer the ball to George Graham and the big cool Scot accurately placed a shot to the far end of the line.

The odds still favoured a draw—until Charlie George received that John Radford pass in the sixth minute of the second half of extra time.

ROCKET

George summoned up all the startling, awesome power at his command to lash the ball in a blur past Clemence.

It was a marvellous moment. It contributed directly to an even more marvellous moment for one man — Arsenal skipper and Footballer of the Year, Frank McLintock.

This was the fifth time he has played in a Cup Final at Wembley and the first time he has been on the winning side.

Yet all the emotions and

From an inside left position, the man who had replaced Alun Evans halfway through the second half slid a ball out to centre forward Steve Heighway on the left.

Heighway, until then anonymous, ineffective, submerged by the occasion, suddenly produced a flash of the dynamic, dramatic running that has become his trademark.

He accelerated past full-back Pat Rice and cut in to slash a shot that went across diving keeper Bob Wilson and slammed inside the far post, bulging the side netting

congratulations cannot and must not be allowed to obscure the fact that this game was decided in an atmosphere of drama it did not deserve.

To put it bluntly, for its first ninety minutes it was the worst Cup Final I have seen. And I have seen more than twenty.

It was ruined by two teams more obsessed by fear of failure than hunger for victory—until they became too tired to dredge up the energy for efficiency, so tired that they had to take chances and concede chances.

And that is NOT what this great game is supposed to be all about.

The first half was marked—or perhaps marred would be more appropriate—by the uncompromisingly ruthless tackling of Peter Storey.

A less tolerant referee than Norman Burtenshaw would not have allowed a couple of tackles on Heighway to go unnoticed.

And one hurtling foul on goalkeeper Clemence went right over the borderline, which separates acceptable hardness from roughness

Still it must also be conceded that Storey was the man who did most to ensure Arsenal a command of the midfield that they did not sufficiently exploit

STALEMATE

For all the sparring and occasional breakaways, it was not until the thirty-ninth minute that the crowd rose and roared to the game's first great shot.

It was fired by Charlie George from fully thirty yards and it skimmed just over the bar

Liverpool were attacking only on the left. Arsenal were thrusting mainly down a middle inevitably sealed. It was a war of attrition: a stalemate. Very stale, mate.

Tommy Smith was not dominating for Liverpool. Neither were Simpson nor McLintock for Arsenal.

Chances arrived so rarely that it was remarkable to see George Graham involved in two near misses in the seventy-eighth minute.

I was beginning to think there would be no winner—and only one loser. The game itself when extra time arrived to leave the fans with something to savour.

George Graham received Man of the Match award

Johnstone a Celtic jinx

CAERPHILLY Grammar School Old Boys, expertly led by Cyril Evans, beat Cardiff High School Old Boys 17—13 in an exciting final to the Old Penarthians Sevens tournament.

Caerphilly led 14 points to three at one stage. But Cardiff fought back and with only one point separating the sides, Evans ran seventy-five yards to put Caerphilly's win beyond doubt.

Caerphilly reached the final by beating Cwmtawe, the holders, 14—5.

Offering a magnificent defence, Caerphilly took their chances well to unset the favourites. Gwilym Davies took two tries, and all the cunning of Cary Samuel failed to stop Caerphilly

Cardiff High School defeated Old Illtylians, 13—8, in a hard semi-final match.

The scores were level at the interval with one try for Roberts and Rhys Williams to add tries. Colan converted both, to take his points to twenty-one for this tournament.

RESULTS

First Rnd.: Old Cantonians 6, Caerphilly GSOB 13; St. David's OB 8, St. Joseph's OB 11 (extra time); Cwmtawe 8 CSOB 10; Mountain Ash CSOB 6; Old Howardians 11, Old Penarthians "B" 8 (extra time); Amman Valley CSOB 10, Cardiff HSOB "A" 16; Old Barians 6, St. Peter's OB 9; Cardiff HSOB 8, Old Penarthians "A" 10; Newport HSOB 6, Old Illtydians 10.

Second Rnd.: Caerphilly 11, St. Joseph's 6 (extra time); Cwmtawe 21, Old Howardians 6; Cardiff HSOB "A" 23, St. Peter's 0; SEMI-FINALS: Caerphilly CSOB 14, Cwmtawe 5; Cardiff HSOB 13 0, Illtylians 0.
FINAL: Caerphilly 17, Cardiff 13.

Rangers 1, Celtic 1: By RODGER BAILLIE

DEREK JOHNSTONE, the glamour teenager whose goal took the Scottish League Cup to Ibrox, is the hero of Rangers again. After only a seventeenth-minute FA Cup final appearance

The Scottish cup, in all its eighty-four years can rarely have seen a finish as dramatic as this one, which snapped Rangers right back into the reckoning.

For with only three minutes to go, it seemed that the green-and-white Celtic ribbons were wrapped firmly round the cup

Then Johnstone, brought on as a substitute in seventy-three minutes for Andy Penman suddenly struck.

A long, hopeful ball from keeper Peter McCloy was

crossed on by left winger Willie Johnston and there was the 17-year-old centre

He should have been stopped by either keeper Evan Williams or twin centre half Connelly, but incredibly they allowed him to step in.

His header rolled over the line for that vital equaliser.

As Celtic skipper Billy McNeill appealed vainly for some infringement, referee Wharton pointed to the centre and the Rangers end went wild.

A solid army of overjoyed fans, chanting their team's name with a fervour as fierce as if they had won the Cup.

At the finish the sad, yellow-jerseyed figure of

Williams, who had played so well until that fatal boob, walked slowly off the pitch, the loneliest man in that massive Hampden crowd.

Three successive times he has been on the losing Cup finals for Celtic. He must have thought his hoodoo had gone at last . . . until the fatal eighty-seventh minute.

Celtic had so carefully guarded their snap forty-minutes lead, a goal which had covered their game with a gloss which it had lacked until then.

It was as hard a final as any old-firm game can ever be, with three players booked—Tom Callaghan and Alex Macdonald of Rangers after vendetta in the first-half, and Celtic's Jim Brogan right after Rangers' goal

BRIDGEND HAMMER POLICE

BRIDGEND beat South Wales Police 31—8 in a magnificent final to the Bridgend Sevens tournament.

In the other semi-final, Bridgend overcame St Luke's College, 20—3 with Des Jenkins getting a hat-trick of tries.

Bridgend's star winger, John Williams, raced in for a hat trick of tries. Further Bridgend tries came from Viv Jenkins (two), George Patterson and Gordon Collier. Centre Norman Lang converted four tries and Jenkins one try.

The police replied with two tries by Alec Finlayson and Mike Knill with one conversion by Terry Diaper.

Cardiff College of Education, the holders, were surprisingly beaten 14—10

in the semi-final by South Wales Police.

Bridgend, the current Welsh champion club also showed tremendous form when they outplayed Swansea in the opening round.

BRILLIANT

Brilliant running and handling proved too much for Swansea with first half tries coming from Gordon Collier John Lloyd and John Williams, and two conversions by Norman Lang.

There was no stopping the Welsh sprinter, John Williams when he again outpaced the opposition to cross for a try, converted by Lang who also added another

Winners of the Open section were Aberavon Quins, playing in the tournament for the first time.

They defeated their neighbours Cwmavon by 11 points to eight with tries coming from Alan John (two), and George Glover. Cardiff Youths proved far too smart for the South Wales police cadets in the final of the youth section

Martin Pengilly scored 18 pts. with two tries and six conversions.

Results:
FIRST ROUND: Cardiff Coll. of Education 18, Maesteg 6; S. Wales Police 18, Tredegar 15; Swansea 0, Bridgend 21; St. Luke's Coll. 6, Penarth 13.
SEMI-FINALS—S. Wales Police 14, Cardiff Coll. 10; Bridgend 20, St. Luke's Coll. 3.
FINAL—Bridgend 31, S. Wales Police 8

CRICKET TOUR

A youth cricket team from England will visit the West Indies in July and August next year.

The tour will be largely sponsored by the Sir Frank Worrell memorial fund in Britain, and will be in return for one made by the West Indies youth team to England last year.

GORDON IS ALL GLOOM

COVENTRY 3, EVERTON 2

GLOOM settled over Gordon Lee's Christmas yesterday, as the sparkling Sky Blues shattered Everton's hopes of topping the First Division table.

Ian Wallace produced a goal of the spectacular quality needed to open a crack in the longest unbeaten run of the season.

And the Merseysiders' 19-game sequence was seemingly smashed beyond repair when teenager Garry Thompson and Steve Hunt completed a sensational burst of three Coventry goals in 25 minutes of the second half.

Yet a game that defied analysis as it twisted one way and then the other, ended with Everton frantically close to saving their record.

Clear

Lee made it clear both before and after the game he wasn't happy playing on a mixture of mud, ice and a large snow-covered strip along one wing.

But the pitch couldn't be blamed for a memorable goal by Wallace. Receiving a headed flick-on by Thompson, he turned on Colin Todd, then found the top corner with a lethal right-foot volley.

Thompson got the second, arriving at the back of Everton's defence to head home a long cross by Tommy Hutchison.

By MIKE BEDDOW

Everton should still have come back into the game as Coventry had three escapes in one dramatic attack. A header from Lyons simply hit keeper Les Sealey on the legs, a shot from Thompson bounced off a defender, then Andy King's stab was blocked.

Then in the 75th minute, Hunt, the ex-New York Cosmos winger, was left completely free on the left to place a simple shot under George Wood's body.

A breath of hope came to Everton in the 81st minute. Martin Dobson and Latchford worked well on the left and Coventry were wide open as Lyons scored easily at the far post.

Three minutes later, Sealey made an awful mess of going for a centre from King and Latchford beat him with a firm header.

Man of the Match: Ian Wallace (Coventry).

Larry's so cheeky!

MAN CITY 0, NOTTINGHAM FOREST 0

NOTTINGHAM FOREST'S Larry Lloyd accused Manchester City's Ron Futcher of striking him in the face towards the end of this exciting match.

Lloyd alleged: "I was running upfield to protest to the referee about a Paul Futcher tackle on Archie Gemmill.

"I brushed past Ron Futcher and he turned round and took a swing at me. You can see the mark on my cheek."

Lloyd dropped to the ground in the final minute and after a few seconds stood up rubbing his face.

Barnsley referee Keith Styles consulted a linesman and went over to Lloyd. No action was taken.

"The referee came over and apologised because he had not seen anything," said Lloyd afterwards. "I told him to leave it."

By VINCE WILSON

Ron Futcher was reluctant to talk about the incident, saying only: "I have no idea what happened."

Forest manager Brian Clough said: "Lloyd told me that he had been whacked across the jaw. The referee had had a magnificent match, and did not see it."

City manager Tony Book didn't see the incident, either.

"I can only take Ron Futcher's word for it, and he told me that Lloyd ran into him," he said.

The match was a magnificent draw with Clough claiming: "We should have won because we played well enough to win.

Book can claim the same, for both teams having clear goal chances.

The best for Forest fell to England striker Tony Woodcock who was sent away in the 54th minute with a beautiful through pass from Robertson only to carelessly shoot wide with keeper

Corrigan helpless. The miss had Clough out of his dug out and glaring at the guilty man. His anger wouldn't be about Woodcock missing the goal, but the carefree way in which he dealt with the situation.

Man of the match: Archie Gemmill (Forest).

BIG MATCH SOCCER PARADE

MASTER

ARSENAL can now spend Christmas celebrating the biggest thrashing they've given Spurs in more than forty years.

Triumph was clear in the smiling faces of players and officials as they drove gleefully away to their own patch of North London.

There is, of course, a special sort of shame for the losers in a fixture always loaded with local rivalry.

It is as much about pride as points and stunned Spurs fans were leaving in waves before the end, muttering darkly about the inadequacies of their team and its management.

"How many more players are you going to let Arsenal have?" roared one of them down at the directors box, where Spurs manager Keith Burkinshaw sat suffering the second half misery.

Arsenal had Jennings, Young and Walford in their team and all three were once at White Hart Lane.

It was destined to be a black Christmas for Spurs before the match was a minute old, when John Pratt miscued a back pass to give Alan Sunderland a present.

Sunderland, sensing a gift-wrapped chance sped in on the blind side of Lacy and his shot went in off the underside of the bar for the first goal of his hat-trick.

Gift

Stunned by that 38 second goal, Spurs fought their way back, managing with enthusiasm and skill to conceal the prospect of sensation.

At that stage, Arsenal had settled for using four men in midfield, where Spurs were expected to be strongest.

So for a while, there was no real opportunity to make the obvious comparison between Ardiles and Liam Brady, who Arsenal claim is the best in the business.

And then, just when it seemed that Spurs would be rewarded for a prolonged period of urgent pressure, Brady came marvellously alive.

From the old inside left area, where Arsenal are

■ GIVE us a cuddle! Well it is Christmas as Arsenal's Steve Walford lets us know exactly who is his Man of the Match (Liam Brady, of course)

encouraging him to play, Brady looked up and hit a long diagonal pass that spelt disaster for Spurs.

It caught them flatfooted, finding Sunderland wide and free. He came past Gorman on what was then a familiar line and once more his shot went in off the underside of the bar.

Suddenly there was a scowl on the game and referee Spencer didn't look equipped to wipe it away.

Walford cut down Lee and deserved more than an angry glance. Perryman suffered first himself and then avenged himself on young Gatting.

But Brady was beginning to dominate, enjoying the room he began to find, as Spurs were forced to push more players forward.

It was then, too, that glaring flaws in Spurs' defensive play began to show up.

SPURS 0 ARSENAL 5

Great

Sunderland was close to his hat-trick with a header that came out off the bar, then he had Kendall leaping to reach a cleverly curled shot.

Brady, using his close control and acceleration to attack from midfield, broke away on the left to gather a pass from Rix.

He was finally boxed in by three defenders, but he found a way out and found Stapleton.

It was Brady himself who did most to warm us on an afternoon when a winter chill turned colder. From fully twenty five yards and with his left foot, he rifled a shot into the top far corner.

There was another to come. Stapleton flicked on and Sunderland on a day when it seemed he just couldn't miss, drove in Arsenal's fifth.

Arsenal greeted the final whistle with upraised arms. Glen Hoddle of Spurs volleyed the ball into the crowd. For the losers it was indeed a bad day.

Man of the Match: Liam Brady (Arsenal).

KEN JONES

DERBY 0 A VILLA 0

By MERVYN ROBILLIARD

DERBY, who cannot stay out of controversy for long, were involved in a bizarre goal that never was.

And as the arguments raged the one man who could have said why Gordon Cowans' ninth minute goal for Villa was disallowed wasn't talking.

The best for Forest fell to England striker the end of a John Deehan cross he beat the advancing David McKellar a yard inside the far post

As they danced a jig of joy, the ball went through a hole in the bottom corner and for two minutes confusion reigned. After examining

the net, Richardson called a ground staff man to effect repairs.

And after appeals by Derby defenders the ref consulted a linesman and rubbed out the goal. It was Villa's turn to protest.

As the game was resumed with a free kick near the penalty spot the referee, presumably adjudged Cowans offside.

Villa manager Ron Saunders said: "It looked a good goal to me and until half time I had no idea why it was disallowed.

"My players said the referee told them it was for offside. That can't be right, as the linesman did not raise his flag."

Man of the Match: Steve Buckley (Derby).

The net result!

■ Larry Lloyd ... apology from the referee.

BORO RAGE

LEEDS 3, MIDDLESBRO 1

By TED MACAULEY

ANGRY Middlesbrough boss John Neal last night tackled referee Ron Bridges about Leeds' controversial equaliser which left his goalkeeper Jim Stewart concussed.

Bridges and the scorer John Hawley, who forced the ball home during a goalmouth melee, both insisted there was no contact with the keeper during the 43rd minute incident.

But as Stewart lay in the back of the Middlesbrough coach, Neal — who had raced onto the pitch to steer his players away from the referee — said he had been assured his player had been fouled.

Leeds, however, unbeaten in their last eight games, have their own

injury worries as they strive for a place in Europe.

Paul Hart and Brian Flynn received knocks against Boro and Ray Hankin, still injured, is likely to miss the tough Boxing Day clash with Aston Villa.

Leeds' hero yesterday was that temperamental genius Tony Currie. He provided the cross for the first goal and hammered in a 20-yarder.

But otherwise he was often ill-tempered and combative. Eddie Gray scored Leeds' second goal and young Mark Proctor was on target for Boro.

Man of the Match: Tony Currie (Leeds).

ACTION ∤ PLUS ∤ KEN JONES

BRADY

ALI What a Life

PICTURES : KENT GAVIN

■ Christmas comes early for Arsenal hero Alan Sunderland after his demolition job on sorry old Spurs.

MARINELLO DEAL

PETER MARINELLO, who first strode on to the English Soccer scene in 1970 in a blaze of publicity as a £100,000 Arsenal signing, looks like returning to London, writes RODGER BAILLIE.

Fulham's £30,000 bid has been accepted by Motherwell and they hope to have him in their side for the Boxing Day game with Cambridge at Craven Cottage.

Marinello, now 27, never settled at Arsenal, was transferred to Portsmouth in 1973 and returned north of the border two years later. Now he could be ex-Scotland's boss Ally MacLeod's first sale as Motherwell manager.

CESAR MENOTTI, the man who steered Argentina to victory in the World Cup in June, has quit as national coach in a row over money. He wanted £75,000 for a four-year contract plus about £5,000 a month.

SOME of us remember them well, those privileged hours spent in the company of Muhammad Ali.

So we'll stay tuned to ITV tomorrow night, waiting for Eamonn Andrews to announce: "Muhammad Ali, This Is Your Life."

But how can anyone hope to portray the life of this amazing man in forty-five minutes of viewing time?

Ali's fights, his friends, half-forgotten faces from his past, a father who christened him Cassius Clay but who didn't really care until his son won an Olympic gold medal.

Winners and losers, well practiced users, some who are simply hangers on.

But there will be Ali's smile, and when it comes to a smile no one does better.

Television will opt for the obvious. Joe Frazier, who was the first man to beat him when it counted. Henry Cooper, who became famous when he knocked Ali down.

But they won't get to the real Ali because no one ever will.

There was that day in London when Ali, appearing on the Mike Parkinson Show, appeared to lose his head.

Lean

Ali, embarrassed by the sudden prospect of having to read from a book, settled swiftly for an extravagant diversion because he doesn't read or write very well.

Will they tell us about that night at Lake Tahoe, Nevada, when the tall, lean but not really there Bob Foster managed, uniquely, to cut one of Ali's eyes?

Ali cringed from the doctor's needle, proving that in some ways he was like most of us.

Will they ask the famous trainer, Angelo Dundee, why he knew that Ali had all the courage that many people thought he lacked?

"What will happen the day someone puts him down?" we once asked Angelo, remembering that Cooper really hurt the big man.

"When his backside hits the floor, he'll be on his way up," said Angelo. "Don't worry about my guy, there ain't no one braver in this business."

It turned out exactly that way when Joe Frazier, successfully defending the heavyweight championship of the world in New York, dropped Ali with a classic, murderous left hook.

Ali bounced up, his jaw visibly swelling, the concussive effect of the punch clear in eyes that were blank with the hurt.

Despite the erosive effect of three years in the wilderness, following his refusal to be recruited into the American forces, Ali wasn't finished.

"Loser and still champion," wrote Budd Schulberg, of "Waterfront" fame. And as much as we admired 'Smokin' Joe we liked Budd for that.

But Schulberg's anxiety was clear some years later in Zaire as Ali prepared to challenge a brooding, awesome George Foreman for the title.

Long

It was a long night before the night ahead and we sat and wondered about Ali's destiny deep into a Kinshasa dawn.

"Don't want to see Ali left for dead, not smeared on the canvas," said Schulberg, and to be fair that's how most of us thought it would be.

Then the fight. "Get off the ropes, move and jab," screamed Ali's handlers as Foreman waded in with those massive arms.

But Ali was his own man. He took the blows and did it his way.

Within fifteen minutes of the fight Ali was naked. Some of his handlers had stolen everything. His gown, his gloves, his boots, his socks, even the protector he'd worn around his groins.

"These guys are amazing," said Ali's ring doctor, Ferdie Pacheco, a man who knows him better than most.

"That stuff will fetch a lot of money. They steal from Ali but he doesn't care."

Pacheco, a man of various talents, provides the most genuine and accurate assessment of Ali, the fighter and the man.

Pacheco, artist and author, backed away from the circus two years ago, convinced that Ali, then 35, should retire.

In his book, "Fight Doctor," he says: "I am asked 'what is Ali really like? It is an unanswered question for the simple reason that Ali defies description.

Logic

"Although I do not believe Ali capable of any great prolonged intellectual thought process, I do feel that he has a quality that is so mysterious and inaccessible to 90 per cent of the human race—of doing the right thing by gut feeling alone. The most infuriating thing is that he intuitively does the right thing, but for the wrong reason.

"Is Ali a smart man? He barely reads and is hopeless about mathematical things. He cannot reason in a logical fashion. He is not a great thinker.

"He is a genius at publicity. A genius at saying the right thing. He could address a Ku Klux Klan rally and come away with an honorary degree bestowed by a cheering majority. He is the ultimate hero."

THAT, I THINK, IS MUHAMMAD ALI AND I'LL TAKE TIME OUT TO WATCH HIM ON CHRISTMAS NIGHT.

JAZZY BLUES

CHELSEA 0, BRISTOL CITY 0

A WEEK of nursing and rehearsing by Danny Blanchflower brought a dogged Chelsea performance which may yet launch a rebirth of the Blues.

By KEN MONTGOMERY

Danny's boys are still the length of Basin Street from First Division survival.

But this point gave them something over which they can at least blow some tiny trumpets.

It certainly eased memories of their 7—2 mauling the week before at Middlesbrough.

Perfectionist Blanchflower quickly admitted: "It's a point — and that must be better than nothing. We still have a long way to go and not a lot of time to get there.

"But at least that was a big improvement from last week.

"We've had little time to work, so I'm pretty satisfied with our draw. Bristol are hard to play against. They must be the biggest team I've seen in my life."

There was some soul again in Chelsea's performance, with an encouraging defensive debut by 18-year-old Londoner Mickey Nutton.

Young Nutton took a leaf from veteran Norman Hunter's book, played it cool, and just edged out City's ex-England defender for man-of-the-match honours.

"The youngster will do for me," said Blanchflower. "All he needs is experience. Duncan McKenzie did quite well, too."

It was never nice to watch.

But a point against businesslike City, who mastered mighty Liverpool the week before, brought not just Chelsea's first home clean sheet of the season, but also the sweet music of applause.

It also took Danny's boys off the foot of the table — a Christmas present in itself for strained Stamford Bridge fans.

Man of the Match: Mickey Nutton (Chelsea).

POOLS CHECK SEE PAGE 42

★

THE FINAL WORD From all

What the players thought about it

GLORY,

ARSENAL

BRIAN TALBOT, who collected his second successive winner's medal with different teams, said: "I'm not worried about who scored our opening goal.

"Alan Sunderland says it was his shot but I know I got a touch. And after all, there was no disputing that Alan got the winner—a great winner

"The feeling this year is just the same as last ... elation. We felt we had thrown it away when we let them come back from two goals down but our winner showed what character there is in the side

"Physically it was a harder final than last year, although not dirty. And it was nice to be told by Prince Charles when I collected my medal: 'Well played'."

DAVID PRICE, who was substituted seconds before United made their dramatic comeback, said: "I was a little bit tired but not tired enough that I couldn't have lasted the last few minutes.

"I still don't know why I was taken off. Nobody said anything to me. I was really choked when United got one but when their second went in I really couldn't believe it."

Skipper **PAT RICE,** called himself a "history maker."

"That's four finals in the '70s — two winners and two losers. My little girl is going to get the medal this time."

LIAM BRADY, who made all three Arsenal goals, said: "I was dreading extra time. I was cut on my feet and we had already brought on the sub."

One of the two men behind the Arsenal magic, coach **Don HOWE,** said: "It was a storybook ending. If an author had written that, nobody would have believed it.

"I thought we had thrown it away. If it had gone into extra time, they would have held the initiative."

Both he and **TERRY NEILL** were desappointed with the way Arsenal played when 2–0 up.

Neill said: "We were bitterly disappointed after last year." He felt the seeds for this year's victory were sown with the long series of replays with Sheffield Wednesday.

"It's been a long road and a difficult road and I've been concerned with our form ver recent matches.

"But now we've won the Cup, I want to say that I don't want this to be just a one-off affair. This is just the start."

MAN. UTD

GORDON McQUEEN: "The blood was pumping in our heads after scoring those two goals in two minutes. I suppose we should have concentrated on getting through to extra time.

"But we kept going at them for a winner. Unfortunately, it came against us.

"All season United have been accused of having no character. We disproved that today by battling on after being down from the very beginning.

"No blame for any of Arsenal's goals can be attached to our 'keeper Gary Bailey. The kid was tremendous.

"I honestly felt we had more of the play in the first half but couldn't get a break."

STEVE COPPELL said: "We felt we were on top at half time, even though we were 2–0 down.

"We thought we could come back and we proved it — but Arsenal proved something else in the final minute."

Skipper **MARTIN BUCHAN** said: "I always thought we might get the draw and force extra time but I don't begrudge them their victory."

Manager **DAVE SEXTON** said: "It was a remarkable achievement to fight back as we did. We earned the right to a replay.

"We were the better side in the first half but Pat Jennings produced fine saves at vital times.

"Even when we were in the dressing room two down at half time I felt we could still come back given the breaks.

"And it was very cruel to climb the hill then lose it all with our moment of lost concentration.

"We didn't expect to win in normal time but it seemed justice that we would get a breather and have another go."

■ Cup of joy . . . as Arsenal's Sunderland and Stapleton celebrate the Gunners' first goal.

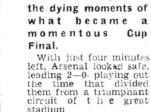

By KEN JONES

WEMBLEY has staged no greater drama than that which erupted in the dying moments of what became a momentous Cup Final.

With just four minutes left, Arsenal looked safe, leading 2–0, playing out the time that divided them from a triumphant circuit of the great stadium.

It was then that United suddenly came bursting out of nowhere, dredging up one last surge of energy and spirit to astonish us with a unique Wembley comeback.

Arsenal had just brought off the flagging Price and replaced him with Walford.

Almost immediately, United struck, the giant McQueen taking Jordan's low cross to drive it past Jennings.

They were playing into the faces of their own fans banked high on the terraces behind Arsenal's goal.

And that bank came fully alive again, as though sensing that there was more drama to come.

United celebrating that goal with exhorting fists, lanced forward again.

Macari sent McIlroy through on the left flank of Arsenal's defence and the slim Irishman, eeling square across field, stroked an equaliser into the far corner.

Salvation for United—or so it seemed—as their manager, Dave Sexton, and his compatriots on the touchline bench leapt in jubilation.

But the joy was short-lived, as Liam Brady applied his genius once more to Arsenal's cause.

From deep in the right-hand corner of United's half and just when we were rolling off the seconds to extra time, Brady sent an immaculate pass to Rix, who crossed perfectly from the left for Sunderland to convert triumphantly from wide of the far post.

Slump

That was it and as Arsenal gave themselves up to an explosion of joy, the United players slumped to the turf in tearful despair.

Three goals in three minutes. Heart-stopping stuff that erased the memory of what had been until then a largely dull and often shoddy Final.

Rising above all that was Brady, the Irishman who is now fully established as one of the great natural talents in the game.

A year ago, Brady

What a fairy tale for Alan in

limped forlornly out of the Final against Ipswich, a half-fit failure promising to do better the next time.

That promise was emphatically fulfilled as he produced two flashes of genuine class to make the two goals that by half time had seemed to have won the Cup for Arsenal.

United's dilemma all week had been whether to try and contain Brady within the overall pattern of their play, or to detail one man to keep him quiet.

They settled for giving the responsibility to Macari, but it was neither one thing nor the other. Brady began quietly as though determined to get the true feel of a pitch soft enough to send the most balanced players slithering embarrassingly on their backsides.

Then in the 12th minute Brady produced a run that was to tear United apart. Three men tried to smother him, but the ball stayed close to that educated left foot.

It went then to Staple-

the BIG names at WEMBLEY

ARSENAL

First blood . . . Brian Talbot (No. 4) and Alan Sunderland Swoop in unison for Arsenal's opening goal,

wunderland

ton, then to Price who, keeping his head, drove a low pass amidst the flailing feet in United's penalty area.

Sunderland and Talbot piled in. Sunderland got the first touch but it looked like Talbot who sent the ball into the roof of Bailey's net.

It was Brady's first significant contribution, but now he began to impress that he was the most important figure in the match.

Nevertheless, United had their moments and, in fact, the better chances in the first half.

Thomas, close in, struck a first-timer from McIlroy's pass that flew straight at Jennings.

Jordan, who looked at times as though he was capable of leaping right out of the stadium, raked the crossbar with a header.

And then after Rice, Arsenal's captain, had been booked for obstructing McIlroy, United produced their most effective combined effort of the first half.

Slow

It was almost in slow motion as he looked up, measured the distance and found Stapleton, who, criminally unmarked on the far post, headed an easy goal.

United for much of the second half looked to have given themselves up to defeat and Arsenal, inspired by Talbot's relentless energy, seemed to have the game well in hand.

For a while we were

were involved and Greenhoff was only inches away from what would have been a spectacular goal as, on the turn, he drove just over the top.

Then it was Macari's turn with a header that once again found Jennings perfectly placed to deal with the threat.

That combination of expert positioning and good fortune was to prove decisive on the day. Even more so was the goal that came in the 44th minute as Brady flowered once more.

treated by Brady to examples of his talent. The dribble, the pass slotted immaculately between defenders.

Arsenal might have gone further in front when Stapleton sent in a header that Bailey only just got to with his knees.

Jennings saved Macari's header, pushing it over the bar brilliantly one-handed.

Talbot made an important tackle on McIlroy. Macari hooked over and Jennings, that combination of skill and luck working for him again, was right in line when Coppell volleyed fiercely.

Even so, there was no hint of the drama to come and Nicholl only just managed to foil Sunderland when the Arsenal forward dived at a Rice centre.

Then suddenly it all happened — almost a bizarre happening.

Whenever Cup Finals are talked about, the finish to this one won't be forgotten.

Man of Match: Liam Brady (Arsenal).

THE OTHER FINAL

Hibs 0, Rangers 0: By RODGER BAILLIE

THE longest hoodoo in Scottish soccer can still be beaten this season. Hibernian, the team no one outside Edinburgh gave a ghost of a chance to win this Scottish Cup Final, can still capture a trophy they last one 77 years ago.

They never looked 4—1 outsiders in a confrontation which can only be better the second time around on Wednesday.

Scotland's Cup Final has so often been criticised for lack of presentation. This time the Scottish FA got that right . . . it was the teams who got the game wrong.

Only in the last ten minutes did the pride and the passion begin to flow.

But certainly there was effort and endeavour in the second half with Rangers always looking more likely to snap into the lead.

Substitute Alex Miller, brought on after fifty minutes for Alex MacDonald, who was injured by an early Ally MacLeod tackle, unleashed a full-blooded drive which somehow Hibs 'keeper Jim McArthur tipped over.

Then in sixty-eight minutes Derek Parlane's header as he zoomed on to a Davy Cooper cross smashed off the underside of the bar.

But the Hibs defence,

AGONY FOR SCOTS

expertly organised by sweeper Jackie MacNamara, who had Des Bremner in front of him blunting the Rangers attack, were never in such danger again.

And in the last ten minutes Hibs suddenly began to believe they could be the winners.

Striker Colin Campbell had three chances which could have brought his team that historic winner.

Now the fans must wait until Wednesday for the deadlock to be broken . . . and for the excitement which was missing for so long yesterday.

HOW THEY PLAYED..

STAR RATINGS FROM TOP SOCCER BOSS

BOB PAISLEY

ARSENAL

PAT JENNINGS: He had more to do in the the last five minutes than in the rest of the game. His vast experience showed when he handled the big men Gordon McQueen and Joe Jordan without panicking

PAT RICE (captain): He played the sensible kind of role you would expect from a captain. The only threat to his composure came from Mickey Thomas, but really he never looked like blowing up.

DAVID O'LEARY: He had a quiet game but really contained Jimmy Greenhoff without too much trouble. He was never in any danger.

WILLIE YOUNG: Not the most elegant of players but he'll be satisfied about coming out on top in his tussle with Joe Jordan. He was run ragged last year but this time he won his duel.

SAMMY NELSON: There was no threat at all down the right flank, so all he had to do was to sit tight. Sensibly, he didn't take any chances when he was presented with so much space.

BRIAN TALBOT: He worked hard in the early part of the game with Liam Brady, then ran out of steam. But, having said that, he kept his head, especially in the tussles with Sammy McIlroy. Overall, a hardworking, competent display.

LIAM BRADY: My man of the match and Arsenal's player of the day. He had a hand in all three goals but didn't try to hog the game. He was content to let play come to him, and when the moment was right he was the butcher who carved them up. Most heads would have fallen at 2—2 but he kept his —the sign of a truly great player.

DAVID PRICE: If there was nothing wrong with him when he was substituted then Arsenal were wrong to take him off. It nearly proved fatal. Price was doing a good job when he left the field and United quickly exploited the mistake.

ALAN SUNDERLAND: He also had a quiet game and didn't cause many problems to Martin Buchan. He's played in far better games for Arsenal. But he'll be well satisfied with his display and, of course, that killer goal at the end.

FRANK STAPLETON: His biggest contribution was that he spread himself among the United back four and didn't let any one defender mark him. He caused immense problems and took his goal well.

GRAHAM RIX: He was involved early and later on in the game but in between he was quiet. He showed one or two nice touches but basically he could have done more.

MAN. UTD

GARY BAILEY: might better for the first goal have covered himself and again he was caught out for the winner. Possibly if Jennings had been in a similar poston the goals wouldn't have been scored. He never really had time to settle although you couldn't blame him solely for United's defeat.

JIMMY NICHOLL: I was disappointed when Nicholls found himself with no one to mark yet didn't try and get involved in the game. I would have liked to have seen him join the midfield. He was too content to sit back.

GORDON McQUEEN: He scored a timely goal but really could have played a bigger part. Along with Joe Jordan he was guilty of wasting chances when they were both jumping to head the same ball.

MARTIN BUCHAN (captain): I feel very sorry for him because he did all he could. He was steady and sensible. He knew he had to stay back while McQueen tried his luck up front late in the game. A very disciplined performance.

ARTHUR ALBISTON: Again he was as guilty as Nicholl. He could have supported the midfield men a lot more. But he was content to stay back

without committing himself to the game.

MICKEY THOMAS: My man of the match for United. I thought he worked as hard as any player on the pitch. If I had to criticise him it would be for not making his final pass tell. Four times he was through into dangerous positions but wasted the ball every time.

JIMMY GREENHOFF: Another player who disappointed me. Mind you, this wasn't the type of game to face when you've been injured.

JOE JORDAN: He scratched a few headers without any real control. He knew as well as anyone else that Young was probably still carrying an injury but he didn't give him the run around you would have expected.

SAMMY McILROY: He let himself get involved in a personal duel with Talbot. He got rattled and in the end it spoiled the game.

LOU MACARI: He tried to close down on Brady and was never able to get the amount of space his game demands. His game is all about causing problems, not trying to contain a problem player.

STEVE COPPELL: He was the player on the pitch that impressed me the most. I've never seen him so quiet.

WEMBLEY SPECIAL   NICHOLAS GRABS CUP

CHARLIE'S

Arsenal's prince

Arsenal 2

■ IAN RUSH takes to the air after putting Liverpool ahead.

Liverpool 1

ARSENAL manager George Graham will have to come up with a king's ransom to make Bonnie Prince Charlie stay at Highbury after his startling two-goal winning performance.

Charlie Nicholas brought a touch of London pride to Wembley, yet he began this Littlewoods Cup final with his future in doubt and his reputation at stake with no offer of a new contract on the table.

Now Graham will have to set before this super Scot the sort of financial incentives that will persuade him not to join up with the team he put to the sword —Kenny Dalglish's Liverpool.

Nicholas' contract ends this summer and he proved his credentials for a handsome new deal when he handed Arsenal their first taste of success for eight years in their centenary season.

He may not have been a huge success in four years at Highbury, with Graham his third manager, but he chose the perfect place to prove he has not been an almighty flop.

By **HARRY HARRIS**

Tear

The hyped-up Nicholas grabbed the goals that finally killed off the most fabled statistic in soccer, that Liverpool never lose when Ian Rush scores.

In 144 games stretching over six seasons, with 122 victories, Liverpool had never lost when Rush has scored.

Well, Rush was on target here, and it was the opening goal of one of the best and most fascinating of recent Wembley finals, yet Liverpool lost.

It was not the way Rush had dreamed his last Wembley appearance before leaving for Juventus would end.

He shed a tear, his head slumped as he bid a sad and emotional farewell,

but he can count all his winners' medals as compensation — four Championships, four League Cups, one FA Cup and one European Cup.

But, while Liverpool slumped away in despair, no one can deny Arsenal their triumph.

Wembley belonged to Charlie.

His equaliser showed all the trademarks and instincts of a true goal scorer.

Luck

It also brought Arsenal back to life after Liverpool's emphatic powerful start, and gave the north London team the vital belief they could actually win.

Charlie's late winner required a huge dose of luck as the deflection off Ronnie Whelan beat goalkeeper Bruce Grobbelaar as much as the Arsenal striker.

Now Liverpool have to

lift themselves to retain their title, the only trophy left to them, while the Gunners have tangible reward for an outstanding first season under Graham.

Jan Molby and Steve McMahon opened up the Arsenal defence for Rush to sidefoot his 35th goal of the season.

A Paul Davis 20-yard

great save from Craig Johnston.

Liverpool's grip on the game was underlined by their superb opening strike in the 23rd minute.

Rush missed a chance as early as the second minute that he normally gobbles up and five minutes later goalkeeper John Lukic produced a

angled shot struck the outside of the post before he began the move that led to Nicholas' equaliser in the 30th minute.

Davis hit a free-kick against the defensive wall, skipper Kenny Sansom swept it back, Adams had a shot blocked and Nicholas struck the post and when

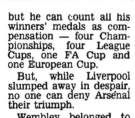

PICTURES by ALBERT COOPER

NICE ONE NEVILLE

By NIGEL CLARKE: Chelsea 1, Everton 2

KERRY DIXON became the latest in a long line of strike stars who have found Neville Southall a heartbreaker.

Dixon beat him once, and thought he had for a second time with a point-blank header until the goalkeeper somehow produced a breath-taking reaction save.

"That could be the difference between winning or losing the League," Dixon said afterwards.

Chelsea would have led 2-1, instead Everton broke away from the clearance, and Alan

Harper exploded their winner.

The keeper himself wasn't so impressed. "I didn't think much of it," he said. "Dixon shouldn't have put the ball where I could get it."

In a match with an undercurrent of bad feeling — four players sent off in the last six meetings between the clubs—Chelsea were unlucky to be beaten.

Joe McLaughlin, who turned a Harper corner into his own net, said: "I didn't think that much of Everton. I still believe Liverpool will end up champions."

GLORY WITH DOUBLE STRIKE

CROWN JEWELS

■ CHARLIE NICHOLAS turns in jubilation after scoring the equaliser. Tony Adams shares his delight.

GUNNERS JOY DAY

■ WINNING feeling from Nicholas and Perry Groves, who laid on the decider.

CRYING SHAME

By TONY STENSON

IAN Rush brushed away the tears and vowed last night to return to Wembley. "I'll be back, even if it's only for Wales," he said after an emotional goal-scoring farewell for Liverpool.

The Merseyside giants hadn't lost in 144 previous games when Rush had scored. But the Juventus-bound star was delighted the burden had finally been lifted from his shoulders.

"It had begun to weigh me down, and I hoped it would go some time," he said. "They say records are there to be broken—and if it had to go there's no better place than Wembley."

Liverpool manager Kenny Dalglish said: "I'm not disappointed because I thought we did well—but all credit to Arsenal for their fightback."

Arsenal skipper Kenny Sansom said: "I can't remember too much about the game. I've been here many times in my career but today was something special. It was a marvellous occasion."

Liverpool's midfield powerhouse Jan Molby said: "I wanted to leave the pitch in the final 20 minutes because I felt very tired and was feeling my injury.

"We thought when Ian scored we would win again . . . now we've got to give the fans the League."

Arsenal's winner was laid on by substitute Perry Groves. He said: "I was going to shoot, but then saw Charlie out of the corner of my eye and I knew he would give me a mouthful if I didn't pass to him."

Viv Anderson turned it back Nicholas provided the vital touch from close range.

Photographers massed behind Lukic's goal in the second half expecting the inevitable Liverpool victory.

But after David O'Leary's trip on Nigel Spackman produced a free-kick that Molby

chipped narrowly wide, Arsenal surprisingly began to gain control.

Nicholas might well have had a penalty just after the hour when tripped by Gary Gillespie, but not even the substitution of Liverpool player-manager Dalglish could change the course of the match.

In fact, it was Graham's

substitution of Perry Groves for Niall Quinn that sealed Arsenal's destiny.

The speedy Groves, eight minutes from the end, skipped past a lunging tackle from Gillespie and his cross set up the winning goal.

And Nicholas was confirmed as the darling of the Arsenal fans.

and MONTE FRESCO

A Sher thing!

By HARRY HARRIS

Charlton 4 Watford 3
STEVE SHERWOOD believes he is saving up all his luck to inflict a shock FA Cup semi-final defeat on Spurs this Saturday at Villa Park to take him back to Wembley.

There, in the FA Cup final three years ago, he was blamed for the Andy Gray goal that gave Everton victory.

A freak training accident to Tony Coton has catapulted 33-year-old keeper Sherwood into the Watford team within reach of a Cup Final return.

Manager Graham Taylor refused to blame Sherwood for any of the four goals at Selhurst Park and the keeper said: "I don't seem to have any luck at the moment—I'm saving it for next week.

"No one will ever let me forget that Andy Gray goal at Wembley, but I'd love to get back and show what I really can do."

Allen's a splash

By JACK STEGGLES

CLIVE ALLEN forced Bobby Robson to eat his words by splashing through a monsoon for a hat-trick, as Spurs beat Norwich 3-0.

Robson left Allen, last night voted the PFA player of the year, sitting in the stand for England's game in Spain six weeks ago claiming: "Clive is not at his best in heavy going."

Allen made nonsense of that. In quagmire conditions, he took his tally for the season to 43.

That left him needing three for an all-time Spurs scoring record and had teammate Nico Claesen enthusing: "Clive is the best finisher I have ever seen."

Coming from a man with Claesen's pedigree, that is some praise. The Belgian international—a big success in last year's World Cup—has played with and against some of the game's greats.

Hot-shot Archie

A CRACKING goal by Steve Archibald paved the way for Barcelona's 4-0 win at Atletico Madrid yesterday.

Gary Lineker later completed the rout of the Madrid side, racing through to slot home the fourth, and his 18th League goal of the season.

Barcelona's finest away performance in the last League match of the regular season closed the gap with leaders Real Madrid to just one point.

Real Madrid drew 0-0 with Espanol on Saturday evening and the stage has now been set for a 10-match play-off between the six top clubs to decide the championships.

SPORTS SUMMARY

LITTLEWOODS CUP FINAL
Arsenal........(1) 2 Liverpool.....(1) 1
Nicholas 2   Rush
Att: 96,000   Rec: £1,000,000

THIRD DIVISION
Middlesbro ..(0) 1 Darlington ..(0) 1
Slaven   Roberts
                   Att: 11,969

FA TROPHY: Semi-final, first leg: Kidderminster 0, Fareham 0.

ITALIAN LEAGUE: Ascoli 0, Verona 1; Atalanta 0, Juventus 0; Avellino 2, AC Milan 1; Empoli 0, Napoli 0; Inter 1, Como 0; Roma 1, Fiorentine 1; Sampdoria 0, Udinese 0; Torino 2, Brescia 2.

GOLF
£400,000 GREATER GREENSBORO OPEN (North Carolina)—Leading scores after third round (US unless stated): 212 S Simpson 69; 213 T Byrum 72. Other scores: 222 J-M Olazabal (Spa) 75, N Faldo (GB) 75.

WARWICK POOLS
COMPETITION A—Pool 1: £2,000. 15 winners each receive £133.33. 02, 52,

with any two from 03, 05, 09, 11, 13, 31, 40, 41.
COMPETITION B—Pool 2: £400. Four winners each receive £100. 08, 21, 35, with any one from 14, 16, 25, 27, 30, 31, 39, 40, 43, 48, 49, 51. Pool 3: £215. Three winners each receive £71.67. Any four from 14, 16, 39, 40, 43. Pool 4: £215. Two winners each receive £107.50. 08, with any three from 25, 29, 31, 35. Pool 5: £215. One winner 13, 26, 28, 36. Pool 6: £300. One hundred and fifty gift winners.

TOP DOG'S BEST
CATFORD (16 races): 9.15 Tradeline Steve, 9.45 Ballaugh Echo, 10.00 Sneaky Prince. CRAYFORD (12): 8.35 Willie Wonka, 9.09 Rhebuck, 9.43 Ardent Lad, 10.00 Blue Falls Boy. HARRINGAY (10): 9.25 Lade Lane, 9.42 Run On Dusty, 10.00 Go Spencer Again (Nap). WEMBLEY (12): 8.30 House Hunter, 9.00 Sambuca, 10.00 Holloways Magic, 10.15 Gortroe Jack.

TONIGHT'S SOCCER
FIRST DIVISION
Watford v Q.P.R. (7.45) ....

It's Arsenal's crown as king Thomas

THE GREATEST

SKIP TO IT!
ARSENAL skipper Tony Adams keeps out Liverpool's ace striker Ian Rush in the championship thriller at Anfield last night

Graham night of triumph

Liverpool 0, Arsenal 2

ARSENAL last night pulled off a soccer miracle to deny Kenny Dalglish a place in history.

Dalglish was bidding to become the first manager to win the double twice, following his triumph three years ago.

Instead, in one of the most dramatic climaxes to any championship season, the Gunners proved they are worthy champions.

The North London glory boys stole the title from the clutches of the FA Cup winners with almost the last kick of this sensational and traumatic season.

Michael Thomas, who had earlier missed a golden chance, made no mistake with an injury-time goal that put the two giants level on points and goal difference, with the Gunners taking the title by scoring more goals.

Thrown

George Graham's team seemed to have thrown the championship away at least twice in recent months, but their 73 goals outstripped Liverpool's 65.

It is 90 years since two teams last went into the final match each with a realistic chance of taking the title. And this time the exhilarating climax was shared by millions of TV viewers.

ITV are paying £50 million for an exclusive contract and they got their money's worth as Arsenal clinched their first title for 18 years — the last time their current manager Graham was in their line-up.

At 10.19 last night, Graham walked off the Anfield pitch with the championship trophy firmly in his grasp, writing his name in the Highbury Hall of Fame just as he always wanted to do.

Graham had joined in Arsenal's lap of honour as some of the Arsenal players broke down with tears of joy, while some Liverpool players wept in despair.

Many Liverpool supporters stayed on the Kop to sportingly applaud the new champions as the Arsenal fans sang "You'll Never Walk Alone" and triumphantly chanted "Champions".

They also mockingly bellowed "Boring, boring, Arsenal", sarcasti-

---

SPORTS SUMMARY

BARCLAYS LEAGUE FIRST DIVISION

Liverpool......(0) 0 Arsenal......(0) 2
41,718   Smith, Thomas

INTERNATIONAL

N Ireland......(0) 0 Chile............(1) 1
2,500
(Windsor Park, Belfast)

GREYHOUNDS

ROMFORD.— 7.30 Lesley Honey 3-1jf (2-1, £23.07). 7.45 Triumph 11-4f (3-6, £11.85). 8.00 Monroe Sailor 2-1f (4-5, £14.96). 8.16 Edwards Surprise 3-1 (2-3, £18.67). 8.32 Barrowboys Town 4-1 (3-6, £20.44). 8.48 Precious Chimes 100-30 (6-2, £20.56). 9.04 Silkys Parade 4-1 (6-4, £35.31). 9.21 Poor Form 4-1 (2-5, £28.03). 9.39 Borris Nap 5-2f (1-3, £14.53). 9.56 Ballymoth Lad 10-11f (1-3, £8.44). 10.13 River Loch 5-4 (1-2, £6.25). Nr: King Paddy (3), Orlas Wish (6). 10.30 Welview Wendy 12-1 (5-1, £54.60).

WEMBLEY.— 7.30 Quality Prince 4-1 (1-5, £20.44). 7.45 Florin Bob 6-1 (9-1, £32.32). 8.01 Fargo 5-4f (6-4, £8.72). 8.17 Moon Sapphire 11-4 (6-2, £8.22). Nr: My Tex (1). 8.33 Peaceful Hero 4-1 (1-5, £49.00). 8.49 Premier Prince 9-2 (1-2, £22.78). 9.05 Daleys Sail 10-11f (2-4, £5.83). 9.22 Quainton Lane 9-2 (3-4, £22.78). 9.39 Botany Girl 8-1 (1-6, £22.18). 9.56 Kingswell Rover 2-1f (4-5, £17.01). 10.13 Lucky Reflection 8-1 (3-1, £35.91). 10.30 Parks Pleasure 6-1 (3-5, £26.88).

WIMBLEDON.— 7.30 Mick And Dick 7-2 (3-2, £9.25). 7.45 Halfway Gent 2-1jf (5-1, £3.27; 5-3, £7.48). 8.00 Personal Views 9-2 (5-1, £9.45). 8.15 Lulus Zola evensf (2-5, £12.54). 8.30 Fancy Note 9-4f (2-1, £25.60). 8.45 Cloverhill June 5-1 (6-4, £58.91). 9.00 Rathbeg Sue 10-1 (1-2, £29.59). Nr: Sunny Outlook (3). 9.15 Chicita Banana 1-2f (6-4, £8.30). 9.30 Sign On Fisher 4-1 (3-1, £11.01). 9.45 Cygnet Man 5-2 (3-1, £14.53). 10.00 Domalle 2-1f (6-2, £17.01). 10.15 Diamond Lady 3-1 (3-4, £11.10).

PONTEFRACT:
Good to firm

6.45:CHAMPAGNE GOLD (T Ives, 5-2f) 1; Croft Imperial (4-1) 2; Tadeus (9-2) 3, 5 ran. 2½, 2 (Denys Smith) Tote: £3.10; £1.50, £1.90; Df: £5.50; Csf: £11.25.

7.15: MY DIAMOND RING (R Fox, 6-1f) 1; Chic-Anita (20-1) 2; My Concordia (20-1) 3; Weffie (9-1) 4. 21 ran. 1½, 1½ (M Usher) Tote: £5.30; £1.80, £2.90, £3.30, £2.30; Df: £49.60; Csf: £112.93; Tricast: £2,057.06. Nr: Cretan Boy.

7.35: ROSEATE LODGE (W Carson, 11-10f) 1; Mystery Band (10-1) 2; Choral Sundown (9-2) 3; Bachelor's Pet (50-1) 4. 16 ran. 4, sh hd (J Watts) Tote: £2.40; £1.10, £1.90, £1.60, £10.50; Df: £11.60; Csf: £15.64; Tricast: £45.60.

8.05: REGAL REFORM (Dean McKeown, 9-1) 1; Austhorpe Sunset (4-1jf) 2; Sunset Reins Free (11-1) 3; Quip (33-1) 4. Amazing Silks 4jf. 17 ran. 6, ½ (G Moore) Tote: £11.10; £1.80, £1.60, £3.60, £4.70; Df: £28.20; Csf: £45.08; Tricast: £376.68. Nr: Dual Capacity.

8.35: COWLEY (Paul Eddery, 11-2) 1; Polar Boy (8-15f) 2; Petavious (33-1) 3, 9 ran. ½, 10 (G Wragg) Tote: £5.80; £1.50, £1.10, £3.20; Df: £2.70; Csf: £8.28. Nr: Bluebird Lady.

9.05: PRINGIPOULA (W Swinburn, 4-1) 1; Green's Seascape (6-4f) 2; Acquatic (13-2) 3. 9 ran. 6, sh hd (C Brittain) Tote: £5.10; £1.90, £1.20, £2.20; Df: £4.00; Csf: £9.89.
Placepot: £21.50

GOLF

VOLVO PGA CH'SHIP.— (Wentworth) 1st rnd leaders (GB & Ire unless stated): 67— N Faldo, I Woosnam; 68— 2 Curry, B Ogle (Aus), C Parry (Aus); 69— M Roe, B Longmuir, N Hansen, C Mason; 70— J Anglada (Spn), J Morgan, S Lyle, M McNulty (Zim), B Lane, A Murray, A Saavedra (Arg), R McFarlane, J Bland (SA).

Ace Pat sacked

By IAN GIBB

● PAT VAN DEN HAUWE was sacked by Wales last night — and manager Terry Yorath stormed: "He'll never play for me again."

● Van Den Hauwe, one of Everton's best players in last Saturday's FA Cup final defeat by Liverpool, is struggling with a hamstring injury.

● But Wales boss Yorath is fuming that he wasn't told early enough before Wednesday's World Cup qualifying game against West Germany at Cardiff.

● Yorath raged:"He has let down his country. This is not something a player can do and expect to get picked again."

● Wales will be left disastrously short of a top class player against West Germany in a game they must win.

CHELSEA PENSION

By IAN GIBB

STAMFORD BRIDGE boss Bobby Campbell can stay at Chelsea until he draws his pension, says chairman Ken Bates.

Following the club's glorious return to the First Division Bates has told Campbell: "You've got a job for life — if you want."

Campbell has been awarded a new improved deal from July 1 — on top of his two-year contract agreed before Chelsea's relegation last season.

His record reads 30 wins and 17 draws in 54 games, with 104 goals scored.

Campbell's No.2 Ian Porterfield is also rewarded with a new three-year deal.

Chairman Bates said: "What Bobby has done so far speaks for itself."

CAMPBELL: Offer

Palace storm

● CRYSTAL Palace have upset Blackburn by switching the home leg of their Second Division play-off final for a second time.

● Originally set for Saturday June 3, it was put back 24 hours because it clashed with England's World Cup tie against Poland at Wembley.

● But it has now reverted to the Saturday on police advice.

● Rovers boss Don Mackay said: "I don't know what Palace are playing at. We could well do without this hassle."

● Yesterday Mackay complained to the Football League and was astonished to find that they were unaware of the latest move.

TODAY'S SOCCER

ROUS CUP
Scotland v England.................
(Hampden Park, 3.00)

'The

flattens sad Liverpool in injury time

STORY EVER TOLD!

MIRACLE MEN KOP TITLE

By HARRY HARRIS

cally turning on everyone who has accused them of negative tactics.

The Gunners have won the championship by scoring eight more goals than Liverpool, with Graham putting the emphasis on entertaining football.

Arsenal dropped home points against Sheffield Wednesday, Millwall, Nottingham Forest and Charlton, but really looked to have thrown away the title with self-inflicted wounds — squandering five points in their last two Highbury games, losing to Derby and drawing with Wimbledon.

Spirit

When Liverpool thumped West Ham 5-1 to send the East Enders down, no-one gave the Gunners a prayer of winning by two.

They had not scored two goals at Anfield since 1974, when Alan Ball scored twice and Liam Brady once. They had lost their last seven First Division games here.

There were more omens in Liverpool's favour. John Aldridge and Ian Rush had never been on a losing side in partnership, while goalkeeper Bruce Grobbelaar had not been on a losing

side in 28 games this season, keeping 13 clean sheets.

It was stacked against Arsenal, but there was an amazing spirit within the camp. They actually believed they could pull it off.

Graham said before the game he was very optimistic. David Rocastle revealed that none of the players was frightened by the daunting task ahead of them.

Even without two of their best players, Brian Marwood and Paul Davis, Arsenal clinched their ninth championship with a remarkable performance.

They strode out with each player holding a bouquet which they presented to the fans.

The Gunners were determined not to leave Anfield empty-handed, while Liverpool were favourites to add the title to the FA Cup they had won at Wembley by overwhelming Everton in another exciting match.

Graham began the game sitting in the directors' box alongside his chairman Peter Hill-Wood and vice-chairman David Dein.

By the start of the second half he was down on the bench.

The Gunners might have taken an early goal

when a cross from Thomas was misjudged by Grobbelaar and Steve Bould's header was goalbound until Steve Nicol headed it over his own bar.

Although Bould was recalled as Graham gambled by reinstating his sweeper system, Arsenal were always ready to attack.

A breakthrough goal after 52 minutes, 13 seconds put the championship on a knife-edge.

Liverpool skipper Ronnie Whelan fouled Rocastle and Nigel Winterburn's free-kick was headed into the corner by Alan Smith.

Booked

Liverpool fervently protested that Smith's 25th goal of the season — his 23rd in the League — should not have counted because referee David Hutchinson had raised his arm for an indirect free kick and the Liverpool camp were insistent that Smith had not got a touch.

Dalglish was on the touchline as both sets of players surrounded the referee in his consultations with the linesman. But the goal was given and suddenly Arsenal took total command.

Thomas stabbed a 74th minute chance created by Kevin Richardson straight at Grobbelaar from close range, and Arsenal's hopes seemed to falter.

Graham pulled off Paul Merson, bringing on Martin Hayes. A few minutes later he brought off Bould, substituting him with Perry Groves.

Richardson was booked for a foul on

Ray Houghton and Rocastle was shown the yellow card for dissent.

Houghton was put in the clear by Aldridge with just seven minutes to go, but blasted his shot over when he could have picked his spot.

As the minutes ticked away, Arsenal were so much on the offensive that John Barnes was forced to play centre-half, heading out a Groves cross as Liverpool were pinned back in their own half.

Liverpool broke and Beardsley and Aldridge faced just one defender. But Aldridge, with 29 goals this season, lacked the technique to control the ball as it bounced away from him.

As the game spilled into injury time Barnes robbed Arsenal skipper Tony Adams, setting off on a dribble which never came off. Lukic threw the ball out to Lee Dixon, his long ball was knocked on by Smith and there was Thomas in the clear.

Thomas had so much

space and time it seemed to take an eternity before he struck the championship-deciding shot past a helpless Grobbelaar.

Aldridge dropped to his knees, Barnes lay on his back and David O'Leary was in tears. The Gunners' longest-serving player had finally tasted championship success.

The Barclays title comes to London and no one in the 41,718 crowd or the millions watching at home can begrudge the Gunners their greatest triumph.

MIRACLE

● From Back Page

match because although it was hard it was never a dirty game.

"Thomas got our vital goal and he deserves an awful lot of credit. He has grown up in the latter part of the season not only as a player but also as a man."

Thomas said: "I can't put it into words exactly how I feel. It is just so wonderful for everybody that we did it in style.

"It is tremendous to score a goal like that, but most of all it was a team performance tonight and to think that no-one gave us a chance makes it even sweeeter."

CHAMPION! Alan Smith (left) and Michael Thomas get their reward.

players were weeping tears of joy

MIRROR SPORT
Graham's amazing boast
I'LL STEAL THE TITLE!
DEFIANT KENNY

Graham lives up to his bold title promise

MIRACLE

ON THEIR WAY!
ARSENAL'S Alan Smith scores with a 52nd-minute glancing header to put the Gunners 1-0 ahead.
Pic: JOHN POWELL

MEN

MAGNIFICENT Arsenal snatched the most dramatic championship triumph of all time at Anfield last night when Michael Thomas struck after 91 minutes and 26 seconds to deny Liverpool a record second League and Cup double.

It was Arsenal's first title success for 18 years — and it ended Merseyside's seven-year First Division domination.

Arsenal had to win by two goals and they could not have left it any later than the closing seconds of a dramatic season.

Heartbroken Liverpool players sank to the turf in disbelief as Thomas tore the League title from their grasp.

The Kop took the blow like true champions, warmly applauding as ecstatic Arsenal paraded the trophy in an emotional lap of honour.

England striker Alan Smith had provided the platform for Arsenal's amazing performance with a 52nd-minute goal.

Even then, all the odds were still stacked against Arsenal taking the title to North London.

Liverpool have not lost at home by two goals for more than three years and they were unbeaten in their last 24 games.

By ALEC JOHNSON
Liverpool 0
Arsenal 2

Jubilant Arsenal manager George Graham said "It is the greatest night of my football life! Who gave us a hope in hell of winning by two goals at Anfield? Certainly nobody outside Highbury!

"This is the fairytale of football and it is what makes it such a wonderful game.

"This was an answer to those people who say Arsenal can only play a kind of kick and rush game. We really planned this one and it all went according to the script.

"We came here determined to control things and once we got the first goal I always believed we could do it.

"I never gave up hope even as it got later and later. If you give up hope in this sport you shouldn't be in the game of football. But I suppose that chance which fell to Thomas was our last gasp.

"This was one of my great ambitions to win the championship for Arsenal. I have a tremendous feeling for the club and an enormous pride in the team I have built here.

"Now I have a piece of history. I am so proud of what we have done and especially by the way we did it against all the odds.

"We were not given a chance either by the critics or by the bookies.

"Yet in a way the critics in giving us so little chance at Anfield made my job easier. I didn't really have to give my team an incentive.

"They were told they had no hope but they've gone out and shown just what they can do.

"All credit to Liverpool for making it a wonderful

● Turn to Page 35

TOP OF THE TABLE

	P	W	D	L	F	A	Pts
Arsenal	38	22	10	6	73	36	76
Liverpool	38	22	10	6	65	28	76

KENNY AGONY

DALGLISH: Praise

By BERNIE LOVETT

● DEJECTED Liverpool manager Kenny Dalglish despaired last night: "Our whole season was condensed in just a few seconds. It was agonisingly close."

● Dalglish praised George Graham's warriors, admitting: "Arsenal are worthy champions — and all credit to them.

● "They have won the championship after 38 games — and on a better goal total. That's what it is all about.

● "But we can put some of the defeat down to us. We made it difficult for ourselves.

● "Arsenal like to play a certain way. You can put your own interpretation on that.

● "We tried to compete with them on the night but it didn't work out."

Published by Mirror Group Newspapers (1986) Ltd. at 33 Holborn, London EC1P 1DQ (01-353 0246) and printed by British Newspaper Printing Corporation (London) Ltd., Watford WD2 5RD.
Serial No. 26,779 ©The Daily Mirror Newspapers, Ltd., 1989. Saturday, May 27, 1989. ★

MIRROR SPORT GEORGE THE SECOND

GLORY GUNNERS! Arsenal's back line of David O'Leary, Steve Bould and skipper Tony Adams celebrate with the Barclays Trophy

Picture: ARNOLD SLATER

What a party!

ARSENAL celebrated their League Championship success last night – and North London went wild.

The champagne flowed in the dressing-room and in the pubs around their Highbury ground. And manager George Graham admitted: "I'm so proud of my team."

But Graham refused to join his team in an emotional lap of honour after skipper Tony Adams had been presented with the Barclays Trophy at the final whistle.

Instead he stayed in the tunnel as the cheers and the chants of just over 40,000 fans ran gloriously around the ground.

Graham, who had won his second title in three seasons, said:

ARSENAL 3 MAN UTD 1

NIGEL CLARKE reports from Highbury

"The players did it. I can bask in the reflected glory. They deserve all the credit, not me.

"Last November we were six points behind Liverpool. Then had two points deducted after the Manchester United affair.

"Everybody wrote us off. They didn't think we had a chance of getting back into the chase. But we did. Now we've won it.

"I didn't think anybody believed that would ever happen. There was no turning point in the season for us. We just got on with the job. But tonight we showed once again that we are professional enough to handle the carnival atmosphere of what was a great night for the club and its supporters."

Now the Gunners need only to avoid defeat against Coventry at Highbury on Saturday to become the first team for a century to go through a League programme with just one defeat.

But Arsenal's big night was so nearly ruined by fans who swarmed onto the pitch and caused the presentation of the Barclays Trophy to be delayed for nearly ten minutes.

Players angrily pushed spectators away and pleaded with them to leave the pitch, while sections of the Arsenal crowd jeered the party-poopers.

Adams had to cut short the moment when he held the trophy to the adoring spectators until police had restored some semblance of order.

But when the lap of honour got

➡ **Turn to Page 26**

19

Published by MGN Ltd. at 33 Holborn, London EC1P 1DQ (071-353 0246) and printed by Mirror Colour Print Ltd. at Watford ©The Daily Mirror Newspapers Ltd., 1991. Tuesday, May 7, 1991. Registered as a newspaper at the Post Office Serial No. 27,383

9 770956 805011

HARRY ★ HARRIS (CHIEF SOCCER WRITER) salutes

'You blew title' rap

By DAVID MOORE
Nottm F 2, L'pool 1

SCOUSER Ian Woan buried Liverpool's last, flickering championship hopes with a 65th minute winner.

And winger Woan's sweet, left foot volley, also sent a message for the future — Nottingham Forest could be title contenders this time next year.

Brian Clough's FA Cup finalists buried the dreams of Graeme Souness that he could somehow rekindle Liverpool's hope of their 12th First Division crown

Woan's winner left Souness, who stepped into the Anfield hot seat following the sensational resignation of Kenny Dalglish, reflecting bitterly: "I was disappointed in certain players.

"I want to know how much a result like this hurts them. I want anybody who plays for me to hurt.

"It was my 38th birthday today ... some celebration!

"I have to say, over the season, I would think that Liverpool have lost the title rather than somebody else has won it. In 12 months time, I hope that things will be different.

"Right now, I don't know how I feel. I've had a five-game assessment, and I know that I need to bring new people into the team."

Nigel Clough and Jan Molby exchanged penalties before Woan's winner.

Glory night

➜ **From Back**

under way, police were still unable to cope with fans who poured onto the pitch.

Earlier, when the news had reached Highbury that Liverpool were losing at Nottingham Forest, the Highbury ground and its surrounding streets became a party area.

Fans clustered around car radios following the progress of the match, and Forest's winning goal was rapturously greeted by 10,000 fans already on the terraces.

Coach Stewart Houston said: "When Tony Adams had his misfortune, everybody thought Arsenal would take a dip. But we were held together by Steve Bould and Anders Limpar. They were magnificent."

Daily Mirror PICTURE POWER

Pictures: BRENDAN MONKS and ARNOLD SLATER

Arsenal—the Kings of English Soccer

CHAMPIONS

Smith treble cheer

ARSENAL 3
MAN UTD 1

THE glorious Gunners were last night crowned champions in style with skipper Tony Adams lifting the Barclays League trophy for the second time in three seasons – and now manager George Graham will take Europe by storm.

After a gap of six years, Arsenal will be England's first representatives in the European Cup. And they will be one of the most efficient and hard-to-beat sides ever to leave these shores.

Graham is the link in an Arsenal dynasty that has superseded Liverpool as the dominant force of soccer in this country.

The £100,000 prize from sponsors Barclays is the start of a gold mine that will yield £5 million in the European Cup.

As the door re-opened to Liverpool only a few weeks ago as UEFA lifted their six-year ban, it is the Gunners who will walk through it, seven points ahead, and with a goal difference of 16 more than the dethroned champions.

Little wonder the Arsenal fans verbally raised two fingers to the FA, who had deducted two championship points after the brawl at Old Trafford earlier this season.

With Liverpool ten points clear at one stage, the Gunners have come back from adversity, includ-

HOME AND DRIED

	P	W	D	L	F	A	Pts
Arsenal	37	23	13	1	68	17	80
Liverpool	37	22	7	8	75	40	73
C Palace	37	19	9	9	47	41	66
Leeds U	36	18	7	11	60	42	61

ing the loss of skipper Tony Adams during his imprisonment for drink driving.

Adams blew kisses to the fans, shook their hands, wore their scarves and waved an Arsenal flag.

No championship captain has come through such personal torment to lead his side to such glory.

Adams was also the perfect diplomat in urging the happy Arsenal supporters to return to the terraces before he could lead his team on a triumphant lap of honour.

The Gunners won the title two years ago at Anfield with a last-gasp winner, but last night, on home territory, they took the championship without having to kick a ball.

The title was theirs after Liverpool crashed to their fourth defeat in their last eight games at Nottingham Forest just over an hour before the Gunners kicked off.

But over the course of the season, Graham's team have proved worthy champions. And Graham will deservedly be crowned Manager of the Year.

His team have lost just one League game and if they don't lose against Coventry at home on Saturday that will set a magnificent record in modern times.

The statistics are breathtaking. The Gunners have conceded just 17 League goals and goalkeeper David Seaman has kept 24 clean-sheets in the League, 29 all season.

It sums up perfectly Graham's contention that Arsenal had cracked the secret of ending the Merseyside monopoly with "consistency."

Arsenal are so far unbeaten at Highbury in the League and have lost only three games all season, a 6-2 Rumbelows Cup knock-out by Manchester United, an FA Cup semi-final heartbreak against Spurs that has deprived them of the double, and the only League defeat at Chelsea.

Arsenal's 10th championship in their history puts them second in the all-time list behind, you guessed it, Liverpool.

But Graham's ideal is not to derive absolute satisfaction from even this championship success, but to go on and win it time and time again.

United took a cautious approach with three key players out of a side, including Lee Sharpe, who personally demolished Arsenal in

GOAL No 1

GOAL 2

GOAL 3

Arsenal — VICTORIA CONCORDIA CRESCIT

HAT-TRICK HERO! Arsenal No 9 Alan Smith puts the ball past the United defence for his first goal (top). Then it's a hug for his second goal and a wave to acknowledge his third

Ready to rule Europe

the Rumbelows Cup with a hat-trick.

And after just 13 minutes a worried United manager took off his skipper Bryan Robson and sent on his son Darren.

Earlier, Robson pulled up after being kicked on the back of his heel by Anders Limpar.

Robson took the knock on the precise spot where he needed surgery on his Achilles tendon after limping out of the World Cup in Italy.

Alan Smith scored his first hat-trick of the season to fully justify his return to the England fold and Graham Taylor's assertion that he is the best all-round centre-forward in the country.

Smith's treble brought his season's haul to 26, and the first came after 18 minutes when he swept in Lee Dixon's low cross.

Smith then kept a cool head, collecting Kevin Campbell's pass in his stride before side-stepping a defender on the edge of the box and sliding his shot home in the 40th minute.

Steve Bruce was harshly adjudged to have handled a shot by Adams that went straight at him and Smith was given the job, normally reserved for Dixon, to complete his hat-trick from the penalty spot after 57 minutes.

Dampen

Seaman saved from Brian McClair from close range and pushed over a 25-yarder from Paul Ince.

But England's new No 1 keeper was deprived of yet another clean-sheet when Mark Robins latched on to a pass from Neil Webb and when he tried to skip round the keeper was clipped over.

Bruce scored from the penalty spot in the dying moments for his 19th goal of the season.

But nothing could dampen the spirits of a frenzied Highbury crowd of just over 40,000.

The deduction of two points will never be forgotten or forgiven by Arsenal's supporters, and it is a remarkable achievement that the Gunners have still finished so far ahead of Liverpool.

In a season of controversy, the row over the price for possible live TV coverage of this match ensured that the League's historic and precious piece of silverware remained locked away at Lytham St Annes.

At least Barclays persuaded the League to allow the presentation of their trophy last night.

United were bit part players on a night that belonged to Arsenal.

GUNNERS GOAL STAR PAYS

Morrow joy and Morrow mourning

ISN'T that just great! Steve Morrow is suddenly a big noise after he has hit the Gunners' winning goal at Wembley. But Morrow's passion turned to pain later as Arsenal's on-pitch celebrations went badly wrong and he was left on a stretcher and in agony.

GOAL! Morrow begins his victory dance after putting Arsenal ahead

WHAT'S happened? asks hero Morrow, as doctors examine his injured arm.

OUCH! Morrow tells manager George Graham just how painful the injury is.

HEAVY PRICE FOR CUP GLORY

What a way to treat a HERO!

Well done, Merson

PAUL MERSON, the man-of-the-match, leads Arsenal's celebrations. It was quite a week for the top Gunner – his wife Lorraine presented him with their second son just a few days before the final.

Hero Steve in Final agony

➡ From Back Page

TONY ADAMS strode the Wembley steps to collect the season's first trophy – looking back in horror as match-winner Steve Morrow was stretchered off with an oxygen mask over his face.

Adams forced a smile he received the Cup from guest of honour Tom Finney. But the Arsenal skipper's celebrations had gone hideously wrong after he grabbed Morrow, the man whose goal won the Coca-Cola Cup for Arsenal.

Adams tossed Morrow over his head and the 22-year-old – who marked John Sheridan out of the match and who found the energy to blast the decisive goal – crash-landed head first.

He fractured his right arm as he broke his fall.

Morrow had scored the first goal of his career – and what a time and place to do it! But he was the centre of concern as Wembley held its breath and the medics crowded around him.

Potential

Morrow struck in the 70th minute when Paul Merson broke past Wednesday's hero Viv Anderson. Merson's cross was cut out by Carlton Palmer, but it fell weakly to Morrow, who beat Chris Woods from seven yards.

Morrow didn't even merit a biography note in the Wembley programme – but the bit-part player was an important cog in George Graham's team plan.

Morrow shadowed

By HARRY HARRIS
Arsenal 2, Sheff Wed 1

Sheridan, who was earmarked as Trevor Francis's potential matchwinner. And he did a fine job.

Chris Waddle tried in vain to use the Wembley stage to underline his England claims. Instead it was Merson, a player with whom Graham Taylor has kept faith, who turned on the magic.

American John Harkes began to raise the stars and stripes over Wembley, blasting Wednesday into a tenth-minute lead.

But Merson, with his ambitions trained also on the World Cup in the US in 1994, rescued Arsenal from their slow start.

Merson collected the Alan Hardaker man-of-the-match award. He was worth it, being both a goal-taker and a goal-maker.

Once again Ian Wright was out of luck

Merson scored his first Cup goal of the season – and it brought Arsenal back to life.

Graham picked Paul Davis to play in midfield and he chipped a free-kick in the 19th minute into the heart of the Wednesday defence to cause mayhem.

The ball spun off Mark Bright's head, under pressure from Andy Linighan, and it dropped tantalisingly to Merson. He hit a vicious curler for 1-1 which shocked his England colleague Woods.

Merson's mobility looked in doubt as he went down injured before half-time. If he was restricted in his movement, it never showed when he burst past Anderson to play the vital role in Morrow's goal.

Wednesday romped into an early lead when Ray Parlour conceded a free-kick and Arsenal feared a blast from Waddle similar to his spectacular goal

against Sheffield United.

In a clever movement Phil King ran over the ball. As the Arsenal defence watched for Waddle, Sheridan found the unmarked King, who had sneaked behind the Gunners defensive wall.

O'Leary stretched to knock out King's cross. But Harkes pounced with a low drive into the corner.

Wright mistimed a diving header from Merson's cross before Merson grabbed the all-important equaliser.

Bright edged in front of Adams but his header was just wide. As play switched to the other end, Campbell's angled shot beat Woods, hit the post and Woods gratefully caught it.

Palmer was booked for blatantly hauling back Wright on the break just before half-time. And Waddle and Wright were lectured by Alan Gunn after a bust-up.

Waddle gestured to

Wright, who pushed him off. But it all finished with a handshake.

On the hour Anderson was whacked on the forehead in an aerial battle with Wright, whose elbow accidentally connected. The referee had a quiet word with Wright as the Wednesday skipper was bandaged up.

Before the end Bright was also cautioned for a lunging tackle as Adams cleared the ball just after the Gunners had gone ahead.

Wright chipped the ball over Woods but his effort disallowed for a foul on Anderson, although Anderson looked as though he slipped.

And Francis threw on sub David Hirst for the final 15 minutes in search of a goal.

By the end the blood was seeping through Anderson's bandage, and trickling down his face. When the final whistle sounded, Anderson sat inconsolable. His display had not been far behind Merson's.

Corner

Paul Warhurst struck the woodwork twice in the FA semi-final against Sheffield United and he hit the post once again at Wembley after four minutes.

the final whistle he jubilantly jumped into Adams' arms.

● The big centre-half incredibly flipped Morrow over his head and he landed awkwardly. It was immediately clear he was distressed.

● Irish team-mate David O'Leary said: "He badly broke his arm. I was right there when it happened. He was in terible pain and I feel so sorry for him."

● Reserve goalkeeper Alan Miller also revealed that Morrow attempted to put the bone back as he lay in agony on the turf that only minutes earlier had supported his greatest day in football.

● His thoughts were not about his medal, nor the victory over Sheffield Wednesday, but if his wife Fiona, watching from the crowd, was all right.

● Morrow will now be out for the rest of the season. But Arsenal boss George Graham refused to condemn what Adams did and said: "It was a bit of horseplay and it has taken away the pleasure of victory a little.

● "It was an unusual thing to happen, but you can't take away a player's right to celebrate. That's what football and winning is all about."

● But there seemed little reason for Adams to behave so boisterously at the final whistle. He said later: "I can't talk – my wife is ill and I'm going home to see her."

● Graham added: "If it is at all possible we will take the Cup in to show off to Steve, and give him his medal as well."

PICTURES BY KENT GAVIN AND BRENDAN MONKS

MIRROR SPORT ON THE CUP

WEMB-

Frank gets Lewis boost

By IAN GIBB

● FRANK Bruno seized on a Stateside vow by former undisputed world heavyweight champion Evander Holyfield to try and force Lennox Lewis into a September showdown.

● Bruno, upset that Lewis was looking more towards a WBC world title defence against Holyfield, was boosted by Evander's pledge to secure a re-

BRUNO: Eager

turn with WBA and IBF champion Riddick Bowe first.

● Bruno, who still has his sights set on a domestic argument with Lewis in September, said: "They are looking to duck the issues and put obstacles in my way.

● "But when they sit down and work it all out, they'll realise that a fight with me will be the best move.

● "Lewis has said that I need him more than he needs me – and he's right in that he has a championship and I need his belt."

● Bruno added: "Lewis committed himself to defend his title against me on September 14, providing he came through the Tony Tucker fight."

CUP FINAL DELAY

LAST night's kick-off in the FA Cup final replay between Arsenal and Sheffield Wednesday was delayed for half-an-hour after a serious accident on the M1 motorway held up fans travelling to the game.

BATTLE DAVID Hirst struggled to find his touch

HOT GUNNER PAUL MERSON made a bright start for Arsenal – despite squandering a great early chance against Wednesday

Wright stuff stuns Owls

IAN Wright, love him or hate him, is the man for the big occasion – and he proved it again by maintaining his incredible record of goalscoring when it really matters.

Just as in the first game on Saturday, Wright opened the scoring with a piece of class opportunism in last night's replay at Wembley.

It was his fourth goal in FA Cup finals, adding to his two for Crystal Palace against Manchester United, with a slick effort after 33 minutes.

Alan Smith, who was restored to the Gunners' attack from the start after coming off the bench in the first match, laid on the most delicate and precise of volleyed passes to breach the Sheffield Wednesday rearguard and send the dashing Wright racing menacingly towards Chris Woods.

The England keeper came to confront his adversary but Wright coolly clipped the ball over him.

It struck Woods, but still found the corner of the net.

He's volatile, most certainly – but there are few contenders better qualified to fill the goalscoring gap left by Gary Lineker than Wright.

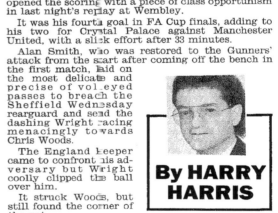

By HARRY HARRIS

Boost

He's still awaiting his first goal for his country, but there can be no better boost for England manager Graham Taylor than the sight of Wright scoring at Wembley twice in the space of six days.

But before Wright was the hero he almost became the villain, lectured by Keren Barrett for a trip on defender turned striker and back to defender Paul Warhurst.

But, that was one of the tamer incidents in a red raw cruncher of a match.

The tackles were flying in all directions, exaggerated by the treacherous, rain-sodden surface.

Dane John Jensen was the culprit for two tackles in the opinion of the Sheffield Wednesday players.

As early as the second minute Jensen slid into Chris Waddle, as the Sheffield Wednesday danger man and Footballer of the Year nipped the ball away.

The referee allowed the play to go on as Waddle spun into the air and fell awkwardly. He clearly needed treatment and that incensed Owls captain Carlton Palmer.

Shortly before half-time Palmer had to be pulled away from the midfield star whose goal helped win the European championship for Denmark.

Jensen's crunching tackle on David Hirst left the £5million striker needing treatment and Palmer gesticulating angrily at the Dane.

The illegal use of the elbow was the most ugly feature of this highly competitive replay.

Arsenal centre half Andy Linighan was the first to feel the full force of Mark Bright's elbow

That finally convinced the referee to issue the first yellow card as early as the 18th minute.

Bright clearly whacked Linighan

FINAL SHOOT-OUT
GLEE!

WOODS: Well beaten by Wright

SEAMAN: Cool for the Gunners

ARSENAL 2
SHEFF WED 1
After extra time

straight in the nose and lower lip with his elbow, and play was held up for three minutes before Linighan recovered.

He bravely carried on, even though at half-time it was revealed he had broken his nose.

Next it was the turn of Waddle to crash to the floor again, this time holding his face.

But Waddle provoked the 28th minute incident when he tried to run past his marker, Nigel Winterburn, tugging the full back in an effort to gain an advantage.

Winterburn shoved him away Gazza style, catching Waddle – though not necessarily in the face – with his elbow.

But the Arsenal fans closest to the incident felt that Waddle had exaggerated the effect of the blow, and Waddle found himself booed for the rest of the match, suffering taunts of "Cheat".

There were so many hold-ups to treat players that the referee needed eight minutes of first half injury time.

After the disappointment of Saturday's game, both teams were hyped up – but instead of raising the entertainment level, it only sparked a feud on the pitch.

Tackle

There were precious few goalscoring attempts in the first half.

Paul Merson, man of the match in the Coca-Cola Cup final between these two teams, had the best chance after just 16 minutes.

Wright picked up a loose ball after a Sheffield Wednesday attack broke down. His dribble ended when he was tackled, but Smith spread the play to Merson in a wide position.

He wriggled past Palmer but his finish was flat as he shot straight at Woods.

Linighan was just off target with a powerful header from Lee Dixon's cross after 25 minutes but only Wright's goal livened up the proceedings.

Wright collected his 30th goal of the season, his 15th in Cup competitions, his tenth in the FA Cup – and it left him just one goal adrift of Ian Rush's record of five goals in finals.

All that – and he had needed painkilling injections before the match on his painful broken little toe.

Smith's selection proved another tactical success for George Graham.

He twice came close in the first half when Sheffield Wednesday hardly had a chance.

From a Dixon throw Kevin Campbell headed on and Smith's first time shot landed in the side netting.

Sheffield Wednesday manager Trevor Francis tried to step up the tempo of his side in the second half.

Post

Wednesday stepped up the pace, and with 68 minutes gone they equalised.

John Harkes crossed from the right, and although Bright failed to reach it with his head, it spun through to Waddle, moving in from the left.

His low drive clipped the heel of Lee Dixon and eluded Seaman's despairing dive.

Moments later the game almost turned on its head as Bright's shot beat Seaman and clipped the post.

Defender Warhurst drove forward menacingly, chased by Wright – but then Arsenal skipper Tony Adams came across to challenge.

Warhurst landed painfully on his already badly damaged left hand.

The official attendance of 62,267 will go down in the record books as the lowest ever for a Cup final at Wembley.

GIVE YOUR VERDICT NOW!

ARSENAL 2 SHEFF WED 1

GEORGE'S CUP OF GLORY!

WINNER: Arsenal's George Graham

LOSER: Wednesday's Trevor Francis

GOALDEN TOUCH

⚽ Wednesday's Chris Waddle survived rough handling in the first half to turn on the magic and stun Arsenal with a magnificent equaliser.

ARSENAL last night gave George Graham the FA Cup in a clean sweep of all the domestic titles.

At rain-sodden Wembley, Gunners defender Andy Linighan headed the winner in this FA Cup replay a minute from the end of extra time.

As on Saturday, star striker Ian Wright gave the Gunners the all-important breakthrough with a 34th-minute goal.

Manager Graham has now won all three trophies – the League title, League Cup and the FA Cup – as a player and a manager. It also means Arsenal will compete in the European Cup-Winners' Cup next season – and opens the door to the UEFA Cup for Norwich City.

The match was studded with controversy from the second minute onwards and continued throughout the first half.

And never more so than in the 18th minute when Mark Bright might well have been sent off for a nasty foul on Arsenal defender Andy Linighan.

As Bright and Linighan went up for a ball, the Wednesday striker held his elbow head-high and caught Linighan across the face with a blow that pole-axed him.

Referee Keren Barratt immediately booked Bright and for a minute

By NIGEL CLARKE

there were ugly scenes as Arsenal angrily protested.

Linighan, an old English oak at the centre of the Gunners' defence, needed three minutes of treatment for a broken nose.

That came after Wednesday fans were outraged when Arsenal's Danish international John Jensen floored Chris Waddle with a late tackle.

Tackle

The ref took no action, clearly believing that Jensen's tackle had been more a case of miscalculation on the skating-rink surface.

But once Wright had put Arsenal ahead, tempers simmered down.

Arsenal claimed the lead they deserved in the 34th minute – almost inevitably through Wright.

Alan Smith was the provider with a delicate touch through the middle, Wright's speed took him beyond Paul Warhurst and he swerved away from the challenge of Chris Woods to slot home his 30th goal of the season.

Defender Warhurst raced forward in search of an equaliser but fell painfully on his damaged left hand after a challenge by Tony Adams.

The crowd of 62,267 was the lowest for an FA Cup final at Wembley.

Waddle levelled in the 68th minute when his shot deflected in off Lee Dixon.

Two minutes later Bright hit the post in a goalmouth scramble.

The match went into extra time.

WEMBLEY SPECIAL Pages 50-51

Published by MGN Ltd. at 33 Holborn, London EC1P 1DQ (071-353 0246) and printed by Mirror Colour Print Ltd. at Watford. Registered as a newspaper at the Post Office. Serial No. 28,013 ©MGN, Ltd., 1993. Friday, May 21, 1993

9 770956 805257

20

By GEORGE

WE'VE DONE IT!

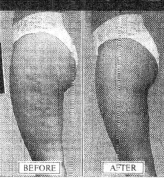

UP IN ARMS: Captain Marvel Tony Adams celebrates

GLAD HATTER: Ian Wright gets his hands on the trophy

Arsenal 1, Parma 0

Words: NIGEL CLARKE Pictures: ARNOLD SLATER

GLORY, Glory! Those glorious Gunners made it a magnificent night for British football in Copenhagen.

Alan Smith's 20th-minute volley won them the European Cup Winners' Cup and set off a red and white extravaganza of celebration

Arsenal did it the hard way, with four first-team men out through injury and keeper David Seaman struggling with damaged ribs. But at the final
⬅ Turn to page 36

Published by MGN Ltd. at One Canada Square, Canary Wharf, London, E14 5AP (071-293-3000) and printed by Mirror Colour Print Ltd. at Watford
©MGN, Ltd., 1994, Thursday, May 5, 1994

Serial No. 28,311

Registered as a newspaper at the Post Office

18>

9 770956 805240

ARSENAL 1

EURO HEROES

IT'S

EURO HERO: Campbell and Merson salute scorer Smith

PARMA 0

PARMA A.C.

EURO HEROES

SMITH blasts Arsenal's winning goal past Parma goalkeeper Bucci

WONDERF-AL

George the first

HARRY HARRIS REPORTS FROM COPENHAGEN

GEORGE GRAHAM wrote his name into Arsenal's Hall of Fame last night – and restored the pride in English football.

Alan Smith got the goal that brought Graham his first European trophy as Arsenal manager and heralded the resumption of England's conquests on foreign soil.

Apart from Manchester United's triumph in this tournament three years ago, English football's status on the Continent had evaporated after five years in the wilderness following the Heysel disaster.

The slow recovery has now been turned into a rapid heartbeat by the Gunners' pulsating success here on a night that was certainly wonderful, wonderful Copenhagen for the North London club.

Glittering

They methodically and marvellously took the Cup Winners' Cup, and skipper Tony Adams deservedly held the glittering trophy aloft.

Forget about "boring" Arsenal. They were brilliant and brave, and battled with the bulldog spirit.

The nation can take them to their hearts at last — the sole survivors in European football who delivered the goods against all the odds.

They were missing suspended topscorer Ian Wright and depleted by injuries to John Jensen, Martin Keown and David Hillier. If that were not enough, England goalkeeper David Seaman needed three pain-killing injections to subdue the discomfort of his injured ribs.

Seaman also had to endure the one ugly moment in Arsenal's night of glory.

The giant keeper went to the aid of his stricken team-mate Nigel Winterburn, whose committed tackle had ended with him getting a ball in the face.

The Parma fans close to the touchline pelted Winterburn and physio Gary Lewin with missiles. As Seaman looked on he was struck on the back of the head.

But Seaman didn't flinch — and he didn't all night despite his rib injury. But that unhappy incident could not mar a night of undiluted celebration.

Seaman was last to leave the scene of the Gunners' triumph here in the Parken Stadium after 20 minutes of wild jubilation in front of their ecstatic fans.

As he did so, the precious piece of silverware was in Seaman's safe hands.

Wright, stripped of his jacket and tie, was one of the first to leap off the bench at the end, and certainly the first to congratulate Seaman on his heroics.

Strain

Steve Bould, magnificent in the heart of defence alongside Adams, and young Ian Selley limped off showing the strain of their endurance, while Jensen hobbled around to join the singing throng of his team-mates.

The Gunners' first European trophy for 24 years was achieved with Seaman refusing to concede a goal for the fifth time in nine matches on the trail to the trophy.

It was wrested from holders Parma's grasp by a performance of passion, patience and finally a penetrative goal from Alan Smith.

Smith, who once led England's forward line, was the lynchpin of this victory with his ability to hold up the ball for his profusion of midfield players to supplement the attack.

Galaxy

Otherwise, the more sophisticated possession football of Parma's galaxy of stars might have maintained possession for virtually the entire game.

The Gunners lost this final 14 years ago on the heartbreak of a penalty shootout. But this time fortune favoured the underdogs, whose policy was to snap and bite at the heels of Parma's array of attacking world-class stars.

The little bit of luck came the Gunners' way when Thomas Brolin, who destroyed Graham Taylor's and England's European championship aspirations in Sweden, struck the upright with an angled drive in the 14th minute.

Parma's best chance originated from an Arsenal attack. Paul Davis, so influential in midfield, fed Kevin Campbell. But the powerful striker dwelt too long, the ball running loose to Selley, whose shot was blocked.

Colombian Astina Asprilla then launched a devastating raid, linking with Gianfranco Zola to create the chance for Brolin.

Six minutes later, Smith struck what turned out to be the decisive blow.

A Lee Dixon throw to Smith was passed back to the right back, whose centre was cleared by captain Lorenzo Minotti straight to Smith, lurking menacingly just outside the box.

Smith showed his vast experience, coolly and deliberately waiting for the ball to drop to the optimum height to crack an unstoppable volley in off the post.

Splendid

The predicted menace of Asprilla, Brolin and Zola failed to materialise because of the splendid organisation and tactical awareness of Graham's side.

Steve Morrow was drafted in and it hardly seemed noticeable that so many of Arsenal's key players were missing.

The use of Smith as the target man, with Paul Merson and Campbell wide and three midfield players supporting them certainly worked for the Gunners.

There could have been more goals. A corner by Davis in the 42nd minute produced a near-post header by Campbell which was blocked on the line by Gabriele Pin.

Before Smith's goal, Campbell got in another header, this time from Merson's corner, which just cleared the far post.

The 15,000 Arsenal fans made Copenhagen a home from home as they loudly urged on their team.

And they even predicted the score. "One-nil to the Arsenal," has been their forecast — and their team didn't let them down.

It was a night of glory and guts by Arsenal. Graham can bask in the glory of his sixth trophy in his eight-year reign as manager and the fifth in the last five years.

Pictures: BRENDAN MONKS

LESSON IN STYLE BY MAN IN THE KNOW

John DILLON

THE banner hanging from the West Stand read simply "Arsene knows".

Exactly what Arsenal's French coach Wenger knows wasn't indicated but, last night at Highbury, the best answer to that one was probably — just about everything.

Tactics. Transfers. Style. Man-management. Training. Diet. Languages. Economics. Nuclear physics. Next week's winning Lottery numbers . . .

Really, honestly, who can say the fella has put a foot wrong since the turn of the year?

Yesterday, he even got Nigel Winterburn playing at times like the absent Dennis Bergkamp.

And that says to me there really may be no limit to the talents of the methodical, quietly-spoken coach who has revolutionised the Gunners in around half the time it took Alex Ferguson to get Manchester United on the winning path.

As Tony Adams lifted the championship trophy, the tall, lean Wenger stood slightly back from the celebrations taking place in the warm, evening sunshine (yes, he even managed that, too, just when it seemed we were in for the coldest, dreariest Bank Holiday for years).

That was all perfectly in keeping with the style of a man who is something uniquely fresh in the English game.

Admire

Wenger is more likely to admire a teacup for its exquisite craftmanship and decoration than sling it across the dressing room like his fiery Scottish predecessor at the top of the table.

Even when Emmanuel Petit was scythed out of the game by a nasty challenge from Don Hutchison, Wenger's protests seemed calm and collected in comparison with most of the histrionics performed by bosses.

But rarely has a manager had such a profound effect in such a short space of time — 19 months at the helm.

Wenger has shifted the whole foundation upon which the institution that is Arsenal is built.

It was illustrated brilliantly by the stylish manner in which the Gunners ascended the last few steps to glory last night. A goal from Tony Adams, veteran standard bearer of the stout English yeomanry Wenger so shrewdly cajoled to new heights, started the party rolling.

Then two quite brilliant strikes from Marc Overmars provided the flamboyant continental taste with which Wenger has transformed a club once as dry and flavourless as old bones. And about as popular, too.

All the while, Arsenal played with such pace, such domination, such a delightful flourish, that Everton's battle for survival was reduced to nothing more than a very small afterthought.

That underlined what is perhaps Wenger's biggest achievement — winning the title and reaching the FA Cup final apart, of course. In one sweet season he has banished a whole host of rancid ghosts from the old marble halls.

The George Graham scandal? History. The year-long Bruce Rioch fiasco. So what? The booze, the drugs, the gambling. Sorted, mon ami, sorted.

Now everybody loves the Arsenal.

Partly because of Manchester United's dominance, but just as much because of the cavalier way in which they claimed the prize even without the injured Bergkamp yesterday, their football was a joy. The manner of their performance once more pointed out another of the priceless qualities Wenger brought with him when he made his arrival in England, little known and little regarded, from Japan.

They swaggered to victory yesterday because Wenger has given his team a big, big conviction that they are the best around.

As the beer flowed in the boozers of N5 last night, glasses of lager were raised to Wenger.

I'd imagine he allowed himself a small tipple of champagne. But his team certainly injected a big case of the bubbly stuff into the Premiership.

SILVER SMILES: Gunners boss Arsene Wenger and skipper Tony Adams celebrate with a firm grip on the trophy

WENGER v GRAHAM
HOW THE TOP GUNS COMPARE

1988/89
P38 W22 D10 L6 Pts76
Top League scorers: Alan Smith 23, Paul Merson 10, Brian Marwood 9.
Ever-presents: John Lukic, David Rocastle, Nigel Winterburn.
Captain: Tony Adams
Manager: George Graham

1990-91
P38 W24 D13 L1 Pts83 (2pts deducted)
Top League scorers: Alan Smith 22, Paul Merson 13, Anders Limpar 11.
Ever-presents: David Seaman, Nigel Winterburn, Steve Bould, Lee Dixon.
Captain: Tony Adams
Manager: George Graham

1997-98
P36 W23 D9 L4 Pts78
Top League scorers: Dennis Bergkamp 16, Ian Wright 10, Marc Overmars 12.
Captain: Tony Adams
Manager: Arsene Wenger

AGONY: Petit hobbles for help to his gashed leg

I thought he'd broken my leg

FRENCH midfielder Emmanuel Petit thought he was out of the FA Cup final and the World Cup after his shin was sliced open by a horror tackle from Everton's Don Hutchison.

Petit said last night: "I feared the worst. I thought he'd broken my leg.

"But after an X-ray I've been reassured there's no damage, just a bad gash.

"I'm furious at the referee. He should have sent off John O'Kane for elbowing me in the face and he did nothing when Hutchison tackled me.

"I thought it was all over – the Cup final and the World Cup with France.

"But I don't want to dwell on it now. I just want to celebrate my second championship in two years because I also won with Monaco last season."

Assault

Hutchison's assault on the French international also brought a stinging response from Gunners boss Arsene Wenger.

He said "It was a bad, bad tackle. The gash on his leg is very impressive.

"It didn't even get a yellow card, but it should have got a lot more."

Referee Gerald Ashby

By MIKE WALTERS

admitted he didn't see the tackle by Hutchison.

He said: "I didn't see the incident, and neither did the linesman. We were badly positioned.

"The best view of it was from the dug-outs."

Petit had only minutes before been elbowed in the face by Everton's John O'Kane, who was booked.

And he gestured angrily at referee Ashby and Hutchison after the tackle which put him out of the game.

Petit joined in the post-match celebrations with his leg in bandages but, although he'll miss Wednesday trip to Liverpool, he is likely to be fit for the FA Cup final against Newcastle on May 16, when Arsenal chase an historic double.

Fergie wants to sign off in style

By STEVE MILLAR

ALEX Ferguson last night handed over the Premiership crown with special congratulations to Arsene Wenger.

The Manchester United boss and his Arsenal counterpart have had their run-ins in the past, and their mind games of this season have added extra spice to the scrap for the 1998 title.

But Ferguson was quick to toast the Gunners on their first Premiership championship.

In the process, they robbed Fergie of a record-busting third successive title which would have been his fifth in a decade of dominance.

But the United boss spoke from the heart when he said: "I want to congratulate Arsenal.

"At Manchester United we know what it takes to be champions, and I want to send special congratulations to Arsene Wenger and his staff."

Tributes came thick and fast from across the country with Mark Lawrenson praising Arsenal's achievement.

He said: "They have been magnificent. The bookies would have given 25-1 in January on Arsenal winning the title.

"Now the Gunners have won 10 games on the trot and the championship is theirs. The way they have played is an added enjoyment. They have come from 11 points behind and scored from everywhere on the pitch."

Fellow BBC pundit Trevor Brooking said: "My congratulations go to Arsenal and Arsene Wenger, the first manager from overseas to win the Premiership.

"I am delighted that they have won it in such style."

STARS PAY TRIBUTE TO

John Gregory

❝ THERE have only been two purposely-full teams all season — Barnsley and Arsenal. Barnsley fought hard to stay up. Arsenal had their sights on the title and they never faltered. ❞

George Graham

❝ FOR the first two thirds of the season, United were best in the country. Arsenal have come on strong in the last third, proving they are worthy of being called the best. ❞

Alan Shearer

❝ I FULLY expected them to do it. They've played some great football and produced some great results, and you can't take that away from them. Good luck to the Gunners. ❞

Ron Atkinson

❝ BEST of luck to Arsenal and Arsene Wenger. They've won the title and won it in style. They have deserved it. Wenger has built a team in the great Arsenal tradition. ❞

LOVELY BUBBLY: Ian Wright sprays the Highbury fans with celebration champagne   Pictures: CHRIS TURVEY and KENT GAVIN

I have waited 7 years for this moment

IAN WRIGHT EXCLUSIVE

SEVEN years – that's how long I've waited for this moment and it could not be sweeter.

I joined Arsenal a few months after they won the title in 1991 and I've had to listen to Tony Adams, David Seaman and the other senior pros telling me how fabulous it felt ever since.

So I make no excuses, offer no apologies, for finding it hard to contain myself because this is easily the most emotional moment of my career.

They often say your name is on the FA Cup, and I'm convinced my name has been on this medal for a long time and you don't know how much it means to me.

When the moment came for me to come on as a substitute for the last 20 minutes, the emotion was overwhelming, thrilling. Absolutely thrilling.

Tunnel

The last four months have felt like I was stranded in a dark tunnel, and to say I'm glad I regained fitness in time to be a part of this triumph is an understatement.

It was entirely fitting that Tony Adams should have rounded off a perfect day with the final goal. Actually, I was a bit disappointed he didn't square it to me!

But, seriously, I've known Tony for seven years now and the man is a colossus, a giant among footballers and a fantastic leader of men.

On Saturday the team stayed in a hotel in Chelsea Harbour, and his presence around the dinner table was inspirational. A quiet word here, a tap on the shoulder there. He is a Captain Fantastic in every sense.

The mood was the usual sense of quiet determination. There was the usual, nutritious food pasta, broccoli, mineral water. And the boss gave his usual, calm team talk. There was no banging the table, no chest-beating from him. I can't pay tribute to his man-management skills enough.

We could hear the fans partying in the street outside more than a couple of hours after the final whistle yesterday and it was difficult to tear myself away from Highbury.

At 8pm, I took another walk across the pitch and showed off my medal to the punters in the Clock End executive boxes.

When you've waited seven years for a championship medal, you don't need an excuse for another curtain call.

It's hard to think about the FA Cup final, the World Cup or the Champions' League next season — at least it should be this morning, because all the boys were going out as a group last night to celebrate.

But the Champions' League is something I really want to have a crack at.

We have so many experienced players, so many internationals that we should be able to look forward to it with relish.

Formula

The last time Arsenal were in the European Cup, it was still in its old knockout formula and the journey was over almost before it had begun when we lost to Benfica.

But that's all in the future. This is for now, and it was hugely satisfying to clinch the title in such style.

When the first three goals went in, I just grabbed the nearest Arsenal blazer or track-suit and gave it a hug.

And when I finally came on, I just had to take a couple of seconds to stand on the touch-line, look skywards and say a quick word of thanks that I had recovered in the nick of time.

I'm lucky that the boss is a patient man who never encouraged me to cut any corners on the road to recovery.

He has been a revelation from day one, and a quick glance at the League table is one in the eye for those who doubted him when he went out and bought young players from abroad instead of paying through the nose to buy British.

This has been a triumph for his system.

Interview: MIKE WALTERS

THE HEROES OF HIGHBURY

Kenny Dalglish

" ARSENAL have finished top on merit. Arsene Wenger had a tough time at the start but has proved people wrong. He was under pressure but has been very astute. "

Frankie Dettori

" WHEN I came back after winning the Guineas on Cape Verdi I heard the first goal and knew they were on the way. What an absolutely fantastic day for me. Now for the Cup. "

Paul Merson

" I'M looking forward to meeting them next season. With Middlesbrough going up it is a super double for me. Arsenal have shown phenomenal form since Christmas. "

Bryan Robson

" The players he has brought in, like Petit and Vieira, have been top quality. And if you only get beaten four times over a season, you deserve to end up with the championship. "

WENGER BREAKS

GREAT PASS: Steve Bould

Now let's make it a double

FROM BACK PAGE

not a man who knows how to show his emotions or speak about them. I haven't done that since school.

"I have also kept them in check because I didn't want to say anything as we were chasing the title because I knew that people were waiting to see what a foreign coach could do.

"But I am proud to be the first foreign coach to have won the championship here.

"I have now won everything in every country I have worked, in France and in Japan."

Wenger confessed for the first time that he thought Arsenal's chances of lifting the title were doomed when they were 13 points behind rivals Manchester United in December.

He said: "I couldn't say it then, but I thought it was over. I thought even a place in the Champions' League had gone.

"That is why I am so proud that we have come from behind to win it.

"Team spirit has been the real star this season. That was never better shown than when Tony Adams scored.

Halled

"It was Steve Bould who gave him the ball and they have both been here a long time."

Wenger hailed Adams and said: "We have seen the real Tony Adams since January.

"As things went on, you got the feeling he was becoming more and more influential.

"You could feel his determination coming through."

Wright, who has missed most of the title run-in through injury, was sent on to get a taste of glory in the 70th minute and launched into wild celebration dances at the end.

Wenger said: "You could see how happy he was. You always can."

Wright was one of the last to leave the dressing room and he added: "This really could be an unbelievable finish to the season for me.

"We're at Wembley and have won the Championship — and, hopefully, it's the World Cup for me. I certainly believe we can win it.

"This is the happiest day of my life. This side is a joy to play in.

"But I'm not unhappy that Nicolas Anelka has been playing while I've been injured.

"There has got to be people coming through."

MOMENT OF TRIUMPH: The months of pent-up emotion are forgotten as Arsenal manager Arsene Wenger finally knows the championship is his *Picture: CHRIS TURVEY*

TITLE MOULD

Arsene earns place among legends

ARSENE WENGER and Tony Adams almost bumped into each other by accident during the melee on the pitch as the exuberance, tears and emotion spilled out as Arsenal were crowned champions.

As they posed in front of photographers, they epitomised Arsenal's success story.

Wenger became the first foreign coach to win the title, and his secret was not a French revolution at Highbury, but combining his continental philosophy with the backbone of the team founded on the British bulldog spirit.

No-one sums up that camaraderie better than Adams, such a reformed character these days.

With Ruud Gullit winning the FA Cup with Chelsea a year ago, foreign coaches are in the Premiership to stay, and Wenger's success is sure to prompt other big teams to consider going continental.

The Frenchman arrived as "Arsene Who?" and while it seemed a bizarre turn of events to sack Bruce Rioch after just one season, when he got Arsenal into Europe, it was appropriate that vice-chairman David Dean was highlighted on the club's jumbo screen as the driving force in bringing Wenger to the club.

Even without their record goalscorer Ian Wright, Arsenal put together a phenomenal run of 10 straight wins to haul back a deficit of 13 points and succeed Manchester United as champions.

Sunshine

At precisely 4.30 on the famous Arsenal clock, Everton had caved in, following Marc Overmars first goal to make it 2-0.

Arsenal had no doubts that this game was all over and the title was theirs with an hour still to go against Everton, and two games left in the season.

Let's face it, Wenger knew the championship was Arsenal's even before his team stepped out into the glorious Arsenal sunshine, and he wasn't alone.

The bookies were no longer taking any bets (although that tactic had backfired before) and the entire Premiership sponsors' entourage had brought all the Carling championship paraphernalia to Highbury.

To their eternal discredit, Everton didn't disappoint anyone.

If Howard Kendall's idea of motivation when his club discovered the plans had already been made to present the trophy was to kick lumps out of the opposition, then no-one will mourn the relegation of a club that was once regarded, along with Arsenal, as a member of the exclusive Big Five club.

Emmanuel Petit was the main target, whacked in the face by John O'Kane and later the victim of a reckless two-footed tackle by Don Hutchison.

If the FA pursue Alan Shearer for kicking an opponent in the head, then they should call for video evidence on a succession of incidents throughout the

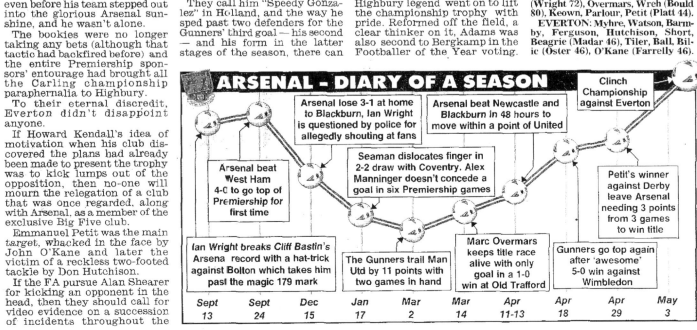

DOUBLE DUTCH: Marc Overmars got two goals and Dennis Bergkamp the trophy   Pictures: CHRIS TURVEY and KENT GAVIN

Harry HARRIS

Arsenal 4 Everton 0

season, especially the X-rated lunge by Hutchison that sent panic around Highbury that the pony-tailed Petit had broken his leg. It s bad enough that the Everton team had been a shambles. Worse, that they were a disgrace at Highbury.

I don't want to waste my time concentrating too much on a club whose proud 44 unbroken years in the top flight has been put at peril with survival hinging on their final game against Coventry when sympathy will now lie with Bolton surviving at Stamford Bridge.

Instead, the Gunners' fans' faith in their team was amply rewarded

I predicted before the start of the season that the £5million signing of Overmars was enough to bring the title to Highbury.

They call him "Speedy Gonzalez" in Holland, and the way he sped past two defenders for the Gunners' third goal — his second — and his form in the latter stages of the season, there can be no doubt he is in great nick as the World Cup finals approach.

Even without double footballer of the year Dennis Bergkamp, Arsenal were full of goals from the moment Adams bamboozled Slaven Bilic from a seventh-minute corner by Petit, and the former West Ham centre-half headed past his own keeper, Thomas Myhre.

It was an own goal, but Adams deserved the credit, and he completed the scoring a minute from the end.

Substitute Steve Bould, of all people, threaded through the perfect pass to find Adams rampaging forward to crack a half-volley into the corner.

It was the perfect finale. The Highbury legend went on to lift the championship trophy with pride. Reformed off the field, a clear thinker on it, Adams was also second to Bergkamp in the Footballer of the Year voting.

TOP OF THE TABLE

	P	W	D	L	F	A	Pts
Arsenal	36	23	9	4	68	28	78
Man Utd	36	21	8	7	68	26	71
Liverpool	36	17	11	8	64	41	62
Chelsea	37	19	3	15	69	43	60
Leeds	36	17	7	12	56	42	58
Blackburn	37	15	10	12	56	52	55

While his place in Glenn Hoddle's World Cup is assured Ian Wright will be given the next two games by Wenger for a last attempt at proving to the England coach his form and fitness.

Wright came on for the last 18 minutes in place of Nicolas Anelka and although he hardly got a touch no-one was more effusive than Wright - - claiming his first championship   as the medals were handed out.

At times it seemed as if he would have to be surgically removed from the trophy.

Herbert Chapman, George Allison, Tom Whittaker, Bertie Mee and George Graham are now joined by Wenger as managers in Arsenal's illustrious history to bring the title to the club.

How ironic it is for such a traditional club, with its famous marble halls, the last club in the country to consider shirt sponsorship and advertising boards, that it can now boast the first foreign coach to win the championship.

ARSENAL: Seaman, Dixon, Winterburn, Vieira, Adams, Anelka (Wright 72), Overmars, Wreh (Bould 80), Keown, Parlour, Petit (Platt 44).

EVERTON: Myhre, Watson, Barmby, Ferguson, Hutchison, Short, Beagrie (Madar 46), Tiler, Ball, Bilic (Oster 46), O'Kane (Farrelly 46).

SHUT OUT: Petit and Adams foil Everton's Ferguson

Awful Everton face the drop

Mike WALTERS

THEY came to Highbury to crown Arsenal rather than bury Everton. But the undertakers are on stand-by and the coroner had asked to be kept informed.

Unless Howard Kendall's men can extricate themselves from the tightest corner since Harold Lloyd found himself dangling from the town hall clock, the blue half of Merseyside will be in mourning – just like the city of Manchester – this time next week.

On the evidence of yesterday's Arsenal cakewalk to the title, Everton couldn't wriggle their way out of a granny-knot.

And, unlike silent movie star Lloyd, they haven't a clue about hanging on for dear life when a terrible drop beckons.

Plank

If their finale against Coventry next Sunday is laced with as much spite and as little nous as this derisory stab at salvation, Kendall's next signing could be down at the Job Centre.

A decent type who has served Everton with distinction in previous incarnations, Kendall yesterday bore the marks of a drowning man when he named his team.

A side overpopulated by central defenders confirmed that the priority was to choke the life out of the game.

It took Slaven Bilic just five minutes to put through his own goal – and to think he quit West Ham a year ago, protesting that Goodison was a more likely source of silverware. They must have been in stitches in the East End.

Don Hutchison, the midfielder Kendall recruited inexplicably from Sheffield United as the antidote to an ailing side, should walk the plank for his atrocious lunge at Emmanuel Petit.

Hutchison is a loser, discarded with few regrets by Liverpool and West Ham among others.

His career has few redeeming features and if his disgraceful assault on Petit costs the Frenchman his FA Cup final place, it's just as well Everton's next League match in North London is more likely to be at Barnet than Highbury.

Of course, Hutchison wasn't the only waster on parade along the thin blue line that Arsenal breached with ease.

Duncan Ferguson seemed more intent on picking a fight with Tony Adams and Martin Keown than leading by example.

And Nicky Barmby's only notable contribution to a vacuous afternoon for Evertonians was to gormlessly get himself booked.

Kendall could not conceal his desperation and he resorted to a triple half-time substitution in the hope Arsenal might take their foot off the pedal. Some hope.

He left Mickael Madar on the bench for 45 minutes, a curious concession to negativity. But, as they say in Frank Spencer territory, some Madars do 'av' 'em.

Everton's nosedive to the brink of Nationwide League obscurity is quite astonishing.

Just ten years ago, they

DANGER ZONE

Bolton	37	9	13	15	41	59	40
Everton	37	9	12	16	40	55	39
Barnsley	37	10	5	22	37	80	35
Crystal Pal	36	7	8	21	33	68	29

smashed the British transfer record to buy £2.2million striker Tony Cottee.

And, would you believe it, Arsenal was the club Cottee spurned in favour of a move to Goodison.

Cottee could only shake his head and mutter unprintables under his breath as he watched from a radio commentary box yesterday as his former club was humiliated.

Everton's fate now rests on that home match against Coventry.

It is a mark of Everton's decline that Coventry have breezed this season, while Goodison chairman Peter Johnson has failed to deliver the big names he promised.

For all Everton's failings on the pitch perhaps their greatest let-down of all has been the emptiness of Johnson's promises.

Big names? Well, Crewe and Bury may not be what Johnson had in mind.

ARSENAL – DIARY OF A SEASON

Clinch Championship against Everton

Arsenal lose 3-1 at home to Blackburn, Ian Wright is questioned by police for allegedly shouting at fans

Arsenal beat Newcastle and Blackburn in 48 hours to move within a point of United

Seaman dislocates finger in 2-2 draw with Coventry. Alex Manninger doesn't concede a goal in six Premiership games

Arsenal beat West Ham 4-0 to go top of Premiership for first time

Petit's winner against Derby leave Arsenal needing 3 points from 3 games to win title

Ian Wright breaks Cliff Bastin's Arsenal record with a hat-trick against Bolton which takes him past the magic 179 mark

The Gunners trail Man Utd by 11 points with two games in hand

Marc Overmars keeps title race alive with only goal in a 1-0 win at Old Trafford

Gunners go top again after 'awesome' 5-0 win against Wimbledon

| Sept 13 | Sept 24 | Dec 15 | Jan 17 | Mar 2 | Mar 14 | Apr 11-13 | Apr 18 | Apr 29 | May 3 |

JOY & PAIN

Boro stage Premiership party but sad City slump to new depths on day of despair

SEE Mania FOR ALL THE FOOTBALL DRAMA

CHAMPIONS

CARLING CHAM

THAT CHAMPION FEELING: The Arsenal players show off the FA Carling Premiership trophy after their crushing win over Everton yesterday

Pic: KENT GAVIN

NOW LET'S MAKE IT A DOUBLE

Wenger toasts title and sets sights on FA Cup glory

ARSENAL claimed the Premiership crown in spectacular style and then set their sights on the double.

The Gunners clinched the title with a glorious, fitting finale from veteran skipper Tony Adams which launched wild celebration parties across North London.

Adams scored the last goal in the awesome 4-0 destruction of Everton which took the title to Highbury for the first time since 1991.

By JOHN DILLON

And Arsenal's French coach Arsene Wenger became the first foreign manager to win the championship in his first full season in charge of the club.

The Gunners face Newcastle at Wembley on May 16 and Wenger spelled out his team's determination to repeat the 1971 achievement by declaring: "This is the biggest satisfaction of my career so far — but now we have to prepare well for the Cup final."

Delighted Ian Wright said: "It could be a fantastic end of the season for me. We've won the title and now the Cup final is coming up so we could do the double. That would be great for London as well as for Arsenal."

Adams held aloft the Premiership trophy for the first time in his career amid emotional scenes on the pitch.

And Wenger was given a massive cheer by the 38,000 crowd in acknowledgement of his unique achievement. He continued: "I am

TURN TO PAGE 38

CAPTAIN MARWEL: Tony Adams hoists the trophy

Published by MGN Ltd. at One Canada Square, Canary Wharf, London, E14 5AP (0171-293 3000) and printed by Mirror Colour Print Ltd. at Watford   Registered as a newspaper at the Post Office   Serial No. 30,440   ©MGN, Ltd., 1997. Monday, May 4, 1998

19

9 770956 805516

The UK's top sports web site: http: www.sporting-life.com

FA CUP FINAL

Double diamonds

Shearer's apology to Adams

By BRIAN McNALLY

ALAN SHEARER sought out Tony Adams after the match to apologise for the crude challenge which earned the England skipper a booking just before half-time.

And Shearer paid tribute to the Gunners, saying: "They have a very good manager and a good team. Give credit to them for not allowing us to play in the first half.

"They are worthy Double winners.

"When you look back on the season and see the silverware they have got, then congratulations to them."

Shearer added: "We had a mountain to climb after that first-half performance.

"But the difference between success and failure is an inch — because I felt if my shot had gone in instead of hitting the post we would have had them on the rack."

Disappointed Newcastle boss Kenny Dalglish insisted his side couldn't have given any more.

He said: "My players gave everything they had. They went in with a very positive mind.

"The turning-point in the game came midway through the second half, when we hit both the bar and the post.

"Sometimes you need a little bit of luck in the Final, and we didn't get it.

"But I'm pleased that my players kept going right until the end, although the second goal by Anelka finished us off.

"There is no disgrace in losing to a very good side like Arsenal. We've got to remember who we were playing against and what they have achieved.

"Arsenal deserved to win the Championship and they deserved to win the Cup.

"But we also can take credit from the fact that we are back in Europe next season and we have reached an FA Cup Final."

Dalglish, whose side have been assured of a Cup-Winners' Cup place ever since Arsenal clinched the title, admitted that Newcastle's failure to equalise during the spirited second-half fightback had been crucial.

"That was probably the best part of the game for us but, unfortunately, we couldn't get any benefit from it," he said.

Dalglish saluted the Toon Army for the manner in which they got behind their side throughout the match.

He said: "This is the first time I've come to Wembley when both sets of fans thought they were winners on the day.

"They sang their appreciation for the effort put in by the players, who gave it everything they had, and it washes away the pessimism that people say is around the club."

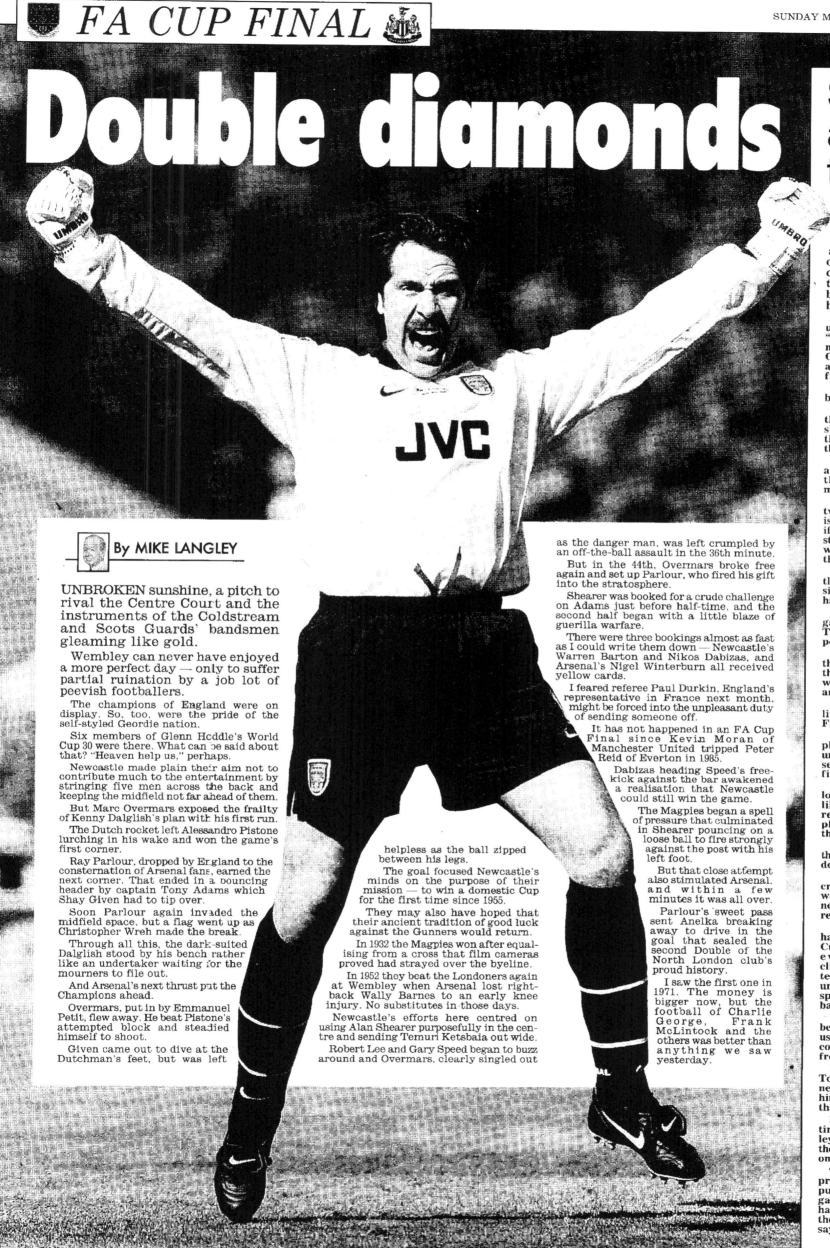

By MIKE LANGLEY

UNBROKEN sunshine, a pitch to rival the Centre Court and the instruments of the Coldstream and Scots Guards' bandsmen gleaming like gold.

Wembley can never have enjoyed a more perfect day — only to suffer partial ruination by a job lot of peevish footballers.

The champions of England were on display. So, too, were the pride of the self-styled Geordie nation.

Six members of Glenn Hoddle's World Cup 30 were there. What can be said about that? "Heaven help us," perhaps.

Newcastle made plain their aim not to contribute much to the entertainment by stringing five men across the back and keeping the midfield not far ahead of them.

But Marc Overmars exposed the frailty of Kenny Dalglish's plan with his first run.

The Dutch rocket left Alessandro Pistone lurching in his wake and won the game's first corner.

Ray Parlour, dropped by England to the consternation of Arsenal fans, earned the next corner. That ended in a bouncing header by captain Tony Adams which Shay Given had to tip over.

Soon Parlour again invaded the midfield space, but a flag went up as Christopher Wreh made the break.

Through all this, the dark-suited Dalglish stood by his bench rather like an undertaker waiting for the mourners to file out.

And Arsenal's next thrust put the Champions ahead.

Overmars, put in by Emmanuel Petit, flew away. He beat Pistone's attempted block and steadied himself to shoot.

Given came out to dive at the Dutchman's feet, but was left helpless as the ball zipped between his legs.

The goal focused Newcastle's minds on the purpose of their mission — to win a domestic Cup for the first time since 1955.

They may also have hoped that their ancient tradition of good luck against the Gunners would return.

In 1932 the Magpies won after equalising from a cross that film cameras proved had strayed over the byeline.

In 1952 they beat the Londoners again at Wembley when Arsenal lost right-back Wally Barnes to an early knee injury. No substitutes in those days.

Newcastle's efforts here centred on using Alan Shearer purposefully in the centre and sending Temuri Ketsbaia out wide.

Robert Lee and Gary Speed began to buzz around and Overmars, clearly singled out as the danger man, was left crumpled by an off-the-ball assault in the 36th minute.

But in the 44th, Overmars broke free again and set up Parlour, who fired his gift into the stratosphere.

Shearer was booked for a crude challenge on Adams just before half-time, and the second half began with a little blaze of guerilla warfare.

There were three bookings almost as fast as I could write them down — Newcastle's Warren Barton and Nikos Dabizas, and Arsenal's Nigel Winterburn all received yellow cards.

I feared referee Paul Durkin, England's representative in France next month, might be forced into the unpleasant duty of sending someone off.

It has not happened in an FA Cup Final since Kevin Moran of Manchester United tripped Peter Reid of Everton in 1985.

Dabizas heading Speed's free-kick against the bar awakened a realisation that Newcastle could still win the game.

The Magpies began a spell of pressure that culminated in Shearer pouncing on a loose ball to fire strongly against the post with his left foot.

But that close attempt also stimulated Arsenal, and within a few minutes it was all over.

Parlour's sweet pass sent Anelka breaking away to drive in the goal that sealed the second Double of the North London club's proud history.

I saw the first one in 1971. The money is bigger now, but the football of Charlie George, Frank McLintock and the others was better than anything we saw yesterday.

WEMBLEY RATINGS

DAVID SEAMAN

COOL as a cucumber in the Wembley sunshine. One first half save off Ketsbaia but had his woodwork rattled twice in the second half when Newcastle staged a brief but goalless comeback **Rating 7**

LEE DIXON

SHOWED his passing ability as well as his stout defending. Has he ever let Arsenal down? How Dalglish could have done with a class fullback like this, instead of the fumbling Pistone. **Rating 8**

MARTIN KEOWN

A GREAT foil for his skipper Adams – always around to tidy up. Must have had his heart in his mouth when he let Shearer in for Newcastle's best chance – but the post saved him **Rating 8**

TONY ADAMS

WHAT did they make this guy out of – pure rock or stainless steel? Another great display and he didn't flinch when Shearer put in a cruel late tackle on his England pal. What a guy, what a captain **Rating 8**

NIGEL WINTERBURN

SERIOUSLY punted as a possible Footballer of the Year, and who could have complained if he'd got the vote? Put in an incredible last-ditch tackle on Shearer and should be going to France '98 at 34 **Rating 8**

RAY PARLOUR

WERE you watching Glenn Hoddle? Man of the Match yesterday and he's been a revelation all season. But he's not in the England squad. Cruel. Made Anelka's goal and could have scored himself **Rating 9**

PATRICK VIEIRA

PADDY has single-handedly destroyed the myth about Frenchmen being big softies. Hard in the tackle, strong on the run. Best foreign buy in years. Hope he doesn't play in the World Cup! **Rating 7**

EMMANUEL PETIT

CREATED the Overmars opener and never stopped working next to Vieira. Monaco must be missing him and certainly Arsene Wenger knew what he was doing when he filched him from his old club **Rating 7**

MARC OVERMARS

FRIGHTENED Newcastle to death with his pace. But then he does that every week. Tired a little in the second half but by then, the job had been done. What was Pistone doing for the goal? **Rating 8**

NICOLAS ANELKA

MISSED a first-half sitter with his head, but kept his cool to score a magnificent second goal to raise the Wembley roof. Pace is phenomenal. If the French are clever, they'll use him in the summer **Rating 8**

CHRISTOPHER WREH

NEVER really got into the game though he did enjoy some useful touches. Don't forget who scored in the semi-final against Wolves though. Replaced by David Platt in the second half. **Rating 7**

SUB: Platt : Worked hard, helped Arsenal's general shape. Good substitution **Rating 7**

THEY'VE GUN

DUTCH OF CLASS: Marc Overmars is joined by later scorer Nicolas Anelka after (inset) beating Shay Given for Arsenal's Wembley opener

AND DONE IT

Overmars and Anelka make it torture for the Toon Army

By David Barnes

ARSENE WENGER kept just the right distance beyond the limelight in which Arsenal's Double winners pranced happily with the FA Cup at Wembley.

And, correct in impeccable dark suit, he reserved his warmest hug for Pat Rice, a little man in droopy shorts.

It will be an enduring image for two men unaware of each other's existence not too long ago and now sharing the emotions only Rice had experienced with Arsenal's first Double 27 years ago.

Marc Overmars and Nicolas Anelka scored the goals that left England captain Alan Shearer with just a yellow card to go with his broken dreams.

Overmars, the ready-made Dutch international from Ajax, and Anelka, the 19-year-old rookie from Paris St Germain, are both shrewd acquisitions from opposite ends of the transfer scale by Wenger.

But, for me, his genius for management can be better seen at work elsewhere.

In the formidable strength and resilience of Tony Adams, who was able to hoist his second FA Cup as Arsenal captain in a career that once drove him to drink, despair and almost to retirement.

Hoddle must add Parlour to his World Cup squad

And in the inexhaustible energy of Ray Parlour who, like Adams, once tested his stamina only by the hours he could stand against a late-night bar.

If I were England boss Glenn Hoddle, who was watching from the stand, I would reach for my World Cup squad sheet and append the name of Parlour in the hope I could pass it on to FIFA on June 2.

It was natural for men to wilt in heat recorded at pitch level at 90 degrees. Parlour never lost a scrap of momentum on his long charge towards a deserved Man of the Match Award.

That's a quality England may find of great value in the sweltering South of France next month — especially when it is allied to such destructive surges.

Shearer, socks rolled down, trudged off a deeply unhappy figure. Yet a courageous one for whom the FA Cup brought his first start of an injury-stricken season back in February.

The luck he enjoyed to escape censure by the FA over the Neil Lennon boot-in-face incident did not extend to this final.

He was cautioned for a reckless and frustrated challenge on Adams and, when he finally found a chance to score, his left-foot shot struck the inside of the post with David Seaman, his England team-mate, well beaten.

STRIKING COUPLE: Marc Overmars and Nicolas Anelka scored the goals and grabbed the Cup yesterday

Arsenal (1) 2
Overmars 23, Anelka 69.

Newcastle (0) 0

Att: 79,183

At least Shearer and Newcastle boss Kenny Dalglish can feel the first stirrings of pride in a season that had heaped so much contempt on their club from boardroom to bootroom. Dalglish won many hearts by clutching the hand of a heavily-limping youngster in the black-and-white stripes of Newcastle on a long, slow march onto the pitch.

What that brave kid saw, though, was a scenario that must have filled him and the rest of the Toon Army with apprehension.

Overmars' first race with Alessandro Pistone showed him to be the far faster man.

The ability of so many players to perform at great pace has been one of the corner-stones of Arsenal's unforgettable exploits.

So has the educated left foot of Frenchman Emmanuel Petit.

It was Petit's measured pass that first undid Newcastle in the 22nd minute, to the obvious embarrassment of Italian Pistone.

As the back-spin bit Overmars ducked under Pistone, moved clear with a little nod of the ball and drove it left-footed between the legs of keeper Shay Given.

Arsenal fans have taken Overmars to their hearts. His manner remains unassuming, though many of his 16 goals for Arsenal this season have carried crucial importance.

Like the one at Old Trafford that gave Arsenal victory and their first belief that they could overhaul Manchester United and win the Premiership title.

And the two he struck at Highbury against Everton to make this improbable dream come true.

Now here he was allowing Arsenal to lightly bear the loss of his Dutch compatriot Dennis Bergkamp to a hamstring injury.

No doubt Bergkamp will thank him for being able to meet the Duchess of Kent and get his hands on a trophy he had done too much to earn in other rounds.

Newcastle's most lively performer was Temuri Ketsbaia, the Georgian who had spoken on the eve of the game of his anger at spending so much time sitting alongside Dalglish in the dugout.

He responded superbly to Dalglish's decision to promote him, though an Arsenal defence that has taken a decade to carefully construct was too thick to pierce.

Green defender Nikos Dabizas almost achieved that when going up for a Rob Lee free-kick and heading against the bar.

You sensed, especially with Shearer striking the post in quick succession, that the red-and-white ribbons could already be applied to the trophy.

And, sure enough, Parlour cleverly sprang the offside trap to allow Anelka a clear run on goal. Anelka might have squandered the chance earlier this season when his inexperience of English conditions made him look a little short of Premiership quality.

Wenger, against the wishes at times of more impatient Gooners, retained faith in Anelka and it must have satisfied him greatly to see what happened next.

For Anelka's impressive pace took him clear and an assured right-foot shot flew like an arrow across Given into the corner.

There was time for Parlour, himself, to try to get his name on the score-sheet.

Platt came on for a lasting souvenir

A searing surge took him through the heart of the defence. Steve Howey was pulled down and received a yellow card.

Referee Paul Durkin had a good game, also booking Warren Barton and Dabizas of Newcastle and Arsenal's Nigel Winterburn.

That's a triumph too for Wenger who has worked hard on a disciplinary image that has often veered wildly out of his control.

Ian Wright must have hoped that Wenger would give him a few minutes to remember, but he remained on the bench and now may never get the chance again.

David Platt, instead, came on as a sub for young Christopher Wreh and so will have a lasting souvenir if he leaves this summer for a career in management.

The Toon Army did itself no favours by booing Stevenage whose officials collected a £5,000 cheque as FA Cup giantkillers.

Wenger walked down the tunnel ahead of his men already plotting a Champions League campaign next season.

It may be a long time till Newcastle can once again find a place at such rare heights.

MATCH FACTS

REFEREE: Paul Durkin, Portland

Arsenal		Newcastle
13	Fouls committed	18
1	Yellow cards	4
0	Red cards	0
6	Offside	3
4	Corners	2
3	Shots on target	1
9	Shots off target	1

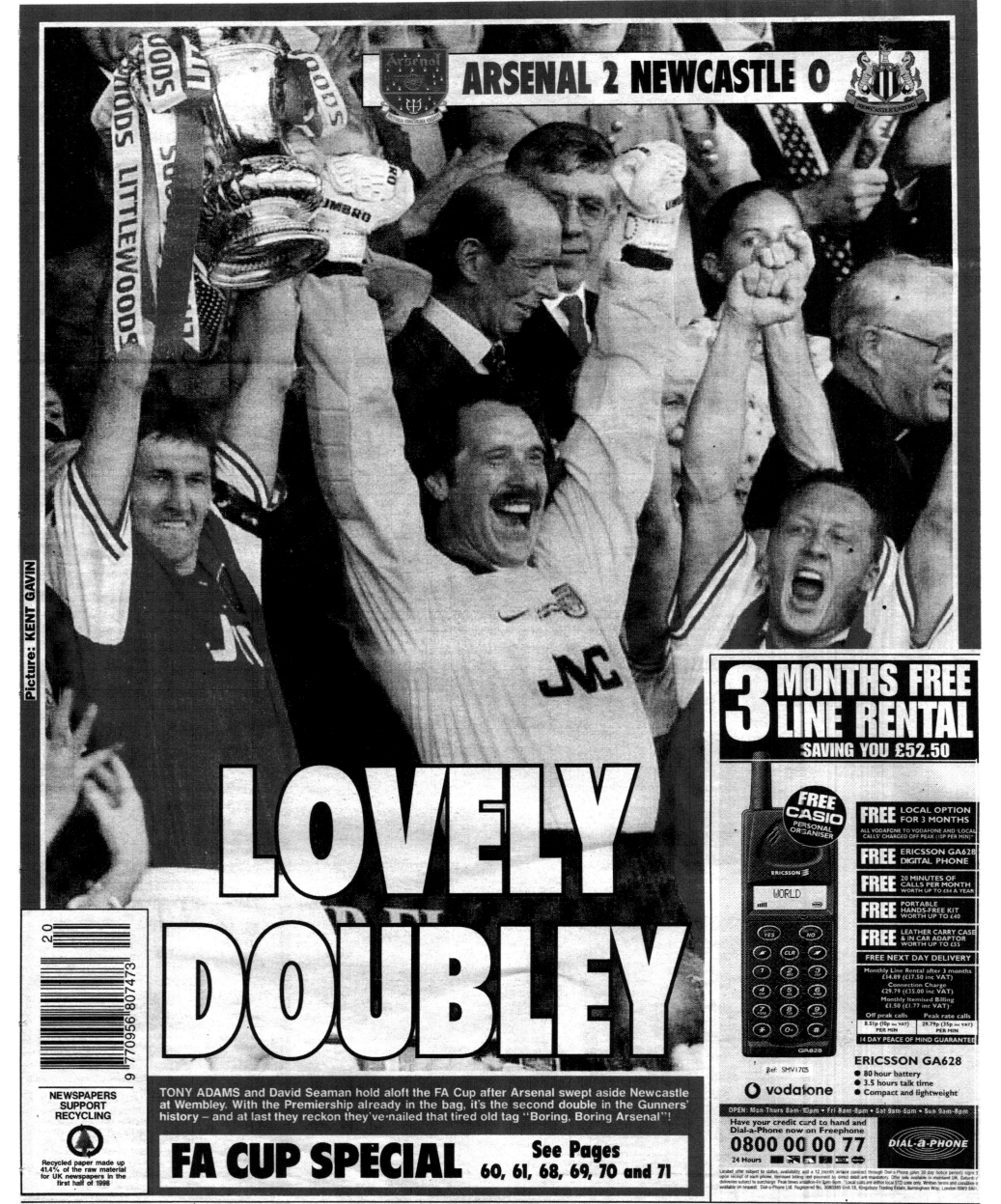

Picture: KENT GAVIN

ARSENAL 2 NEWCASTLE 0

LOVELY DOUBLEY

TONY ADAMS and David Seaman hold aloft the FA Cup after Arsenal swept aside Newcastle at Wembley. With the Premiership already in the bag, it's the second double in the Gunners' history – and at last they reckon they've nailed that tired old tag "Boring, Boring Arsenal"!

FA CUP SPECIAL See Pages 60, 61, 68, 69, 70 and 71

Published by MGN Ltd. (0171-293 3000) and printed by Mirror Colour Print Ltd. Registered at the Post Office as a newspaper. **Serial No. 1727** ©MGN Ltd., 1998.   LO

Henry is Wenger's new Anelka... on the pitch that is

ARSENAL scorer Kanu with the Charity Shield

HOW ALEX LOURDED IT

By LEE WEST

ARSENE WENGER refuses to accept that Treble winners United were superior to his team.

"I don't believe United were any better. They had a bigger squad," said Wenger, launching the opening shots of this season's psychological warfare with United.

Wenger, whose team beat Alex Ferguson's men 2-1 to win the Charity Shield, is convinced that luck played a big part in United's Treble.

He said: "They must have gone via Lourdes. That takes nothing away from the quality of what they did, which was extraordinary, but they did need a lot of luck.

"Take their final against Bayern, and the games against Inter Milan and Juventus when Del Piero and Montero were missing, and Zidane was on one leg.

Miss

"And then there was us missing a winning penalty in the last minute of our Cup semi-final against United.

"Fans do not forget the difference in our budgets. United spent £29million to buy Stam, Blomqvist and Yorke to finish two points ahead of us. That works out at around £15million a point."

Wenger, if given the choice of United players, would go straight for David Beckham.

He said: "I like him a lot. He was the player of the year. The one who made the most progress from the season before.

"I like his effectiveness in delivering the ball. His quality in the long game and in his centres. He has become a complete player. He will develop in the middle of the park, a little like Zidane."

HE is young, fast, hungry for goals and Parisian. And, to be honest, as Thierry Henry arrived at Highbury he was wearing an all-too-familiar blank expression on his face as well.

But Arsene Wenger promised last night that although he intends to fashion Henry into a new Nicolas Anelka, his next creation will soon wear a smile rather than a scowl.

Wenger, the shrewd Frenchman, will reconvert Henry from a winger into the fastest forward in England, having been the very man who switched him out wide when they were together at Monaco five years ago.

Wenger said: "We had to replace Anelka. And Thierry has pace, youth and is a good finisher.

"So I would like to emphasise his qualities as a central striker. He began in that role. He was the top scorer for the French Under-17 team.

"Since then, he has played wide on the right and wide on the left. I put him out there at Monaco because I had too many players in the middle.

"Now it is time for him to come back to a role as a target striker.

"He gives us so many options. Everything is possible when he has the ball at his feet. We had

HOORAY HENRY

FIRST AGAIN
How Mirror Sport revealed he was joining on July 21

John DILLON

Anelka and we have Marc Overmars. But we needed more pace if were are going to have a successful season.

"Now we have got it."

Ironically, Henry is Anelka's best pal. And while Arsenal might hope for his style on the pitch, off it, they will be glad to hear, he is a different character.

Wenger said: "They are two different characters even if they are good friends. Thierry is more of an extrovert than Nicolas."

And Henry said: "Nicolas has his life. I have mine. Even if we are friends, everyone has their own choices to make.

"I will just live normally and try to integrate as quickly as possible.

"I've no real definite plan about how I am going to settle here. I will live my life well.

"I want to work hard because I'm very happy and lucky to join a club like Arsenal. I have wanted to join them for a long time and it is a good opportunity for me."

The satisfactory conclusion to the long quest to sign 21-year-old Henry followed swiftly upon the lightning-fast move to capture Davor Suker from Real Madrid on Monday. And Wenger

---

now has the four forwards he knew he needed to mount a twin challenge for the title and Champions League.

And this less than a week after it looked like all his preparations had been blown sky-high by the sorry saga of Anelka.

Suker, Dennis Bergkamp and Kanu will rotate Stamford Bridge-style as and when the demands of fixtures, travel and exhaustion dictate.

Any Arsenal fans who were worrying about exactly where Henry is going to play after his £10million arrival from Juventus last night, can now stop.

Henry, one of the more exciting members of the dour French World Cup-winning squad, is perfectly built to surge on to those sweet balls from the feet of Bergkamp, Kanu and Emmanuel Petit.

His biggest problem will be facing up to the inevitable comparisons with Anelka.

But Wenger added: "If you do not want to be compared with anyone, you might as well stay at home.

"If you want to be a big player, you have to accept such comparisons."

£10M THIERRY TO PLAY

FROM BACK PAGE

official club photo-call after flying home from Heathrow but club officials are desperate to rush him back in time for the big kick-off.

After a difficult summer, manager Arsene Wenger is delighted that he has signed both Henry and Suker. Wenger said: "We had a lot of news this summer that was not positive for the club. It didn't send any message about ambition. It made the fans feel down.

"But in 48 hours, we have signed a very experienced striker and now a very young talent too."

It also emerged that Henry has been part of an illegal and acrimonious transfer wrangle involving Real Madrid, like the one surrounding Anelka earlier this summer.

He was fined £40,000 by UEFA last year for signing an improper pre-contract with Real while he was with Monaco of France.

TEENAGE PALS: Henry and Anelka were team-mates in the French Under-17 side
Main picture: CHRIS TURVEY

FA CUP FINAL 2002: Double-chasing Gunners

THE BIG INCIDENTS

KEY MOMENTS IN THE MATCH

2min Graeme Le Saux is soon in trouble with hard-line referee Mike Riley who books the Chelsea defender for a kicking Lauren to the ground.

14min Arsenal carve out the first real scoring opportunity. Thierry Henry feeds Sylvain Wiltord inside the Chelsea box but the shot is blocked by Marcel Desailly.

17min Chelsea find their feet and composure after a sticky start and Le Saux tests David Seaman with a dipping low shot the England keeper saves at the second attempt.

18min Patrick Vieira's mistake at an Arsenal free-kick gifts the ball to Frank Lampard but the Blues midfielder's 25-yard shot is comfortably kept out by Seaman.

22min Bergkamp wastes glorious chance to score. His lofted header when unmarked from Vieira's cross flies over Carlo Cudicini but a yard wide.

27min Riley decides to clamp down again on flying tackles. This time Vieira puts his foot in hard on Eidur Gudjohnsen and receives a yellow card.

35min Le Saux — getting more joy down the left in support of his strikers — finds Gudjohnsen but the Icelander's volley is saved by Seaman.

37min Cameroon star Lauren almost makes Chelsea pay dearly when getting onto the end of Wiltord's cross only to head agonisingly inches over from six yards out.

46mi A superb ball from Vieira cuts open a sleepy Chelsea defence only for the usually lethal Henry to see his weak shot saved by Cudicini.

58min Gudjohnsen's quick-thinking nearly breaks the deadlock. The blond striker, wide on the right of the Arsenal box, hits a powerful shot which Seaman just manages to tip over.

60min Chelsea begin to look the sharper and more positive in attack. Melchiot's ball and Jesper Gronkjaer's pass ends in Le Saux blazing over the bar.

65min Henry's cheeky backheel puts fellow Frenchman Wiltord free and in on goal. But the World Cup star shows little composure in slicing wide of target.

68min Hasselbaink — struggling throughout with a calf strain and mainly ineffective — is finally replaced by Gianfranco Zola who is given a rapturous applause by his adoring Chelsea's fans.

69min Ray Parlour pounces to put Arsenal ahead. Collecting Wiltord's pass he unleashes a curling 25-yard shot which a diving Cudicini cannot stop flying into the top right-hand corner of his net.

76min John Terry — on at half-time as substitute for Gallas — and Henry are booked after a clash. The two go head to head and Riley acts.

FINAL-LY: Bergkamp rues a missed chance but enjoyed his first full FA Cup Final victory

78min Boudewijn Zenden replaces Melchiot but Arsenal almost make it 2-0 when Cudicini saves Henry's shot after Wiltord breaks clear.

79min It's ready, Freddie go time! Swede sensation Ljungberg completely kills off Chelsea. Racing 30 yards he shrugs aside Terry and coolly and calmly curls a shot passed Cudicini and into the far corner.

ANTHONY CLAVANE

NO WONDER Arsenal fans were wearing Cup Final T-shirts bearing the legend: "May The Fourth Be With You."

For May 4 will surely go down in history as the turning-point in modern English football, when Manchester United's dominance was replaced by the all-conquering Gunners.

The force is certainly with Arsene Wenger's men who are now on course for another astonishing Double following yesterday's triumph.

Two exquisitely-taken goals by Ray Parlour and Freddie Ljungberg gave them their first trophy in four years.

And 11 straight wins in the League has left them a mere 90 minutes away from the title.

Lucky Arsenal? Perhaps. Chelsea were, for most of the game, the better side.

But Wenger's men, who drew the so-called winners' changing room, will argue that they deserved this win after being robbed by Liverpool in last year's final.

With both teams already in Europe, Arsenal in the Champions League, Chelsea in the UEFA Cup – the first-half confirmed fears this would be more of a spectacle than a contest.

Hopefully, the competition will recover from Manchester United pulling out two seasons ago.

And with modern Cup finals having a tendency to disappoint, the FA was desperately hoping that two of the game's more glamorous sides would restore the fading lustre of the famous old pot.

But the second-half fireworks were on a par with the pre-match rocket display.

Wenger and Ranieri must have put something in their players' drinks at the interval.

The tempo was upped as both teams flew out of the traps.

Henry missed a good chance, Seaman tipped Gudjohnsen's stinger over the bar, Lampard squandered a magnificent opportunity, Ljungberg started making runs,

Wenger's boys are now best in Britain

Gronkjaer gave Cole a torrid time on the right and Wiltord blasted wide from close range.

Then Parlour struck and Freddie did it again to hit back at Wenger's critics.

The only time Mr Calm has threatened to turn into Mr Angry is when journalists have called Arsenal underachievers.

Not anymore. The FA Cup is their first trophy since the Double in 1998, but fans should expect another one within a matter of days.

Either at Old Trafford on Wednesday or at Highbury three days later, the Gunners should clinch the title and finally put and end to all those jibes.

After being bridesmaids for so long – three times in the League and once before in the FA Cup Wenger's men were determined to get hitched.

And it's all thanks to Arsene, the Frenchman who taught the English how to combine style and substance, the foreign coach who paved the way for Houllier and Eriksson.

Wenger is the history-maker who is now within one game of pulling off a miraculous double Double. Not that Sir Alex Ferguson will be rolling out the red carpet when Wenger's charges take to the field at Old Trafford on Wednesday.

It's more likely to be red-hot coals.

Wenger's attempt to out-psyche the master of mind games with his "everyone thinks he has the prettiest wife" jibe will not have gone down well with the Laird of Govan.

Although two London teams contested yesterday's showpiece, for the first time in 20 years, it was hardly a Cockney Final, in truth it was more of a cosmopolitan one.

ARSENAL RATINGS   MANAGER ARSENE WENGER   opta opta.co.uk

DAVID SEAMAN (7)
Mins on pitch	90	Dropped crosses	0
Goals conceded	0	Catch success %	100
Shots saved	5	Passes to teammates	14
Shots saved %	100	Passes to opposition	10
Catches	5	Distribution accuracy	58%

LAUREN (6)
Mins on pitch	90	Passes on target	36
Goals	0	Passes to opposition	11
Shots on target	0	Fouls given	1
Shots off target	1	Fouls conceded	0
Assists	0	Clearances	5

TONY ADAMS (6)
Mins on pitch	90	Passes on target	31
Goals	0	Passes to opposition	3
Shots on target	0	Fouls given	2
Shots off target	0	Fouls conceded	2
Assists	0	Clearances	11

SOL CAMPBELL (6)
Mins on pitch	90	Passes on target	29
Goals	0	Passes to opposition	8
Shots on target	0	Fouls given	0
Shots off target	1	Fouls conceded	1
Assists	0	Offsides	0

ASHLEY COLE (6)
Mins on pitch	90	Passes on target	37
Goals	0	Passes to opposition	9
Shots on target	0	Fouls given	3
Shots off target	0	Fouls conceded	1
Assists	0	Clearances	6

SYLVAIN WILTORD (7)
Mins on pitch	89	Passes on target	28
Goals	0	Passes to opposition	11
Shots on target	0	Fouls given	0
Shots off target	1	Fouls conceded	0
Assists	0	Clearances	0

RAY PARLOUR (7)
Mins on pitch	90	Passes on target	33
Goals	1	Passes to opposition	8
Shots on target	1	Fouls given	2
Shots off target	1	Fouls conceded	4
Assists	0	Offsides	0

PATRICK VIEIRA (6)
Mins on pitch	90	Passes on target	42
Goals	0	Passes to opposition	17
Shots on target	0	Fouls given	1
Shots off target	0	Fouls conceded	2
Assists	0	Offsides	0

FREDDIE LJUNGBERG (9)
Mins on pitch	90	Passes on target	18
Goals	1	Passes to opposition	10
Shots on target	1	Fouls given	0
Shots off target	0	Fouls conceded	2
Assists	0	Clearances	0

DENNIS BERGKAMP (6)
Mins on pitch	71	Passes on target	19
Goals	0	Passes to opposition	8
Shots on target	0	Fouls given	1
Shots off target	1	Fouls conceded	2
Assists	0	Clearances	0

THIERRY HENRY (6)
Mins on pitch	81	Passes on target	10
Goals	0	Passes to opposition	13
Shots on target	0	Fouls given	2
Shots off target	2	Fouls conceded	1
Assists	0	Offsides	0

SUBSTITUTES
Substitute	Replaced	On pitch	Rating
Edu	Bergkamp	19 mins	6
Kanu	Henry	9 mins	6
Keown	Wiltord	1 mins	6

take Manchester United's title of football kings

SECOND TIME LUCKY: Freddie Ljungberg is joined by Sylvain Wiltord, Edu and Thierry Henry after a happier ending to his goal in this year's final   *Picture: Kent Gavin*

The teams were led out on Welsh soil by Frenchman Wenger and an Italian Roberto Di Matteo, not Claudio Ranieri.

And only seven of the 22 players starting were actually English.

At least the pride of St George was restored when Parlour curled in the first goal.

But it had to be the man with the cockatoo quiff who finished Chelsea off.

A cross between Johnny Rotten and Marge Simpson, Ljungberg has been inspirational in the last few weeks.

They should have put Freddie's red flashes on the Cup alongside the red ribbons.

The 25-year-old midfielder has notched 17 goals already this campaign.

When he's scored this season, Arsenal haven't lost.

It looks like the footballer of year awards were cast too early.

Thierry Henry should have had his 31st goal of the season, immediately after the restart.

Henry badly wanted to make amends for the 2001 final. But, as with last season, he was too casual in front of goal.

Dennis Bergkamp, a substitute in last season's final defeat, injured in 1998's destruction of Newcastle, should have opened the scoring after 21 minutes when he headed Vieira's cross over Cudicini but past the post.

But these are minor quibbles.

For Arsenal at last produced the goods, Old Trafford awaits.

As for Chelsea, they will feel hard done by.

Despite being written off, their Cup final record has been excellent. With two FA, one League, a Cup Winners and European Super Cup to their credit their supporters were hoping their inconsistency in the League would be banished by another big-game performance.

But the team with the split personality badly needed World Cup winners like Emmanuel Petit to play like World Cup winners and convince everyone they haven't been saving themselves for the Far East.

They desperately needed to have Hasselbaink fully fit.

They needed Frank Lampard and Graeme Le Saux to make Mr Eriksson regret leaving them out of his World Cup squad when it is announced on Thursday.

I don't think Sven will be losing any sleep after seeing Le Saux's wild foul on Lauren which almost got him sent off.

And Chelsea still badly need Claudio Ranieri to deliver the first trophy of his reign at Stamford Bridge if he is to silence the doubters who still can't understand why the Cup-laden Luca Vialli was so unceremoniously ditched.

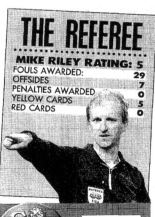

THE REFEREE

MIKE RILEY RATING: 5

FOULS AWARDED:	29
OFFSIDES	7
PENALTIES AWARDED	0
YELLOW CARDS	5
RED CARDS	0

CHELSEA RATINGS

MANAGER CLAUDIO RANIERI

opta.co.uk

CARLO CUDICINI — 7

Mins on pitch	90	Dropped crosses	0
Goals conceded	2	Catch success %	100
Shots saved	2	Passes to team mates	17
Shots saved %	50	Passes to opposition	12
Catches	1	Distribution accuracy	59%

MARIO MELCHIOT — 6

Mins on pitch	76	Passes on target	23
Goals	0	Passes to opposition	6
Shots on target	0	Fouls given	3
Shots off target	0	Fouls conceded	2
Assists	0	Clearances	0

MARCEL DESAILLY — 8

Mins on pitch	90	Passes on target	37
Goals	0	Passes to opposition	7
Shots on target	0	Fouls given	1
Shots off target	0	Fouls conceded	0
Assists	0	Clearances	7

WILLIAM GALLAS — 7

Mins on pitch	90	Passes on target	39
Goals	0	Passes to opposition	3
Shots on target	0	Fouls given	0
Shots off target	0	Fouls conceded	1
Assists	0	Offsides	0

CELESTINE BABAYARO — 6

Mins on pitch	45	Passes on target	10
Goals	0	Passes to opposition	6
Shots on target	0	Fouls given	0
Shots off target	0	Fouls conceded	0
Assists	0	Clearances	1

JESPER GRONKJAER — 7

Mins on pitch	90	Passes on target	18
Goals	0	Passes to opposition	16
Shots on target	0	Fouls given	2
Shots off target	0	Fouls conceded	1
Assists	0	Clearances	2

FRANK LAMPARD — 7

Mins on pitch	90	Passes on target	47
Goals	0	Passes to opposition	8
Shots on target	1	Fouls given	2
Shots off target	1	Fouls conceded	3
Assists	0	Offsides	0

EMMANUEL PETIT — 6

Mins on pitch	90	Passes on target	34
Goals	0	Passes to opposition	16
Shots on target	0	Fouls given	1
Shots off target	0	Fouls conceded	0
Assists	0	Offsides	0

GRAEME LE SAUX — 7

Mins on pitch	90	Passes on target	30
Goals	0	Passes to opposition	14
Shots on target	0	Fouls given	4
Shots off target	1	Fouls conceded	1
Assists	0	Clearances	0

EIDUR GUDJOHNSEN — 8

Mins on pitch	90	Passes on target	17
Goals	0	Passes to opposition	13
Shots on target	0	Fouls given	4
Shots off target	1	Fouls conceded	2
Assists	0	Clearances	0

JIMMY HASSELBAINK — 6

Mins on pitch	67	Passes on target	10
Goals	0	Passes to opposition	13
Shots on target	0	Fouls given	1
Shots off target	0	Fouls conceded	4
Assists	0	Offsides	0

SUBSTITUTES

Substitute	Replaced	On pitch	Rating
Terry	Babayaro	45 mins	6
Zola	Hasselbaink	23 mins	6
Zenden	Melchiot	14 mins	6

It's Freddie steady go for Arsenal

From Back Page

that if we beat Chelsea it would be the perfect boost for us going to Old Trafford. The players were already confident but this will give us extra belief.

"It would be nice to wrap up the title at Old Trafford. But if we don't there is still the home game with Everton.

"We have a celebration dinner tonight but that will stop at midnight when we must start thinking of the Championship. That's always been our No1 goal this season. This Cup is an added bonus. It certainly feels nice to be close to achieving the Double for the second time since I became manager.

Thierry Henry said: "We are now confident we can go on and win the Double.

"This makes up for last year's defeat by Liverpool when Michael Owen beat us with an amazing goal. We scored two amazing goals today and it feels like a dream. Chelsea are a good side and it was tough out there.

"You can lose a Cup Final so easily but we were desperate to win this one."

The lucky North dressing room at the Millenium Sta-

WENGER: Cup of joy

dium struck again as the Gunners out-fought their bitter rivals.

Chelsea, with Jimmy Floyd Hasselbaink only half-fit after passing a fitness test on his calf problem, had chances to take the lead.

But once Parlour struck with a superb 25-yard shot and then Ljungberg scored one of the great Cup Final goals, Arsenal's record-equalling 15th appearance in the final was always going to end in glory.

Parlour did his chances of being picked by Sven Goran Eriksson for the World Cup no harm with his performance. He said: "I haven't scored as many goals as I would have liked this season but this one makes up for it. You dream of doing it when you're a kid."

Ljungberg is the first player in 40 years to score in successive Cup Finals. He said: "I aim to keep my hair red from now on. It has brought me lots of luck. That was one of the best goals I have ever scored."

A dejected Hasselbaink, who had to be substituted, said: "I am very disappointed. We had our chances but the first goal was always going to be crucial.

"My injury was a problem. It was a massive gamble to play and it didn't come off."

Pictures by Kent Gavin and Dale Cherry

FA CUP FINAL 2002: Super strike puts

ACE PARLOUR

GUNDERFUL MOMENT: Millennium celebrations for Thierry Henry and Freddie Ljungberg following the stylish strike from the Swede which put Arsenal two up

Gunners on course and Ljungberg seals it

RAYSES ROOF

ARSENAL 2
CHELSEA 0

PAUL SMITH
At the Millennium Stadium

ARSENAL completed the first leg of the Double with two stunning second-half strikes at the Millennium Stadium.

Carbon-copy goals from Ray Parlour and Freddie Ljungberg in the space of 10 minutes destroyed Chelsea in the Cardiff sunshine yesterday.

The sheer quality of those goals lifted a game seemingly heading towards extra-time — until first Parlour dispatched a 70th-minute 30-yarder of pure class to grace this domestic showpiece final.

And not to be outdone, Sweden international Ljungberg, capping a man-of-the-match performance, ensured victory with a sweet right-foot effort which was every bit the equal of Parlour's opener.

If the omens were to be believed this first final between two London sides in 20 years favoured an Arsenal victory from the outset.

No side occupying the North dressing-room had ever lost a final at this magnificent venue.

The full-strength Gunners, chasing the first leg of another Double, predictably restored England keeper David Seaman to their line-up.

And while Chelsea got a boost with striker Jimmy Floyd Hasselbaink overcoming a late fitness scare, goal-scoring semi-final hero John Terry was not so lucky, starting on the bench with an ear infection that was affecting his balance.

The clash exploded as early as the second minute when Chelsea's temperamental defender Graeme Le Saux went in high on Lauren, prompting Leeds official Mike Riley to brandish an early yellow card.

It was Arsenal who had the better of a frantic opening 10 minutes, despite forcing just the one early corner and failing to get a shot on goal with their superior possession.

When Thierry Henry did set up strike partner Sylvain Wiltord 16 minutes into the game, Celestine Babayaro's timely intervention snuffed out the danger.

Against the run of play it was Le Saux who unleashed the first shot on target from 25 yards, and after Seaman failed to handle it cleanly he was fortunate not to find another player in a blue shirt cashing in on his fumble.

Seaman then showed greater authority as he dived low to save an awkward shot from

FRED AND BURIED: Ljungberg giving Carlo Cudicini no chance with his clincher in Cardiff   *Picture: Reuters*

ARSENAL		CHELSEA
56%	Possession	44%
4	Shots on target	5
4	Shots off target	5
2	Blocked shots	0
5	Corners	4
15	Fouls conceded	15
5	Offsides	5
2	Yellow cards	3
0	Red cards	0

ATTENDANCE: 73,963

SCORERS: Parlour (70 mins)
Ljungberg (80 mins)

Frank Lampard. Arsenal's response was a move that saw Patrick Vieira crossing from the right and Dennis Bergkamp looping a header that grazed the outside of the post with Chelsea keeper Carlo Cudicini caught in two minds.

Tempers flared again in the 27th minute as Vieira's late tackle on Eidur Gudjohnsen saw him also enter the referee's book.

And referee Riley was briefly in danger of losing control, as one nasty tackle followed another — all somehow going unpunished.

All this failed to stop a spirited run by Gudjohnsen, who exchanges passes with Le Saux but failed to get enough power on his final shot.

At the other end panic ensued in the Chelsea defence with seven minutes of the first half remaining. Wiltord reached the byline and crossed for Lauren, who headed fractionally over the bar when it seemed easier to score.

While Chelsea had come more and more into the game, the below-par service provided for strikers Gudjohnsen and Hasselbaink invariably denied them a real cutting edge in front of goal.

The teams returned for the second half and with defensive frailties concerning Claudio Ranieri, Terry stepped off the bench to replace Babayaro who had looked vulnerable at times during the first 45 minutes.

Within a minute Henry should have opened the scoring. Turning Mario Melchiot in the Chelsea penalty area, though, his shot lacked any real conviction and Cudicini saved.

The tough tackling persisted, notably from Arsenal duo Parlour and Ashley Cole. But Riley consistently overlooked some obvious offences.

Chelsea forced a succession of corners, but their delivery continued to undermine some good approach play.

But in the 57th minute Hasselbaink rode a succession of challenges and threaded the ball out to Gudjohnsen and from 30 yards out the Icelander sent a curling shot towards the top corner of Seaman's goal — requiring the England keeper to tip over at full stretch.

Within two minutes Le Saux had evaded Cole's challenge to reach the byline, centring to the unmarked Lampard whose shot went woefully wide.

Suspect defending by Sol Campbell paved the way for another Chelsea attack when he gifted Le Saux the ball in his own half. However, he made

amends with a telling challenge on Hasselbaink as he turned to shoot deep inside the Arsenal penalty area.

Arsenal found themselves under a sustained period of pressure before Wiltord squandered a golden opportunity from a breakaway attack when Henry sent him clean through on goal and he blasted his first-time shot wide.

In the 69th minute Chelsea sent on Gianfranco Zola to replace the tiring Hasselbaink — and within a minute they found themselves behind.

Adams played the ball through to Wiltord and when he found Parlour with a telling pass the midfielder skipped two challenges before unleashing a right-foot curling shot into the top corner from 30 yards.

While his touch in front of goal has eluded him in the

League, Parlour's only other goal this season came in the same competition, against Gillingham in the fifth-round clash at Highbury.

Arsenal could so easily have been two up in the 77th minute when Cole broke away and shot tamely at Cudicini, but two minutes later the Gunners did put the game beyond reach of their rivals with an identical effort to their first goal.

Substitute Edu's through-ball was picked up by Ljungberg, and the in-form midfielder rode a challenge from Terry, cut inside and unleashed a right-foot shot beyond Cudicini to signal party time for the Arsenal fans.

MAN OF THE MATCH

FREDDIE LJUNGBERG - ARSENAL
The Swede has been an absolute inspiration for the Gunners since replacing the injured Robert Pires. Yesterday he fired home his seventh goal in the last six games to kill off Chelsea and seal the first half of the Double.

SHOCK: Wes Brown

Wes is set for World Cup spot

EXCLUSIVE
By PAUL SMITH

MANCHESTER United defender Wes Brown will be the shock inclusion in England's final squad of 23 for the World Cup finals, to be announced by Sven Goran Eriksson on Thursday.

The squad will also contain the name of West Ham's Joe Cole who has won a dramatic reprieve after his second-half performance against Paraguay last month.

Brown's selection, forced by the withdrawal of Gary Neville, means Arsenal's Martin Keown and Middlesbrough's Ugo Ehiogu will be left out.

Eriksson hasn't yet decided whether to take Manchester United's Phil Neville, heartbroken when left out by Glenn Hoddle for France '98, or West Ham winger Trevor Sinclair.

That issue aside, Eriksson has already picked 22 of the 23 players who will leave for Dubai a week tomorrow.

It is Brown's inclusion that will raise the most eyebrows. The United youngster, who has had a succession of injuries over the past two years, has literally crawled through the back door.

It is his versatility that has undoubtedly won him favour with Eriksson, Brown being equally comfortable in the centre or right of defence.

Cole's inclusion came after a dramatic reprieve. Following his mistake against Italy Eriksson had virtually made up his mind to omit the talented midfielder but a good display against Paraguay sees him go at the expense of Michael Carrick, Danny Murphy and Frank Lampard.

Although Eriksson refused to rule out Steve McManaman earlier in the week, the former Real Madrid star will not be surprised to find that he has not made the plane.

Tottenham's Darren Anderton, who has made a habit of gaining an 11th-hour place, has also been overlooked.

LIKELY SQUAD

Keepers

David Seaman	Arsenal
David James	West Ham
Nigel Martyn	Leeds

Defenders

Rio Ferdinand	Leeds
Wayne Bridge	Southampton
Sol Campbell	Arsenal
Danny Mills	Leeds
Ashley Cole	Arsenal
Gareth Southgate	Middlesbro
Wes Brown	Man Utd

Midfield

Nicky Butt	Man Utd
David Beckham	Man Utd
Steven Gerrard	Liverpool
Paul Scholes	Man Utd
Owen Hargreaves	B Munich
Joe Cole	West Ham
Kieron Dyer	Newcastle

Strikers

Teddy Sheringham	Spurs
Michael Owen	Liverpool
Emile Heskey	Liverpool
Darius Vassell	Villa
Robbie Fowler	Leeds

Picture: REUTERS

FREDDIE STEADY GO!....

Ljungberg puts Gunners on course for the Double

ARSENAL 2 CHELSEA 0

By PAUL SMITH

ARSENAL were on course for a dream double last night after breaking Chelsea's hearts in Cardiff.

Boss Arsene Wenger claims his Gunners can can now get the result they need at Old Trafford on Wednesday.

The North Londoners only need a draw against Alex Ferguson's men to finish off a superb season having seen Tony Adams lift the FA Cup for the third time in his long career yester-

day. Stunning second-half strikes from Ray Parlour and Freddie Ljunberg completed the first part of the Gunners' twin mission at the Millennium Stadium.

Now Wenger believes the second part is just a matter of when and not if.

The Frenchman insisted: "We knew

◄ **Turn to Page 86**

Veron storms out

£28M STAR THREATENS TO QUIT AFTER ROW WITH TEAMMATES

JUAN Sebastian Veron has walked out on Manchester United, vowing never to play for the club again.

It follows a massive bust-up with five leading United stars after United's Champions League exit against Bayer Leverkusen.

The row erupted in the dressing room almost immediately

EXCLUSIVE

By PAUL SMITH
Sports Reporter of the Year

after last Tuesday's 1-1 draw in Germany and spilled over to the airport where a group of players continued to vent their anger at the Argentinian star, claiming his indifferent performances for the club

had cost United dearly. Two United stars had to physically restrain their team-mates as the row got increasingly heated.

Veron stood his ground but later stormed off, insisting he would never pull on a United shirt again.

On Thursday he flew to Rome with his family and has remained in the Italian capital refusing to come back.

And last night there was further evidence that he may have played his last game in the Premiership.

It was revealed that Lazio's new

◄ **Turn to Page 77**

Published by MGN Ltd. (0207-293 3000) and printed by Mirror Colour Print Ltd. Registered at the Post Office as a newspaper. **Serial No. 1929** ©MGN Ltd., 2002. ■■■■■■■■■

Austria €3.30, Belgium €2.20, France €3.00 (19.68 FrF), Germany €3.00, Greece €2.50 (852 Dr), Italy €2.00, Netherlands €2.30, Portugal €2.00, Spain €2.00, Turkey (5.1m L)

A

18

9 770956 807770

THREE AND EASY: Patrick Vieira, Ashley Cole and Sol Campbell celebrate a memorable victory last night
Pic: BRADLEY ORMESHER

WE'VE TAKEN AWAY THEIR TITLE

Wenger wins Double at United and says: There is now a shift in power

By DAVID McDONNELL

ARSENE WENGER hailed a shift in the balance of Premiership power last night as Arsenal completed a record-breaking Double in Manchester United's backyard.

Sylvain Wiltord's 56th minute strike at Old Trafford secured the title with the Gunners' 14th and most important away win of the season.

Arsenal have gone through the entire season unbeaten away from home – the first time it has been done since 1889 – and have scored in every League game.

The triumph came just four days after the FA Cup success in Cardiff, and Wenger predicted his side will go on to dominate in the manner of United.

The Frenchman said: "This is an unbelievable feeling. We wanted there to be a shift in power and to bring the Premiership trophy back home to Highbury is fantastic.

"This team has been incredible all season and the spirit has been unbelievable. This is much sweeter than winning the Double four years ago because we've had to endure so many disappointments since then.

"To win it at Old Trafford is extra special and means a lot.

Manchester United are the team we wanted to beat because they have dominated for so long.

"There is a lot of rivalry between myself and Alex Ferguson but there is also respect and he congratulated me at the end.

"We have 84 points, completed the Double, not lost away from home and won 14 away games – and scored in every game this season. It is absolutely tremendous. The

TURN TO PAGE 62

UNITED ARE EVEN STRUGGLING TO FINISH SECOND..

	P	W	D	L	F	A	Pts
ARSENAL	37	25	9	3	75	33	84
Liverpool	37	23	8	6	62	30	77
Man Utd	37	24	4	9	87	45	76
Newcastle	37	21	8	8	73	49	71
Chelsea	37	17	13	7	65	35	64

LAST DAY FIXTURES
Saturday: Arsenal v Everton, Manchester United v Charlton, Liverpool v Ipswich

MARTIN LIPTON'S MATCH REPORT PAGES 62 & 63 OLIVER HOLT'S ANALYSIS PAGES 60 & 61

Published by MGN Ltd. at One Canada Square, Canary Wharf, London, E14 5AP (020-7293 3000) and printed by Mirror Colour Print Ltd.
Registered as a newspaper at the Post Office   **Serial No. 31,496**   ©MGN Ltd. Thursday, May 9, 2002   Oldham.
Austria 2.50 EUR, Belgium 1.60EUR, France 2.00EUR/FFR 13.12, Germany 2.00EUR, Greece 1.80EUR/613Dr, Italy 1.70EUR/3292Lire, Netherlands 1.80EUR, Portugal 1.70EUR (continent) 341Esc, Spain 1.70EUR/283 Pta.

9 770956 805844

BARCLAYCARD FA PREMIERSHIP >> PREMIERSHIP TITLE SHOOT-OUT:

WE ARE THE CHAMPIONS: Jubilant Arsenal players celebrate in style last night
Pics: BRADLEY ORMESHER and CHRIS TURVEY

Fergie must swallow pride and axe Veron

David McDonnell
AT OLD TRAFFORD

IT HAS been a tortuous first season for the most expensive player in British football and the misery continued for Juan Sebastian Veron last night. Manchester United's £28m signing lasted less than an hour after another unconvincing display which could prove to be his last for the club.

The meek applause for Veron as he trudged from the pitch summed up the miserable season he has endured since his move from Lazio.

It later emerged that Veron was at the centre of a training ground incident which left Nicky Butt's World Cup hopes in doubt.

The pair collided during training and Butt is now sidelined with knee ligament damage for at least a fortnight.

How ironic that Veron played an unwitting part in further injury misery to England – just a month before they meet his Argentina side in the World Cup.

However, thoughts of the World Cup were distant last night as the debate raged about Veron. Daily Mirror readers made their feelings clear in yesterday's phone poll, 61 per cent claiming Veron has been a flop at Old Trafford.

Sir Alex Ferguson may suffer from myopia with regard to Veron's form, but it seems the rest of the world disagree with him.

Defence

After Fergie's impassioned and foul-mouthed defence of his record buy earlier in the week, it remained to be seen how the Old Trafford faithful would react to the man charged with bringing to an end their domestic dominance.

Initial support when Veron's name was read out and applause when he took an early corner gave way to howls of derision as he repeatedly lost possession. For much of the first half he loitered on the side, arm raised pleading for the ball, although he would have been more effective hailing a cab.

Fergie was right. Veron is a f****** great player, but only in the right team and in the right role. With Argentina he is a class apart, only because the team is built around his unique talent.

With the colossus that is Keane at United, that is simply not going to happen at Old Trafford. Veron will have to be fitted in around the man Fergie has hailed the greatest player in United's history.

Keane was also right. Good players don't make good teams. You hardly need to be Hercule Poirot to work out who the United skipper was aiming his pre-match salvo at. And, indulging in the detective theme, the evidence for Keane's onslaught was there for all to see last night. Fierce pride may prevent Fergie from off-loading Veron, but the United boss can no longer defend the indefensible.

Veron, great player he undoubtedly is, has failed to make the impact required to justify his record-breaking transfer fee.

Fergie must now swallow his pride, accept he has made a rare error in the transfer market and put everyone – particularly Veron and the suffering United fans – out of their misery.

SYLVA LINING: Wiltord's goal that clinched the title

ARSENE HAS THE POWER
FROM BACK PAGE

turning point was the victory at Liverpool just before Christmas. We were down to 10 men but still won. That's when I knew we had the mental strength to win the title."

Defeat for United has left them empty-handed for only the third time in 12 years. And they slipped into third place last night as Liverpool beat Blackburn 4-3. The Merseysiders will guarantee the runners-up spot with a win at home to relegation favourites Ipswich in the final fixtures on Saturday, leaving United outside the top two for the first time in Premiership history.

United would then face the humiliation of having to play a qualifying match to reach the opening phase of next season's Champions League.

Boss Sir Alex Ferguson said: "People react to adversity. I've always done that and we will be more determined than ever next season. Our home form this season has come back to haunt us. We've had six defeats at home which is our worst record for 12 years.

"We have to change that and there will be changes in the summer."

YOUR VERDICT ON VERON: Just 39% agreed with Fergie.. and a whopping 61% disagreed

MANCHESTER UNITED 0 ARSENAL 1

DOZEN IT MAKE YOU PROUD

12 wins on the trot..
12 titles.. and a double that will live for ever

Martin Lipton CHIEF FOOTBALL WRITER AT OLD TRAFFORD

PERFECTION comes in many forms. For Arsenal last night, its shape was Sylvain Wiltord, its impact one that will resonate through the summer.

Not since 1889, when Preston avoided defeat in 12 games, has a team gone through an entire top-flight campaign unbeaten away from home.

But that is what Arsenal's 12th successive win, to claim a 12th championship and a second Double under Arsene Wenger, have now achieved. And deservedly so.

It may not have had the sheer electrifying drama on Anfield in 1998, nor the glittering climax of the first Wenger Double four years ago.

Yet this was even more glorious, a night Arsenal will never forget.

Crown

They did not simply usurp United's crown in front of a disbelieving Old Trafford, they did it with a performance of unyielding resolve without arguably their four most influential players.

Arsenal won at Old Trafford without Tony Adams, Dennis Bergkamp, Thierry Henry and Robert Pires.

Could any other team have done that? No, as even Sir Alex Ferguson, acknowledging Wenger's triumph with a cursory pat, must now accept.

After all, take David Beckham, Gary Neville, Nicky Butt and Ruud van Nistelrooy out of the United side – although the latter was Ferguson's bemusing choice – and what you have left was plain to see.

The Gunners claimed the Double by displaying every element that has set them apart from their Premiership rivals and summed up exactly where, for all Ferguson's churlish comments, United have fallen short.

At no stage during the campaign, as Ferguson fiddled with his tactics, have United's back-line demonstrated even a glimpse of the determination epitomised by Sol Campbell and Martin Keown. Neither, for all the drive of Roy Keane, do they possess anybody else able to fight and scrap for every ball in the manner of Patrick Vieira.

Nor, when it came to the crunch, a player on the sort of streak that Sven Goran Eriksson must hope Freddie Ljungberg will leave behind on the jet to Japan.

No real surprise, given the run of form he has been on over the past month, that Ljungberg should play a pivotal point in the overthrow of United's three-season reign.

United's anxieties to keep the title dream alive led to shocking challenges and rightful bookings for Paul Scholes, Phil Neville and Roy Keane.

They always looked exposed to one quick counter, and it came with brutal simplicity 11 minutes into the second half on an evening that had that feeling of inevitability, from the moment Ferguson's bloody-mindedness had surfaced in his selection of Juan Sebastian Veron.

Mikael Silvestre, under no pressure, gifted the ball to Ray Parlour. Swiftly, like everything Arsenal do at their best, the ball was transferred to Wiltord. Instantly, Ljungberg sensed the moment.

His run, angled across from the left, was typical of a man who has proved in the space of barely a month that there is life after Pires.

Blanc was favourite. Or so it seemed.

But Ljungberg wanted it more, just like Arsenal wanted it more, and he rode the challenge of the former France skipper, and set himself for another glory goal.

For once, Ljungberg was denied, Fabien Barthez plunging to his right. The save was excellent, but where United stood still, Wiltord continued his run, and he made no mistake as he slotted the most important goal of his club career. It was the crucial moment, but this had been a victory forged by the spirit Wenger has engendered in his team this season.

The Frenchman has transformed a side that had become scared of winning into one that cannot contemplate defeat.

United had plenty of possession, but to little effect, as Veron tried to influence but served only to exasperate.

Vieira, augmented by Edu, blotted out Keane.

With Ryan Giggs peripheral, Diego Forlan demonstrating why he is still awaiting his first United goal, and Scholes overly wound-up, the on-field spats served only to fire up Arsenal.

Scholes, teed up by Forlan, saw a shot flick the resolute Campbell on its way over the bar, and then Kanu of all people got the vital second touch after Wes Brown made the first contact to Silvestre's driven cross. Yet that was it, with the exception of a Veron free-kick straight at David Seaman.

Ashley Cole's development as a defender has never been more evident, while Lauren ensured Giggs never broke out of his shell.

Most importantly, shielded by Vieira and Edu, and with Ljungberg and Parlour unrelenting in their efforts, Campbell and Keown stood firm, repelling all would-be boarders.

Wiltord's strike saw Ferguson belatedly recognise the folly of his way, sacrificing Veron in favour of van Nistelrooy.

It was too late, as United were reduced to hit and hope, Arsenal sucked them on to the ropes and then struck as their fans sang victory songs.

Arsenal were exultant. They had every right to be. They are the masters now.

The fact that United are likely to finish third – their first time out of the top two since 1992 – will make it all the more beautiful for them.

Sorry Sir Alex, what was that about the best team in the country?

MAN UTD: Barthez, P Neville, Blanc, Brown, Silvestre, Scholes, Keane, Veron (van Nistelrooy 58), Giggs, Solskjaer, Forlan (Fortune 68).

ARSENAL: Seaman, Lauren, Keown, Campbell, Cole, Ljungberg, Parlour, Vieira, Edu, Wiltord, Kanu (Dixon 89).

Match stats

Man Utd		Arsenal
3	SHOTS ON TARGET	3
5	SHOTS OFF TARGET	4
4	CORNERS	5
4	YELLOW CARDS	2
0	RED CARDS	0

ATTENDANCE: 67,580
MAN OF THE MATCH: Parlour

THE SEASON SO FAR

— Man Utd
— Arsenal

REPRODUCED FROM THE OPTA INDEX

SHOOTING STAR: Robert Pires scores at Leeds

HOW ARSENAL RAN AWAY WITH CHAMPIONSHIP

ARSENAL became the first team since Preston in 1889 to go an entire season unbeaten away from home.. this is how their awayday dream unfolded

AUGUST 18: MIDDLESBRO 0 ARSENAL 4
Ray Parlour was sent off, but they still managed to ruin manager Steve McClaren's debut.

SEPTEMBER 8: CHELSEA 1 ARSENAL 1
A controversial penalty from Jimmy Floyd Hasselbaink ruined Arsenal's hopes of a victory.

SEPTEMBER 15: FULHAM 1 ARSENAL 3
Two goals from Thierry Henry and Dennis Bergkamp in the last eight minutes stunned Fulham.

SEPTEMBER 29: DERBY 0 ARSENAL 2
The Gunners went top with this win at Pride Park after Henry scored twice from set-pieces.

OCTOBER 13: SOUTH'PTON 0 ARSENAL 2
Rarely tested by a struggling Saints side, with Henry and Robert Pires finding the target.

OCTOBER 27: SUND'LAND 1 ARSENAL 1
Kanu seemed to have ended a 35-year run without a win in Sunderland only for Stefan Schwarz to level.

NOVEMBER 17: TOTTENHAM 1 ARSENAL 1
Manager Arsene Wenger was left frustrated after an injury-time equaliser from Gustavo Poyet.

DECEMBER 1: IPSWICH 0 ARSENAL 2
Freddie Ljungberg got the Gunners off to a flyer with a fourth-minute goal, and they never looked back.

DECEMBER 15: WEST HAM 1 ARSENAL 1
A rare goal Ashley Cole secured a point at Upton Park.

DECEMBER 23: LIVERPOOL 1 ARSENAL 2
First win at Anfield in nine years despite Giovanni van Bronckhorst being sent off in the 36th minute.

JANUARY 20: LEEDS 1 ARSENAL 1
Went a goal behind after six minutes when Robbie Fowler scored, only for Robert Pires to equalise.

JANUARY 23: LEICESTER 1 ARSENAL 3
Victory saw them move to within a point of United, and Wenger declared the title race well and truly on.

JANUARY 30: BLACKBURN 2 ARSENAL 3
Arsenal equalled Liverpool's league record of scoring in 25 consecutive games.

FEBRUARY 10: EVERTON 0 ARSENAL 1
Sylvain Wiltord scored the vital goal, with Wenger declaring: "We had to dig deep."

MARCH 2: NEWCASTLE 0 ARSENAL 2
A wonder goal from Bergkamp was the highlight of this crucial victory over their title rivals.

MARCH 17: ASTON VILLA 1 ARSENAL 2
England goalkeeper David Seaman came to the Gunners' rescue with a marvellous penalty save.

APRIL 1: CHARLTON 0 ARSENAL 3
Wenger saw his side improve their title credentials against a side with a great record in London derbies.

APRIL 29: BOLTON 0 ARSENAL 2
Freddie Ljungberg made it six goals in five games to take them five points clear, Sylvain Wiltord adds a second.

MAY 8: MANCHESTER UNITED 0 ARSENAL 1
Wiltord's strike last night clinches the Double in style.

WHY THEY ARE THE TOP GUNNERS

ARSENAL not only won the Double for the third time in their history, after similar successes in 1971 and 1998, but they set a whole host of new milestones.

☐ In domestic football they are unbeaten since December 18, when they lost at home to Newcastle. That run now stretches to 28 matches and encompasses just four draws.

☐ At Bolton, Arsenal set a Premiership record of scoring first in 26 games this season, which became 27 at Old Trafford last night.

☐ Arsenal set a new club record of 12 consecutive league victories in beating United, equalling the Premiership record set by the deposed champions in 2000.

☐ Sylvain Wiltord's goal extended Arsenal's run of scoring in successive league games to 37. The all-time record is 46, set by Chesterfield in the old Third Division (North) over two seasons between 1929-31.

☐ This was only the third time that Arsenal have won at Old Trafford in the 15 clashes there since Sir Alex Ferguson took charge. On the other two times, in 1990-91 and 1997-98, the Gunners also went on to win the title.

CAPTION: IT'S A HUGS GAME: Arsene Wenger, David Seaman and Lauren celebrate last night

---

'IT'S BRILLIANT, WE PROVED WE'RE THE BEST'

ARSENAL'S Double-winning heroes last night told of their delight at clinching the title.

Midfielder Ray Parlour, a scorer in Saturday's FA Cup triumph, said: "It's brilliant. It's been a long season, we've had our ups and downs but the lads stuck together and to win it here at Old Trafford is amazing."

Striker Freddie Ljungberg, who had a part in last night's goal, added: "We've been waiting for this for three years. United are a great side but we've proved we've been the best all season".

And France World Cup star Patrick Vieira said: "I've proved the club means a lot to me, I hope I've given the club back what it deserves.

"This is tremendous. We showed how badly we wanted to win it here. From the start of the season we knew we could win the Premiership and had the players to do so."

Veteran defender Lee Dixon said: "It just gets better and better. I'll be hanging up my boots soon but I'm going to enjoy this while I can. This is the best squad since I've been at Arsenal."

Goalkeeper David Seaman added: "We're enjoying the moment. We played really well and deserved the win."

FA CUP FINAL 2003: Passion of Pires is proof enough

ARSENAL SHOW

THE expression on Robert Pires's face told its own story.

So, the FA Cup's a Mickey Mouse competition, is it?

Arsenal's foreign legion couldn't care less about the romance of this "devalued" tournament, could they?

After he scored the winning goal, Pires momentarily lost his famous Gallic cool.

He might have won the World Cup and European Championship with France, the Double with Arsenal, and been voted Player of the Year last season.

But, as he put it: "That goal meant everything to me."

It meant, of course, that the Gunners weren't going to finish the campaign empty-handed. That their season hadn't gone completely belly-up.

On a personal level it made up for missing last season's showpiece, and the World Cup in Japan, with a cruciate ligament injury.

But most of all it meant he and his team-mates actually had the stomach for a fight.

This had been doubted by critics since the draw at Bolton last month.

True, Arsene Wenger's men were the overwhelming favourites yesterday.

But since the debacle at the Reebok they had been savaged for lacking commitment, hunger and desire.

There were even rumblings in Highbury's marble halls. We were told the Cup meant more to journeymen like Marsden, Ormerod and Oakley than to the "showboating" sorcerers of Arsenal.

But the Londoners were just as pumped up for this one.

ANTHONY CLAVANE

It was an old-fashioned scoreline – 1-0 to the Arsenal – and an old-fashioned display of resilience in the face of adversity.

A patched-up Arsenal, despite the absence of their talisman Vieira and rock Campbell, stood their ground and delivered an emphatic two-fingered gesture to their detractors.

It wasn't always pretty. At the beginning and end of the second half they were on the rack.

But George Graham must have smiled as previously scorned figures like Oleg Luzhny and Lauren revived memories of the legendary back four.

In fact, thanks to those two plus Martin Keown and Ashley Cole, David Seaman only had one save to make – albeit a breathtaking one.

It has still been a season of under-achievement.

After an awesome start to the campaign, their temperament let them down.

Never mind the injuries and bad luck. As Wenger admits, they kept taking their eye off the ball.

But in their third successive final, they were refreshingly gritty without sacrificing the exquisite quick-passing game that is their trademark.

There was a lot of nonsense written in the pre-match build-up about how a Saints win would be good for football. And how important it was for David to slay Goliath.

All neutrals were supposedly hoping the South Coast yeomen would topple the cocky aristocrats.

But the reason the old pot has lost its gleam is not because there haven't been any real upsets.

Southampton repeating their famous 1976 triumph over Manchester United would have cheered up the old romantics.

But, ever since United pulled out three seasons ago, we have been given the distinct impression the big boys don't take it seriously.

They don't come much bigger than the Gallic genius whose goal rescued Arsenal's season.

And Pires's celebrations – not to mention his post-match comments – were unequivocal.

Who could doubt Arsenal's seriousness after witnessing the sublime Henry dancing majestically past the mesmerised Claus Lundekvam time and again?

Who could doubt they were up for it after watching Lauren block Jo Tessem's goal-bound strike and Ashley Cole clear James Beattie's header off the line in the final seconds?

And what about old Safe Hands?

In possibly the final act of an amazing stint between the sticks, he pulled off another career-defining save to deny Brett Ormerod an equaliser with seven minutes remaining.

"He's an institution," raved Pires. "The best keeper in England," said Wenger. Try telling Ormerod he's a busted flush.

It was important for the pony-tailed one to go out with a bang rather than a whimper.

Now he'll hopefully be remembered for his achievements, not his mistakes.

Of course, the Cup was a consolation prize for the Gunners. No one can pretend the Champions League and the Premiership weren't their priorities.

But reports of the death of their season have been greatly exaggerated.

From the moment they linked arms for the national anthem to their team hug at the final whistle, they showed great camaraderie.

Let's not forget the bewitching beauty and high-speed grace of their football this season, especially early on when they got our pulses racing and were hailed as the dominant force in English football.

OK, a certain red-nosed Scot in Manchester had other ideas.

And Fergie won't have been too troubled about the "Are you watching, Manchester?" chants at the end.

But Arsenal are hardly finished as a force in the English game.

In fact, yesterday they gave us a glimpse of how they might be resurrected next season as a new, hungrier and more pugnacious outfit.

FINAL BOW: Seaman, Pires, Cole and Campbell lead the

THE REFEREE

GRAHAM BARBER

RATING	7
FOULS AWARDED	28
OFFSIDES	6
PENALTIES AWARDED	0
YELLOW CARDS	6
RED CARDS	0

ARSENAL RATINGS

MANAGER ARSENE WENGER

david SEAMAN — 6

Mins on Pitch	90	Drops	0
Goals conceded	0	Catch Success %	100
Saves	3	Distribution own player	16
Shots Saved %	100	Distribution opp player	16
Catches	1	Distribution %	50

LAUREN — 7

Mins on Pitch	90	Passes on target	38
Goals	0	Passes to opposition	10
Shots on target	0	Fouls given	0
Shots off target	0	Fouls conceded	0
Assists	0	Clearances	7

martin KEOWN — 7

Mins on Pitch	90	Passes on target	22
Goals	0	Passes to opposition	8
Shots on target	0	Fouls given	0
Shots off target	0	Fouls conceded	1
Assists	0	Clearances	14

oleg LUZHNY — 7

Mins on Pitch	90	Passes on target	33
Goals	0	Passes to opposition	6
Shots on target	0	Fouls given	2
Shots off target	0	Fouls conceded	3
Assists	0	Clearances	10

ashley COLE — 7

Mins on Pitch	90	Passes on target	27
Goals	0	Passes to opposition	14
Shots on target	0	Fouls given	0
Shots off target	0	Fouls conceded	0
Assists	0	Clearances	3

robert PIRES — 7

Mins on Pitch	90	Passes on target	39
Goals	1	Passes to opposition	13
Shots on target	1	Fouls given	5
Shots off target	1	Fouls conceded	1
Assists	0	Clearances	2

ray PARLOUR — 7

Mins on Pitch	90	Passes on target	30
Goals	0	Passes to opposition	10
Shots on target	0	Fouls given	3
Shots off target	1	Fouls conceded	1
Assists	0	Clearances	2

gilberto SILVA — 6

Mins on Pitch	90	Passes on target	52
Goals	0	Passes to opposition	8
Shots on target	0	Fouls given	2
Shots off target	0	Fouls conceded	0
Assists	0	Clearances	9

freddie LJUNGBERG — 7

Mins on Pitch	90	Passes on target	26
Goals	0	Passes to opposition	6
Shots on target	0	Fouls given	1
Shots off target	1	Fouls conceded	2
Assists	0	Clearances	1

thierry HENRY — 8

Mins on Pitch	90	Passes on target	20
Goals	0	Passes to opposition	11
Shots on target	0	Fouls given	1
Shots off target	5	Fouls conceded	2
Assists	0	Clearances	0

dennis BERGKAMP — 7

Mins on Pitch	77	Passes on target	15
Goals	0	Passes to opposition	18
Shots on target	0	Fouls given	3
Shots off target	1	Fouls conceded	0
Assists	0	Clearances	0

SUBSTITUTE

Mins on Pitch	13	Passes on target	7
Goals	0	Passes to opposition	2
Shots on target	0	Fouls given	1
Shots off target	0	Fouls conceded	0
Assists	0	Clearances	0

opta

that this prize really matters to Wenger's superstars

CUP CLASS

celebrations after a committed Gunners performance at the Millennium Stadium

THE KEY MOMENTS

23secs Freddie Ljungberg's pass down the right releases Thierry Henry on the edge of the penalty area. He shakes off the challenge of Claus Lundekvam and has a great chance to score the fastest goal in FA Cup Final history, but Antti Niemi makes an important save with his legs.

7min Henry cuts inside from the right and hits a low shot from 15 yards which is spilled by Niemi. Dennis Bergkamp pounces on the loose ball and, after being forced wide, his shot from the angle is cleared off the line by Chris Baird.

10min A superb 30-yard cross-field pass from Bergkamp sets up Henry on the left edge of the box. It's another good chance for the French striker, but this time he shoots weakly at Niemi.

29min Referee Graham Barber shows the game's first yellow card, to Martin Keown, and his decision is spot-on after the Arsenal defender clattered into Brett Ormerod on the touchline.

30min Saints striker James Beattie is booked for a high challenge on Oleg Luzhny as tempers flare.

38min Robert Pires punishes Saints' failure to clear the ball by sliding home the opening goal to give Arsenal the lead. Bergkamp's perfectly weighted cross sees Ljungberg's shot blocked, but the ball bounces free and Pires pounces to steer it into the bottom right-hand corner.

43min An escape for Southampton as Bergkamp drills in an angled drive from the right and Anders Svensson and Lundekvam combine to clear the ball off the line.

53min Bergkamp shows his genius by slipping his marker and curling a teasing shot towards goal which Niemi manages to palm away, and Ljungberg fires the loose ball into the side-netting.

57min Pires releases Henry and he carries the ball to the left edge of the box before hitting a low shot that Niemi tips around his left-hand post.

59min Paul Telfer is the third player to be cautioned after leaving his foot in on Pires.

64min Niemi, who has only just recovered from a knee injury to reclaim his place in the Southampton side, injures himself as he kicks a clearance and has to be carried off on a stretcher. He is replaced by Paul Jones.

74min Saints boss Gordon Strachan tries to shake things up by introducing Jo Tessem in place of Anders Svensson. It almost works as the sub's first touch is a half-volley that Lauren does well to block.

76min Marsden goes into the book for a foul on Pires, and before play restarts Bergkamp is replaced by Sylvain Wiltord.

CREATIVE TALENT: Bergkamp

83min David Seaman to the rescue as Ormerod flashes in a fierce angled drive and the 39-year-old goalkeeper manages to claw the ball to safety.

86min Strachan takes his last throw of the dice as he sends on Fabrice Fernandes for Chris Baird.

90min Michael Svensson joins the list of players who have been booked, for a foul on Ljungberg.

93min Drama to the end as Beattie's header from a corner is cleared off the line by Ashley Cole.

94min After four minutes of added time, Arsenal celebrate becoming only the third team ever to retain the FA Cup.

SOUTHAMPTON RATINGS

MANAGER GORDON STRACHAN

antti NIEMI — 6

Mins on Pitch	66	Drops	0
Goals conceded	1	Catch Success %	100
Saves	5	Distribution own player	10
Shots Saved %	83	Distribution opp player	9
Catches	1	Distribution %	53

chris BAIRD — 7

Mins on Pitch	87	Passes on target	23
Goals	0	Passes to opposition	10
Shots on target	1	Fouls given	0
Shots off target	1	Fouls conceded	2
Assists	0	Clearances	8

claus LUNDEKVAM — 6

Mins on Pitch	90	Passes on target	13
Goals	0	Passes to opposition	2
Shots on target	0	Fouls given	2
Shots off target	0	Fouls conceded	1
Assists	0	Clearances	8

michael SVENSSON — 6

Mins on Pitch	75	Passes on target	16
Goals	0	Passes to opposition	8
Shots on target	0	Fouls given	0
Shots off target	0	Fouls conceded	1
Assists	0	Clearances	0

wayne BRIDGE — 6

Mins on Pitch	90	Passes on target	25
Goals	0	Passes to opposition	21
Shots on target	0	Fouls given	1
Shots off target	0	Fouls conceded	0
Assists	0	Clearances	1

paul TELFER — 6

Mins on Pitch	90	Passes on target	21
Goals	0	Passes to opposition	13
Shots on target	0	Fouls given	1
Shots off target	2	Fouls conceded	3
Assists	0	Clearances	0

matt OAKLEY — 6

Mins on Pitch	90	Passes on target	31
Goals	0	Passes to opposition	11
Shots on target	0	Fouls given	0
Shots off target	0	Fouls conceded	2
Assists	0	Clearances	0

anders SVENSSON — 5

Mins on Pitch	90	Passes on target	18
Goals	0	Passes to opposition	5
Shots on target	1	Fouls given	0
Shots off target	2	Fouls conceded	2
Assists	0	Clearances	7

chris MARSDEN — 6

Mins on Pitch	90	Passes on target	18
Goals	0	Passes to opposition	5
Shots on target	0	Fouls given	0
Shots off target	0	Fouls conceded	4
Assists	0	Clearances	2

brett ORMEROD — 6

Mins on Pitch	90	Passes on target	10
Goals	0	Passes to opposition	4
Shots on target	0	Fouls given	1
Shots off target	2	Fouls conceded	0
Assists	0	Clearances	1

james BEATTIE — 6

Mins on Pitch	90	Passes on target	10
Goals	0	Passes to opposition	12
Shots on target	1	Fouls given	4
Shots off target	3	Fouls conceded	1
Assists	0	Clearances	2

SUBSTITUTES

Mins on Pitch	42	Passes on target	10
Goals	0	Passes to opposition	6
Shots on target	0	Fouls given	0
Shots off target	0	Fouls conceded	2
Assists	0	Clearances	0

opta index

FA CUP FINAL 2003: Pires pounces for the

Gunners rescued by sweet FA Cup

ARSENE WENGER

Wenger: He's still the best

From Back Page

Highbury. The week ended better for him than it started. I've been speaking with him about the future. He is 40 soon and it will be hard for him to play 60 games a season at that age.

"He could easily have gone and complained publicly about it but he is a super professional and showed just how good he is on the field.

"I still want him at the club. He can still do a job for Arsenal, even at worst as cover for another keeper."

Seaman helped Arsenal reach the final with a stunning save in the semi-final to deny Sheffield United.

And he was the hero again when he denied Ormerod. Seaman said: "I got something on it, it stayed out and we have a trophy at last. There's life in the old dog yet!

"We were so determined to win it. We believed in ourselves and that helped us. It wasn't a great final, but it's fantastic to win it."

Highbury goalkeeping coach Wilson believes Seaman wants to carry on. He expects him to make a decision in the next 48 hours and has advised him not to hang up his gloves just yet.

Wilson said: "It was great for David to keep a clean sheet today and he genuinely deserves it. It could well be his last game – at Arsenal anyway – but I think he will carry on playing, I think he really wants to play.

"David has got a real dilemma because I think there will be an offer to take over from me on the goalkeeping front at Arsenal.

"I had to finish when I was 33 and I think he should carry on. He was born to be a great goalkeeper and I just think he should play as long as he can play like that."

The Gunners were lifting the FA Cup for the ninth time in their history. And it was a perfect occasion for Pires, sidelined for seven months by an injury suffered in the sixth round of last season's FA Cup. The winger laid his tournament ghosts to rest with a 38th-minute strike to ease the Gunners' pain of surrendering their title to Manchester United.

Wenger added: "The team was under pressure today because we were scared to finish without a trophy. The last few weeks have been difficult, I suppose. We got the trophy we wanted today.

"We are disappointed not having won the title but we won the FA Cup and we were very, very close to a double Double. Considering the opposition, that's not bad."

Thierry Henry – who signed a new contract yesterday morning – said: "To win nothing would've been a massive disappointment. People have wondered whether I would still be here next year, but my desire is still the same and when I hear the fans singing my name I don't want to leave."

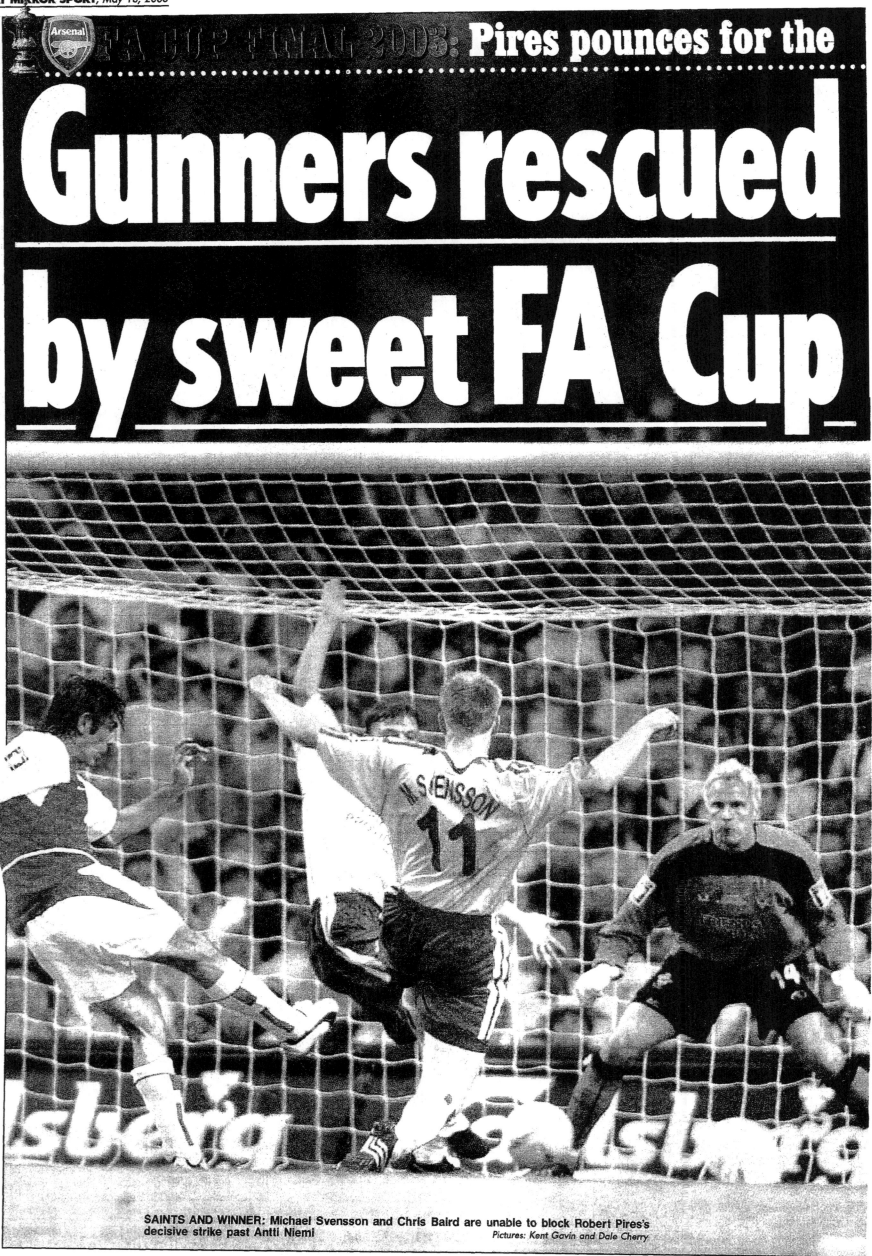

SAINTS AND WINNER: Michael Svensson and Chris Baird are unable to block Robert Pires's decisive strike past Antti Niemi

Pictures: Kent Gavin and Dale Cherry

winner as Arsenal end season on a high

HOW ironic that for all their boasts about being disciples of the beautiful game, Arsenal should get finally their hands on a trophy with the scoreline that is closest to all Gooners' hearts.

The FA Cup may have been low on Arsene Wenger's list of priorities when he was making declarations of intent about Premiership and Champions League domination a few months ago, but in the end it proved to be his saving grace.

That oldest footballing pot of them all, rescuing Mr Wenger and his Foreign Legion from the humiliation of finishing with nothing at the end of a season which was meant to bring a place in history.

No one who saw Robert Pires salute his winner, Thierry Henry jig a dance of joy or the red-and-white hordes celebrate David Seaman as he lifted the trophy in Cardiff yesterday could have been left in any doubt about the solace this triumph provided.

And while the summer will probably be spent dreaming of what could

ARSENAL 1
Pires 38
SOUTHAMPTON ...0
Attendance 72,500

SIMON MULLOCK

have been, the bottom line is that this 122nd FA Cup Final has provided Arsenal with the reality check they so desperately needed.

The roof that closed on the Millennium Stadium yesterday afternoon would have probably fallen in on them had the Gunners been humbled by Southampton's outsiders.

And while the margin of victory should have been much wider than that provided by Pires' 38th-minute strike, it will be no bad thing that in the end Arsenal were left to rely on those old Highbury virtues of guts, determination and character to repel a late Saints onslaught.

Seaman, captain for the day in the absence of Patrick Vieira and with his future in doubt as he approaches his 40th birthday, produced a save that harked back to his England pomp to deny Brett Ormerod six minutes from time. And when James Beattie finally escaped the clutches of Martin Keown deep into injury-time, he was thwarted by Ashley Cole's goal-line clearance.

Maybe this was the day when Arsenal discovered that there is a place for the legacy of the past in Wenger's grand scheme for the future. The manager himself admitted: "It would have been unthinkable for us to finish the

season without a trophy. It was a big, big blow for us, losing the Championship like we did, and it meant winning today was very important.

"The players have shown great mental strength. They have proved to everyone just how strong they are."

That Arsenal needed to produce fight along with the fantasy was down to their inability to put Gordon Strachan's men down and keep them there.

It was only two years ago that the Gunners gave Liverpool a footballing lesson – only to fall victim to two late Michael Owen goals and watch the Cup go to Merseyside.

They must have feared it was Groundhog Day when they failed to take any of the three chances that would have put them out of sight with the contest barely 10 minutes old.

There were only 23 seconds on the clock when Strachan's men enjoyed an amazing double escape.

Freddie Ljungberg delivered a raking ball that exploited Henry's pace perfectly and Claus Lundekvam was reduced to grabbing a handful of the Frenchman's shirt to keep up.

Henry admirably stayed on his feet when a fall would have brought a penalty and a likely red card for the Saints defender, but after finally breaking free of the stranglehold, he could only guide his shot at the legs of Antti Niemi.

Henry's speed of thought and movement left Lundekvam floundering again in the eighth minute and when Niemi spilled his low drive, Dennis Bergkamp's follow-up from a tight angle was cleared off the line by the alert Baird.

A third chance went begging when Bergkamp threaded a dream pass in behind Lundekvam and this time Henry's drive with his unfavoured left foot didn't carry enough power to trouble the Southampton keeper.

Those Saints fans fortunate enough to remember the club's FA Cup triumph against Manchester United at Wembley 27 years ago will have recalled that Final taking similar shape.

There was to be no happy ending this time, but Southampton still had their heroes, with 21-year-old defender

Chris Baird outstanding in only his third start for the club and keeper Niemi denying Arsenal an emphatic victory with a string of saves.

Indeed, it was Ballymena-born Baird who was the first to threaten for the Saints with a long-range drive that forced Seaman to scramble desperately across his line to save at the expense of a corner.

Michael Svensson was then too high with a volley before namesake Anders caused panic in the Arsenal defence with a twinkle-toed dash into the penalty area only for his shot to be deflected behind.

But Arsenal scored the goal they had been threatening in the 38th minute – and it was to prove to be enough.

Ray Parlour's ball into the feet of Henry was despatched into the path of Bergkamp to cross for Ljungberg. The Swede's attempt to shoot was blocked by Lundekvam, but Pires was loitering close by and the Frenchman controlled before despatching his drive between Niemi and his near post from 10 yards.

It was a sweet moment for Pires, who missed last year's title run-in and the FA Cup Final after rupturing a cruciate ligament and was recovering from surgery as Chelsea were beaten in Cardiff.

Moments later, another breathtaking example of Henry's pace and precision almost brought a second Pires goal, but he directed his shot too high when his fellow Frenchman crossed from the right.

Southampton escaped again when Lundekvam hacked clear from close to his own goalline after Bergkamp's shot had been blocked by Paul Telfer.

Arsenal continued to hold the upper hand after half-time

and Ljungberg should have done better than lift his shot into the sidenetting after Bergkamp's drive had been beaten out by Niemi.

Southampton's Finnish keeper excelled again to get a fingertip on another Henry effort that was destined for the bottom corner.

It was to be Niemi's final intervention and he was carried off in the 66th minute after pulling a calf muscle to be replaced by Paul Jones.

Referee Graham Barber booked Henry for diving in a bid to win a penalty before Arsenal's nerves started to fray when the Saints finally galvanised themselves for a sustained period of late pressure.

The thousands of Southampton fans – decked out in unfamiliar yellow and blue – thought their moment had arrived in the 84th minute when Ormerod let fly with an angled drive only to see Seaman turn the ball away spectacularly.

Those same supporters were on their feet again deep into extra time when, with keeper Jones even making a sortie into the Arsenal box for a Matt Oakley corner, Beattie jumped to connect with a downward header that was chested off the line by Cole.

Southampton still have a place in the UEFA Cup to cherish for their efforts this season and Gordon Strachan was right to be proud of his men afterwards.

He said: "On a good day or a lucky day we might have got something near the end. I thought both Ormerod and Beattie had scored.

"But I have no complaints. We were giving away strength, speed, skill and experience to Arsenal. The one thing we had was big hearts.

"We won't enjoy getting beat, but the players can be proud of themselves. I know I am. They have come off the pitch with no regrets – and that's all a manager can ask."

MAN OF THE MATCH

Thierry Henry The Frenchman was Arsenal's most potent threat and could have had a hat-trick to go alongside his Man of the Match award.

From the moment he threatened a goal inside the first minute, he didn't give Southampton's defenders a moment's peace.

Henry signed a new Arsenal contract before the Final and there will surely be many more honours to come for him over the next four years.

ARSENAL		SOUTHAMPTON
7	Shots on target	4
5	Shots off target	10
4	Shots blocked	2
4	Corners	8
10	Fouls conceded	18
3	Offsides	3
2	Yellow cards	4
0	Red cards	0

REPRODUCED FROM THE OPTA INDEX

HERO SANDWICH: Scorer Pires celebrates in the company of Ashley Cole and fired-up Gunner Thierry Henry at the Millennium Stadium

THUMBS UP: Ljungberg

MISERY: Beattie looks on

PARTY: Jeffers joins in

JOY: Campbell and Keown

CUP-LIFTING: Pires

SAD EXIT: Hero Niemi

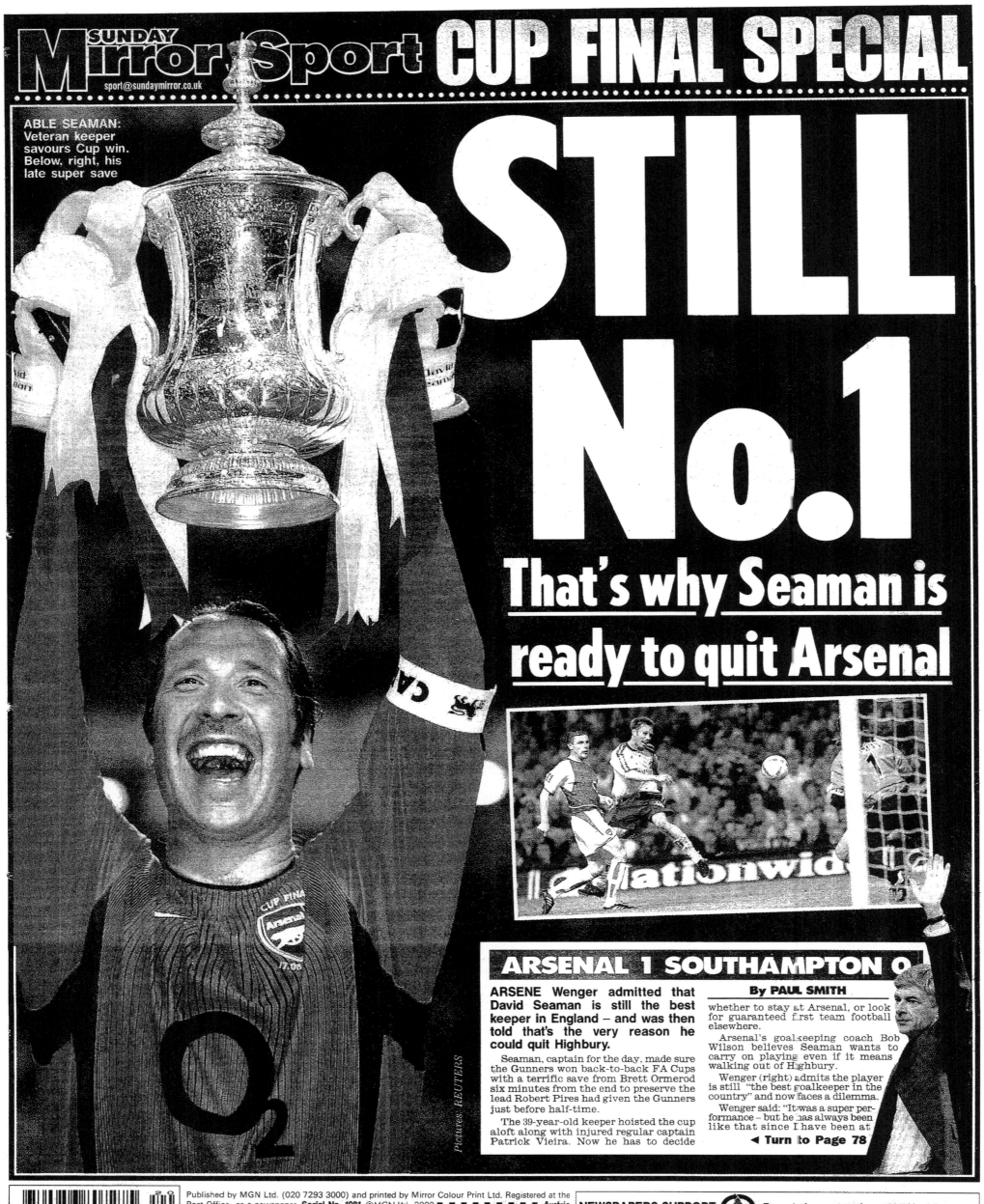

ABLE SEAMAN: Veteran keeper savours Cup win. Below, right, his late super save

STILL No.1

That's why Seaman is ready to quit Arsenal

Pictures: REUTERS

ARSENAL 1 SOUTHAMPTON 0

By PAUL SMITH

ARSENE Wenger admitted that David Seaman is still the best keeper in England – and was then told that's the very reason he could quit Highbury.

Seaman, captain for the day, made sure the Gunners won back-to-back FA Cups with a terrific save from Brett Ormerod six minutes from the end to preserve the lead Robert Pires had given the Gunners just before half-time.

The 39-year-old keeper hoisted the cup aloft along with injured regular captain Patrick Vieira. Now he has to decide whether to stay at Arsenal, or look for guaranteed first team football elsewhere.

Arsenal's goalkeeping coach Bob Wilson believes Seaman wants to carry on playing even if it means walking out of Highbury.

Wenger (right) admits the player is still "the best goalkeeper in the country" and now faces a dilemma.

Wenger said: "It was a super performance – but he has always been like that since I have been at

◀ **Turn to Page 78**

Published by MGN Ltd. (020 7293 3000) and printed by Mirror Colour Print Ltd. Registered at the Post Office as a newspaper. **Serial No. 1981** ©MGN Ltd., 2002 ■ ■ ■ ■ ■ ■ ■ ■ Austria e3.30, Belgium e2.20, France e3.00 (19.68 FrF), Germany e3.00, Greece e2.50 (852 Dr), Malta 80c, Italy e2.00, Netherlands e2.30, Portugal e2.00, Spain e2.00, Turkey (6.75m L), Cyprus £1.20 L0

ALIVE

THIERR-IFIC: Henry celebrates his second goal, and Arsenal's third, with Ray Parlour

GOTCHA: Webb Ellis trophy joins the Twickenham goodies

Bill's back where he belongs

By KEVIN GARSIDE

THE World Cup was added to England's trophy collection at Twickenham yesterday.

The golden cup, nick-named Bill after William Webb Ellis, the founder of rugby, was placed along-side the Six Nations trophy and the Calcutta Cup in the Museum of Rugby.

It was earned by blood and sweat in Australia on Saturday and has spent the last few days being passed around at functions and even on the flight that brought the team home.

But when it was finally put into position at HQ yesterday it was by gloved hands.

The museum's curator, Jed Smith, said the trophy will spend most of its time in the cabinet, but will also be taken on tour around the country.

He said: "We now have every trophy England could possibly win right here at Twickenham."

PEOPLE'S CHAMPIONS: PAGES 62-65

Henry revives Arsenal Euro dream

From MARTIN LIPTON Chief Football Writer

RAMPANT Arsenal ripped Inter to shreds last night with a record-breaking rout that represented the greatest European performance in their history.

Thierry Henry's double led the charge with further strikes from Freddie Ljungberg, Edu and Robert Pires which left the Gunners on the verge of a remarkable Champions League escape act.

And thrilled boss Arsene Wenger

Inter Milan 1
Arsenal 5

admitted that it could hardly have been sweeter.

Wenger, whose side were without skipper Patrick Vieira, Lauren, Dennis Bergkamp and Sylvain Wiltord said: "That was the most satisfying result I've had in Europe.

"I could not have expected that but I'm so proud of my players, the spirit they showed and the quality of our display."

Christian Vieri's fluked equaliser could have destroyed

Arsenal's self-belief after 12 months without an away win in Europe.

But boosted by Ljungberg's goal four minutes into the second half, the Gunners roared on to complete their best-ever win in the Champions League and leave them a win over Lokomotiv Moscow away from the knock-out phase, despite picking up just one point from their first three games.

Wenger added: "At half-time the players feared it was going against them

TURN TO PAGE 71

WENGER: Night to remember

Published by MGN Ltd. at One Canada Square, Canary Wharf, London, E14 5AP (020-7293 3000) and printed by Mirror Colour Print Ltd. at Watford and Oldham. Registered as a newspaper at the Post Office. **Serial No. 31,975** ©MGN Ltd. **Wednesday November 26, 2003** ■ ■ ■ ■ ■ ■ ■ ■ ★ Austria 2.50 EUR, Belgium 1.60 EUR, France 2.00 EUR, Germany 1.85 EUR, Greec 1.80EUR, Italy 1.70 EUR, Netherlands 1.80 EUR, Portugal 1.70 EUR (continent) 341Esc, Spain 1.70EUR, Malta 50 cents, Turkey 3,000,000Lire and Cyprus £1

CHAMPIONS LEAGUE GROUP B: INTER

The famous five steps to glory

ALL Arsenal's European doubts were dispelled with these five sensational goals in the San Siro Stadium last night.

Despite Christian Vieri's first-half equaliser of Thierry Henry's opening goal the Gunners never lost faith and after Freddie Ljungberg put them back in the lead early in the second half, the floodgates opened.

0-1 Henry's slide rule finish opens the scoring

1-2 And Henry's brilliance sets up Ljungberg

1-3 By the left Henry scores his wonder goal

1-4 And it's Edu's turn to score from the left

1-5 Pires' coup de grace with Inter in tatters

JUMP START: Thierry Henry takes to the air to celebrate his 25th-minute opener — and went one better with a stunning third

IT WAS a long 12 months. But don't tell any Arsenal fan that it was not worth the wait.

All the misery, all the anguish and all the pain that Arsene Wenger and his side have put themselves through were obliterated in 90 minutes of sheer joy at the San Siro last night.

This was the sort of display Arsenal have been promising but failing to deliver for too long, a night that rewrote the history books, not only recording their biggest away win in the Champions League, but also inflicting the heaviest home defeat an Italian side has ever suffered in the competition.

Just as Chelsea took Lazio apart three weeks ago, so the Gunners took Inter to the cleaners, arguably in even more beautifully cold-blooded fashion.

Thierry Henry was simply unstoppable, Freddie Ljungberg was back to his brilliantly inventive best, Ashley Cole and Sol Campbell proved that Englishmen can defend, and the industry of Ray Parlour and Edu meant that Patrick Vieira was not missed.

Perfection

It was footballing perfection, seven shots bringing five goals, each one a stiletto through the heart of the Italians who had stolen away from Highbury hailed as assassins themselves two months ago.

But more importantly, it was with the fusion of desire and devastation, total commitment and glorious finishing that sent out a message that will reverberate across the whole continent this morning.

Of course, Arsenal have experienced false dawns before, most spectacularly after Henry's magnificent hat-trick saw off Roma

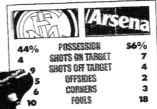

44%	POSSESSION	56%
4	SHOTS ON TARGET	7
9	SHOTS OFF TARGET	4
5	OFFSIDES	2
6	CORNERS	3
10	FOULS	18

ATTENDANCE: 44,884
MAN OF THE MATCH: Henry

REPRODUCED FROM THE OPTA INDEX · opta

GROUP B TABLE

	P	W	D	L	F	A	Pts
L Moscow	5	2	2	1	7	5	8
Arsenal	5	2	1	2	7	6	7
Inter Milan	5	2	1	2	7	10	7
D Kiev	5	2	0	3	7	7	6

Results so far: D Kiev 2 L Moscow 0; Arsenal 0 Inter Milan 3; L Moscow 0 Arsenal 0; Inter Milan 2 D Kiev 1; L Moscow 3 Inter Milan 0; D Kiev 2 Arsenal 1; Inter Milan 1 L Moscow 1; Arsenal 1 D Kiev 0; L Moscow 3 D Kiev 2; Inter Milan 1 Arsenal 5.
To play: Dec 10: Arsenal v L Moscow, Dynamo Kiev v Inter Milan.

last November. Arsenal had only won one Champions League game since, and that courtesy of Cole's escape-from-jail last-minute header against Dynamo Kiev earlier this month.

But after scoring just three goals in four-and-a-half games, they exploded into life with four in 45 minutes that left the San Siro stunned and humbled.

It was a night on which Arsenal obeyed Wenger's game-plan to the letter, making light of the clutch of absences.

Against a team with the firepower of Obafemi Martins and Christian Vieri they had to defend well, with Campbell brilliantly helping Pascal Cygan endure his trial by fire and Cole outstanding.

Yet once they settled, and Henry consigned his hamstring strain to the back of his mind, Arsenal were different class.

Their opener, brilliantly finished by Henry – who else? – on 25 minutes summed up what these Gunners can do.

Cole linked with Edu and carried

NEW-FOUND FAITH TO ROCK RIVALS

From MARTIN LIPTON

FIRST Chelsea at Lazio, now Arsenal in the San Siro. A second-class league? I don't think so.

If ever two games were designed to shatter the footballing superiority of the aristocrats of Serie A, these were they.

But more importantly than Arsenal's confirmation of the message Chelsea rammed home in the Eternal City three weeks ago will be the impact being felt across Europe this morning.

In Madrid and Turin, Munich and La Coruna, there will have been a sense of awe as they watched Arsenal's tactical triumph, a feeling English football has to be respected.

We've been told the Premiership still has much to learn from Serie A and La Liga. Yet with Arsenal now odds-on to join Chelsea and Manchester United in the knockout phase, we can truly begin to take pride in what we are developing.

Yes, all three standard bearers are lucky to have great foreign talent and any of their Champions League rivals would love to have Thierry Henry, Patrick Vieira, Ruud van Nistelrooy, Claude Makelele or Hernan Crespo in their ranks.

But Arsenal's marvellous night in Milan was equally built on Ashley Cole and Sol Campbell, just as Glen Johnson, John Terry and Frank Lampard have shone for Chelsea and Paul Scholes, Rio Ferdinand and the Nevilles stand out for United.

What is clear as never before is Premiership sides are learning how to take on the giants at their own game, wait for the weaknesses to appear and expose them to brutal effect.

Arsenal, Chelsea and United can take on the cream of Europe on better than even terms.

That is not an idle boast. It is a truth the whole of football would acknowledge.

No one wants to play them – and that is exactly how we should want it to be.

MILAN 1 ARSENAL 5, SAN SIRO

SIRO TO HERO

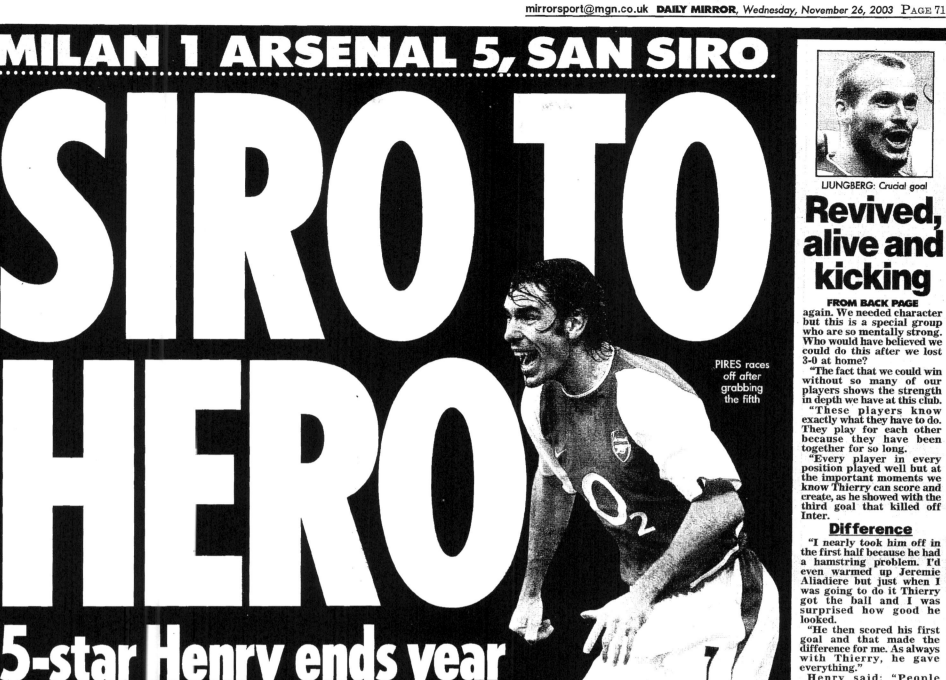

PIRES races off after grabbing the fifth

5-star Henry ends year of living dangerously

LJUNGBERG: Crucial goal

Revived, alive and kicking

FROM BACK PAGE

again. We needed character but this is a special group who are so mentally strong. Who would have believed we could do this after we lost 3-0 at home?

"The fact that we could win without so many of our players shows the strength in depth we have at this club.

"These players know exactly what they have to do. They play for each other because they have been together for so long.

"Every player in every position played well but at the important moments we know Thierry can score and create, as he showed with the third goal that killed off Inter.

Difference

"I nearly took him off in the first half because he had a hamstring problem. I'd even warmed up Jeremie Aliadiere but just when I was going to do it Thierry got the ball and I was surprised how good he looked.

"He then scored his first goal and that made the difference for me. As always with Thierry, he gave everything."

Henry said: "People speculated about our commitment but before this we didn't have all the luck.

"We didn't show the true face of Arsenal in the Champions League. Everyone was waiting for us to do something in Europe and tonight we did."

Ljungberg added: "It's easy to build on things once you get a lead and, in the second half, we relaxed a bit and played like we can.

"They had to come forward and we are a bit quick on the break. We punished them."

Martin Lipton reports from Milan

CHIEF FOOTBALL WRITER

on running as Pires took up the baton and fed Henry who turned the ball on first time towards Cole.

The England defender was dumped to the ground from behind by Javier Zanetti – although the German referee did not show any interest – but when the ball ran free Henry coolly picked his spot from 14 yards, low, right-footed and emphatic.

But Arsenal made a potentially fatal mistake when Edu sold skipper Ray Parlour horribly short in the centre-circle.

Cristiano Zanetti was away, with Vieri peeling off to his left to receive the pass and while Campbell closed the Aussie-raised striker down the ricochet off his heel caught Jens Lehmann flat-footed as the ball looped in off the bar.

That was the moment when, as Wenger conceded, he feared his players might fold and Lehmann made a vital stop to keep out Marco Materazzi's free-kick.

Conviction

But four minutes after the break Arsenal were back in front. Cygan's interception sent Henry one-on-one with Materazzi.

It was no contest and when Henry found Ljungberg unmarked the Swede took his time before slipping home past Francesco Toldo.

From then on Arsenal had to defend with conviction, but always looked likely to take the game out of Inter's reach on the break as Henry galloped away down the left, twice testing Toldo.

Five minutes from time Henry once again showed Inter a clean pair of heels as he bore down on goal to stroke his 13th of the season into the bottom corner.

Arsenal were rightly ecstatic, Inter utterly destroyed, and the last two minutes summed up how swiftly a match can be transformed into an unforgettable classic. First Cole's long ball put Henry away again, and when Pires and Ljungberg dummied, Brazilian midfielder Edu was left with an open goal.

So was Pires a minute later after substitute Jeremie Aliadiere had cruised down the right wing, the Frenchman keeping his feet to find the target and set off another chorus of "Swing Low, Sweet Chariot".

Of course, as Wenger warned, his men cannot stumble again against Lokomotiv Moscow in a fortnight.

But now, perhaps, they will believe in themselves properly in the biggest competition of all. And nobody, anywhere, will take them lightly.

INTER MILAN: Toldo, Cordoba, Javier Zanetti, Cannavaro (Pasquale 59), Materazzi, Brechet, Cristiano Zanetti, Lamouchi (Almeyda 57), Van der Meyde (Cruz 69), Martins, Vieri.

ARSENAL: Lehmann, Cole, Campbell, Toure, Cygan, Ljungberg, Parlour, Edu, Pires, Kanu (Silva 73), Henry (Aliadiere 89).

Celts stay on course

Celtic 0 Bayern Munich 0

MANAGER Martin O'Neill was delighted to have secured the point which means Celtic now have to go to French champions Lyon needing a draw to progress to the last 16.

"I think you saw at the end of the game how Bayern celebrated – they were delighted to get something out of this game," he said.

"I'm not disappointed. I thought we did terrifically well. We were magnificent.

"At the start of the campaign we all thought Bayern would be the side which went away and Celtic, Anderlecht and Lyon would battle for the remaining spot, but it is not like that.

"We will go with plenty of confidence to Lyon."

WINSTON'S A WINNER

L Moscow 3 Dynamo Kiev 2

SUBSTITUTE Winston Parks grabbed Lokomotiv's 89th-minute winner to put them top of Group B.

Lokomotiv defender Vadim Evseev, who was hailed a national hero after scoring the only goal in last week's Euro 2004 play-off between Russia and Wales, was key to their win and he must now try to tame Arsenal's Thierry Henry in the decider at Highbury on December 10.

By NEIL KERBER AND DAVID BLACK
FOR MORE GREAT CARTOONS LOG
ON TO: www.cantkickwontkick.com

GROUP A TABLE

	P	W	D	L	F	A	Pts
Celtic	5	2	1	2	6	4	7
Anderlecht	5	2	1	2	4	5	7
Lyon	5	2	1	2	4	5	7
B Munich	5	1	3	1	5	5	6

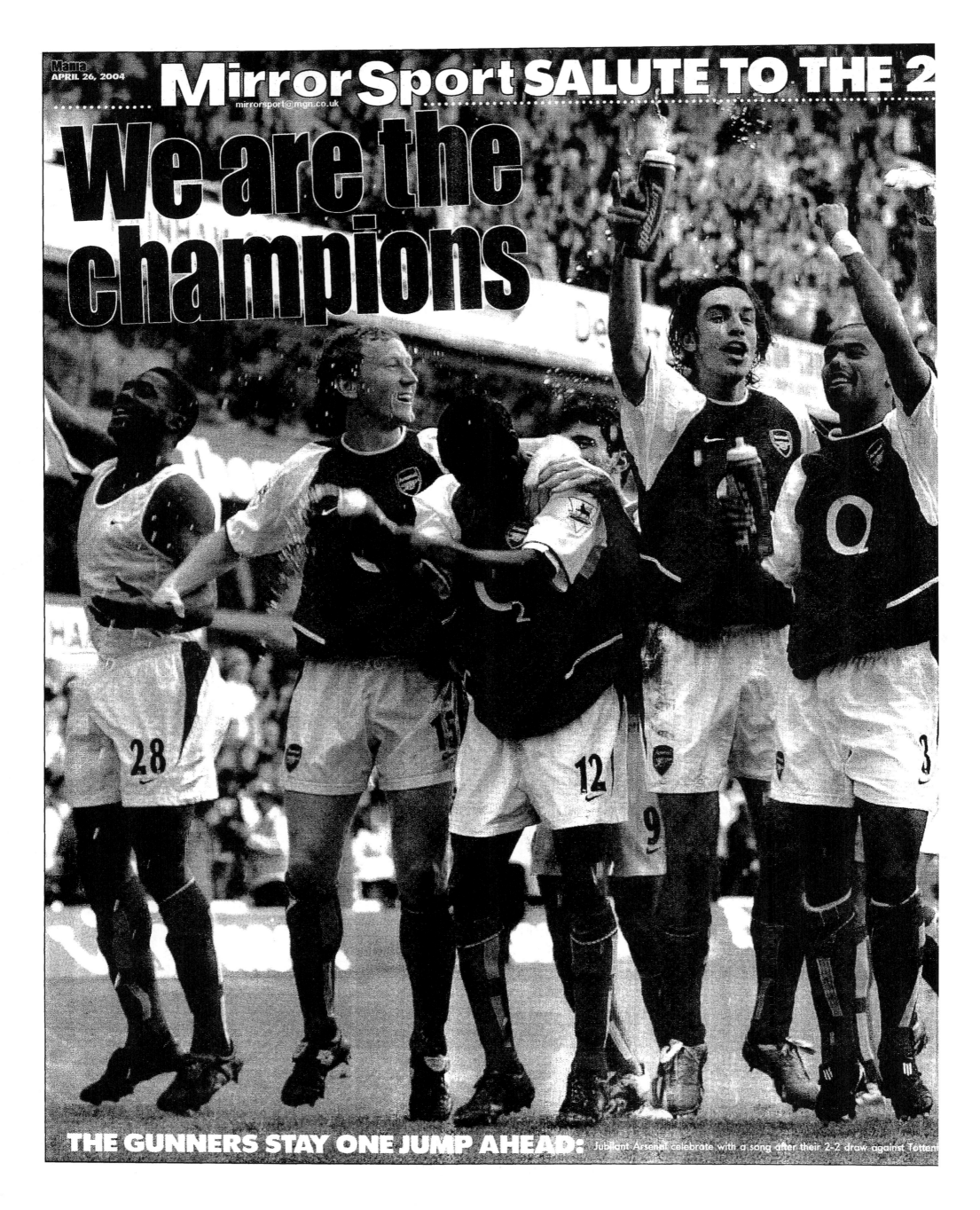

MirrorSport SALUTE TO THE 2

mirrorsport@mgn.co.uk

Jubilant Arsenal celebrate with a song after their 2-2 draw against Tottenham

We are the champions

THE GUNNERS STAY ONE JUMP AHEAD: Jubilant Arsenal celebrate with a song after their 2-2 draw against Tottenham

Gunners' scroll of honour

Championships (13)
1931, 1933, 1934, 1935, 1938, 1948, 1953, 1971, 1989, 1991, 1998, 2002, 2004

FA Cups (9)
1930, 1936, 1950, 1971, 1979, 1993, 1998, 2002, 2003

League Cups (2)
1987, 1993

Cup Winners Cup (1)
1994

Fairs Cup (1)
1970

League & FA Cup Double (3)
1971, 1998, 2002

FA Cup & League Cup Double (1)
1993

Appearances in FA Cup Final (16)
1927, 1930, 1932, 1936, 1950, 1952, 1971, 1972, 1978, 1979, 1980, 1993, 1998, 2001, 2002, 2003

Appearances in League Cup Final (5)
1968, 1969, 1987, 1988, 1993

Cup Winners Cup Final Appearances (3)
1980, 1994, 1995

Appearances in UEFA (Fairs) Cup Final (2)
1970, 2000

Arsenal

...ham at White Hart Lane clinched their THIRD Premiership title under the managership of Arsene Wenger.

Picture: KENT GAVIN

.. Portsmouth 5 Middlesbrough 1.. Blackburn 1

IT'S GUNNER

THE BIG STORIES

DEFOE GETS SVEN CALL

PAGE 92

HARRY: I'M STAYING

PAGE 89

FIRST AGAIN

IT'S been another great week for Sunday Mirror Sport readers as our rivals caught up on some of the stories we've brought you in the last three months.

Some papers finally told their readers about Manchester United's preparations for a summer swoop for Wayne Rooney – we told you about it on February 15.

Then there was the revelation that Teddy Sheringham would not be staying at Portsmouth. Paul Smith broke that story on March 21.

Some of our rivals got very excited about Ruud van Nistelrooy's declaration that he would not be moving to Italy or Spain – we brought you that story on April 18.

Along with our superlative PREMplus pull-out, it all makes for a brilliant service.

ROONITED
Fergie to lead chase for Wayne as Everton prepare to sell star

EXCLUSIVE: Rooney

Walk out on United! What a load of rubbish

EXCLUSIVE: Van Nistelrooy

SHERI'S SKY ROUTE

VETERAN England striker Teddy Sheringham is finally considering retirement.

Regardless of whether Portsmouth stay up or not, manager Harry Redknapp has decided...

EXCLUSIVE: Sheringham

THE PREMIERSHIP	P	W	D	L	F	A	GD	Pt
Arsenal	38	26	12	0	73	26	47	90
Chelsea	38	24	7	7	67	30	37	79
Man Utd	38	23	6	9	64	35	29	75
Liverpool	38	16	12	10	55	37	18	60
Newcastle	38	13	17	8	52	40	12	56
Aston Villa	38	15	11	12	48	44	4	56
Charlton	38	14	11	13	51	51	0	53
Bolton	38	14	11	13	48	56	-8	53
Fulham	38	14	10	14	52	46	6	52
Birmingham	38	12	14	12	43	48	-5	50
Middlesbro	38	13	9	16	44	52	-8	48
South'mptn	38	12	11	15	44	45	-1	47
Portsmouth	38	12	9	17	47	54	-7	45
Tottenham	38	13	6	19	47	57	-10	45
Blackburn	38	12	8	18	51	59	-8	44
Man City	38	9	14	15	55	54	1	41
Everton	38	9	12	17	45	57	-12	39
Leicester	38	6	15	17	48	65	-17	33
Leeds	38	8	9	21	40	79	-39	33
Wolves	38	7	12	19	38	77	-39	33

GUN FIRE: Patrick Vieira hits Arsenal's winner

INSIDE: YOUR GREAT PULL-OUT
PREMplus

Bolton 0 Fulham 2 .. Wolves 0 Tottenham 2..

Birmingham 1.. Charlton 2 Southampton 1

GET BETTER

Wenger's chilling warning as awesome Arsenal make history

ARSENAL stormed into the record books as the first English side in modern-day history to go through the season without a League defeat.

After beating Leicester City 2-1 and lifting the Premiership trophy in front of their ecstatic fans, skipper Patrick Vieira said: "This team will be remembered forever.

"I'm really proud of our achievement. It was our intention from the start of the season not to lose a game in the Premiership and we have done that. It is an absolutely magnificent feat."

Vieira scored the winning goal after Paul Dickov had given the Foxes a shock first-half lead and Thierry Henry had equalised from the spot immediately after the restart.

Arsenal manager Arsene Wenger said: "This is a fantastic moment for us. I did not believe it was possible but we have done it.

"I have always had that dream and we have fulfilled it. This is the best title win for me.

"We have always been at the top of the table and it is very tough when you are leading throughout the season.

"But I have fantastic players who have made it possible and to not lose is amazing.

"There is always room to get better and this team want to improve. They are a set of players who are hungry for more.

"We started off badly but, in the end, we were focused on winning. We wanted to finish the season on a good note and they wanted to finish at home with a win.

"We wanted everything to be perfect and the only way we could do that was by beating Leicester.

"They were dangerous opponents because, having been relegated, they could relax and it was a difficult game to go into psychologically."

Leicester boss Micky Adams paid tribute to the Gunners. He said: "We gave a good account of ourselves but in the end we lost another match.

"We tried to come to Highbury and spoil the party but what they have achieved is amazing.

"They will go down in the annals of history as one of the greatest teams ever."

Claudio Ranieri admitted he was on the verge of tears after CHELSEA'S 1-0 win over LEEDS.

His four-year reign is expected to end this summer, despite leading the club to second in the Premiership

ARSENAL 2
LEICESTER 1
By ANTHONY CLAVANE

and the last four of the Champions League.

After a ten minute standing ovation from a packed Stamford Bridge – which included applause from Peter Kenyon and Roman Abramovich – Ranieri's players gave their manager a fitting send off.

The squad formed a guard of honour towards the tunnel and applauded as the Italian made his way off the pitch fighting back the tears.

Ranieri said: "It was emotional for me, especially when my players clapped me off like that.

"I may be a professional but I'm Latin and can be emotional and this club will always have a special place in my heart.

"The supporters have been fantastic to me and I want to thank them all for backing me. Even you journalists have killed me before but have helped me to live again.

"It has been a fantastic season and now Chelsea need to improve on what they have done this year. The basis is there to do that."

Sir Bobby Robson hailed his NEWCASTLE team after they grabbed a place in next season's UEFA Cup after a 1-1 draw at LIVERPOOL.

He said: "We have had to play four games in 10 days – nobody else has had to do that – and we were on our knees at the end."

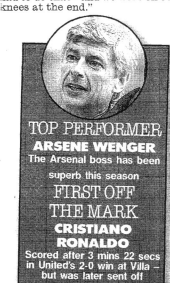

TOP PERFORMER
ARSENE WENGER
The Arsenal boss has been superb this season
FIRST OFF THE MARK
CRISTIANO RONALDO
Scored after 3 mins 22 secs in United's 2-0 win at Villa – but was later sent off

LIVERPOOL 1 NEWCASTLE 1

NEWCASTLE boss Sir Bobby Robson blasted the "ungrateful people" who have criticised his side's form.

Robson said: "We have had a difficult two weeks.

"But I've been in deep water before and come through it.

"We have ungrateful people around the place. But we get on with our lives without those sort of people."

See PREMplus

ASTON VILLA 0 MAN UTD 2

ASTON Villa boss David O'Leary attempted to put a brave face on his team's UEFA Cup heartache by admitting he would be delighted if the Midlanders missed out by one place next year as well.

He said: "We were outclassed by a top team.

"If I am talking about the team finishing sixth in 12 months' time, I would be delighted."

See PREMplus

CHELSEA 1 LEEDS 0

CLAUDIO RANIERI revealed how he said 'goodbye' to his Chelsea players after their victory over Leeds – in case he does not get another chance.

He said: "I wanted to say goodbye just in case I don't have another opportunity.

"When my players clapped me it was very emotional, and also when the fans shouted my name."

See PREMplus

FOOTBALL LATEST

South Africa win World Cup

MABBUTT

SOUTH AFRICA will stage the 2010 World Cup.

They beat off a challenge from Morocco in the first round of voting to become the first nation from the continent to be awarded the World Cup.

The decision will heal the heartbreak suffered by the South Africans after they lost the 2006 Finals by a single vote to Germany.

Gary Mabbutt, who has been an ambassador for the South African bid, was overjoyed.

He said: "This is a wonderful gift to the people of South Africa."

UNITED PLOT MILNER RAID

MANCHESTER UNITED will test James Milner's resolve to drop into the First Division with Leeds.

The England Under-21 international rejected the chance to move to Spurs during the week despite Leeds accepting a £4.5m bid.

Ferguson is set to move in on the Yorkshire club for a player he has admired since he first broke into the Leeds team as a 16-year-old.

And United are certain that Milner will find it impossible to reject the chance to stay in the Premiership at Old Trafford.

Walt's snub to Chelsea

SAMUEL

WALTER SAMUEL has warned Roma that he will stay if they try to sell him to Chelsea ahead of Real Madrid.

Stamford Bridge chief executive Peter Kenyon has had a £15m offer for the Argentine hardman accepted by the Roman giants – and that is £7m more than the bid tabled by Real.

But Samuel has set his heart on moving to Spain ahead of England.

Roma president Franco Baldini said: "We have received many good offers for Samuel but it is Real Madrid who have the advantage because they are the choice of the player."

VAN'S THE MAN FOR O'LEARY

ASTON VILLA are poised to win the race to sign dominant Dutch midfielder Mark van Bommel.

Villa manager David O'Leary wants Van Bommel as his key summer signing after appearing to miss out on Muzzy Izzet.

Several other Premiership clubs, including Tottenham, have been chasing van Bommel, who still has a year remaining on his current contract with Dutch club PSV Eindhoven.

Dion lined up for Coventry return

DUBLIN

DION DUBLIN is being lined up for a emotional return to Coventry City – after being axed by Aston Villa.

The veteran striker has been told his contract at Villa Park will not be renewed.

And his former club are poised to offer him the chance to extend his playing career.

O'Leary reckons Dublin has at least two more seasons in him outside the top flight.

He said: "In a Division One team that is progressive and ambitious, Dion would do a fantastic job. He is a massive influence."

GUNNERS ON

TOTTENHAM 4
Naybet 37, Defoe 61, King 74, Kanoute 88

ARSENAL 5
Henry 45, Lauren 55 (pen), Vieira 60, Ljungberg 69, Pires 81

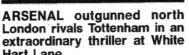

paul SMITH

ARSENAL outgunned north London rivals Tottenham in an extraordinary thriller at White Hart Lane.

In a match described by both club coaches as the crazy version of what is normally a tight game, nine goals hit the back of the net – scored by as many different scorers, for the first time in the Premiership.

There was little evidence of what was to follow in a subdued first half which brought just two chances – and two goals.

Noureddine Naybet opened the scoring for Tottenham but an injury-time equaliser by Thierry Henry saw the teams go in level.

What was to follow bordered on complete madness as two defences lost their heads.

After Lauren had put Arsenal ahead from the spot and Patrick Vieira had extended the visitors' lead six minutes later, you suspected the game was as good as over.

But one defensive error after another was punished as Spurs reduced the deficit through Jermain Defoe and Arsenal restored their two-goal cushion through Freddie Ljungberg to make it 4-2.

When Ledley King headed home Spurs' third of the afternoon and Robert Pires ran rings round the Spurs defence to make it 5-3 you thought surely that had to be the lot.

But Fredi Kanoute stepped off the bench to set up a nail-biting finish that almost brought an equaliser for the hosts when Michael Carrick shot inches wide in injury time.

Arsene Wenger said: "Derby games are normally tight with few chances

VERDICT

If you're a fan, you might see a game like this in the flesh once in a lifetime if you're lucky. If you're a manager, once in a lifetime is quite enough

ATTENDANCE: 36,095

but I have to say this was the crazy version today. Naturally I was pleased that we had come from behind and the team showed tremendous character – but I wasn't best pleased with the goals we conceded.

"It was bordering on madness – but I would have been very disappointed if we hadn't left with the three points.

"I thought we were rather subdued in the first half and Tottenham showed great fighting spirit. But the equaliser at the end of the half changed the balance of the game.

"We played to our strengths after the break and the goals followed. But it wasn't easy on the eye. I relaxed briefly when we had those two-goal

advantages – but they didn't last that long."

Spurs boss Martin Jol would have been far happier if the game had finished at half-time. He said: "The way we played in the first half pleased me and if I can take anything from the game there were encouraging signs before the break.

"I can't even begin to explain what happened afterwards. I would have to agree with Arsene Wenger, it was slightly crazy out there.

"I think my players had birds flap-ping around in their heads – it was extraordinary. I have dealt with players losing the ball in midfield but three of Arsenal's goals came when we gave the ball away at the back.

"If someone had said we would score four goals against one of the best teams in Europe and still lose the game I would have said they were mad. But this was no ordinary game."

Spurs began brightly as Arsenal appeared content to sit deep and soak up home pressure. And barely six minutes had passed when keeper Jens

Spurs left reeling as Reds win a thriller

SUCCESSFUL LAUR FIRM: Lauren celebrates his penalty – which made it 2-1 to the Gunners – with Thierry Henry
Picture: Reuters

1-0 | 1-1 | 1-2 | 1-3

Lehmann was called into vital action.

Defoe's pace took him beyond Lauren and when his cross fell for Pedro Mendes, Arsenal's German keeper saved well at the near post.

For all their possession, though, Jol's side didn't threaten again un-til the 17th minute when Robbie Keane's shot on goal was blocked.

The breakthrough eventually came in the 36th minute. Carrick's free-kick eluded a clutch of players be-fore falling kindly for Naybet to fire home – although his decision to cel-

ebrate with the crowd didn't please referee Steve Bennett who immedi-ately booked him.

A minute had barely passed before Lehmann was called into action again when he prevented Pascal Cy-gan from heading into his own net.

Arsenal's French defender almost made amends a minute later when Paul Robinson saved his towering header from a Dennis Bergkamp free-kick.

As Spurs looked good for an interval lead, though, their defence

CLOUD NINE

MAN OF THE MATCH

PATRICK VIEIRA
A sublime display from the Arsenal captain. While all around him appeared to be losing their heads, he stayed calm

TOTTENHAM		ARSENAL
6	Shots on target	7
3	Shots off target	4
13	Shots blocked	0
20	Corners	4
5	Fouls conceded	11
3	Offsides	5
0	Yellow cards	0
	Red cards	0

RATINGS

TOTTENHAM: Robinson 7, Naybet 6, Mendes 7 (Davies 7), Keane 7 (Gardner 6), Brown 6 (Kanoute 7), Edman 7, Ziegler 7, Pamarot 7, Defoe 8, Carrick 7, King 7.

ARSENAL: Lehmann 7, Cole 7, VIEIRA 9, Ljungberg 8, Reyes 7 (Pires 7), Bergkamp 7 (Van Persie 7), Lauren 7, Henry 7, Fabregas 7, Cygan 7, Toure 7.

MANAGER RATINGS: Jol 7, Wenger 7.
REFEREE: S Bennett 8.

Robert Pires had scored in the previous three encounters between these rivals and it came as no surprise when he made it four in as many games yesterday

2-3 · **2-4** · **3-4** · **3-5** · **4-5**

went to sleep and Henry latched on to Lauren's long pass to score.

No one could have predicted what was to follow. Arsenal came out firing on all cylinders and when Ljungberg was dragged down in the box, Lauren stepped up to make it 2-1.

On the hour Vieira strode through the Spurs defence like a knife through butter to make it 3-1.

But barely a minute later Defoe left a static Arsenal defence dead and unleashed a thunderous shot into the top corner.

You could barely draw breath before Ljungberg capitalised on another horrific defensive howler and made it 4-2.

Then King rose unopposed in the area in the 74th minute – and it was 3-4.

Surely the goals had come to an end? Not so. Pires came off the subs' bench and made a mug of Noe Pamarot before making it 5-3.

But there was still somehow time for Kanoute to set up that nail-biting finish.

NO WAY JOSE: White Hart pain for Reyes from a high challenge by Erik Edman
Picture: Kent Gavin

BARCLAYS PREMIERSHIP GUNNERS GO GOAL CRAZY:

MAGNIFIQUE

ROBIN VAN PERSIE gets the rout in motion

1-0 8 MINS

ROBERT PIRES nods home his first of the night

2-0 12 MINS

PIRES grabs his second as Arsenal take control

4-0 50 MINS

3-0 37 MINS PATRICK VIEIRA lobs Richard Wright

EDU scores a penalty on his final appearance

5-0 70 MINS

BERGKAMP is rewarded for his super show

6-0 77 MINS

MATHIEU FLAMINI rounds off the scoring

7-0 85 MINS

WENGER HAILS WONDER SHOW

FROM BACK PAGE

that I'm not in the thick of it – but then maybe I would spoil it! It was superb to watch.

"Our team spirit and belief is back and the togetherness is there.

"It was a great performance because there was always something sharp going on with some fantastic touches. Every game is a new challenge but we have shown also that we have improved defensively. A season is a long time but this team is growing together and improving all of the time."

Wenger was glowing in his praise for Bergkamp who made three goals and scored one which left the crowd chanting: "One more year" as they made it clear they want him to stay.

But Wenger was reluctant to commit himself over whether Bergkamp will be given a new one-year contract.

Wenger said: "If it was a referendum then yes he would be staying! But we will sort it out together. But he has shown again his class and his contribution.

"Dennis is 36 and you cannot base a whole season on his contribution. He cannot play 50 games because he will be 37 next year. Dennis accepts that already but he wants to play a part.

"I can understand the fans. He is highly loved here and deserves it."

WELL DEN: Wenger congratulates Dennis Bergkamp

Arsenal 7 Everton 0 from Highbury

SEVEN

Arsenal fire frightening FA Cup Final warning to Fergie's men

Martin Lipton

ARSENAL'S message to Manchester United could not have been louder: Be afraid. Be very afraid.

At the end Highbury stood in tribute to Arsene Wenger's men, saying goodbye to Edu and the famous red shirts but begging for a final season from pass master Dennis Bergkamp with the chasm between the best and the rest truly gaping.

As the Arsenal players were enjoying a delirious lap of honour, shamed Everton deserved to be on the receiving end of the verbal drubbing from David Moyes that was just as fearful as the pasting they had taken on the pitch.

It may have been Chelsea who have been setting all the records, rightly taking the Gunners' crown and proclaiming themselves the best in the business.

But last night at least it was awesome Arsenal's turn to break a couple of their own, the biggest win under Wenger and their best since the Premiership began 12 years ago, earned by a display of dazzling brilliance.

They were worth it too, a class apart from the side that will accompany them into the Champions League next season, although the fact Arsenal are 22 points ahead of the Toffees speaks volumes about the true quality of the Premiership.

This was why Wenger insists his team are the best attacking unit in the country – the runs electric, the passes instinctive, the finishing immaculate, a fitting farewell to the shorts that will be exchanged for the club's original redcurrant for their final year at their spiritual home. Of course it helps when you have a player with the vision of Bergkamp, who was the orchestrator-in-chief of a night of sustained and sublime genius.

It is made easier when you can add in the intelligence of Edu, who said his own goodbyes with a display that suggests Wenger may live to regret his departure, the drive of skipper Patrick Vieira, and the zest of Robin van Persie and Jose Antonio Reyes.

Of course, the brutal truth is it will count for nothing and the season will be remembered only as a disappointment if they do not lift the FA Cup at Cardiff in nine days' time.

But more importantly, more chillingly for Sir Alex Ferguson and his team, Wenger was able to ease Sol Campbell and Thierry Henry back into harness ahead of their trip to the Millennium Stadium and their morale could not be higher.

Everton's humiliation could not have been deeper, as boss Moyes' admission of being "totally embarrassed" made clear.

Yet even had they been bang on the button and completely committed, it would not have made much difference. Arsenal were simply outstanding.

Maybe it helped, too, they were given a wake-up call when Mikel Arteta shot straight at Jens Lehmann after waltzing into the box after three minutes.

Within another nine, as Bergkamp took up the baton, the only question was how many.

The beautiful angled pass delivered beyond the Everton centre-backs for van Persie to rifle home first-time belonged in an art gallery. The ball that released Reyes in the build-up to the second would have had a "priceless" tag attached to it.

When Reyes pulled back, the beneficiary was Robert Pires, steering his rebound header in off the bar after former Gunner Richard Wright made the first of many top drawer saves.

Everton had no answers, the mesmerising movement too much for them and if there was a surprise it was that Arsenal had to wait for the 37th minute to get their third. It was worth the wait in every aspect, arguably the team goal of the season, with Edu's surge followed by an instant flick by Reyes, true genius from the outside of Bergkamp's boot, and Vieira's cultured dinked finish.

Everton looked punch-drunk, but if they thought things could not get any worse, the arrival of Henry in place of van Persie at the interval suggested otherwise.

Arsenal cut loose despite Vieira making way for Mathieu Flamini, with Lee Carsley playing an inadvertent part in the next two goals.

When the midfielder tried to cut out Henry's pass, it turned into a perfect through-ball for Pires' 17th of the season and 20 minutes from time the Irish international midfielder handled the French substitute's chipped cross.

Edu calmly rolled home the spot-kick into the North Bank net as Everton prayed for Alan Wiley's final whistle.

Not surprisingly, the biggest cheer came when Bergkamp charged down David Weir's clearance and strolled on before rolling home what was only his seventh of the season, the demands for Wenger to offer the Dutchman a last 12 months echoing round the ground.

There was time for one more. Henry crossing from the left, Cesc Fabregas turning back and Flamini slotting home.

It will not be that easy in Cardiff. But Arsenal have to win something. And if Bergkamp is not around next season, he is in the mood to make sure he goes out with a bang.

ARSENAL: Lehmann, Lauren, Campbell, Senderos, Cole, Pires (Fabregas 64), Vieira (Flamini 45), Edu, Reyes, Bergkamp, Van Persie (Henry 45).
EVERTON: Wright, Hibbert, Weir, Yobo, Pistone, Carsley, McFadden, Watson, Arteta (Ferguson 75), Kilbane, Beattie (Bent 45).

DUTCH OF CLASS: Philippe Senderos embraces hero Dennis Bergkamp

65%	POSSESSION	35%
13	SHOTS ON TARGET	3
7	SHOTS OFF TARGET	5
3	OFFSIDES	3
4	CORNERS	2
9	FOULS	14
2	YELLOW CARDS	0
0	RED CARDS	0

ATTENDANCE: 38,073
MAN OF THE MATCH: Bergkamp

TOP OF THE TABLE

	P	W	D	L	F	A	Pts
(C) Chelsea	37	29	7	1	71	14	94
Arsenal	37	25	8	4	86	34	83
Man Utd	37	21	11	5	56	25	74
Everton	37	18	7	12	43	43	61
Liverpool	37	16	7	14	50	40	55
Bolton	37	15	10	12	46	42	55

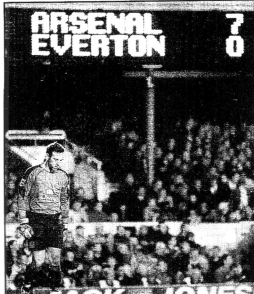

ARSENAL 7
EVERTON 0

WHAT A LOVELY SCORE.. but not if you're Richard Wright

BIGGEST WINS IN THE PREMIERSHIP

Man Utd 9 Ipswich 0 March 1995
Andy Cole led the way with five goals, with Mark Hughes (2), Paul Ince and Roy Keane also netting for United against an Ipswich team who finished bottom at the end of the season.

Newcastle 8 Sheff Wed 0 Sept 1999
Alan Shearer bagged five – including two penalties – as relegation-bound Wednesday were routed. Aaron Hughes set the ball rolling, while Kieron Dyer and Gary Speed netted in the second half.

N Forest 1 Man Utd 8 Feb 1999
Ole Gunnar Solskjaer came off the bench to fire four goals in the last 10 minutes. Andy Cole and Dwight Yorke each got two. Alan Rogers briefly levelling matters for Forest, who went down at the end of the campaign.

OTHERS
Arsenal 7 Everton 0 - May 2005. Blackburn 7 N Forest 0 - Nov 1995 (Shearer 3, Bohinen 2, Newell, Le Saux). Man Utd 7 Barnsley 0 - Oct 1997 (Cole 3, Giggs 2, Scholes, Poborsky).

Football Latest

City want Stewart

MARCUS Stewart is poised to fulfil a lifelong dream by joining Bristol City on a free transfer – the club he supported as a boy. Brian Tinnion, boss of the League One outfit, wants Sunderland striker Stewart to lead his side's bid for promotion next season after they failed to make this year's play-offs. Tinnion, in talks with Stewart this week, said: "He is real quality."

STEWART: Hopes

RITCHIE'S SIT IN

ANDY RITCHIE, who has impressed at Barnsley since taking over from Paul Hart in March, will sit down with chairman Gordon Shepherd in the next 48 hours with a view to taking the job permanently.

Ritchie said: "I'm very pleased with the way it's gone – we'll see what comes out of the talks."

Hold out for Hierro

BOLTON boss Sam Allardyce has told Fernando Hierro to rip up his retirement plans after claiming only Frank Lampard has outshone him this year.

HIERRO: Backed

Bolton star Hierro, 37, has said he will quit next month, but Allardyce who wanted to hand him a new 12-month deal, said: "After Lampard, he has been the best midfielder in the country since Christmas."

FULHAM WANT LEW

FULHAM boss Chris Coleman wants former Watford manager Ray Lewington to join his coaching staff.

Coleman and his assistant Steve Kean have struggled this season and they want the former Fulham star to help steady the ship. Lewington has been out of work since being axed by Watford earlier this season.

Macca to cash in

FORMER England midfielder Steve McManaman will have one last big pay day in Dubai.

McManaman, a bit-part player for Manchester City this season, has received several offers to play in the Middle East and will quit the Premiership this summer.

McMANAMAN

City, meanwhile, are leading the chase for Scunthorpe defender Andy Butler, 21, who is valued at £1m.

COPP NEW CLUBS

READING boss Steve Coppell has told Les Ferdinand and Martin Keown they have no future with the Royals.

The former England internationals will not have their contracts renewed.

COVENTRY have made injury plagued midfielder Tim Sherwood available on a free transfer after he made only 11 appearances this season.

Don't sign big-Wigs!

WIGAN boss Paul Jewell has been warned not to sign any "big-time Charlies" by keeper John Filan.

JEWELL: Warning

The Aussie fears bringing in the wrong characters could destroy the harmony in the Latics camp. Filan said: "The team spirit and the mix of players here is great and we wouldn't want to break that up. We need good quality players who are not going to cause any hassle."

NIKOS PAYS PRICE

NIKOS Dabizas insists there are no hard feelings towards Leicester boss Craig Levein after he was shown the door at the Walkers Stadium.

"I would like to have stayed," said Dabizas, who has now set his sights on Italy. "But I understand the club have to reduce their wage bill and that it was a financial decision."

7-UP FOR IT

Arsenal in goal bonanza.. but Bergkamp faces axe

By JOHN CROSS Arsenal 7 Everton 0

ARSENE WENGER last night toasted his biggest-ever win as Arsenal manager after his seven-goal Gunners sent out an FA Cup warning to Manchester United.

Wenger hailed his team as "fantastic" and he was also given a major boost as leading scorer Thierry Henry proved his fitness by coming on as a half-time substitute.

But Wenger still refused to commit himself on whether he will give 36-year-old Dennis Bergkamp a new contract even after the Dutch veteran admitted he was "upset and frustrated" by the club stalling on a new deal.

Wenger said: "We are enjoying our play and I'm a little envious

TURN TO PAGE 71

DUTCH OF CLASS: Bergkamp and Henry celebrate

SVEN'S TALL STORY

By MARTIN LIPTON

BEANPOLE striker Peter Crouch will be handed a shock England call-up today — even though he could be a Coca-Cola Championship player by the end of the week.

The 6ft 7in Southampton frontman will become the tallest-ever player capped by England

TURN TO PAGE 66

Published by MGN Ltd. at One Canada Square, Canary Wharf, London, E14 5AP (020-7293 3000) and printed by Trinity Mirror Printing Ltd. at Watford and Oldham. Registered as a newspaper at the Post Office **Serial No. 32,419** ©MGN Ltd. Thursday, May 12, 2005 ■■■■■■■■ ★ Austria 2.50 EUR, Belgium 1.60 EUR, France 2.00 EUR, Germany 1.85 EUR, Greece 1.80EUR, Italy 1.70 EUR, Netherlands 1.80 EUR, Portugal 1.70EUR (continent) 341Esc,-Spain 1.70EUR, Malta 53 cents, Turkey: 3,400,000 TL & 3.40 YTL, Cyprus £1.05, Denmark 20DK

SUNDAY Mirror SPORT
sport@sundaymirror.co.uk

O'NEILL SET TO QUIT
EXCLUSIVE: PAGE 72

CHAMPIONS LEAGUE FINAL
RIJKAARD HAILS SCOUSE POWER
EXCLUSIVE: PAGES 76, 77

HARRY GOES BACK TO HELL
SEE PAGE 74

Gunners' spot of luck
PAT KEEPS COOL TO STEAL CUP

CAPTAIN FANTASTIC: Patrick Vieira lifts the Cup after his spot-kick sent United crashing — but it's agony for Paul Scholes (above right), whose miss was crucial

ARSENAL 0 MAN UTD 0
Arsenal win 5-4 on pens

By DUNCAN WRIGHT

LUCKY Arsenal made football history at the Millennium Stadium after the destiny of the FA Cup was decided by a penalty shoot-out for the first time.

Never before in the 133 years of the world's most famous knock-out competition had the outcome been decided by the lottery of spot kicks.

Arsenal had been outplayed for the bulk of yesterday's titanic clash with Manchester United and needed an heroic display from goalkeeper Jens Lehman to ensure the final remained goalless after extra-time. But there was no doubting the cold, clinical eye of the

◄Turn to Page 79

Published by MGN Ltd. (020 7293 3000) Printed by Trinity Mirror Printing Ltd at Watford and Oldham. Registered at the Post Office as a newspaper. **Serial No. 2085** ©MGN Ltd., 2002 ■■■■■■■■■ Austria €3.30 Belgium €2.20, France €3.00 (19.68 FrF), Germany €3.00, Greece €2.50 (852 D-), Malta €4c (Inc VAT), Italy €2.00, Netherlands €2.30, Portugal €2.00, Spain €2.00, Turkey TL5.65, Cyprus £1.25 (Inc VAT).

NEWSPAPERS SUPPORT RECYCLING
Recycled paper made up 75.5% of the raw material for UK newspapers in 2003

ARSENAL RATINGS

jensLEHMANN 8

Did well to save twice from Rooney but nearly caught out at his near-post after the break. Looked dodgy with crosses late on – but saved the crucial penalty brilliantly.

LAUREN 6

Vulnerable against the trickery of Cristiano Ronaldo down United's left side. Temper started to boil in the second half as Ronaldo's runs tested him defensively.

koloTOURE 6

Had a fairly comfortable time against the lone striker formation favoured by Sir Alex Ferguson. No frills and no fuss as usual from the Ivory Coast defender.

philippeSENDEROS 7

The biggest test yet for the Swiss youngster who kept out Sol Campbell and didn't let anyone down with an assured performance at the back.

ashleyCOLE 6

Rash challenge on Rooney earned an early booking and trod a tightrope from then on. Tireless as ever but pushed to the limit by United's precocious teenager.

cescFABREGAS 5

Has been a revelation this season for a player so young but on the big stage he struggled to impose himself on the game as Arsenal's attacking moves faltered.

patrickVIEIRA 6

Started the game intent on stamping his authority but his influence lessened as the game wore on. Calmness personified with the penalty which clinched the Cup.

gilbertoSILVA 7

A vital player, breaking up play and covering ground as United pushed forward in the second half. Showed what a huge miss he has been for much of the season.

robertPIRES 5

Should have been a key attacking outlet for Arsenal up against Wes Brown at full-back but the Frenchman was strangely subdued and wasteful in possession.

dennisBERGKAMP 5

Not helped by Arsene Wenger's decision to play him as a lone striker. Crowded out as the Gunners struggled to find their rhythm and was replaced after an hour.

joseREYES 5

The only genuine pace in the Arsenal attack and looked happier when facing the physical challenge. But was easily dealt with – and he couldn't dispute his late red card.

MANAGER

ARSENE WENGER

Poor tactical decision left Arsenal blunt in attack and without ideas. A lucky Cup winner.....................................5

SUBSTITUTES

Ljungberg (for Bergkamp 65) Worked hard as usual down the right.....................................6

Van Persie (for Fabregas 87) Little opportunity to make an impact in normal time.......6

Edu (for Pires 103) Too late for impact.......6

IT'S PAUL O

Misery for Scholes as

ARSENE WENGER will no doubt savour the irony that, at the end of a season which brought the Battle of the Buffet, he got to enjoy a dish best served cold.

Revenge was sweet for the Arsenal boss in Cardiff as the Gunners claimed a place in FA Cup history by becoming the first team to claim the trophy in a penalty shoot-out.

This time it was Sir Alex Ferguson who was left to choke on sour grapes after Jens Lehmann's heroics and Patrick Vieira's clinching strike from the spot took salvation to Highbury.

Lehmann defied United with a string of saves as Ferguson's men did everything but score in 120 minutes of almost complete domination. And when the keeper blocked Paul Scholes' penalty with the score tied at one apiece, it gave the Gunners an advantage they were never to surrender.

ARSENAL............0
MAN UTD.............0
AET: Arsenal won 5-4 on penalties

simon MULLOCK

They were even able to overcome the loss of penalty-taking striker Jose Antonio Reyes – sent off in the last few seconds – with Lauren, Freddie Ljungberg, Robin van Persie, Ashley Cole and finally Vieira all giving Roy Carroll no chance.

But United probably complained all the way home that they didn't get what they deserved – and they would be dead right. With Wayne Rooney living up to his tag as England's golden boy, Cristiano Ronaldo running riot and Roy Keane bossing Vieira in the midfield battleground, they were in control for most of the afternoon.

But when it came to bottle the Gunners were not found wanting.

Vieira missed a penalty in a UEFA Cup Final shoot-out when Arsenal were beaten by Galatasaray in Copenhagen five years ago this week. But he still had the courage to step up to the mark when his team needed him.

What Malcolm Glazer made of it all as he watched his £800m investment from the safety of his Florida home is anybody's guess.

But for the United fans dressed in black to mirror the team's away strip and the mood in Manchester following Glazer's unwanted takeover, it was pure agony.

Ref Rob Styles was kept busy – he booked five players as well as making sure Reyes became only the second man in 133 years to be dismissed in an FA Cup Final.

But while there were niggles, it rarely got nasty – despite a couple of touchline flare-ups between Wenger, Ferguson and Carlos Queiroz as the tension mounted.

Ronaldo's first excursion past the bemused Lauren should have brought the opening goal in the

THE PENALTY SHOOT-OUT

Man Utd		Arsenal
1	Van Nistelrooy ✓	✓ Lauren
2	Scholes ✗	✓ Ljungberg
3	Ronaldo ✓	✓ Van Persie
4	Rooney ✓	✓ Cole
5	Keane ✓	✓ Vieira

SPOT THE DIFFERENCE: Jens Lehmann makes the match-winning save from Paul Scholes's penalty in the shoot-out, capping an excellent performance by the German keeper

OVER NOW

Lehmann saves pen

sixth minute, but Scholes headed wastefully over from six yards.

In the 27th minute, United were certain they had taken the lead.

Scholes and Darren Fletcher worked a short free-kick back to Rooney and when his low blast came back off Lehmann's legs, Rio Ferdinand drilled in the rebound only for a borderline offside decision to go against him.

In the second half Keane rolled back the years with a rampaging run that took him past Cole only for Kolo Toure to hack his cross behind. Then Rooney surprised Lehmann, choosing to shoot instead of crossing only to see his effort come back off the post.

The introduction of Freddie Ljungberg brought a little more menace to the Londoners' attack, but they had an almighty double escape with five minutes left.

Lehmann flapped at a Ronaldo corner and was grateful to see Vieira block Keane's shot. And when Scholes' flag-kick bounced to Van Nistelrooy at the far post, the Dutchman's instinctive nod flew off the head of Ljungberg and bounced away off the crossbar.

When Rooney sent another long-range drive just over the game was destined for extra time.

Sub Robin van Persie forced Carroll into his first serious save of the game with a free-kick that the Irishman tipped behind. But it needed another Lehmann save to keep out Scholes's shot on the turn and from Giggs's corner, Van Nistelrooy mistimed a header when he seemed certain to score.

Reyes, already booked for a needless foul on Mikael Silvestre in normal time, was dismissed in the last few seconds of extra time for hacking down Ronaldo.

But just as United had survived the sending-off of Kevin Moran to beat Everton at Wembley in 1985, so Arsenal were to triumph with 10 men yesterday.

Van Nistelrooy, Ronaldo, Rooney and Keane all kept their nerve from the spot, but once Lehmann had foiled Scholes, Wenger could begin licking his lips in anticipation.

Match stats

ARSENAL		MAN UTD
14	Shots on target	8
3	Shots off target	12
3	Shots blocked	2
30	Corners	12
3	Fouls conceded	23
3	Offsides	6
1	Yellow cards	2
	Red cards	0

REFEREE WATCH
ROB STYLES

The ref kept a lid on most things and generally enjoyd a decent game – especially when tempers began to fray in extra time.

ATTENDANCE: 71,876

roy CARROLL 6
Nearly caught out by an early Jose Reyes break but after that hardly had a save to make as the Gunners' attack was snuffed out by United.

wes BROWN 7
Seen as a possible weakness by the Arsenal bench, Brown stuck to his task and came out on top in his personal duel with Pires.

rio FERDINAND 6
Composed and comfortable dealing with the threat of Bergkamp. Did his job quietly and allowed others to sparkle on the ball.

mikael SILVESTRE 6
Got an early whack in the face from Bergkamp and was assured even when the pace of Reyes was pushed further forward following the Dutchman's substitution.

john O'SHEA 6
Still not playing in his preferred position, O'Shea performed as well as his manager would have wanted to keep Arsenal's attacks down the right to a minimum.

cristiano RONALDO 8
A constant threat for United all match. Great skill created two chances in the first half and was too much for Lauren to handle at times.

darren FLETCHER 6
Did the donkey work in midfield as United crowded out the Gunners in the important area of the field. Also helped out Brown to counter any Arsenal attacks.

roy KEANE 8
The legs may be ageing but Keane rolled back the years with a non-stop display breaking up attacks, starting forward moves and making searching runs himself.

paul SCHOLES 6
Fairly quiet afternoon before the late drama. Headed off target with a good early opportunity but still helped link up well with his forwards. Didn't deserve his spot-kick misery.

wayne ROONEY 9
Rose to the occasion once again. Tested Ashley Cole to the limit and on another day could have scored a hat-trick. Unlucky to hit a post.

van NISTELROOY 6
Not the easiest of roles on his own but never ducked out of a challenge. Should have scored with far-post header which Ljungberg cleared away.

MANAGER
SIR ALEX FERGUSON
Got his tactics spot on to frustrate Arsenal with United clearly the better side. But it was all in vain..............8

SUBSTITUTES
Fortune (for O'Shea 71) Helped to snuff out threat of Ljungberg down Arsenal right.....7
Giggs (for Fletcher 90) Couldn't engineer the breakthrough in extra time......................6

CUP OF CHEER: Patrick Vieira lifts the hallowed trophy after the drama of Cardiff

Arsenal 0 Man Utd 0

Arsenal win 5-4 on penalties

By JOHN CROSS

NIL-NIL to the Arsenal! Arsene Wenger's team saw their grim determination rewarded with a dramatic victory in the FA Cup Final's first penalty shoot-out.

German keeper Jens Lehmann was the Gunners' hero with a superb save from Paul Scholes's spot-kick. That left Patrick Vieira to stroke home the decisive penalty.

The irony of an English star seeing a penalty saved by a German was lost on Lehmann. "I was not aware at this particular moment of an English opponent," he said stoically.

"We played a bit more not to lose, rather than to win," said Gunners boss Wenger.

Pictures: BRADLEY ORMESHER, CHRIS TURVEY and KENT GAVIN

FULL COVERAGE – PAGES 2 TO 9

OUR HERR-O! Jens Lehmann, whose penalty save won the Cup, celebrates

ESCAPE TO

WE LOVE FOOTBALL

Mania

Daily Mirror

FA CUP SPECIAL

SEASON 2004–2005, MAY 23, 2005

VICTORY

CHAMPIONS LEAGUE KNOCKOUT STAGE, 1ST LEG:

Burned up at the Bernabeu.. those who tried & failed

Arsenal last night became the first English team to beat Real Madrid at the Bernabeu. Previous failed bids:

April 8 2003, Champions League: Manchester United lost 3-1

March 3 2001, Champions League: Leeds United lost 3-2

April 4 2000, Champions League: Manchester United drew 0-0

March 20 1985, UEFA Cup: Tottenham Hotspur drew 0-0

November 5 1975, European Cup: Derby County lost 5-1

October 3 1973, UEFA Cup: Ipswich Town drew 0-0

May 15 1968, European Cup: Manchester United drew 3-3

April 11 1957, European Cup: Manchester United lost 3-1

HENRY THE FIRST: Thierry Henry avoids the challenge of Sergio Ramos to give Arsenal a lead they thoroughly deserved on a magical night for the Londoners

Oliver Holt
CHIEF SPORTS WRITER

THE hard-core Real Madrid fans unfurled a giant banner behind one of the goals before the game.

"The Spirit Is Back," it said. It was supposed to be a tribute to their team's recent resurgence.

Instead, it acted as a beacon to an Arsenal team who had arrived here cast in a role as playthings of the galacticos.

After a terrible, traumatic season, full of injuries and mediocrity and the troubles of Sol Campbell, it was Arsenal who got their spirit back.

It was a remarkable victory at a time when the club seemed to be at its lowest ebb since Wenger's arrival nearly a decade ago.

The result was enough, the first time an English side has ever won in the magnificent steep-sided cathedral of the Bernabeu.

But Arsenal played such beautiful football it seemed as though we were watching the return of an old friend. They cut Madrid to shreds

	Real Madrid	Arsenal
POSSESSION	65%	35%
SHOTS ON TARGET	6	6
SHOTS OFF TARGET	10	4
OFFSIDES	1	4
CORNERS	5	2
FOULS	15	25
YELLOW CARDS	2	2
RED CARDS	0	0

ATTENDANCE: 80,000
MAN OF THE MATCH: Toure

with intricate, passing football and a wonderful solo goal from Thierry Henry who, of course, was imperious.

And a team that has lost to West Brom and West Ham and others, in the Premiership, handed the mighty Madrid a football lesson.

All of the team was superb, from stand-ins like Emmanuel Eboue and Mathieu Flamini to established stars like Henry Kolo Toure and Freddie Ljungberg.

Cesc Fabregas was brilliant at the heart of the team. Jose Antonio Reyes found his form again. Alexander Hleb showed at last why Arsene Wenger bought him.

And yes, Philippe Senderos helped to mark Ronaldo out of the game.

From their eerie high in a corner of the arena as the

CROCKED AGAIN, WOOD YOU

AGONY: Woodgate comes off

John Cross

SVEN GORAN Eriksson always makes a habit of leaving games early to catch a flight, so football does not interfere with his busy social diary.

But the England manager's loyal assistant Tord Grip might just as well have left the Bernabeu after only nine minutes last night in favour of a nearby tapas restaurant.

Grip went to Madrid to watch the supposed second coming of Jonathan Woodgate.

Sure as hell he wasn't there to spy on Arsenal, who did not include a single Englishman in their starting line-up. It was left to David Beckham and Woodgate to fly the English flag – until the defender's desperate injury curse struck once again.

This time it was even more cruel than usual, Woody lasting just those nine minutes before pulling up with a suspected muscle tear in his left thigh.

Far worse than the month on the sidelines he will require to recover are the doubts raised as to whether Eriksson can gamble on his fitness for the World Cup.

The former Newcastle and Leeds centre-half's injury record has been more depressing than an episode of Casualty for the past two years.

Woodgate has a reputation for being injury-prone – the worst possible condemnation of any player's hopes of getting back into the England set-up. Yet he is potentially still the most gifted English central defender of his generation, which is why Real paid £13.4m to Newcastle for him 18 months ago.

Woodgate has the composure on the ball of Rio Ferdinand, Sol Campbell's defensive instincts and John Terry's dogged grit. That potent mix

★

REAL MADRID 0 ARSENAL 1

FROM THE BERNABEU

IT'S REAL 0.. THE REAL ARSENAL 1

Historic Gunners back to best

minutes ticked away to their famous victory the visiting fans sung "You've only come to watch the Arsenal."

And when the final whistle went, Henry and David Beckham embraced and swapped shirts.

Beckham left the field with Henry's jersey tucked down the back of his shorts but it was Arsenal who had had Madrid in their pockets all night.

They could have been two goals up in the first 10 minutes as they stunned their hosts with the kind of authoritative, flowing football they have been searching for all season in the Premiership.

Iker Casillas saved from Reyes in the second minute after Henry had played the Spain winger through on goal and then Ljungberg took the ball round Casillas following another Henry through ball only to be denied by a late, lunging tackle from Roberto Carlos.

In the first half, Henry was untouchable and Arsenal played neat triangles of passing football that left Madrid chasing shadows.

Real were shockingly bad. They contributed to their own demise by standing off Arsenal and allowing them to play something

Premiership opposition no longer do. They were not helped when the luckless Jonathan Woodgate limped out with a hamstring injury after nine minutes but the pattern of Arsenal's dominance had been established.

Roberto Carlos gave away possession almost every time he touched the ball. Ronaldo was peripheral, Zidane was fitful and the new Brazilian wonderboy. Cicinho, was run ragged by Reyes.

Beckham, Real's best player, should have scored 12 minutes before half time after he dispossessed Senderos on the edge of the Arsenal box.

The loose ball ran to Ronaldo. Ronaldo played it back to Beckham and even though the England skipper shot on target, Jens Lehmann blocked it with his legs.

Henry finally got the goal Arsenal deserved two minutes into the second half. It was a yet another strike of supreme individual brilliance from the Frenchman, who had picked the ball up just inside the Madrid half.

He shrugged off the challenges of Ronaldo and Thomas Gravesen, skipped past Guti and then eluded Sergio Ramos before sliding his shot

past the left hand of Casillas and into the far corner It would be wrong to introduce a note of pessimism on such a magical night for the club but Henry's performance is bound to encourage clubs like Real and Barcelona to redouble their efforts to prise him away from north London.

The whistles from the crowd that Ronaldo dreads began soon after Henry's goal.

Their spirits were lifted briefly by the introduction of Raul, but not even their talisman could help Madrid recover their fluency

In fact, he spurned Real's best chance when he rose unmarked to meet a Beckham free-kick but headed over

The last image of a mesmerising performance came when Henry highstepped his way past two flailing challenges of desperate Madrid defenders like a balletic hurdler

He put his foot on the ball just before it ran out of play and stood there alone for a moment, the king of all he surveyed.

REAL MADRID: Casillas, Cicinho, Sergio, Woodgate (Mejia 9), Carlos, Gravesen (Julio Baptista 76), Beckham, Guti, Zidane, Robinho (Raul 63), Ronaldo.
ARSENAL: Lehmann, Eboue, Toure, Senderos, Flamini, Ljungberg, Hleb (Pires 76), Silva, Fabregas (Song Billong 90), Reyes (Diaby 80), Henry.

HENRY

HUGS GAME: David Beckham embraces Thierry Henry at the final whistle
Pictures:
BRADLEY ORMESHER

Henry is the hero of Madrid

FROM BACK PAGE

them mature. This is a result that will help us come together.

"My only regret is that there were one or two opportunities for more goals and unfortunately we could not take them."

French striker Henry, who has seen his team struggle away from home in the Premiership this season, said: "It's been a long time since I have seen an Arsenal team play like that.

"We were brilliant defensively and the most important thing is that we were not scared to play, and when we are not scared to play we are superb.

"We were tremendous, and what the young players achieved at their age in the Bernabeu was amazing.

"I knew I would get one chance. We had wasted chances in the first half and I told myself I had to take the next one and I did that.

"Because I scored people will put me ahead of the team, but the whole team was tremendous tonight.

"But we have to stay calm and focused. We have only won one game and we are not there yet."

It was a devastating defeat for Real Madrid, for captain David Beckham and Jonathan Woodgate, who limped off after only nine minutes with a torn left hamstring.

Beckham said: "I could tell after the first five minutes that we were not going to play well. I feel so sorry for Jonathan. It is devastating for him."

So Andriy for Milan

CHAMPIONS LEAGUE ROUND-UP

ANDRIY Shevchenko put AC Milan in the driving seat against Bayern Munich.

The first leg of their knock out tie ended 1-1, wrecking the German side's perfect home record.

Michael Ballack gave Bayern a first-half lead with a stunning half-volley. But a needless handball gave Shevchenko the chance to equalise from the spot on 57 minutes.

Bayern, who had won all 15 of their previous home matches since a move into their new stadium, were without goalkeeper Oliver Kahn, hurt in the warm-up.

Former Liverpool boss Gerard Houllier's Lyon continued their march in Europe thanks to Juninho's goal at PSV Eindhoven. He struck in the 65th minute to give Lyon an away goal in a repeat of last year's quarter final, won by the Dutch.

CREDIT IT?

of qualities should make him the most complete defender.

His departure did nothing to settle the Real defence. But Arsenal's menace was down to the incisive play of Thierry Henry, Jose Antonio Reyes and Freddie Ljungberg.

Arsene Wenger claimed they had never been such big underdogs in Europe during his 10 years at the club. But the Gunners did not play like

it. Ljungberg was reinvigorated, perhaps the top man in a display full of defensive grit, belief and flair.

Yet not even that could have prepared Arsenal for what happened in the 47th minute when Henry fired home his 41st Champions League goal.

Henry delivered on the big stage and in doing so revived Arsenal's turbulent season.

BENFICA V LIVERPOOL REPORT: PAGES 52 & 53

ARSENAL 2 JUVENTUS 0 UEFA

ABSOLUTELY

GIFT OF THE FAB:
Teenager Fabregas
celebrates his 40th-
minute opener
at Highbury

Pictures:
KENT GAVIN
and **CHRIS TURVEY**

THE Old Lady of Italian football was left humbled and humiliated by Arsenal's young European upstarts on another Champions League night of glory at Highbury.

Cesc Fabregas, 18, graduated from being Patrick Vieira's midfield pupil into teaching his former captain a cruel and painful lesson as Arsenal took a giant step towards unchartered European territory.

Fabregas hit a magnificent 40th-minute opener and set up Thierry Henry's clincher as Arsenal's youngsters came of age with a victory that marks them down as genuine contenders to win the trophy.

Arsene Wenger has never reached the Champions League semi-finals in his 10-year reign at Highbury and this must also go down as one of the most memorable nights in the famous old stadium's history.

The Gunners not only beat Juventus, but they gave them a footballing lesson which bore out Wenger's much-derided decision to put his faith in this brilliant crop of youngsters.

His biggest gamble was to sell Vieira to Juventus for £13.7 million, which has looked rash and foolhardy at times this

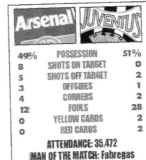

Arsenal		Juventus
49%	POSSESSION	51%
8	SHOTS ON TARGET	0
5	SHOTS OFF TARGET	2
3	OFFSIDES	1
4	CORNERS	2
12	FOULS	28
0	YELLOW CARDS	2
0	RED CARDS	2

ATTENDANCE: 35,472
MAN OF THE MATCH: Fabregas

season as Arsenal have floundered in the Premiership.

But the likes of Fabregas, Jose Antonio Reyes, Mathieu Flamini and Philippe Senderos seem to love the European stage and these exciting nights.

They worked tirelessly, played some superb pass-and-move football and generally outclassed Juventus.

It left Vieira so annoyed he stupidly got himself booked for a rash late foul on Reyes which rules him out of the second leg, while Juventus finished the game with nine men following two dismissals.

Mauro Camoranesi and Jonathan Zebina were dismissed in the 87th and 89th minutes respectively as they picked up second yellow cards, with the latter lashing out at his school friend Henry.

That was a measure of Juve's frustration at being humbled by Arsenal as Vieira's return to Highbury ended in jubilation for his former team-mates.

They beat Real Madrid in the last round but this victory over a team eight points clear at the

CHAMPIONS LEAGUE QUARTER-FINAL, 1ST LEG

FABREGAS

Wenger boys in sight of the semi after young Gun sees off Italy's Old Lady

John Cross

CAP GUN: Arsenal skipper Henry after firing in the second

top of Serie A shows they can dream of emulating Liverpool's heroics of last season.

But there can be no more exciting prospects in Europe than Fabregas and he showed last night he is every bit as good as Barcelona's prodigious 18-year-old Lionel Messi, who tore Chelsea apart in the last round.

His vision, passing and pace gave Vieira and his midfield partner, Brazilian captain Emerson, the runaround and he led the way for Arsenal to dominate and overrun Juventus.

KISS OFF: Camoranesi blows kisses to Highbury crowd after his red for a foul on van Persie

It was also ironic that Vieira, the former hardman of Arsenal's midfield, should be the Juventus player who was tackled by Robert Pires in the build-up to the opening goal. Pires, noted for his flair rather than aggression, slid in and stole the ball from Vieira before passing to Henry who threaded the ball through to Fabregas.

It was then that Fabregas showed his class by selling a dummy to French veteran Lillian Thuram before firing a low shot which left keeper Gianluigi Buffon wrong-footed.

Henry, Fabregas and Alexander Hleb saw second-half shots brilliantly saved by Buffon while the hugely impressive Kolo Toure's pace helped ensure Juventus did not have a shot on target. Finally the priceless second goal came in the 69th minute.

Hleb's through ball released Fabregas and a less composed and talented player would have gone for goal himself, but the Spaniard squared the ball for Henry who fired into the empty net with Buffon stranded.

Highbury erupted again amid amazing celebrations as this display proved Arsenal have left Vieira behind and can start enjoying Wenger's breathtaking vision for the future.

JUVE LEFT GASPING BY CESC

FROM BACK PAGE

was a great night for us. We wanted to play well defensively and score goals – and we managed to do that.

"The technical quality was very high and that shows the team is improving.

"The regret is I thought there was one more goal in this match, especially with some of the chances we had in the second half and the number of set-pieces.

"I believe we can go through now.

"We have to keep our feet on the ground and continue to play our game. Juventus will try to come at us but we will go at them and try to score goals.

"Patrick suffered because we dominated the game. Fabregas has great quality and gets stronger.

"My thinking is not about being vindicated on selling Patrick. He is a tremendous player and when you lose one like him you will suffer a little bit and another team is born.

"I didn't speak to him but maybe I will get the chance to talk later because he is a winner and when he does not win he is not happy."

Fantastic

Fabregas said: "If you look at the way we played, we've dominated and could have scored more.

"Everyone played 100 per cent. We're getting better and better. We still can improve but it was a great performance from every player."

Henry added: "I think he (Fabregas) did brilliantly, not only playing against Patrick Vieira but also Emerson, Camoranesi and Adrian Mutu."

Vieira endured a miserable night as he struggled to make an impact for the Serie A giants and misses the second leg after he was booked for a second-half foul on Jose Antonio Reyes.

Midfielder Mauro Camoranesi and defender Jonathan Zebina were sent off on a disastrous night for Juventus but boss Fabio Capello warned: "This tie is still alive. Considering the way we played in the second half, the result is good."

☐BARCELONA missed several chances as last night's other quarter-final against Benfica ended goalless in Lisbon.

1-0 Fabregas shoots past Buffon to put the Gunners ahead last night

2-0 Henry hammers home following more good work from Fabregas

OLIVER HOLT'S VERDICT: PAGES 52 & 53 ● **TEAMS & RATINGS: PAGE 53**

ARSENAL 1 VILLARREAL 0 ✪ CHAMPIONS

Magical mystery the Yellow

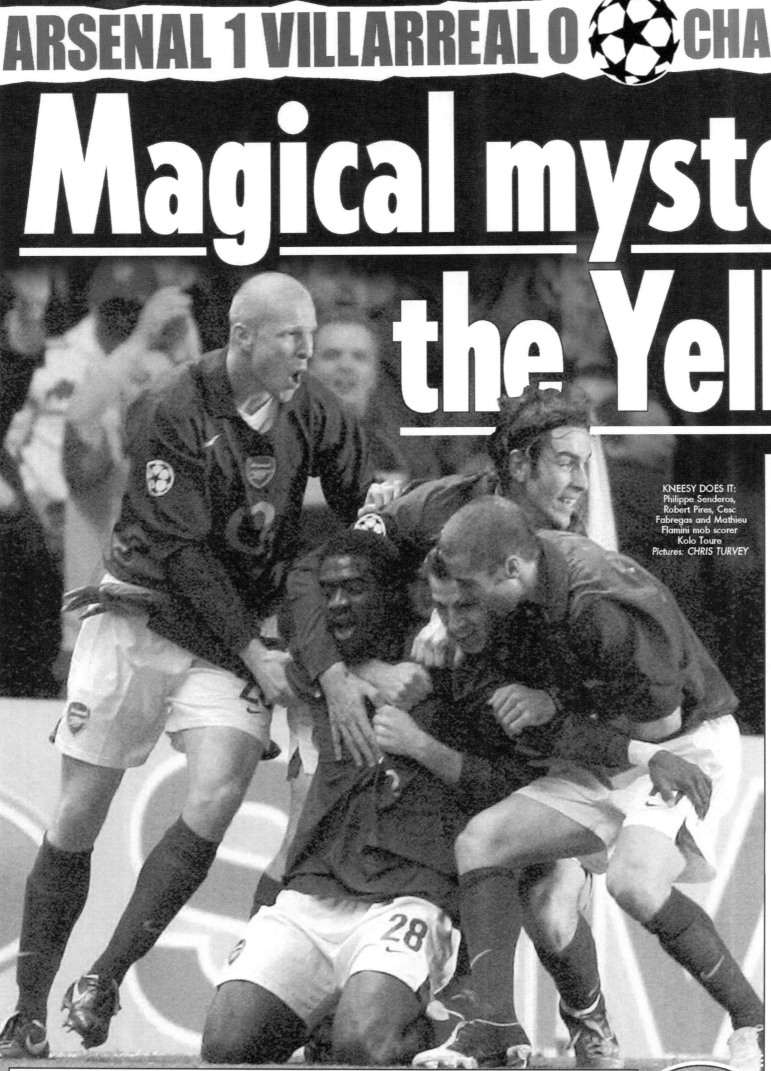

KNEESY DOES IT: Philippe Senderos, Robert Pires, Cesc Fabregas and Mathieu Flamini mob scorer Kolo Toure
Pictures: CHRIS TURVEY

THEY DID it at the cathedral that is the Bernabeu and the rust-bucket that is the Stadio Delle Alpi.

And now after waving a European goodbye to their own piece of hallowed ground, Arsenal know they have to keep another clean sheet at El Madrigal on Tuesday to fulfil their Champions League destiny.

Highbury has witnessed more emotive nights, as the tension of the prize at stake appeared to grip the whole ground, yet it has never seen one as important.

For once, the hero was not Thierry Henry. By his standards, Arsene Wenger's skipper had a night when things didn't quite come off – a bit like the squirrel which had roamed around the pitch for much of the first half.

But this was a victory chiselled out by a solid team performance, confirmed by the one moment when they showed the requisite quality in front of goal. And while Wenger and his players

Arsenal		V		
55%	POSSESSION		45%	
5	SHOTS ON TARGET		3	
7	SHOTS OFF TARGET		4	
8	OFFSIDES		7	
5	CORNERS		2	
17	FOULS		17	
0	YELLOW CARDS		5	
0	RED CARDS		0	

ATTENDANCE: 35,438
MAN OF THE MATCH: Toure

were surely ruing the narrowness of the advantage they earned, it was fitting that the precious gem Arsenal will take with them to southern Spain was mined by the player who has stood as a shining beacon at the back, who has been the leader of a defensive line that has defied all expectations.

Kolo Toure began the season as the novice in Wenger's back division. Yet in the absences of Sol Campbell, Ashley Cole and Lauren the smiling man from the Ivory Coast has emerged as the cornerstone on which Wenger's entire rebuilding job has been founded.

Last night, apart from one slip when he lost his footing, Toure was immaculate to ensure Arsenal's record run without conceding was extended to nine Champions League matches.

But it was his close-range contribution at the other end, four minutes from the interval,

ARSENAL OWE IT TO GOALO

FROM BACK PAGE

more goal in the match. We want a great performance. We need to be strong defensively and sharp on our counter-attacks and if we can do that then I believe we can go through."

Arsenal captain Thierry Henry, who saw a 12th-minute effort flagged offside when TV replays suggested the goal

should have stood, said: "This was a big result because we did not concede and we have already shown that we can keep clean sheets away from home.

"They will need to come at us a bit more because they did not attack us even at 1-0."

Wenger admitted that he was disappointed not to win more comfortably on Arsenal's

last European night at Highbury.

He added: "It was a difficult situation between keeping a clean sheet and finding another goal which made it hard for us to find our flow."

Wenger also revealed that he is ready to gamble on rotating his players for Saturday's north London derby with

Tottenham – a shoot-out for the fourth Champions League place – to keep them fresh for the Villarreal return.

He said: "You might look at it and think it will be a gamble but I believe I might have to rotate players to make sure they all stay fresh and ready for the challenge."

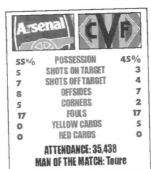

NICE WON SQUIRREL: This fury creature stopped play last night

LEAGUE SEMI-FINAL, FIRST LEG

Toure sinks Submarine

BUT GUNNERS STILL FACING A FIGHT FOR FINAL PLACE

Martin Lipton
CHIEF FOOTBALL WRITER

SIMPLY THE CHEST: Toure celebrates his crucial strike

that may prove to be the most important goal he will ever score.

Toure had snatched an earlier opening, stabbing the ball wide from eight yards.

Yet when he was handed a second opportunity, as Alexander Hleb read Henry's mind to sprint down the inside-left channel and squirt the ball across, Toure's instinctive prod for his first of the season was certain and unanswerable. It was the minimum the Gunners required from a night which does not look decisive by any means.

Doubt

Arsenal nerves were demonstrated when Jens Lehmann greeted the final whistle by rucking with Emmanuel Eboue for conceding a free-kick that never got to be taken.

But Wenger's men know they got the rub of the green on the biggest decision of the match by Austrian referee Konrad Plautz.

That came in first half stoppage time, seconds after Jens Lehmann had fisted away a swerving free-kick from Juan Roman Riquelme, the most dangerous weapon in the battery of the 'Yellow Submarines'.

When the clearance was knocked back to the edge of the Arsenal box, Gilberto's wild lunge ploughed through Jose Mari without coming close to the ball.

It looked a stone-cold penalty but the referee turned his back on the Villarreal appeals.

The Spanish side were not alone in casting doubt over the officials. When Henry had accepted Robert Pires' slide-rule pass to find the net on 12 minutes, television replays suggested he was level, rather than in front, of the last defender.

After Toure's early miss, Gilberto and then Philippe Senderos could not hit the target with headers, as Arsenal failed to take advantage of the hesitancy of the makeshift Villarreal back-line.

When Hleb's trickery freed Emmanuel Eboue to drill in from the right, Henry could only muster a weak effort which Cesar Arzo headed off the line.

And then, deep in stoppage time, substitute Dennis Bergkamp looked certain to nudge home when Gilberto nodded back across goal only for Javi Venta to take the ball off the Dutchman's toe.

ARSENAL RATINGS
COMPILED BY JOHN CROSS

 JENS LEHMANN **8/10**
Made two great saves from danger man Riquelme's driven free-kicks. Deserves much credit for Champions League record of nine clean sheets.

 EMMANUEL EBOUE **8/10**
Rampaging runs down the right have been a feature of Arsenal's European run. Last night was more about defending and his aggression and strength.

 KOLO TOURE **9/10**
What a time to score your first goal of the season. Was excellent and he looks every inch the elder statesman of this defence. Man of the match.

 PHILIPPE SENDEROS **8/10**
Great early chance which he headed over. Defensively strong and kept Villarreal's strikers under control. Sat tightly on Diego Forlan throughout.

 MATHIEU FLAMINI **8/10**
Strong runs down the left were a major part of Arsenal's attacking play. Fit-again Ashley Cole may struggle to regain his place.

 FREDDIE LJUNGBERG **8/10**
Live wire down the left even if sometimes his final ball let him down. Energy and pace gave Villarreal problems and made up for Jose Antonio Reyes' absence.

 GILBERTO **8/10**
Got away with a blatant penalty for a foul on Jose Mari. Otherwise he had an excellent game in which he sat deep and did a superb job on Riquelme.

 CESC FABREGAS **8/10**
Looked bright in the early stages with some good runs even if he looked subdued. Has been struggling with a foot injury which maybe restricted him.

 ALEXANDER HLEB **8/10**
Work rate was outstanding. Ran himself ragged in midfield and then made a superb run and fired in a low cross for Kolo Toure's opener.

ROBERT PIRES **8/10**
Despite his indifferent form in the Premiership, Pires seems to relish big nights at Highbury. Starred against Juventus and was passing to good effect.

 THIERRY HENRY **8/10**
His pace frightened the life out of Villarreal's shaky defence. He was a constant threat to prove there is no more committed Arsenal player.

ARSENAL SUBSTITUTES

DENNIS BERGKAMP: (for Hleb 75). Not even the mercurial Dutchman could conjure another goal for Arsenal last night. Rating 6
ROBIN VAN PERSIE (for Ljungberg 75): Did not have enough time to cause problems for the Villarreal defence. 6

VILLARREAL LINE-UP

Barbosa, Javi Venta, Quique Alvarez, Arzo, Arruabarrena, Senna, Tacchinardi, Sorin (Josico 72), Riquelme, Jose Mari (Franco 55), Forlan (Calleja 90).

WANTED: Gerrard

Ruud's 'offered' to Real

FROM BACK PAGE

Inter Milan's wantaway Brazilian Adriano. Flores said: "I have recommended to President Fernando Martin the highest priority is the signing of a powerful central striker, and Adriano is my choice.

"We also need a midfielder of that elite class, in case Zinedine Zidane leaves. Gerrard is the player I have included in that list."

Flores' public statement about Gerrard will infuriate Liverpool who have had to fend off the Madrid giants, as well as Chelsea, for the past two summers.

But the Italian is new President Martin's closest advisor and his words indicate another concerted bid.

That will worry England boss Sven Goran Eriksson after the midfielder admitted his Euro 2004 performances were affected by Chelsea's drawn-out pursuit.

Liverpool will not be interested in selling whatever the bid – but a move for Van Nistelrooy could be successful.

One insider said: "Real were told that Van Nistelrooy has analysed what has gone on over the last few months and decided it is time to leave.

"Of course he is a player that interests Real, but only at the right price. The fact is that he is 30 in July and has suffered with knee injuries."

HIGHS AND LOWS: Thierry Henry goes for the spectacular as Gilberto battles with Diego Forlan

OLIVER HOLT'S VERDICT: PAGES 68 & 69

RESULT!

He's just not Roed worthy

"WE HAVE had applications from top managers all over the world but we have decided to go for this guy with no coaching badges and all the charisma of a pork pie."

Those are the words Newcastle chairman Freddy Shepherd will have to use if yesterday's plunge on Glenn Roeder to get the Toon job was based on substance rather than whisper.

From 25-1, Roeder was still being backed at 4-6 yesterday, at which time befuddled bookies decided to suspend betting. Betting wasn't the only thing suspended. Disbelief was too.

Roeder (right) is still not in possession of the coaching badge necessary to manage any top Premiership side and won't get one in time for next season (interestingly enough, though, he WAS allowed to coach West Ham for two years).

Backing Roeder to get the job is like backing Ghana to win Eurovision. You've got to be in it to win it and all the rules say Roeder ain't in it. Punters – and bookies – are as baffled as Adam on Mother's Day. Roeder is the manager, remember, who took a West Ham side containing Kanoute, Carrick, Cole, Defoe, Sinclair, James and Johnson into the First Division.

A manager who paid £5million for Don Hutchison and a similar amount for Tomas Repka. A man who was born to be caretaker – of the local school.

Roeder was still trading at around 6-4 on Betfair yesterday, suggesting that an awful lot of punters don't believe the Toon smoke signals.

Betfair betting (Newcastle job): 6-4 Roeder, 6-1 O'Neill, 12-1 Curbishley, Houllier.

PARIS IS BENT ON REVENGE

WHEN you mention the words 'poker' and 'Paris Hilton' together the obvious reaction is 'yes please'. PartyPoker.com are offering blonde minx Paris the chance to win her £100,000 Bentley back after reports she lost it in a game of poker at her family's casino in Las Vegas.

It's hard to believe the high society girl actually managed to lose a car during a game of cards? Surely it's more likely she forgot where she parked it. Paris has to go heads-up against poker legend Mike Sexton (insert your own joke) and, in the unlikely event Paris takes Sexton, PartyPoker will hand her the keys to a brand spanking new Bentley.

Thing is, I've heard Paris (left) is such a snob she won't even sit in the same car as her chauffeur.

Albert's aiming for Costa bravo

BY rights Albert Costa shouldn't have an earthly against Dominik Hrbaty in today's Barcelona Open second round – but prepare for a massive plunge on the Spaniard.

Costa, you see, is quitting tennis after this event – and Barcelona is HIS manor.

One Betfair punter staked £5,000 on underdog Costa (right) winning a tough first-round match against American Vince Spadea. He buried Spadea in three sets. Who's to say a tide of goodwill won't sweep Barcelona hero Costa (a 2-1 chance today) to victory in the Spanish city this week?

Finalists play cat and mouse

A JOBBING actor in a theatre production of The Mousetrap has been an understudy to the lead character for the last eight years.

Try telling him life's not a dress-rehearsal.

It's an FA Cup Final dress-rehearsal tonight when West Ham host Liverpool in the Premiership.

In what is likely to be the phoney war to end all phoney wars, Hills go just 4-1 that of tonight's starting line-ups, no more than 11 will start next month's Cardiff showpiece.

Pires for Villarreal a Racing cert

THERE are rumours among disgruntled punters on the Betfair chatroom that odds-savvy national newspaper journalists are influencing betting markets for their own gain.

A story written with authority about the impending move can have a major impact on odds.

Here's an example. On Monday, Ladbrokes offered 4-1 about Arsenal midfielder Robert Pires playing for Villarreal next season. Yesterday, without laying a single bet, they slashed those odds to 7-4.

The reason? A comment made by respected Spanish journalist Guillem Balague in the Racing Post.

"As far as I know it's a done deal," wrote Balague yesterday.

Here's the latest Betfair Champions League betting: **4-5** Barcelona; **15-8 Arsenal; 10-1** Milan.

VILLARREAL 0 ARSENAL 0

Oliver Holt
SPORTS WRITER OF THE YEAR

THE ARSENAL players celebrated wildly at the end. They ran to Jens Lehmann and leapt on him.

When they had finished hugging each other, they trotted to the two opposite corners of El Madrigal where their fans were corralled.

They took off their shirts and flung them to the supporters, many of whom were so overcome that they were in tears.

In those moments, this 0-0 draw in a small town north of Valencia, felt like a glorious triumph for Arsenal.

In those moments, it felt every bit as uplifting as this season's previous Champions League victories over Real Madrid and Juventus.

As the realisation began to sink in that they would play against AC Milan or Barcelona for club football's top prize in Paris on May 17, they began to blot out the memory of the 90 minutes they had just endured.

It seems incongruous to criticise them on such a momentous night, on a night when such a fine old club

TOURE: Superb

experienced a proud moment in its history by advancing to its first European Cup Final.

But they played so poorly that that kind of parsimony is impossible to avoid.

This triumph was altogether different from the triumphs that have gone before in this competition this season.

Because this was not really a triumph at all. It was a great escape, a gift from the gods of good luck to a team that froze.

Arsenal have played some enchanting football since the turn of the year but last night they were dreadful.

In the past, they have deserved good luck for the beauty of their play but here they did not deserve anything.

If Juan Roman Riquelme had scored the last-minute penalty harshly awarded against Gael Clichy, it would have been the least Villarreal deserved. If Lehmann had not performed his heroics and Villarreal had been preparing for a trip to Paris next month, no one could have begrudged them their victory.

Arsenal played as though they were paralysed by nerves. Only Lehmann and Kolo Toure did themselves justice.

Even then, if Villarreal had had better forwards than the desperately ordinary Diego Forlan and Guillermo Franco, there would have been nothing Toure and Lehmann could have done. As for the rest of them, Thierry Henry was fretful, Jose Antonio Reyes was ineffective and Alexander Hleb squandered possession with reckless regularity.

Sol Campbell looked desperately ill at ease and Gilberto Silva granted Riquelme the freedom of El Madrigal in the opening half.

Campbell's performance, in fact, was another reason for the strange feeling of ambivalence that accompanied such a momentous result for Arsenal. He did not crack as some had feared he would after all the troubles and the doubts that have assailed him this season. But he did nothing to suggest he would be able to cope with forwards of the quality of Andrei Shevchenko or Samuel Eto'o.

His painful uncertainty was a symbol of Arsenal's unexpected lack of assurance and a reminder of the fragility that accosted them so often earlier in the Premiership season.

Campbell, of course, had played only once since the night of February 1 when he walked out of Highbury at half-time after being

HE'S THE MANN! Arsenal keeper Jens Lehmann makes a sensational late penalty save

A happy Gunners'

CHAMPIONS LEAGUE SEMI-FINAL, 2ND LEG

ARSENAL WIN 1-0 ON AGGREGATE

from Riquelme to put the Gunners into the Champions League Final last night   *Pictures: BRADLEY ORMESHER*

ending can't conceal Spanish fright night

embarrassed by Bobby Zamora. In that solitary appearance, he broke his nose against Portsmouth and had to be substituted.

It was hardly the ideal preparation for the most important game in Arsenal's history.

But an injury to Philippe Senderos against Spurs on Saturday meant that Arsene Wenger had no choice but to throw Campbell into the fray.

Yet in a nervous side Campbell looked more awkward and unsure than the rest. Whereas once Arsenal would have been bolstered by his return, last night they seemed unnerved by it.

Leader

The England defender's first touch was a panicky clearance from an attempted Riquelme through-ball, but for much of the first half Campbell was a bystander.

The game went on around him. It bypassed him. It also became obvious that he is no longer the leader of this Arsenal defence. That mantle has passed to Toure and it was he who took the responsibility of organising those around him, he who gave Hleb a long lecture about his defensive duties.

Twice in the opening nine minutes of the second half, Arsenal's nine-game run without conceding a goal in the competition nearly came to an end, both times when Franco beat Campbell to headers but directed the ball wide when he should have scored. That Arsenal were able to cling on owed much more to Villarreal's profligacy than any defensive excellence.

At the end, the Arsenal fans broke into a chant. "Que sera sera," they yelled, "whatever will be will be, we're going to gay Paris, que sera sera."

As a rhyme, it worked nicely. But unless the real Arsenal stand up in the Stade de France, the attractions of Paris in the springtime will be lost on them.

SHAKY SOL: Campbell endured a nervous night – but still ended up in the final

Results & fixtures

UEFA CHAMPIONS LEAGUE SEMI-FINAL, SECOND LEG
Villarreal ....(0) 0   Arsenal ....(0) 0
                         23,000
(Arsenal win 1-0 on aggregate)

BARCLAYS PREMIERSHIP
Aston Villa..(0) 0   Man City ......(1) 1
26,422   Vassell 71

COCA-COLA LEAGUE TWO
Rochdale.....(1) 1   Barnet ....(1) 1
Dagnall 23   Hendon 28 (pen)
                      1,769
Torquay ......(2) 4   Stockport .....(0) 0
Thorpe 4, 18   3,565
Kuffour 23
Hollands 48

	P	W	D	L	F	A	Pts
Carlisle........	43	24	10	9	81	40	82
North'mptn..	44	21	16	7	61	36	79
Grimsby......	44	22	10	12	62	42	76
Leyton O	44	20	15	9	62	48	75
Wycombe....	44	17	17	10	70	55	68
Cheltenham..	44	17	15	12	58	53	66
Lincoln City ..	44	14	20	10	63	52	62
Peterboro....	44	17	11	16	56	45	62
Bristol R......	44	17	9	18	57	62	60
Darlington ..	44	15	14	15	56	51	59
Shrewsbury..	44	15	13	16	54	54	58
Wrexham......	44	15	12	17	59	52	57
Boston Utd...	44	14	15	15	48	60	57
Chester......	44	14	12	18	53	57	54
Mansfield....	44	13	14	17	59	61	53
Rochdale......	43	13	13	17	63	66	52
Bury..........	44	12	15	17	43	55	51
Notts C.......	44	12	15	17	46	59	51
Macclesfld...	44	11	17	16	56	68	50
Barnet.......	44	11	17	16	42	56	50
Stockport....	44	11	17	16	57	78	50
Oxford Utd...	44	11	15	18	40	53	48
Torquay	44	12	12	20	51	65	48
Rushden & D .	44	11	12	21	43	72	45

NATIONWIDE CONFERENCE
Burton........(2) 2   Dag & Red ...(1) 2
Clare 14   Moore 3
Harrad 23   Akurang 72
                      1,235
Exeter ....(2) 4   Crawley......(0) 0
Mackie 34   1,782
Seaborne 38
Farrell 41
Moxey 62
Grays..........(0) 1   Southport.....(0) 1
DeBolla 49   Pickford 67
                      918
Halifax........(0) 2   Gravesend.....(0) 0
Sugden 52, 54   1,680
Woking........(1) 2   Forest Green.(1) 1
Evans 15   Brough 38 (pen)
Richards 55 (pen) 890

	P	W	D	L	F	A	Pts
Accrington ...	41	28	7	6	76	43	91
Hereford	41	21	14	6	56	32	77
Grays	41	21	13	7	93	53	76
Halifax......	41	21	12	8	55	38	75
Morecambe ..	41	21	8	12	66	40	71
Stevenage...	41	19	12	10	62	45	69
York.........	41	17	12	12	62	45	63
Exeter	41	18	8	15	64	47	62
Burton Albn	41	15	12	14	49	52	57
Dagenham....	41	15	10	16	61	58	55
Cambridge ...	41	15	10	16	50	55	55
Woking	41	13	14	14	55	46	53
Aldershot ...	41	15	6	20	60	74	51
Gravesend...	41	13	10	18	45	56	49
Canvey Is ...	41	12	12	17	45	58	48
Kidminster...	41	12	11	18	37	55	47
Crawley	41	12	10	19	48	55	46
Southport....	41	10	10	21	36	67	40
Tamworth ...	41	8	13	20	32	63	37
Scarboro	41	9	9	23	39	65	36
Forest Green.	41	7	14	20	47	62	35
*Altrincm....	41	10	11	20	39	68	23

* 18pts deducted

NATIONWIDE NORTH: Stalybridge 2 Barrow 1; Worksop 2 Lancaster 0.
NATIONWIDE SOUTH: Cambridge City 0 Havant and W 0; Hayes 4 Weston-S-Mare 1.
UNIBOND PREMIER: Farsley Celtic 5 Runcorn 0; Matlock 1 Blyth Spartans 1; Ossett Town 0 Burscough 0.
UNIBOND PRESIDENT'S CUP, Final: Ilkeston 0 Bradford P A 1.
PREMIER RES: Coventry 1 Spurs 3; Southampton 2 Norwich 0; Blackburn 4 Wigan 0; Leeds 1 Middlesbrough 1.
PONTIN'S COMBINATION: Swansea 0 Plymouth 5; Swindon 2 Cardiff 1; Leyton Orient 0 Oxford 0; MK Dons 1 Colchester 1.
MANCHESTER SENIOR CUP, Final: Oldham 2 Manchester United 3.
ERREA CUP, Final, Second Leg: Bromsgrove 1 Hitchin 2 (Agg 1-3).

CRICKET
TOUR MATCH (Fenner's, Day 2 of 3): Sri Lanka 289 & 140-4 (Samaraweera 82 not), British Univs 125 (Vaas 4-34, Zoysa 4-38).

SNOOKER
WORLD CHAMPIONSHIP (Sheffield): Quarter-finals: P Ebdon (Eng) leads S Murphy (Eng) 7-1; R O'Sullivan (Eng) level with M Williams (Wal) 4-4; G Dott (Sco) leads N Robertson (Aus) 10-6; K Doherty level with M Fu (HKg) 8-8.

SPEEDWAY
ELITE LEAGUE: Peterborough 63 (Andersen 14, Sullivan 14) Oxford 31 (Wiltshire 7, Eriksson 7) Peterborough win the bonus point.
PREMIER TROPHY: Isle of Wight 43 (Holder 14) Rye House 50 (Boxall 13) Rye House win the bonus point.
TONIGHT'S FOOTBALL
(7.45pm unless stated)
UEFA CHAMPIONS LEAGUE SEMI-FINAL, SECOND LEG
Barcelona (1) v AC Milan (0) ....
BARCLAYS PREMIERSHIP
West Ham v Liverpool ....
TODAY'S CRICKET
(11.00 unless stated)
LIVERPOOL VICTORIA COUNTY CHAMPIONSHIP
Div 1 (day 1 of 4): **Riverside:** Durham v Lancs; **Rose Bowl:** Hants v Sussex; **Lord's:** Middlesex v Kent; **Edgbaston:** Warwicks v Yorks.
Div 2 (day 1 of 4): **Sophia Gardens:** Glamorgan v Essex; **Grace Road:** Leics v Surrey; **New Road:** Worcs v Somerset.

WE LOVE FOOTBALL
Mania

DAILY Mirror

IN ASSOCIATION WITH ▼ Wickes

Season 2005-2006
May 8, 2006

KING HENRY IS No.1 IN THE WORLD

By MARTIN LIPTON

Arsenal 4 Wigan Athletic 2

ARSENE WENGER lauded Thierry Henry as the greatest attacking player on the planet after the French skipper brought down the Highbury curtain with a hat-trick that saw the Gunners leapfrog Spurs to take the £10million final Champions League spot.

Henry's seventh Arsenal hat-trick in his seven years at the club took his Golden Boot tally to 33 goals this season to end the 93-year Highbury era on a massive high.

Arsenal stars of the past were celebrated as the party

4-PAGE FAREWELL TO HIGHBURY SPECIAL INSIDE

went on for 90 minutes and Wenger said: "I don't know all the players this club has had but Thierry is the best striker in the world.

"Handing him the captaincy this year has given him an extra dimension. He has grown in strength, as a player and as a personality. He has matured a lot this year."

Henry has still to confirm whether he'll be at Arsenal next year and at the end of the closing ceremony the captain and Ashley Cole sat in the centre-circle looking at the deserting stands around them.

It appeared like a gesture of

TURN TO MANIA PAGE 12

FAN CLUB: Thierry Henry celebrates with his team-mates at the end and with boss Arsene Wenger (inset)
Pictures: KENT GAVIN

TAXI FOR VAN

RED RAGE: The Dutch star has been sulking

End of the Ruud at United after Dutch ace storms out

By DAVID McDONNELL

RUUD VAN NISTELROOY'S Manchester United career is over after he stormed out of Old Trafford yesterday when he learned he had been left out of the team.

Sir Alex Ferguson will today tell the United board that he wants van Nistelrooy out of the club after the sulking striker disrupted team spirit following a series of rows with team-mates.

Van Nistelrooy, who clashed with his colleagues in training this week, dashed away from the team hotel in a taxi after Ferguson

TURN TO MANIA PAGE 3

vodafone

▼ Wickes THE FOOTBALL LEAGUE CHAMPIONSHIP   ▼ Wickes THE FOOTBALL LEAGUE CHAMPIONSHIP   ▼ Wickes THE FOOTBALL LEAGUE CHAMPIONSHIP   ▼ Wickes THE FOOTBALL LEAGUE CHAMPIONSHIP

FAREWELL TO HIGHBURY

1913-2006

WAVING GOODBYE: Ian Wright leads the cheers as a host of former Arsenal stars are introduced to the crowd *Pics: KENT GAVIN*

THANKS FOR THE MEMORIES

A HOST of Arsenal legends said an emotional goodbye to Highbury yesterday.

The Thierry Henry-inspired 4-2 victory sparked a party to celebrate 93 years of football at the famous stadium.

Arsenal heroes including Ian Wright, Charlie George, Lee Dixon and George Graham were there to pay tribute at the Gunners' 2010th and final match at their north London home before moving down the hill to the new 60,000-seater Emirates Stadium.

Fans were issued with red and white T-shirts reading "I was there, May 7, 2006".

After the match, former and current players performed a lap of honour and Who singer Roger Daltrey sang specially written song "Highbury Highs."

Picture special: Pages 10-11
Match report: Page 12

RED MASTERS: Henry and Fabregas celebrate

4-PAGE SPECIAL ON THE FINAL HOURS OF FAMOUS THEATRE OF FOOTBALL

SEALED W

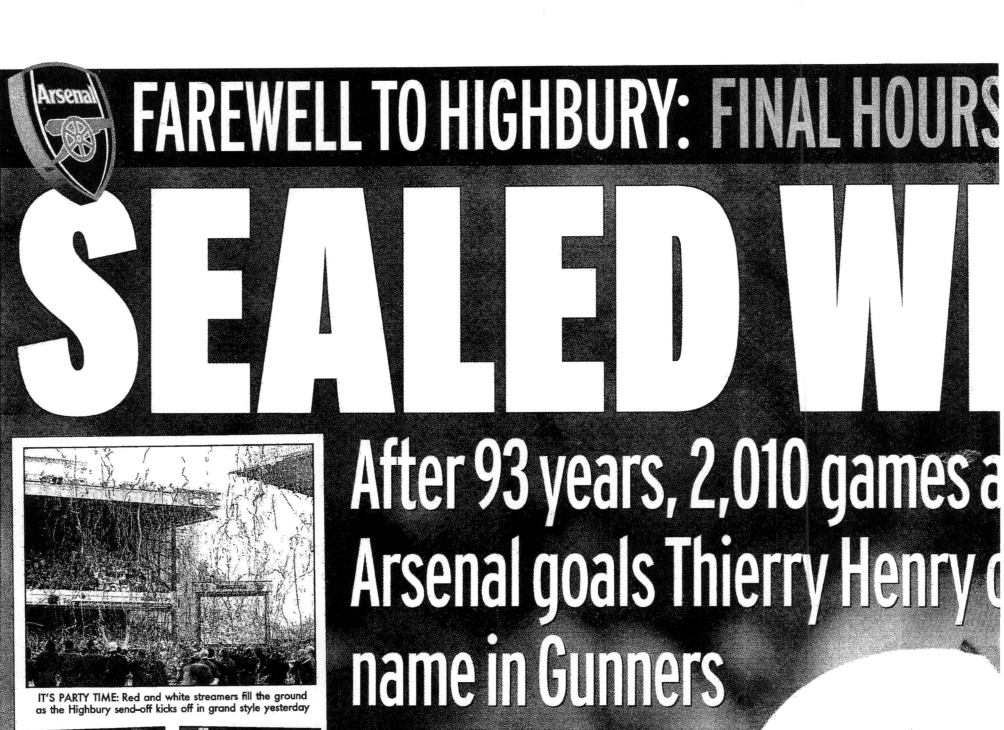

After 93 years, 2,010 games a Arsenal goals Thierry Henry name in Gunners history with a special tribute to Highbury

IT'S PARTY TIME: Red and white streamers fill the ground as the Highbury send–off kicks off in grand style yesterday

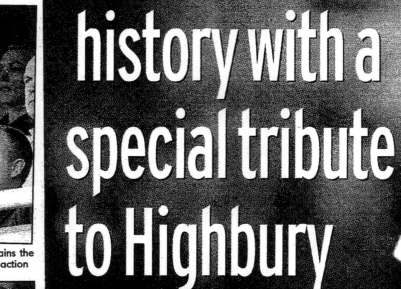

ROGER AND OUT: Arsenal fan Roger Daltrey entertains the crowd at the end and George Michael watches the action

WRIGHT STUFF: Gunners legend Ian Wright acknowledges the fans

TH A KISS

nd 4,038
carves his

THE FINAL ACT:
Who else but
Thierry Henry fires
home the last goal
at Highbury. He
scores a penalty
that sealed a 4-2
win and then
kisses the turf
Pictures:
KENT GAVIN

GIVE HIM A BIG HAND: Boss Arsene Wenger celebrates a
memorable final day at Highbury with adoring Arsenal fans

KING GEORGE: North Bank legend Charlie George
applauds the crowd while this fan pays his own tribute

HIGHBURY GIANTS: Supporters get into the party spirit
with models of Wenger, Henry, Adams and Bergkamp

JUMP START: Robert Pires celebrates after firing the Gunners in front

Henry...he floats like a butterfly and stings like a bee!

Arsenal 4 Wigan 2

By MARTIN LIPTON

CHIEF FOOTBALL WRITER

THE STAGE was set, the theatre full, the performance a sell-out.

So on the pitch that once played home to The Greatest, it was only right that the greatest Arsenal performer of them all was word-perfect to ensure the Highbury era ended in style.

While Muhammad Ali paused only briefly in this corner of north London to put paid to one Henry (Cooper), another Henry has called it home for seven glorious years.

Many legends have worn the famous Arsenal shirt and graced this beautiful stadium.

They were led out for the fans to pay tribute after the game, names like Malcolm McDonald, Frank McLintock, Paul Merson, David Seaman and Ian Wright, all basking in the adulation.

Whether Thierry Henry will be back is impossible to say. We know that Dennis Bergkamp and Robert Pires will not return and that Ashley Cole could be joining them through the exit door.

But on this day, with so much at stake as well as so much to celebrate, there could be only

one hero. Henry's seventh Arsenal hat-trick was not, like some of the previous six, a work of art.

Two simple one-on-one finishes and a penalty represented perhaps three of the easiest of the 142 goals he has scored at the stadium he has turned into a personal shrine.

In what could be his final campaign at Arsenal, with Barcelona waiting not only to end his Champions League dream but also to entice him to the Nou Camp, he

Roar

This was not a vintage Arsenal performance. Indeed, with Wigan determined to put up a fight, the whole afternoon could have turned into a nightmare.

Even after Pires turned home Kolo Toure's knock-down at the second opportunity to fire Arsenal into an eighth-minute lead, events elsewhere were taking over.

The roar that greeted news of Carl Fletcher's opener for

has shone brightest of all. And as so often, when Gunners needed him most, he was there to deliver the goods, his hat-trick ensuring that Arsenal rather than bitter rivals Spurs claimed the fourth Champions League slot.

West Ham against Spurs at Upton Park clearly affected Arsene Wenger's men, who soon found themselves staring at the unthinkable.

Jens Lehmann may not have accepted total blame when Paul Scharner nudged home David Thompson's near-post free-kick to level seconds later

But the German was all over the place when Thompson let fly from 35 yards with another dipping free-kick 12 minutes before the break

Crisis, where it had all seemed so easy. But cometh the hour, cometh the man.

Henry began his assault on Wigan, on Spurs, and on the history books.

Fittingly, perhaps, it was an error by a Spurs player the on-loan Reto Ziegler that

paved the way for Henry's first, although once Pires slipped him through on goal there was only ever going to be one conclusion as the Frenchman side-footed home.

And 11 minutes after the restart, another catastrophic defensive blunder this time Thompson's errant back pass, saw Henry skip round Mike Pollitt and slot home

The ecstatic Arsenal crowd demanded more and 15 minutes from time it came.

Swedes Andreas Johansson and Freddie Ljungberg had followed each other onto the park as substitutes and before either had touched the ball, the Wigan man clearly hauled Ljungberg back in the box.

For once woeful ref Uriah Rennie got one right pointing to the spot and sending off Johansson after just 88 seconds on the pitch

Henry made no mistake to take his club tally to 214, dropping to his knees and kissing the turf in front of the North Bank in celebration.

News of Yossi Benayoun's West Ham winner came as Bergkamp made his final Premiership bow, and the waves of warmth that spread round all four corners summed up the mood. For the Arsenal fans this was not a funeral. It was a joyous celebration of 93 years of history, a day to make memories as well as recall them.

Henry has made many of them. If he is not back next year, he has left a legacy that will never be forgotten. That is the mark of a true genius.

HENRY IS THE WORLD'S No.1

FROM MANIA PAGE 1

farewell from both, but Wenger added: "I don't know who will go or who will stay. I want to keep everybody.

"This will be the last game at Highbury for Thierry but I hope it won't be the last for the club."

Arsenal's win, coupled with Spurs' defeat at West Ham, saw Tottenham – struck down by food poisoning overnight – lose the fourth spot they have held since December 3.

Wenger said: "It will take some of the pressure off when we play Barcelona. I'm confident this team has the character we need.

"I feel that for the history of the club it was important for us to finish at Highbury on a high. I am very proud that we did."

Wigan chairman Dave Whelan was left stunned last night as French defender Pascal Chimbonda marched up to him to hand in a written transfer request before he had even taken off his boots.

A shocked Whelan said he would only grant the transfer if another club paid £6million for the defender.

Arsenal		Wigan
54%	POSSESSION	46%
6	SHOTS ON TARGET	3
6	SHOTS OFF TARGET	5
3	OFFSIDES	2
5	CORNERS	1
13	FOULS	17
1	YELLOW CARDS	1
0	RED CARDS	1

ATTENDANCE: 38,359
MAN OF THE MATCH: Henry

TEAMS AND RATINGS

ARSENAL: Lehmann 6; Eboue 7, Toure 8, Campbell 6, Cole 7; Hleb 7 (Van Persie 80, 6), Fabregas, Gilberto, Pires (Ljungberg 75, 6), Henry 8, Reyes 7 (Bergkamp 79, 6).
WIGAN: Pollitt 7, Chimbonda 6, Jackson 7, Scharner 6, Baines 6, Thompson 7 (Johansson 75, 4), Kavanagh 6, Ziegler 6 (Francis 67, 6), McCulloch 7, Roberts 8, Camara 7 (Connolly 82, 6)
Referee: URIAH RENNIE

FIRST AMONG EQUALS: Thierry Henry slides the ball under Mike Pollitt to level at 2-2

BARCELONA 2 ARSENAL 1 CHAMPIONS LEAGUE FINAL

KICKED UP THE BARCA

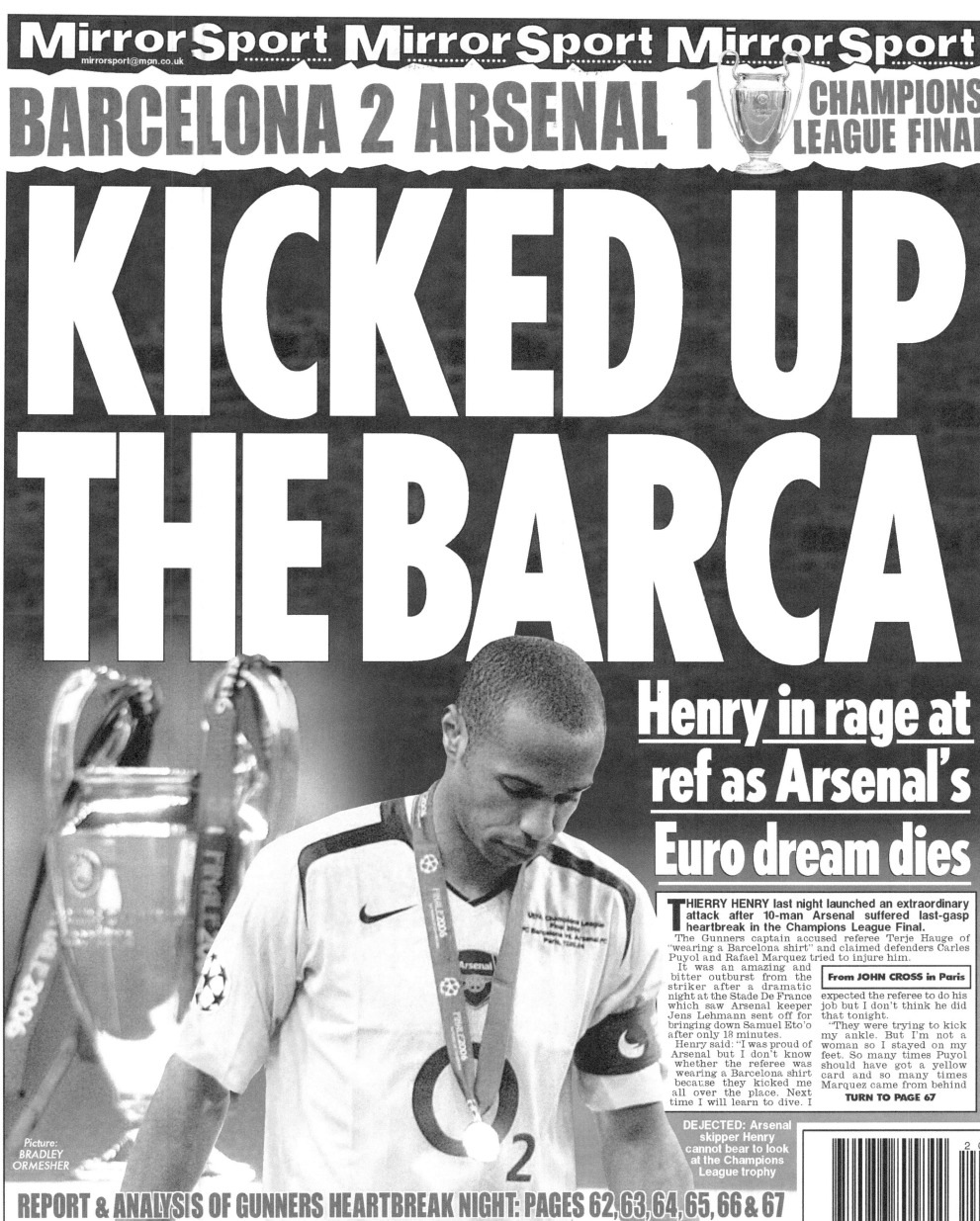

Henry in rage at ref as Arsenal's Euro dream dies

THIERRY HENRY last night launched an extraordinary attack after 10-man Arsenal suffered last-gasp heartbreak in the Champions League Final.

The Gunners captain accused referee Terje Hauge of "wearing a Barcelona shirt" and claimed defenders Carles Puyol and Rafael Marquez tried to injure him.

It was an amazing and bitter outburst from the striker after a dramatic night at the Stade De France which saw Arsenal keeper Jens Lehmann sent off for bringing down Samuel Eto'o after only 18 minutes.

Henry said: "I was proud of Arsenal but I don't know whether the referee was wearing a Barcelona shirt because they kicked me all over the place. Next time I will learn to dive. I

From JOHN CROSS in Paris

expected the referee to do his job but I don't think he did that tonight.

"They were trying to kick my ankle. But I'm not a woman so I stayed on my feet. So many times Puyol should have got a yellow card and so many times Marquez came from behind

TURN TO PAGE 67

Picture: BRADLEY ORMESHER

DEJECTED: Arsenal skipper Henry cannot bear to look at the Champions League trophy

REPORT & ANALYSIS OF GUNNERS HEARTBREAK NIGHT: PAGES 62, 63, 64, 65, 66 & 67

Published by MGN Ltd. at One Canada Square, Canary Wharf, London, E14 5AP (020-7293 3000) and printed by Trinity Mirror Printing Ltd. at Watford, Oldham and Birmingham. Registered as a newspaper at the Post Office **Serial No. 32,734** ©MGN Ltd. Thursday, May 18, 2006 ■ ■ ■ ■ ■ ■ ■ ■ ■ ■ ★ Austria 3.00EUR, Belgium 2.00 EUR, France 2.00 EUR, Germany 2.00 EUR, Greece 2.00 EUR, Italy 2.00 EUR, Netherlands 2.00 EUR, Portuga 2.00 EUR (continent) 341Esc, Spain 2.00EUR, Malta 53 cents, Turkey: 4.25 YTL, Cyprus £1.05, Denmark 20DK

BARCELONA 2 ARSENAL 1 UEFA

FAIRYTALE

ENGLAND & THE EUROPEAN CUP

ARSENAL'S defeat last night was the third for an English side in Europe. Leeds lost 2-0 to Bayern Munich in 1975 and Liverpool were beaten 1-0 by Juventus in 1985.

Scotland's Celtic were, of course, the first British winners back in 1967 and here's England's full roll of honour...

1968, Wembley: **MAN UTD 4** *(Charlton 53, 99, Best 93, Kidd 94)* **BENFICA 1** *(Graca 75)*

1977, Rome: **LIVERPOOL 3** *(McDermott 28, Smith 67, Neal pen 85)* **BORUSSIA M'GLADBACH 1** *(Simonsen 50)*

1978, Wembley: **LIVERPOOL 1** *(Dalglish 64)* **BRUGES 0**

1979, Munich: **NOTTM FOREST 1** *(Francis 45)* **MALMO 0**

1980, Madrid: **NOTTM FOREST 1** *(Robertson 21)* **HAMBURG 0**

1981, Paris: **LIVERPOOL 1** *(Kennedy 81)* **REAL MADRID 0**

1982, Rotterdam: **A VILLA 1** *(Withe 67)* **BAYERN MUNICH 0**

1984, Rome: **LIV'POOL 1** *(Neal 14)* **ROMA** *(Pruzzo 45)* **1 AET** *(Liverpool won 4-2 on penalties)*

1999, Barcelona: **MAN UTD 2** *(Sheringham 90, Solskjaer 90)* **BAYERN MUNICH 1** *(Basler 6)*

2005, Istanbul: **LIVERPOOL 3** *(Gerrard 54, Smicer 56, Alonso 59)* **AC MILAN 3** *(Maldini 1, Crespo 39, 44) **AET** *(Liverpool won 3-2 on penalties)*

CHAMPS: Barca lift the Cup

THE SAM BUSTER: Samuel Eto'o celebrates Barca's 76th-minute equaliser with Arsenal full-back Ashley Cole appealing for offside
Pictures: BRADLEY ORMESHER

CHAMPIONS LEAGUE FINAL FROM PARIS

TURNS SOUR

Final agony for 10-man Arsenal as Barca pinch Euro glory

MARTIN LIPTON

CHIEF FOOTBALL WRITER, AT THE STADE DE FRANCE

DREAMS are not supposed to be ended like this, shattered into a million pieces just as they start to look like reality.

Glory should not be snatched away when it seems so close, stolen from a side that had given everything and believed it could achieve the impossible.

But sometimes even Arsene Wenger cannot conjure a magic night when he needs it.

And while Arsenal left the Stade de France railing against the injustices of the world, as Thierry Henry ranted, Jens Lehmann brooded and Manuel Almunia reflected on how quickly a fairy tale can turn sour, in the end the truth was that the better team won.

Last night, just as Arsenal

ROW: Henry protests to ref Hauge

looked set to pull off the greatest rearguard action that ever was, the irresistible force of the men from the Nou Camp eventually swamped the Gunners.

Despite the best efforts of referee Terje Hauge, who seemed single-handedly set on ruining the game by getting so many decisions wrong, the Stade de France witnessed a worthy Final.

With less than a quarter of an hour to go, Wenger's men appeared to have done the impossible, not only preventing Ronaldinho from weaving his destructive magic, but doing so with 10 men after Lehmann was sent off after just 18 minutes.

That decision summed up the inadequacies of the official who should have waited for just a second to watch Ludovic Giuly roll the ball into the empty net rather than blowing up and leaving himself no option but to dismiss the German keeper.

Yet Arsenal, who had began so brightly with Henry cursing himself as he failed to convert Emmanuel Eboue's cross after skipping away from Carles Puyol in only the third minute, delivered a stunning twist.

It created a remarkable story with Sol Campbell poised to sing a personal redemption song that was reverberating around the stadium.

When Campbell rose superbly to power home Henry's free-kick, it banished the clouds of doubt that have hung over his mind and body since that infamous half-time walk-out against West Ham on February 1.

It did not matter that Eboue's outrageous dive had bought the set-piece as Campbell roared

with glee and the travelling Gooners began to believe. At times afterwards, especially when Samuel Eto'o sprang away from him with that panther-like gait to crash the ball against the post courtesy of Almunia's fingertips, Campbell was rocking.

Yet in his desire and determination, echoed through the yellow-shirted ranks, Arsenal defied all logic and were poised to fulfil their apparent destiny.

But football is the cruellest of games, and it was horribly unfair that Almunia, who had done so much to keep the Gunners in the lead, and Henry of all people were cast in the role of villains.

The captain, with his lightning thrusts and rapier moves, had

IT'S OVER: Barcelona sub Juliano Belletti shoots at Almunia...

END OF THE DREAM

...and the ball flies in off the keeper's leg for their late winner

prevented Barcelona from throwing everything at his men even at the height of their second-half siege.

While Ronaldinho flickered in and out and Eto'o roamed majestically, Arsenal's resolve was conspiring to destroy Catalan hearts.

Brutal

With every block by Campbell, clearance by Kolo Toure, tackle by Ashley Cole or Gilberto or save by Almunia, their frustrations and desperation intensified.

Three times, caught by Arsenal's brilliant counter-attacks, they could have suffered the knock-out blow.

First Alex Hleb, fed by Henry, dragged wide and Freddie Ljungberg

was denied by Victor Valdes. And the best chance of all went to Henry.

It was the sort of opening he normally takes without thought. But when it mattered most, when one swing of that right foot would have brought the ultimate joy, Henry fired straight at Valdes. Within minutes, Barca were level.

Ronaldinho, now hugging his favoured left touchline, dropped deep to feed substitute Henrik Larsson whose sublime touch freed Eto'o.

Arsenal were convinced the flag should have gone up but Eto'o did not care and as Almunia left a gap at his near post the Cameroonian slipped in with all the certainty Henry had lacked shortly beforehand.

Within four minutes it was all over as Larsson picked out defender Juliano Belletti.

Sub Mathieu Flamini could not get there but Belletti's cross-shot would surely have gone out for a goal-kick if Almunia had left it. Instead, the touch off the inside of his right knee diverted the ball into the net as Belletti was submerged under a tide of blue and maroon shirts.

There was no way back, no chance of turning the game back again. Dead on their feet, a man short and shattered, there was nothing left to give. All they had were recriminations and remorse. So harsh, so brutal. Not destiny, just despair.

HENRY'S RAGE AT REFEREE

FROM BACK PAGE

to take my ankles as well." Henry also claimed Barcelona stars Eto'o and Ronaldinho did not play well – and it was supersub Henrik Larsson who turned the game.

"Larsson was the difference," Henry added. "But I did not see Ronaldinho and I did not see Eto'o."

Henry's comments could now land him in trouble with UEFA and were also surprising. Arsenal were lucky when Lehmann was sent off that Hauge did not play the advantage and allow Ludovic Giuly's effort to stand.

Television replays also showed that Emmanuel Eboue dived under Puyol's challenge to win a free-kick which led to Sol Campbell's 37th-minute opener.

Arsenal stayed ahead with reserve keeper Manuel Almunia making a string of saves before Eto'o and Juliano Belletti fired goals in the 76th and 80th minutes.

It was devastating for Arsenal boss Arsene Wenger who also admitted that he was disappointed by Hauge's performance.

Heroes

It also came 24 hours after linesman Ole Hermann Borgan was removed from the game after being photographed in a Barcelona shirt.

"We have lost and it is hard to take because of some of the decisions," said Wenger. "But this team will come back even stronger.

"One of their goals was also offside and with 10 men it's hard to cope against a world-class team like Barcelona.

"I never thought we had it won. I'm not naive enough to believe that with 15 minutes to go, 1-0 up with 10 men that it was won.

"I couldn't have asked for any more. My players were heroes but they are not rewarded."

At the end Eto'o spent several minutes talking with Henry, who could be one of his team-mates next season.

Eto'o was coy about what was discussed, however, adding: "This was our private little thing. I will call him on the phone later. We are friends."

Barcelona boss Frank Rijkaard said: "It was a difficult game because Arsenal sat back after the sending off and when they scored.

"I feel sorry for the fans as the sending off changed the game and made it hard for us."

F.C.B.		Arsenal
71%	POSSESSION	29%
9	SHOTS ON TARGET	5
7	SHOTS OFF TARGET	3
1	OFFSIDES	1
3	CORNERS	4
20	FOULS	16
2	YELLOW CARDS	2
0	RED CARDS	1

ATTENDANCE: 79,500
MAN OF THE MATCH: Eto'o

DREAM START: Sol Campbell outjumps Oleguer to head home Thierry Henry's 37th-minute free-kick

OLIVER HOLT'S VERDICT: PAGES 64 & 65 ⚽ **TEAMS & RATINGS: PAGES 62 & 63**

CARLING CUP ⚽ LIVERPOOL 3 ARSENAL 6 CARLING

BAP BOPS THE

RIGHT OLD KNEES UP: Julio Baptista gets a pat after scoring the sixth for Arsenal, but Jeremie Aliadiere receives all the congratulations from Cesc Fabregas, Abou Diaby and Armand Traore
Pics: BRADLEY ORMESHER

NIGHTMARE: It's grim for Benitez

Kids romp to a record

FROM BACK PAGE

six at Anfield in 77 years, and Baptista became the first visiting player to score four since Wolves' Denis Westcott in 1946. But Arsene Wenger was more concerned with the future than the past as he hailed his fabulous fringe men.

He said: "I have always believed Baptista would deliver. He has great mental strength and a team attitude. He's scored four, might have had a fifth, and I thought he and Jeremie Aliadiere were outstanding up front.

"I did not expect us to get six goals but I am very pleased with the way we tackled the game. It was the way we want to play football. I am tempted to put these players out against Spurs. They have earned the right to play."

Kop keeper Jerzy Dudek had a nightmare and was to blame for two of the goals, even though he saved the spot-kick. The agony for Liverpool was completed by the loss of Mark Gonzalez with a leg injury after five minutes and then sub Luis Garcia with a knee injury.

Aliadiere, Baptista, Alexandre Song and Baptista again tore through the Liverpool defence in one of the worst first halves in Anfield history. Robbie Fowler equalised at 1-1 and skipper Steven Gerrard made it 5-2. Sami Hyypia pulled one back before Baptista completed the rout.

Baptista said: "It was special for me and for the team. We are very strong and I am very happy."

TRUTH HURTS: Anfield scoreboard is painful

Luxury gap real concern for Rafa

Alan Nixon

IT WAS like being at a fashion show or even a motor exhibition – as next year's models were rolled out for inspection before they become known on every high street.

And on this evidence there are plenty of young Gunners heading for the fast lane, while the Liverpool kids spluttered to a halt last night.

Arsenal's Denilson is a wiry-looking Brazilian while Armand Traore, a young master from Paris, has positional sense and quick feet for a left-back. Cameroon's

Alexandre Song is a little raw but could do well out on loan.

Keeping them occupied is Arsene Wenger's dilemma – as Jeremie Aliadiere has proved. The Frenchman was a hero at youth-team level but stagnated as his career drifted. He proved he has the ability with his goal but the hard part is finding somewhere to play. Liverpool have

nobody in their ranks who looks like a future world-beater. There is no Gerrard or even Carragher coming through on last night's showing.

It was further proof to Rafa Benitez that he has to get those Dubai millions in quickly to buy from the smartest showrooms, rather than waiting for the next star to drop off the Anfield assembly line.

Lee Peltier, Danny Guthrie and even the mountainous Gabriel Paletta are a fair distance away from making an impact.

FREDDIE RAGE AT ARSENAL KO

FROM BACK PAGE

at all. He knows he's not had a great season with injuries but he expected to be given time to recover.

"Instead he was told that Arsenal have to sell in order to buy and that he is one of the players to go.

"From what they have said it's not about where he wants to go, but where he's told to go. He was told in no uncertain terms he should take any offer that is on the table, otherwise he will not play again."

Ljungberg was stunned to be told last week that he is surplus to requirements after more than seven years service to the club he joined in 1999.

CUP QUARTER-FINAL FROM ANFIELD

KOP FLOPS

Reds humiliated again as rampant Gunners hit them for six at Anfield

GUNNING FOR BLUES: Tommy Mooney's never forgiven Marcel Desailly

David Maddock

LIVERPOOL suffered their worst humiliation at Anfield in almost 80 years last night, destroyed by four-goal Julio Baptista and the young Gunners.

Not since 1930 have the Reds conceded six goals at home, and it could take almost as long to erase the memory of this truly horrible Carling Cup performance.

A disbelieving crowd had waited almost a month for this tie to be replayed, after the original game had been postponed because of fog.

As it turned out, they'd have seen more had it gone ahead then, because they watched most of the match through their hands.

Late goals from Steven Gerrard and Sami Hyypia clawed a little pride back, but it didn't disguise the fact that the Anfield club trail a worrying distance behind their London rivals.

Shallow

In fact, had the brilliant Baptista not missed a second half penalty then Liverpool would have conceded seven goals here for the first time in their history.

Liverpool manager Rafael Benitez has privately conceded for some time that he simply doesn't have the class in his side, never mind his squad, to mount a serious challenge to England's big three. This confirmed it.

When Arsenal can produce a truly awesome display such as this, after making NINE changes from the team that won here at the weekend, then you know they have got quite outstanding strength in depth.

In reply, Liverpool had only their indomitable skipper Gerrard and veteran striker Robbie Fowler to put up any sort of resistance. Their squad looks very shallow indeed.

From the 26th minute, there was an ominous silence around Anfield as goalkeeper Jerzy Dudek repeated his horror show of the weekend.

He failed to deal with a weak shot from Jeremie Aliadiere, after the Frenchman had been allowed to stroll through a dreaming defence to give Arsene Wenger's youngsters the lead. Fowler showed his

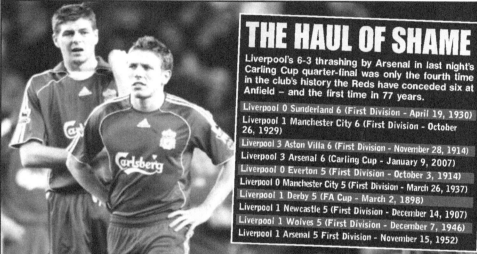

FRIGHT NIGHT: Steven Gerrard and Craig Bellamy find defeat hard to take as Liverpool's season descended into disaster

THE HAUL OF SHAME

Liverpool's 6-3 thrashing by Arsenal in last night's Carling Cup quarter-final was only the fourth time in the club's history the Reds have conceded six at Anfield – and the first time in 77 years.

Liverpool 0 Sunderland 6 (First Division - April 19, 1930)
Liverpool 1 Manchester City 6 (First Division - October 26, 1929)
Liverpool 3 Aston Villa 6 (First Division - November 28, 1914)
Liverpool 3 Arsenal 6 (Carling Cup - January 9, 2007)
Liverpool 0 Everton 5 (First Division - October 3, 1914)
Liverpool 0 Manchester City 5 (First Division - March 26, 1937)
Liverpool 1 Derby 5 (FA Cup - March 2, 1898)
Liverpool 1 Newcastle 5 (First Division - December 14, 1907)
Liverpool 1 Wolves 5 (First Division - December 7, 1946)
Liverpool 1 Arsenal 5 First Division - November 15, 1952)

class and briefly levelled when he cleverly flicked home a cross from substitute Luis Garcia through his legs.

But then Baptista took over as Liverpool were engulfed in a mist of defensive incompetence.

The Brazilian is known as 'The Beast', but there was a beauty about his play as he combined brilliantly with Aliadiere – whose movement was a joy to behold – to rip a woeful home defence and their bumbling keeper to shreds.

On 40 minutes Baptista lofted in a free-kick which Dudek just stood and admired. Then he combined brilliantly with his French sidekick to dance through and

convert with a degree of arrogance.

That goal came in first half stoppage time but, incredibly, it was Arsenal's fourth before the break, because seconds before Dudek flapped like a circus sea lion at a corner from Cesc Fabregas, to allow Alex Song to convert with the use of his own arm and Hyypia's knee.

Dudek offered some respite when he produced his only save of the match to briefly deny Baptista his hat-trick.

But normal service was resumed when the Polish keeper dived all around the Brazilian's shot from the edge of the box on the hour. By then, the statisticians were already reaching for the record books, and even though the home side did make a

LIVERPOOL		Arsenal
48%	POSSESSION	52%
9	SHOTS ON TARGET	7
6	SHOTS OFF TARGET	1
5	OFFSIDES	0
9	CORNERS	3
13	FOULS	16
0	YELLOW CARDS	1
0	RED CARDS	0

ATTENDANCE: 42,614
MAN OF THE MATCH: Baptista

better fist of it in the last half hour, they were still reduced to their biggest home embarrassment since Sunderland won 6-0 here back in the Great Depression.

Gerrard's goal was a beauty, an audacious volley on 67 minutes, and with 10 minutes left Hyypia headed home from a Danny Guthrie cross.

But Baptista fittingly had the last word when he rolled home after Aliadiere had again taken Liverpool apart.

It will now be interesting to see what team Wenger selects for their semi-final against London rivals Spurs.

For Liverpool, Saturday's selection will be rather more straight forward, given the need to extinguish this agonising memory.

LIVERPOOL: Dudek, Peltier, Hyypia, Paletta, Warnock (Alonso 58), Guthrie, Gerrard, Aurelio, Gonzalez (Luis Garcia 11), Fowler, Bellamy (Carragher 75).
ARSENAL: Almunia, Hoyte, Toure, Djourou, Traore (Connolly 88), Walcott (Diaby 74), Fabregas, Song, Denilson, Julio Baptista, Aliadiere.

Can't Kick Won't Kick...

ABRAMOVICH SPEAKS OUT:
HE'S REALLY TERRIBLE! HE'S GONNA HAVE TO GO!!!

YOU'LL HELP ME FIND A NEW MANAGER WON'T YOU ANDRIY?

YESKI!

SHEVCHENKO MOURINHO

SHEVCHENKO MO

Kerber+Black

By NEIL KERBER AND DAVID BLACK

CARLING CUP SEMI-FINAL, 1ST LEG, WYCOMBE v CHELSEA, TONIGHT, 8PM

By MIKE WALTERS

WYCOMBE skipper Tommy Mooney faces the team that "destroyed" his Premiership dream tonight – and nearly ended his career.

And while he holds no grudges against Chelsea, tonight's Carling Cup semi-final first leg opponents, his seven-year-old son Kelsey is even a big fan of Jose Mourinho's team, he will never forgive Stamford Bridge legend Marcel Desailly for the tackle that put him out of the game for seven months.

Mooney was starring for Watford in their last Premiership stopover (when they beat Chelsea 1-0 at Vicarage Road, to widespread hilarity) when French defender Desailly hit him with a brutal tackle.

He said: "I was clattered by Desailly by the corner flag and spent seven-and-a-half months out with a displaced kneecap as a result.

"I needed two operations and by the time I came back, Watford were already down.

"I wasn't happy about the challenge: if you said it showed disregard for a fellow professional's well-being, that covers it quite well – Desailly was a World Cup winner, but he never apologised.

"I don't hold any grudges against Chelsea as a club – in fact, my son Kelsey, is a massive Chelsea fan. We've only been to the Bridge once this season, for the 1-0 win against Barcelona in the Champions League this season, so he's absolutely hooked.

"But I still don't care much for Desailly. I wouldn't stand at the bar and have a shandy with

MOONEY: DESAILLY WRECKED MY CAREER

him, and whenever he came on TV as a pundit at the World Cup last summer, I wanted to put my boot through the screen – although I would rather deliver it in person!

"It's more than seven years ago now, and I wish the disappointment would go away, but it has always been there, gnawing away at me.

"It totally destroyed what should have been the best year of my professional life."

There will be mixed emotions, too, for Steve Brown, hero of Wycombe's run to the FA Cup semis in 2001, who will be reunited tonight with referee Steve Bennett – the clot who sent him off for sending a message to his seriously-ill son Maxwell after scoring in the quarter-finals.

PROBABLE TEAMS

Wycombe	Chelsea
4-4-2	4-4-2
Young	Hilario
O'Halloran	Bridge
Antwi	Essien
Martin	Ferreira
Williamson	Geremi
Bloomfield	Wright-Phillips
Betsy	Diarra
Oakes	Ballack
Torres	Mikel
Mooney	Shevchenko
Easter	Kalou

TV TIMES: Live on Sky Sports 1 from 7.30pm

JOSE'S KEEP-BALL

By MARTIN LIPTON

JOSE MOURINHO last night gave his strongest public backing for Michael Ballack.

The Chelsea boss insisted that the £130,000-a-week German skipper was worth his automatic place in the Blues side on merit, despite scoring just five goals in 24 games since arriving from Bayern Munich.

And Mourinho shot down suggestions that senior Blues stars had confronted him over Ballack's dismal contribution so far.

He said: "Reports about problems in the dressing room are not correct. Do we want more from Ballack in terms of performance? Not from him, from everybody.

"If the objective is to put some kind of pressure on me then no chance because I pick the team, nobody else does it.

"He is in the team not because the fans, the president or journalists pick it, but because I do.

"Michael has not done anything amazing yet, but he is a team player and sacrifices himself for the team. That is another reason why he plays."

THIERRY

Robbo: We back boss

By MARTIN LIPTON

PAUL ROBINSON last night insisted the Spurs players are all behind Martin Jol, but admitted they must keep him in his job.

One win and four points from six games leaves Spurs, who started the season thinking about the top four, in the wrong quartet of clubs at the other end of the table.

But the England keeper maintains the only difference between Tottenham and Arsenal is confidence and Jol is the manager who can turn things around.

Robinson said: "The players are fully behind the manager. We are hopeful that he will be staying and we will dig out the results for him in the next few weeks.

"People are going to talk because of what has happened this season, but we've got a very close, tight ship. We're keeping everything in-house and we're going to get the results for the manager.

"The performance against Arsenal wasn't lacklustre. It wasn't a team that rolled over and accepted defeat, but one that was up for the fight.

"We know they're not streets ahead of us. But there's a mentality, they finish games off."

One month to save job

FROM BACK PAGE

the home defeat by Arsenal that plunged Spurs to 17th in the Premier League table.

But the next five games, in three different competitions, will be used to decide whether or not the Dutchman goes.

But he will be sacked regardless if Sevilla's Juande Ramos decides he wants to take up the White Hart Lane challenge.

The Spurs boss said: "I feel there are two worlds here in London. There are the people who want me out and and then there are the supporters. They are still backing me and that's a great feeling.

"I don't think the board is a problem and as long as the players show me the commitment they showed again, there is no problem."

GLORY BOYS: Arsenal stars Tomas Rosicky, Kolo Toure and Emmanuel Adebayor celebrate victory over Spurs

SHAKER: Wenger and Jol after the match

NO THIERRY, no hope? I think we got that one wrong.

And as Arsene Wenger stared down from the top of the Premiership for the first time since November 2004, the Gunners chief admitted he feels he could be creating his most vibrant Arsenal team yet.

Of the team that started at the ground where the 'Invincibles' claimed their crown three years ago, only Kolo Toure and Gilberto remained.

Thierry Henry's departure this summer, following on from the passing of Patrick Vieira, Dennis Bergkamp, Ashley Cole and Robert Pires, was supposed to signal the end of Wenger's Golden Era, not its glorious rebirth.

It may have taken 66 minutes for Emmanuel Adebayor's header to finally reward Arsenal's beautiful football – cancelling out Gareth Bale's early free-kick – to take the ridiculous out of the north London derby scoreline.

But nobody inside White Hart Lane, including the Spurs fans whose subdued mood throughout bore witness to what they were seeing, would deny that Wenger's men played the purest football on display in the Premiership so far this season.

Sublime goals from the magnificent Cesc Fabregas and Adebayor sealed the victory, a thunderous strike from the Spaniard followed by the African's stunning volley. Yet

MARTIN LIPTON
CHIEF FOOTBALL WRITER

what inspired, thrilled and captivated was the sheer instinctive quality Arsenal showed all over the pitch. At times it tore Spurs to shreds.

No wonder Wenger looks more content than he has for three years. It was a performance worthy of adding a new word to the footballing vocabulary. "I'm very excited with this team because – I don't know if the word exists – they are 'playerish'," said Wenger.

"They love to play and that is something that you feel from the outside. They love to play. Even at 2-1 they don't go to the corner flag, they continue to try to score.

"There is an extra dynamic in there because, maybe, the players feel this is the year in which they have to grow old. The younger players are more experienced."

Nobody sums that up more than the boy-man at the heart of everything. Fabregas may only be 20, but in his head he is already 32, chillingly calm amid the maelstrom and utterly outstanding.

Wenger added: "If it becomes hectic he keeps his head and cools the game down when it becomes a bit nervous.

"Suddenly he finds a good pass and gets you out of tight

EARLY HOPE: Gareth Bale's goal puts Tottenham in front

INSIDE: YOUR No.1 MANIA PULL-OUT

BIRMINGHAM 1 / BOLTON 0 Mania Page 13
CHELSEA 0 / BLACKBURN 0 Mania Pages 4 & 5
EVERTON 0 / MAN UTD 1 Mania Pages 10 & 11
PORTSMOUTH 0 / LIVERPOOL 0 Mania Pages 8 & 9

confidence between London rivals

WHO?

Wenger's awesome kids prove there is life after Henry, firing Gunners to top & putting Jol on brink

ONE OF THE GREATS: Fabregas has put Arsenal on top

LEAP OF FAITH: Adebayor outjumps Paul Robinson to score

THEY'VE AD IT: Adebayor gets his second goal

FAB-ULOUS: Cesc scores a screamer

43%	POSSESSION	57%
2	SHOTS ON TARGET	8
8	SHOTS OFF TARGET	5
	OFFSIDES	14
6	CORNERS	11
13	FOULS	20
2	YELLOW CARDS	0
0	RED CARDS	0

ATTENDANCE: 36,053
MAN OF THE MATCH: Fabregas

TEAMS AND RATINGS
TOTTENHAM: Robinson 6, Chimbonda 7, Dawson 6, Kaboul 5, Lee 5, Malbranque 6 (Bent 82), Jenas 7, Huddlestone 6, Bale 6 (Lennon, 69, 6), Berbatov 6, Keane 5.
ARSENAL: Almunia 6, Sagna 7, Toure 8, Gilberto 7, Clichy 6; Hleb 7 (Song 90), Fabregas 9, Flamini 7, Diaby 5 (Rosicky, 56, 6); Adebayor 8, Van Persie 7 (Denilson 85).

situations." Fabregas himself is revelling in his role as the heartbeat of these new Gunners.

The nervelessness which saw him grab Vieira's No.4 shirt two years ago is being backed up time and again and his fifth goal of the campaign has already bettered last season's tally.

"Thierry was an important player for a lot of years, but now he's not here, he's gone," said Fabregas. "We have to play more as a team like we're doing now. We're playing more collectively, more as a team and this is important.

"Scoring late goals shows we're strong physically and stay in games until the end, which is very important to develop spirit in the team. We never give up."

Weaker teams than Arsenal might have felt it was not meant to be when Bale scored with Spurs' only first-half shot, while Paul Robinson and the woodwork foiled Adebayor, Alex Hleb and Abou Diaby.

The second period was more even. Toure bailed out Manuel Almunia's headless chicken rush which looked to have left Dimitar Berbatov with an open goal before Adebayor made up for a hat-trick of misses by beating Robinson to Fabregas' free-kick.

"Sometimes people have questions about Emmanuel but when you take him out of the team you feel there is a lot of presence gone out," said Wenger. "He can be frustrating because he can miss an easy chance but he has shown today what big chances he can take. And he is a constant threat in the air."

Adebayor caused Michael Dawson and Younes Kaboul ceaseless problems, although Spurs could have gone in front again a minute prior to Fabregas' stunner when Berbatov's volley smashed against Gael Clichy's chest before the Bulgarian nodded the rebound over.

But when sub Darren Bent missed horribly after Jermaine Jenas sent him through on goal, Spurs were deflated, and Adebayor's goal of the season contender was the perfect finale.

"It was one of the best goals of my career, because it was an amazing control and shot so I'm very happy," said the Togo striker, who has now scored five in as many games against Spurs.

"We just have to keep believing in ourselves and keep playing our football."

It sums up Wenger's philosophy beautifully. The big question, of course, is whether they can last the pace.

After all, you don't win anything with kids, do you?

PREMIER LEAGUE TABLE
	P	W	D	L	F	A	Pts
Arsenal	5	4	1	0	10	4	13
Man City	4	4	0	2	5	2	12
Liverpool	5	3	2	0	11	2	11
Man Utd	6	3	2	1	7	6	11
Chelsea	5	3	2	1	7	6	11
West Ham	5	3	1	1	8	3	10
Everton	5	3	1	2	8	6	10
Blackburn	5	3	0	5	6	3	9
Newcastle	4	2	2	0	6	5	8
Wigan	6	2	2	2	7	5	8
Aston Villa	5	2	1	2	5	8	7
Birmingham	6	2	1	3	7	9	7
Middlesbro	6	2	1	3	7	7	7
Sunderland	6	2	1	3	5	9	7
Portsmouth	6	1	3	2	7	8	6
Fulham	6	1	2	3	9	11	5
Tottenham	6	1	1	4	9	11	4
Reading	6	1	1	4	9	11	4
Bolton	6	1	1	4	3	10	4
Derby	5	0	1	4	3	15	1

SUNDERLAND ..2 READING 1	*Mania Page 6*
WEST HAM ....3 MIDDLESBRO..0	*Mania Page 12*
WIGAN ....1 FULHAM 1	*Mania Page 7*
MAN CITY.......1 ASTON VILLA...0	*Mania Pages 2 & 3*

PLUS: ALL THE CHAMPIONSHIP, LGE ONE & TWO ACTION
PLUS: STAN THE MAN.. IT'S COLLYMORE ON MONDAY

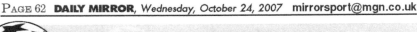

CHAMPIONS LEAGUE GROUP H:

MAGNIFICENT

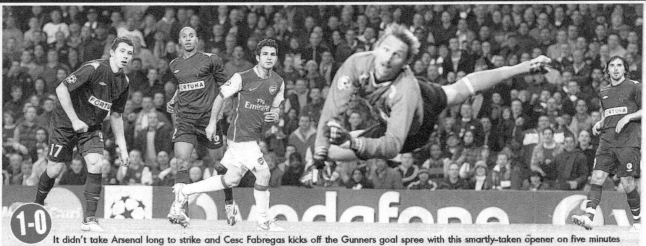

1-0 It didn't take Arsenal long to strike and Cesc Fabregas kicks off the Gunners goal spree with this smartly-taken opener on five minutes

2-0 Slavia's David Hubacek can only divert Alexander Hleb's shot into his own goal

3-0 Theo Walcott puts his mark on the proceedings with the first of two goals

4-0 The visitors do not know what's hit them as Hleb makes it 4-0 on 51 minutes

5-0 Walcott fires home the fifth from a narrow angle just four minutes later

6-0 Free-scoring Fabregas slides home his second of the night as Arsenal run riot

7-0 Substitute Nicklas Bendtner rounds off the rout on 89 minutes *Pictures: KENT GAVIN*

John Cross

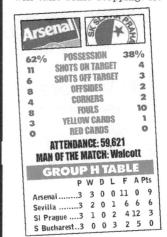

IT WAS a result and a performance which will make the whole of Europe sit up and take notice, let alone the rest of the Premier League.

Slavia Prague are not Champions League heavyweights, but the nature of Arsenal's record-breaking win should serve a notice of intent ahead of two daunting fixtures which will provide the acid test for the Gunners' title ambitions.

Arsene Wenger's youngsters go to Liverpool on Sunday and host Manchester United a week Saturday and you can be sure last night's game will make worrying viewing for Rafa Benitez and Sir Alex Ferguson.

Arsenal were awesome and their 12-match winning run will take some stopping. At

	Arsenal	SK SLAVIA PRAHA
62%	POSSESSION	38%
11	SHOTS ON TARGET	4
6	SHOTS OFF TARGET	4
8	OFFSIDES	2
4	CORNERS	2
8	FOULS	10
3	YELLOW CARDS	1
0	RED CARDS	0

ATTENDANCE: 59,621
MAN OF THE MATCH: Walcott

GROUP H TABLE

	P	W	D	L	F	A	Pts
Arsenal	3	3	0	0	11	0	9
Sevilla	3	2	0	1	6	6	6
Sl Prague	3	1	0	2	4	12	3
S Bucharest	3	0	0	3	2	5	0

the centre of last night's demolition job was Theo Walcott with a two-goal man-of-the-match display which at last justified the hype surrounding the 18-year-old whizzkid.

However, to overlook the contributions of Alexander Hleb and Cesc Fabregas would be criminal.

Walcott combined with the Spaniard, the man from Belarus and substitute Nicklas Bendtner to put Arsenal fans in seven heaven, their second-rate opponents adding an own goal through David Hubacek.

The scoreline equalled the Gunners' biggest win under Wenger and it was also their most emphatic in the competition as they went 22 games unbeaten.

At times they played with such style and freedom it was almost an exhibition. It took

Arsenal 7 Slavia Prague 0 EMIRATES STADIUM

SEVEN

Walcott comes of age with double as Gunners go goal crazy in Europe

NO WONDER THE POOR PRAGUE FANS WERE SCREAMING!

YOU'RE JUST FAB: Adebayor and Walcott celebrate with Fabregas

WONDER WAL: Theo Walcott lead the Prague defenders a merry dance last night

SITTING IT OUT: Jens Lehmann watches the action from the bench last night

Lehmann 'play me' threat to Wenger

By JOHN CROSS

JENS LEHMANN last night warned Arsene Wenger that it would be dangerous to "humiliate" him any longer.

Lehmann, who also launched an attack on his goalkeeping rival Manuel Almunia, promised to speak out against Wenger unless he regains his place in the Arsenal first team.

The German, 38 next month, said: "It's possible that some day I'll feel like talking about the whole issue. But at the moment I'm just swallowing it all as part of the humiliation. That's something one has to take in.

"But I think – and this is aimed at my dear manager – one shouldn't humiliate players for too long. I'm an Arsenal player and I won't just fade away quietly."

Lehmann then hit out at Wenger's assertion that he had three world class keepers.

He said. "One of them must be me. The other two have proved their class by winning titles? If I think about that, I can't recall any. I guess today you're nevertheless world class.

"I'm convinced I'll be playing again. Almunia has not yet showed that he can win matches for us."

Wenger said last night: "It's not my purpose to humiliate Jens – I respect him a lot and I will have a chat with him about it."

Our boy wonder

FROM BACK PAGE

League title rivals Liverpool in irresistible form. Wenger said: "Once Theo scored it settled him down and when the space opened up you could see he is clinical.

"There was a bit of Thierry Henry in the way he took his second goal because he didn't panic, which is the sign of a real finisher.

"I'm convinced he has all the ingredients to be a top striker – talent, fantastic pace, intelligence and technique – but he is still only 18 and you have to be patient."

Walcott said: "My first goal was special as my brother-in-law's brother passed away recently – that one was for him."

Slavia coach Karel Jarolim gasped: "We were powerless to stop Walcott."

---

just five minutes for Slavia to be undone.

Hleb's trickery on the left set up Fabregas who raced into the edge of the box and curled an exquisite shot into the far corner.

Fabregas returned the favour on 24 minutes when his corner created havoc, the ball was not cleared and Hleb's shot was deflected in off Hubacek.

Arsenal were on cruise control and Walcott was presented with another gift on 41 minutes. Daniel Pudil inexplicably played a long pass back to keeper Vaniak, who miscontrolled, and Walcott coolly fired home a simple chance.

Within 13 minutes of the restart Arsenal were out of sight. Fabregas found Hleb who outwitted Vaniak with a 20-yard shot.

Fabregas and Hleb combined again before releasing Walcott down the left and the youngster's pace took him clear before he squeezed home a low shot off the far post.

Then came the move of the match. Hleb started it, found Emmanuel Adebayor who passed to Walcott and his lay-off set up Fabregas to fire into the bottom corner.

With the Gunners strolling, Bendtner simply walked his effort into the net on 89 minutes.

ARSENAL: Almunia 7, Sagna 7, Toure 7, Gallas 7, Clichy 7, Eboue 7, Fabregas 8, Flamini 7 (Gilberto 62,7), Hleb 8 (Rosicky 62,7), Adebayor 8 (Bendtner 62,7), Walcott 9.

SLAVIA PRAGUE: Vaniak, Krajcik, Suchy, Hubacek, Pudil, Senkerik, Svec, Tavares (Belaid 62), Kalivoda (Jablonsky 46), Ivana (Volesak 56), Vlcek.

Can't Kick Won't Kick

By NEIL KERBER & DAVID BLACK

Benitez excited in Turkey!

KEBABS

WOW - LOOK AT THE ROTATION ON THAT!

RAFA

GERRARD TORRES

CHAMPIONS LEAGUE LAST 16,
SAN SIRO

SMILERS: Grant (right) and Lampard

GRANT'S FATE IN BALANCE

Chelsea v Olympiacos, 2nd leg, tonight, 7.45pm

By NEIL McLEMAN

AVRAM GRANT yesterday admitted failure in the Champions League tonight would be catastrophic for Chelsea and for him.

After investing £578million in the club, owner Roman Abramovich is desperate for them to be crowned kings of Europe this season.

And the Russian billionaire has piled on the pressure by already booking hotels and restaurants in Moscow for the final on May 21.

Grant blew the first chance of silverware during his reign when Chelsea lost the Carling Cup Final and needs a win at home tonight to make the quarter-finals after a goalless draw at Olympiacos.

He nodded when asked if it would be a catastrophe to be eliminated tonight. "You can use your own words," said the Chelsea boss. "I agree that until we can be in the final of the Champions League we are missing something.

"All the big clubs were there – even Arsenal, a big club who won many other titles.

"But in football today there is a lot of pressure and at a big club it pushes you to try to achieve the best and I like the pressure."

Didier Drogba will do all he can to make Abramovich's dreams come true. The Blues have three times reached the last four since the tycoon bought the club in 2003, without ever going through to the final.

But Drogba believes they are due a change in fortune.

"We've done three semi-finals and the bad luck is gone," said the striker. "We will go to the final and win it."

☐ CHELSEA were given a lift yesterday when the FA overturned Frank Lampard's three-match ban for his red card at Upton Park on Saturday.

Team-mate Joe Cole said: "That's great news as he is a massively important player for us."

PROBABLE TEAMS

Chelsea	Olympiacos
Cech	Nikopolidis
Belletti	Zewlakow
Carvalho	Julio Cesar
Terry	Antzas
A Cole	Leonardo
Mikel	Torosidis
Lampard	Stoltidis
Ballack	Ledesma
J Cole	Patsatzoglou
Drogba	Djordjevic
Kalou	Kovacevic

TV TIMES: Live on Sky Sports 2, kick-off 7.45pm

SPORT ON TV

FOOTBALL: Champions League last-16 second legs, Chelsea v Olympiacos – Sky Sports 2, 6pm; Real Madrid v Roma – Sky Sports 3, 7.30pm; other matches on Sky Sports Interactive.
CRICKET: Second day of the First Test from Hamilton, New Zealand v England – Sky Sports 1, 9pm.
TENNIS: Barclays Dubai Championships – British Eurosport, 10am, 3.30pm, 5.15pm.
SKIING: World Cup cross country from Norway – British Eurosport, 2pm.

JOHN CROSS
REPORTS FROM MILAN

Cesc and Manu on target as young Guns come of age

ARSENE WENGER watched his young pretenders graduate into Champions League heroes as Arsenal produced one of the best European victories in the history of English football last night.

Arsenal became the first ever English club to beat AC Milan in the San Siro with a performance of real style, maturity and class – which even had the home fans applauding them off at the end.

And it was Cesc Fabregas who typified Arsenal's glorious night as the 20-year-old midfielder ran the show, struck a stunning opener and outclassed AC Milan's top veterans.

The reigning seven-times European champions were simply outplayed on a night when Wenger's "surprise package" emerged as the real deal.

Chance

Just when it seems easy to write off Arsenal as they have stuttered in recent weeks in the Premier League title race, they seem to roar back with a victory of sheer class which marks them down as champions.

Fabregas and Emmanuel Adebayor left it late to break the deadlock but Arsenal dominated the game, with a victory which will make the rest of Europe sit up and take notice. And if ever Arsenal's title challenge needed a shot in the arm then last night provided it.

After being held to a goalless draw at the Emirates, it might have appeared Arsenal's chance had gone.

Manchester United buckled here last season when overwhelmed by AC Milan in the semi-final.

But Arsenal showed maturity beyond their young years as they weathered an early storm to come back and produce a sensational late victory.

Arsenal, with an average age of 24.2, showed no fear against AC Milan's superstars.

This was billed as Wenger's boys against the men of Milan. But when the final whistle blew last night, Arsenal's youngsters had come of age. Fabregas

AD THAT'S YOUR LOT: Emmanuel Adebayor slides in at the far post to slot home Theo Walcott's cross

CESC MAGNIFIQUE: Fabregas lets fly to score the Arsenal opener

stood out as the best player on the pitch and, for a 20-year-old to do that against such experienced and class players, it really is something special.

But Fabregas's midfield partner, Mathieu Flamini, was also outstanding with his work-rate, industry and superb tackling.

Brazilian superstar Kaka is the reigning World Player of the Year, but he was outshone. Maldini, the old man of Milan's team at the grand age of 39, had a deflected header hacked off the line by keeper Manuel Almunia, who also saved well from Pato in the 19th minute. But Arsenal's Adebayor was a constant threat as he led the line brilliantly forcing a superb 28th-minute tip-over from Zeljko Kalac.

Alex Hleb was desperately unlucky to be booked in the 33rd minute for an alleged dive on the edge of the box but TV replays showed that Alessandro Nesta had caught him with his challenge. A minute later, Fabregas fired a warning shot as he blasted a 20-yard shot against the bar.

Wenger went for the jugular after 71 minutes as he threw on Theo Walcott for Emmanuel Eboue and the 18-year-old's pace really troubled AC Milan's old legs.

Walcott might have done better as his cross-shot was saved by Kalac but

DONE IT: Arsene Wenger punches the air after a famous win

Can't Kick Won't Kick ...

AVRAM SPEAKS OUT!

PEOPLE SAY I'M NOT A BIG ENOUGH CHARACTER TO DEAL WITH ALL THE STARS AT THIS CLUB!

C'MON BOSS THAT'S SIMPLY NOT TRUE!

WOW! FRANK LAMPARD SPOKE TO ME!!!

By NEIL KERBER AND DAVID BLACK

2ND LEG: AC MILAN 0 ARSENAL 2

Arsenal win 2-0 on aggregate

HEROES

Warriors restore pride & passion

Oliver Holt
CHIEF SPORTS WRITER

THE agonies of the past fortnight were forgotten here in the San Siro last night and Arsenal's season was born again.

Kaka, Pata, Pirlo, Maldini and the rest of the polished jewels of AC Milan had no answer to a performance of quite stunning technical beauty.

Arsenal passed Milan off the pitch, made them look like novices in the art of possession football and consigned the Champions League holders to an early exit from the competition. So you can forget the idea that the trials and the traumas of their draws with Birmingham City and Aston Villa were the beginning of the end of their campaign.

Because the way they played last night made a mockery of the commonly-held fear that their season was on the brink of implosion, that defeat here would be swiftly followed by being overtaken by Manchester United in the race for the Premier League.

They played like the kings of Europe, let alone England, in this magnificent stadium, and reminded everyone that at their best they are simply peerless.

Suddenly, it appears as if everything is possible again for them now.

Humbled by their FA Cup thrashing at Old Trafford and traumatised by the injury to Eduardo, they seemed desperately vulnerable coming into last night's game.

They all responded magnificently. William Gallas was transformed from a cry-baby to a football warrior, a leader, a captain, holding Milan at bay in a torrid opening 15 minutes.

Cesc Fabregas played wonderfully in midfield. He helped to hurry the normally flawless Andrea Pirlo out of his stride to the point where he made him look limited and ordinary.

Beside him, Mathieu Flamini was tireless, foiling Kaka time and again, hustling Milan into surrendering the ball.

Alexander Hleb was superb, too, relentless in his prompting, and Emmanuel Adebayor was a constant threat.

By the end of the first half, Arsenal were so thoroughly in control that a fusillade of shrill whistles cascaded down from the stands.

It was the sound of the Champions League holders being comprehensively outplayed. To Arsenal, it was the sound of victory.

Match stats

47%	POSSESSION	53%
4	SHOTS ON TARGET	4
7	SHOTS OFF TARGET	5
8	OFFSIDES	9
4	CORNERS	3
17	FOULS	24
3	YELLOW CARDS	3
0	RED CARDS	0

ATTENDANCE: 81,879
MAN OF THE MATCH: Fabregas

that was just a taste of what was to come as Arsenal left it late before sealing their famous triumph.

Midfielder Andrea Pirlo, normally one of the best in Europe, lost possession and Fabregas then side-stepped Gennaro Gattuso before unleashing a stunning 30-yard shot into the bottom corner. He had tears in his eyes as he celebrated.

It stunned the San Siro and even Wenger, normally so cool and unemotional on the touchline, joined in the goal celebrations as the Gunners took a giant step towards the quarter-finals.

Then deep into the second minute of injury time, Walcott used his pace down the right, beat Kakha Kaladze and then sent over a low cross which Adebayor gratefully slipped into the empty net at the far post.

AC MILAN: Kalac 6, Maldini 6, Kaladze 6, Resta 6, Oddo 6, Ambrosini 5, Pirlo 5, Gattuso 6, Pato 6, Kaka 7, Inzaghi 6 (Gilardino 69, 5).
ARSENAL: Almunia 7, Clichy 7, Senderos 7, Gallas 8, Sagna 7, Diaby 7, Fabregas 9, Flamini 8, Eboue 7 (Walcott 71, 7), Hleb 7 (Silva 89), Adebayor 8.

WENGER HAILS KIDS

FROM BACK PAGE

seven-times European champions AC Milan in the San Siro.

Emmanuel Adebayor grabbed a second deep into injury time to cap a victory which Wenger hailed as "perfect" – and it left Fabregas convinced they can go all of the way.

Fabregas said: "We don't have 25 internationals like Chelsea, so we can't challenge for all four trophies. But we are in contention for the two trophies and they are the ones we really want to win.

"We are top of the Premier League and through to the quarter-finals of the Champions League after beating the holders at home, so why not? Why can't we win them both? This is just one more step. But we have done nothing yet. We want to go right until the end in this competition."

Wenger added: "We played with organisation. We never dropped off, closed them down and didn't give them time. We went forward whenever we could with the ball.

"I'm very proud of our performance tonight. We deserved to win. I have a big respect for Milan but to come here and beat them deserves a lot of credit.

"It's similar to winning in Madrid two years ago. We knocked out the holders tonight. It shows that 0-0 at home is not a bad result.

"This team is very young but they've won at the Bernabeu and now at San Siro, and you need some quality to do that."

Keep up to date with all the live action on our brilliant website

Mirror Football
www.MirrorFootball.co.uk

ARSENAL 3
Van Persie 42, 60 Fabregas 43

IT'S FRIGHT V

Horror for Harry on Halloween

PAUL SMITH
sport@sundaymirror.co.uk

ARSENE WENGER claimed his young side are capable of going on and winning the Premier League title following a comfortable victory over their north London neighbours.

A brace from Dutchman Robin van Persie and a wonderful individual goal from captain Cesc Fabregas ensured Arsenal's 16-year unbeaten home record against Tottenham stayed intact.

And Wenger was upbeat about their title chances.

He said: "This side is good enough to win the league title. I've said it from day one.

"We have the opportunity and quality. I accept that it will also come down to our attitude on and off the pitch and whether we can steer clear of injury.

"But if you are asking me if I feel confident? Absolutely.

Digs from both camps invariably lit up an already explosive north London derby, but Wenger was quick to put things into context.

"It's not about opinion it's about what happens on the pitch. That is all that counts.

"People will talk about our goals against Tottenham, but I felt our back five was formidable and we stifled Tottenham's offensive play.

"Goals kill off games, but if you can't defend you're always going to leave yourself open."

With his side leading 3-0 Wenger was captured on camera throwing his jacket to the ground in frustration. But he explained: "I threw

my jacket out of frustration because I couldn't get my message across to the players because of the noise from the crowd, which I'm not use to."

Redknapp meanwhile was at a loss to explain away the manor of his side's defeat.

He said: "It wasn't as if I was sitting there three minutes from half-time worried about anything I had seen. If anything I fancied our chances.

"The crowd were on Arsenal's back and challenging every mis-placed pass. Some of their players were scared to make a pass at that point.

"Then we go and concede two sloppy goals in the space of a minute and the mood around the place completely changes.

"They swagger off the field with their heads up and like they had played us off the park and were trudging off with our heads down.

"After that we faced an uphill battle. Once the third goal went in it was goodnight for us."

Redknapp appeared to erupt with furry at home fans behind him in the first-half and was keen to clear the issue up.

He fumed: "Some guy was swearing with kids around and that is unacceptable.

"I asked the steward to ask him to behave like a decent human being.

"He was swearing at me and setting a very bad example with young children around."

As if the fierce rivalry between these sides wasn't enough the pre-match comments from both managers made for an explosive clash.

While Wenger was writing off Tottenham's chances of breaking into the top four, Redknapp was brutally putting in the boot over their chances of winning the title.

Even so Spurs had their work cut out to secure the points against a Gunners side that have not been beaten at home by their neighbours since 1993.

While Arsenal dominated the early stages of the game it was the officiating by Mark Clattenburg that proved more of a talking point. David Bentley

escaped punishment no fewer than three times in the first 20 minutes and Benoit Assou-Ekotto also seemed to be buying favouritism with the Durham official much to the discuss of the home fans.

The closest we came to seeing the deadlock broken in the first-half was when Andrey Arshavin's shot was deflected into the path of Cesc Fabregas 12 yards from goal.

Although the Spaniard's drive was crisp and clean, Heurelho Gomes continued his fine form by diving at full stretch to his left to keep the ball out.

The evident lack of action on the field was being compensated by the controversy off it.

Redknapp erupted with fury on the visitors' bench calling on stewards to go into the crowd as abuse reigned down on him from home fans behind

the dugout. Sir Alex Ferguson had made similar complaints last season when Manchester United were the visitors.

As the break approached a goal looked unlikely until the game exploded into action with just three minutes remaining.

Bacary Sagna's near post cross was converted home by Robin van Persie, his fifth goal in as many games and within 53 seconds they were 2-0 down.

Spurs barely had time to kick-off after conceding the first goal when Wilson Palacios lost possession and Fabregas raced 50 yards avoiding three tackles before firing the ball home.

The momentum stayed with Arsenal after the break and they put to bed any lingering doubts on the hour. Gomes collided with Ledley King and inadvertently pushed his low cross to into van Persie's path.

▼ THREE STRIKES AND YOU'RE OUT: Tottenham goalkeeper Heurelho Gomes can only look on as Arsenal wing wizard Robin van Persie taps in for Arsenal's third goal and

Spurs have too many Bentleys..ch

MANSION CASINO & PO

MICHAEL CALVIN
sport@sundaymirror.co.uk

BIG MATCH VERDICT

AS Second Comings go, it was distinctly third rate.

David Bentley (left) was an irrelevance, an extra lost in the crowd scenes of a bizarre north London derby.

He once believed that he was born to strut the great stages of the game.

Now, like the Tottenham team that collapsed around him, he's a symbol of crass complacency and exaggerated

talent. In the end, as Spurs subsided to a suicidal defeat, he was barely worth booing.

The home fans taunted him with chants of "Bentley, Bentley, what's the score?"

A look at Harry Redknapp's face, that of a bloodhound kicked once too often, provided the answer.

The sight of Fabio Capello, in the directors' box, merely reminded Bentley of the magnitude of the opportunity he has lost in a calamitous year.

Even his nickname – "Becks" – is an ironic indication of how far, and how fast, he has fallen.

True to form, he didn't earn his latest last chance. It was an

TOTTENHAM 0
AN MAN

...his second of the afternoon at The Emirates yesterday.

...ocolate soldiers that melt in heat of battle

accident of football history, an act of expedience.

Without Aaron Lennon's ankle injury, Bentley would still be in solitary confinement.

His recall was a classic case of a manager making the most of a difficult situation.

Redknapp needs him. For now.

Come January, when more money will be thrown at the memory of the Glory Game, he will be expendable.

Redknapp admitted as much afterwards, when he mourned the loss of Lennon without even bothering to mention Bentley. Spurs are where they always seem to be – outside

the Big Four, looking in. Robbie Keane's pre-match bluster, that they've a depth beyond Arsenal, made him look simply silly.

Arsene Wenger couldn't resist observing: "Football is no about opinion. It's about performance."

The faults are familiar. Tottenham were criminally casual, comically generous. They simply didn't have the character to cope.

Bentley's best chance, a chipped free-kick from the left edge of the box, was tipped over the bar by an under-employed Manuel Almunia.

Wenger deserves to be taken equally seriously when he continues to promote the party line that Arsenal are potential champions.

Bentley's first League game for 10 months was a study of a

man ambushed by a sudden inferiority complex.

Tales seeping out of Spurs' training ground suggest he has been reduced to eating on his own, or with the youth team.

His career is in limbo. His reputation is in tatters. He looked nervous, ill at ease.

That may be true, but they cannot change a man's character.

He has too many men like Bentley, chocolate soldiers who melt in the heat of battle.

fooled no one when he clung to the old managerial cliche that goals change games.

Redknapp, meanwhile,

STAT ATTACK

**at THE EMIRATES STADIUM
ATT: 60,103**

How they rated

 **ARSENAL**

Subs: Eduardo (for Bendtner 37)
Eboue (Arshavin 78)
Ramsey (van Persie 86)

7 Sagna 7 Almunia 7 Clichy
7 Vermaelen 8 Gallas 7
8 Diaby Fabregas Song
6 Bendtner 7 Arshavin Van Persie
6 Keane 7 Crouch
6 Palacios 6 Jenas Huddlestone Bentley
5 Bassong 6 King 6 Corluka
6 Ekotto 6 Gomes

○ **TOTTENHAM**

Subs: Hutton (for Corluka 86)
Bale (Huddlestone 55)
Pavlyuchenko (Keane 65)

Shots

| 6 off target | 4 |
| 8 on target | 4 |

Story of the game

6	Corners	2
14	Fouls Conceded	11
4	Offsides	3
1	Yellow	1
0	Red	0

Possession

 52% — 48%

MAN OF THE MATCH

9 ROBIN VAN PERSIE
Bathed in the glory of the Arsenal's fans' adoration after destroying the arch rivals' with a brilliant brace of goals

MANAGERS

A WENGER 8
Revelled in Arsenal fans' applause

H REDKNAPP 6
Redknapp raged...but not sure if it was at his team or the home fans

REFEREE
M Clattenburg
Warranted a yellow card 6

Even Bentley's nickname 'Becks' is an ironic indication of how far – and fast – he's fallen

Next four games

WOLVES (A)   SUNDERLAND (A)
SUNDERLAND (A)   WIGAN (H)
CHELSEA (H)   ASTON VILLA (A)
BOLTON (H)   EVERTON (A)

▼ **ROYAL MALE STRIKER:** Rasiak savouring a vital victory

McAnuff does right Jobi at the right time

JOBI McANUFF helped ease the pressure on boss Brendan Rodgers as Reading ended their run of four consecutive defeats with victory over Coventry.

The winger, who followed Rodgers from Watford to the Madejski Stadium, scored his first goal for the Royals and set up the other two for Polish forward Grzegorz Rasiak.

And the three points was enough to lift the Royals out of the relegation zone.

Although the hosts scored for the first time in four games, it was of little consequence as Chris Coleman's side made it a winless run of five games.

And Reading, woeful in front of goal against Leicester on Monday, showed the Sky Blues how easy it is to score by taking the lead after just 27 seconds.

McAnuff raced down the right and crossed for Rasiak to head in to the top corner from close range. And in the opening exchanges, the Royals simply ran riot.

Ryan Bertrand tested home keeper Demitrios Konstantopoulos, in place of injured Kieren Westwood, with a left-footed shot. Followed by a feeble effort from Simon Church, when through on goal.

But the Sky Blues found chances. Ben Turner forced a block from Ivar Ingimarsson, returning from suspension, and shot-stopper Adam Federici fielded a Freddy Eastwood volley.

Aussie Federici then did well to deny Jermaine Grandison's forceful header. And defender Grandison was needed at the other end to block Church's 20-yard effort.

Yet Reading continued to look dangerous.

Lively McAnuff threatened to double the lead before half-time, but Konstantopoulos was equal to the left-footed shot.

After the interval, McAnuff again made the

difference. Ingimarsson's corner was cleared by Grandison, but as far as the lurking McAnuff, whose 12-yard shot soared in to the top left corner.

The Royals should have extended their lead, but Rasiak's effort was denied by Konstantopoulos.

Sky Blues chief Coleman was aware that his side were struggling, so brought top scorer Leon Best – returning from injury – off the bench.

And the striker made an immediate impact.

Best picked up possession on the right and picked out strike partner Eastwood, who fired home from 20 yards.

And hopes of an equaliser vanished when Rasiak restored the two-goal lead after pouncing on the rebound off the post from McAnuff's effort. But the strike knocked any ambition out of the Sky Blues who seemed to surrender.

HOW THEY RATED

COVENTRY		READING	
6	Konstantopoulos	Federici	7
6	Clarke	Tabb	6
6	Cranie	Ingimarsson	6
6	Turner	Pearce	6
6	Van Aanholt	Bertrand	6
6	Grandison	McAnuff	8
6	Gunnarsson	Howard	6
6	Cork	Matejovsky	6
5	McIndoe	Sigurdsson	6
6	Eastwood	Church	6
6	Morrison	Rasiak	7

Best (McIndoe) 5, Long (Church) 6,
Hussey (Aanholt) 6, Karacan (Howard) 7
Osbourne (Gunnarsson) 5

MANAGERS
6 **C COLEMAN** — **B RODGERS** 7

MAN OF THE MATCH

JOBI McANUFF 8
A constant menace on the right hand side

REFEREE: E Ilderton 7

▲ **OUTSTANDING:** Phil Jones

Rio looking to call time on England

FROM BACK PAGE

squad for the final Euro 2012 qualifier against Montenegro.

Ferdinand, who has won 81 caps, is believed to be torn between extending his international career, given the succession of injuries he has endured recently, and playing for United.

Rumours have been rife that United boss Sir Alex Ferguson is even considering selling Ferdinand.

He was dropped for yesterday's win at Everton after being heavily criticised for his poor performance in United's 6-1 derby humiliation last Sunday.

Fergie has a proven track record for ruthlessly changing his team. The days when Ferdinand and Nemanja Vidic were his undisputed first-choice central defenders appear to be over.

Yesterday, at Goodison Park, Fergie named Vidic and Jonny Evans as his central defenders, with outstanding new boy Phil Jones used at right-back.

Chris Smalling has also blossomed as a potential right-back, as well as in his favoured central role.

A foot injury will keep him out for the next three weeks.

From being a defensive stalwart for club and country, Ferdinand has suddenly become vulnerable to major selection decisions.

Concentrating solely on club issues could yet help him extend his career – at least with United.

Gomes back off to Brazil

By BILL MILLS

TOTTENHAM Hotspur goalkeeper Heurelho Gomes has revealed he's heading home to Brazil.

Gomes is fed up with a place on the bench behind Brad Friedel and will quit Spurs after Christmas.

Gomes, who joined Spurs in a £7.8 million move from PSV Eindhoven three years ago, said: "The club bought Brad as second keeper behind me but the manager Harry Redknapp chose Friedel as his No1 goalkeeper.

"It is very likely that I will leave London this coming winter. I will go back to Brazil on a loan deal, so I can come back to another club in Europe after that."

Gomes has been reduced to occasional appearances in the Europa League this season, while Redknapp has preferred veteran Friedel for his club's Premier League campaign.

BARCLAYS PREMIER LEAGUE

GUNNERS TRIUMPH IN
ROBIN

▲ **CELEBRATION:** After Chicharito goal

PRAISE FOR MAN UTD'S COMEBACK

EVERTON	0
MANCHESTER UTD	1

By ANTHONY CLAVANE

SIR Alex Ferguson last night hailed a resilient win at Everton as Manchester United bounced back from their derby humiliation.

A week after their 6-1 drubbing by Manchester City, Fergie's men won 1-0 at Everton to keep up the pressure on their noisy neighbours.

After watching a 19th-minute winner by Javier Hernandez give them all three points, Ferguson said: "It was a hard game and we expected that because every time you come to Everton the crowd get behind them and show great enthusiasm.

"But we defended well and the pleasing aspect for me was winning 1-0.

"It was a fantastic performance by Nemanja Vidic. Every ball that came into our box he got it clear – and that's his speciality.

"There have been so many chances against us recently. We have to reduce that if we are going to win the league. Today we didn't have any problems. The goal was a brilliant one by Hernandez, with great build-up and Chicharito does what he does best."

But Everton boss David Moyes felt the home side should have come away with a point. He said: "We were unlucky not to get a draw. We were very surprised by Wayne Rooney playing in midfield. It caused us problems in the first half.

"But we played well in the second half and we felt we had enough chances to get a point."

MAKE MINE A TREBLE
Van Persie salutes Arsenal fans after his hat-trick helps conquer Chelsea

TOP LONDON DERBY BATTLE

GOOD

Van Persie claims Arsenal hat-trick in 8-goal thriller as Chelsea buckle

PUT OUR HEADS TOGETHER
▲ Song, Terry and Ivanovic all clash for ball

CHELSEA	3
ARSENAL	5

By PAUL SMITH
sport@sundaymirror.co.uk

ROBIN Van Persie did nothing to hide his delight after destroying Chelsea with a stunning hat-trick at Stamford Bridge yesterday.

Van Persie's treble took his goal tally to nine in five Premier League games.

It also saw Van Persie's personal tally reach an astonishing 29 goals in 27 league appearances this year alone.

The day of records saw Chelsea concede five goals at home for the first time in the history of the Premier League.

"You could see how happy we were at the end because we fought hard and every one of us showed character," beamed Van Persie.

"It's a big, big win for us today."

On a day when all eyes were on Chelsea's England skipper John Terry following his week in the headlines, he was left cursing himself after a slip let in Van Persie to put Arsenal 4-3 up.

Asked about the goal, Van Persie added: "I was surprised when John

Terry slipped because it was an easy back-pass and I only saw later that he slipped because I was closing him down.

"I suddenly realised I was one-on-one with Petr Cech and a couple of things came to my mind as to what to do, but I did the easiest one.

"It means a lot to get a hat-trick here because this is one of the hardest grounds to play at."

Goalkeeper Wojciech Szczesny, who was fortunate to escape a straight red card in the second half after bringing down Chelsea's Ashley Cole, tweeted: "I don't know why I stayed on the pitch, but what a game! Great spirit, great atmosphere and a great win! RVP needs to start scoring though!"

Midfielder Aaron Ramsey

believes the Gunners are starting to show what they can do after a slow start to the season.

"It was a really good game for us, we showed great character coming back from behind," added Ramsey.

"We deserved it in the end, we created a lot of opportunities and took a lot of them.

"We are finally gelling together now and showing what we are capable of doing and this is just an example of that

"I'm sure the manager will look at some of the defending and work on that, but at the end of the day we're happy to get the win."

Chelsea boss Andre Villas-Boas denied the racism row that has engulfed Terry had any impact on Chelsea's performance.

"Has the situation affected John?

No, not at all," said Villas-Boas. "It hasn't distracted him at all.

"For me, it was never a situation. It's a misunderstanding. It's an FA investigation, so let them investigate. This is just a defeat for a team, a very important defeat and nothing else."

Gunners manager Arsene Wenger said: "Chelsea have been very secure defensively in the games they have played until today, so maybe it is the quality of our play that opened them up. We kept throwing everything forward."

The win saw Arsenal maintain their push for the top four.

Meanwhile, Manchester City stay five points clear at the top after their 3-1 defeat of Wolves.

It wasn't quite the goal frenzy to which City fans have become accustomed to and manager Roberto Mancini reminded the fans that sometimes they have to be patient.

"After the result at Manchester United, I don't want everyone to think it will be easy," he said.

"It is impossible to score four, five and six goals every game. You have to be patient sometimes."

Liverpool cruised to a 2-0 triumph at West Brom last night, with a first-half Charlie Adam penalty and a strike from Andy Carroll.

GREAT WAL OF FIRE
▲ Gervinho & Theo celebrate

PREMIER LEAGUE

	P	W	D	L	F	A	GD	Pts
Man City	10	9	1	0	36	8	28	28
Man Utd	10	7	2	1	27	12	15	23
Chelsea	10	6	1	3	23	15	8	19
Newcastle	9	5	4	0	12	6	6	19
Liverpool	10	5	3	2	14	10	4	18
Tottenham	8	5	1	2	15	13	2	16
Arsenal	10	5	1	4	20	21	-1	16
Norwich	10	3	4	3	14	15	-1	13
Aston Villa	10	2	6	2	13	13	0	12
Swansea	10	3	3	4	12	15	-3	12
Stoke	9	3	3	3	7	11	-4	12
QPR	9	3	3	3	7	14	-7	12
West Brom	10	3	2	5	9	13	-4	11
Sundland	10	2	4	4	14	12	2	10
Fulham	10	2	4	4	13	12	1	10
Everton	9	3	1	5	10	13	-3	10
Wolves	10	2	2	6	9	17	-8	8
Blackburn	10	1	3	6	13	23	-10	6
Bolton	10	2	0	8	13	27	-14	6
Wigan	10	1	2	7	6	17	-11	5

CONGRATULATIONS
▲ Arsene and AVB shake on it

▲ **CONTROVERSY:** Ferdinand and Terry clash during game

AFFAIR TAUNT CAUSED RACE ROW WITH JT

FROM BACK PAGE

he did not racially abuse the QPR defender.

Now, Sunday Mirror Sport understands that Ferdinand's account of events contradicts Terry's version.

Ferdinand, the younger brother of England defensive stalwart Rio, admits that he did not hear Terry's comments that were caught on camera and sparked the heated debate in the wake of last Sunday's west London derby at Loftus Road.

But the Sunday Mirror investigation reveals the players originally exchanged words after a clash.

It is alleged by senior QPR officials and sources close to Ferdinand that Terry said to Ferdinand: "Stop acting like a c***."

Ferdinand immediately retorted: "No, acting like a c***iss****ing your best mate's girlfriend."

This appears to be a reference to Terry's alleged relationship with Vanessa Perroncell, the former girlfriend of his then Chelsea team-mate Wayne Bridge.

Their reported affair was revealed in February

2010, saw Terry stripped of the England captaincy and sparked a furious backlash from Bridge (inset) and other football figures.

Last Sunday, after the verbal exchange, Terry is seen walking away.

He then delivers the comments that are now under scrutiny by the FA.

Anton's brother Rio was appointed England skipper by coach Fabio Capello in the fall-out from the Terry-Perroncell affair.

JT reclaimed the England captain's armband in March this year in controversial manner. Despite saying he'd never reinstate Terry as his skipper, Capello performed a U-turn as Rio – and a string of alternative captains – were hit by injuries.

Last night, a Chelsea spokesman declined to comment on the basis that the incident is now part of an FA investigation and that the club are not making any further comment at the moment.

John Terry's personal adviser Paul Nicholls also declined to comment.

JT row must be resolved for the good of England: Pages 60-61

WENGER IN CITY CARLING CLASH

By BILL MILLS

ARSENE WENGER suffered defeat in the final minute of the Carling Cup Final last season against Birmingham and now the Arsenal manager will have to overcome Manchester City to move a step closer to another Wembley final.

Wenger will pit his wits against Roberto Mancini after the pair were drawn against each other yesterday while there is a mouthwatering clash at Stamford Bridge where Chelsea will face Liverpool.

Sir Alex Ferguson (above) celebrates his 25th anniversary at Manchester United next Sunday and his

side were drawn against Crystal Palace in the Carling Cup quarter-finals.

It is a repeat of the clash that gave him his first Old Trafford trophy in 1990 in the FA Cup Final replay when Ferguson saw his United side beat Palace 21 years ago.

They progressed into the Carling Cup's last eight with an easy 3-0 defeat of Aldershot while Palace beat Southampton 2-0.

Blackburn's last-gasp win of Newcastle earned them a trip to Cardiff.

Quarter-final round draw: Arsenal v Manchester City; Chelsea v Liverpool; Manchester United v Crystal Palace; Cardiff v Blackburn. Ties to be played week of Nov28.

3pm

FOOTBALL'S ANSWER TO THE 3AM GIRLS

Got a story for 3pm?
Email: steve.anglesey
@mirror.co.uk

ANDY CARROLL DRINKS A BARREL AT WEMBLEY

NO chance at Wembley for Liverpool or Cardiff fans to enjoy Arsenal's amazing comeback demolition of Spurs. Despite that game finishing 30 minutes before the Carling Cup final kick-off, the only thing available on the in-stadium monitors was the omnibus edition of EastEnders.

NO matter how many boot camp fitness programmes you go on, there's no outrunning your reputation... as Andy Carroll found out from this Wembley banner yesterday.

HE'S BAD KOMPANY

BOURNEMOUTH owner Eddie Mitchell, dumped from a 606 interview on Saturday for swearing, isn't the only one who was censored this weekend.

Manchester City's groundbreaking live post-match interview with skipper their Vincent Kompany via Facebook and Twitter had to be edited after the Belgian international described one of his duties as "handing out the bollockings".

But that's not the end of the subject of swearing at City. Reports that Porto have reported the Blues to Uefa over supporters' "You're not Incredible" chant at Hulk make no mention of the song fans followed up with.

Which was: "Spider-Man's right - you're f***ing s***e."

PPS: City fans who sit near the club's bench are increasingly amused by Roberto Mancini's habit of munching on fruit pastilles during matches.

He shares his sweets with coach Brian Kidd but wisely never gives one to the increasingly portly assistant boss David Platt.

DOWN THE LIEW

ALL eyes on next month's Sports Journalist Awards, where the exciting Jonathan Liew of the Daily Telegraph is up for young writer of the year.

Should Jonathan win, he'll pick up his award from the evening's master of ceremonies Jim Rosenthal (right), who he recently called a "salesman trying to flog us a second-hand motor" during a piece which delivered this verdict on Rosenthal hosting Europa League football on Channel 5: "You cannot polish a turd."

NOEL HITS BOOS

NOW he's no longer playing alongside brother Liam, has Noel Gallagher calmed down? No, he hasn't.

The former Oasis songwriter's solo tour includes a regular spot in which he dedicates a song to his beloved Manchester City and Mario Balotelli (below).

As you can imagine, this tends to meet with a mixed reaction.

In Newcastle - where Noel is already an acquired taste after saying in 2009, "I don't think there's a greater sight than seeing fat Geordies crying on Match of the Day" - virtually the entire audience booed.

Noel responded: "Go and f*** back off to the Sports Direct Arena"... which didn't go down too well, either.

DAFT QUOTES OF THE WEEK

"You can't bite your nose off to spite your face"
- **PAUL MERSON**

"Not to win is guttering"
- **MARK NOBLE**

"Rolando's been given a second yellow for arguing with the life support.... er, the linesman"
- **CHRIS WADDLE**

"They're not that very good, Napoli"
- **PAUL MERSON**

"That's put a strain on his left-hand knee"
- **JOHN SCALES**

"However people have interpretated that is up to them"
- **EDDIE MITCHELL**

"For us to overtake them has been a massive undertaking"
- **SAM ALLARDYCE**

"He's a good footballer, as in technical-wise"
- **TONY CASCARINO**

WICKED WHISTLE

WHICH unexpectedly successful manager told his players not to get carried away and start driving flash motors... then turned up a few weeks later in a new Bentley?

OG FOR GEOFF

THERE'S an unwritten rule that British actors don't show off their honours on film posters and credits.

So despite both of them being knighted, Oscar winners Michael Caine and Anthony Hopkins drop their 'Sirs'. And staying plain old Judi Dench is the much-loved Dame Judi.

Alas, no one appears to have told the promising young thespian who appears as football agent Adam Aveley in new Brit thriller Payback Season... and who is named on the poster as Sir Geoff Hurst MBE.

Just a surprise he didn't ask for a mention of that hat-trick in brackets.

CONGRATULATIONS to the enterprising salesman outside Carrow Road who yesterday was offering 'half-and-half scarves' that turned out to be just the Canaries' normal green and yellow affair. He explained to puzzled onlookers that they were "half Norwich City, half FC United".

PREMIER LEAGUE: YOU'RE

HE'S A WONDER WAL
Theo Walcott celebrates the double that stunned Spurs after the foul on Gareth Bale (left) that led to the penalty which put Spurs 2-0 up

ARSENAL 5 TOTTENHAM 2

Arsenal

TOTTENHAM HOTSPUR

ARSENAL: Szczesny 7, Sagna 8, Koscielny 7, Vermaelen 7, Gibbs 8 (Jenkinson 75, 6), Song 7, Arteta 8, Rosicky 9, Walcott 8 (Oxlade-Chamberlain 81), Benayoun 8 (Gervinho 88), Van Persie 9. **Goals:** Sagna 40, Van Persie 43, Rosicky 51, Walcott 65, 68

SPURS: Friedel 7, Walker 5, King 5 (Dawson, 82), Kaboul 6, Assou-Ekotto 4, Kranjcar 5 (Van der Vaart 46, 5), Parker 4, Modric 6, Bale 6, Saha 5 (Sandro 46, 6), Adebayor 5. **Goals:** Saha 4, Adebayor 34 pen **REF:** Mike Dean **ATT:** 60,106

GUNBELIEVABLE

STILL A WINNER
Arsene Wenger celebrates during an amazing game at the Emirates

On the ropes at 2-0 down, Arsenal overpower Spurs and show their belief in Wenger remains strong

BAC IN BUSINESS
Sagna heads home to start the Arsenal fightback Pics KENT GAVIN

By JOHN CROSS

REPORTS of Arsene Wenger's demise have been greatly exaggerated.

Robin van Persie led an amazing Arsenal fightback, finished off with a flourish by Theo Walcott to complete an unforgettable derby.

It will also go down as proof that the Arsenal players still believe in Wenger and are determined not to let the power shift across north London.

Arsenal were two down inside 34 minutes, it was the ultimate test of their character and they dug deep in a sensational comeback.

Van Persie typified that spirit, but Walcott, more than any other player, embodied the extremes that have plagued Arsenal's season.

Walcott struggled in the first half largely because the fans got on his back. The mental strength required to score twice and use his pace to tear apart Tottenham's creaking defence was incredible.

That is the story of Arsenal's season. Infuriating and brilliant in equal measure to leave the fans wondering. Yet when Wenger is under siege, the players still dig deep for him.

It was the response Wenger was looking for after the Milan mauling

and, even though it did not happen at Sunderland last week, the players delivered a display that humiliated their neighbours.

Tottenham went to Arsenal as most people's favourites for probably the first time in Wenger's 16-year reign yet they could not take the final step.

The game had barely taken shape when Tottenham took a fourth-minute lead. Gareth Bale found Emmanuel Adebayor, Laurent Koscielny slipped, the Spurs striker found Louis Saha and his shot deflected cruelly into the net off Thomas Vermaelen.

Arsenal fans were shell shocked but stuck with their team – apart from directing stick towards Walcott.

Van Persie missed a sitter, the outstanding Tomas Rosicky saw a header brilliantly saved by Brad Friedel and they had Spurs pinned back.

But Spurs hit Arsenal on the counter attack as Luka Modric released Bale, the Welshman's pace took him past Kieran Gibbs

and he went down under keeper Wojciech Szczesny's diving challenge.

No end of TV replays could end the debate as to whether it was a penalty. But it looked harsh and perhaps that explained why referee Mike Dean did not send off Szczesny.

Adebayor stepped up and powered his shot past Szczesny. Adebayor celebrated and got stick even though he did not receive the same hatred as earlier in the season.

Maybe the Arsenal fans were too busy shouting at their own team to care too much. The Spurs fans were in dreamland but, two down and in desperate trouble, Arsenal responded brilliantly.

Van Persie hit the post and you began to wonder if it was going to be one of those days. But Arsenal got back in it after 40 minutes. Gibbs found Mikel Arteta and his cross was headed home powerfully by Bacary Sagna.

Three minutes later, Van Persie showed sensational skill. He

worked some space, turned on the edge of the box then curled a brilliant left-foot shot beyond Friedel into the top corner.

Arsenal were in charge. Redknapp made a double change at half-time and on came Rafael van der Vaart and Sandro for Niko Kranjcar and Saha respectively. But rather than stem the tide, it handed the initiative to Arsenal.

Friedel had already pulled off a great save from Yossi Benayoun before Arsenal took the lead. Rosicky sent Sagna away down the right and the Czech midfielder raced to get on the end of the cross and fired home.

Walcott showed his intent with a great run and shot which hit the post. The Gunners got another when Rosicky's ball forward found Van Persie, the Dutchman held off two defenders and fed Walcott, who raced through to score.

Walcott scored again as Sagna turned provider and the England winger raced into the penalty box, held his nerve and buried a shot into the far corner.

Tottenham were on the ropes. Their nightmare got worse when Scott Parker was sent off for a second bookable offence after an awful late foul on Vermaelen.

Fourth place is still in Wenger's sights. And Arsenal fans can still dream of finishing above the old enemy.

NOT GUNNER LOSE
Robin van Persie fires home before Tomas Rosicky scores to make it 3-2. Then Theo Walcott increases the Arsenal lead

ARSENAL v TOTTENHAM		
MAN OF THE MATCH		
ROBIN VAN PERSIE Led the fightback. Brilliant goal		
57%	BALL POSSESSION	43%
8	SHOTS ON TARGET	5
8	SHOTS OFF TARGET	6
7	CORNERS	5
0	OFFSIDE	2
16	FOULS	12
3 · 0	CARDS	2 · 1

HARRY: WE'LL COME OUT FIGHTING

By DARREN LEWIS

HARRY REDKNAPP says Spurs face their toughest challenge of the season to bounce back from this crushing defeat.

"We've got to come back like we did earlier in the season," he said. "We need to bounce back and recover.

"The momentum was with Arsenal at half-time. We came in at the break feeling sorry for ourselves having been 2-0 up and pegged back.

"You had to fancy Arsenal to win at that stage. If you

were neutral, you've got to fancy them. They were full of it second half and we couldn't match it.

"Last year we were 2-0 down at half-time and won 3-2. Here I was saying 'let's get to half-time' as I could see them scoring.

"We seemed to buckle after they scored, which isn't like us. We don't do that often. But they're a good side. Van Persie's second goal was amazing.

"When you're 2-0 up, you expect to win the game. We're seven points clear of Arsenal

and Chelsea. It's going to be tight, but we're in a great position.

"If we can finish third, that's a great season for us."

Spurs hit back from defeats in their first two games to both Manchester clubs to go on the run that had taken them into title contention.

But they'll be without Scott Parker to face United next Sunday after the midfielder was sent off for two cautions.

Redknapp (left) added: "We could have done without that."

RESULT!

with sports betting's top tipster DEREK McGOVERN
E-MAIL ME AT: betsguru@aol.com

IN ASSOCIATION WITH *William* HILL

Sack so hard to swallow for Big Mac

JOHN McCRIRICK has just found out what the worst part of getting old is.

In his case, his face.

It's a shame McCririck has been ousted. Watching racing on the telly won't be the same without the prospect of seeing a boozed-up racegoer punching Big Mac among his chins.

McCririck, 72, polarises opinion. He was accused of sexism when he appeared on Celebrity Big Brother alongside feminist Germaine Greer but, in fairness to Big Mac, Greer looks fit for a woman of her age.

He accused C4 of being ageist and said his former colleague Jim McGrath was

the only employee over 50 kept on. "It is so sad Channel 4 have gone down the well-worn path of ageism," said ageing Mac, looking well worn.

And he added: "It is so sad the Channel 4 have gone down the well-worn path of ageism." And

▲ OUT WITH THE OLD
McCririck was axed by C4

responding to barbs that Clare Balding (left) is too hoity-toity for C4 viewers, McGrath said: "She may be hoity but she won't see toity again."

Bookies Paddy Power are betting on what role McCririck will pick up next – almost certainly not one with salad.

He's 3-1 to become official spokesman on the racetrack for a bookmaker and 6-1 to set up a tipping line. It would be as eagerly awaited as mine.

BET OF THE DAY MY mate Mick heard that most accidents take place within two miles of home. So he moved.
Get on Norwich at 7-2 to beat Spurs in the Capital One Cup tonight.

Real London mauling

BOOKIES reckon there'll soon be a London-based team playing in the NFL but I don't share their confidence.

If there's a demand in London for a team of overpaid sportsmen lumbering around looking for someone to assault, then surely it is already being met by QPR.

I once watched a Super Bowl in its entirety – it was the longest year of my life.

It's a game played by overblown hulks and watched by bearded virgins, who sometimes bring their boyfriends along too.

If Derren Brown somehow magically confiscated the ball, neither side would notice for about 20 minutes.

That's how long the adverts last. The behemoths of New England Patriots and St Louis Rams somehow managed to fill Wembley Stadium on Sunday (below) – and that was before the crowds got there.

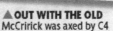

The Pat-riots? I had more fun watching the Tottenham riots.

OK, I'm no NFL expert – but surely there has to be more to a sport than the ability to upend an opponent and/or cheerleader.

Hills offer 4-1 for a London NFL franchise before the end of 2020. I'll let you know if that's a good bet when I find out what franchise means.

Trouble on the cards

TONIGHT'S Stamford Bridge ref will have his work cut out, as opposed to Sunday's Stamford Bridge ref, who has merely had his work cut.

Given the bad blood on Sunday, I predict with utmost confidence that it will all kick off again tonight at 7.45pm if I'm not mistaken. Some are saying boiling point will

not be reached because different personnel will be on the pitch.

Indeed, a look back at United's League Cup sides shows that they rarely find room for a Rooney, a Webb or a Clattenburg.

Clattenburg has been stood down, but Fergie is hoping to have him back in the squad when things blow over. A grudge is a

grudge and I would begrudge no one taking a slice of the 5-2 for a red card to be brandished when the two sides do battle tonight.

Sunday's stormy Premier League clash should have finished two-all, which is 12-1 with Hills tonight. It's 40-1 for a three-all, and about 1-4 for a free-for-all.

ADDITIONAL REPORTING BY JOHN SHAW

Capital One. Cup CAPITAL ONE

▲ ONWARD CHRISTIAN Benteke heads home

BENTEKE'S CRUEL END TO STOREY

| SWINDON | 2 |
| ASTON VILLA | 3 |

By NEIL McLEMAN
n.mcleman@trinitymirror.com

PAUL LAMBERT accused his Aston Villa stars of complacency after finally beating Paolo Di Canio's Swindon last night.

But the Italian still stole the show by staging a one-man pitch invasion at full time to applaud his own fans.

The Robins boss then pointed to the Villa supporters and the ground to suggest that the 17th-placed team in the Premier League will be going down this season.

Two goals in nine minutes from Christian Benteke and Gabriel Agbonlahor eased the visitors into a 2-0 half-time lead.

But the League One side threw on super sub Miles Storey after the break and the 18-year-old striker scored twice – including an outrageous back-heeled equaliser – to set up a thrilling finish.

And with both teams chasing a winner, Benteke converted Eric Lichaj's 90th-minute cross to put Lambert's men into the quarter-finals for the third time in four years.

But the Villa chief was still not happy, saying: "At 2-0 up I thought we were very comfortable and we nearly had another one just before half-time.

"Then we became complacent. I know from experience with Norwich how difficult it is here. They try to play the right way. It will be an eye-opener for some. But it is a big win for us."

Di Canio had launched into a typically outrageous goal celebration after his side's equaliser nine minutes from time – and repeated his flamboyant gestures after the game.

But he insisted he was not taunting the Villa fans about relegation. He said: "That was not the case. I was saying to my fans that they had been brilliant and Villa were below them.

"To see the County Ground full of emotion when we scored the second goal was amazing.

"It was a joke, it was just banter."

SWINDON: Foderingham, Devera, McCormack, Flint, McEveley, Ritchie, Miller, Ferry, Roberts, Benson, Collins.

A VILLA: Given, Lowton, Herd, Vlaar, Lichaj, Weimann Ireland, El Ahmadi, Bannan, Agbonlahor, Benteke.

REF: Stuart Attwell
ATT: 14,434

READING v ARSENAL

MAN OF THE MATCH
CHRISTIAN BENTEKE
Villa's two-goal hero

	SWINDON	ASTON VILLA
BALL POSSESSION	53%	47%
SHOTS ON TARGET	3	3
SHOTS OFF TARGET	3	5
CORNERS	4	5
OFFSIDE	3	2
FOULS	5	8
CARDS	1 0	1 0

4-0 down, Gunners stage an amazing fightback to win 7-5

CUP: LAST NIGHT'S 4TH RD ACTION

REST OF THE GAMES: SEE PAGES 64 & 65

7RACLE

4-4 Walcott cannot believe it as his goal brings Arsenal level

4-1

▲ **GLIMMER OF HOPE!** Walcott slides home Arsenal's first

4-2

▲ **PUNCHY** Giroud adds another after coming on

4-3

▲ **CLOSING IN** Koscielny is mobbed

4-5

▲ **MC HAMMER** Chamakh's goal triggers wild celebrations

5-6

▲ **WONDER WAL** Walcott salutes his hat-trick

5-7

▲ **BEYOND BELIEF** Chamakh scores again

READING 5 ARSENAL 7
After extra time

By DARREN LEWIS
d.lewis@trinitymirror.com

WHAT A MATCH. What a scoreline.

After all the bad blood, recrimination and allegations of racism hogging the headlines, along comes this corker to restore our faith in the game we love.

This was epic and enthralling. A roller-coaster of extreme emotions for both sets of fans at the appropriately-named Mad Stad.

For the first 40 minutes the Reading fans were delirious as their side sliced through Arsenal.

Nobody could believe what they were seeing as Laurent Koscielny's own goal was sandwiched between strikes from Jason Roberts and Mikele Leigertwood in 20 minutes.

When Noel Hunt added a fourth on 37 minutes the angry Arsenal fans let rip.

Chants of 'We want our money back' and 'We want our Arsenal back' came cascading down from the away stands. Some fans headed back down the M4 to London.

Arsenal were being ruthlessly, sensationally, dismantled at the hands of a team promoted last season from the Championship. They were heading for a humiliating exit.

But enter Theo Walcott. Locked in a stand-off with the Gunners over a new deal. Set for the exit door if he doesn't get it sorted.

Maligned by so many over his football ability. And laughed at over his desire to be a striker for the Gunners.

Nobody of an Arsenal persuasion was doubting him last night as he smashed a hat-trick that led Arsenal to a remarkable victory.

His first goal came just before half time, Walcott racing clear to slot the ball past Adam Federici.

The 4-1 half-time deficit was still, however, Arsenal's worst since February 2001 when they were 5-1 down to Manchester United. And when the two teams re-emerged it was still Reading who looked sharper with Hunt, Hal Robson-Kanu and Leigertwood failing to take their chances.

But then Arsene Wenger sent on Olivier Giroud for Emmanuel Frimpong and young Thomas Eisfeld for Serge Gnabry. And the game changed completely.

Three minutes after coming on Giroud netted from Walcott's corner. Arsenal were a different team and Reading just could not contain them.

Giroud had another header saved low by Federici on 77 minutes.

But a minute from time Koscielny headed in from Walcott's corner to make it 4-3. And deep into stoppage time Walcott rammed home at the second attempt to spark delirium in the away stands. But the drama hadn't ended there. No chance.

When Marouane Chamakh was teed up by Andrey Arshavin on 103 minutes he made no mistake, burying a low drive into the corner. And that seemed to be that.

But substitute Pavel Pogrebnyak, who had come on with 17 minutes remaining of normal time, headed in from Chris Gunter's cross to make it 5-5.

A renewed surge rocketed around the stadium. Could Reading find a last rally against the odds?

We soon found out. With the clock moving into stoppage time at the end of extra time, Arshavin burst down the left, twisting and turning. His ball into the six-yard box caused all sorts of chaos and, at the second attempt, Walcott lashed it high into the middle of the goal.

Back came Reading. Pinging in crosses, flinging bodies into the box. But they committed so many men forward they had no answer when Chamakh burst through to lob Federici.

A crazy result. A crazy night.

READING: Federici 6, Gunter 6, Gorkss 6, Morrison 5, Shorey 6, Tabb 6, McCleary 6 (McAnuff 73, 6), Leigertwood 7, Robson-Kanu 7, Roberts 6 (Church 90), Hunt 6 (Pogrebnyak 73, 6).
ARSENAL: Martinez 6, Jenkinson 7, Koscielny 6, Djourou 7, Miquel 5 (Meade 105), Arshavin 7, Frimpong 5 (Giroud 62, 8), Coquelin 6, Walcott 9, Chamakh 6, Gnabry 5 (Eisfeld 62, 7).
REFEREE: Kevin Friend **ATT:** 23,980

Shirt changed

CONFUSED Olivier Giroud and Francis Coquelin were left as red as their shirts after throwing them to away fans after 90 minutes, thinking they were set for a replay. They had to ask for them back after being told extra time was to be played.

▲ **BARE CHEEK** Giroud last night

READING v ARSENAL
MAN OF THE MATCH
THEO WALCOTT
Outstanding hat-trick sealed win

READING		ARSENAL
35%	**BALL POSSESSION**	65%
9	**SHOTS ON TARGET**	13
8	**SHOTS OFF TARGET**	10
11	**CORNERS**	11
9	**OFFSIDE**	0
14	**FOULS**	18
2 0	**CARDS**	6 0

WENGER GOES MAD

FROM BACK PAGE

started very sloppy and had to wake up. The boss told us it wasn't good enough. It wasn't Arsenal. We showed everyone what we can do. We're absolutely knackered."

Wenger admitted the remarkable comeback had saved him from suffering one of his worst-ever defeats.

He said: "Had we gone out, and the way we could have gone out in the first half, that would not have been one of my proudest moments."

Reading became the first team EVER in the history of either the League Cup or the FA Cup to score five goals and lose.

Boss Brian McDermott admitted: "It feels like a funeral. It was the worst result of my career because we were 4-0 up against a top team and we lost the game.

"I don't think I will be looking at the DVD of this one. I think it will go straight into the bin and we'll move on."

▲ **ART ATTACK** Boruc is facing the sack at Saints

BORUC IN THE DOCK FOR RANT

By ALEX CROOK

ARTUR BORUC faces the sack after being reported by stewards for swearing at his own Southampton fans.

Boruc, 32, thought he had escaped punishment after video evidence cleared him of throwing a water bottle into the crowd following Clint Dempsey's winning goal in the 2-1 defeat against Tottenham on Sunday.

Saints yesterday confirmed they had launched an investigation after several staff members came forward to accuse the Pole of launching an F-word rant and making crude hand gestures to supporters.

A club source said: "We are treating the matter extremely seriously and sanctions could be imposed.

"We watched the CCTV and it is clear Artur threw the bottle at advertising hoardings and not into the crowd so there was no case to answer.

"However we have received a lot of complaints from supporters saying he swore at them."

Boruc only joined Saints last month on a short-term deal from Fiorentina and has conceded six goals in two Premier League games.

▲ **SHAKY** Lee Clark faces uncertain Blues future

BID COULD HIT CLARK

By JAMES NURSEY

LEE CLARK faces an uncertain future at Birmingham as Gianni Paladini steps up his bid for the cash-strapped Championship club.

Mirror Sport revealed on September 11 that former QPR chairman Paladini wants to acquire Brum.

The Italian is in talks over an improved £30million bid to buy out embattled Blues president Carson Yeung.

The fallen Hong Kong tycoon faces a money-laundering trial next month and his assets have been frozen.

City are still cutting back on coaching and playing staff after relegation in 2011.

Paladini and pal Flavio Briatore got through 12 bosses at Loftus Road. And if Paladini takes over, Clark will be under instant pressure with the club sitting 17th after being fourth last term.

MATCH STATS at THE EMIRATES ATT: 60,111

STORY OF THE GAME

ARSENAL		TOTTENHAM	ARSENAL		TOTTENHAM
7	SHOTS ON TARGET	3	80	TACKLES SUCCESS	70.6
3	SHOTS OFF TARGET	2	65.8	POSSESSION	34.2
3	BLOCKED SHOTS	3	54.8	TERRITORIAL ADVANTAGE	45.2
6	CORNERS	6	587	TOTAL PASSES	298
13	FOULS	13	27	TOTAL CROSSES	15
4	OFFSIDES	2	138	LOST BALLS	140
1	YELLOW CARDS	2	18	THROW INS	19
0	RED CARDS	1	45	RECOVERIES	45
87.9	PASSING SUCCESS	78.2	66.1	1ST HALF POSS.	33.5
15	TACKLES	17	66.2	2ND HALF POSS.	33.8

EA SPORTS
PLAYER PERFORMANCE INDEX

The total distance in miles travelled
for the team for the entire game

ARSENAL	TOTTENHAM
61.32	**55.38**

Total distance in miles whether the ball is in or out of play

ARSENAL		TOTTENHAM	
1) MIKEL ARTETA	6.52	1) SANDRO	6.29
2) SANTI CAZORLA	6.17	2) GARETH BALE	5.77
3) THOMAS VERMAELEN	5.79	3) JERMAIN DEFOE	5.56
4) THEO WALCOTT	5.66	4) AARON LENNON	5.49
5=) BACARY SAGNA	5.45	5) WILLIAM GALLAS	5.40
6=) OLIVIER GIROUD	5.45	6) JAN VERTONGHEN	5.37
7) PER MERTESACKER	5.35	7) TOM HUDDLESTONE	4.54
8) LUKAS PODOLSKI	5.05	8) CLINT DEMPSEY	3.43
9) LAURENT KOSCIELNY	4.99	9) MICHAEL DAWSON	3.09
10) JACK WILSHERE	4.93	10) HUGO LLORIS	2.68
11) WOJCIECH SZCZESNY	2.76	11) KYLE NAUGHTON	2.43
12) AARON RAMSEY	1.77	12) KYLE WALKER	2.39
13) SANTOS	0.93	13) TOM CARROLL	1.91
14) ALEX OXLADE-CHAMBERLAIN	0.48	14) EMMANUEL ADEBAYOR	1.03

▲ TOP: Arteta (right) covered most ground

Highest speed in mph when the ball is in or out of play where
the player achieves a minimum of 7 metres per second for at
least 5 metres

ARSENAL		TOTTENHAM	
1) LUKAS PODOLSKI	21.39	1) TOM CARROLL	5.44
2) THEO WALCOTT	19.77	2) CLINT DEMPSEY	4.61
3) AARON RAMSEY	19.15	3) TOM HUDDLESTONE	4.41
4) JACK WILSHERE	18.28	4) SANDRO	4.29
5) BACARY SAGNA	18.07	5) EMMANUEL ADEBAYOR	4.16
6) OLIVIER GIROUD	17.74	6=) MICHAEL DAWSON	3.98
7) THOMAS VERMAELEN	17.40	6=) GARETH BALE	3.98
8) SANTI CAZORLA	17.34	8=) JERMAIN DEFOE	3.80
9) LAURENT KOSCIELNY	16.84	8=) WILLIAM GALLAS	3.80
10) ALEX OXLADE-CHAMBERLAIN	16.71	10) AARON LENNON	3.69
11) PER MERTESACKER	16.49	11) JAN VERTONGHEN	3.56
12) MIKEL ARTETA	16.31	12) KYLE WALKER	3.47
13) SANTOS	14.23	13) KYLE NAUGHTON	3.42
14) WOJCIECH SZCZESNY	10.29	14) HUGO LLORIS	1.74

Average speed in mph of player during
the game when the ball is in play

ARSENAL		TOTTENHAM	
1) SANTOS	5.12	1) TOM CARROLL	5.44
2) AARON RAMSEY	4.99	2) CLINT DEMPSEY	4.61
3) JACK WILSHERE	4.85	3) TOM HUDDLESTONE	4.41
4) MIKEL ARTETA	4.43	4) SANDRO	4.29
5) SANTI CAZORLA	4.25	5) EMMANUEL ADEBAYOR	4.16
6) ALEX OXLADE-CHAMBERLAIN	4.16	6=) MICHAEL DAWSON	3.98
7=) LUKAS PODOLSKI	4.07	6=) GARETH BALE	3.98
7=) OLIVIER GIROUD	4.07	8=) JERMAIN DEFOE	3.80
9) THOMAS VERMAELEN	3.89	8=) WILLIAM GALLAS	3.80
10) THEO WALCOTT	3.80	10) AARON LENNON	3.69
11) BACARY SAGNA	3.71	11) JAN VERTONGHEN	3.56
12) PER MERTESACKER	3.49	12) KYLE WALKER	3.47
13) LAURENT KOSCIELNY	3.33	13) KYLE NAUGHTON	3.42
14) WOJCIECH SZCZESNY	1.72	14) HUGO LLORIS	1.74

EA SPORTS Player Performance Index is the official player
rating index of the Barclays Premier League

OPTA MATCH FACTS

13 Spurs have failed to keep a clean sheet at Arsenal since November 1998, in both league and cup action, for the past 13 seasons

30 There have been a total of 30 goals netted in the past five PL games between Arsenal and Spurs at The Emirates

50 Adebayor's red card was the 50th marching order that Spurs have been shown in the PL – and Adebayor's third red from referee Howard Webb

REF: HOWARD WEBB

Played an excellent advantage for Cazorla ahead of Arsenal's third goal

TEAM RATINGS PAGE 18

ARSENE'S

2-1 Podolski puts his side ahead

3-1 Giroud slides in for another

4-1 Cazorla caps a great game

5-2 Walover as Theo adds his

ARSENAL **5**
Mertesacker 24, Podolski 42,
Giroud 45, Cazorla 60, Walcott 90

TOTTENHAM **2**
Adebayor 10, Bale 71

By MATT LAW
Twitter: @Matt_Law_SM
sport@sundaymirror.co.uk

EMMANUEL ADEBAYOR might not have had a better game for Arsenal... it's just a shame he is employed by Tottenham these days.

Spurs manager Andre Villas-Boas is not a man who inspires a lot of sympathy, especially after he tried to claim his team controlled the game. But you had to feel for him at the Emirates.

Villas-Boas tried to be bold and give the Tottenham fans what they want, but Adebayor let him and the club down.

His goal and sending-off is exactly why Arsenal manager Arsene Wenger agreed to sell Adebayor to Manchester City in 2009. The bad usually outweighs the good.

Arsenal had already seen their former striker in headless chicken mode three years ago, when he scored against the Gunners for City, ran the length of the pitch to celebrate in front of their fans and stamped on Robin van Persie.

Adebayor's antics for Spurs yesterday were every bit as mental and this time he did not escape a red card.

It looked as though Adebayor had rewarded the brave decision by Villas-Boas to team him with Jermain Defoe when he opened the scoring after just 10 minutes.

It was Defoe's shot that had been stopped by Arsenal goalkeeper Wojciech Szczesny and Adebayor pounced from close range.

Never one to shirk the

▲ **BALE THE HERO:** AVB with Spurs scorer

> **Arsenal badly needed a confidence boost and they got it**

limelight, Adebayor danced in front of the Arsenal fans in celebration, but the 28-year-old soon had egg on his face.

Just seven minutes later, Adebayor made a wild lunge on Santi Cazorla and left referee Howard Webb with no option but to send him off. Spurs might have been winning, but it was effectively game over.

Cazorla lifted himself off the floor to produce another mesmerising display, Theo

PER-ING

Wenger laps up being the cream of north London

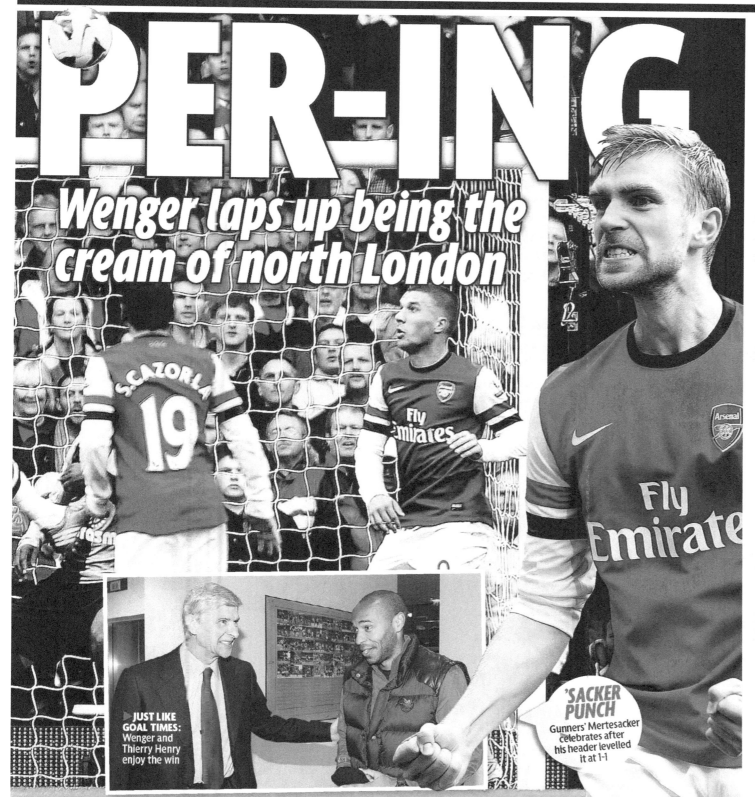

JUST LIKE GOAL TIMES: Wenger and Thierry Henry enjoy the win

'SACKER PUNCH
Gunners' Mertesacker celebrates after his header levelled it at 1-1

MATCH RATINGS

Compiled by Matt Law

ARSENAL

WOJCIECH SZCZESNY 6
Returned from injury and could do nothing about Adebayor's opening goal. Otherwise a relatively quiet day for the Pole.

BACARY SAGNA 7
Dangerous going forward and provided a good cross for Per Mertesacker's goal, but his defending remains a little suspect at times.

PER MERTESACKER 6
Redeemed his costly early error for Adebayor's opener by levelling the scores with a good header, his first goal at the Emirates.

LAURENT KOSCIELNY 6
A pretty comfortable game for the Frenchman once the Arsenal defence had only one striker to look after and more time on the ball.

THOMAS VERMAELEN 7
Enjoyed getting the opportunity to move forward from left-back as an attacker, as 10-man Tottenham posed little attacking threat.

MIKEL ARTETA 8
Bounced back from his terrible display against Fulham with a much more characteristic performance, full of control and calm assurance.

JACK WILSHERE 7
Again proved his fitness by getting up from several heavy challenges and, along with Arteta, confidently bossed the midfield.

THEO WALCOTT 8
How is there even a debate whether the winger deserves a new contract and a pay rise? Another assist and another goal. Enough said.

SANTI CAZORLA 9
Survived Adebayor's moment of madness to produce a brilliant piece of play to set-up Arsenal's third goal before also scoring himself.

LUKAS PODOLSKI 8
Scored via a deflection off Gallas and set up a goal for Cazorla. Couldn't be blamed for thinking that north London derbies are easy.

OLIVIER GIROUD 8
The Frenchman is really starting to find his feet in England and is developing a good relationship with Walcott. Scored Arsenal's third goal.

TOTTENHAM

HUGO LLORIS 6
Made a wonderful save from a Giroud header in what eventually became a very tough afternoon for the Tottenham rearguard.

KYLE WALKER 4
Not at his marauding best and struggled once Spurs were reduced to 10 men. Along with Naughton, he was replaced at half-time.

WILLIAM GALLAS 4
Unfortunate to see Podolski's shot deflect off him and past Lloris, but it soon became apparent he could not cope with the Arsenal attack.

JAN VERTONGHEN 4
The teamwork of Giroud, Walcott and Podolski proved just too hot for Vertonghen and his Tottenham defensive team-mates.

KYLE NAUGHTON 4
Substituted at the break after suffering a tough time up against the speed of Walcott and the overlapping of right-back Bacary Sagna.

AARON LENNON 5
Nearly doubled Tottenham's lead moments after Adebayor had scored, but proved otherwise too quiet and ineffective.

SANDRO 5
Lucky to escape early bookings for repeated fouls on midfielder Wilshere. Couldn't live with the England man or with his team-mate Arteta.

TOM HUDDLESTONE 5
Lost Mertesacker for the German defender's goal and failed to get in a decisive block in the run-up to Podolski's deflected effort.

GARETH BALE 6
Spent more time defending than attacking. Scored a good goal, but opponents Arsenal were already well out of sight by then.

EMMANUEL ADEBAYOR 2
His dance in celebration after scoring looked pretty ridiculous, but his sending-off that gave Spurs no chance was positively stupid.

JERMAIN DEFOE 6
Had the shot saved from which Adebayor scored on the rebound, but struggled without reward on his own up front with little service.

ARSENAL SUBSTITUTES

RAMSEY (on for Wilshere 72) 7 – Performed well for the final 18 minutes.
SANTOS (on for Podolski 81) 6 – Sensibly decided against asking any Spurs players for their shirt.
OXLADE-CHAMBERLAIN (on for Giroud 86) 8 – Set up the fifth goal for Walcott.

TOTTENHAM SUBSTITUTES

DAWSON (on for Walker, 46) 5 – Impossible situation for him to be thrown into.
DEMPSEY (on for Naughton 46) 5 – No chance of turning the game for the visitors.
CARROLL (on for Huddlestone 72) 5 – Did better than Huddlestone, but could not have been much worse.

Walcott underlined the fact he deserves a new contract and a pay rise, and Olivier Giroud and Lukas Podolski gave encouragement they are settling into life in England.

Of course, it was not much of a contest once Spurs went a man down, but Arsenal badly needed a confidence boost and they got it.

Having been at fault for Adebayor's opener, Per Mertesacker redeemed himself by heading Arsenal's equaliser from a Walcott cross and two goals in the final three minutes of the first half wrapped up the victory.

First, Tom Huddlestone failed to clear and Podolski turned in the area before seeing a shot deflect off William Gallas and squirm past Hugo Lloris.

Then, Webb played a brilliant advantage as Cazorla rode a late challenge, drifted left and crossed for Giroud to fire a deserved goal.

Villas-Boas took off both his full-backs at half-time and moved to three at the back. But there was nothing he could do to turn the tide.

The home side's fourth came with half-an-hour left, as Cazorla deservedly got on the scoresheet by tapping in from close range after good work from Walcott and Podolski. Gareth Bale pulled a goal back for Spurs, but Alex Oxlade-Chamberlain stepped off the bench to help hammer home Arsenal's advantage.

He wriggled his way into the penalty area and crossed for Walcott to score from eight yards. The goal meant Arsenal beat their north London rivals by the exact same scoreline as last season.

Wenger's men used their 5-2 victory over Spurs in February to inspire a turnaround in form and surge up the table past their enemies.

They will clearly be hoping the latest thrashing has the same effect.

LAW'S VERDICT

Andre Villas-Boas tried to be bold and was badly let down by Adebayor. Arsenal took full advantage and the win should do wonders for their confidence.

ADEBAYOR SHOWS HOW TO GO FROM HERO TO ZERO IN JUST A MATTER OF MINUTES
▲ Spurs striker puts away the opener, but then loses it in his brutal challenge on Cazorla, which led to Howard Webb showing him the red card

OUR RATINGS

COMPILED BY STEVE STAMMERS

FABIANSKI
5 Hull's two early strikes came from set-pieces. Could have been more commanding in his area

SAGNA
6 Supported the attack when he could and showed the kind of commitment lacking in some

MERTESACKER
6 With only one striker, a test of concentration for a player who must have suffered flashbacks

KOSCIELNY
6 Excellent in defence when called on. Was alert to the Hull break. Scored the crucial equaliser

GIBBS
6 Like Sagna, supplemented the attack when he could. But missed a sitter late on

ARTETA
5 Struggled against the massed ranks of the Hull midfield. Not his finest performance

★ STAR MAN

SANTI CAZORLA

PASSES	79
PASS COMPLETION	89.9%
TOTAL SHOTS	2
GOAL ASSISTS	1
GOALS	0

RAMSEY
6 His brilliant winner made up for a game where, like Arteta, he struggled for long spells.

CAZORLA
7 Arsenal's most influential player. The one man able to open up a determined Hull side

OZIL
5 Unable to get on the ball and create for the front men until late in the contest

PODOLSKI
4 Totally anonymous. He survived until the 51st minute before he was substituted

GIROUD
6 Worked hard enough and only had support when Sanogo came on for Podolski

SUBSTITUTES
Sanogo 6 (Podolski, 51) At last an ally for Giroud
Wilshere (Ozil, 107)) Finally got on to pick up medal
Rosicky (Cazorla, 107) Almost set up another goal
Subs not used: Szczesny, Vermaelen, Monreal, Flamini

ARSENAL		HULL CITY
7	Shots on Target	4
11	Shots off Target	8
7	Blocked Shots	0
7	Corners	3
17	Fouls	18
0	Offsides	4
1	Yellow Cards	3
0	Red Cards	0
85.7	Passing Success	76.2
21	Tackles	20
76.2	Tackles Success%	80
64.7	Possession%	35.3
54.4	Territorial Advantage%	45.6
796	Total Passes	425
24	Total Crosses	12
178	Lost Balls	156
72	Recoveries	78
59.3	1st Half Poss%	40.7
71.1	2nd Half Poss%	28.9

Att: 89,345

ARSENAL
Cazorla 17, Koscielny 71, Ramsey ˙09

HULL CITY
Chester 4, Davies 9

3
2

Aar....a cup at last!

RAMSEY ENDS NINE-YEAR WAIT FOR WENGER IN EXTRA-TIME

By DAVE KIDD
at Wembley

AS Arsene Wenger finally toasted a first trophy in nine years, there was no more fitting scorer of the winning goal than Aaron Ramsey.

For Arsenal have shown uncommon patience in their manager, while Wenger has shown uncommon patience in his young midfielder.

And, even in a footballing age of instant judgement and knee-jerk sackings, they proved good things come to those who wait.

A year ago, Ramsey had become the whipping boy of the Emirates crowd

And it seemed the Welshman would never recapture the early promise that preceded the horrific leg break he suffered at Stoke in 2010. Yet, Wenger's faith in the kid never wavered and, had Ramsey not suffered another injury at West Ham on Boxing Day, Arsenal might have won the Premier League as well as the FA Cup.

Back at Christmas, the ex-Cardiff player was in such outstanding form that Arsenal were top of the League and their revitalised midfielder was favourite to be Footballer of the Year.

Still, this was no bad consolation. An extra-time winner to cap one of Wembley's greatest comebacks in a modern classic of a Cup Final.

After such a lengthy wait, it was never likely to be easy for the Gunners to get their hands on the new FA Cup.

James Chester and Curtis Davies had sent Steve Bruce's men hurtling towards dreamland early on, but Santi Cazorla soon clawed one back with a free-kick, before Laurent Koscielny's second-half leveller. But then, they are not exactly early risers when it comes to big matches, this Arsenal side.

Three down after 15 minutes at Stamford Bridge, four down after 20 minutes at Anfield and, here at Wembley, again that familiar old feeling.

Wenger's men had tossed away two goals almost before Leona Lewis had piped down from singing Abide With Me.

You wonder sometimes how Wenger prepares his team for such red-letter days.

It does not seem to involve any mention of the opposition – because Hull love a set-piece and they love a wing-back bombing down the flank, yet Arsenal appeared clueless about defending against either.

Wenger had stuck with semi-final shoot-out hero Lukasz Fabianski ahead of Wojciech Szczesny and, inside nine minutes, he was retrieving leather from onion bag – twice.

First, Ahmed Elmohamady won a corner, Stephen Quinn played it deep to Tom Huddlestone, whose scuffed volley was cutely diverted in by Chester.

Then Quinn crossed from the left, Alex Bruce's header cannoned off the post and Davies fired in from a tight angle.

The Hull fans were cavorting in the Wembley aisles after eight minutes of mayhem and euphoria. Smiles as wide as Steve Bruce's waistline.

Their club had waited 110 years for a major Cup Final and it seemed as if the whole of the East Riding was here. Old ladies in tiger-print replica shirts were dancing like Bet Lynch at an acid-house rave in the Rovers.

Kieran Gibbs soon

Hull fans were cavorting in Wembley aisles, smiles wide as Bruce's waistline

REFEREE:
LEE PROBERT
Not his best game after an impressive season. Missed two clear-cut penalties

OPTA'S BIG-MATCH FACTS

Arsenal became the first side since 2006 to bounce back from a 2-0 deficit in the Final and triumph

The Gunners had only conceded two goals in their previous five FA Cup Finals combined

The last time an FA Cup Final went into extra time was in 2007, when Chelsea beat Man United 1-0

Hull scored more than one goal during a game against Arsenal for the first time since September 2008

COMPILED BY STEVE STAMMERS

OUR RATINGS

McGREGOR
6 Should have done better with the Cazorla free-kick that brought Arsenal back into it

DAVIES
6 Excellent in defence, but lucky not to concede a penalty for lunge at Cazorla

BRUCE
7 He defended with determination and grit and he epitomised the Hull spirit. Limped off

CHESTER
6 Showed composure in defence and was a threat at set-pieces, grabbing the first goal

ELMOHAMADY
5 A bright start but pushed further back as Arsenal pressure increased later on

LIVERMORE
5 More destructive than inventive. More creation needed. He was content to spoil

HUDDLESTONE
6 Like Livermore, was needed to smother Arsenal's midfield. Better than he showed

MEYLER
5 Contributed muscle more than anything else. A key man in the Hull strategy.

ROSENIOR
6 Was not exposed and was resilient at the back. Not able to break forward regularly

QUINN
5 Hardly made any positive contribution. Ran, chased and harried. That's about it

FRYATT
6 A lonely man at Wembley after that dramatic opening for Hull. Competed fiercely

SUBSTITUTES

McShane (Bruce, 66) Stuck to his task as Arsenal pushed
Aluko (Fryatt, 76) Major impact and almost scored
Boyd (Rosenior, 102) Went to wing back. More effective up front.
Subs not used: Figueroa, Koren, Sagbo, Harper

SO NOW YOU'RE GUNNER BELIEVE US: Arsenal's victorious team celebrate their Cup triumph, as does manager Arsene Wenger (right)

WITH STUNNING GUNNERS STRIKE

headed off the line to avert a total early meltdown. And then, perhaps out of embarrassment, Arsenal decided to join in.

Bruce fouled Cazorla 25 yards out and the Spaniard clambered up to curl home the free-kick.

Yet, until half-time, there was little purpose about Arsenal's play, Mesut Ozil wafting about like a £42million apparition, miskicking when he should have scored from a Lukas Podolski

centre. After the break, though, Hull were under the cosh.

And, on 71 minutes, Bacary Sagna won a header from Cazorla's corner and the ball cannoned off a defender for Koscielny to turn in.

Gibbs then skied a sitter from Olivier Giroud's cross and Arsenal were appealing – in vain – for a penalty when David Meyler clattered into Cazorla.

Then, in extra-time, Giroud crashed a header off the bar from

Ramsey's cross before the Welshman slammed home his 109th-minute winner after Arsenal's outstanding sub Yaya Sanogo created space and Giroud applied a cunning back-heel.

There was still time for a kamikaze dash from Fabianski, letting Sone Aluko (below) shoot wide across the face of goal.

It was cruel on Hull, whose players had summoned such an early whirlwind and whose fans were magnificent.

But, finally, the waiting was over for Arsenal – thanks their gutsy comeback and their own Comeback Kid.

KIDD'S *VERDICT*

After the worst possible start, the Gunners showed they had the spirit and belief to come back and clinch victory, despite a brilliantly defiant performance from the Tigers.

IT'S RAMSEY S

Midfielder takes centre stage again to save Arsenal wit

By SIMON MULLOCK
at Wembley

ARSENE WENGER will forever be indebted to Aaron Ramsey.

For 70 minutes, it seemed the only way Arsenal's players would be taking a ride on an open-topped bus this weekend was if Wenger took them to Southend.

After going two goals down inside eight minutes, it took the Gunners an age to recover from the shock of finding themselves staring into the teeth of one of the FA Cup's biggest shocks.

Even Santi Cazorla's free-kick goal midway through the first period failed to provide the catalyst for Wenger's men to restore natural order.

Arsenal's onslaught grew in both intensity and desperation with every passing second-half minute. And when

referee Lee Probert turned a blind eye to two penalty appeals, lesser teams may have crumbled.

Hull's Tom Huddlestone was fortune that Probert failed to spot him grab Olivier Giroud around the neck as the Frenchman challenged for a cross.

But there was no excuse for the official to dismiss Cazorla's plea that he had been upended by Curtis Davies, because the Spaniard had clearly been fouled.

Then the Gunners got the kind of good fortune that makes this grand old competition so famous.

Huddlestone leapt unchallenged to clear, only for the ball to strike the back of James Chester's head and loop back towards goal.

Defender Laurent Koscielny still had work to do, but he swivelled in an instant

to hook a shot past City keeper Allan McGregor, and the eruption of relief at the West End of Wembley said it all.

Suddenly, the driver of the liveried bus that had been primed to take the Gunners squad on a triumphant tour of Islington today was looking forward once again to the possibility of a few more precious hours of overtime.

Arsenal were supposed to stroll to their first trophy in nine years.

After less than eight minutes, Wenger would have been tempted to lock his players in the stocks outside the town hall so they can be pelted with rotten fruit.

There would have been no shortage of fans willing to bring the oranges and apples.

More that 50,000 of them gave Arsenal a numerical advantage in the stands,

> **His celebration harked back to Charlie George's strike of legend 43 years ago**

paying through the nose to land (Wembley seats when the official alloca inevitably ran out.

Yet where in mattered most – ou the pitch – it was the Londoners seemed outnumbered.

Every time an Arsenal player possession of the ball, he was immedia surrounded by one or more Hull shir

Perhaps there is some sense in chairman Aseem Allam's desire to rebr City as the Tigers.

This was the day when Steve Bru side hunted Arsenal down in packs.

Bruce went with three at the back, Alex standing in between James Che and Davies.

They were there to defend.

Yet they were fated to make and the goals that put the City fans

GOALS GALORE

3-2
109 MINS
Aaron Ramsey
ends Hull's dreams

0-1
4 MINS
James Chester
nets the opener

0-2
9 MINS
Curtis Davies
fires home

1-2
17 MINS
Santi Cazorla
gets one back

SWEET
h dramatic late winner

2-2
71 MINS
Koscielny
equalises

Club dreamland. Just 183 seconds in, Chester, the Manchester United reject who has come of age on Humberside, swooped to steer Huddlestone's volley past Lukasz Fabianski.

Then, when Bruce's brave header came bouncing back off the post, there was Davies to produce a finish that was just as assured.

Arsenal were supposed to hold all the tactical and technical aces, but Wenger was being out-manoeuvred by the Hull boss.

The Gunners weren't helped by the jaded efforts of Giroud or another flat performance by £42million Mesut Ozil.

But at least Cazorla looked up for the fight.

And when Bruce took the Spanish midfielder out with a clumsy tackle in the 16th minute, Cazorla took full retribution by lifting a glorious free-kick high past McGregor's left hand from 25 yards.

Kieran Gibbs could have won the cup in normal time, but blazed over from 10 yards.

But perhaps it was fitting that Ramsey should score the winner 11 minutes from the end of extra time.

The Welsh midfielder was pivotal in Arsenal topping the Premier League for much of the season before he was stricken by injury and the Gunners failed to keep up with the pace.

His exquisite finish from Giroud's back-heel was worthy of a Wembley winner.

Ramsey's celebration harked back to Charlie George's strike of legend 43 years ago.

It had been a long time in coming.

2014 WI

FA C GUNNER

PARTY TIME ..AT LAST
Jubilant Arsenal celebrate, while (left) Cazorla, Koscielny and Ramsey pose with the trophy

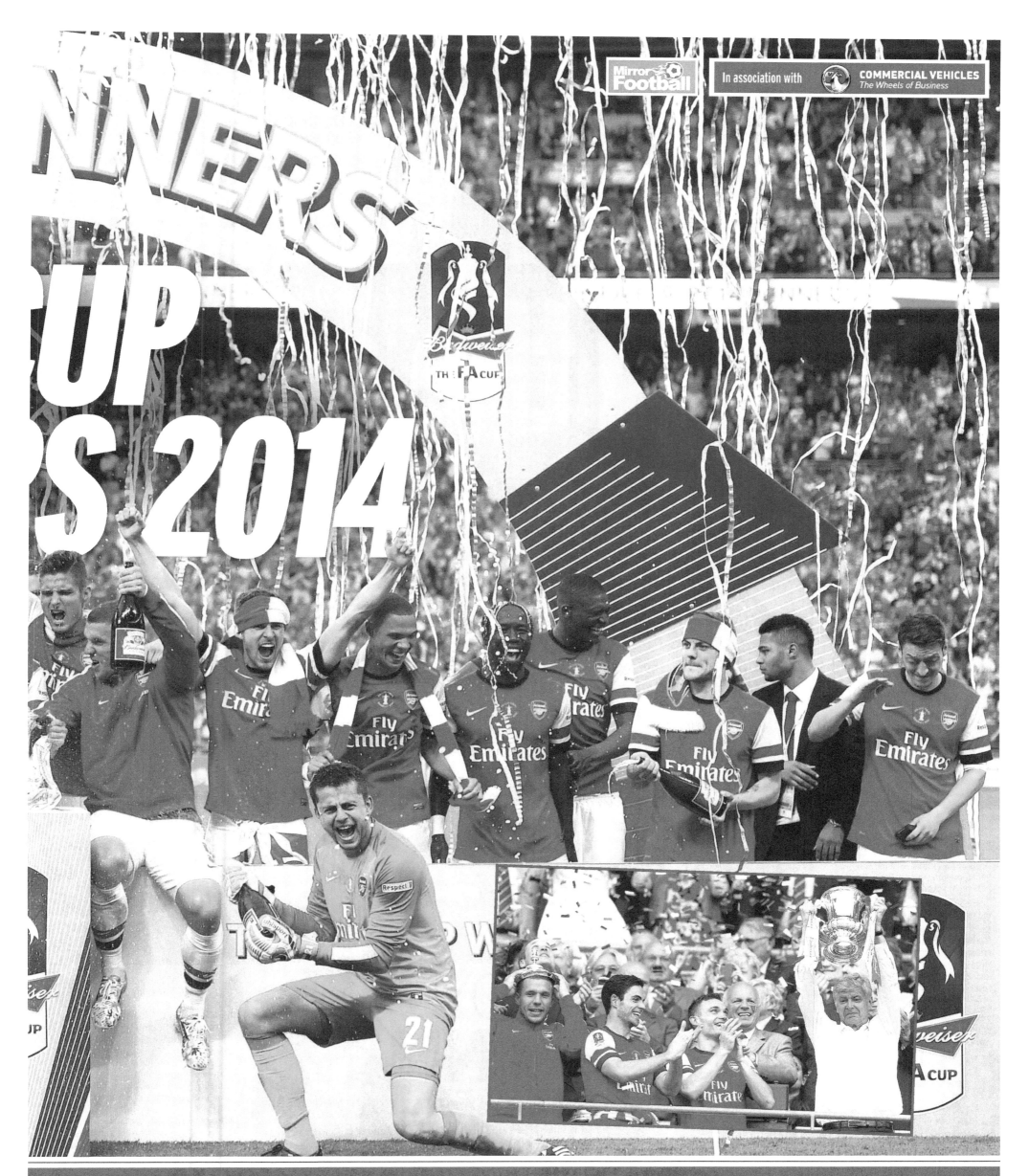

WINNERS' CUP S 2014

CRUNCH TIME FOR RODGERS

EXCLUSIVE BY **SIMON MULLOCK**

BRENDAN RODGERS' Liverpool future will hinge on the assurances he gives to the club's American owners this month.

The Kop boss will meet with Fenway Sports Group president Mike Gordon in the next two weeks to undergo a debrief of a season that promised much and delivered little.

Sunday Mirror Sport has been told by a senior Anfield source that Rodgers' (below) future will NOT be on the agenda, despite reports that Jurgen Klopp is waiting for a call from Anfield after quitting Borussia Dortmund.

But it is understood that Gordon won't just be demanding answers about Liverpool's sixth-placed finish.

He will also look for proof from Rodgers that he is the right man to take the club forward.

The Ulsterman's stock has fallen in the 12 months since he took the Reds tantalisingly close to the Premier League title – but the end-of-season review is now a normal procedure under FSG and there is a belief that Rodgers deserves more time.

YAYA STAYS

FROM BACK PAGE

Sport that Toure now feels he is being given the respect he deserves after being told by Sheikh Mansour that he wanted him to stay.

Seluk (below) said: "Yaya is staying – because Sheikh Mansour told him he must stay.

"Mansour told Yaya that he is still a very important player and that he was the first big player to join City after the takeover.

"He told him that City wouldn't even discuss a possible sale now.

"This is good. People have tried to say that Yaya only wanted more money, but it was never about money. It was only about respect."

It is unique for Mansour to personally intervene in a football-related matter, despite investing more than £1billion of his personal fortune into transforming City over the past seven years.

LLET ME GO!

FROM BACK PAGE

United. They appear to be fighting a losing battle to keep David de Gea, who seems set to join Real Madrid.

Lloris will be top of United's wanted list to replace De Gea (below). The 28-year-old has spent three seasons at White Hart Lane and has a good working relationship with Pochettino.

But he is desperate to play in the Champions League as he prepares to lead his country in their home Euros next summer.

The asking price will be at least £25million. There is no buy-out clause in Lloris's contract, so Spurs chairman Daniel Levy can drive a hard bargain.

And Levy is aware that Lyon – the club that sold Lloris to Spurs in 2012 for £12m – are entitled to 20 per cent of any transfer fee in excess of what they received.

FA CUP FINAL 2015

Super Walcott still the centre

OFF AND RUNNING
Walcott wheels away to celebrate after firing his side ahead with a stunning left-foot volley

ANDY DUNN
BRITAIN'S BEST COLUMNIST FROM WEMBLEY

NO better place to prove a point. No finer way to forget physical agony. No grander stage to showcase a talent undermined at every turn.

Theo Walcott had heard the whispers, clocked the knowing looks: Hasn't kicked on, a body bonded with injury, his finishing shy of world class, pretty much the same now as he was when a beard was out the question.

Lightning quick, capable of the spectacular but short on game intelligence.

You know the stuff. He does.

But if Walcott needed one final emphatic response to the nonsense – and he didn't – he delivered it from the perfect pulpit.

This crushing Arsenal triumph was a collective, stylish amble through Aston Villa's wafer-thin armoury of sheer mediocrity.

Yet frustration was festering before Walcott's world-class – yes, world-class – finish five minutes before half-time.

It was a finish stitched together by balance, composure and technique.

It was a finish that should keep him central and keep Raheem Sterling from the Emirates.

It was a finish that should see his new contract stamped 'URGENT'.

Sure, missed opportunities preceded and followed. Some could be filed under 'wasteful', some unfortunate to involve an inspired veteran in Shay Given. But Walcott is a middle man. Villa could not handle much at Wembley – they certainly could not handle Walcott.

After his sorties through the physical mill, few would begrudge Walcott days like these.

And when, on his return from that cruciate ligament injury, he found himself on the tracksuit side of the touchline, he never bleated.

This was not a reward from Arsene Wenger. This was a realisation that Walcott's potency through the centre might just be greater than Olivier Giroud's. The reward from Wenger came when he sat Theo down 15 minutes from the end.

Walcott headed for his seat, the yellowed legions rose from theirs.

Those in claret and blue could only

ARSENAL 4
Walcott 40, Sanchez 50
Mertesacker 62, Giroud 90

ASTON VILLA 0

THE FA CUP

shows he is of attention

> **If** was a finish that should keep Raheem Sterling from the Emirates... and see Theo's new contract marked 'URGENT'

SUITED & BOOTED
Villa manager Tim Sherwood is consoled by Arsenal counterpart Arsene Wenger

headshake their despondency at their team's woeful performance.

They were fortunate to concede only goals from Walcott (below with Gunners legend Ian Wright), Alexis Sanchez, Per Mertesacker and Giroud.

Only Given – assuming you don't blame him for the Sanchez jaw-slackener – emerged with any worthwhile sliver of credit. But at least Villa's fans contributed to a fine occasion.

After the poison served up in Zurich, this was the palate-clear ser – football's happy boil-wash after a week in FIFA's sewers.

It did not scale any great heights of exhilaration or tip bodies towards

seat-edge. It was far too one-sided for that. But it was a football match of good sportsmanship and some style, with the monopoly on style enjoyed by an Arsenal team as bent on painting pictures as puncturing defences.

Wembley was Mesut Ozil's canvas.

Pummelling Ozil for his work-rate is the equivalent of hammering Picasso for forgetting to whitewash the garden wall.

He was simply dreamy. He doesn't kick the ball, he whispers in its ear. Liquid genius.

Sanchez has a more bristling demeanour but only marginally less panache.

And between them, they conjured

up an exhibition of elaborate torture. Sanchez, though, can be as copybook as picture book – the headed assist for Walcott's opener one example, his wonderfully violent goal another.

Wenger's summer must now be consumed by supplementing the elite talent of those two with high-quality additions to his formation's peak and base.

But that can wait for a moment or two.

The FA Cup Final is about celebration and tears, elation and stomach-knotting deflation.

It is about players shining in the brightest spotlight as the season's curtains close.

And Arsenal and Theo Walcott did just that.

WHERE THE CUP WAS WON & LOST
BY STEVE STAMMERS

MESUT OZIL V JACK GREALISH

A WORLD Cup winner with 64 caps for Germany against a 19-year-old still to declare his international intentions. Only one winner there. The occasion seemed to get to Grealish in the battle between proven class and immense potential.

Ozil wriggled into spaces that seemed not to exist. Grealish ran, too often, into blind alleys. Ozil had composure. Grealish took time to settle.

The Villa youngster gave the ball away too easily through over-eagerness to impress on such a huge occasion. Ozil created at a stroll.

In the long term Grealish will be a major asset to his club, and whichever country he opts for. Ozil is proven quality and it showed. Grealish's time will come - it just wasn't yesterday.

VERDICT: OZIL BY A MILE

PER MERTESACKER V CHRISTIAN BENTEKE

SUCH was the dominance of the other German World Cup winner in the Gunners side that he had one of his most comfortable games of the season.

Benteke won a handful of aerial duels but they amounted to nothing. The occasional flick on, the odd ball back to his midfield. But nothing for him to launch himself at in the Arsenal area.

In his defence, there was little ammunition coming in from the flanks. Mertesacker rubbed salt into the wound in the 62nd minute when he headed home a corner from Santi Cazorla. Surely it was supposed to be the other way round?

The big Belgian was short of allies up front and starved of a supply of crosses. The bigger German had the proverbial cigar on as a result.

VERDICT: BENTEKE SUBBED - ENOUGH SAID

SANTI CAZORLA V TOM CLEVERLEY

SOMETHING of a mismatch that in many ways summed up the game. Cazorla is the heartbeat of Arsenal. He is brave - not just physically but in the areas where he is happy to take possession of the ball and then use it to some effect.

Cleverley has been reborn under the management of Tim Sherwood but was left chasing shadows around the Wembley pitch. Cazorla dictated the pace of the game, the flow of Arsenal's attacks.

Cleverley, for all his industry, could not get close enough to snuff out the danger. No one could question the application of the Villa midfield man.

It was simply that Cazorla had too much class for him. Just as his team-mates had too much class for Villa. One of many battles lost.

VERDICT: CAZORLA WAY TOO CLEVER

FA CUP FINAL 2015

ALL GUNS

WONDERWAL: Theo Walcott

Walcott: Now for the title

FROM BACK PAGE

league next season." Boss Arsene Wenger also goes into the record books – as he moves alongside Villa's old boss George Ramsay by winning the cup for a sixth time.

Jubilant Wenger crowed: "I am very proud. This was a continuation of how we have played recently, and it shows we have made progress and can deal with pressure.

"My hunger is great and I want to win more."

Walcott repaid Wenger for showing faith in him at Wembley – and then vowed to lead Arsenal back to Premier League glory.

Gunners boss Wenger gave Walcott the nod to start ahead of Olivier Giroud, and he responded by breaking the deadlock.

Walcott said: "I thank the manager for having faith and picking me – and I have paid him back for that.

"There needs to be more of those goals next year. We are very close to challenging for the league. We just need

ANDY DUNN VERDICT Pages 76-77

to start the season well. I have been here for a long time and this is one of the best squads I have been part of. It is fantastic – but we should be achieving much more. The Premier League is the next target."

Walcott missed last year's success here over Hull, and added: "I miss this feeling.

"Last year I was at home. I would like to thank the physiotherapists – this is massive for me."

Aston Villa manager Tim Sherwood said: "I can't make any excuses, Arsenal were too good.

"We couldn't impose ourselves on them or nullify what they had. They had too much quality.

"When you've had your midfield booked and your right-back, obviously you're walking a tight-rope. It's a learning curve. You have to learn and we need to build a new team. We have a losing mentality here.

"They've been scraping relegation for the past four years. We need to try and change that. We gave the fans nothing to cheer about today but I can promise them it will get better."

San's the man as Arsenal produce a performance fit for a prince

A SHAY TO FORGET One of Villa's few heroes, Shay Given, looks dejected after their crushing defeat

BY SIMON MULLOCK
Chief Football Writer at Wembley

ARSENAL were good enough to reduce princes and prime ministers to tears.

The Gunners lifted the FA Cup for a record 12th time with a performance of such superiority that it was Aston Villa who were flattered by the final scoreline.

Theo Walcott, Alexis Sanchez, Per Mertesacker and Olivier Giroud scored the goals that took the famous old pot back to the Emirates for the second successive season.

Such was the level of humiliation, honorary Villans Prince William and David

Cameron might have been tempted to flick through the statute books for some ancient English law that allows them to lock up troublesome Frenchmen in the Tower.

No manager has won the Cup more than Arsene Wenger, whose sixth triumph was never in doubt once his side found their range in the closing minutes of a first half they dominated. At least Cameron wasn't there to witness the carnage.

Poor old William was forced to hand over the trophy to Mertesacker and injured club captain Mikel Arteta though gritted royal teeth.

That 39-year-old keeper Shay Given was Villa's best performer said everything about the way Tim Sherwood's side froze on a day that should have been a celebration for the Midlands club. Given, beaten by Wenger's

Poor William was forced to hand over the trophy with gritted teeth

ARSENAL 4
Walcott 40, Sanchez 50
Mertesacker 62, Giroud 90

ASTON VILLA 0

THE FA CUP

BLAZING

ALL ONE WAY
Sanchez fires home a wonder goal (above), Mertesacker heads home the third and Giroud celebrates the fourth

MATCH STATS

ARSENAL		ASTON VILLA
9	Shots on Target	0
4	Shots off Target	0
3	Blocked Shots	2
8	Corners	0
9	Fouls	15
5	Offsides	2
0	Yellow Cards	5
0	Red Cards	0
86.6	Passing Success %	83.5
68	Duels Won	53
56.2	Duel Success %	43.8
18	Tackles	20
83.3	Tackles Success %	85
57.6	Possession %	42.4
53	Territorial Advantage%	47
499	Total Passes	370
27	Total Crosses	20
133	Lost Balls	115
71	Recoveries	47
62	1st Half Poss %	38
53.6	2nd Half Poss %	46.4

Att: 89,283

HOW THEY RATED
COMPILED BY DEAN JONES

Arsenal

SZCZESNY 6 — Little to do on the day. Toughest part of his cup final was a row with his dad on social media

BELLERIN 6 — Probing runs down the right flank caused problems but Grealish never gave him any trouble

MERTESACKER 7 — Could not believe his luck as he scored one of the easiest cup final goals in history

KOSCIELNY 6 — Would never have imagined that dealing with Benteke in a cup final could be so simple

MONREAL 6 — Still improving and will have been surprised by the fact Villa failed to test him out more often

COQUELIN 7 — Nicknamed Columbo and he worked hard to detect trouble and protect his defence

CAZORLA 8 — Incredible array of passing left Villa unsure whether they were coming or going

RAMSEY 7 — Pushed forward whenever possible and cut Villa open with probing balls in behind

OZIL 7 — Lovely moments of skill. Villa's midfield struggled to cope with his awareness and creativity

SANCHEZ 8 — Rounded off the season by scoring an absolute belter that will forever be replayed

WALCOTT 7 — Natural finisher and repaid Wenger's faith by breaking the deadlock with clinical strike

SUBSTITUTES
Giroud 6 (on for Walcott, 77) Scored fourth goal
Wilshere 6 (on for Ozil, 77) Kept things neat and tidy
Oxlade-Chamberlain (on for Sanchez, 89) Crossed for late goal
Subs not used: Gibbs, Gabriel, Flamini, Ospina.

Aston Villa

GIVEN 6 — The 39-year-old made a few decent stops but could do little about the Arsenal goals

HUTTON 5 — Gave his all but booking for hacking down Sanchez summed up his evening

OKORE 6 — Known as 'Concrete Ron' at Villa Park but unfortunately he didn't settle at Wembley

VLAAR 5 — Scoreline could have been worse without him but just could not cope with barrage of attacks

RICHARDSON 6 — Block halfway through first half denied Walcott a certain goal but ultimately it meant little

WESTWOOD 5 — Struggled to take control of any midfield battles. Caught chasing shadows

DELPH 5 — Has had a great season but just could not reproduce his top form on biggest stage

CLEVERLEY 5 — Booking for cynical trip on Monreal gave indication of just how hard Villa found occasion

GREALISH 5 — Struggled to get into game and confidence began to wane when he started losing possession

N'ZOGBIA 4 — Could not make any positive impact. Decision making was poor and passing too sloppy

BENTEKE 5 — At fault for Mertesacker goal – this could prove to be his last game for club

SUBSTITUTES
Agbonlahor 5 (on for N'Zogbia, 53) Rarely troubled the Arsenal defence
Bacuna 5 (on for Richardson, 68) Anonymous
Sanchez 5 (on for Westwood, 71) No impact
Subs not used: Baker, Sinclair, Cole, Guzan.

Arsenal when he played for Newcastle at the old Wembley 17 years ago, produced a fine save to keep out Laurent Koscielny's close-range header.

Aaron Ramsey, the Gunners' extra-time hero against Hull last year, then wasted two glorious opportunities.

And when Kieran Richardson threw himself into a brilliant block to prevent Walcott volleying Arsenal ahead from six yards, Wenger must have feared the worst.

However, five minutes before the break, the Villa defence hesitated fatally as Sanchez soared above Nacho Monreal's cross and Walcott was there in a flash, beating Given with a half-volley of power and precision. Game over.

The only ones to turn up for Villa were the 40,000 who packed the west end of Wembley. Those who didn't pay to get in were beyond awful.

Sanchez settled any needless Arsenal nerves with a 50th-minute goal that will go down as one of the finest in the Cup's 143-year history.

There was no disguising what the Chilean's intentions were when he cut in from the left at pace, but Given was left floundering by a shot from 30 yards that carried too much swerve and pace.

Mertesacker then only had to shrug his shoulders to shake off Christian Benteke and head home Santi Cazorla's corner in the 62nd minute. And although Villa saw a furious

penalty appeal waved away by referee Jon Moss when Jack Grealish was felled by Hector Bellerin's challenge, by now the final whistle couldn't come quick enough.

Giroud was feeling no pity after starting on the bench, though, and when Alex Oxlade-Chamberlain threaded a cross into the Villa six-yard box in injury time, the Frenchman applied the coup de grace.

Mertesacker said: "We deserved this. We played on the front foot from the start and that makes a massive difference. It is a great way to finish off the season and I can look forward to my first holiday since retiring from international football."

Arsenal's FA Cup victory meant Southampton qualified for the Europa League. Saints star James Ward-Prowse tweeted: Thanks Gunners!

HELLO, MY OLD CHINA

FLASHBACK: Friday's Mirror revealed Rooney has mega offers from China

Show us the love, Rooney

FROM BACK PAGE

that there is a two-year contract worth £50million waiting for him in China as he weighs up his options after being told he is surplus to requirements at Manchester United.

Koeman will also seek assurances that a player who has won every club honour in 13 years at United is still hungry for success before sanctioning any move.

United would prefer for Rooney to move abroad – a number of clubs in the United States are also monitoring his situation – because it is likely to cost them money if he moves back to Merseyside.

The former England captain also has two years left on his Old Trafford contract, and United will have to offer him a pay-off as compensation for reduced earnings if he goes to Everton.

New deal for Pep...

FROM BACK PAGE

much longer-term project after targeting a raft of the world's best young players.

City have already spent £43million on Monaco's 22-year-old midfielder Bernardo Silva since clinching a Champions League place last weekend.

And the Blues are now looking to wrap up deals for Benfica keeper Ederson and Monaco duo Fabinho and Benjamin Mendy.

That would take City's summer spending spree past the £150m mark – and they also want Tottenham's £40m-rated Kyle Walker.

And it is unlikely that the recruitment will stop there.

Guardiola is confident that he can land Arsenal's Alexis Sanchez, despite the Gunners' reluctance to allow the Chilean forward to move to another Premier League club.

The rebuild is a huge statement of intent by the club – and they reckon that Guardiola will want to be around when the team he is building hits its peak in four or five years' time.

ARSENAL 2 CHELSEA 1

Sanchez 4, Ramsey 79   Costa 76

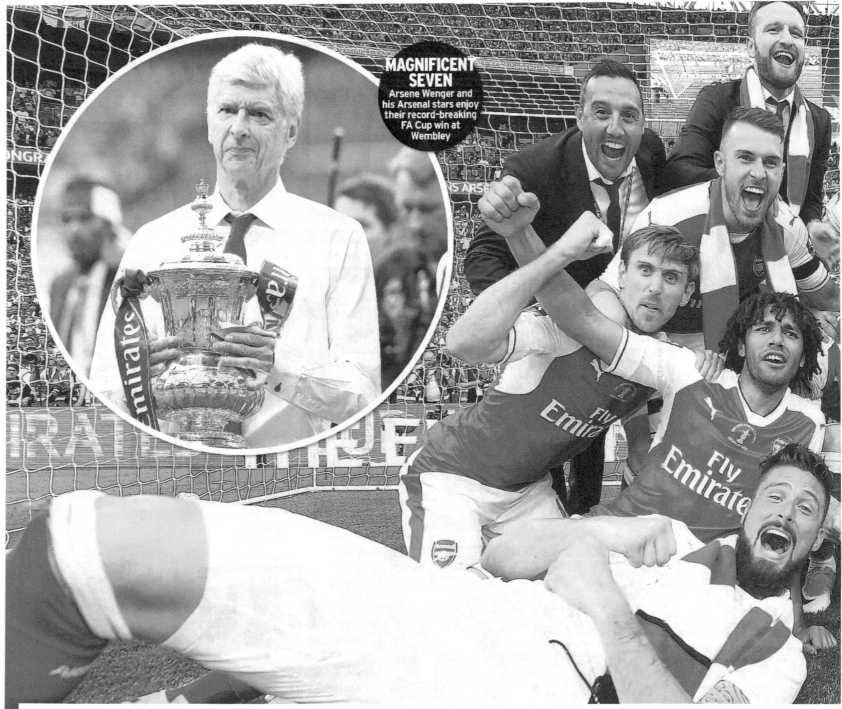

MAGNIFICENT SEVEN
Arsene Wenger and his Arsenal stars enjoy their record-breaking FA Cup win at Wembley

Arsene, you deserve all our respect

RESPECT. It seems it is all he wants and it is all he should get.

Total, final respect.

At times at Wembley, Arsene Wenger was bent double in psychological pain, hands on knees, barely able to look.

Despite the controversial Alexis Sanchez opener, despite seeing Victor Moses dismissed after diving, despite watching Aaron Ramsey's header make Diego Costa's equaliser irrelevant, there was probably not one second of this victory he enjoyed.

He should enjoy it now, enjoy the respect that should come with a 10th Arsenal trophy, 16th if you go by Jose Mourinho's book.

Go on holiday and enjoy it.

Enjoy how Arsenal deserved this victory, enjoy how he managed to turn a personnel crisis into a personal triumph.

This was a proud moment for a proud man.

He had de-jacketed symbolically early, stripped for yet another tussle with those who believe his reputation is tarnished, those who this managerial statesman considers to have treated him with unforgivable disrespect. Not that he

MOST FA CUP WINS BY A MANAGER...		...AND THE MOST SUCCESSFUL TEAMS	
7 Arsene Wenger	Arsenal	13 Arsenal	
6 George Ramsay	Aston Villa	12 Manchester United	
5 Alex Ferguson	Man Utd	8 Tottenham	
Thomas Mitchell	Blackburn	7 Liverpool, Aston Villa, Chelsea	
4 John Nicholson	Sheffield Utd	6 Newcastle, Blackburn	
3 Bill Nicholson	Spurs	5 Everton, Manchester City,	
Charles Foweraker	Bolton	West Brom, The Wanderers	

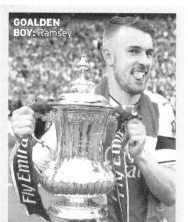

GOALDEN BOY: Ramsey

RAMSEY: WE OWE WENGER

FROM BACK PAGE

the job. It would be ridiculous if 20 years, or the future of the club, depended on one game. Overall we will know more next week.

Wenger's fate will now be decided at a Board meeting on Tuesday. But the Frenchman insisted that Arsenal will have to back him or sack him because he will not walk away from his 21-year reign at the club.

He said: "We have a board meeting on Tuesday and on Wednesday or Thursday it will be clearer. But I'm proud to have won seven of these cups. I'm proud having done this – winning the championship without losing and winning seven FA Cups."

Wenger added: "I just want to do well for this club. It's down to the Board members if I am the right man to lead this club further. It's not about popularity. It's about competence.

"I am in a public job and I accept people don't agree me. But once the game starts and you are a fan, you stand behind the team. That's what I did not accept during the season, and I will never accept it.

"This club has special values. What has happened is not acceptable.

"I don't know what will happen. I know in my own mind what I want to happen, but tonight I will enjoy this win and not worry about the future."

Aaron Ramsey, who scored the 77th-minute winner, added: "I'm really happy for the manager. He deserved this. Hopefully, he'll be here next season. We all owe him a lot."

Arsenal went ahead after three minutes when Alexis Sanchez scored his 30th goal of the season with Ramsey stood in an offside position.

The champions were also reduced to 10 men when Victor Moses was handed a second yellow for diving.

Chelsea boss Antonio Conte said: "The goal after three minutes should have been disallowed. But then, our start wasn't good enough – Arsenal started better than us."

ANDY DUNN

Britain's best columnist from Wembley

could brandish his team-sheet with any sort of belligerence.

Circumstances coerced him into the selection of Per Mertesacker, but the David Ospina decision almost smacked of mischievous defiance.

With Cesc Fabregas, imperious in the title run-in, unable to command a starting place for Chelsea, the paper contest looked a walkover.

That does not account for Chelsea starting at a walk.

This is an outstanding Chelsea team, but it is not one that can afford to have any of its moving parts out of sync.

Particularly the perpetually-moving part that is N'Golo Kante.

To see him struggle like this was eye-rubbingly unreal, the treadmill of award-collection clearly taking its toll.

When Antonio Conte (right) has the Champions League front to fight

on, there is little no doubt he will need reinforcements.

This was the 14th time he had fielded this starting 11, a luxury the law of professional football averages says is unlikely to be afforded to him next season.

But Arsenal's first-half domination was not driven solely by Kante's and his comrades' incompetence and sluggishness.

This was a Wenger team with an unrecognisable intensity.

On one Chelsea attacking occasion, three defenders raced each other to deny Diego Costa.

Mesut Ozil executed a sliding tackle on Eden Hazard.

Let me repeat that.

Mesut Ozil executed a sliding

tackle on Eden Hazard. Granit Xhaka was granite-tough and Danny Welbeck was a persistent, limb-whirring pest.

When Arsenal perform like they did here, Wenger's insistence this group of players has what it takes to emulate Conte's Chelsea goes from risible to reasonable.

That is the thing with Wenger.

He appears to be an incurable optimist, he is an incurable optimist.

He probably thinks Mertesacker has got a couple more seasons in him.

The likeable German's performance was one of the stories of this peculiar, but hugely enjoyable, contest. It was a lesson in

positioning. Wenger, though, if he stays, will need defensive extras.

The remain route now looks likeliest, for sure.

Conte is certainly staying, even if those Inter Milan stories carried emphatic credence.

One specific area he will have to address is upfront, where Costa will be an underestimated loss if he leaves.

After simulation cost Moses a second yellow, Costa stepped up, his deflected finish levelling matters.

Following Ramsey's immediate response, Costa would only be denied a second equaliser by some Ospina inspiration.

Even though Ospina was limp-wristed for the Costa goal, it was a measure of how much it was Wenger's day that his reserve keeper could eventually count himself a hero.

Bear in mind a coupe of efforts against the woodwork and a raft of squandered opportunities, nothing about this Arsenal win was undeserved.

It was deserved for its defiance, for its spirit and for its quality.

And now for Wenger, the respect he deserves.

Total respect.

RARE SIGHT THIS SEASON: Arsenal supporters wanting their boss to stay

SM1

OUR RATINGS
mirror.co.uk/sport/football

ARSENAL
BY STEVE STAMMERS

OSPINA
7 Swansong for the Colombian and he did not let team down

HOLDING BOOKED
7 Mature performance beyond his years and his experience

MERTESACKER
7 Commanding and kept tight grip on the troublesome Costa

MONREAL
7 Efficient and tidy. Grew into back-three role, read the game well

BELLERIN
7 Defensive knack of a full-back and speed of a winger. Impressive

RAMSEY BOOKED
6 Energy to spare, casual in possession at times, but scored the winner

XHAKA BOOKED
7 Solid. Appears to have erased the reckless streak from his game

CHAMBERLAIN
7 Adapting rapidly to new responsibilities and demands

STAR MAN

ALEXIS SANCHEZ

Minutes Played	89
Goals	1
Attempts On Target (inc Goals)	1
Attempts Off Target	1
Blocked Shots	2
Total Passes	33
Accurate Passes	27
Pass Completion	81.8
Accurate Forward Half Passes	16
Forward Half Pass Completion	66.7
Goal Assists	0
Key Passes (Assists for Attempts)	1
Duels	15
Duel Success%	13.3
Tackles	0
Tackles Won %	0
Clearances	0
Lost Balls	20
Recoveries	9
Free Kicks Won	2
Fouls	1
Offsides	0

SANCHEZ
8 Outstanding, elusive, brave. Stroke of luck with goal, but earned it

OZIL
6 Flashes of brilliance combined with his usual spells of anonymity

WELBECK
7 Chosen ahead of Giroud and his mobility gave Chelsea problems

SUBSTITUTES

Giroud 78 (for Welbeck) **6**
Set up the second goal with his first touch

Coquelin 82 (Oxlade-Chamberlain) Booked **6**
Brought on to add steel and booked after one minute!

Elneny 90+3 (Sanchez)
6 Came on right at the end, just to kill time

Subs not used:
Perez, Walcott, Iwobi, Cech

ARSENAL 2 CHELSEA 1
Sanchez 4, Ramsey 79   Costa 76

RAM RAID

Aaron scores winning Cup Final goal just like he did to beat Hull in 2014

HEADING FOR GLORY
Aaron Ramsey's brilliant header rockets into the net despite Courtois' despairing dive

THE EMIRATES FA CUP

BY **SIMON MULLOCK** from Wembley

IT was fitting that Aaron Ramsey scored yet another goal to rescue Arsenal's season.

When the Welsh midfielder stooped to head home Olivier Giroud's 79th-minute cross to once again claim the FA Cup for Arsene Wenger's team, the joy in his celebration said it all.

Ramsey has been one of the players who has taken plenty of grief for a season of Premier League underachievement at the Emirates.

Troy Deeney even accused him of faking injury when Watford inflicted a painful defeat on Wenger's men.

But when it mattered most – after Arsenal had suffered the shock of Diego Costa volleying Antonio Conte's 10-man champions level – there he was scoring the goal that gave those same supporters joy.

Back in 2014, at the same end of Wembley, Ramsey scored the extra-time winner as the Gunners recovered from two goals down to beat Hull.

Perhaps, Arsenal's fans should think twice before getting on his back next time his standards slip.

Chelsea were reduced in numbers when Victor Moses was sent off for trying to con a penalty out of referee Anthony Taylor when they were trailing to Alexis Sanchez's early opener.

But they showed real character to level through Costa.

However, just three minutes later, Ramsey was once again Arsenal's Wembley hero.

It was a bitterly disappointing end to the season for Conte.

But at times, Chelsea looked like they had been on a two-week bender since clinching the title – and that enabled Arsenal to play the kind of champagne football their fans demand.

This was Arsenal's best performance since the number they did on Chelsea at the Emirates in September promoted Conte to have a tactical rethink that turned into a title-winning masterstroke. After a minute's silence for the victims of the Manchester bomb had been impeccably observed, Arsenal should have been out of sight by the break.

Yes, Sanchez was fortunate to get the benefit of offside and handball decisions before ramming the Gunners into a fourth-minute lead.

Sanchez started and finished the move for his 30th goal of the season.

Ramsey was standing in an offside position when the Chilean's attempt to find him with a clipped pass was cut out by the head of David Luiz.

And Ramsey was still beyond the last man when N'Golo Kante tried to complete the clearance only for Sanchez to charge the ball down and ease the ball low past Thibaut Courtois.

Chelsea didn't know whether to appeal for offside or handball. They had valid cases for both. Assistant referee Gary Beswick raised his flag, but the referee consulted him before awarding the goal.

Injuries to Shkodran Mustafi and Gabriel, as well as Laurent Koscielny's suspension, forced Wenger to ask the ageing Per Mertesacker and Rob Holding to keep the champions at bay. Mertesacker, given the captain's armband for his first start in more than a year, was a rock when Chelsea launched a second-half rally. And Holding was just as impressive.

But, by then, it should have been game over.

Mesut Ozil should have scored when Sanchez sent him clear, but the German took a slightly heavy first touch and when he managed to clip a clever finish over the sprawling Courtois, there was Gary Cahill to backheel off the line.

Danny Welbeck's header hit the post and Ramsey's chested follow-up struck the same upright.

Conte's men were a different beast on the restart.

David Ospina was fortunate that a deflection on Kante's shot

...AGAIN!

MATCH STATS — opta

ARSENAL		CHELSEA
6	Shots on Target	5
7	Shots off Target	7
3	Blocked Shots	6
7	Corners	5
15	Fouls	11
0	Offsides	0
4	Yellow Cards	1
0	Red Cards	1
82.1	Passing Success	78.9
23	Tackles	25
82.6	Tackles Won %	80
52.3	Possession	47.7
44.5	Territorial Advantage	55.5
487	Total Passes	432
13	Total Crosses	19
55.1	1st Half Poss.	44.9
49.8	2nd Half Poss.	50.2

MATCH FACTS

■ Arsenal have won their 13th FA Cup, more than any other side.

■ **Arsene Wenger has won the FA Cup seven times, more than any other manager in history.**

■ The Gunners have lifted the trophy in each of their last six FA Cup final appearances.

■ **Arsenal have beaten Chelsea twice in a season (in all competitions) for the first time since 2003/04.**

■ This was just Chelsea's third defeat against Arsenal in their last 14 clashes in all competitions, but the second of those to come at Wembley (also in the 2015/16 Community Shield).

■ **At 3 minutes 49 seconds, Alexis Sanchez's opening goal was Arsenal's fastest ever in an FA Cup final.**

■ Alexis Sanchez has scored in five successive games for Arsenal in all comps for the first time ever.

■ **Alexis Sanchez has been directly involved in 45 goals in 51 appearances for Arsenal this season (30 goals, 15 assists).**

■ Victor Moses is the fifth player to be sent off in an FA Cup final (Smalling 2016, Zabaleta 2013, Reyes 2005, Moran 1985).

■ **Diego Costa netted his 22nd goal of the season for Chelsea in all competitions, his best-ever return in a single campaign for the Blues.**

■ Aaron Ramsey has scored two goals in his last three FA Cup final appearances, with both of them winners (also v Hull in 2014).

OUR RATINGS
mirror.co.uk/sport/football

CHELSEA
BY STEVE STAMMERS

COURTOIS — **7**
Could do nothing about goals, made outstanding save from Bellerin

AZPILICUETA — **6**
Quiet and was given immense problems by Welbeck and Sanchez

LUIZ — **6**
Was thankful to have an authentic defender in Cahill alongside him

CAHILL — **7**
Chelsea's best defender. One vital clearance and played a captain's role

MOSES SENT OFF — **5**
Made little impression. Blatant dive earned him a second yellow card

KANTE BOOKED — **6**
Only glimpses of the form that won him the plaudits and awards

REFEREE
ANTHONY TAYLOR:
Decisive when he had to be and replays showed the second Moses card was correct

MATIC — **6**
Not his day. Failed to make any impact. Hauled off on 61 mins

ALONSO — **6**
Unable to supplement attacks like he has done for much of the season

PEDRO — **6**
Promised more than he delivered. Flattered to deceive too often

COSTA — **6**
Could not unsettle an old pro like Mertesacker with his aggression

HAZARD — **6**
Looked as though the efforts of the season had caught up with him

SUBSTITUTES
Fabregas 61 (Matic) **5**
Failed to restore Chelsea's superiority in midfield
Willian 72 (Pedro) **5**
Tried to add zest to the Blues' attack, but to no avail
Batshuayi 88 (Costa)
Came on too late to have any impact on the game

Subs not used:
Begovic, Zouma, Ake, Terry

---

took the ball straight to him. And Mertesacker's brilliant intervention thwarted Costa.

Moses, booked for a 56th-minute foul on Welbeck, tumbled theatrically over Alex Oxlade-Chamberlain's challenge as he cut into the box and was given a second yellow, followed by the red.

Yet, amazingly, the Blues were level 14 minutes from time.

Substitute Willian fed a lofted cross into the box and Costa scuffed a deflected volley that carried too much power for Ospina.

Chelsea's fans were still celebrating when Ramsey (left) struck.

Giroud span and fed a cross that the Welshman stooped to head home.

Even then, it took a brilliant save by Ospina to prevent Costa from levelling.

And Ozil wasted the chance to kill off the game when he struck the post with a chance he should have taken.

THAT'S HANDY: Sanchez just before he scores the first goal

5 KEY MOMENTS

BY **STEVE STAMMERS**

Key Moment 1:
Four minutes and Alexis Sanchez appears to handle a clearance. Not given. Linesman Gary Beswick flags Aaron Ramsey offside, but Sanchez keeps running, scores and referee Anthony Taylor gives the goal after consulting his colleague.

Key Moment 2:
Sixteen minutes and Gary Cahill is alert as David Luiz takes the pace off a shot from Mesut Ozil and

clears the ball off the line. Two goals down would have been a massive blow for Chelsea.

Key Moment 3:
Twenty minutes and another escape for Chelsea as a Danny Welbeck header looks goalbound, but the post comes to the rescue. And, as the rebound comes out, the ball hits Ramsey just two yards out and goes wide.

Key Moment 4:
Sixty-eight minutes and Victor Moses - already

booked - dives and is shown a second yellow card by referee Taylor. He can have no complaints at the decision.

Key Moment 5:
Between the 76th and 79th minute. First Diego Costa equalises after his shot is deflected past goalkeeper David Ospina by a combination of Per Mertesacker and Rob Holding. Enter Olivier Giroud from the bench and it is from the Frenchman's cross that Ramsey restores the lead.

DM1ST

ARSENAL 5   BURNLEY 0

Aubameyang 14, 75, Lacazette 45, Kolasinac 54, Iwobi 64

Ratings by JOHN CROSS
mirror.co.uk/sport/football

ARSENAL

CECH   **7**
Commanding even if sometimes back passes put him under cosh

BELLERIN   **7**
Good rampaging forward runs, provided good assists

CHAMBERS   **7**
Positive and determined, took his good display in Madrid into this

MAVROPANOS   **8**
Proper old-school defending here. Gutsy tackles and headers

KOLASINAC   **7**
Looks like a tank-storming forward, terrific goal

WILSHERE   **8**
Always wants the ball, lively and creative. Arsenal must keep him

XHAKA   **7**
Much better as he put his foot in and was tenacious

MKHITARYAN   **8**
Impressive display as he was busy, drove forward, made things happen

IWOBI   **7**
Just when you question if he's good enough... he rifles one home

AUBAMEYANG   **9**
Scored twice and made one, plus partnership with Lacazette good

LACAZETTE   **8**
Scored - and you can see how much it means to him

SUBS: Ramsey (Wilshere 72)   6
Welbeck (Lacazette 72)   6
Mertesacker (Chambers 77)   6

MOTM
AUBAMEYANG

BURNLEY

POPE   **6**
Didn't stand much of a chance and actually made some decent saves

LOWTON   **5**
Got ran ragged by Aubameyang and did not get much protection

LONG   **5**
Exposed defensively at times as Burnley's defence left creaking

TARKOWSKI Booked   **5**
Forgot the basics and even got caught dribbling into his own box

WARD   **5**
Struggled against Mkhitaryan's movement and quality

LENNON   **4**
Had a subdued game, offered little protection and less going forward

CORK   **6**
Busy, put in the hard yards but struggled to find a way through

WESTWOOD   **6**
Arguably Burnley's best player (not saying much) for composure

GUDMUNDSSON   **5**
Got very little change out of Bellerin and did not create enough

HENDRICK   **5**
Did so little that you barely noticed him. Hugely disappointing

BARNES   **5**
Substituted early on after hurting his arm in nasty clash with Xhaka

SUBS: Vokes (Barnes 22)   5
Nkoudou (Lennon 71)   5

CRAVAT'S

Emotional Wenger takes his final bow at Emirates after 22 years.. but vows he won't cut his ties with his beloved Gunners

ARSENE, CAN I PLEASE HAVE YOUR TIE

SMART WAY TO GO OUT
Wenger relaxed and smiling as he enjoys a wonderful send-off following a superb home victory

BY JOHN CROSS
Chief Football Writer

WHAT felt like it was going to be a sad day turned into a joyous one.

The scoreline set up Arsene Wenger's farewell party, but the mood really summed up the true feelings around one of English football's all-time greats.

Not one fan left early before the post-match celebrations and he was given a send-off to make the hairs on the back of your neck stand up.

The chorus of "One Arsene Wenger" rang around the Emirates for one last time as Arsenal's greatest-ever manager said an emotional farewell.

There was a real lump-in-the-throat moment when Wenger rounded off his speech on the pitch by saying: "I would like to finish with a simple word – I will miss you."

It takes the bigger man to forgive and forget the bad times to remember the good, glorious moments of his 22 years in charge of Arsenal.

They chanted his name at the end, formed a guard of honour before and after – a wonderful reminder of the good days.

Arsenal chairman Sir Chips Keswick was booed (he had been dismissive of fans at the AGM), kitman Vic Akers and Per Mertesacker got great send-offs, and club-legend Bob Wilson made a wonderful speech calling Wenger the best manager the club had ever had.

There were big banners on the pitch of the trophies won, huge balloons and letters spelling out "Merci Arsene", which the club have tried to make the buzz words since announcing he will leave at the end of the season.

There have been empty red seats throughout the campaign, but there was not one to be had for the farewell party

and instead the stadium was decked out in red from the "Merci Arsene" T-shirts left on every seat for the fans.

The club put on one hell of a party and have handled the departure with grace and class – and the players also put on a show to remember.

It would be easy to get swept up by the emotion of the day and the fact Burnley knew winning would put Arsenal under pressure for sixth place and the potential ignominy of having to enter the Europa League at the third qualifying stage in July.

But the Gunners tied it up with a classy send-off, which Wenger would have enjoyed far more because the football was terrific, and that, rather than pomp and ceremony, is what he really loves.

It was a beautiful sunny day and, rather in keeping with recent seasons, Arsenal put on a five-star performance when the pressure is off and it does not really matter.

What a great shame that Mesut Ozil was missing, the £350,000-a-week Germany star went AWOL in Madrid, legend Martin Keown (left) said he would "have an emotional breakdown" and would not play again this season. He might just be right.

But the rest did their manager proud. Alexandre Lacazette and Pierre-Emerick Aubameyang showed again that maybe they can play together up front, while Henrikh Mkhitaryan and Jack Wilshere drove forward from midfield.

Arsenal got their first after 14 minutes after Hector Bellerin and Alex Iwobi combined nicely, Lacazette's cross-shot was then turned in by Aubameyang.

The Clarets never showed up, maybe it was one game too far, and their striker Ashley Barnes went off injured with a suspected broken collar bone.

Arsenal had it sewn up by half time

when Iwobi released Bellerin down the right, and his cross was turned in by Lacazette in first-half injury time.

Sead Kolasinac, set up by Wilshere, drove home the third after 54 minutes. Kolasinac has shown promise this season, but maybe needs a fresh start under a new manager, while Konstantinos Mavropanos produced another promising display at centre-half.

Arsenal got a fourth after 64 minutes when Iwobi rifled into the net and Aubameyang made it five after 75 minutes following more good work from Bellerin.

Mertesacker, who will retire to take over the academy, got a great reception as the game almost had a testimonial feel to it.

The post-match celebrations – featuring legends like Pires, Keown, Petit and Ljungberg – gave it a wonderful feel, but there was no better way for it to end at the Emirates than with a wonderful win.

MATCH STATS

64%	POSSESSION	36%
8	SHOTS ON TARGET	2
5	SHOTS OFF TARGET	2
4	CORNERS	5
0	OFFSIDE	0
6	FOULS	7
0 0	CARDS	1 0

REF: Andre Marriner ATT: 59,540

JOY Noble after netting in West Ham's 2-0 victory

ALL FOLKS

NO REST FOR THE BEST OF THE REST

BY **JOHN CROSS**

BURNLEY boss Sean Dyche hailed his players for their "remarkable achievement" in reaching Europe – and then warned them that pre-season training will start early.

Dyche (above) made it clear that he intends to take the Europa League seriously even though Burnley will enter the third qualifying round stage as early as late July.

"It's a remarkable achievement. There's a genuine gap to the top six so to be considered the best of the rest is a fine achievement," Dyche said.

"No-one would have called that at the beginning of the season.

"We've gone from 40 points last season to 54 points, without getting a penalty, and now into European competition so that is a remarkable achievement.

"Pre-season has shifted closer to give us more time to make sure they're fit and well but for now let's enjoy the fact we've made it into Europe. There's the kudos, then the finance, and the feel in the town. But our focus will still be on the Premier League."

Dyche admitted that having little to play for yesterday was the reason behind their heaviest defeat of the season.

Dyche added: "They had something to play for – the legend that is Arsene Wenger.

"There was a big shift in the performance. They were clinical. Their passing and movement was good and when they do that they're very good. They've done that to better teams than us. They can hurt teams.

"We've been exceptional so I'm not going to criticise anyone. But it's difficult without the edge you need when there's something on the game."

Puel out, Wagner in for Foxes

FROM BACK PAGE
upturn when he was appointed in October.

Just as happened when he was at Southampton, the Frenchman's style of football has proved unpopular with both players and fans at Leicester.

The Foxes have won only two of their last 12 Premier League games, including four defeats in the last five – to leave Puel in danger of being axed.

Leicester were booed off at the end of both halves of their 2-0 home defeat to West Ham on Saturday, when Mark Noble scored a stunning volley for the Irons.

And Puel was taunted with chants of "You don't know what you're doing" and "You're getting sacked in the morning".

Leicester have begun looking around for potential successors to Puel – and Wagner has emerged as a leading target.

The Terriers' Premier League survival hopes are in the balance, with two games – against Chelsea away and Arsenal at home – to go.

But former Borussia Dortmund reserves boss Wagner won admirers after leading Huddersfield into the top flight for the first time in 45 years on one of the smallest wage budgets in the Championship.

His current contract runs until 2019 after he penned a new two-year deal, following the Terriers' promotion last season.

Sarri says 'sack me'

CHELSEA target Maurizio Sarri has told Napoli's president to sack him if he is not happy with his work.

Napoli drew 2-2 at home with Torino yesterday to end their hopes of winning the Serie A title. Aurelio De Laurentiis blamed the coach for not rotating the squad enough, naming Antonio Conte and Carlo Ancelotti as potential replacements.

But Sarri said: "If the president is not happy he can always take the exit option. I've always tried to do my best and, if I have to leave, it's not because of what the president has said. If the era is over, that's down to the club."

De Laurentiis said: "I tell Sarri to stay calm because this is his home. We want him with us."

CROWD PLEASING Wenger guard of honour and Aubameyang netting opener

I'LL BE BACK.. AND I'LL BOO

BY **JOHN CROSS**

ARSENE WENGER promised to return to Arsenal as a fan – and joked he would shout at his successor.

Wenger received a wonderful send-off, a guard of honour and tributes from club legends on an emotional day.

The Gunners boss, 68, admitted he is struggling to know what to do next, but was clearly moved by the tributes after his final home match following 22 years in charge. He said: "I would be happy to sit in the North Bank. It depends on if I work somewhere else or not.

"In the job I do, will I be free on the day Arsenal plays I will be happy to be in the North Bank if you can get me a ticket. The positive of that is that I can shout at the next manager!

"Sometimes to make people happy is to go somewhere else. I want to make people happy, I have this certain idea of football to be played.

"My ambition was to win with style, when you're at a big club you have that responsibility and for the supporters to have a special experience when they come to the club. That was always my target.

"I have to deal with it. It is a story that ends. I see it in one way. Guys that manage 22 years a club of this stature, you have not many. So I can only say, My friend, you have been very lucky. I will cherish every moment I was here, but it's a new start for me."

PREMIER LEAGUE TABLE

	P	W	D	L	F	A	Pts
Man City (C)	36	30	4	2	102	26	94
Man Utd	36	24	5	7	67	28	77
Liverpool	37	20	12	5	80	38	72
Tottenham	36	21	8	7	68	32	71
Chelsea	36	21	6	9	61	34	69
Arsenal	36	18	6	12	72	48	60
Burnley	37	14	12	11	35	37	54
Everton	37	13	10	14	43	55	49
Leicester	36	11	11	14	49	54	44
Newcastle	36	11	8	17	36	46	41
Crystal Palace	37	10	11	16	43	55	41
Bournemouth	37	10	11	16	43	60	41
Watford	37	11	8	18	44	63	41
Brighton	36	9	13	14	33	47	40
West Ham	36	9	11	16	45	67	38
Huddersfield	36	9	9	18	27	56	36
Southampton	36	6	15	15	36	55	33
Swansea	36	8	9	19	27	53	33
West Brom	37	6	13	18	31	54	31
Stoke (R)	37	6	12	19	33	67	30

ARSENAL 4 TOTTENHAM 2

Aubameyang 10 pen, 56, Lacazette 74, Torreira 77   Dier 30   Kane 34 pen

RATINGS by DARREN LEWIS
mirror.co.uk/sport/football

ARSENAL

LENO 6
Crucial saves from Son. But should have done better from Dier's header

MUSTAFI Booked 5
Started well but those old mistakes began to creep in

PAPASTATHOPOULOS 5
Another to begin well but eventually opened up at will

HOLDING 5
He will protest but his challenge on Son merited a penalty

BELLERIN 6
Unlucky to have his first-half shot blocked by Davies

TORREIRA Booked 8
Led the fight from the outset but his defence let him down

XHAKA Booked 7
Followed the Torreira example and stepped up when the going got tough

KOLASINAC 7
Set up Iwobi among other chances but they couldn't convert

MKHITARYAN 7
Took the early fight to Spurs with his willingness to scrap

AUBAMEYANG 9
Scored two, set up the other. Fantasy team gold

IWOBI 6
He will know that he should have scored with his 19th-minute chance

SUBS:
Lacazette (Iwobi 45) 7
Ramsey (Mkhitaryan 45) 7
Guendouzi (Mustafi 89)

MOTM
PIERRE-EMERICK AUBAMEYANG

TOTTENHAM

LLORIS 5
Fine saves from Iwobi and Xhaka at crucial moments. At fault for Lacazette goal

AURIER Booked 5
Decent going forward. Still so suspect defensively

VERTONGHEN Sent off 4
Gave away that early penalty. Sent off for that late tackle

FOYTH 6
Actually played well overall but learned a tough lesson in his first derby

DAVIES 6
Terrific first-half block to deny Hector Bellerin

DIER Booked 6
Mixed it in the middle, headed Spurs back into it but then overrun in midfield

SISSOKO 6
Now Tottenham's midfield general. But Arsenal had too much for him today

ALLI Booked 5
Just not enough from him as Arsenal dominated

ERIKSEN 6
Led the first-half fightback but couldn't respond in the second

KANE 7
Unerring as ever from the spot with the pressure on

SON HEUNG-MIN 6
Arsenal simply could not cope with his direct running in the first half. Snuffed him out in the second

SUBS:
Moura (Son 79) 5
Winks (Alli 79) 5
Rose (Davies 82)

GUNNERS FULL FOUR-CE Lacazette leads the celebrations after his goal. Far right: Aubameyang and Torreira

LONDUN

Unai was the true hero of this blockbuster, his tough

BY **DARREN LEWIS**
@MirrorDarren

ARSENAL'S real Man of the Match in this epic? Unai Emery.

Never mind ruthless, two-goal Pierre-Emerick Aubameyang and the manner in which he broke Tottenham's hearts.

Look to the man who has brought the fire back to the red half of north London.

The man who decided lightweight Mesut Ozil could be nowhere near a contest for

gladiators and streetfighters. The man under whom the club's unbeaten run was extended to 19 matches with the biggest win of his time in charge.

If Arsene Wenger wonders why – after all he had done for the club – they finally wanted him out last season, he need only look at the dynamism with which his successor ripped apart the Gunners' bitter rivals.

Spurs were demolished. Put back in their box after two seasons of finishing higher in the table. Just one win now at

the home of their neighbours in 26 seasons.

Mauricio Pochettino and his men will point to the fact they were tired after a tough week and that they still have Champions League football.

But they are no longer above Arsenal, who appear to be coming for them.

The hosts were ahead after 10 minutes. Jan Vertonghen handled at a corner and referee Mike Dean pointed immediately to the spot.

Aubameyang converted and

Emery whipped up the crowd. The tempo was relentless. But Spurs fought back superbly.

Son Heung-Min forced two fine saves from Arsenal keeper Berndt Leno before Eric Dier

MATCH STATS

59%	POSSESSION	41%
7	SHOTS ON TARGET	6
11	SHOTS OFF TARGET	3
8	CORNERS	5
5	OFFSIDE	2
15	FOULS	17
3 0	CARDS	3 1

REF: Mike Dean ATT: 59,973

headed in from a corner. Game on. Especially after it kicked off as the England midfielder celebrated. Arsenal substitute Stefan Lichtsteiner shoved Dier, Moussa Sissoko raced over to protect his team-mate and Pochettino raced down the pitch as the tension boiled over.

Arsenal had lost their heads. Spurs kept theirs to go in front a minute later. Son raced into the box and Rob Holding brought him down. Penalty.

Harry Kane (celebrating right) sent Leno the wrong way. The

PREMIER LEAGUE TABLE

	P	W	D	L	F	A	Pts
Man City	14	12	2	0	43	6	38
Liverpool	14	11	3	0	27	5	36
Chelsea	14	9	4	1	30	11	31
Arsenal	14	9	3	2	32	18	30
Tottenham	14	10	0	4	25	15	30
Everton	14	6	4	4	20	16	22
Man Utd	14	6	4	4	22	23	22
Leicester	14	6	3	5	20	17	21
Bournemouth	14	6	2	6	23	21	20
Watford	14	6	2	6	17	19	20
Brighton	14	5	3	6	16	20	18
Wolves	14	4	4	6	13	17	16
West Ham	14	4	3	7	17	22	15
C Palace	14	3	3	8	10	17	12
Newcastle	14	3	3	8	11	19	12
Cardiff	14	3	2	9	13	27	11
Huddersfield	14	2	4	8	9	24	10
Southampton	14	1	6	7	12	26	9
Burnley	14	2	3	9	13	29	9
Fulham	14	2	2	10	14	35	8

STOMACH FOR THE FIGHT Arsenal and Tottenham players in a scuffle

A mystery after Ozil goes AWOL

BY **PAUL BROWN**

MYSTERY surrounded Mesut Ozil's absence from Arsenal's thumping North London derby win over Tottenham yesterday.

The Gunners insisted Ozil was ruled out of the game by back spasms, but he was nowhere to be seen at the Emirates.

And Arsenal boss Unai Emery later admitted he did not know where the former Germany star was.

Asked about Ozil after his team's 4-2 win, Emery said simply: "He has backache." Asked when he got it, Emery replied: "I don't know."

And when pressed on whether Ozil was at the game, the Gunners boss said: "I don't know. The players who played deserve the headlines."

Emery and Ozil are understood to endure a difficult relationship, with the Spaniard forced to deny claims of a bust-up between the pair earlier this season. Ozil later tweeted: "Proud of the whole team. North London is red!"

DERBY DISGRACE

FROM BACK PAGE

were hurled into the away end, and the incident involving Aubameyang.

He had just put the Gunners in front from the penalty spot when a banana was thrown at him.

A man was arrested. The FA will also be investigating.

Missiles were thrown during a melee which broke out as Eric Dier celebrated his 30th-minute equaliser for Spurs by running to the home fans and putting his finger to his lips.

Dier, who was booked, said: "It's a derby. Football is all about emotion and I don't understand how I could get a yellow card in that situation."

A Met Police spokesman said there were seven arrests at the game for public order offences, one relating to an object thrown on to the pitch. It is understood two others involved the lighting of smoke canisters.

Both teams face an FA charge over the brawl.

PRIDE
calls putting fight into Gunners

Gunners, from a position of strength, were falling apart.

It took the intervention of Emery to persuade his men to stay calm. He threw on Alexandre Lacazette and Aaron Ramsey for the start of the second half. Eleven minutes later it was level again.

Hector Bellerin sent the ball down the line, Ramsey squared and Aubameyang gave Hugo Lloris no chance.

On the hour, with Arsenal rampant, Dele Alli cleared off the line from Shkodran Mustafi before Juan Foyth lost the ball in midfield, Lacazette was sent into the box and the Frenchman's shot deflected off Dier and past Lloris.

Emery, with his fists clenched, turned to his fans and coaching staff, screaming out in triumph.

Arsenal knew they still needed a knockout punch. They found it when Aubameyang slipped the ball inside Dier and Lucas Torreira powered it past Lloris.

By the time Jan Vertonghen received a second yellow for his foul on Lacazette, Spurs were done anyway. Arsenal had passed the biggest test of their unbeaten run.

They now go to a Manchester United side with one of the worst defensive records in the Premier League this season. A nightmare campaign could be about to get even worse for Jose Mourinho.

BRINGING BACK THE FIRE Emery masterminded a battling demolition of Tottenham

DML1

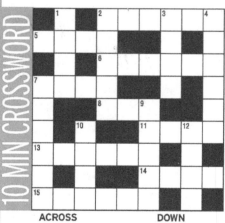
10 MIN CROSSWORD

ACROSS
2 Feeling of resentment (6)
5 — Moore, GI Jane? (4)
6 Although (6)
7 Crop such as maize (4)
8 Tag (3)
11 Medicinal herb, — vera (4)
13 Short-sighted (6)
14 Kiln for drying hops (4)
15 Character created by Edgar Rice Burroughs (6)

DOWN
1 Roman emperor (4)
2 Huge mythical being (5)
3 Antlered animal (4)
4 Tempt (6)
7 Carry out (6)
9 Breakfast rasher (5)
10 Entrance to a room (4)
12 Remove from power (4)

FRIDAY'S SOLUTIONS ACROSS: 6 Heave, 7 Leo, 8 Ill at ease, 13 Deterrent, 18 Sun, 19 Elite. **DOWN:** 1 Thai, 2 Haul, 3 Wept, 4 Ulna, 5 Ooze, 9 Lie, 10 Awe, 11 Err, 12 Son, 13 Dose, 14 Tony, 15 Reel, 16 Eric, 17 T-rex.

Brought to you by CROSSWORDS

CORONAVIRUS CRISIS:

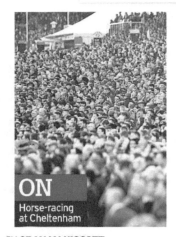

ON
Horse-racing at Cheltenham

BY **GRAHAM HISCOTT**
Head of Business and **BEN GLAZE**
Deputy Political Editor

THE mass suspension of football games and sport events has sparked fears of big job losses and clubs being driven to the wall.

All elite football in England was yesterday called off until April 3 in a bid to tackle the worsening outbreak of the coronavirus.

Wales's Six Nations match against Scotland today has been postponed as has tomorrow's Premiership Rugby Cup final between Sale and Harlequins.

Others sports, from cricket and golf to motor racing, have also either been ditched or delayed.

Next month's Virgin Money London Marathon was postponed until Sunday, October 4 and the Manchester marathon on April 5 was also called off.

It means thousands of fans could lose cash on travel tickets already booked to go to events.

But yesterday's Gold Cup at Cheltenham, which was attended by 60,00 people, still went ahead.

Later, sources said the Government will officially ban all mass gatherings across Britain from next weekend in the fight against the deadly virus – which has killed 11 people here. The number of confirmed cases yesterday leapt from 590 to 798.

Ministers yesterday pushed for more people to work from home.

The unprecedented delay of so many sports events could prove a crippling blow to clubs' finances, and the firms that rely on sports for their livelihood.

Swathes of businesses, from food stalls to pubs, hotels, coach firms, and printers will be hammered.

Others, including airlines, cinemas and restaurants, have either suffered a slump in sales or are braced for the worst as the virus spreads across the UK.

Dale Vince, chairman of League Two club Forest Green Rovers, feared the suspension will mean the rest of the season being axed.

He said: "It will blow a hole in our finances. It won't sink us but it may be more devastating for some of the other clubs to deal with."

Shrewsbury Town's chief executive Brian Caldwell warned it could cost the League One club between £200,000 and £250,000 in lost ticket sales. He said: "I look at some of the others in League One and Two who haven't paid their wages on time and it will have a devastating effect."

The Football Association, Premier League, EFL, Barclays FA Women's Super League and FA Women's Championship collectively agreed to postpone their games in England. UEFA has put off next week's Champions League and Europa League fixtures. England's March friendlies with Italy and Denmark are also off.

Top-flight clubs, benefitting from TV rights money will not be affected as badly.

Sky and BT Sports confirmed they would not be refunding customers as a result of the delays.

But both outfits revealed they would broadcast any postponed games when they are rescheduled. Which? consumer rights expert Adam French said fans with tickets for games will be entitled to refunds if they cannot make the new date.

But he added: "It could be harder to get a refund on any travel or accommodation booked for the match, unless it was purchased as part of a package."

The devolved government in Scotland has advised against gatherings of more than 500, meaning football will be played

GAME

» **Fears over clubs going to the wall and big job losses**

» **Large gatherings banned next week & work at home push**

OFF
No games at the Emirates

UK LATEST	
Cases (up 208):	**798**
Deaths (up 1):	**11**

WORLD LATEST	
Cases:	**145,336**
Deaths:	**5,416**

SPORTS FIXTURES CANCELLED

CHANGER

OFF Wales won't play Scotland

WE ARE LIVERPOOL

OFF No games at Anfield stadium

REDUCTION BA has warned staff

BA tells staff to prepare for job cuts, groundings

BY **GRAHAM HISCOTT**
Head of Business

BRITISH Airways yesterday told staff it expected to make job cuts and ground more planes, calling the crisis "worse than 9/11".

Unions fear redundancies at Edinburgh Airport which warned it could be facing "close to zero" passenger demand.

In a message titled "the survival of BA", chief executive Alex Cruz said: "Please do not underestimate the seriousness of this for our company."

He said BA, which has 45,000 staff, is under "immense pressure" and will "have to react fast and definitively in response to the worsening situation".

As a result, jobs would be lost "perhaps for a short period, perhaps longer term" and BA is in discussions with trade unions.

A BA spokeswoman declined to comment when asked how many jobs could go.

Meanwhile global stock markets staged a rally yesterday – a day after the worst crash for more than 30 years.

The FTSE 100 closed the day up 128.63 at 5366.1, with the 2.5% rise clawing back £32billion of the £160bn shed on Thursday.

Russ Mould, investment director at City firm AJ Bell, said: "That truly was a nightmare of a week for savers and investors."

Germany's Dax gained 0.8% and France's Cac had a 1.8% win.

---

behind closed doors from Monday. It is the first time there has been such a widespread suspension of sport since Princess Diana's funeral in 1997.

No10, which has faced criticism for its slow response to the virus crisis, announced mass gatherings such as sports events, gigs and conferences, will be banned.

A Whitehall source said the move will help free up emergency services rather than curb the virus spread.

The insider declined to say how many constituted a mass gathering but added: "Ministers are working with the Chief Scientific Adviser and Chief Medical Officer on our plan to stop various types of public event. We are also talking to businesses and other bodies about the timing of moving towards much more widespread working from home.

"We are concerned about the burden large events put on public services, including the NHS and police, from dealing with coronavirus.

"We drafted emergency legislation to give the Government the powers to deal with coronavirus, including powers to stop mass gatherings and compensate organisations."

Public tours of Parliament will be banned and MPs were also urged not to invite guests into the building and to axe official visits abroad. Trade body UK Hospitality warned coronavirus "could put millions of jobs at risk" in the sector. Chief executive Kate Nicholls said the numbers of people using pubs and restaurants fell 26% in the past 10 days. And hotel bookings for the next two months have crashed by 50%.

Kate added: "Some of the firms affected will not survive. I have been through economic crashes and

> ❝ **It will blow a hole in our finances. It may be more devastating for other clubs**
>
> **DALE VINCE** CHAIRMAN OF FOREST GREEN ROVERS

foot-and-mouth, but I have never seen anything like this in terms of its severity." Sport Relief host Gary Lineker last night kicked off this year's event by declaring the UK is going through "unprecedented times". He promised "a chunk" of the money raised from the charity telethon will go to help victims of the coronavirus pandemic. Former rugby World Cup winner Mike Tindall yesterday called for calm as sporting events were being axed or delayed.

As he arrived at the Cheltenham festival, he said: "Do I feel cancelling everything is going to solve it, I'm not sure. Keep calm and carry on, that's what British do, don't they?"

graham.hiscott@mirror.co.uk
🐦 @Grahamhiscott

VOICE OF THE MIRROR: PAGE 10

- Football, rugby, and London Marathon are postponed
- BA warns of jobs losses and aircraft grounded

AT A GLANCE

- Large gatherings to be banned, home-working to be encouraged
- Experts predict that

coronavirus will now return every winter

- Trump declares national emergency as 150m could be infected in the US

BACK YEAR AFTER YEAR: PAGES 4&5   WHAT'S OFF: SEE SPORT

THE Emirates FA CUP

RATINGS by Darren Lewis

ARSENAL

MARTINEZ 7
Less to do than his City counterpart. Commanded his area

BELLERIN 7
Played part in the build-up to first goal. Good all-round display

MUSTAFI 7
Lucky not to see his side concede after he was robbed by Sterling

LUIZ 8
Superb through-ball to set up Aubameyang for a sitter

TIERNEY 8
Vital early clearance from Sterling's low ball in from the left

XHAKA 7
Good day at the office for the Swiss who mucked in

CEBALLOS 7
Some moments of creativity amid dogged defensive display

MAITLAND-NILES 8
Stuck to his defensive duties to help keep the door shut

PEPE 8
Peach of a cross to set up Aubameyang for his first-half goal

AUBAMEYANG 9
Fine finish for first, ice in his veins for that second – end product was the difference

LACAZETTE 7
Caused problems throughout with his movement and his work rate

SUBS: Willock (Pepe 72) 7
Torreira (Lacazette 78) 7
Holding (Mustafi 87)
Kolasinacat (Ceballos 88)

MAN OF THE MATCH

PIERRE-EMERICK AUBAMEYANG

MAN CITY

EDERSON 6
Fine first-half saves from Mustafi. No chance with Auba's brace

WALKER 6
Rampaging runs down the right but no trademark delivery

GARCIA 6
AWOL on a couple of occasions as Aubameyang found way through

LAPORTE 5
Nowhere near as Mustafi managed to get in first-half header

MENDY 6
Had Bellerin's measure down the left but needed to do much better

GUNDOGAN 4
Lucky that Aubameyang didn't do more damage after he conceded

DE BRUYNE 7
Pinged passes all over the place. Unlucky to see free-kick fly wide

MAHREZ 4
All left foot and not much else in the way of creativity

SILVA 7
Classy yet again. Unlucky not to score with 66th-minute chance

STERLING 6
Hat-trick last week, missed a hat-trick of chances here

GABRIEL JESUS 4
Just couldn't impose himself like Aguero has done so often for City

SUBS: Rodri (Gundogan 65) 5
Foden (Mahrez 65) 5
Fernandhino (Silva 87)

ARSENAL 2 MANCHESTER CITY 0
Aubameyang 19, 71

MATCH FACTS

■ Arsenal have reached the FA Cup final a record 21 times and won it more than any other side (13).
■ Manchester City have been eliminated from a domestic cup tie (League Cup and FA Cup)

AUBA POPS

Gunners grab first slot in FA Cup Final

GUNNER GLEE
Pierre-Emerick Aubameyang broke deadlock

By **HARRY PRATT**
at Wembley

PIERRE-EMERICK Aubameyang usually needs only one chance to hit the back of the net.

Give him three, though, and you are asking for trouble, as Manchester City discovered at Wembley last night when they suffered a shock semi-final exit.

Having missed one early sitter, prolific Gunners skipper Aubameyang bagged a deadly double.

Mikel Arteta's underdogs are into their 21st final at the expense of Pep Guardiola's holders – and what a magnificent evening for the young Emirates coach as he masterminded a truly stunning triumph over the manager he used to stand alongside in the City dugout .

It will have left Guardiola feeling a nasty sense of deja-vu at the national stadium. The last time his City side had lost here was in the 2017 semis – against Arsenal.

Arguably, the most important stat of all for this showdown was City had beaten Arsenal seven times in row. The last of those had come in the first Premier League game after coronavirus.

Poor that evening, Arteta's men had improved markedly since.

That upturn, including beating champions Liverpool in midweek, meant there was genuine optimism they could end their long losing streak against City.

Yet it was Guardiola's men who flew out of the blocks and could have been two up inside 10 minutes.

Only a timely clearance by Kieran Tierney denied David Silva a tap-in

■ for the first time since February 2018, with this their 22nd tie since that game.
■ Arsenal have eliminated the holders of the FA Cup the last six occasions they've faced them.

■ Manchester City had just one shot on target in this match, their fewest in a game since April 2018 in the Champions League against Liverpool (0).

■ Pierre-Emerick Aubameyang has now netted 66 goals for Arsenal in all competitions. Since his debut for the club, only Mo Salah (68) has scored more among Premier League players.

PEP'S BUBBLE

VITAL STATS opta

ARSENAL		MAN CITY
2	Shots on Target	8
2	Shots off Target	7
2	Blocked Shots	8
6	Corners	8
9	Fouls	16
1	Offsides	1
0	Yellow Cards	0
2	Red Cards	0
75.4	Passing Success %	86.9
51	Duels Won	51
50.0	Duel Success %	50.0
7	Tackles	11
57.1	Tackles Won %	45.5
42.5	Possession %	57.5
27.0	Territorial Adv %	73.0
354	Total Passes	464
10	Total Crosses	35
121	Lost Balls	107
48	Recoveries	49
56.4	1st Half Poss %	43.6
31.4	2nd Half Poss %	68.6

REFEREE: Jonathan Moss

CAPITAL GAINS
Aubameyang finished off a brilliant Arsenal move to make it 1-0 on 19 minutes

after Dani Ceballos was robbed and Raheem Sterling crossed into the danger area.

Then Sterling should have had another following a howler by Shokdran Mustafi. Yet the England ace hesitated.

Having barely got out of their own half, the Gunners stepped up a gear – or three. They had the ball in net on 13 minutes but Alexandre Lacazette was offside. Then David Luiz sent Aubameyang through – only for the normally-lethal hitman to blast straight at Ederson.

It mattered not. For soon after the Gabon ace was perfectly placed at the far post to squeeze in Nicolas Pepe's cross.

Aubameyang was less clinical 15 minutes before the break.

City's defence was in disarray, it needed only a five-yard pass into Pepe's path, but the Arsenal skipper under-hit it and the opportunity passed.

That felt like a crucial moment. It was hard to imagine City would not be better in the second half – no doubt having been given a rocket by Guardiola (left).

They were better, yet within three minutes of the resumption Guardiola was once again holding his head in

hands as Sterling wasted another glorious opening. How did he drag his shot wide from 10 yards, following Kevin De Bruyne's cut back?

Resilient, back-to-the-wall defending was the name of the game for the Gunners thereafter.

Mustafi survived a VAR penalty check when Sterling went tumbling on the hour, before the latter fluffed a point-blank header from a corner.

The drinks break came at the perfect time for the Gunners, who immediately countered to make it 2-0 and left City reeling.

Tierney's chip sent Aubameyang clear and he coolly tucked in.

SUCKER PUNCH Aubameyang is in for 2-0 after City had piled on pressure

SMLO

REDS STAY IN BUBBLE

BY STEVE BATES

MANCHESTER UNITED will keep their Aon Training Complex a first-team bio-bubble going into the new season.

Club bosses banned all development or academy teams from their Carrington training complex when lockdown was eased to allow Project Restart to get under way.

And they have decided to keep their training ground exclusively for first-team use only – possibly until the end of the year – with worries over a new wave of coronavirus cases causing concern at Old Trafford.

Only the senior squad of Ole Gunnar Solkjaer (above) are allowed to enter Carrington, with strict monitoring still in place for United's stars. All players have to follow stringent guidelines on socialising, spending time with family outside their own household and interaction with anyone outside their bubble.

United are determined to keep their first-team squad out of harm's way with games still to come in Germany in the Europa League this month.

And that means youth teams will be split between sites at their old Cliff training ground in Salford and nearby Littleton Road.

While some Premier League stars have been seen on holiday in Ibiza and other destinations, there is a fear they could get exposed to Covid-19.

It's a worry for leading Premier League officials, who believe their strict protocols have worked well.

Pope is a Blues target

BY HARRY PRATT

CHELSEA are stepping up their efforts to land Burnley keeper Nick Pope.

Blues boss Frank Lampard appears to have lost all faith in Spanish stopper Kepa Arrizabalaga – and wants a world-class replacement.

He sees Pope, 28, who just missed out on the Golden Glove this season after keeping 15 Premier League clean sheets - one less than Manchester City's Ederson - as the best choice.

The England keeper, capped twice by Gareth Southgate, still has three years left on his contract with Burnley and will not come cheap.

ARSENAL 2 CHELSEA 1
Aubameyang 28 pen, 67   Pulisic 5

WINNING

Mikel lifts trophy in first season as boss... thanks to Aubameyang

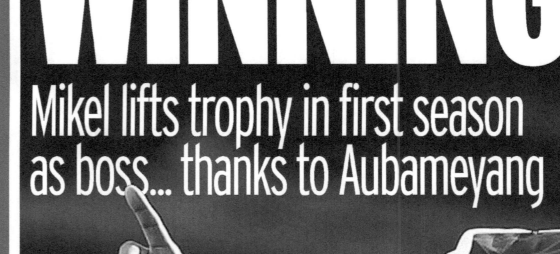

VITAL STATS opta

ARSENAL		CHELSEA
3	Shots on Target	3
4	Shots off Target	3
4	Blocked Shots	3
6	Corners	4
2	Fouls	14
3	Offsides	0
1	Yellow Cards	4
0	Red Cards	1
78.7	Passing Success	85.0
42	Duels Won	49
46.2	Duel Success %	53.8
11	Tackles	14
45.5	Tackles Won %	57.1
40.3	Possession	59.7
53.6	Territorial Adv %	46.4
356	Total Passes	545
19	Total Crosses	13
132	Lost Balls	124
53	Recoveries	52
45.5	1st Half Poss	54.5
34.5	2nd Half Poss	65.5

BY SIMON MULLOCK
From WEMBLEY

IT won't matter to Mikel Arteta that his players didn't get to climb the 107 steps to Wembley's Royal Box to collect the Cup.

Pierre-Emerick Aubameyang's two goals served notice that the Gunners are going places under their Spanish manager.

It has taken Arteta just 28 games to lift his first trophy for the club he served with such distinction as a player.

A two-time winner of the famous old silverware when he patrolled Arsene Wenger's midfield, the 38-year-old has another medal to add to his collection.

Now the Emirates hierarchy have to back their young boss in the market. And the first piece of business must be to try to persuade Aubameyang to sign a contract that will keep him in north London for the remainder of his career.

It will cost them £20million to trigger an extension – but that's cheap at the price.

Aubameyang has scored 29 goals this season for a team that was going nowhere until Arteta left Pep Guardiola's side at Manchester City to answer their SOS call.

The Gunners have now lifted the FA Cup trophy a record 14 times.

The last time that they were beaten in a final at Wembley was 40 years ago when Frank Lampard senior was playing left-back for West Ham and the Hammers defeated them 1-0. It

PROVING HIS POINT Arteta gives out his instructions on way to victory

---

SMLO

Arsenal — Chelsea

**HEADS UP
FA CUP FINAL**

IS AN ART

PRIDE LONDO

DINK, IT'S ALL OVER Aubameyang cleverly scores winner past Caballero

CAPTAIN'S SPOT ON
Skipper Aubameyang celebrates after firing home his penalty equaliser (right)

What the managers said...

BY **TOM HOPKINSON**
and **HARRY PRATT**

MIKEL ARTETA was in Wembley heaven as he hailed Arsenal's latest FA Cup success – and tipped skipper Pierre-Emerick Aubameyang to stay.

Arteta, celebrating his first trophy seven months into his first managerial job, said: "If you ask my opinion, I think Auba will stay.

"He knows what I think and that I want to build the squad around him.

"Everything is based on my discussions with him and his people – nothing is done yet, but I hope we will hear something soon.

"The players all admire him here and we value him so much."

Arteta added: "Big games require big players to do it. He's done it in the semis and now in the final.

"People questioned that he couldn't do it in big games, but here we have it."

With a Europa League place secured, Arteta added: "It's a great start. This is a trophy for the fans.

"This is the first trophy I've won as a manager and it's probably the greatest day in my career so far."

> **I think Auba will stay. I want to build the squad around him**

Chelsea boss Frank Lampard said: "We shouldn't become too stuck on this defeat. We need to look at the season as a whole and what we have managed to do to come where we've come in the league.

"This would have been the icing on the cake, but it wasn't to be. We didn't play well enough, we know that in our dressing room.

"But we went into the game with Willian pulling out in the last 24 hours or so, same as Ruben Loftus-Cheek, we then suffered two hamstrings and a dislocated shoulder with Pedro maybe.

"It has been a very busy period for us and the players have given everything – and playing with 10 men in the last 20 minutes was a really difficult challenge for them.

"We had a great start, we had control of the game and then we started to get sloppy. We got slower in our game and it changed the tone of it.

"But, in terms of football, we didn't play well enough."

RATINGS by John Cross

ARSENAL

EMILIANO MARTINEZ 8
No chance on the goal and was otherwise solid and commanding

HECTOR BELLERIN 7
Exposed a few times defensively, but crucial run on second goal

ROB HOLDING 6
Must rediscover his form and confidence to get back to his best

DAVID LUIZ 8
Won ding-dong battle with Giroud, barely gave Chelsea striker a kick

KIERAN TIERNEY 8
Since the restart has shown he is a top-quality player. Huge potential

AINSLEY MAITLAND-NILES 8
Justified Arteta's faith, was their best player early on. Excellent

GRANIT XHAKA 7
Marshalled midfield. Twice fouled by Kovacic, who was sent off

DANI CEBALLOS Booked 7
Sets the tempo for Arsenal in midfield, makes it tick

NICOLAS PEPE 7
Had a wonder goal ruled out for offside. So hit-and-miss

PIERRE-EM AUBAMEYANG 9
Top quality striker. Priceless goals. Arsenal can't afford to lose him

ALEXANDRE LACAZETTE 7
Still searching for his first FA Cup goal, but incredibly hard-working

SUBS: Nketiah (Lacazette 82); Sokratis (Luiz 88); Kolasinac (Tierney 90+13).

MAN OF THE MATCH

AUBAMEYANG

CHELSEA

WILLY CABALLERO 6
Kept his place, which must spell the end for Kepa

REECE JAMES 6
Has come back to the fore in recent weeks, given a stern test

CESAR AZPILICUETA Booked 5
Conceded a penalty and then went off injured soon after

KURT ZOUMA 6
Was often Chelsea's best defender, but got turned for the winner

ANTONIO RUDIGER Booked 6
Chelsea's defence looked a weak spot and he was unsettled

MARCOS ALONSO 6
Better going forward as Arsenal found room down his flank

JORGINHO 6
Blues miss a fully fit Kante, but worked hard in midfield

MATEO KOVACIC Sent off 5
Saw a yellow card early on, then lost his head and booked again

MASON MOUNT Booked 7
Involved in the build-up for opening goal. Industrious

CHRISTIAN PULISIC 7
Terrific opening goal, outstanding until hamstring went. Top quality

OLIVIER GIROUD 6
Led the line well, played a part in first goal and caused problems

SUBS: Christensen (Azpilicueta 35) 5; Pedro (Pulisic 48) 6; Barkley Booked (Mount 78); Hudson-Odoi (Rudiger 78); Abraham (Giroud 78).

---

seemed like that might happen again when the Chelsea team managed by his son (below) took a fifth-minute lead through attacking midfielder Christian Pulisic.

But this was to be Aubameyang's evening – while Chelsea ran into a mountain of problems.

The Blues lost captain Cesar Azpilicueta, Pulisic and Pedro through injury.

They played the last 17 minutes with 10 men when Mateo Kovacic was shown a second yellow card for a foul on Granit Xhaka.

And their number was reduced again in injury time when sub Pedro had to be carried off. Pulisic's opening goal was a beauty.

The American collected Jorginho's pass and kept moving after immediately working the ball to Mason Mount on his left.

Mount's low cross into the box was flicked on by Olivier Giroud and Pulisic lifted a glorious finish over Gunners keeper Emiliano Martinez.

The Blues were bossing the opening exchanges and had plenty of possession, but the drinks break gave Arteta a chance to rally his players.

Pepe thought he had scored one of the great cup final goals – only for the glorious 25-yarder that he sent arcing over Blues keeper Willy Caballero to be ruled out because team-mate Ainsley Maitland-Niles had strayed offside.

But it did not matter too much because moments later the Gunners were level.

Aubameyang got goal-side of Azpilicueta and then felt an arm on his shoulder as the Blues defender tried to recover.

That was all the excuse the striker needed to take a tumble and referee Anthony Taylor had no doubts – a penalty for Arsenal and a yellow card for the Chelsea skipper.

Both decisions were dubious.

But both were upheld by VAR Stuart Attwell – and Aubameyang sent Caballero the wrong way for the equaliser.

Now it was Arsenal in the ascendancy, while Chelsea suffered another blow when Azpilicueta limped off with a knee injury.

Lampard was forced to reorganise again when Pulisic sent a shot wide after the break and suffered a hamstring strain that ended his evening.

As the contest drifted from end to end, it seemed the next goal would win it.

So it proved.

Hector Bellerin's rampaging run was halted by Marcos Alonso's thumping tackle.

But Pepe worked the loose ball across to Aubameyang and he fooled Kurt Zouma with a dip of his shoulder before dinking the ball over Caballero.

Kovacic was unlucky to be sent off for a second challenge on Xhaka, but it illustrated Chelsea's misfortune perfectly.

FA CUP FINAL ARSENAL 2 CHELSEA 1

RATINGS by JOHN CROSS
mirror.co.uk/sport/football

ARSENAL

MARTINEZ
Wonderful FA Cup story. Fought so hard for his chance and took it — **8**

BELLERIN
Big summer ahead but Arsenal need him. Made crucial run on second goal — **7**

HOLDING
Showed big heart. Every team needs characters and he is one — **7**

LUIZ
No grey areas with Luiz but this was a day to cherish, dominated Giroud — **8**

TIERNEY
A defiant, determined character. Top quality player and a winner — **8**

MAITLAND-NILES
No sign of nerves and he was Arsenal's best player early on. Big future — **8**

XHAKA
His fortunes have completely changed under Arteta. Bossed it — **8**

CEBALLOS
Has been so important in second half of the season. They must keep him — **7**

PEPE
There are flashes of brilliance and quality but needs to be consistent — **7**

AUBAMEYANG MotM
Incredible class.. Priceless goals. Arsenal can't afford to lose him — **9**

LACAZETTE
His work rate, non-stop running was so important in the victory — **7**

SUBS: Nketiah (Lacazette 82), **Sokratis** (Luiz 87), **Kolasinac** (Tierney 90)

CHELSEA

CABALLERO
His selection must be the end for Kepa. Not really at fault — **6**

JAMES
Has won back his place in recent weeks, but struggled here — **6**

AZPILICUETA
Awful day for Chelsea skipper. Conceded pen, went off injured — **4**

ZOUMA
Is a pure defender, did OK generally but got turned on the winner — **6**

RUDIGER
Would he be better surrounded by better defenders? Exposed — **6**

ALONSO
Arsenal found room down his flank. They need to strengthen at left-back — **6**

JORGINHO
Worked hard but they missed Kante's quality and work ethic — **6**

KOVACIC
Sent off. Deserved the first yellow card but second was so harsh — **5**

MOUNT
Booked. One of Chelsea's few bright spots, worked hard and did well — **7**

PULISIC
After his slow start at Chelsea, has come good. Chelsea's best player — **7**

GIROUD
Played a part in opening goal, led the line but Luiz won the battle — **6**

SUBS: Christensen (Azpilicueta 35) **5, Pedro** (Pulisic 48) **6, Barkley** (Mount 78), **Hudson-Odoi** (Rudiger 78), **Abraham** (Giroud 78)

TIERNEY: IT IS ALL FOR OUR FANS

BY **JOHN CROSS**

KIERAN TIERNEY dedicated his FA Cup winner's medal to the fans who have helped him through the "toughest year of his life."

Tierney (above) thanked the Arsenal supporters for their backing during a turbulent first year at the club when he has struggled with injuries, form and confidence.

He said: "It's been so high and so low at different times but everyone at the club and the fans have been brilliant with me and this one is for them.

"It's been the toughest year of my life and I couldn't have picked a better ending for the season.

"There's so many people I want to thank... my family, my friends and the manager for putting his trust in me and I shared a moment with him at the end. We're building something, and all trust in this process 110 per cent."

BBC DOING IT WRIGHT WAY

BY **JOHN CROSS**

THE FA Cup Final was the most-watched game of the 2019/20 season with 8.2million tuning in on the BBC to watch.

BBC share the rights with BT Sport but - with help from Ian Wright (above) - got a far bigger audience on terrestrial TV.

Sky had revealed that 5.5m watched the Merseyside derby in June when that Premier League game was shown free to air.

It is a huge thumbs-up for the FA Cup that it still draws huge audiences, with the obvious advantage that games are shown on the BBC rather than on a subscription channel.

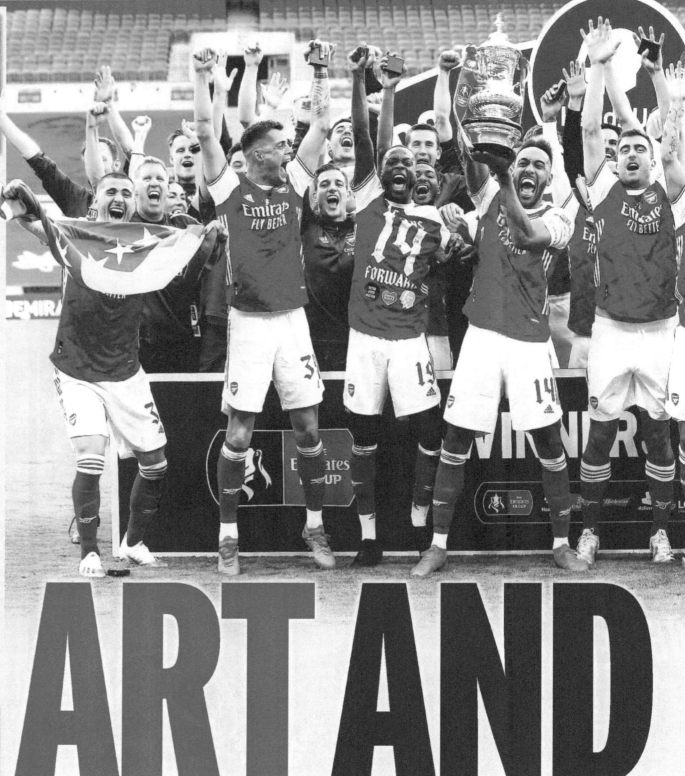

ART AND

Arsenal could have crumbled at 1-0 down but Arteta

BY **JOHN CROSS**
Chief Football Writer
@johncrossmirror

MIKEL ARTETA set about making a culture change when he took over as Arsenal manager.

To bring in a stronger mentality, a togetherness, to make them harder to beat, more resilient and better defensively after years of being a soft touch.

This FA Cup success shows that in the space of eight months Arteta is making inroads, but there is one thing he has not changed and that is the club's love affair with the FA Cup, emphasised by this record 14th triumph in the competition.

Lifting the trophy underlines the progress the Spaniard has made, but bigger proof was in the way that after going 1-0 down,

they did not crumble. The FA Cup was vital in terms of being a passport into Europe and providing funds and fresh hope of rebuilding this squad.

But the way they achieved it, from outsmarting Manchester City in the semi-final to having too much for Chelsea in the final, shows the Gunners are moving in the right direction.

The respect the players have for Arteta was there for all to see in the togetherness of the post-match celebrations and the way they listened to his instructions in the first drinks break when the momentum changed.

"I am so proud of how we have been able to get through it," said Arteta. "When you win things, it creates a great spirit for the staff and players.

"Hopefully they can see what

we are trying to do and they can be involved even more. There is still a lot of work to do. But I am proud of what the players have done and how far they have come. It is a great group of lads to manage. We know our strengths and weaknesses, but we know the effort and commitment we have put in every training session and game."

There were many big performances. Pierre-Emerick

Aubameyang's coolness from the spot and his supremely composed second goal (below). David Luiz dominated Olivier Giroud, who had been such a driving force in the closing weeks of the season.

Ainsley Maitland-

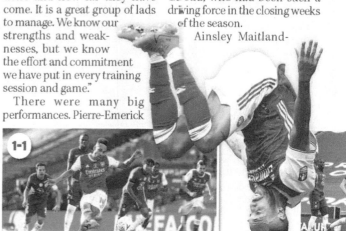

1-1

MARTINEZ'S FAMILY KEPT APART FOR CRYING GAME

BY **JOHN CROSS**

EMILIANO MARTINEZ has revealed that his family could not even be together to watch the FA Cup Final.

His native Argentina is still in a strict lockdown and his brother could not be in the same house as his parents to watch the 27-year-old enjoy the proudest moment of his career.

The Arsenal keeper broke down in tears of joy after the game as he dedicated the win to his family back in his home country – but it was reward for not giving up.

Martinez said: "I never wanted to go back to Argentina with empty hands.

"After a decade, to win the FA Cup with Arsenal, playing a key role in the game, I could not be prouder.

"My family are in lockdown now. My brother watched it in a different house to my parents. It is tough for them as they wanted to be here and it is tough for me because it has been a long time.

"I wanted to see them here and give them a hug after a long, long fight.

"I always do it for them. My family supported me all the way, I have a family here in Europe and I do it for

them – I never do it for myself. I was just crying for the first five, 10 minutes after the game.

"Now I am relaxed I might get a replica to put in the cabinet at home. I came from a long way to get here."

Martinez also revealed how a players' meeting after Arsenal lost at Brighton in their second game back after lockdown changed the course of their season.

That Seagulls defeat was a huge blow to their hopes of reaching the Champions League places, but they have salvaged the season with the FA Cup.

Martinez added: "You can see that we changed. After the restart, when we lost against Brighton, we sat down ourselves and thought, 'We need to change – we need to trust the manager, we need to trust ourselves'.

"I was saying to the players before kick off: trust yourselves, trust everyone.

"We have got a clever manager, he will know what to do in the future. I just wanted to win the FA Cup for the fans.

"Obviously, we had a bad season in terms of playing style, we changed the manager twice which has not happened at Arsenal for a long period."

THE FA CUP SPECIALISTS

There have been 140 FA Cup finals and Arsenal have now won exactly 10 per cent of them.

14 Arsenal
12 Manchester United
8 Chelsea, Tottenham
7 Liverpool, Aston Villa
6 Newcastle, Manchester City, Blackburn
5 Everton, West Brom, Wanderers
4 Wolves, Bolton, Sheffield United
3 Sheffield Wednesday, West Ham

TEAR WE GO
Emotional Martinez is comforted by two-goal Arsenal hero Aubameyang

SOUL

has changed the way they all think

Niles was an unsung hero, Hector Bellerin's charge forward for the winning goal, Kieran Tierney and Emiliano Martinez were excellent again and yet, quietly but assured, it was another player who perhaps best embodies Arteta's turnaround.

Granit Xhaka was on his way out when Arteta arrived, unpopular after his fall-out with the fans and as ostracised as Mesut Ozil and Matteo Guendouzi are now. But Xhaka is proof that if

you buy into Arteta's philosophy anything is possible.

Xhaka is now the player that Arsenal thought they were buying. A commanding midfielder, who is clearly being coached and drilled. His midfield axis with Dani Ceballos has become a key component.

Arteta added: "Granit is a really good example, but the players have to be willing and they have to have the personality and the workrate he has.

"You need to have faith and courage to face the problem and slowly start to knock down the wall and start to enjoy the profession in the way he deserves.

"We were just there to support him a little bit and give him advice. The rest was up to him and he deserves credit for that."

Anything that could go wrong

for Chelsea, did. Christian Pulisic was outstanding early on, scored the opener and Arsenal found him impossible to pick up, but he went off injured just after half-time.

Cesar Azpilicueta made a clumsy challenge to concede a penalty, then got injured. Mateo Kovacic was sent off for two bookings – the second ridiculously harsh – and Pedro suffered a nasty shoulder injury late on.

The luck was with Arsenal, but they had fought hard since the restart to earn it.

MATCH STATS

ARSENAL		CHELSEA
40%	POSSESSION	60%
3	SHOTS ON TARGET	3
4	SHOTS OFF TARGET	3
357	TOTAL PASSES	546
78%	PASS SUCCESS	85%
4	BLOCKED SHOTS	3
6	CORNERS	4
3	OFFSIDE	3
2	FOULS	14
1	0 CARDS	4 1

£250K FOR AUBA

FROM BACK PAGE
Aubameyang and now it is down to the club to find the right deal.

But he also reckons the 31-year-old can become of the Arsenal greats in the tradition of Thierry Henry, Ian Wright and Dennis Bergkamp, after his two-goal FA Cup final heroics.

Arteta said: "We always had incredible strikers at this club and Auba deserves to be named and compared with the big names.

"By winning trophies he will be closer to that the longer he stays. Hopefully we can have him for longer.

"The biggest problem was to convince him to work the way he was working. He was

going to get more reward and respect, and our respect would go to admiration – from his team-mates and the people who have been with him and from the fans.

"Goalscoring is the most difficult thing in football, he makes it look simple."

Aubameyang's £180,000-a-week deal expires next summer but his contract includes a 12-month extension clause which must be triggered by December 31 which would see his wages go up significantly and, with a bonus, would cost the club around £20million for a season.

Arsenal want to give him a deal to remove that financial penalty but the player is in a strong bargaining position.

Sunday Mirror Sport

mirror.co.uk/sport

HOWE QUITS CHERRIES

EDDIE HOWE has left his job as Bournemouth boss - and plans to take a break.

The 42-year-old failed to keep the Cherries in the Premier League despite a final-day win over Everton. Howe said: "I think now is the right time for the club to have a change."

SHOW ME THE MONEY

EXCLUSIVE
BY **TOM HOPKINSON** and **JOHN RICHARDSON**

MIKE ASHLEY has told American TV mogul Henry Mauriss to show him the colour of his money - and Newcastle United will be his.

The American is understood to be "incredibly focused" to get a deal done and willing to pay £350million to take control at St James' Park.

Chris Ronnie, a long-time associate of Newcastle owner Ashley (left) and, ironically, an old school friend of Magpies boss Steve Bruce, is leading negotiations. Ashley has set a deadline of August 14 to give Newcastle clarity ahead of the 2020-21 season - and an agreement on a price could be reached within the coming weeks.

Should Ashley and Mauriss get that far, the bid **TURN TO PAGE 66**

TURN TO PAGE 66

50 GREATEST OLYMPIANS

INSIDE
50 GREAT OLYMPIANS PULL-OUT

ARSENAL 2 CHELSEA 1

HEADS UP FA CUP FINAL AT WEMBLEY

AUBA THE MOON

MATCH REPORT Pages 70&71
ANDY DUNN Pages 68&69

BY **TOM HOPKINSON**

PIERRE-EMERICK Aubameyang broke Chelsea hearts as Arsenal won the FA Cup for the 14th time.

Auba scored twice after Christian Pulisic had given Blues the lead. Gunners boss Mikel Arteta said of his match-winner: "I think he wants to stay. It's just about getting the deal done."

Cup-winning boss Arteta says his matchwinner 'wants to stay'

Published by MGN Ltd. (020 7293 3000). Printed by Trinity Mirror Printing Ltd at Watford, Oldham, Birmingham and Glasgow. Registered at the Post Office as a newspaper. Serial No. 8177. MGN Ltd 2020. Austria €4, Belgium €2.20, France €3 (€9.68 FrF), Germany €3, Greece €2.95, Malta €2.70, Italy €2.20, Netherlands €250, Portugal €3.30 (CONT), Spain €2.30, Turkey YTL 13, Cyprus €2.75, Egypt EGP 17.00   LSL

NEWSPAPERS SUPPORT RECYCLING
The recycled paper content of UK newspapers in 2017 was 64.6%

SMLO 020820

9 770956 807671